# SEX AND DIFFERENCE I
## GREECE AND ROME

EDINBURGH READINGS ON THE ANCIENT WORLD

GENERAL EDITORS

Michele George, *McMaster University*; Thomas Harrison, *University of St Andrews*

ADVISORY EDITORS

Paul Cartledge, *University of Cambridge*; Richard Saller, *University of Chicago*

This series introduces English-speaking students to central themes in the history of the ancient world and to the range of scholarly approaches to those themes, within and across disciplines. Each volume, edited and introduced by a leading specialist, contains a selection of the most important work, including a significant proportion of translated material. The editor also provides a guide to the history of modern scholarship on the subject. Passages in ancient languages are translated; technical terms, ancient and modern, are explained.

PUBLISHED

*Sparta*
Edited by Michael Whitby

*Sex and Difference in Ancient Greece and Rome*
Edited by Mark Golden and Peter Toohey

*Greeks and Barbarians*
Edited by Thomas Harrison

*The Ancient Economy*
Edited by Walter Scheidel and Sitta von Reden

*Roman Religion*
Edited by Clifford Ando

IN PREPARATION

*Ancient Slavery*
Edited by Keith Bradley

*Ancient Myth*
Edited by Richard Gordon

*Alexander the Great*
Edited by Simon Hornblower

*Athenian Democracy*
Edited by P. J. Rhodes

*The 'Dark Ages' of Greece*
Edited by Ian Morris

*The Age of Augustus*
Edited by Jonathan Edmondson

# SEX AND DIFFERENCE IN ANCIENT GREECE AND ROME

*Edited by*
Mark Golden and Peter Toohey

EDINBURGH UNIVERSITY PRESS

© Editorial matter and selection Mark Golden and Peter Toohey, 2003

Edinburgh University Press Ltd
22 George Square, Edinburgh

Typeset in Sabon MT
by Servis Filmsetting Ltd, Manchester, and
printed and bound in Great Britain by
Antony Rowe Ltd, Chippenham, Wilts

A CIP record for this book is available from the British Library

ISBN 0 7486 1319 6 (hardback)
ISBN 0 7486 1320 X (paperback)

# Contents

# Acknowledgments

## EDITORS' ACKNOWLEDGMENTS

Conceived when the new millennium was some years off, this book finally appears when the new millennium is some years off. We thank all those who have helped us complete the journey. (You others know who you are.) In particular, we are grateful to Amy Richlin for taking time out from a tour of Winnipeg's curling rinks to critique an early draft of our table of contents; to our translators; to our home universities, New England, Calgary, and Winnipeg, for funding travel which eased the strains of long-distance collaboration; to the Faculty of Humanities, University of Calgary, for providing funds to aid in the book's production; and to the staff of the Interlending and Document Supply department at the University of Winnipeg Library (Heather Mathieson, Lynne Schultz) for obtaining so many of the books and articles from which our eventual selection was made.

To spend so much time on ancient women must encourage reflection on others who are gone but not forgotten. This book is dedicated to the memory of Sari Golden (1954–83).

For permission to reprint the articles included in this volume, we would like to thank the following: Professor C. Schnurr-Redford and Akademie Verlag; the editors of *Jahrbuch für Antike und Christentum* (for H. Herter's article); Professor B. Wagner-Hasel and the editors of *Die altsprachliche Unterricht*; Professor F. Frontisi-Ducroix and Gallimard; Professor E. Lieber and Olms Weidmann.

## PUBLISHER'S ACKNOWLEDGMENTS

Marilyn Katz, "Ideology and 'the status of women' in ancient Greece," in A.-L. Shapiro (ed.), *History and Feminist Theory* (*History and Theory* Beiheft 31) (1992), pp. 70–97. © Wesleyan University.

H. D. F. Kitto, *The Greeks*, Penguin Books 1951, rev. edn 1957. © H. D. F. Kitto, 1951, 1957. Reproduced by permission of Penguin Books Ltd.

K. J. Dover, "Classical Greek attitudes to sexual behavior," *Arethusa* 6 (1973), pp. 59–73 © The Johns Hopkins University Press. Reprinted with permission of The Johns Hopkins University Press.

D. Halperin, "The social body and the sexual body," © 1990 from *One Hundred Years of Homosexuality* by D. Halperin. Reproduced by permission of Taylor & Francis, Inc./Routledge, Inc., http://www/Routledge-ny.com

David Cohen, "Law, society, and homosexuality in classical Athens," *Past and Present*, vol. 117 (1987), pp. 3–21. Reproduced by permission of Oxford University Press.

L. Foxhall, "Pandora unbound," in *Dislocating Masculinity*, eds A. Cornwall and N. Lindisfarne, pp. 133–46. London: Routledge, 1994. Reproduced by permission of Routledge Publishers.

L. Dean-Jones, "The cultural construct of the female body," in *Women's History and Ancient History*, ed. by Sarah B. Pomeroy. © 1991 by the University of North Carolina Press. Used by permission of the publisher.

A. Richlin, "Gender and rhetoric," in *Roman Eloquence*, ed. by W. J. Dominik, pp. 90–110. London: Routledge, 1997. Reproduced by permission of Routledge Publishers.

J. Clarke, *Looking at Lovemaking in Roman Art: Constructions of Sexuality in Roman Art, 100 B.C.—A. D. 250*, pp. 91–118. © 1998 The Regents of the University of California. Used by permission of the publisher.

Nancy Demand, *Birth, Death, and Motherhood in Classical Greece*, pp. 121–30. © Johns Hopkins University Press, 1994

I. Morris, "Archaeology and gender ideologies in early archaic Greece," *Transactions of the American Philological Association (TAPhA)*, 129 (1999), pp. 305–17. Reproduced by permission of the American Philological Association.

B. Kellum, "Concealing/revealing: gender and the play of meaning in the monuments of Augustan Rome," pp. 158–81 in T. Habinek and A. Schiesaro (eds), *The Roman Cultural Revolution*, 1997. Reproduced by permission of Cambridge University Press.

L. E. Talalay, "A feminist boomerang: the Great Goddess of Greek prehistory," *Gender and History*, 6 (1994), pp. 165–83. © Blackwell Publishers Ltd.

Reprinted from Michael Jameson, "The asexuality of Dionysus," in *Masks of Dionysus*, ed. by Thomas H. Carpenter and Christopher

A. Faraone. © 1993 by Cornell University. Used by permission of the publisher, Cornell University Press.

Barbara Gold, "'Vested interests' in Plautus' *Casina*," from *Helios* 25.1. Reproduced by permission of Texas Tech University Press.

# Note to the Reader

The articles and excerpts included in this book were originally published in a range of different journals and books. A degree of uniformity has been imposed (for example, in the abbreviations used), but many of the conventions of the original pieces have been preserved. This applies to spelling (UK or US) and to different modes of referencing: chapters using the Harvard (i.e. name and date) system are followed by individual bibliographies; those using 'short titles' usually have footnotes and no bibliography.

The final bibliography contains books and articles abbreviated in the footnotes of the articles which could not otherwise be easily identified, together with those referred to in the introduction and further reading. Book information (particularly those edited volumes in which articles are to be found) is very easily available on the web. Students, unlike their teachers, will know this already and that, for books, checking the authors' designation on easily accessible sites such as www.melvyl.ucop.edu will quickly provide the details they need.

Editorial notes and translations of ancient texts are introduced either within square brackets [ ] or in daggered footnotes †. Some Greek terms, especially those in use in English, have been transliterated.

All abbreviations of ancient texts, modern collections, books and journals, used either in the chapters or in the editorial material, are listed and explained on pp. xii–xvi.

# Abbreviations

(For ease of use, abbreviations to ancient sources and to journals and modern editions have not been distinguished.)

There are many abbreviations in the notes to Herter's article (Chapter 4). We believe that these notes are so useful that they deserve to be preserved in their entirety. Their extent, however, makes their listing here impossible. Many may be found in *The Oxford Classical Dictionary* (3rd edn). For others, see (for Greek authors) Liddell, Scott, and Jones, *A Greek–English Lexicon*; G. W. H. Lampe, *A Patristic Greek Lexicon*; L. Berkowitz and K. A. Squitier, *Canon of Greek Authors and Works* (Oxford, 1990); and (for Latin authors) Lewis and Short, *A Latin Dictionary* and *The Oxford Latin Dictionary*.

| | |
|---|---|
| *ABSA* | *Annual of the British School at Athens* |
| *ABV* | J. D. Beazley, *Attic Black-Figure Vase Painters* (Oxford 1956) |
| *ACF* | *Annuarie du Collège de France* |
| *AE* | *Année épigraphique* |
| Aes. | Aeschylus |
|   *Eum.* | *Eumenides* |
| *AHR* | *American Historical Review* |
| *AJA* | *American Journal of Archaeology* |
| Am. | *Amores* (Ovid) |
| Amic. | *De Amicitia* (*On Friendship*) (Cicero) |
| Anth. Pal. | *Anthologia Palatina* (*Palatine Anthology*) |
| Ar. | Aristophanes |
|   *Lys.* | *Lysistrata* |
|   *Thes.* | *Thesmophoriazusae* |
| Ars Am. | *Ars Amatoria* (Ovid) |
| *ARV²* | J. D. Beazley, *Attic Red-Figure Vase Painters*, 2nd edn (Oxford 1963) |

| | |
|---|---|
| *Ath. Pol.* | *Athenaion Politeia (Athenian Constitution)* (Aristotle) |
| *AU* | *Der altsprachliche Unterricht* |
| *BCH* | *Bulletin de correspondance hellénique* |
| *BdA* | *Bollettino d'Arte del Ministro della Pubblica Istruzione* |
| *Brut.* | *Brutus* (Cicero) |
| *Cael.* | *Pro Caelio* (Cicero) |
| Cic. | Cicero |
|   *Att.* | *Letters to Atticus* |
|   *Orat.* | *Orator* |
| *CIL* | *Corpus Inscriptionum Latinarum* |
| *CMG* | *Corpus Medicorum Graecorum* |
| *CML* | *Classical and Modern Literature* |
| *Controv.* | *Controversiae* (Seneca the Elder) |
| *CPh* | *Classical Philology* |
| *Demon.* | *Demonax* (Lucian) |
| Dio | Dio Cassius |
| Dion. Hal. | Dionysius of Halicarnassus |
|   *Ant. Rom.* | *Roman Antiquities* |
| *Diss. Ut.* | *De Dissectione Uteri* |
| *DW* | *Diseases of Women* (Hippocrates) |
| *EMC* | *Echos du monde classique* |
| *Ep.* | *Epistulae (Epistles)* (Seneca the Younger) |
| Eur. | Euripides |
|   *Bacch.* | *Bacchae* |
|   *Hec.* | *Hecuba* |
|   *Hipp.* | *Hippolytus* |
|   *Or.* | *Orestes* |
|   *Tr.* | *Troades* |
| *Fast.* | *Fasti* (Ovid) |
| *FGr Hist* | F. Jacoby (ed.), *Die Fragmente der griechischen Historiker* (Leiden 1957–present) |
| *FHG* | C. Müller and T. Müller (eds), *Fragmenta Historicorum Graecorum.* (Paris 1851) |
| *G&R* | *Greece and Rome* |
| *GA*, also *de gen. an.* | *Generation of Animals* (Aristotle) |
| Gell. | Aulus Gellius |
|   *NA* | *Noctes Atticae (Attic Nights)* |
| *Gen.* | *On Generation* (Hippocrates) |

| | |
|---|---|
| *GRBS* | *Greek, Roman and Byzantine Studies* |
| *Gyn.* | *Gynecology* (Soranus) |
| *HA* | *History of Animals* (Aristotle) |
| *Harv. Stud. Class. Phil.* | *Harvard Studies in Classical Philology* |
| Hes. | Hesiod |
|   *Op.* | *Opera et Dies* (*Works and Days*) |
|   *Theog.* | *Theogony* |
| Hor. | Horace |
|   *Carm.* | (*Carmina*) (*Odes*) |
| Hyg. | Hyginus |
|   *Fab.* | *Fabulae* |
| *ICS* | *Illinois Classical Studies* |
| *IG* | *Inscriptiones Graecae* (Berlin 1873–present) |
| *Il.* | *Iliad* |
| *ILS* | H. Dessau, *Inscriptiones Latinae Selectae* (Berlin 1892–1916) |
| *JAC* | *Jahrbuch für Antike und Christentum* |
| *JHB* | *Journal of the History of Biology* |
| *JHS* | *Journal of Hellenic Studies* |
| *JRA* | *Journal of Roman Archaeology* |
| *JRS* | *Journal of Roman Studies* |
| *Lac. Constitution* | *Spartan Constitution* (Xenophon) |
| *LIMC* | *Lexicon Iconographicum Mythologiae Classicae* (Zurich 1981–present) |
| *L.L.* | *De Lingua Latina* (*On the Latin Language*) (Varro) |
| *LSS* | F. Sokolowski (ed.), *Lois Sacrées des Cités Grecques: Supplément.* (Paris 1962) |
| Lucr. | Lucretius |
| Macrob. | Macrobius |
|   *Sat.* | *Saturnalia* |
| *MDAI (A)* | Mitteilungen des Deutschen Archäologischen Instituts. Athenische Abteilung |
| *MDAI (R)* | Mitteilungen des Deutschen Archäologischen Instituts. Römische Abteilung |
| *NC* | *On the Nature of the Child* (Hippocrates) |
| *Nigr.* | *Nigrinus* (Lucian) |
| *NSC* | *Notizie degli scari di antichità* |
| *NW* | *Nature of Women* (Hippocrates) |

| | |
|---|---|
| *Od.* | *Odyssey* |
| *OED* | *Oxford English Dictionary* |
| PA | *Parts of Animals* (Aristotle) |
| *PA* (in Lieber's article, Chapter 20) | "Airs, Waters, Places" (Hippocrates) |
| *PCG* | R. Kassel and C. Austin (eds), *Poetae Comici Graeci* (Berlin 1983–present) |
| Pind. | Pindar |
| *Ol.* | *Olympians* |
| Pl. | Plato |
| *Phaedr.* | *Phaedrus* |
| *Symp.* | *Symposium* |
| *Theaet.* | *Theaetetus* |
| *PLG* | T. Bergk (ed.), *Poetae Lyrici Graeci* (Leipzig 1882) |
| Plin. | Pliny |
| *NH* | *Natural History* |
| Plut. | Plutarch |
| *Alcib.* | *Life of Alcibiades* |
| *Ant.* | *Life of Antony* |
| *Lyc.* | *Life of Lycurgus* |
| *Mor.* | *Moralia* |
| *Quaest. Conviv.* | *Quaestiones Conviviales* |
| *PMG* | D. L. Page (ed.), *Poetae Melici Graeci* (Oxford 1962) |
| *Prob.* | *Problemata* |
| Prop. | Propertius |
| Quint. | Quintilian |
| *Inst.* | *Institutio Oratoriae* |
| *Res Gest.* | *Res Gestae* (Augustus) |
| *Rhein. Mus.* | *Rheinisches Museum* |
| *Rhet. Her.* | *Rhetorica ad Herennium* |
| *SAWW* | *Sitzungsberichte der Österreichischen Akademie der Wissenschaft in Wien, Philos.-Hist. Klasse* |
| *SEG* | *Supplementum Epigraphicum Graecum* (Leiden 1923–present) |
| Sen. | Seneca |
| *Tranq.* | *De Tranquillitate Animi* |
| Serv. | Servius |
| *Ecl.* | *Eclogues* (Virgil) |
| Serv. Dan. | Servius Danielis |

| | |
|---|---|
| *Suas.* | *Suasoriae* (Seneca the Elder) |
| Suet. | Suetonius |
| *Aug.* | *Augustus* |
| *Claud.* | *Claudius* |
| *Iul.* | *Julius Caesar* |
| *Vit. Hor.* | *Life of Horace* |
| Tac. | Tacitus |
| *Dial.* | *Dialogus* |
| TAP*h*A | *Transactions of the American Philological Association* |
| Theoc. | Theocritus |
| *Tr.*, also *Trist.* | *Tristia* (Ovid) |
| TrGF | B. Snell and S. Radt (eds), *Tragicorum Graecorum Fragmenta* (Göttingen 1971–present) |
| Val. Max. | Valerius Maximus |
| Vell. | Velleius Paterculus |
| Virg. | Virgil |
| *Aen.* | *Aeneid* |
| Vitr. | Vitruvius |
| Xen. | Xenophon |
| *Oec.* | *Oeconomicus* |
| ZPE | *Zeitschrift für Papyrologie und Epigraphik* |

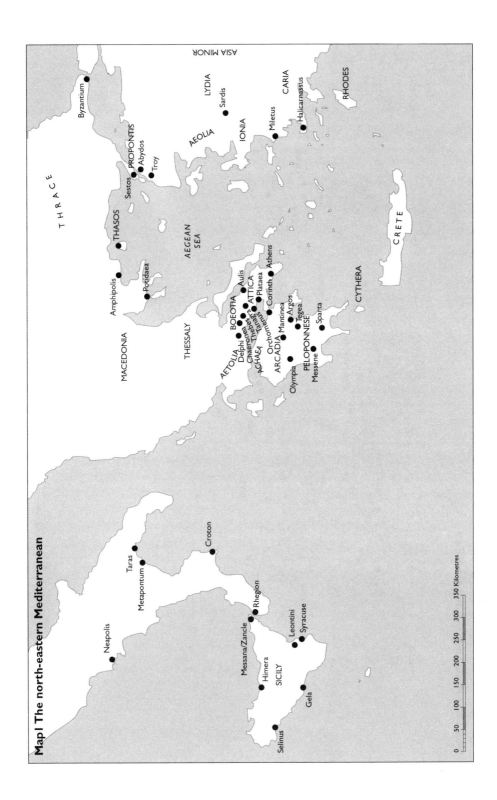

Map1 The north-eastern Mediterranean

ASIA MINOR

THRACE

Byzantium

PROPONTIS
Sestos
Abydos
Troy

THASOS

Amphipolis

Potidaea

MACEDONIA

THESSALY

AEGEAN
SEA

AEOLIA

LYDIA
Sardis

IONIA
Miletus

CARIA
Halicarnassus

RHODES

CRETE

CYTHERA

AETOLIA
Delphi
Chaeronea
Thebes
Tanagra
Orchomenus

BOEOTIA
Aulis
ATTICA
Plataea
Athens
Corinth

ACHAEA
ARCADIA
Mantinea
Tegea
Olympia
Messene
PELOPONNESE
Argos
Sparta

Neapolis

Taras
Metapontum
Croton

Rhegion
Messana/Zancle
Himera
SICILY
Selinus
Gela
Leontini
Syracuse

0   50  100  150  200  250  300  350 Kilometres

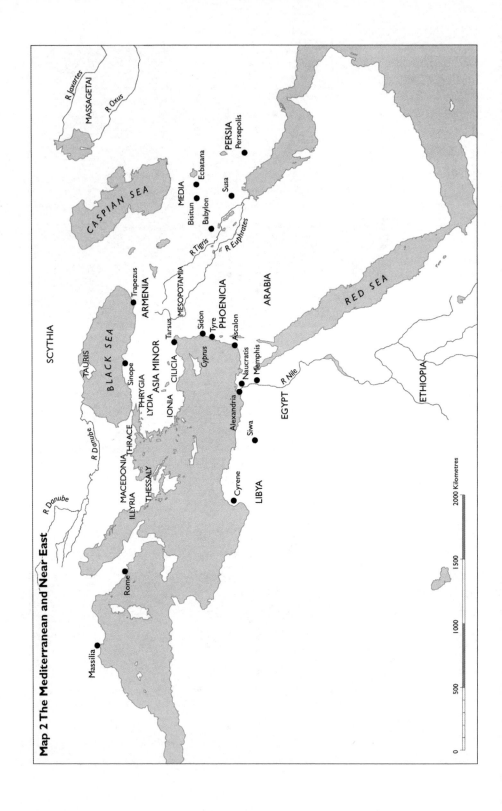

Map 2 The Mediterranean and Near East

# Introduction

"Look, Johanna," I said apologetically …
"SSHHHH!" she said. (There are certain instruments which seem to exercise an unaccountable fascination on female human beings. Did you know, for instance, that in ancient Athens there was a law against chaps playing flutes under girls' windows? There was nothing about giving them bunches of flowers, boxes of chocolates or mink coats, but playing the flute was reckoned to be taking an unfair advantage; even *clever* girls succumbed to it. I'm not making that up, I'm really not; ask any Greek Historian. Ask him in that lucid interval between the after-luncheon nap and the cocktail hour.)

Kyril Bonfiglioli, *After You With the Pistol* (1979)
(= *The Mortdecai Trilogy* [London 1991] 237–8)

No one would take Charlie Mortdecai for an expert on Greek history, let alone Greek historians. Still, it is true enough that students of classical antiquity face more questions on sex and gender than they used to. They also have a lot more authorities besides Charlie to help them find answers—so many, perhaps, that a guide to the guides (like this one) will have some value. We offer here a selection of scholarship on sex and gender in Greece and Rome, organized so as to provide a historical overview. The predominance of relatively recent work is, in part at least, a reflection of the extraordinary upsurge in the pace of research and publication in the past twenty years and of the range of approaches now available.[1] It is not meant to guarantee that all will prove as enduring as some pioneers.

Anyone who has prepared an anthology like this one will be all too aware of the process which led to our final roster. Readers disturbed by the absence of old favorites may well share our own disappointment. Some likely candidates were inaccessible, others costly, still others all too readily available, recently reprinted in collections of a different kind. Furthermore, some seminal studies are so focused on

---

[1] Earlier work is more prominent in a collection published in the German series *Wege der Forschung*: A. K. Siems (ed.), *Sexualität und Erotik in der Antike Welt* (Darmstadt 1988).

the explication of Greek and/or Latin texts as to be unsuitable for the audience (generalists, undergraduates) we have in mind.

This book traces a development over time. For many years, discussions of gender—"what a group at a given time thinks males and females are like in nature and behavior"[2]—focussed on the delineation of separate spheres within Greek and Roman societies. Men, especially citizen men, occupied the public sphere of the community, both literally—they alone ranged freely throughout the Greek and Roman worlds—and metaphorically, as participants in politics, litigants in courts, theater audiences. Women, contrariwise, were restricted to the home. Meanwhile, sex occupied a separate sphere of its own, sometimes the province of specialists in ancient medicine, at others the pastime of collectors of *curiosa*, of investigators into sexual positions, sex sellers, the erotic vocabulary. These amassed much material of interest; but their work had few points of contact with the established debate on gender roles, and still fewer with mainstream ancient history.

These fields have been transformed by the work of the past forty years, first Kenneth Dover's, then, following in his footsteps, that of Michel Foucault. A sexual act, penetration, became the main means of defining gender. Men penetrated, women were penetrated. As a result, not all males were men; subordinate groups—boys, slaves—could forego or lose that status. But to say only so much is to oversimplify: for one thing, men who desired to penetrate too many women or boys, or who desired to do so too much, might also lose status, subject to the power of their own passions as much as were their partners. The public and the private thus became knit together in a web of power. This marriage of sex and gender, especially in Foucault's work, has been both championed and challenged. At the same time, the older model of the separation of spheres has been called into question on other grounds; and marginal or transgressive categories (eunuchs, cross-dressers, gods) have taken a turn at center stage. Men too, once accepted without question as part of the background against which others stood out, now appear to wear masks and play roles like any actors. What follows is an elaboration of this sketch. For convenience, we have marked items excerpted in the present collection with an asterisk (*). We have made no effort to make references to the vast literature anything like comprehensive.

---

[2] J. Henderson, "Greek attitudes toward sex," in M. Grant and R. Kitzinger (eds), *Civilization of the Ancient Mediterranean: Greece and Rome* (New York 1988) 1250.

I

Later assumptions have always complicated the understanding of sex and gender in the ancient world, contaminating even the texts which are our main sources of information. Justinian's *Code* contains a rescript of Diocletian and Maximinian to Firminus, a slave who petitioned to avenge his master's death. It seems, however, that it is a female slave, Firmina, who seeks vengeance; compilers of the code, or those who copied the manuscript later on, changed her name "on the assumption that only a man could be capable of such *fides* and fortitude."[3] Similarly, one source of our knowledge of an Olympic victory by Bilistiche, Ptolemy Philadelphus's girlfriend, calls her Philistiakhos. During the seventeenth century, when scholars began to collect the mass of literary evidence which still forms the foundation for most studies of antiquity, later ancient writers (themselves struck by the difference between Greek and Roman customs) were taken to reflect earlier times too. During the eighteenth century, travellers' tales of contemporary Greek and Turkish domestic arrangements were thought to illuminate ancient texts and what they left obscure.[4]

Our story, however, starts only toward the end of the eighteenth century, a time of turmoil and ferment, when the political structure of the *ancien régime* was under attack and (in France and the Thirteen Colonies of North America) even overthrown. Civic space lay open. Who could occupy it? The American Declaration of Independence asserted that all men were created equal; Tom Paine proclaimed the Rights of Man. Some voices (Condorcet and Olympe de Gouges in France, Mary Wollstonecraft in England, and the German Theodor von Hippel) spoke for women too. But the loudest or more authoritative directed them toward a different destination, the domestic sphere. Here too there was honor to be earned: as Rousseau had expressed it in *Émile* (published in 1762), woman was meant to be man's helpmeet, not his handmaid. But an equal share of civil society was out of the question. Justification for this view was found in the original democracy, one of the models which inspired so many of the intellectuals and activists of the day, classical Athens.[5]

[3] J. Evans Grubbs, "The slave who avenged her master's death: *Codex Justinianus* 1.19.1 and 7.13.1," *Ancient History Bulletin*, 14 (2000) 81–8 (quotation: 82).
[4] *C. Schnurr-Redford, *Frauen in klassischen Athen: Sozialer Raum und reale Bewegungsfreiheit* (Berlin 1996) 15–21.
[5] *M. A. Katz, "Ideology and 'the status of women' in ancient Greece," in A.-L. Shapiro (ed.), *History and Feminist Theory* (Middletown 1992) 70–97 (*History and Theory* Beiheft 31).

Confirmation was at hand in Rome, source of so many symbols for French and American revolutionaries alike. There also (it was argued) women had had a role to play in great and admirable civilizations, but one which did not challenge men's primacy in public life or monopoly of political power. Established in this charged context, the model of separate spheres dominated discourse on gender roles and relations in classical antiquity for the next two centuries, giving rise to debates in many areas which, on the surface at least, would seem to carry little threat to prevailing patriarchy. (The earliest, in fact, concerned whether or not women made up part of the audience for Athenian drama.)[6]

Nineteenth-century social theorists, differ as they did on much else, nevertheless accepted the model of separate spheres.[7] According to the tenor of the times, their perspective was evolutionary. The territorial state arose at the expense of the family, men's domain depended on the relegation of women to the home. Bachofen, Maine, Fustel de Coulanges, Morgan, Engels: they were educated in various traditions, lived far apart, spanned the political spectrum from imperial administrator to ally of the Iroquois to revolutionary socialist. Yet the model of separate spheres underlay each man's account of antiquity and continued to prevail through much of the succeeding century.[8] It certainly animates *Kitto's The Greeks (1951), a bestseller which brought women's privacy to a wider public than ever. This is not to suggest that women's status itself was settled. The Greeks, again, is sufficient proof that it wasn't. Even in respect to what was universally regarded as part of their province—reproduction—opinions could differ on how their contributions were valued. Take Greek women: some scholars stressed the Hippocratic attribution of much of the active role in birthing to the fetus and the tendency to regard philosophy (with Socrates as midwife) or pederasty as essential to creating men;[9] for others, the importance of motherhood in making Athenian citizens after Pericles' law of 451/0 carried

---

[6] M. A. Katz, "Did the women of ancient Athens attend the theater in the eighteenth century?," *Classical Philogy*, 93 (1998) 105–24.

[7] J. J. Bachofen, *Das Mutterrecht* (Basel 1861); Henry Maine, *Ancient Law: Its Connection with the Early History of Society and its Relation to Modern Ideas* (London 1861); N. D. Fustel de Coulanges, *La cité antique: Étude sur le culte, le droit, les institutions de la Grèce et de Rome* (Paris 1864); L. H. Morgan, *Ancient Society* (Chicago 1877); F. Engels, *Der Ursprung der Familie, der Privateigentums und des Staats* (Zürich 1884); See C. B. Patterson, *The Family in Greek History* (Cambridge MA 1998) 5–28.

[8] J. Blok, "Sexual asymmetry: a historiographical essay," in J. Blok and P. Mason (eds), *Sexual Asymmetry: Studies in Ancient Society* (Amsterdam 1987) 1–57.

[9] N. Demand, *Birth, Death and Motherhood in Classical Greece* (Baltimore and London 1994) 19, 134–40.

more weight. (It might also be argued that Athenian law would not have forbidden marriages between siblings with the same mothers if women's contribution didn't count.) In general, however, it was the model of separate spheres which generated questions and organized thought on gender. Very little of this, mind you, took on men, except by implication: their roles and reputations were too much in accord with those of classicists and the worlds they inhabited to require research, to say nothing of explanation.

Scholars of the time were no more likely to mix their own public and private lives. Wilamowitz's memoirs, for example, contain next to nothing about his wife. They ascribed a like reticence to the Greeks and Romans; so Athenian vases displaying sexual acts—sometimes very vividly—were assumed to portray slaves or prostitutes (an assumption only recently assailed).[10] Consistently, it was the activities of those marginalized by the social and sexual norms of the day who attracted notice in print—prostitution and pederasty in particular. This attention might be painstaking; some retains its value today.[11] Hans Herter's account, here translated for the first time into English, still leads the list of authorities in the article on secular prostitution in the latest edition of the *Oxford Classical Dictionary*.[12] The survey of sexual vocabulary by Euios Lênaios (organized by body parts, sex acts, foreplay, and defecation) held the field until the studies by Jeffrey Henderson and James Adams;[13] the compilation of references to sexual positions assembled by F. K. Forberg has not been supplanted

[10] Against the asumption: M. F. Kilmer, *Greek Erotica on Attic Red-Figure Vases* (London 1993) 159–67.

[11] See the survey in D. M. Halperin, J. J. Winkler and F. I. Zeitlin (eds), *Before Sexuality: The Construction of Erotic Experience in the Ancient Greek World* (Princeton 1990) 7–13. The valuable research of Werner Krenkel, made available largely in articles published in *WZ Rostock*, is a contemporary continuation of this tradition. See, e.g., "Tonguing," *WZ Rostock*, 30 (1981) 37–54, and "Transvestismus in der Antike," *WZ Rostock*, 39.9 (1990) 144–57.

[12] *H. Herter, "Soziologie der antiken Prostitution im Lichte der heidnischen und christlichen Schrifttums," *JAC*, 3 (1960) 70–111. Significant studies in a recent flurry include M. Henry, *Menander's Courtesans and the Greek Comic Tradition* (Frankfurt 1985); C. Reinsberg, *Ehe, Hetärentum und Knabenliebe im antiken Griechenland* (Munich 1989); M. Beard and J. Henderson, "With this body I thee worship: sacred prostitution in antiquity," *Gender and History*, 9 (1997) 480–503; L. Kurke, "Inventing the *hetaira*: sex, politics and discursive conflict in archaic Greece," *Classical Antiquity*, 16 (1997) 106–50; J. Davidson, *Courtesans and Fishcakes: The Consuming Passions of Classical Athens* (London 1997); T. McGinn, *Prostitution, Sexuality and the Law in Ancient Rome* (New York 1998); B. Stumpp, *Prostitution in der römischen Antike* (Berlin 1998); R. Flemming, "*Quae corpore quaestum facit*: the sexual economy of female prostitution in the Roman Empire," *JRS*, 89 (1999) 38–61; J. DeFelice, *Roman Hospitality: The Professional Women of Pompeii* (Warren Center 2001).

[13] E. Lênaios, *Aporrhêta* (Thessalonica 1935); J. Henderson, *The Maculate Musè: Obscene Language in Attic Comedy* (New Haven 1975); J. N. Adams, *The Latin Sexual Vocabulary* (Baltimore 1982).

by Carole Marks's dissertation;[14] Theodor Hopfner's study of what
Greeks and Romans wrote about the human genitalia has no rival.[15]
But even this was often published pseudonymously (Euios Lênaios
was K. Kharitonides; Paul Brandt's *Sittengeschichte Griechenlands*
(1928), translated into English as *The Sexual Life of the Ancient
Greeks*, appeared under the name Hans Licht) or in languages which
were not widely read (Kharitonides' Modern Greek) or left unfinished
(both Hopfner and Kharitonides originally intended to extend their
studies). This was not the path to scholarly success.


II

A few pages based on a section of a Platonic dialog opened up a new
era.[16] Kenneth Dover was already a distinguished scholar, Professor
of Greek in the University of St Andrews and soon to deliver the
Sather Lectures on ancient literature at Berkeley. His article displayed
all his formidable philological rigor, examining vexed passages of
Aristophanes and disputed readings in Hesychius and Photius as well
as Plato. No less characteristically, it also demonstrated Dover's wide-
ranging reading and uncompromising common sense. ("It is possible
that Bethe's theory ... shows the influence ... of the belief in which
most modern Europeans have been brought up, that the choice
between different physical contexts for the sexual act is morally
important and that to prefer boys to girls, unlike a preference for
(e.g.) Turkish coffee, is an enrolment in the forces of darkness ... The
belief itself is neither universal nor inescapable" (42 n. 35).) Already
in 1964 Dover sounded the themes of his later publications: the centrality of Athenian law-court speeches; due attention to painted
pottery; distinctions of genre, context, class, between beliefs and
behaviors; the tendentious use of terms of personal abuse (such as
"prostitute") in political propaganda; and, above all, the contrast
between the older, active *erastês* and his passive junior partner in a

---

[14] F. K. Forberg, *Apophoreta* (Coburg 1824), originally published as a kind of loot- or
doggie-bag (*apophorêta*) to the main meal of a commentary on a mélange of Renaissance
Latin epigrams. A bilingual Latin and English version, *Manual of Classical Eratology*, was
published in a limited edition of 100 copies for Viscount Julian Smithson and friends at
Manchester in 1884. Lest one worry about the viscount and his friends, "Who may peruse it
as a means of awakening voluptuous sensations will be severely disappointed. Here we have
no curious erotic story born of a diseased mind, but a cold, relentless analysis of those human
passions which it is ever the object of Science to wrestle with and overthrow" (vi); M. C.
Marks, "Heterosexual Coital Position as a Reflection of Ancient and Modern Cultural
Attitudes", Dissertation (SUNY, Buffalo 1978).
[15] T. Hopfner, *Das Sexualleben der Griechen und Römer*. 1 (Prague 1938).
[16] K. J. Dover, "Eros and nomos (Plato, *Symposium* 182A-185C)," *Bulletin of the Institute
of Classical Studies*, 11 (1964) 31–42.

homosexual pair, the *erômenos*. These Dover saw as essentially two stages in the social development of a Greek citizen rather than as life-long identities. (In a later article, a contribution to an important *Arethusa* special issue on sex in antiquity, Dover followed his friend, the practising psychoanalyst George Devereux, in referring to "pseudo-homosexuality".)[17] All this reappeared fifteen years later in his magisterial *Greek Homosexuality* (London 1978, second edition 1989). The reduction and removal of social and legal hostility toward homoerotic acts, feminism and allied movements for which "the personal is the political"—these and the environment which engendered them obviously encouraged acceptance of Dover's approach. It would be wrong, however, to understate the authority afforded by his professional prestige. Dover's themes soon echoed, in Roman studies as well as Greek.[18] But his influence was nowhere more significant than in—and through—the work of Michel Foucault.[19]

In 1976, Foucault published the first of the six projected volumes of his history of sexuality.[20] Here he argued that sexuality is not an ahistorical constant but an invention of the eighteenth century. There is nothing natural about sexual instincts, their repression is a myth. On the contrary, sexuality, the idea of sex, is a cultural creation which imposes itself on bodies, a means to force individuals into predetermined categories in order to control them. (As in his earlier work, Foucault is interested in the dialectic of knowledge and power.) The body parts, sensory phenomena, and moral issues which make up sexuality for us today belong, in different places and times, to other, often quite separate discourses, which may combine sex with apparently unconnected areas of life. For the Greeks and Romans, for example, sex posed problems like those linked to hunger, thirst, the desire for sleep. By the time he narrowed his focus to the classical Greek world, Foucault had read Dover and assimilated many of his conclusions: homosexual and heterosexual desire were identical in kind (so that the use of this modern terminology can only mislead); excess (lack of

---

[17] *K. J. Dover, "Classical Greek attitudes to sexual behaviour," *Arethusa*, 6 (1973) 59–73; G. Devereux, "Greek pseudo homosexuality and the 'Greek miracle,'" *Symbolae Osloenses*, 42 (1967) 69–92.

[18] See, e.g., for the active/passive distinction, M. B. Skinner, "Parasites and strange bedfellows: a study in Catullus' political imagery," *Ramus*, 8 (1979) 137–52; for the interaction of sexual self-presentation and political policy, J. P. Hallett, "Perusinae glandes and the changing image of Augustus," *American Journal of Ancient History*, 2 (1977) 151–71.

[19] For a critical account of Dover's work and of its influence on Foucault, see J. Davidson, "Dover, Foucault and Greek homosexuality: penetration and the truth of sex," *Past and Present*, 170 (2001) 3–51.

[20] M. Foucault, *Histoire de la sexualité. 1. La volonté de savoir* (Paris 1976) = *The History of Sexuality. 1. An Introduction* (trans. R. Hurley: New York 1978).

self-control) and passivity (falling under another's control) were the main forms of sexual immorality for men.[21] For their part, the Romans of the Empire were troubled by romantic attachments with citizen boys, and so elevated the reciprocal relationship of the married couple.[22] (Here, Foucault owed much to his colleague at the Collège de France, Paul Veyne.)[23] Each, for Foucault, represented a turning point in the career of the hero of his story, man the desirer.

Made his own by "one of the greatest thinkers of our age," "one of the great intellectual figures of the twentieth century," these ideas were in turn taken over and transmitted by gifted and engaged scholars like Jack Winkler and David Halperin.[24] As Marilyn Skinner put it, "Foucault's account of ancient sexual protocols became all but universal among specialists in Graeco-Roman culture on this side [the US] of the Atlantic ... Classicists now found themselves unexpectedly poised on the cutting edge of radical philosophic inquiry. It was a heady feeling, and it galvanized the field."[25] Dominance and submission were now the marks of gender; and behaviors, real or imagined, in what was once regarded as private life were seen to mirror or establish public position. Sexual intercourse, then, took on a new significance as a guide to gender definition in antiquity. Men and women were no longer self-evidently distinct; they were created and confirmed through intimate interactions. These tended to replicate all too visible public patterns. But a boy or even an adult male could be feminized by penetration; and too much virility—Heracles', Marc Antony's—could pass over into its opposite, service to a women's strength.[26] Behavior might betray biology. So much for separation. No wonder, then, that ancient medical

[21] M. Foucault, *Histoire de la sexualité. 2. L'usage des plaisirs* (Paris 1984) = *The History of Sexuality. 2. The Use of Pleasure* (trans. R. Hurley: New York 1984).

[22] M. Foucault, *Histoire de la sexualité. 3. Le souci de soi* (Paris 1984) = *The History of Sexuality. 3. The Care of the Self* (trans. R. Hurley: New York 1986).

[23] P. Veyne, "La famille et l'amour sous le haut-empire romain," *Annales,* 33 (1978) 35–63; "L'homosexualité à Rome," *Communications,* 35 (1982) 26–33.

[24] Quotations: J. J. Winkler, *The Constraints of Desire: The Anthropology of Sex and Gender in Ancient Greece* (New York 1990) 3; D. Larmour, P. A. Miller and C. Platter, "Situating *The History of Sexuality,*" in D. Larmour, P. A. Miller and C. Platter (eds), *Rethinking Sexuality: Foucault and Classical Antiquity* (Princeton 1998) 3–41 (at 34). Halperin's presentation of Foucault's ideas in *One Hundred Years of Homosexuality and Other Essays on Greek Love* (London and New York 1990) is the *locus classicus.*

[25] M. B. Skinner, "Zeus and Leda: the sexuality wars in contemporary classical scholarship," *Thamyris,* 3.1 (1996) 103–23 (at 106). The "sexuality wars"—and classicists' combat in them—sometimes spilled over into the courts, as when details of Greek lexicography and the correct reading of Plato's *Laws* figured in the Colorado Gay Rights Case; D. Mendelsohn, "The stand: expert witnesses and ancient mysteries in a Colorado courtroom," *Lingua Franca,* 6 (1996) 34–46.

[26] N. Loraux, "Herakles: the super-male and the feminine," in Halperin et al., *Before Sexuality,* 21–52; B. F. Russell, "The emasculation of Antony: the construction of gender in Plutarch's *Life of Antony,*" *Helios,* 25 (1998) 121–37.

science and biological theory insisted (sometimes in the teeth of the evidence) that there really was a distinctively male body, or even that there was only one real body type, the male, and that women's was a deviation and a deformity; a case of the gentleman doth protest too much.[27] A focus of feminist research—Ann Ellis Hanson contributed a translation of Hippocrates to the first volume of *Signs*—the medical writers, voluminous but overlooked during much of the twentieth century, came to the fore through Foucault's focus on the body.[28] Socialization too came in for study: how boys were taught to be men and why not to be women. Performance played an important part, the delivery of words as much as their drift.[29] At the same time, sex and gender emerged as never before as central concerns of classical scholarship. Now, male and female were everywhere entwined: gender-specific codes and hierarchies were seen to operate in each aspect of ancient culture. In the *Iliad*, direct oral transmission was male, mediated speech (written or oral) female; in Greco-Roman Egypt, men and women both transformed their bodies, but in different ways (men more permanently); women's spells were meant to retain affection, while erotic magic to arouse lust was the instrument of men (a status courtesans, women of initiative, might claim as they used it to attract clients); ancient botanists ascribed gender to trees differently than we do today, on the basis not only of which produce fruit, but also of the character of their wood: male trees are tougher and knottier, females easier to warp and control (and therefore—an interesting consequence—more useful).[30]

---

[27] E.g., *L. Dean-Jones, "The cultural construct of the female body in classical Greek science," in S. B. Pomeroy (ed.), *Women's History and Ancient History* (Chapel Hill and London 1991) 111–37.

[28] A. E. Hanson, "Hippocrates: Diseases of Women 1," *Signs*, 1 (1975) 567–84. Other important work of this period includes A. Rousselle, "Observation féminine et idéologie masculine: le corps de la femme d'après les médecins grecs," *Annales(ESC)*, 35 (1980) 1089–115, S. Campese, P. Manuli, and G. Sissa (eds), *Madre materia: sociologia e biologia della donna greca* (Turin 1983), D. Gourevitch, *Le mal d'être femme* (Paris 1984). See the discussion in N. Demand, "Gender studies and history: participation and power," in S. M. Burstein, R. MacMullen, K. A. Raaflaub, and A. M. Ward, *Current Issues and the Study of Ancient History* (Publications of the Association of Ancient Historians 7: Claremont, CA, 2002) 31–43.

[29] M. W. Gleason, *Making Men: Sophists and Self-Presentation in Ancient Rome* (Princeton 1985); *A. Richlin, "Gender and rhetoric: producing manhood in the schools," in W. J. Dominik (ed.), *Roman Eloquence: Rhetoric in Society and Literature* (London and New York 1997) 90–110; A. M. Keith, *Engendering Rome: Women in Latin Epic* (Cambridge 2000).

[30] K. Bassi, "Orality, masculinity and the Greek epic," *Arethusa*, 30 (1997) 315–40; D. Montserrat, *Sex and Society in Graeco-Roman Egypt* (London and New York 1996) 61–79; C. Faraone, *Ancient Greek Love Magic* (Cambridge, MA, 1999); C. G. Tortzen, "Male and female in Peripatetic botany," *Classic et Medivalia*, 42 (1991) 81–110; L. Foxhall, "Natural sex: the attribution of sex and gender to plants in ancient Greece," in L. Foxhall and J. Salmon (eds), *Thinking Men: Masculinity and its Self-Representation in the Classical Tradition* (London and New York 1998) 57–70; M. Negbi, "Male and female in Theophrastus's botanical works," *Journal of the History of Biology*, 28 (1995) 317–32.

There is no question, then, of the influence of Foucault and his many followers. But there have been skeptics too. Some, inevitably, have charged that the master has been misunderstood; hostile critics claim that Foucault has been trivialized to be made palatable, admirers refine his purpose—the history of formal discourses and institutions rather than of popular attitudes or acts, philosophical speculation rather than history at all.[31] ("The French themselves realize that Parisian theory is an art form; the Americans, poor lambs, take it seriously.")[32] More telling for us are responses which affect our understanding of the Greek and Roman worlds; sometimes, of course, these have more far-reaching implications as well. Already in *Before Sexuality*, the 1990 volume which brought together some of the most attractive studies Foucault influenced or inspired, Peter Brown argued that early Christians conceived of sexuality as the inmost secret of the human heart in a way much more modern than Foucault's periodization would allow.[33] Thomas Habinek later located the invention of homosexuality in the ancient precursor of the modern metropolis—Augustan Rome. In this cosmopolitan environment too we find an exchange economy, "the isolation of sex as a topic for analysis, the privileging of sexual pleasure as a criterion of personal fulfilment, the constitution of distinctive sexual identities based on object choice, the association of sex with privacy, the professionalization of advice about sex."[34] Foucault missed this, but then Foucault, insofar as he got Rome at all—a sore spot for specialists— got it wrong. So the supposed shift from pederasty to married partnership is an artefact of Foucault's selection of sources and chronological vagueness.[35]

In this case, Foucault may postulate a change which did not occur; in general, however, it is his failure to draw distinctions which vitiates his work—he was after all sketching in broad strokes. Athens was not all of Greece; even there, the classical period diverged from the archaic, the fourth century from the fifth; vases and literary sources

---

[31] E.g., B. Thornton, "*Idolon theatri*: Foucault and the classicists," *CML*, 12 (1991) 81–100; D. M. Halperin, "Forgetting Foucault: acts, identities, and the history of sexuality," *Representations*, 63 (1998) 93–120; Larmour et al., "Situating *The History of Sexuality*."

[32] R. Wright, *A Scientific Romance* (Toronto 1997). For the record, this volume's editors are Australian and Canadian.

[33] P. Brown, "Bodies and minds: sexuality and renunciation in early Christianity," in Halperin et al., *Before Sexuality*, 479–93; cf. D. Cohen, "Sex, gender and sexuality in ancient Greece," *Classical Philology*, 87 (1992) 145–60 (at 159).

[34] T. Habinek, "The invention of sexuality in the world of Rome," in T. Habinek and A. Schiesaro (eds), *The Roman Cultural Revolution* (Cambridge 1997) 23–43 (at 27).

[35] D. Cohen and R. Saller, "Foucault on sexuality in Greco-Roman antiquity," in J. Goldstein (ed.), *Foucault and the Writing of History* (Oxford 1994) 35–59, especially 44–55.

conflict; varying views prevailed in terrain which was contested as it is today; class counts.³⁶ Above all, Foucault assimilates Rome to Greece. Yet the late Republic may (as Habinek suggests) have witnessed the development of a homosexual subculture, self-conscious and identifiable, flamboyantly flaunting distinctive dress, hairstyles, gestures, with its own haunts and habits. Some in this demi-monde were pathics; others, perhaps many others, enjoyed reciprocal relationships in which patterns of penetration were not essential markers of status but irrelevant or transitory.³⁷ The dichotomy of active and passive and the hierarchy it expressed have been called into question elsewhere too. Symmetrical pairings may appear in the ancient novel.³⁸ Even in classical Athens, supposedly passive partners perhaps derived pleasure from vigorous and active movement.³⁹ It may be that a more nuanced formulation is needed for Greece too; "Greek values are better thought of as a multidimensional grid rather than as a simple dichotomy."⁴⁰ But it is only for Rome from the late Republic on that the subjectivity of a sexual subculture can be perceived as a challenge to contemporary norms as well as to modern constructions of them.

Finally, in the process of refashioning gender, Foucault elides women. Modern feminists find their work ignored or incorporated without acknowledgment.⁴¹ Ancient women are not desiring subjects

³⁶ Athenocentrism: Cohen and Saller, "Foucault," 37–8; Periodization: J. Boardman, "The phallos-bird in archaic and classical Greek art," *Revue archéologique*, 1992 (2), 227–42; E. C. Keuls, "The Greek medical texts and the sexual ethos of ancient Athens," in P. J. van der Eijk, H. E. J. Horstmanshoff, and P. H. Schrijvers (eds), *Ancient Medicine in its Socio-Cultural Context. 1* (Amsterdam and Athens, GA, 1995) 261–73; R. W. Wallace, "On not legislating sexual conduct in fourth-century Athens," in G. Thür and J. Vélissaropoulos-Karakostas (eds), *Symposion 1995* (Cologne 1997) 151–66. Genre: M. F. Kilmer, "Painters and pederasts: ancient art, sexuality and social history," in M. Golden and P. Toohey (eds), *Inventing Ancient Culture: Historicism, Periodization and the Ancient World* (London and New York 1997) 36–49; C. Calame, *The Poetics of Eros in Ancient Greece* (trans. J. Lloyd: Princeton 1999) 65–88. Varying views: *D. Cohen, "Law, society and homosexuality in classical Athens," *Past and Present*, 117 (1987) 3–21; J. Roy, "An alternative sexual morality for classical Athens," *Greece and Rome*, 44 (1997) 11–22. Class: *J. R. Clarke, *Looking at Lovemaking: Constructions of Sexuality in Roman Art 100 B.C.–A.D. 250* (Berkeley and Los Angeles 1998) 91–118.
³⁷ Much of the debate here has focused on those described as *cinaedi*: see especially A. Richlin, "Not before homosexuality: the materiality of the *cinaedus* and the Roman law against love between men," *Journal of the History of Sexuality*, 3 (1993) 523–573; R. Taylor, "Two pathic sub-cultures in ancient Rome," *Journal of the History of Sexuality*, 7 (1997) 319–71; H. N. Parker, "The teratogenic grid," in J. P. Hallett and M. B. Skinner (eds), *Roman Sexualities* (Princeton 1997) 47–65; C. A. Williams, *Roman Homosexuality: Ideologies of Masculinity in Classical Antiquity* (New York and Oxford 1999) 175–93, 206–18.
³⁸ D. Konstan, *Sexual Symmetry: Love in the Ancient Novel and Related Genres* (Princeton 1994); S. Goldhill, *Foucault's Virginity: Ancient Erotic Fiction and the History of Sexuality* (Cambridge 1995).
³⁹ Davidson, *Courtesans and Fishcakes*, 168–82, 253–5.
⁴⁰ Demand, *Birth*, 128.
⁴¹ A. Richlin, "Zeus and Metis: Foucault, feminism, classics," *Helios*, 18 (1991) 160–80; cf. her *The Garden of Priapus*, 2nd edn (New York 1992) xiii–xxxiii.

like men, or are too much so, taken to experience and configure sex just like them, as a masque of power and position.[42] So women, like men, valued the virginity of their partners.[43] Female homoeroticism may fail to register because penetration has no (or less) place; besides, women have no status and so aren't relevant in themselves to a discourse of dominance.[44] In response, Sappho and her friends have figured as prototypes of reciprocal relationships; Sulpicia uses the story of Dido to subvert the protocols of sexual conduct for Roman women.[45]

Sappho and Sulpicia, of course, are two of the very few ancient women who can speak for themselves on this subject. Others' voices may be available nevertheless. Myths of goddesses and their mortal lovers can be read as parallels to the ritual celebration of women's sexual and reproductive power at the Greek Thesmophoria; the belief that women must emit a seed at orgasm to ensure conception may seem simply to mimic men's sexuality—but it has a surprising origin, in wives' wish to persuade their husbands to care for their sexual pleasure.[46] These suggestions should be placed in the broader context of work to recover women's sentiments and ideas:[47] in the goods they likely deposited in graves, in an alternative version of the myth of the Lemnian women, in the story of the midwife Hagnodice, in the use of the metronymic and other turns of speech, in Plutarch's *Lives* of

[42] M. A. Katz, "Sexuality and the body in ancient Greece," *Metis*, 4.1 (1989) 155–79 (especially 167–77); L. Dean-Jones, "The politics of pleasure: female sexual appetite in the Hippocratic Corpus," *Helios*, 19 (1992) 72–91.

[43] J. Triantaphyllopoulos, "Virginité et défloration masculine," in B. G. Mandilaras (ed.), *Proceedings of the XVIII International Congress of Papyrology, Athens, 25–31 May 1986. 2* (Athens 1988) 327–33.

[44] H. King, "Sowing the field: Greek and Roman sexology," in R. Porter and M. Teich (eds), *Sexual Knowledge, Sexual Science: The History of Attitudes to Sexuality* (Cambridge 1994) 29–46 (especially 30–1). Foucault here replicates the silence of our sources, who generally ignore sexual relations between women or stress their strangeness—long ago, literally outlandish (the Romans thought them Greek), dependent on physical deformations. See J. P. Hallett, "Female homoeroticism and the denial of Roman reality in Latin literature," *Yale Journal of Criticism*, 3.1 (1989) 209–27 (= Hallett and Skinner, *Roman Sexualities*, 255–73).

[45] E. S. Stigers, "Sappho's private world," in H. P. Foley (ed.), *Reflections of Women in Antiquity* (New York 1981) 45–61; A. M. Keith, "*Tandem venit amor*: a Roman woman speaks of love," in Hallett and Skinner, *Roman Sexualities*, 295–310.

[46] Winkler, *Constraints*, 180–209; Rousselle, "Observation féminine"; cf. Rousselle, *Porneia: On Desire and the Body in Antiquity* (trans. F. Pheasant: Cambridge, MA, 1988) 27–9. A passage from Boswell's diary indicates that mutual sexual pleasure need not challenge the dominance of the male partner: "[T]here cannot be higher felicity on earth enjoyed by man than the participation of genuine amorous affection with an amiable woman. There he has a full indulgence of all the delicate feelings and pleasures both of body and mind, while ... he exults with a consciousness that he is the superior person." (F. A. Pottle [ed.], *Boswell's London Journal 1762–1763* [London and New Haven 1950] 84).

[47] *L. Foxhall, "Pandora unbound: a feminist critique of Foucault's *History of Sexuality*," in A. Cornwall and M. Lindisfarne (eds), *Dislocating Masculinity: Comparative Ethnographies* (London and New York 1994) 133–46.

Agis and Cleomenes, in ritual laments.[48] Even their silences have been made to speak for them (in David Schaps's argument that women, unlike slaves, did not rebel or run away when their cities were threatened by war).[49]

These examples are Greek. How much more might we wish for the words of the Roman women who schooled their sons in political leadership (Cornelia), demonstrated against the Oppian Law, took on the triumvirs ("Thuria"), spoke in court (Hortensia), raised armies and appeared at their head (Fulvia).[50] But this brings us back to the relation of the public and the private, an old issue on which much has since been said.

## III

The model of separate spheres—women relegated to private space, the public a male preserve—never worked particularly well for Rome. The system of nomenclature, by which women bore a form of their birth family's name throughout their lives, is emblematic of the porosity of the divide. In addition, their control of property combined with high mortality and delay in both male marriage and eligibility for high office to ensure that they influenced electoral coalitions and political alliances in the public world from which they were formally excluded. Their *imagines* were displayed at family

[48] Grave goods: S. Houby-Nielsen, "Grave gifts, women and conventional values in Hellenistic Athens," in P. Bilde, T. Engberg-Pedersen, L. Hennestad, and J. Zahle (eds), *Conventional Values of the Hellenistic Greeks* (Aarhus 1997) 220–62. Lemnian women: S. Jackson, "Myrsilus of Methymna and the dreadful smell of the Lemnian women," *ICS*, 15 (1990) 77–83. Hagnodice: H. King, "Agnodike and the profession of medicine," *Proceedings of the Cambridge Philological Society*, 32 (1986) 53–75. Women's speech: M. B. Skinner, "Greek women and the metronymic: a note on an epigram by Nossis," *Ancient History Bulletin*, 1 (1987) 39–42; J. N. Adams, "Female speech in Latin comedy," *Antichthon*, 18 (1984) 43–77; A. H. Sommerstein, "The language of Athenian women," in F. De Martino and A. H. Sommerstein (eds), *Lo spettacolo delle voci* (Bari 1995) 2.61–85; L. McClure, *Spoken Like a Woman: Speech and Gender in Athenian Drama* (Princeton 1999); A. Lardinois and L. McClure (eds), *Making Silence Speak: Women's Voices in Greek Literature and Society* (Princeton 2001). Plutarch: A. Powell, "Spartan women assertive in politics? Plutarch's *Lives* of Agis and Cleomenes," in S. Hodkinson and A. Powell (eds), *Sparta: New Perspectives* (London 1999) 393–419. Laments: G. Holst-Warhaft, *Dangerous Voices: Women's Laments and Greek Literature* (London and New York 1992).

[49] D. M. Schaps, "The women of Greece in wartime," *Classical Philology*, 77 (1982) 193–213. The argument would be more convincing if Archidamus's army had advanced on Athens with banners taken from an International Women's Day march. In this case, silence is indeed telling.

[50] Cf. M. B. Skinner, "Introduction: *quod multo fit aliter in Graecia* …," in Hallett and Skinner, *Roman Sexualities*, 3–25. For two interesting attempts to uncover women's words in male-authored texts, see A. Richlin, "Julia's jokes, Galla Placidia, and the Roman use of women as political icons," in B. Garlick, S. Dixon, and P. Allen (eds), *Stereotypes of Women in Power* (New York 1992) 63–91, and her "Pliny's brassiere," in Hallett and Skinner, *Roman Sexualities*, 197–220.

funerals, funerals at which eulogies of their own qualities might be made the basis of their male relatives' appeals for prominence. Even their homes had public areas, the *atrium* which welcomed clients and allies, the *cubiculum* which did duty both as a place for interaction with outsiders and as the most intimate and secret of hideaways.[51] This was a world in which politics invaded the home. Conversely, male genitalia were paraded in public spectacles and incorporated into the design of the city (as in Augustus's Forum); "the physical expression of phallocracy was thus at all times potentially monumental, tangible or ubiquitous."[52]

For Greece too the model is increasingly problematic.[53] Archaeology cannot substantiate literary traces of the *gynaikôn* or *gynaikônitis*, the women's quarters, where they were once believed to be kept closely confined. Space within the house was more fluid, separation a matter of cues rather than keys, male visitors controlled instead of the women of the house;[54] and, as always, the more members of this society understood the conventions, the more they could play with or against them (as vase painters do).[55] In some respects, in fact, house design may have brought women out into the open, on the roof tops where they tended the gardens of Adonis ("a stage for female privilege within sight, but beyond the reach, of the dominant society"), on the balconies which brought access to the air and the eyes of others.[56] Not that Greek

[51] A. Wallace-Hadrill, "The social structure of the Roman house," *Papers of the British School at Rome*, 56 (1988) 43–97; A. M. Riggsby, "'Public' and 'private' in Roman culture: the use of the *cubiculum*," *JRA*, 10 (1997) 38–56.

[52] *B. Kellum, "Concealing/revealing: gender and the play of meaning in the monuments of Augustan Rome," in T. Habinek and A. Schiesaro (eds), *The Roman Cultural Revolution* (Cambridge 1997) 158–81; cf. E. C. Keuls, *The Reign of the Phallus: Sexual Politics in Ancient Athens* (New York 1985) especially 65–97; quotation: D. Montserrat, "Reading gender in the Roman world," in J. Huskinson (ed.), *Experiencing Rome: Culture, Identity and Power in the Roman Empire* (London 2000) 153–81 (at 170).

[53] D. Cohen, *Law, Sexuality and Society: The Enforcement of Morals in Classical Athens* (Cambridge 1991) 70–97; J. Roy, "*Polis* and *oikos* in classical Athens," *Greece and Rome*, 46 (1999) 1–18.

[54] L. Nevett, "Separation or seclusion? Towards an archaeological approach to investigating women in the Greek household in the fifth to third centuries B.C.," in M. Parker Pearson and C. Richards (eds), *Architecture and Order* (London and New York 1994) 98–112, and "Gender relations in the classical Greek household: the archaeological evidence," *ABSA*, 90 (1995) 363–81; *I. Morris, "Archaeology and gender ideologies in early archaic Greece," *Transactions of the American Philological Association*, 129 (1999) 305–17; L. Nevett, "Continuity and change in Greek households under Roman rule: the role of women in the domestic context," in E. N. Ostenfeld (ed.), *Greek Romans and Roman Greeks* (Aarhus 2002), 81–97.

[55] *F. Lissarrague, "Satyres chez les femmes," in P. Veyne, F. Lissarrague, and F. Frontisi-Ducroux, *Les mystères du gynécée* (Paris 1998) 179–98.

[56] J. D. Reed, "The sexuality of Adonis," *Classical Antiquity*, 14 (1995) 317–47 (at 346); C. M. Antonaccio, "Architecture and behavior: building gender into Greek houses," *Classical World*, 93 (2000) 517–33.

women were housebound; Aristotle knew that this was impossible for poor families—the vast majority—and modern scholarship has finally caught up.[57] Class is not the only relevant factor: women must have been more prominent in wartime (a few months of almost every year), country women surely worked their families' fields.[58] Distance from the metropolis and the fashions it brought into being must have contributed here. Why does Cnemon's daughter (almost alone among the women of Greek literature) help her father farm in Menander's *Dyscolus*? Yes, she needs to be outside so that the passing stranger can fall in love with her at first sight, and her willingness to pitch in does her credit. It is also relevant, however, that Cnemon's property is at the very edge of Attica, far from neighbors and the norms they might try to uphold.

More fundamentally, much depends on just how the public sphere is defined; we should not forget the tendentious context of its modern origins. It suits us, in our largely secular societies, to begin an investigation of public life with politics, law, the economy, and then to touch on religion as an afterthought, an exception. Even Sarah Pomeroy's *Goddesses, Whores, Wives and Slaves* (New York 1975), a pathbreaker which is still a stimulating synthesis, leaves religion to the end of the chapter on women and the city of Athens and to the last of the chapters on Rome. Yet the gods and their worship pervaded the ancient city; Athens had some 150 festival days a year. And women were inseparable from Greek religion, not just as participants (as in the Panathenaea, where their domestic arts of cooking, weaving, cleaning were shown to serve the *polis*'s patron deity), but in central roles, as priestesses.[59] To be sure, men monopolized the sacrificial act and might choose priestesses and manage their cults. But (despite some modern doubts) women could share in the sacrificial meal.[60] Nor were they cyphers—the priestess Theano refused to curse Alcibiades despite a decree of the people (Plut. *Alcib.* 22.4); others merited proud memorials, conspicuous on the roads that led

---

[57] *B. Wagner-Hasel, "Frauenleben in orientalischer Abgeschlossenheit? Zur Geschichte und Nutzamwendung eines Topos," *AU*, 32.2 (1989) 18–29; Cohen, *Law*, 149–54.

[58] W. Scheidel, "The most silent women of Greece and Rome: rural labour and women's life in the ancient world," *Greece and Rome*, 42 (1995) 202–17, 43 (1996) 1–10.

[59] M. R. Lefkowitz, "Women in the Panathenaic and other festivals," in J. Neils (ed.), *Worshipping Athena: Panathenaia and Parthenon* (Madison 1996) 78–91; U. Kron, "Priesthoods, dedications and euergetism: what part did religion play in the political and social status of Greek women?," in P. Hellström and B. Alroth (eds), *Religion and Power in the Ancient Greek World: Proceedings of the Uppsala Symposium 1993* (Uppsala 1996) 139–82 (BOREAS 24).

[60] R. Osborne, "Women and sacrifice in classical Greece," *Classical Quarterly*, 43 (1993) 393–405.

Introduction

to the center of Athens. And in some cases, such as that of the Delphic oracle, male managers may have had a more minor role than modern scholars presume.[61] Perhaps our definition of democracy itself should be broadened to let women in, as full members of the households which made it up and the families which knit it together.[62] One effect of Pericles' law is worth noting here: its recognition of women's role in creating citizens brought them new prominence on Attic grave reliefs, where private, domestic activities were now more frequently offered up for public view.[63] One last consideration: this is a realm in which women's subjectivity is bound to matter a great deal. Did Athenian women (for example) think of themselves as citizens?[64] Did ancient women separate public and private like their men? After all, Athenian husbands apparently tended to think of their wives as outsiders in the *oikos* and, by the late Republic, most wives were not members of their husband's *familia* according to that most masculine of discourses, Roman law.[65] For all that, divorce was not a casual matter at Athens and family sentiment at Rome was not dictated by the law; on the contrary, it modified it in some respects.[66] Women must have had a hand in shaping these realities. But how? And how much?

While the public and private spheres have been brought closer together and seen to interpenetrate in more recent research, the bipolar model of two starkly opposed genders has come in for question as well. For a start, one of the poles, long taken as a fixed point against which the other was measured, now appears just as notional, contingent, and man-made. To the many collections devoted to women in Greece and Rome we can now add a few on men and masculinity, though not enough yet to fill a shelf (much less a room of their own).[67] Far from being fixed, the male ideal now seems to shift

---

[61] L. Maurizio, "Anthropology and spirit possession: a reconsideration of the Pythia's role at Delphi," *Journal of Hellenic Studies*, 115 (1995) 69–86.
[62] M. A. Katz, "Women and democracy in ancient Greece," in T. M. Falkner, N. Felson, and D. Konstan (eds), *Contextualizing Classics: Ideology, Performance, Dialogue. Essays in Honor of John J. Peradotto* (Lanham 1999) 41–68.
[63] R. Osborne, "Law, the democratic citizen and the presentation of women in classical Athens," *Past and Present*, 155 (1997) 3–33.
[64] D. M. Schaps, "What was free about a free Athenian woman?," *Transactions of the American Philological Association*, 128 (1998) 161–88.
[65] J. Gardner, "Aristophanes and male anxiety—the defence of the *oikos*," *Greece and Rome*, 36 (1989) 51–62.
[66] L. Cohn-Haft, "Divorce in classical Athens," *Journal of Hellenic Studies*, 115 (1995) 1–14; S. Dixon, *The Roman Family* (Baltimore and London 1992) 45–60.
[67] See especially the two edited by L. Foxhall and J. Salmon: *When Men Were Men: Masculinity, Power and Identity in Classical Antiquity* and *Thinking Men: Masculinity and its Self-Representation in the Classical Tradition* (both London and New York 1998).

over time: weeping unashamed in Homer, bidden to check unmanly tears at Socrates' deathbed, now a commander and man of action, now a cultured rhetorician.[68] It may also spill over from one social class to another.[69] As with women, cultural blinkers may sometimes impair the view: in our desire to envisage ancient medicine as gendered in ways we are used to, we may both read imaginary midwives into Hippocratic texts and overlook the evidence for caregiving men.[70]

Equally important in the work of the last ten years are the various strategies researchers have identified to blur or transcend the polarity itself. For instance, the dead have no gender: men and women are owed the same ritual and an identical period of mourning (whereas adults and children are treated differently and living mourners have very clear gender roles).[71] Divinities play by their own rules. Athena is a warrior, Demeter a loving mother only to Kore and Hera an indifferent one to Hephaestus; "a goddess is not an incarnation of the feminine yet she often represents a purified, and even more often a displaced, form of femininity."[72] Even one of the most famous figures of nineteenth-century scholarship on gender, the mother goddess of Mediterranean matriarchy, may be less maternal and more multifaceted than she once seemed.[73] As for gods, Dionysus is associated with the phallus, freedom from social constraints, and the sex play of satyrs, but he is himself asexual or bisexual or anyhow unaffected by

---

[68] H. van Wees, "A brief history of tears: gender differentiation in archaic Greece," in Foxhall and Salmon, *When Men*, 10–53; R. Alston, "Arms and the man: soldiers, masculinity and power in Republican and Imperial Rome," in Foxhall and Salmon, *When Men*, 205–23; cf. H. Moxnes, "Conventional values in the Hellenistic world: masculinity," in Bilde et al., *Conventional Values*, 263–84.

[69] R. Osborne, "Sculpted men of Athens: masculinity and power in the field of vision," in Foxhall and Salmon, *Thinking Men*, 23–42.

[70] H. King, *Hippocrates' Woman: Reading the Female Body in Ancient Greece* (London and New York 1998) 172–87; R. H. Steinberg, "The nurturing male: bravery and bedside manners in Isocrates' *Aegineticus*," *Greece and Rome*, 47 (2000) 172–85.

[71] R. Lizzi, "Il sesso e i morti," in F. Hinard (ed.), *La mort au quotidien dans le monde romain: Actes du colloque organisé par l'Université de Paris IV (Paris—Sorbonne 7–9 octobre 1993)* (Paris 1995) 49–68.

[72] N. Loraux, "What is a goddess?," in P. Schmitt Pantel (ed.), *A History of Women in the West. 1. From Ancient Goddesses to Christian Saints* (trans. A. Goldhammer: Cambridge, MA, 1992) 11–44 (quotation: 43). Cf. Sparky Anderson's description of the statuesque slugger José Canseco: "He has the body of a Greek goddess."

[73] *L. E. Talalay, "A feminist boomerang: the Great Goddess of Greek prehistory," *Gender and History*, 6 (1994) 165–83. See also M. W. Conkey and R. E. Tringham, "Archaeology and the Goddess: exploring the contours of feminist archaeology," in D. C. Stanton and A. J. Stewart (eds), *Feminisms and the Academy* (Ann Arbor 1995) 199–247; L. Meskell, "Goddesses, Gimbutas and new age archaeology," *Antiquity*, 69 (1995) 74–86; B. A. Olsen, "Women, children and the family in the late Aegean Bronze Age: differences in Minoan and Mycenaean constructions of gender," *World Archaeology*, 29 (1998) 380–92; L. Goodison and C. Morris (eds), *Ancient Goddesses* (Madison 1999).

the desires and doings of his devotees.[74] Nicole Loraux's interest in psychoanalysis has made her one of the most interesting essayists in this area. She puts the issue as follows: "Greek formulations of the difference between the sexes must be approached via the notion of exchange: all exchange between the sexes, and not only inversion ... or even the exchange that operates by the mixing of opposites and the blurring of all boundaries."[75]

Dionysus, of course, is a cross-dresser. His playing the other may reflect an initiation rite for young men; adults, bearded symposiasts adorned as women on Attic vases, perhaps strive for social distinction.[76] Such transgendered disguise is a staple of Roman erotic elegy, where male poets often put on the *persona* of their female lovers.[77] It was once most prominent on the ancient stage: women's parts were regularly played by men.[78] This practice may have allowed Athenian playwrights to present powerful women more persuasively (or more palatably) than they might otherwise do, and might make it easier for the men who made up all, most, or the most important part (the judges) of the audience to feel and be cleansed of the appropriate emotions. On this reading, it is essentially conservative.[79] Need this always be so? The actors, after all, are not the only ones for whom gender is a performance; we have already noted that this is widely accepted as characterizing Greeks and Romans in general. The play of gender, then, may challenge normative roles too.[80] Ironically, postmodern readings of this kind invite the response that they themselves merely reinforce a present-day orthodoxy of subversion.

It would be misleading to leave the impression that the study of sex

---

[74] *M. Jameson, "The asexuality of Dionysus," in T. H. Carpenter and C. A. Faraone (eds), *Masks of Dionysus* (Ithaca, NY, and London 1993) 44–64.

[75] N. Loraux, *The Experiences of Tiresias: The Feminine and the Greek Man* (trans. P. Wissing: Princeton 1995) 7.

[76] J. N. Bremmer, "Transvestite Dionysos," *Bucknell Review*, 43 (1999) 183–200; M. C. Miller, "Reexamining transvestism in archaic and classical Athens: the Zewadski stamnos," *American Journal of Archaeology*, 103 (1999) 223–53.

[77] M. B. Skinner, "*Ego mulier*: the construction of male sexuality in Catullus," *Helios*, 20 (1993) 107–30; M. Wyke, "Taking the woman's part: engendering Roman love elegy," in A. J. Boyle (ed.), *Roman Literature and Ideology: Ramus Essays for J. P. Sullivan* (Bendigo 1995) 110–28; S. Raval, "Cross-dressing and 'gender trouble' in the Ovidian corpus," *Helios*, 29 (2002) 149–72.

[78] The essential starting point is the work of Froma Zeitlin, now conveniently available in *Playing the Other: Gender and Society in Classical Greek Literature* (Chicago 1996) 341–416. See now S. O. Murray, "Gender-mixing roles, gender-crossing roles, and the sexuality of transgendered roles," *Reviews in Anthropology*, 31 (2002) 291–300.

[79] Cf. M. S. Cyrino, "Heroes in d(u)ress: transvestism and power in the myths of Herakles and Achilles," *Arethusa*, 11 (1998) 207–41.

[80] *B. Gold, "'Vested interests' in Plautus' *Casina*: cross-dressing in Roman comedy," *Helios*, 25 (1998) 17–29.

and gender in Greece and Rome is all image and representation.[81] Sometimes it is nature which blurs the categories. Perhaps one in 300,000 live births today is hermaphroditic, displaying a mixture of primary sexual determinants; our own unease and modern medicine work together to correct such anomalies at birth. The Greek and Roman myths and rituals of hermaphroditism are in part a kind of cover-up of a reality which must have had profound effects for some at least.[82] Eunuchs made up another third sex, most, in this instance, made, not born. Their services were real as well as symbolic.[83] The *galli*, castrated priests of Cybele, excited horror because of their transgression of sexual boundaries but nevertheless figured in a cult which was widely recognized and widespread. On the basis of parallels elsewhere (the priests of Inanna, the Native American *berdache*), it is suggested that they take on new social and economic roles which developed as communities with rigid divisions of labor according to gender became more complex.[84] Our final selection also attempts to link anomalies in sex and gender with reality, though here the cross-dressing eunuchs are Scythians and the realities are environmental and biological.[85] This again represents an old question reopened, the truth (if any) behind ancient traditions; Bachofen believed that matriarchy had given rise to myth. It may also reflect a reaction against the Foucauldian stress on discourse alone. This

[81] Cf. the comments on prostitution, a matter of sex and money whatever its symbolic weight for the Athenian citizen body, by E. E. Cohen, "'Whoring under contract': the legal context of prostitution in fourth-century Athens," in V. Hunter and J. Edmondson (eds), *Law and Social Status in Classical Athens* (Oxford 2000) 113–48.

[82] The classic treatment is M. Delcourt, *Hermaphrodite: Myths and Rites of the Bisexual Figure in Classical Antiquity* (trans. J. Nicholson: London 1961) (originally published in 1956). More recently: e.g., L. Brisson, *Le sexe incertain: androgynie et hermaphroditisme dans l'Antiquité gréco-romaine* (Paris 1997); A. Ajootian, "The only happy couple: hermaphrodites and gender," in A. O. Koloski-Ostrow and C. L. Lyons (eds), *Naked Truths: Women, Sexuality, and Gender in Classical Art and Archaeology* (London and New York 1997) 220–42; A. M. Keith, "Versions of epic masculinity in Ovid's *Metamorphoses*," in P. Hardie, A. Barchiesi, and S. Hinds (eds), *Ovidian Transformations: Essays on the Metamorphoses and its Reception* (Cambridge 1999) 214–39; G. Crifò, "'Prodigium' e diritto: il caso dell'ermafrodita," *Index,* 27 (1999) 113–20; K. Waldner, *Geburt und Hochzeit des Kriegers: Geschlecterdifferenz und Initiation in Mythos und Ritual der griechischen Polis* (Berlin 2000).

[83] P. Guyot, *Eunuchen als Sklaven und Freigelassene in der griechisch-römischen Antike* (Stuttgart 1980); W. Stevenson, "The rise of eunuchs in Greco-Roman antiquity," *Journal of the History of Sexuality,* 5 (1995) 495–511; Gleason, *Making Men,* 131–58; C. E. Dessen, "The figure of the eunuch in Terence's *Eunuchus*," *Helios,* 22 (1995) 123–39; A. Traina, "L'ambiguo sesso: il c.63 di Catullo," in N. Criniti (ed.), *Commune sermioni: Società e cultura della "Cisalpina" dopo l'anno mille* (Brescia 1998) 189–98.

[84] W. Roscoe, "Priests of the goddess: gender transgression in ancient religion," *History of Religions,* 35 (1996) 195–230.

[85]* E. Lieber, "The Hippocratic 'Airs, Waters, Places' on cross-dressing eunuchs: 'natural' yet also 'divine,'" in R. Wittern and P. Pellegrin (eds), *Hippokratische Medizin und antike Philosophie: Verhandlungen des VIII. Internationalen Hippokrates-Kolloquiums in Kloster Banz/Staffelstein vom 23. bis 28. September 1993* (Hildesheim 1993) 451–76.

article stands at the end, then, as a reminder of what a survey of scholars' ideas may too easily obscure: people as real as ourselves (somehow) experienced the pleasures and pains about which we theorize.

# PART 1

*Before Foucault: Prehistory*

# *1 Women in Classical Athens— Their Social Space: Ideal and Reality*†

## CHRISTINE SCHNURR-REDFORD

### translated by Hanne Sigismund Nielsen*

One path leading to the source of the topos of the seclusion of Greek women takes us back to the work of the Archbishop of Canterbury, Queen Anne's personal priest and primate of the English Church, John Potter (1674–1747). His *Archaeologia Graeca, Or The Antiquities of Greece* was published in English in 1699 and, in an unauthorized Latin translation, in Leiden in 1702. In the same year this version was included in the *Thesaurus antiquitatum Graecarum* by J. F. Gronovius. Which sources did Potter use? In the 1715 English edition he mentions the works of I. Meursius, Sir George Wheler, Isaak Tzetzes, C. Sigonius, Francis Rous, and the *Leges Atticae* of Samuel Petitus (1594–1643). It is evident from his mention of the latter three scholars and Meursius that he bases his discussion on the very first scholars who, by slowly working through the huge compilation of known sources, established the field of Greek antiquities. For this reason the list of primary literature in Potter's book is both abundant and diverse: his sources stretch from Homer to late antiquity and include the Bible. The thirteenth chapter, concentrating on Greek women, is written exclusively on the basis of (late) ancient sources. The frequent editions of Potter's work give a clear impression of its importance.

The topos of the seclusion of women was brought to the attention of scholars in continental Europe by the much-criticized German translation of Potter's work by the Protestant theologian J. J. Rambach (Halle 1775–1778). But Potter's English edition is very different from

---

† Originally published as *Frauen im klassischen Athen: Sozialer Raum und reale Bewegungsfreiheit* (Berlin 1996) 15–21.

* Professor Sigismund Nielsen wishes to acknowledge the assistance of the author of this article and of Milo Nikolic.

Rambach's German translation. The differences appear not only in the
additional appendices but also in the scholarly literature used. There
had been much German literature on this subject during the 76 years
between the two. For example, Rambach refers to a study by Ludwig
Wilhelm Iunius/Georg Heinrich Antastius, *De gynaeceis Graecorum*, a
dissertation from Leipzig (1745) that already relied heavily on Potter,
and to two other important earlier works. One is the dissertation
by Christoph Rahnisch entitled *De cura virginum apud veteres*
(Koenigsberg 1672), which should be considered the very first work on
the seclusion of Greek women. The other is Johann Philipp Pfeiffer's
*Antiquitatum Graecarum gentilium sacrarum, politicarum, militar-
ium et oeconomicarum* (1689), which came into being by unabashedly
copying Rahnisch. This is the first book to make an explicit mention
of the *Oriental* living conditions of Greek women.

   Potter, in his English edition of 1699, gives the impression that he is
influenced only by sources from (late) antiquity and that, where the
question of women is concerned, in the end we must go back to
Cornelius Nepos ("nor does she reside anywhere but within the interior of a house, which is called the *gynaeconitis*, where no one enters
except close relatives" (*Praefatio* 7)) and Plutarch: Potter begins his
chapter 13, "On the Confinement and Employments of their Women",
in the following way: "the barbarious Nations, and amongst them the
Persians especially, (saith ... Plutarch) were naturally jealous, clownish
and morose towards their Women, not only their wives, but their Slaves
and Concubines; whom they kept so strictly, that never any one saw
them beside their own Family: When at home they were cloyster'd up;
when they took a Journey, they were carried in Coaches, or Waggons,
close cover'd at the Top and on all sides". Although Potter distinguishes the Greeks from the "Persian rigor", Greek women were,
according to him, nevertheless confined to the remotest part of the
house in order to keep them away from male company. "To this end the
Grecian Houses were usually divided into two Parts ...", a presumption that excluded all other ways to explain the Greek habit of letting
the two sexes live apart. Likewise, the habit of having the women's
quarters on the second floor could only be thought of as a "Means to
keep them from Company". The room of young unmarried women
was equipped with "Locks and Bolts". If their husbands were jealous,
married women were kept in "perpetual Imprisonment". Finally,
women were guarded by *Gynaikonomoi* and eunuchs. This shows that
already in Potter's work all elements of the topos existed, but it had not
yet been reduced to a specific phrase or slogan.

   Rambach's work is a direct translation of Potter's study, plus appendices, and, particularly, references to scholarly literature. However, the errors in the translation are particularly significant, because they underscore a clear bias. The most serious misunderstanding, although it reinforces Potter's obvious conviction concerning the supervision of Greek women, is Rambach's equation of the English "guardian" with the German "Aufseher" (guard) instead of "Vormund" (guardian), even though in this context it is absolutely clear that only the legal expression "Vormund" is possible. Rambach's addendum, which states "that huge dogs were put on guard close to the *gynaeceum* in order to scare adulterers", has not been without effect. Molossian dogs have ever since been part of the argument concerning female seclusion. Likewise as well Rambach's newly added explanation that 'the Greeks found it necessary to watch over women and to reduce their possibilities of free movement because Greek men understood the frailty and many faults of the female sex' and that therefore it was very easy for it to become victims of seduction. This insertion was not likely to raise doubts about Potter's opinions.

All this, however, does not explain why C. de Pauw, in his *Recherches philosophiques sur les Grecs* (1787), finally formulated the idea of "clôture Asiatique", i.e. "Oriental seclusion". He seemed to be in need of scholarly precedent. Although Rambach is called upon as de Pauw's witness, the specific formula "Oriental seclusion" is not found at all — neither in Rambach's work nor in Potter's. Here seclusion has not yet taken on "Oriental" connotations. A closer reading of de Pauw's list of secondary literature is revealing. With the exception of the compilators S. Petitus, Sigonius, Meursius, Ubbo Emmius, and the *Thesaurus* of J. F. Gronovius, the major part of the list consists of authors of contemporary travel descriptions (*Reiseliteratur*). R. Chandler, R. Pococke, J. Spon, G. Wheler, von Riedesel, M. Guys, N. E. Kléman or Kleeman, M. Tournefort, and many others contributed significantly to a picture of Greece that described the conditions of the eighteenth century rather than those of ancient Greece. De Pauw did this because it was believed that the ancient sources could be supplemented by a comparison with contemporary sources. It would be interesting to study to what extent the idea of "Oriental" seclusion in scholarly works on ancient Greece was influenced by contemporary English, French, and later German travellers in Greece. It must be emphasized that these, for the most part, very subjective views found their way into scholarly discussion through the back door and yet were considered as important as the existing academic literature. Even Potter, who in his English edition very scrupulously based his study on ancient sources, refers to Sir George Wheler's *A Journey into Greece* dating to 1682.

To understand how the topos originated and solidified one has to acknowledge that contemporary travel literature drifted in and left an indelible mark.

If Richard Chandler's description of his travel to Athens under Turkish rule in *Travels in Asia Minor and Greece* (translated into German by Voss and Boie 1777) is taken into consideration, it is easy to imagine why ideas such as the following were proclaimed by the academic community in Germany:

> The liberty of the fair sex in Athens matches almost to the same degree that of the Turks. High walls guard their houses; the windows do not turn towards the street and are barred or shut with planks so that all sorts of communication, even eye contact, are avoided. The harem, or container of the Turkish women, is not only impossible to enter, but should not even be looked on from the street. If anyone approaches a Turkish woman when she goes out, he would offend. If an encounter cannot be avoided in the city, then the usual thing is to turn oneself towards the wall and stand still until she has passed without even looking at her. This is considered decent behaviour in Athens.

In this description it is almost impossible to determine whether these rules only apply to Turkish women. The emphasis on Greek women's lack of freedom in the initial part of the quote suggests strongly that they too lived in a container or a harem. Of young Greek women it is said: "neither prudence nor modesty allow the girl to be seen by men before she is married...and the Greek man would dismiss her with contempt if she by accident unveiled her face in his presence."

In Chandler's description of the Athenians of his own days three more interesting references to ancient times are found: "once in a while a Greek man invites a traveller to his *gynaeceum* or the room where the women of his household live. Inside the house they have, so to speak, been taken out of their shells and behave quite differently to how they do on the street. Now the young woman looks like Thetis ...." Using these ideas and descriptions in an eighteenth-century traveller's account facilitated the contamination of the classical sources. In eighteenth-century Athens there seems to have been a special part of the Greek house reserved for women. As these houses were found closely neighbouring the harems of the Turkish families, it seemed logical for the traveller to equate the *gynaeceum* and the harem. Moreover, this equivalence was most likely extrapolated to the ancient Athenian room, the *gynaikonitis*, and this would strongly influence its characterization as a prison etc.

In the following description of female education it is likewise not possible to find out whether Greek or Turkish women are at issue. It can hardly be accidental that we read:

in Athens the improvement of the soul and heart is not considered important for female education. Girls learn how to dance ... they learn to play the Turkish zither, the tympanon, ... and how to embroider ... It is looked upon as a miracle of cleverness and diligence to hear about a woman who could read and write. The Turk Osman Aga's mother ... was feared for her learning so that even her relative Achmet Aga was terrified of her when she paid her yearly visit to him.

Since the following bracketed quotation from Chandler could equally describe the conditions of ancient Athens ("normally a wife serves her husband and when she has prepared the dinner she eats perhaps with a female slave. Her husband does the shopping. He takes his dinner alone or in the company of other males"), it is quite understandable that, especially in the late eighteenth century, classical Athens was more and more closely identified with the East and its Oriental customs. At that time it was quite openly assumed that "the ancient sources could be supplemented ... by being compared with contemporary habits" (as Boeckh said as late as 1886).

Although it should not be considered part of classical scholarship, the book I am about to mention does represent the timbre of the historical scholarship of its time. I am speaking of Montesquieu's *De l'esprit des lois* (1748). This work was of major importance for the Enlightenment and for European *Geistesgeschichte* in general. It is, together with the travel literature, responsible for the change in how the life of Greek women was described as well as for the new *vocabulary* that in later times became dominant in the discussion of ancient Greek woman. Montesquieu's work forms a link between the very early works of Rahnisch, Pfeiffer and Potter from the seventeenth century (where all components of the later topos are found and the seclusion of women is actually described, although the formula of "Oriental seclusion" is not yet to be found) and the works of the late eighteenth century, which use the elaborated topos readily. In sum: De Pauw is the first to use the formulation "Oriental seclusion" and Rambach is not the inventor. De Pauw knows Montesquieu's writings, which describe the phenomenon of confining Oriental women.

How is the new idea that Montesquieu brings into the discussion to be described? It is not what he says about Athenian women as citizens of a republic, but more what he says about their counterparts, namely women living under a despotic rule. According to Montesquieu these women not only introduced luxury but were themselves luxury articles [...] Within the boundaries of his seemingly new teaching concerning the influence of the climate (he believes he can trace Nature even in the most recondite of legislation)

he examines the character of the Orient and its inhabitants. The heat
in Oriental countries, Montesquieu maintains, makes women ready
for marriage at the age of eight, nine or ten years. Therefore childhood and marriage coincide. This implies that beauty and maturity
only infrequently coexist in women. This again meant that there was
a permanent state of inequality between the sexes, that polygamous
marriages existed, and that men were encouraged to treat women like
children or slaves. Montesquieu in *De l'esprit des lois* associates
domestic rule with politics. In a republic where all citizens were equal
it would be difficult to subject women to male dominance (xvi.9): "to
the contrary, women's servitude matches the temper of despotic
government … in Asia domestic and governmental despotism march
apace. In a state where one above all requires tranquillity, and where
extreme subordination is termed peace, women must be enclosed;
their intrigues would be fatal for their husbands." The main emphasis of the two following chapters is on the additional reasons for
the "seclusion within the house" and here finally is mentioned again
the (warm) climate, which encouraged nymphomania, faults and the
vices that therefore motivate the seclusion of women.

In order to examine the effects of the drifting sands of contemporary travel literature, let us review Montesquieu's sources. In Book
xvi.14, which concerns domestic rule in the Orient, he mentions that
he has his information from Chardin's comprehensive four-volume
work, *Voyages en Perse* (1735). Many other travellers to the Orient are
found in Montesquieu's notes. We may therefore conclude with
caution that the creation of the topos of the seclusion of women in
*ancient* times builds on a misunderstood interpretation of European
descriptions of travels in Greece during the Turkish occupation as
well as on a clear interest in the exotic during the eighteenth century.

It is obvious how the idea of the secluded woman of the Orient
evolved into that of the secluded woman of the classical period. First,
the scholarly tradition which maintained that Athenian women had
very limited freedom of movement was already 100 years old by the
end of the eighteenth century—it had existed since Rahnisch's work
of 1672. Second, there is a good, early example of how Montesquieu's
thoughts were applied to ancient history with methodological slop-
piness in *An Essay on the Original Genius and Writings of Homer*
(1769) by Robert Wood. So we read, "we must acknowledge that this
most pleasing feature, in a portrait of Heroic, Patriarchal and
Modern Oriental life, is sadly contrasted by a gloomy part of the
picture, which produces the most striking differences between our
manners and theirs; I mean, that unnatural separation of the sexes,

which precludes the female half from that share in the duties and amusements of life, which the common interests of society seem to demand." The heroic period of Oriental life is, according to Wood, identical with Homeric Troy; in that period "the female sphere of actions … was then confined to the uniformity of servile domestic duties … employing royal beauty in the meanest offices of domestic drudgery…". The conditions, described by Wood as tyrannical prescription, suggest a "despotic origin" which leads us back again to Montesquieu's political vocabulary. It was up to Cornelius de Pauw to bring the "neutral" seclusion of the ancient historians together with the form of confinement of Oriental women that was described by early travellers, Montesquieu and ethnographers. De Pauw coined the term "clôture Asiatique" in 1787 and from then on the formula was repeated and petrified as a topos in Ancient History.

# 2 Ideology and "the Status of Women" in Ancient Greece[†]

## MARILYN KATZ

Is a "History of Women" possible? Does Woman exist? The first of these provocative questions was the title of a 1984 collection of essays by French feminists;[1] the second was addressed recently by the British feminist Denise Riley.[2] With some exceptions, such challenges to the category of research have not disrupted the smooth surface of the study of women in antiquity, which, as Marilyn Skinner observed in 1986,[3] was incorporated readily into the field of classics, and defined according to existing parameters of scholarly investigation.[4]

The dominant research question in the field, centered around the "status" of women in ancient Athens, has in fact only recently been fully redefined, but without developing an adequate historiographic basis for it. That is to say, we now know that the status question is the wrong one, but we have not made clear why this is so, nor do we have

[†] Originally published in A.-L. Shapiro (ed.), *History and Feminist Theory* (*History and Theory* Beiheft 31) (Middletown, CT, 1992), 70–97.
    [1] *Une Histoire des femmes est-elle possible?*, ed. Michelle Perrot (Paris, 1984).
    [2] Denise Riley, *"Am I That Name?" Feminism and the Category of "Women" in History* (Minneapolis, 1988).
    [3] Marilyn Skinner, "Classical Studies, Patriarchy and Feminism: The View from 1986," *Women's Studies International Forum* 10 (1987), 181–186.
    [4] In the following essay I have not attempted to be comprehensive: some books or articles are discussed in detail; many other important items are omitted altogether. My discussion is restricted to works which I consider representative of the principal analytic approaches, and which are useful for demonstrating the theoretical and ideological premises of the various interpretive methods. For a survey of women's studies in classics, readers may consult one or more of a number of older and more recent review articles: M. B. Arthur, "Review Essay: Classics," *Signs: Journal of Women in Culture and Society* 2 (1976), 382–403; P. Culham, "Ten Years after Pomeroy: Studies of the Image and Reality of Women in Antiquity," *Helios* n.s. 13 (1986), 9–30; E. Fantham, "Women in Antiquity: A Selective (and Subjective) Survey 1979–84," *Echos du monde classique. Classical news and views* 30 (1986), 1–24; M. Skinner, "Classical Studies vs. Women's Studies: *Duo moi ta noêmmata*," *Helios* 12 (1986), 3–16; M. Skinner, "Rescuing Creusa: New Methodological Approaches to Women in Antiquity," *Helios* n.s. 13 (1986), 1–8; and Amy Richlin, "Hijacking the Palladion," *Helios* 17 (1990), 175–185 (= *Gender and History* 4 [1992], 70–83).

a clear understanding of why the study of women in Greek antiquity was originally formulated around this issue. The object of this essay is to provide this missing historiography, to identify the ideological parameters that informed the constitution of the original research question, and to suggest that the new reformulation, centered around women in Greek society, must itself be modified in order to incorporate an analysis of female sexuality in ancient Greece.

I first investigate the constitution of the dominant research question in the field, under the heading of "Patriarchy and Misogyny." I trace the origins of this question back to the late eighteenth century, and I take note of the continuing force of this paradigm. In section II, "Women in Civil Society," I examine the ideological basis of this hegemonic discourse, arguing that it derives from the eighteenth-century debate over women's place in civil society, where the example of the women of ancient Athens served a legitimating function within a wider political framework. I conclude this section with a treatment of recent challenges to the traditional interpretive paradigm for the study of women in ancient Greece.

In the last section, "Race, Culture, and Sexuality" [not reprinted here,] I begin with an analysis of the phrase "oriental seclusion." I then take up the theory of the constitution of woman as a separate race, based on eighteenth-century reevaluations of ancient medical theory, within the context of the development of racial theory overall. I go on to argue that the subsequent development, at the end of the eighteenth and beginning of the nineteenth centuries, of a separate discourse on sexual pathology was initially concerned almost exclusively with women and homosexuals, and was only extended to other groups subsequently. In the development of this discourse, too, the men and women of ancient Greece figured prominently; I discuss the current controversy over homosexuality in ancient Greece in the context of the historiographic parameters that have defined it. I conclude the essay with some remarks concerning the direction of future research.

## I PATRIARCHY AND MISOGYNY

The hallmark of the approach I shall examine is its focus on "woman" as a category and its preoccupation with the question of status. I have classified it under the heading of "patriarchy and misogyny" in order to highlight the concern with dominance and subordination which informs it throughout, but which is often hidden from view.

In a famous polemic the historian A. W. Gomme in 1925[5] described
the then prevailing orthodoxy as the view that the status of women
in ancient Athens in the classical period was an "ignoble" one by
comparison with their position in the Dorian states of the same
period, and with that in the earlier, archaic period (89). Most contemporary discussion of the question has taken its start from this
essay and from the similar chapter on "Life and Character" in Kitto's
*The Greeks* (1951).[6]

A more complete account of the *communis opinio* of the time,
however, may be gleaned from the sections on "Die Frauen" in the
second edition of Beloch's 1893 *Griechische Geschichte*.[7] The
Ionians, according to Beloch, under the influence of the neighboring
peoples of Asia Minor, inaugurated the exclusion of women from the
public sphere and their confinement to the home and to the company
of female friends. The Athenians adopted the practice from their
fellow Ionians, but among non-Ionian Greeks women retained the
freedom they had enjoyed in Homeric times. Prostitution—inspired
by the example of the Lydians—sprang up among the Ionians as the
inevitable corollary to the seclusion of well-born women, and the
practice of homosexuality developed along with it (I.1, 406–408).

The Ionian practice of seclusion became more widespread in Athens
during the fifth century, at just the time when democratic ideals of
liberty were institutionalized: "it was as if the women had wanted to
devise a counterweight to their husbands' boundless strivings for
freedom" (II.1, 159). Athenian men now turned to the company of hetairas ("female companions"[8]) for the female intellectual stimulation
which they had "sought at home in vain" (*ibid.*). These "emancipated"

[5] A. W. Gomme, "The Position of Women in Athens in the Fifth and Fourth Centuries B.C.,"
here cited from the reprint in Gomme, *Essays in Greek History and Literature* (Oxford, 1937),
89–115.
    [6] H. D. F. Kitto, *The Greeks* (Harmondsworth, Eng., 1951). For contemporary discussion,
see D. C. Richter, "The Position of Women in Classical Athens," *Classical Journal* 67 (1971),
1–8; Sarah B. Pomeroy, *Goddesses, Whores, Wives, and Slaves: Women in Classical Antiquity*
(New York, 1975), 58–62; R. Just, "Conceptions of Women in Classical Athens," *Journal of
the Anthropological Society of Oxford* 6 (1975), 153–170; Arthur, "Review Essay: Classics";
J. Gould, "Law, Custom and Myth: Aspects of the Social Position of Women in Classical
Athens," *Journal of Hellenic Studies* 100 (1980), 38–59; E. Cantarella, *Pandora's Daughters:
The Role and Status of Women in Greek and Roman Antiquity* [1981], transl. Maureen B.
Fant (Baltimore, 1987); P. Walcot, "Greek Attitudes towards Women: The Mythological
Evidence," *Greece & Rome* 32 (1984), 37–47; and D. Cohen, "Seclusion, Separation, and the
Status of Women in Classical Athens," *Greece & Rome* 36 (1989), 3–15.
    [7] Karl Julius Beloch, *Griechische Geschichte*, 2nd ed. Here cited from the second edition as
follows: I.1 (Strassburg, 1912); II.1 (Strassburg, 1914); III.1 (Berlin, 1922); IV.1 (Berlin, 1925).
    [8] The term is the feminine of *hetairos* meaning "companion"; the Greek plural is *hetairai*,
sometimes Latinized to *hetaerae*. Gomme suggests the translation "*demi-mondaine*" (*Essays
in Greek History*, 105); and Beloch renders *hetairai* as "Damen der Halbwelt" (III.1:434).

women flourished especially among the Ionians, their aspirations toward freedom nourished by the Ionian exaltation of learning and instigated by the cloistered lives of ordinary free women (*ibid.*, 160).

By the fourth century, under the influence of their fathers and husbands, a few women rejected traditional roles and turned to the study of philosophy; the notion of marriage for the sake of children began to yield to an ideal of companionate union for mutual fulfillment. This development was resisted vigorously, and it gave rise to expressions of misogyny, but mostly from "crybabies [whose] wives were too good for them." Hetairas continued to play an important role, and functioned as companions for almost all of the important men of this period (III.1, 434).

In the Hellenistic period the lives of ordinary women remained restricted, and hetairas retained a prominence in Athens which was later transferred to Alexandria. But the hetaira in her role as symbol of female emancipation was eclipsed by a new type of woman—the Hellenistic queen of the Macedonian and Alexandrian realms (IV.1, 416–420).[9] The example of her life of complete freedom within the court influenced the Greek world at large, leading to such developments as the extension of citizenship rights (proxeny), the institutionalization of education for women, the possibility of unaccompanied travel abroad, and the refinement of manners in social intercourse between the sexes.

Gomme was not the first to dispute what came to be regarded as the orthodoxy on women in ancient Greece. The principal elements of his perspective may already be found in Friedrich Jacobs's *Beiträge zur Geschichte des weiblichen Geschlechtes*, which was published in 1830.[10] Jacobs remarked that in his own time the question of women's status among the ancient Greeks was a debated issue: "Some have regarded women's position in Greece as demeaned, in the manner characteristic of barbarians; others have disputed this interpretation; and a third group thinks that the housewife was little esteemed and loved, but that hetairas by contrast, because of their education, enjoyed love and respect" (161). Jacobs divides his own treatment of the issue into an introductory section on marriage, followed by a discussion of "the Greek woman," and concludes with a lengthy section on "The Hetairas."

[9] For the most recent discussion of these women, see S. B. Pomeroy, *Women in Hellenistic Egypt: From Alexander the Great to Cleopatra* (New York, 1984).
[10] Friedrich Jacobs, *Beiträge zur Geschichte des weiblichen Geschlechtes*, in *Abhandlungen über Gegenstände des Alterthums* (Vermischte Schriften vol.4; Leben und Kunst der Alten vol. 3 [Leipzig, 1830]), 157–554.

In disputing the claim that ancient Greek, and especially Athenian, women were (1) regarded with contempt, (2) secluded, (3) uneducated (with the exception of the hetairas), and (4) unfree and unequal until the advent of Christianity (228), Jacobs cites the evidence of "Christian" sentiments among the pagans, and expressions of misogyny by the Church fathers. Thus, he argues, the disparagement of women was no more characteristic of pagan thinking than was their high regard inherent in Christianity. Jacobs goes on to discuss Homer and Hesiod, characterizing the *Odyssey* as "a love song to Penelope" (234), and arguing in general that the archaic picture gives us representations of both good and bad women. If the latter predominate in Hesiod, this has to do both with the poet's view of life, in which evil predominates over good, and with "the nature of things," rather than with "a contempt for the gender predominating in his time" (241). It is in "the nature of things," Jacobs argues, that as long as there are two sexes there will be two kinds of women, but praise of the good woman will be remarked less frequently than blame of the bad (229, 242).

Concerning the claim that women in ancient Greece were secluded and uneducated, Jacobs argues that restriction to home life was a matter of custom rather than law (254, 273), and that similar practices have been the rule all over western Europe up to the present time. Furthermore, if seclusion originated in the Orient, it was nonetheless consistent with Christian belief and practice, albeit in a milder form (255). The housebound life of the Athenian matron, and the tradition attested in Thucydides of silence about even her virtues, means that we have little evidence about women's education. But girls' training was in all likelihood entrusted to their mothers, who instructed them in the domestic arts and "womanly wisdom"; and their education was completed by their husbands, as Hesiod and, above all, Xenophon make clear (248ff.).

Overall, Jacobs insists, the Greek woman's intelligence and moral sensibility was sufficiently developed so that she was not an object of her husband's contempt (251), and he cites Xenophon's *Oeconomicus* in defense of his claim that the Athenian wife was regarded with respect (205–206). And while recognizing the existence of a misogynistic and antimarriage tradition,[11] he nevertheless concludes that the ancient Greeks in Athens and elsewhere recognized the moral worth of wives and marriage and honored the "sanctity" of this union (314).[12]

---

[11]  See especially his discussion of Meiners, 206–210.

[12]  For the argument that "die Ehe bei den Hellenen als ein unter göttlicher Obhut gestelltes Institut, sein Gedeihen von den Göttern erwartete," see 180–183.

The interpretive framework which guides Jacobs's judgments on ancient Greek women is set forth in his first chapter, "A General View of Marriage," in which he defends the general proposition that marriage is ideally a social institution representing "a union and interpenetration of the physical and moral strivings of human nature" which finds its fullest and most complete realization in society at large, but whose first elements are represented by the marital union (165–166). To the man belongs the right of rule, derived from the fact of his physical and intellectual superiority, and to the woman, on account of her sense for order and beauty, as well as her capacity for detail, belongs both "the authority and duty to execute the laws set down by the man" (167–168). And he concludes: "it is a general rule that it is proper for the woman to obey the man" (187).[13]

If one compares the premises and conclusions of Jacobs's essay with those of Gomme and Kitto, the similarities are striking. All agree that, as Gomme puts it, "Athenian society was, in the main, of the normal European type."[14] Jacobs would not have disputed Gomme's contention that "there is no reason to suppose that in the matter of the social consequence and freedom of women Athens was different from other Greek cities, or the classical from the Homeric age" (114). Like Gomme, Jacobs subscribed to the view that "Greek theory and practice [did not] differ fundamentally from the average ... prevailing in mediaeval and modern Europe" (115). Gomme claims, "when Theognis said, 'I hate a woman who gads about and neglects her home,' I think he expressed a sentiment common to most people of all ages" (115). This is similar to Jacobs's comments on a fragment of Menander in which a husband admonishes his gadabout wife that the courtyard door is the customary limit of a freeborn woman's realm: "in Berlin and Vienna, in Paris and London a husband in such a situation would say to his wife: 'within the limits of your house your tongue may have free rein; beyond the door your realm ends.'"[15]

Kitto remarks, "The Athenian had his faults, but preeminent among his better qualities were lively intelligence, sociability, humanity, curiosity. To say that he habitually treated one-half of his own race with indifference, even contempt, does not, to my mind, make sense."[16] Jacobs found the view that ancient Greek women were

---

[13] "Das es der Frau gezieme dem Manne zu gehorchen, galt allgemein."

[14] Gomme, "The Position of Women," 99, n.2.

[15] Jacobs, *Beiträge*, 264. Compare Gomme's statements about this same fragment, in "The Position of Women," 99.

[16] Kitto, *The Greeks*, 222.

tolerated only as a necessary evil, and that romantic love was directed only toward the educated hetaira, similarly incredible: "such is the harshness then, with which, it is claimed, the stronger sex exercised its mastery; such is the ignominy that the weaker sex tolerated in a land which we have been accustomed from childhood to revere as the cradle of culture, among a people whom we have been accustomed to regard as the patrons of all that is beautiful, great and masterful."[17]

There is striking continuity, then, in both the tone and the terms in which the argument against the orthodoxy of women's seclusion in ancient Athens was formulated over the course of the century which lies between Jacobs and Gomme. I shall suggest below that this continuum is even longer, stretching across the two hundred years from 1775 to 1971 and beyond. But how did the orthodoxy itself come into being, and on the basis of what evidence?

Jacobs in 1830 was concerned, at the most general level, to refute the contention of Christoph Meiners that "Homer makes it incontestably clear that women in the earlier period were as little regarded as in the later, and no less secluded [then] than later," a notion which Meiners explained on the basis of a postulated kinship between Greeks and Slavs.[18] Jacobs regarded as similarly misguided Thöluck's idea that "the female sex, whose status among the pagans was low, was first through Christendom accorded a human dignity similar to that of men" (224). And he objected as well to de Pauw's claim "that the hetairas, who were accustomed to attend the schools of the philosophers, were infinitely better educated than the women of standing, who perhaps never spoke [their] language correctly" (246), and to Böttiger's contention "that Athenian men kept their wives secluded; that this was a dominant custom; that Athenian women sighed under 'oriental harem-slavery'" (224).[19]

Karl August Böttiger, who served as Director of the Museum of Antiques in Dresden in the early nineteenth century, was the author of *Sabina, or Morning Scenes in the Dressing-Room of a Wealthy Roman Lady* (Leipzig, 1806), and thereby the founder of the genre of

[17] Jacobs, *Beiträge*, 243–244.
[18] *Ibid.*, 224. I discuss this idea more fully below [not reprinted here].
[19] Jacobs appears to be referring to Böttiger's claim, in his 1796 essay, "Waren die Frauen in Athen Zuschauerinnen bei den dramatischen Vorstellung?," that the question should be referred to the Greeks' general practice of secluding their women and confining them "zur orientalischen Haremssclaverei," a practice which, Böttiger says, "no one who [has read Lucian] would regard as exaggerated" (*Kleine Schriften*, ed. Sillig, vol. I [Leipzig, 1837], 295); Böttiger also cites Meiners ("Betrachtung über die Männerliebe der Griechen, nebst einem Auszuge aus dem Gastmahle des Plato," in *Vermischte Philosophische Schriften*, vol. I [Leipzig, 1775]), who there remarks on the similarities between certain Greek and Oriental customs, including seclusion of women in the harem (68).

"antique domestic literature."[20] His novel was adapted to the Greek situation in 1840 by Wilhelm Adolf Becker, who in *Charicles* recounts the adventures of an Athenian youth of the same name who, in the waning years of the fourth century BCE, having been ensnared as an adolescent by a hetaira in Corinth, goes on as a young adult to marry the young and beautiful heiress, Cleobule.

Becker appended to *Charicles* an excursus on "The Women," in which he acknowledged that "a variety of views have been entertained on the social position of the Greek women, and their estimation in the eyes of the men. The majority of scholars have described them as despicable in the opinion of the other sex, their life as a species of slavery, and the gynaeconitis [women's quarters] as a place of durance little differing from the Oriental harem; while a few writers have stoutly contended for the historic emancipation of the fair sex among the Greeks" (462).

While arguing overall that "the truth lies between the contending parties," Becker goes on to defend, on the basis of an extensive consideration of the evidence from the poets, orators, and philosophers, and from vase-paintings as well, the view that the women of the classical period "were less respected and more restrained [than in the heroic era], and that the marriage relationship was less tender and endearing" (462).

Becker's picture, although tempered in many cases by qualifications, may be summarized as follows: in the classical period "the women were regarded as a lower order of beings, neglected by nature in comparison with man, both in point of intellect and heart; incapable of taking part in public life, naturally prone to evil, and fitted only for propagating the species and gratifying the sensual appetites of the men" (463). "The only *arete* [virtue] of which woman was thought capable ... differed but little from that of a faithful slave" (464). "[Women's] education from early childhood corresponded to the rest of their treatment ... their whole instruction was left to the mother and the nurses, through whose means they obtained, perhaps, a smattering *en grammasi* [of letters], and were taught to spin and weave, and similar female avocations. ... Hence there were no scientific or even learned ladies, with the exception of the hetaerae" (465). "The gynaeconitis, though not exactly a prison, nor yet an everlocked harem, was still the confined abode allotted, for life, to the female portion of the household" (465). "Marriage, in reference to

[20] According to Frederick Metcalfe, in the "Translator's Preface" to Becker, *Charicles or Illustrations of the Private Life of the Greeks* (London, 1866), vii. All subsequent citations of *Charicles* are from this translation.

the procreation of children, was considered by the Greeks as a necessity enforced by their duties to the gods, to the state, and to their
ancestors. ... Until a very late period, at least, no higher considerations attached to matrimony, nor was strong attachment a frequent
cause of marriage. ... Sensuality was the soil from which ... passion
sprung, and none other than a sensual love was acknowledged
between man and wife" (473). As to the wife's household duties: "the
province of the wife was the management of the entire household,
and the nurture of the children; of the boys until they were placed
under a master, of the girls till marriage" (490). At another point, he
notes: "still it is an unquestionable fact that in many cases the wife
was in reality the ruling power in the house, whether from her mental
superiority, domineering disposition, or amount of dower" (493).
Becker concludes with a consideration of the "double standard": "the
law imposed the duty of continence in a very unequal manner" (494),
noting that "infidelity in the wife was judged most sharply," and that
the law required an adulterous wife to be divorced (494).

This is, then, the nineteenth-century orthodoxy on the status of
women in ancient Greece, formulated on the basis of an extensive
consideration of the evidence. The matter was, of course, far from
settled. In the second half of the nineteenth century and in the first
half of the twentieth, articles, dissertations, and monographs on the
subject of women's status proliferated, and a complete bibliography
on the topic for this century would run to more than fifty items.

In section II, I shall argue that beneath both the question of women's
emancipation in ancient Greece and that of their purported seclusion we
can detect the operation of a specific politico-philosophical framework.
The lineaments of this ideological perspective, however, particularly in
the years after 1850, have most often lain hidden from view. This, I
suggest, is because, once the orthodoxy gained widespread currency, its
origins in a specific philosophical discourse were ignored, and the scholarly dispute was conducted on the basis of its particulars. [...]


## II  WOMEN IN CIVIL SOCIETY

In recent years, feminist political scientists like Carole Pateman[21] and
Susan Moller Okin[22] have argued that the theory of the liberal demo-

---

[21] Carole Pateman, *The Disorder of Women* (Stanford, 1989). For a recent discussion of
Pateman's work overall in the context of political theory, see Anne Phillips, "Universal
Pretensions in Political Thought," in *Destabilizing Theory: Contemporary Feminist Debates*,
ed. M. Barrett and A. Phillips (Stanford, 1992), 10–30.
[22] Susan Moller Okin, *Women in Western Political Thought* (Princeton, 1979).

cratic state, the study of which has flourished recently in mainstream political science, has remained unaffected by feminist theory. This is not to say that "women's issues" have not been addressed. But, as Pateman notes, "the underlying assumption is that questions which have been taken up as 'women's issues' can be embraced and incorporated into mainstream theory" (1989, 2). She goes on to argue that feminist theory introduces a new and challenging perspective into this discourse. For "feminism does not, as is often supposed, merely add something to existing theories and modes of argument" (1989, 14). Rather, feminist theory demonstrates that "a repressed problem lies at the heart of modern political theory—the problem of patriarchal power[23] or the government of women by men" (1989, 2).

To be more specific: classical social contract theory, on which the contemporary theory of civil society is based, is founded on the Lockean premise of freedom and equality as a birthright. This birthright constitutes men as individuals possessing a natural political right, and "as 'individuals' all men are owners, in that they all own the property in their persons and capacities over which they alone have right of jurisdiction."[24] These free and equal individuals form a political association through a social contract which establishes obligations and to whose authority its members accede by means of their consent to be governed.

Women, by contrast, are understood to agree to subordinate themselves to their husbands, a subjection which has "a Foundation in Nature,"[25] and though husband and wife "have but one common Concern; ... it being necessary that the last Determination, *i.e.* the Rule, should be placed somewhere, it naturally falls to the Man's share as the abler and stronger."[26] As Pateman observes: "the contradiction between the premise of individual freedom and equality, with its corollary of the conventional basis of authority, and the assumption that women (wives) are naturally subject has ... gone unnoticed. ... [Yet] if women are naturally subordinate ... then talk of their consent or agreement to this status is redundant."[27]

[23] I shall not embark here upon a definition of the term "patriarchy," an understanding of which, despite its widespread popular currency, requires a thoroughgoing historiographic and political analysis. For some preliminary remarks on a contrast between "paternal" and "fraternal" patriarchy, see Pateman, *Disorder*, 35–36.

[24] *Ibid.*, 10.

[25] John Locke, *Two Treatises of Government*, ed. Peter Laslett, 2nd ed. (Cambridge, Eng., 1967), 191–192 (1.47–48).

[26] *Ibid.*, 339 (II.82).

[27] Pateman, *Disorder of Women*, 213. Cf. also her chapters, "Women and Consent" and "Feminism and Democracy," in *Disorder of Women*, 71–89; 210–225. For a theoretical critique of John Stuart Mill's theory of sexual egalitarianism, see Susan Moller Okin, "John Stuart Mill, Liberal Feminist," in *Women in Western Political Thought*, 197–223.

Locke did not specifically theorize women's subordination, but Rousseau's theory of the social contract, based on the premise that man, in passing from the state of nature to civil society, loses his natural liberty but gains both civil liberty and moral freedom,[28] did explicitly justify it. Rousseau, who like other Enlightenment thinkers, as Wagner-Hasel says, "developed the theoretical foundations for the interrelationship between ancient and modern democracy, and regarded as their models Attic generals like Pericles or Roman Senators of Cicero's kind,"[29] modeled his "people's assembly" on the *comitia tributa* ("tribal" or popular assembly) of the ancient Romans, drawing certain additional features from the constitution of the Spartans.

Rousseau generally regarded ancient Sparta as "the example that we ought to follow."[30] But in *Émile*, published, along with *The Social Contract*, in 1762, it was classical Athens that provided the paradigm for the incorporation of women into the ideal state. There, Rousseau expanded upon arguments which he had first advanced in the 1758 "Letter to M. d'Alembert on the Theater," where he remarked that "the ancients had, in general, a very great respect for women."[31] And he explained in more detail:

> Among all the ancient civilized peoples [women] led very retired lives; they did not have the best places at the theatre; they did not put themselves on display; they were not even always permitted to go; and it is well known that there was a death penalty for those who dared to show themselves at the Olympic games. In the home, they had a private apartment where the men never entered. When their husbands entertained for dinner, they rarely presented themselves at the table; the decent women went out before the end of the meal, and the others never appeared at the beginning. There was no common place of assembly for the two sexes; they did not pass the day together. This effort not to become sated with one another made their meetings more pleasant. It is certain that domestic peace was, in general, better established and that greater harmony prevailed between man and wife than is the case today.[32]

Among others, Mary Wollstonecraft, in *A Vindication of the Rights of Woman* (1792), argued against Rousseau's views. There she insisted that the confinement of women's instruction to such frivoli-

---

[28] Jean-Jacques Rousseau, *The Social Contract*, transl. M. Cranston (Baltimore, 1978), 64–65 (1.8).

[29] Wagner-Hasel, "Das Private wird politisch," 26.

[30] Rousseau, "Letter to M. d'Alembert on the Theatre," in *Politics and the Arts*, transl. Allan Bloom (Glencoe, Ill., 1960), 133.

[31] *Ibid.*, 48.

[32] *Ibid.*, 88–89.

ties as Rousseau had envisioned, would produce "weak beings ... only fit for a seraglio!"[33]

The question of women's status in ancient Greece, and of the extent and meaning of their "seclusion," then, did not originate in the nineteenth century, nor was it raised first by scholars of classical antiquity. Rather, as the above citations indicate, it formed part of the intellectual currency of the eighteenth century, and played an important role in the general debate over the form and nature of civil society. Furthermore, some of the specific terms of this discourse were set in the eighteenth century. Rousseau, for example, had remarked in 1758 that women in the ancient world were "respected" and that this was connected with their having led "very retired lives." What is more, the formulation of the question itself relied on a certain circular logic: Rousseau in 1758 cited the example of women in ancient Athens to substantiate his views on women's nature; Jacobs in 1830 relied on the eighteenth-century view of women's nature to authenticate his interpretation of the ancient evidence.

It is only in the last ten years or so that the "status" model has been challenged as a research paradigm, and this has been achieved principally by introducing a discontinuity between the ancient conception of the relationship between *polis* (city-state) and *oikos* (household) and the analogous modern distinction between "public" and "private." The landmark 1979 study on the question, Sally Humphreys's "*Oikos* and *Polis*," treats the opposition in Athenian society and culture overall, showing that such modern distinctions as that between the political and economic spheres are misleading when applied to ancient Athens. Humphreys foregoes discussion of women's status as such, but treats aspects of women's incorporation in and exclusion from the functioning of the sociocultural totality. In addition, she makes the important observation that "the separation of men and women in social life meant that in a sense the public world of the city reached into the house."[34] [...]

## IV  SUMMARY AND CONCLUSIONS

The burden of this essay has been, first, to show that the question of women's status in ancient Greece has continued to be addressed in

---

[33] Mary Wollstonecraft, *A Vindication of the Rights of Woman: An Authoritative Text. Backgrounds. The Wollstonecraft Debate. Criticism,* ed. Carol H. Poston, 2nd ed. (New York, 1988), 10; cf. 29.

[34] S. C. Humphreys, "*Oikos* and *Polis*," in *The Family, Women and Death: Comparative Studies* (London, 1983), 1–21, citation 16. See also D. Cohen, "Public and Private in Classical Athens," in *Law, Sexuality, and Society,* 70–97.

contemporary scholarship in much the same terms as it was formulated in the nineteenth century. Scholars generally, even when they
have acknowledged this history in long and ponderous footnotes,
have generally stopped at this point, availing themselves of what I
shall call the "European seclusion theory"—the notion that their
nineteenth-century predecessors developed the foundations of classical scholarship alone in their studies with their books. (One need
only think here of the frontispieces frequently prefaced to biographies, depicting the scholar poring over his voluminous tomes in soli-
tary concentration.) In the second section above, I have attempted to
demonstrate that the formulation of the question of women's status
in ancient Greece has a far more complex history, and that its terms
were intimately bound up with the eighteenth-century discourse on
freedom, the individual, and civil society.

This history is well known, but within the field of classics it is generally relegated to the subdiscipline known as the history of the classical tradition or the classical heritage.[35] Within this framework, not
only are the ideological specifics of the tradition widely overlooked,[36]
as Martin Bernal lately has made clear,[37] but the discussion of women
and their history is largely left out of account, except where it touches
on themes having to do with Greek mythology and religion.

What I have tried to show, with reference to the study of women in
antiquity, is that its history and historiography are in fact constituted
through a complex intersection between classical scholarship and the
classical tradition, and that this interpenetration was itself significantly conditioned by the contemporary discussions on language,
nationalism, and race. To evaluate this history properly, we must take
into account, therefore, not only Rousseau's reading of antiquity, but
such further considerations as his contribution to the formation of
political theory, and the contemporary rereading and critique of his
influence.[38] Furthermore, the exemption of women from civil society

[35] For example, Frank M. Turner, *The Greek Heritage in Victorian Britain* (New Haven,
1981).
[36] Or relegated to footnotes: see, for example, the remarks on the part played by "contemporary racial thinking" in Matthew Arnold's work, in Turner, *The Greek Heritage*, 20–21, n.4.
[37] Martin Bernal, *Black Athena: The Afroasiatic Roots of Classical Civilization*. Volume I:
*The Fabrication of Ancient Greece* (London, 1987). I shall not comment on the extensive
dispute to which this book has given rise, other than to say that I regard the general burden
of the historiographic account as largely correct, notwithstanding the fact that Bernal has
sometimes been careless with the evidence.
[38] See, for example, the recent discussion by A. Koppelman, "Sex Equality and/or the
Family: From Bloom vs. Okin to Rousseau vs. Hegel," which contrasts Susan Okin's and Allan
Bloom's views on the implications of Rousseau's theory of the family to contemporary feminist debate on the place of women in the social order. (*Yale Journal of Law and the
Humanities* 4 [1992], 399–432.)

in political theory should be understood, not only in terms of the perseverance of patriarchy and a motivated nostalgia for the ancient Greek past, but within the context of eighteenth-century medical inquiry, its rereading of the ancient theory of biology, and its eventual intersection in the nineteenth century with the discourse on language, race, and nationality.

It should be clear that what has interested me here is not the history of ideas, although I do regard it as important to know that a certain continuity can be found among the ideas of, for example, Rousseau, Jacobs, and A. W. Gomme, and that this continuity is based on a shared notion, inherited from the eighteenth century, of women's proper sphere and its correlation with their "nature." Rather, I have been concerned to make clear how the terms of the discussion themselves came into being, and to identify their ideological valences.

Thus, from the historiographic point of view, there is not a "history of women" as such. But there is a history of women in society, as Wagner-Hasel and others have shown, and there is also a history of the gendered individual, as recent studies on sexuality in ancient Greece have demonstrated. In this essay, I have concentrated on the history of the history of women, which, as I have tried to show, still awaits reconstruction in its fullest particulars. This can only be achieved, not by dismissing as outdated what has gone before, but by exposing the ideological foundations of a hegemonic discourse that has dominated the discussion of ancient women, and that continues to make its powerful influence felt in the discussion of women generally as part of civil society at the present moment in history.

# 3  *The Athenian Woman*

## H. D. F. KITTO[†]

Most men are interested in women, and most women in themselves.
Let us therefore consider the position of women in Athens. It is the
accepted view, challenged, so far as I know by nobody except A. W.
Gomme,[1] that the Athenian woman lived in an almost Oriental seclusion, regarded with indifference, even contempt. The evidence is partly
the direct evidence of literature, partly the inferior legal status of
women. Literature shows us a wholly masculine society: domestic life
plays no part. Old Comedy deals almost entirely with men (but for the
extravaganzas of the *Lysistrata* and *Women in Parliament*); in Plato's
dialogues the disputants are always men; the *Symposium* both of Plato
and Xenophon make it quite plain that when a gentleman entertained
guests the only women present were those who had no reputation to
lose, except a professional one: indeed, in the Neaera case testimony
that one of the wives dined and drank with her husband's guests is
given as presumptive evidence that she is a prostitute. The Athenian
house was divided into the "men's rooms" and the "women's rooms":
and the women's part was provided with bolts and bars (Xen., *Oec.*).
Women did not go out except under surveillance, unless they were
attending one of the women's festivals. Twice in tragedy (Sophocles'
*Electra* and *Antigone*) girls are brusquely told to go indoors, which is
their proper place: Jebb, commenting on *Antigone* 579, quotes a poetic
fragment: "Nor permit her to be seen outside the house before her marriage", and he quotes from the *Lysistrata* of Aristophanes: "It is difficult for a (married) woman to escape from home." It was the man who
did the shopping; he handed what he bought to his slave to carry. (The
"mean man" in Theophrastus carries it all home himself.) In the comedies of Menander (third century B.C.) the young man who has roman-
tically fallen in love with a girl has invariably met her at a festival—the

[†] Originally published in *The Greeks* (Harmondsworth 1951), 219–34.
[1] In *Essays in Greek History and Literature* (Blackwell, 1937).

44

implication being that he has little chance of incurring this malady in ordinary social life. (Though we may remember that the staid Ischomachus "chose" his young wife, so that presumably he had at least seen her, and we shall hear from Theophrastus that a young man might serenade his sweetheart.) Indeed, the romantic attachments that we do hear of are with boys and young men, and of these we hear very frequently: homosexual love was regarded as a normal thing and treated as frankly as heterosexual love. (Like the other sort, it had its higher and its lower aspect.) Plato has some fine passages describing the beauty and the modesty of young lads, and the tenderness and respect with which the men treated them.[2] Marriages were arranged by the girl's parent [;|...] Xenophon's Ischomachus [...] took no very ecstatic view of matrimony. The wife is the domestic manager and little more: indeed, he expressly says that he prefers his young wife to be entirely ignorant, that he himself may teach her what he wishes her to know. The education of girls was omitted; for intelligent female company the Athenian turned to the well-educated class of foreign women, often Ionians, who were known as "companions", hetaerae, women who occupied a position somewhere between the Athenian lady and the prostitute: Pericles' famous mistress Aspasia belonged to this class—her name, incidentally, meaning "Welcome"! So we read in Demosthenes: "Hetaerae we keep for the sake of pleasure: concubines (i.e. female slaves) for the daily care of our persons, wives to bear us legitimate children and to be the trusted guardians of our households." And finally, no account of the position of women in Athens is complete without a reference to Pericles and Aristotle. Pericles said in his Funeral Speech: "The best reputation a woman can have is not to be spoken of among men either for good or evil": and Aristotle holds (in the *Politics*) that by nature the male is superior, the female inferior, therefore the man rules and the woman is ruled.

Therefore, as I have said, it is almost unanimously held that the Athenian woman had very little freedom, some writers going so far as to speak of "the contempt felt by the cultured Greeks for their wives". It is orthodox to compare the repression of women in Athens with the freedom and respect which they enjoyed in Homeric society —and in historical Sparta.

This seems to be confirmed when we turn to the legal evidence. Women were not enfranchised: that is, they could not attend the Assembly, still less hold office. They could not own property: they

---

[2] Those who find this topic interesting or important are referred to Hans Licht, *Sexual Life in Ancient Greece*.

could not conduct legal business: every female, from the day of birth to the day of her death, had to be the ward, so to speak, of her nearest male relative or her husband, and only through him did she enjoy any legal protection. The "guardian" gave the woman in marriage—and a dowry with her: if there was a divorce, the dowry returned with the wife to the guardian. The legal provision most foreign to our ideas related to the daughter who was left sole heir to a father who had died intestate: the nearest male kinsman was entitled to claim her in marriage, and if married already he could divorce his own wife in order to marry the heiress. (It should be explained that in any case Attic law recognized marriage between uncle and niece, even between half-brother and half-sister). Alternatively, the nearest male kinsman became guardian to the heiress, and must give her in marriage, with a suitable dowry. In fact, a man who had no son and was not likely to have one, normally adopted one—not a male baby but a grown man —for example, a brother-in-law; for the purpose of the adoption was not to indulge a sentiment or cure a psychosis, but to leave behind a proper head of the family to continue its legal existence and religious rites. But obviously many a man died before the adoption of a son appeared necessary: heiresses were left, and Isaeus (an orator who specialized in cases of disputed inheritance) assures us—or rather assures his audience, which may not be the same thing—that "many a man has put away his wife" to marry an heiress. Apart from this special case, the laws of divorce applied to husbands and wives with reasonable, though not complete, impartiality: for instance—I quote Jebb's careful wording—"a childless union could be dissolved at the instance of the wife's relatives".

Does any more need to be said? When the legal evidence is added to the literary—and I think my necessarily brief summary represents both not unfairly—is it not quite clear that the Athenian treated his women with considerable indifference, for which "contempt" may not be too harsh a substitute? Can we doubt on the evidence that in this pre-eminently masculine society women moved in so restricted a sphere that we may reasonably regard them as a "depressed area"?

In detective stories there often comes a point where the detective is in possession of the facts, and sees that they lead to one conclusion. There is no doubt at all—except that we are still ten chapters from the end of the book. Accordingly, the detective feels a vague uneasiness: everything fits, yet it seems all wrong: there must be something, somewhere, which he has not yet discovered.

I confess that I feel rather like that detective. What is wrong is the picture it gives of the Athenian man. The Athenian had his faults, but pre-eminent among his better qualities were lively intelligence, sociability, humanity, and curiosity. To say that he habitually treated one-half of his own race with indifference, even contempt, does not, to my mind, make sense. It is difficult to see the Athenian as a Roman paterfamilias, with a greater contempt for women than we attribute to the Roman.

To begin with, let us take a few general considerations that may induce in us a certain hesitation. As far as Greece is concerned, the most Hellenic of us is a foreigner, and we all of us know how wide of the mark even an intelligent foreigner's estimate can be. He sees undeniable facts—but misinterprets them because his own mental experience is different. Other facts he does not see. For example, I once had the advantage of having an analysis of the English character from a young German who was not a fool, and knew England tolerably well, both town and country. He told me, as something self-evident, that we play cricket for the good of our health: and when I mentioned in the course of the discussion the flowers which every cottager loves to grow, I found that he had supposed them to be wild flowers. Naturally, his picture of the Englishman was exceedingly funny. Similarly, every Frenchman has his mistress (evidence: French novels and plays), no Frenchman loves his wife (all French marriages are "arranged"), there is no home-life in France (men congregate in cafés, which respectable women do not use); and the Frenchwoman's legal status is much lower than the Englishwoman's. Women in France therefore are less free, less respected and less influential than in England.—We used to hear this argument, and know how silly it is. The foreigner so easily misses the significant thing.

Another general point: the fallacy of assuming that anything for which we have no evidence (viz. home-life) did not exist. It may have existed, or it may not: we do not know.—But is it possible that Greek literature should be so silent about domestic life if domestic life counted for anything? The answer expected is No: the true answer is Yes. In a modern literature the argument from silence would be very strong: in Greek literature it amounts to very little. [...] Homer refrains from painting in the background which we expect, and gives us one which we do not expect; [...] the dramatists are constructional rather than representational. In the *Agamemnon* Aeschylus does not show us the streets and the market, ordinary citizens' houses, goatherds, cooks and scullions about the palace. We do not infer that these did not exist, nor that Aeschylus had not an interest in such things. We can see at once that these things do not come into his play because there was no reason why they should. All classical Greek art had a very austere standard of relevance.

A related point is the subject-matter of the literature of the period. Unless we are on our guard, we instinctively think of Literature as including novels, biographies, letters, diaries—literature, in short, about individuals, either real or fictive. Classical Greek literature does not revolve around the individual; it is "political". Practically the only informal literature we have is Xenophon's *Memorabilia* and *Table Talk* (the *Symposium*), and these do not profess to give an intimate biography of Socrates, but deal explicitly with Socrates the philosopher. We find Xenophon's Ischomachus rather unromantic? To what has been said above on this point we may now add this, that Xenophon was not writing about Athenian married life; like Mrs Beeton, he was writing on Household Management.

Then there is a point very shrewdly made by Gomme, that our evidence is scanty, and we may easily misinterpret what we have. Gomme puts together some dozen dicta about women and marriage selected from nineteenth-century writers which would give a very false impression if we could not see them—as we can—against the whole background, and read them accordingly. Take Pericles' dictum, which has come re-echoing down the ages. It is typical of the disdain which the Athenians felt for women. Possibly. But suppose Gladstone had said, "I do not care to hear a lady's name bandied about in general talk, whether for praise or dispraise": would that imply disdain, or an old-fashioned deference and courtesy?

Again, it is pointed out that it was common form in Athens to refer to a married woman not by her name (as it might be, Cleoboulê) but as "Nicanor's wife". The Athenian woman, poor thing, did not even have a known name, so obscure was she. Quite so: but among ourselves, when Sheila Jackson marries she becomes Mrs Clark: Sheila to her friends indeed, but Sheila Jackson to nobody.—We must be cautious.

My last general point is perhaps the most important. In discussing this topic, what are we really talking about? Are we comparing the position of women in Athens with the position of women in Manchester? Or are we trying to estimate the character of the Athenian, and of his civilization, on the basis (partly) of the position he allotted to his women? It makes a very great difference. If the former, then it is pertinent to say that the Manchester woman can vote and take a part in political life, while the Athenian woman could not. But if we say that because we give women the vote we are more enlightened and courteous than the Athenian, we are talking nonsense. We are comparing details in two pictures and ignoring the fact that the pictures are utterly different. If a woman in Manchester wants to go to London, she can do it on precisely the same terms as a man: she can buy her ticket, summer or winter, and the fare is the same for all. If an Athenian (male) wanted to go to Thebes, he could walk or ride a mule, and in winter the journey across the mountains was exhausting and perilous. If a woman wanted to go—it might be possible, by waiting for the proper season, but it would be a serious undertaking. It is perfectly reasonable, in a modern state, that women should be enfranchised. In the first place, civilization—to use the word for once in its improper sense—has made the physical differences between the sexes of very little political importance: women can use the train, bicycle, telephone, newspaper, on the same terms as men; and conversely the bank-clerk or don, provided that he is healthy, need not be stronger in muscle than the normal woman; he knows that there is no chance of his being required next week to march twenty miles under a baking sun in heavy armour, and then to fight as stoutly as the next man—or else imperil the next man's life. In the second place, the substance of politics and administration has changed. It is true that political decision then, as now, affected everyone regardless of age and sex, but the field which government covered was very much smaller, and concerned, in the main, matters which, inescapably, only men could judge from their own experience and execute by their own exertions. One reason why women have the vote today is that in many matters of current politics their judgement is likely to be as good as a man's, sometimes better, while in important matters their ignorance is not likely to be greater. Nor should we forget what is probably an even more important difference. We think that it is normal to regard society as an aggregate of individuals. This is not normal from the historical point of view: it is a local development. The normal view is that society is an aggregation of families, each having its own responsible leader. This conception is not Greek only: it is also Roman, Indian, Chinese, Teutonic.

It is open to anyone to say that not for untold wealth would he have been a woman in Ancient Athens: perhaps one would not regret not having been an Athenian man either; for the polis, not to mention the ordinary conditions of life, made some extremely uncomfortable demands on him too. What is not sensible is to say to the Athenian: "We treat women much better in Golders Green. Aren't you a bit of a blackguard?"

After this general discussion let us look at the evidence again. We will try to keep in mind the two separate questions: does the orthodox view correctly state the facts? and, if so, does it draw the correct deductions from them? That is, was the life of the Athenian woman restricted and stunted? and, if so, was the reason that the men regarded them with indifference or disdain?

We have seen that the literary evidence is too scanty, and, in a certain sense too one-sided, to give us any confidence that we have in it the complete picture. When a man gives a dinner, his wife does not appear. The Athenian gentleman liked masculine company—unlike the gentlemen of London, who have never even heard of a club which did not freely admit ladies. But did the Athenian play the host or the guest every evening of the year? And did the women not have their social occasions? Euripides was under the impression that they did: more than once he says things like, "What an evil it is to have women coming into the house gossiping!" Did the Athenian, when he had no guests, dine alone, like some Cyclops in his cave? Did he never dream of talking to his wife about anything except the management of the household and the procreation of lawful children? Stephanus and Neaera once more raise their disreputable heads. Their prosecutor says, in his peroration, to the one, two or three hundred jurymen:

> Gentlemen, if you acquit this woman, what will you say to your wives and daughters when you go home? They will ask where you have been. You will say, "In the courts". They will say, "What was the case?" You of course will say, "Against Neaera. She was accused of illegally marrying an Athenian, and of getting one of her daughters—a prostitute—married to Theogenes the archon…"
>
> You will tell them all the details of the case, and you will tell them how carefully and completely the case was proved. When you have finished they will say, "And what did you do?" And you will reply, "We acquitted her".—And *then* the fat will be in the fire!

It is perfectly natural—and that is the reason why I quote the passage. It is one of the very few scraps of evidence we have bearing on the ordinary relations of a man with his wife and daughters, and what happens is precisely what would happen today. The juryman is not expected to reply to his women: "You forget yourselves! You are Athenian women, who should rarely be seen and never heard."

Another literary scrap. In Xenophon's *Table Talk* one of the guests, Niceratus, has recently married. Niceratus knows Homer by heart, and explains to the company how much Homer has taught him—strategy, rhetoric, farming: all sorts of things. Then he says, turning pleasantly to his host, "And there's another thing I've learned from Homer. Homer says somewhere: 'An onion goes well with wine'. We can test that here and now. Tell them to bring in some onions! You will enjoy the wine very much more." "Ah!" says another guest, "Niceratus wants to go home smelling of onions so that his wife shall think that no one else has so much as thought of kissing him!" It is of course very slight, but it is precisely the sort of good-natured jest that one might hear any evening in an English club or a public-house.

But there is evidence, not yet mentioned, which is not so slight. It points in the same direction, and is unintelligible on the orthodox view. We happen to possess a large number of painted vases (fifth century) that portray domestic scenes, including some funerary-urns representing a dead wife as living, and taking farewell of her husband, children and slaves. There are also sculptured tombstones—quite ordinary ones—showing similar scenes. These, in their noble and unaffected simplicity, are among the most moving things which Greece has left us. They rank with the Andromache passage in the *Iliad* which I paraphrased earlier. I quote from Gomme's essay a sentence which he quotes from an article on certain Athenian tombs.[3] "Damasistratê and her husband clasp hands at parting. A child and a kinswoman stand beside the chair, but husband and wife have no eyes save for each other, and the calm intensity of their parting gaze answers all questionings as to the position of the wife and mother in Attic society." Homer says, in a notable verse. "There is nothing finer than when a man and his wife live together in true union"—ὁμοφρονέοντε, "sharing the same thoughts". If an illustrator of Homer wanted to illustrate this verse, he would automatically turn to these paintings and sculptures—made for a people who held women, especially wives, in slight esteem!

I will say no more about vases, but turn to Attic tragedy. One of its notable features is its splendid succession of tragic heroines—three Clytemnestras, four Electras, Tecmessa, Antigone, Ismene, Deianeira, Iocasta, Medea, Phaedra, Andromache, Hecuba, Helen. They differ in character, naturally, but all are vigorously drawn: none is a dummy. What is more, the vigorous, enterprising and intelligent character is commoner than the other sort. This, it may be said, is natural enough in drama. Perhaps so: but it is not inevitable that in Euripides the women, good or bad, should so often be more enterprising than the men. The clever woman who contrives something when the men are at a loss is almost a stock character in Euripides—Helen, for example, and Iphigenia (in the *Iphigenia in Tauris*). As for enterprise— "Come!" says the old slave to the ill-used Creousa in the *Ion*, "you must do something womanly. Take to the sword! Poison him!"[4] It is hard to believe that the dramatists never, even by accident, portrayed

---

[3] By J.S. Blake-Reed in the *Manchester Guardian*.
[4] *Ion*, 843.

the stunted creatures among whom (we are to suppose) they actually lived, and got these vivid people out of books—from Homer. As if a modern dramatist turned from his despised contemporaries, drew his women from Chaucer or Shakespeare—and made a success of it. Euripides indeed makes women complain of what they suffer at men's hands—much of it as relevant to modern society as to ancient: he also makes many of his men suffer at the hands of vengeful and uncontrollable women. Some moderns accuse Euripides of being a feminist; ancient critics—with more reason, I think—called him a misogynist. At least, he did not think them negligible: nor did Aeschylus and Sophocles.

Now that we have positive reason for doubting at any rate the extreme doctrine of repression and disdain, let us, like the uneasy detective aforementioned, examine some of the evidence again. "It is difficult for women to get out," says Jebb, quoting Aristophanes, in a note which otherwise deals with the very careful supervision of unmarried girls. The suggestion is that married women too were carefully kept indoors: and any classical scholar would remember that Xenophon speaks somewhere of putting bolts and bars on the door of the women's quarters. But if we actually turn up the passage in Aristophanes we get a rather different impression. It runs (a married woman is speaking): "It's difficult for women to get out, what with dancing attendance on one's husband, keeping the servant-girl awake, bathing the baby, feeding it…" We have heard not dissimilar things in our own time: the ogre has disappeared from this passage at least.

But she was not allowed out unless she had someone to keep an eye on her? The lively Theophrastus helps us here. With his habitual fineness of distinction Theophrastus describes three characters all of whom we might call "mean". The first of them is straightforwardly "stingy": it is characteristic of him to come before quarter-day to collect sixpence due to him as interest on a loan, to turn the whole house upside-down if his wife has lost a threepenny bit, and to prevent a man from helping himself to a fig from his garden, or from picking up a date or olive in his orchard. Then there is, literally, "the man of base gain", who gives short measure, feeds his slaves badly, and sponges on his friends in petty ways. But it is the third who concerns us at the moment. He does the family shopping, as the men regularly did, but instead of handing it to his slave to carry home, he carries it home himself, meat, vegetables and all, in a fold in his tunic: moreover, although his wife brought him a dowry of £5,000, he does not allow her to keep a maid, but when she goes out he hires a little girl from the women's market to attend her. This kind of meanness is "aneleuthe-

ria", or "conduct unbecoming a gentleman": Theophrastus defines it
as "a lack of self-respect where it involves money". That is to say, for a
lady to be properly attended when she went abroad was only her due.
And I may add here, with a conventional apology for its coarseness,
another detail from Theophrastus which contributes something material to our argument. One of his Characters is the Coarse Buffoon,
"who will stand by the door of the barber's shop and tell the world at
large that he means to get drunk … and when he sees a lady coming he
will raise his dress and show his privy parts". There were all sorts in
the streets of Athens. There were perhaps very good reasons for not
allowing girls to go about unguarded.

Then if we actually look at the bolts and bars passage, we find that
their purpose is "that the female slaves may not have babies without
our knowledge,[5] and to prevent things being improperly taken out of
the women's quarters": which may serve to remind us to what an
extent the Greek home was also a factory. Quite apart from what we
regard as "domestic work", there was the making of clothes—from
the raw wool, the grinding as well as the baking of the flour from the
corn which the husband had brought in, the provision of food for the
winter. We have in fact to think away most of our shops and the things
that come in packets. Clearly the wife's position was one of great
responsibility. Hollywood demonstrates to us, both by precept and
example, that romantic love is the only possible basis for a happy and
lasting marriage: was the Greek necessarily dull or cynical because he
thought differently? He was aware of the force of "romantic" love—
and generally represented it as a destructive thing [...]

But this is all very well: the man had his hetaerae and worse. What
about that passage in the Neaera-speech?—what indeed? It is sometimes used as if it had all the authority of a state-document—but
what is it? A remark made, in a disreputable case, by a pleader who
is very much a man of the world to a jury of a hundred or more ordinary Athenians, very many of whom are there because the seven-and-
sixpenny juror's fee pays the fishmonger's bill at the end of the week.
"Hetaerae indeed! Pretty slave-girls! Too expensive for the likes of us
—but thank you for the compliment!" And in any case, what is the
speaker actually saying? His whole argument is concerned to bring
out the enormity of Stephanus' offence in foisting upon the body-
politic alien and even tainted stock. This is not snobbery: it has its
roots in the conception that the polis is a union of kinsmen.

---

[5] Both Xenophon and Aristotle remark that to have children made a decent slave more well
disposed to his owner. But a man does like to have some idea who is likely to be born in his
house.

Therefore he says, "Hetaerae and slave-girls are all very well, but when we come down to bed-rock, on which the existence of our polis depends, and the sustenance of our individual households, to whom do we turn? To our wives." Far from implying contempt for the wife, this passage raises her beyond the reach of other women. It is in fact entirely in keeping with the evidence of the vase-paintings. It is our entirely different material and social background, and our inheritance of centuries of romance, which make us misread passages like these and then to try to argue away the evidence from painting and drama. Even so lively and sensitive a scholar as T.R. Glover represents Socrates as saying this to a friend: "Is there anybody to whom you entrust more serious matters than to your wife—or to whom you talk less?"[6] But the plain meaning of the Greek is "... to whom you entrust more serious things, and with whom you have fewer arguments?" And the reason why he has fewer arguments with his wife is (by implication) that they are working together in partnership and understanding.

Boys were sent to school, taught to read and write, and educated in poetry, music and gymnastics: girls did not go to school at all—another proof that the Athenian despised women and preferred dolts. The Athenian woman was illiterate and uneducated—so that when she went to the theatre and heard Antigone talking so nobly and intelligently, she must have opened her dull eyes in astonishment, wondering what sort of a creature this was, and how Sophocles could ever have imagined that a woman could be like that! It is obviously grotesque. It comes, again, from our confusing Athens with Manchester.

First, we are making an assumption which may or may not be true when we argue that because a girl did not go to school she was illiterate. Children have been known to pick up the art of reading at home, and what we know of Athenian intelligence and curiosity suggests that our assumption is unsafe. Secondly, those who cannot read today are sub-human, but that is not true of a society in which books are comparatively rare things. To the ordinary Athenian the ability to read was comparatively unimportant; conversation, debate, the theatre, much more than the written word, were the real sources of education. The boy was not sent to school to work for a certificate and thereby given "educational advantages" (that is, qualifications for a job better than the manual work which we admire so much more than the Greeks). The Greek, in his perverse and limited way, sent the boys to school to be trained for manhood—in morals, manners and

---

[6] Glover, *From Pericles to Philip*, 346; Xenophon, *Oec.*, III, 12.

physique. Reading and writing were taught, but these rudiments could not have taken very long. The rest of the elementary curriculum was the learning of poetry and singing (mousikê), and physical training: mousikê was prized chiefly as a training in morals and in wisdom, and the moral influence of "gymnastikê" was by no means overlooked.

What was the girl doing meanwhile? Being instructed by her mother in the arts of the female-citizen: if we say "housework" it sounds degrading, but if we say Domestic Science it sounds eminently respectable; and we have seen how varied and responsible it was. To assume that she was taught nothing else is quite gratuitous, and the idea that her father would never discuss anything political with her is disproved by the Neaera-passage.

But did women have any opportunity of sharing in the real education that Athens offered? In the Assembly and law-courts, no—except at second-hand. What about the theatre? Were women admitted? This is a very interesting point. The evidence is various, clear and unanimous: they were. [...]

The evidence is decisive, but "in the treatment of this matter scholars appear to have been unduly biased by a preconceived opinion as to what was right and proper. Undoubtedly Athenian women were kept in a state of almost Oriental seclusion. And the old Attic comedy was pervaded by a coarseness which seems to make it utterly unfit for boys and women. For these reasons some writers have gone so far as to assert that they were never present at any dramatic performances whatsoever. Others, while not excluding them from tragedy, have declared that it was an impossibility that they should have been present at the performance of comedy."[7] Impossible; *ganz unmöglich!* That is the end of the matter. But [...] the evidence disproves the notion that women could attend Tragedy but not Comedy. And even if we violate the evidence, we gain nothing, because the tragic tetralogy itself ended with the satyric play, of which the one surviving example (Euripides' *Cyclops*) contains jokes which would make the Stock Exchange turn pale. In this matter, then, there was an equality and a freedom between the sexes inconceivable to us—though not perhaps to eighteenth-century Paris.[8]

It seems then—to sum up this discussion—that the evidence we have hardly warrants such phrases as "kept in almost Oriental seclusion". Scholars have not made a clear enough distinction between

---

[7] Haigh, *The Attic Theatre*, 3rd edition (by A. W. Pickard-Cambridge).
[8] It is true that comedy and the satyric drama were associated with "religion"—and that it often removes all difficulties to call the same thing by a different name.

girls and married women, nor between conditions of life in Athens and Manchester, nor between Classical Greek and modern literature. Theocritus, in the early third century B.C., writes a lively mime describing how a Syracusan lady in Alexandria visits a friend and goes with her through the streets to a festival: and we are told, "These are Dorian ladies: see how much more freedom they had than the Athenians." The inference seems illegitimate. We ought rather to say, "This poem was written in Alexandria, a cosmopolitan city, in an age when the city-state had come to an end, and politics were the concern of kings and their officials, not of the ordinary citizen. See therefore what different subjects the poets now write about. No longer do they confine themselves to matters which touch the life of the polis: instead, they actually begin to write about private and domestic life."

# 4 *The Sociology of Prostitution in Antiquity in the Context of Pagan and Christian Writings*

## HANS HERTER[†]
### *translated by Linwood DeLong*

One reason for writing an additional article on the delicate topic of prostitution, given that an article on this topic already exists[1] (*RAC* 3, 1154–213), is that in this existing article the author's attitudes toward this phenomenon overshadow the subject matter and a gap in scholarship has developed that should be filled. The second reason is that one is dealing with a phenomenon that simply cannot be overlooked in more developed societies and that was certainly more prominent in antiquity than it is today. This is not the place to search for the causes or impacts of prostitution, or to investigate the significance of *hetairai* [prostitutes] in the intellectual history of classical antiquity, or to study the artistic aspects of the different topics that emerge from a study of prostitution.[2] I cannot become involved in an examination of details. Rather, like the author of the aforementioned article, I intend to concentrate only on the attitude of Christianity toward prostitution compared with the way that prostitution was regarded in secular antiquity, no matter how tentative may be my results.

One can gauge how serious this problem was for the Church Fathers by their references to it not only in texts that focus on this topic but also

---

[†] Originally published as "Die Soziologie der antiken Prostitution im Lichte des heidnischen und christlichen Schrifttums," *Jahrbuch für Antike und Christentum*, 3 (1900), 70–111.

[1] For further literature on this topic, which is cited here in abbreviated form, see *RAC* 3, 1212f and F. Hauck—S. Schulz, *pornê*, *Theologisches Wörterbuch zum Neuen Testament* 6.579–95. The most recent, definitive work known to me that discusses this topic in a general manner (W. Bauer, *Geschichte und Wesen der Prostitution* [Stuttgart 1956]) provides adequate space to study the convergences between conditions in antiquity and in modern times, but it offers a totally distorted picture of the conditions in antiquity. Regarding texts from antiquity, see K. Schneider, *Het.* (= "Hetairai," *RE* 8.2, 1331–72) 1361f.

[2] In the case of such topics it was, from a practical point of view, unsatisfactory to restrict oneself to those places that dealt specifically with *hetairai*. In the article entitled "Prostitute" it was not, nor should it have been, possible to discuss the whole phenomenon of fornication.

in their frequent passing references to it elsewhere. Not infrequently they discuss this topic with a surprising openness, though always with an *honoris praefatio* [respectful introduction], that can only be explained by the situation that existed in antiquity.[3] In general one could say that Christianity opened up a new approach to this topic with a determination that surpasses the approach of some strictly observant Stoics, though it betrays a strong Israelite influence: *porneia* [prostitution] is placed beside *moikheia* [adultery] once and for all, even though (to the extent that it is expressed) it is viewed as a less serious misdeed and is attributed to both parties. The paralleling of both sins is clearly an indication of Christian origin.[4] As a result of this re-evaluation many of the generally recognized motives for committing adultery became applicable to prostitution, a process that is less clearly observable in this article than in a previous one and that must be dealt with in a systematic examination of the whole phenomenon of adultery. In spite of my desire to concentrate on the topic at hand, I have not been totally able to withstand the temptation to introduce a wide variety of material from pagan perspectives for which there was no direct Christian counterpart. I trust that I will not annoy future scholars who investigate this topic. I do so primarily in asides and do not wish to create the impression that I have completely exhausted this topic.

## I THE SPREAD OF PROSTITUTION AND THE CENTERS OF PROSTITUTION

Because Christians have a very fixed value judgment concerning prostitution, the factual information that they provide on this subject is somewhat colored by their attitudes. This can be seen in their comments concerning the spread of this evil. Prostitutes belonged chiefly, if not exclusively, to urban centers[5] but they often came from outside the cities and they moved to other places of residence, as was the case with the frequently mentioned Neaera.[6] Naturally prostitutes were primarily attracted to large centers of population and activity, and in Greece the primary centers were Athens[7] and

---

[3] One should consult the sermon by John Chrysostom regarding the acts of Synesius.

[4] E.g. *PTeb.* 2.276.16. See also *RAC* 3, 1190f.

[5] Hor. *Epist.* 1.14.21f; Antip. Thess. *Anth. Pal.* 6.208; Lib. *Comp.* 5.6 and elsewhere. Regarding prostitutes in villages, see for example Dio Chrys. 5.25. Regarding this topic in general, see *Anacreontea* 14.

[6] [Dem.] 59.107f; see Firm. Mat. *Math.* 6.31.90; regarding *peregrina* [(resident) foreigner] = prostitute: Donat. Ter. *An.* 146, 469.

[7] Men. *Sam.* 175–82; Heraclid. Pont. *Opp. Graec.* 1, 5; Turpil. 186; Lucian *Musc. enc.* 11; Ath. 12.532CD, 547D, 13.583D etc. For writings concerning Athenian *hetairai* see Ath. 13.567A.

Corinth.[8] Other cities were significant in this connection: Epidamnus,[9] Epidaurus,[10] Cyzicus,[11] Lesbos,[12] Megara,[13] Miletus,[14] Samos,[15] and Tanagra,[16] just to name a few examples. Byzantium is also mentioned quite early.[17] Some geographical regions were important in this connection, such as Thessaly[18] and Sicily.[19] No less important were the regions in Egypt[20] such as Alexandria, Canopus, Elephantine, Naucratis.[21] In Italy everything converged on Rome,[22] the center of evil,[23] but the *meretrix* [whore] of Cumae[24] and of Naples[25] retained reputations of their own, as did the *Lucana amica* [Lucanian girlfriend].[26] The situation in Pompeii in particular was well known.[27] Frequently the prostitutes came from the Orient[28] and were referred to as Lydians,[29] Syrians,[30] Phoenicians,[31] or even Thracians.[32] After passing through Egypt, these living wares were introduced on the coast of the Red Sea, or in the case of more distant countries, through Coptus and were taxed with a special

---

[8] Schneider, *Het.* 1339; M. Goebel, *Ethnica.* Diss. Breslau (1915) 36–8. See also Pl. *Resp.* 3.404D; Eub. fr. 54; Strattis, fr. 26; Plut. *Tim.* 14; *Mor.* 767F–8A; Lucian *Am.* 51; Philostr. *Ep.* 47; Alciphr. 3.24.3; Ath. 8.351CD; Schol. Ar. *Lys.* 91.

[9] Plaut. *Men.* 261f, 553.

[10] Plaut. *Epid.* 540f, 554f.

[11] Eup. fr. 233; see W. Süss, *RhM* 97 (1954) 122.

[12] Pherecr. fr. 149. Mytilene: *Hist. Apoll. Tyr.* 33–6, 39–47 (modern Greek version 535–606, 626–793).

[13] Goebel 28f; Hauschild *AJP* 74 (1953) 10; see also Plaut. *Pers.* 137f, Lucian, *Catapl.* 6.

[14] Eub. fr. 42.

[15] T. Lenschau, *RE* 21, 1732; Diph. fr. 50; Clearch. fr. 44W. = Ath. 12.540F–1A; Plut. *Mor.* 753D; see also Alex. Sam. fr. 1 J.

[16] Goebel 63f.

[17] Theopomp. fr. 62 J.; Procop. *Aed.* 1.9.4; Agath. *Anth. Plan.* 80; Anon. *Anth. Pal.* 7.221 (?); Psellus, *Ep.* 97f K.-Dr. Even Sparta was not totally unaffected (Polemo, Ath. 13.574CD; see also Nic. *ibid.* 592A).

[18] Theopomp. fr. 49J.; Theophr. fr. 147 (Ath. 10.435A); Pers. Ath. 13.607 C.

[19] Plaut. *Rud.* 53–6, 540–4.

[20] Schneider, *Het.* 1339; Bringmann 120f; F. Cumont, *L'Égypte des astrologues* (Brussels 1937) 180f.

[21] Hdt. 2.135; Ath. 13.596B–E.

[22] F. Leo, *Plautinische Forschungen zur Kritik und Geschichte der Komödie*[2] (Berlin 1912) 140; K. Schneider, *Mer.* (="Meretrix," *RE* 15.1, 1018–27) 1022f; for example Cass. Dio 79.13.3 [465 B.].

[23] Sen. *Dial.* 12.6.2f.

[24] Furius Bibaculus fr. 4 M.

[25] Afran. 136.

[26] Hor. *Epist.* 1.15.21.

[27] M. Della Corte, *Case ed abitanti di Pompei*[2] (Pompei-Scavi: Presso l'autore 1954), Index (see for example 48f, 122f, 140–2, 168f, 366f, 390).

[28] Prop. 2.23.21f; Juv. 3.65f; Philostr. *Ep.* 47; W. Schubart, *IMS* 10 (1916) 1533f; *Excavations at Dura-Europos* 1935–6 (New Haven 1944) 258.

[29] Anon. *iamb. in turpilucr.* 40 D.; Stat. *Silv.* 1.6.70; Ath. 13.597A.

[30] Plaut. *Truc.* 530–5, 633f; *Copa* 1; Suet. *Ner.* 27. 2; see also Plut. *Crass.* 32.3 and n. 517.

[31] Herod. 2.18. Philostr. *Ep.* 47.

[32] Hdt. 2.134. Ath. 13.576C, 577A, 595A. Philostr. *Ep.* 47; Phot., *Suda* s.v. *Rhodôpidos anathêma.*

levy.[33] On the other hand, King Straton of Sidon used to acquire his prostitutes from Greece.[34] Dio Chrysostom (7.134) mentions that during his time Greek women served much more frequently as prostitutes than had been the case earlier.

The Leporello index is a substantial one, right from the beginning, and with little effort it could be made much longer, but the summary judgment that the whole world was full of prostitution was first made by Christian writers.[35] All or almost all cities, it was stated, had an overabundance of prostitutes.[36] Even Jerusalem[37] and other places within the Holy Lands[38] were no exception. The large cities of the world were particularly strongly criticized,[39] specifically Alexandria[40] and Constantinople,[41] where speeches about whores were in vogue and where a murdering hand directed at whores was needed,[42] but also eastern cities in general.[43] An actress in Antioch who had converted, and whose reputation extended from Cilicia to Cappadocia, was born in the most infamous city in Phoenicia;[44] according to F. J. Dölger she was from Heliopolis.[45] In Corinth the Apostle Paul had special reasons for attacking all forms of sexual perversions.[46] Salvian (*Gub. Dei* 7.15) says about Aquitania: *paene unus gurges omnium gula, paene unum lupanar omnium vita* [Gluttony, so to speak, is a capacious sink for all, and life just everyone's brothel]. Egypt is a country of vice[47] and Africa, especially Carthage, abounds with fornication.[48] According to Augustine,[49] there were many prostitutes in Bulla but in the surrounding area, for example in Hippo, "almost" none.

[33] Tariff of Coptus, 90 A.D., Ditt. *OGI* 674, 16f; see also Schubart, *IMS* 10 (1916) 1533f; L. Fiesel, *GGN* 1925, 100f.

[34] Theopomp. fr. 114 J. See also Ter. *Ad.* 224–31; Strabo 2.99. Ship's cargoes consisting of *hetairai*: Antiphil. *Anth. Pal.* 9.415; Phil. *Anth. Pal.* 9. 416. W. W. Tarn, *The Greeks in Bactria and India* (Cambridge 1938; ²1951) 373–5. See below note 154.

[35] Clem. Al. *Paed.* 3.22.2 who also thinks about pederasty in the same way as Lib. *Or.* 64.81 does.

[36] Clem. Al. *Paed.* 3.31.2f.; Athan. *Gent.* 25.

[37] Gr. Nyss. *Ep.* 2; Jer. *Ep.* 58.4.4, cf. 74.3 (based on *Ezek.* 16); Jo. Mosch. *Prat.* 45. The zealots had made a *porneion* [brothel] out of Jerusalem (Jos. *BJ* 4.562).

[38] Jo. Mosch. *Prat.* 14; Caesarea and Sebaste: Jos. *BJ* 19.357.

[39] Salv. *Gub. Dei* 7.106.

[40] Gr. Nyss. *V. Gr. Thaum.*, *PG* 46.904 and many others.

[41] Mac. Aeg. *PG* 34.221 and many others.

[42] Gr. Naz. *Carm.* 2.1.15.21f.

[43] Gr. Nyss. *Ep.* 2. Edessa: Gr. Nyss. *V. Ephr.* (*PG* 46.833; *PL* 73.321f).

[44] Chrys. *Hom. in Mt.* 67(68).3. Simon's Helena originally came from Tyre (Eus. *Hist. Eccl.* 2.13); see also Jo. Mosch. *Prat.* 186; *RAC* 3, 1210.

[45] *AChr* 3 (1932) 271 no. 34. See also *RAC* 3, 1209f.

[46] See also Pall. *H. Laus.* 148 (65).

[47] E.g. Epiph. *Haer.* 66.2.3f.

[48] Salv. *Gub. Dei* 7.65–108.

[49] August. *Serm.* Denis 17.7–9 (G. Morin, *S. Augustini sermones post Maurinos reperti* [Rome 1930]). See also Dessau, *ILS* 9455.

A similar tendency can be observed in the depiction of the conditions within individual cities. For the purposes of an historical exposition[50] it is sufficient to observe here that in some instances an organized form of prostitution had developed at sites consecrated to Aphrodite. Young girls who served as possessions of the goddess benefitted the temple and indirectly the city, by surrendering themselves to the temple visitors. We are familiar with this situation in Corinth, for it was documented to exist there during the Persian Wars. One can assume, however, that neither the thousand and more *hierodouloi* [temple slaves] whom Strabo refers to nor the ones at the Pontic Comana[51] were the only women who practiced this profession. Apart from this we are familiar with examples of sacred prostitution only in areas on the periphery of Greek territory (Cyprus, both of the Comanas, Eryx, Sicca Veneria) and we can cite counter examples that are clearly un-Hellenic. It seems reasonable to assume that there was an influence from the East, just as F. W. von Bissing has done in his explanations of individual occurrences in Egypt.[52] The Epizephyrian Locrians' dedication in the middle of the fifth century BC and their custom of consecrating a pig to Aphrodite,[53] which was so shamefully misused by Dionysius II, may both be tied to a foreign custom, even if they offered free women and virgins to the goddess. These are simply two unusual cases, from which Clearchus[54] constructed a generalization when he claims that this was a continuous custom not only among the Locrians but also among the Cyprians and Lydians. If Nicander's report is correct,[55] that Solon built the temple of Aphrodite Pandemos in Athens using the proceeds from the brothel that he constructed, then one can observe the influence of an Asian model. The center of this argument, Solon's construction of the first brothel,[56] does not deserve the distrust that it frequently receives.[57] The fact itself, as well as the motivation that is ascribed to him, is consistent with what we know about Solon's concern for the institution

[50] *RAC* 3, 1157–9. According to legend, the Propoetides were the first prostitutes (Ov. *Met.* 10.238–45; Plut. *Mor.* 777D); compare the daughters of Cinyras and Elegeis-Pero.

[51] Strabo 8.378; 12. 559. For each Comana Strabo mentions the fantastic number of 6000 *hierodouloi* [temple slaves] (12.535, 558). See also *RAC* 3, 1175.

[52] *RhM* 92 (1944) 375–81. See especially *PTeb.* 6. Cf. H. Bonnet, *ZÄS* 80 (1955) 4.

[53] Just. 21.3; cf. Clearch. fr. 47 W., Ath. 12.541C–E and Ael. *VH* 9.8; see also Strabo 6.259f; Plut. *Mor.* 821D; *Tim.* 13. S. C. Turano, *ArchClass* 4 (1952) 248–52.

[54] Clearch. fr. 43aW., Ath. 12.516AB.

[55] Nic. fr. 9f Gow-Scholfield. See also U. von Wilamowitz-Moellendorf, *Der Glaube der Hellenen* (Basel 1956) 1.97 n. 1.

[56] Philem. fr. 4, see Ath. 13.569DF.

[57] It is regarded as a joke (A. V. Puntoni, *Studi di mitologia greca ed italica* 1 [Pisa 1884] 75 [not available to the author]; Leo, *Plautin. Forsch.*² 152) or at least as something embellished for the purposes of fiction (W. Judeich, *Topographie von Athen*² (Munich 1931) 285 n. 1).

of marriage.[58] An anecdote from the older Cato confirms that such places existed in Rome.[59]

This essay provides ample indication concerning the number of houses in the cities that opened themselves to the frequent visitors. Dio Chrysostom (7.133, 139) contains a deep lament about this phenomenon, and Tertullian (*Ad. Mart.* 2.7) emphasizes that Christians encounter *loca libidinum publicarum* [places of public lust] everywhere.[60] The situation is further complicated by the tendency for restaurant owners,[61] who generally did not enjoy a good reputation,[62] to function as pimps, even using their wives as prostitutes.[63] It appears that even simple *popinae* [eating houses] and similar kinds of places offered possibilities for prostitution.[64] According to Roman law, waitresses had the same status as prostitutes in a bordello.[65] In a similar vein, *caupones* [taverns] and *lenones* [pimps] are frequently mentioned in the same sentence,[66] as are their corresponding establish-

---

[58] *RE* 3A, 967; cf. *RAC* 3, 1180.

[59] Hor. *Sat.* 1.2.31–5 with Porphyrio and *Schol. Acr.* (*RAC* 3, 1158). See also Aristipp. fr. 59 M., Diog. Laert. 2.69.

[60] For proof, see the following examples: Athenag. *Leg.* 34; Cypr. *Ad. Don.* 10; *Hab. Virg.* 12; *Ep.* 55.26; Lactant. *Div. Inst.* 6.23.7; Arn. 2. 42; Zeno Ver. 1.4.4; Mac. Aeg. *PG* 34.221–4; [Rufin.] *V. Eug.* 14; Chrys. *Virg.* 19; *Stag.* 2.1; *Hom. in Mt.* 28.4; 73.3; *Hom. in Hebr.* 14.4; Isid. *Pel. Ep.* 2. 274; Salv. *Gub. Dei* 7.72; Jo. Mosch. *Prat.* 97. Cf. *Anth. Lat.* 907.9; Plut. *Mor.* 752C; Aeschin. 1.124. There are very many designations (Schneider, *Het.* 1339; Schneider, *Mer.* 1022). Probably the most common Greek term was *porneion*, for which the people from Attica frequently used the euphemism *oikēma* or *oikiskos* (*RE* 17, 2117), as well as *khamaitypeion*. In Latin one finds *lupanar* (later *lupanarium*), as well as *fornix* (literally an arch; see Isid. *Or.* 10.110; *TLL* s.v.) and also *lustrum* (Serv. *Aen.* 3.647). *Effeminatorium domus meretricum* [home of pathic prostitutes]: *Gloss. Lat.* 5. 599.14. *Koineion* probably *PSI* 1055a. *Kasôrion*: see E. Müller-Graupa, *Glotta* 19 (1931) 67. The Christians also speak about *porneia* and *khamaitypeia*, *lupanaria* and *fornices*. Later *phoundax*, see G. Rouillard, *RPh* 68 (1942) 63–6.

[61] L. Friedländer, *Sittengeschichte Roms* 1^10 (Leipzig 1921–3) 351, 387; Schneider, *Het.* 1341; Schneider, *Mer.* 1023; T. Kleberg, *Hôtels, restaurants et cabarets dans l'antiquité romaine* (Uppsala 1957), previously Kleberg, *Värdshus och Värdshusliv* (Göteborg 1934) 111–13; M. Bös, *KJ* 3 (1958) 21f.

[62] Isoc. 7.49; Hyp. fr. 141Bl. = 138J.; Artem. 1.23.

[63] Ar. *Plut.* 426; Theopomp. fr. 62 J.; Hor. *Sat.* 1.5.82–5; *Epist.* 1.14.25f; *Copa* 1; Plut. *Tim.* 14; *Juv.* 8.162 + *Schol.*; Apul. *Met.* 1.7f; Polyaenus, 4.2.3; Philostr. *Ep.* 32f, 60; Ath. 13.566 F–7A; Cass. Dio 79.13.2; Lib. *Or.* 46.19; *CIL* 4.7384, 8442; [Lucian], *Philopatr. dial.* 9 p. 329 Bonn.; cf. Catull. 37; Hor. *Carm.* 3.7.9–22; Plut. *Demetr.* 26 *extr.*; *Syntipas* p. 57 Jernst.; Eustath. *Hysm.* 8.4.3 (240H.). In the inns, traveling pimps would often lodge with their young girls (Strabo 12.578).

[64] Kleberg, 37; Tac. *Hist.* 3.83; regarding *popina = meretrix*, see Kleberg, 16; *thermipolium* [shop selling warm drinks], Kleberg, 24; J. Colin, *Latomus* 15 (1956) 60; *ganeum* ("beneath the earth") = *taberna meretricum* [shop of prostitutes] (*TLL* s.v.).

[65] Ulpian, *Dig.* 23.2.43; see also 3.2.4.2; Alex. *Cod. Iust.* 4.56.3; Constantin. *Cod. Theod.* 9.7.1 and *Cod. Iust.* 9.9.28; see also Kukules, 2.2.130f. Cf. Jos. *AJ* 3.276; from the prostitute Rahab he creates (*AJ* 5.7–15, 30) the female owner of an inn (see Hauck-Schulz, *TheolWb* 6.584 n. 33; K. H. Rengstorf, *ibid.* 588f).

[66] Theopr. *Char.* 6.5; Aur. Vict. *Caes.* 33.6; Kleberg, 82f.

ments.[67] Thus the Lydians were restricted by the Persians, *cauponas et ludicras artes et lenocinia exercere* [to using taverns and the arts of public spectacles and pimping],[68] as were the Babylonians.[69] To visit a tavern, when it could be avoided, was viewed as a discreditable activity, and was placed on the same level as visiting a brothel, even if the purpose of the visit was to satisfy the desires of the stomach.[70] If one could not find private accommodation then inns could not be avoided, but the latter were nevertheless regarded with suspicion.[71] The brothels that were situated on properties (*praedia*) should be viewed as taverns located on roads.[72] There is no lack of dubious signage.[73] The question as to whether the well-known marble bas-relief from Rome, bearing the inscription *Ad sorores IIII* [To the four sisters], should be mentioned here must be put aside.[74] From Christian sources one also gains a picture of regularized prostitution in taverns.[75]

When there are occasional references in these sources to *kapêleia* [retail trade], there is a connection to stores. In fact there are places of prostitution in Pompeii that are linked to places where wares are sold; in one instance there is a connection to a hair salon.[76] The thermal baths, with their female servants and bathing masters who offered various opportunities, justifiably aroused suspicion.[77] In

[67] Hor. *Epist.* 1.14.21; Col. 1.8.2; Plut. *Mor.* 1093F (a comic fragment?); Suet. *Iul.* 49.1; Apul. *De dog. Plat.* 1.13; Just. 21.5.4; Poll. 9.34; Julian. *Or.* 6.186D; Mac. Aeg. *Hom.* 12.2; Jer. *In Os.* 1.4.10–2; *Gloss. Lat.* 5.369.44.

[68] Just. 1.7.12.

[69] Plut. *Mor.* 173C; see also *RAC* 4, 621.

[70] Sen. *Dial.* 7.7.3; see also *RAC* 3, 1164f; Kleberg, 120; A. Alföldi, *ZtschrNum* 38 (1928) 169 n. 4.

[71] In addition to Hor. *Sat.* 1.5.82–5 the other significant example is the well-known bas-relief of Aesernia (*CIL* 9, 2689; Dessau, *ILS* 7478; Dar.-Sag. 1.2 fig. 1258; F. Poulsen, *Römische Kulturbilder* [Copenhagen 1949] 184; Kleberg, 69f, 90). For comic poets, a trip meant *porneia* (Ar. *Ran.* 113).

[72] Ulpian, *Dig.* 5.3.27; see also Navarre 1837 n. 4.

[73] Kleberg, 117. A servant is called Culibonia (*CIL* 4, 8473; Kleberg, 89).

[74] For a description of the ancient statues, see Berlin (1891) 359f no. 890; A. v. Salis, *Antike und Renaissance* (Erlenb.-Zür. 1947) 161 Plate 48c; Kleberg, 57, 66; for a different perspective see A. Rumpf, *AJA* 58 (1954) 177. Even a distinguished establishment, such as the so-called Villa of Good Fortune in Olynthus, which was referred to as a tavern by W. A. McDonald, in G. E. Mylonas (ed.), *Studies Presented to D. M. Robinson on his Seventieth Birthday* 1 (St. Louis 1951) 365–73, shows no clear signs of prostitution, even though it bears the inscription *Aphroditê kalê* [Aphrodite is beautiful].

[75] See Gr. Nyss. *Ep.* 2; Jer. *Virg. Mar.* 21; Jo. Mosch. *Prat.* 31, 188, 194; Symeon Metaphrastes, *V. Abr.* 19–27; A. Thom. 48–55; *V. Thdr.* 3 (T. Ioannis, *Mnêmeia Hagiologika* [Venice 1884] 363f); see also Salv. *Gub. Dei* 7.73; Pall. *H. Laus.* 45; Psellus, *Ep.* 97 K.-Dr.; Kleberg, 95f, *RAC* 3, 1205. Regarding the tradition of viewing Helena as a *stabularia* [inn-keeper], see Kleberg, 138 n. 2.

[76] Della Corte, *Case ed abitanti* ²198; cf. Mart. 2.17.

[77] Ulpian, *Dig.* 3.2.4.2; Mart. 2.48.52; Tac. *Hist.* 3.83; Anon. *Anth. Pal.* 5.81; *Syntipas* p. 36f Jernst.; J. Colin, *RBPh* 33 (1955) 860f.

Ephesus one can find an elegant house of pleasure *paidiskêia* [with young girls], dating from the turn of the first century AD, which continued to operate during Christian times, and was located in the basement of the thermal baths of the Scholasticia.[78] Perhaps the common *alicariae* [spelt-girls, prostitutes][79] were connected to baking and milling operations. In later times there were veritable human traps located in the grain mills of Rome, which Theodosius eliminated,[80] but there were also other infamous *mylônes* [mills].[81] According to Anacreon, even Artemon had contact with female bread peddlers, and in the area of Samos that was under Lydian influence these women did not make a totally positive impression.[82] The female wreath sellers in Eubulus were probably women of easy virtue,[83] as were a flower seller[84] and a seller of ointments[85] who are mentioned elsewhere.

## 2  DEPENDENT AND FREE-MOVING PROSTITUTES

The actual whorehouses generally belonged to pimps, sometimes madams, who are also mentioned in Christian writings and in legal codes. Not infrequently the owners of these prostitutes assigned the management of these women to others,[86] so that the owners themselves could retain their reputation as honest people.[87] There was a fluid transition from larger institutions to the smaller ones where a pimp,[88] or frequently a madam,[89] maintained one or several young women and directed their activities.[90] Former prostitutes were predes-

---

[78] F. Miltner, *JÖAI* 43 (1956–8) Beibl. 20f., n. 14; *AAWW* 1958, 80; *Atlantis* 30 (1958) 309 with illustrations on p. 310; *Ephesos* (Vienna 1958) 51f. The balneum Venerium in Pompeii (*CIL* 4, 1136) was not a disreputable institution, but rather a bath that was worthy of Venus for the upper ten thousand (Kroll, 176 n. 83; A. Maiuri, *PP* 3 [1948] 156–64).

[79] Plaut. *Poen.* 266; Paulus in Festus, 7.11–13 L.; see also Della Corte 397.

[80] Socr. *H. E.* 5.18; Thphn. *Chron.*, PG 108.209; see also Kleberg, 80, 85, 90.

[81] Bas. Sel. *V. Thecl.*, PG 85.488.

[82] Anac. fr. 54, see also 16D.; Clearch. fr. 44W, Ath. 12.540 F–1A, to be explained according to Hsch. s. v. *dêmiourgos*.

[83] Eub. fr. 98–105; see also T. B. L. Webster, *WS* 69 (1956) 114, *Art and Literature in Fourth Century Athens* (London 1956) 71f.

[84] Dionys. Soph. *Anth. Pal.* 5.80.

[85] Asclep. *Anth. Pal.* 5.180.

[86] Isae. 6.19; Ulpian, *Dig.* 3.2.4.3; 5.3.27; see also *PSI* 1055a; *PLond.* 5.1877.

[87] Ulpian, *Dig.* 5.3.27.

[88] Eub. fr. 88; *Com. Adesp.* fr. 804; Stabo 14.648 (W. Aly, *Strabonis Geographica* 4 [Bonn 1957] 43); cf. W. Croenert, *RhM* 64 (1909) 440, Ath. *H. Ar.* 20.

[89] Ar. *Thesm.* 1172–1201; Anon., *Anth. Pal.* 5.100.

[90] Plaut. *Cist.* 374–6; see also *Merc.* 410f; Ath. 13.593f, 595A. The tradition of the *hetairai* school of Aspasia (Plut. *Per.* 24.5, 30.4: Ath. 13.569f) is probably attributable to a joke of Aristophanes (*Ach.* 526f, Schneider, *Het.* 1335f; Navarre 1823f). See also E. Meinhardt, *Perikles bei Plutarch*, Diss. Frankfurt (1957) 54, 78, 217.

tined to this kind of job,[91] and they lived off the earnings of younger women.[92] Not infrequently it was the biological mother,[93] or alleged mother, who was able to derive particular benefit from this pretext.[94] The practice of using one's wife as a prostitute, which was punishable by law,[95] should be mentioned in this connection.[96] When Christian writers condemned such a dismal phenomenon,[97] they believed that they could refer to the examples of Socrates and Cato,[98] but they also had to deal with the issue of Abraham.[99] In private homes in Roman times it was sometimes customary for the host to look after the erotic needs of his guests.[100] It is not possible to deal here with other instances of occasional prostitution. John Chrysostom (*Hom. in 1 Cor.* 30.4) writes about elderly persons of both genders who earned a substantial income in this manner.

In addition to the dependent prostitutes there were many who worked freely and lived off their own earnings. Artemidorus[101] refers to them *a potiori* as *plazomenai* [rovers] in contrast to those *ep' ergastêriôn* [in brothels]. Such women would occupy the brothel,[102] use a rented house or even their own house.[103] One could enter into a long-term relationship with a prostitute,[104] either with

[91] Poll. 4.153.

[92] Hyp. 5.3; Theopomp. fr. 253J.; Claudian. 18.90–7; Synes. *Ep.* 3.

[93] Ath. 13.580F; Plaut. *Asin.*; *Epid.* 555f; Tib. 1.6.57–66; Ov. *Am.* 1.8.91; Marc. Arg. *Anth. Pal.* 5.126; Lucian, *Dial. meret.* 1.3, 6; Aristaenet. 1.19; cf. Plut. *Cleom.* 33.1; Xen. *Mem.* 3.11.4.

[94] [Dem.] 59.18f; Plaut. *Cist.* 89–93 = Men. fr. 382 Körte; Plaut. *Truc.* 401, 802; Ter. *Haut.* 233f, 269–71; Prop. 2.6.11; cf. Men. fr. 361.

[95] Ulpian, *Dig.* 48.4.2.2; 30.3f.; see *Cod. Iust.* 9.9.17; Papinian, *Dig.* 48.5.9; Tryph., *ibid.* 4.4.37; see P. Jörs in *Festschrift Theodor Mommsen zum fünfzigjährigen Doctorjubiläum* (Marburg 1893) 10, 25, G. Kleinfeller, *RE* 12, 1943.

[96] Schneider, *Mer.* 1021; W. Kroll, *WS* 37 (1915) 237f; F. J. Brecht, *Motiv- und Typengeschichte des griechischen Spottepigramms* (*Philologus* Supplementband 22.2) (Leipzig 1930) 58; F. Cumont, *L'Égypte des astrologues* (Brussels 1937) 181 n. 1; see for example Aeschin. 2. 149; [Dem.] 59.41, 68; *Com. Adesp.* fr. 8; Hor. *Carm.* 3.6.29–32; *Sat.* 2.5.75f; Ov. *Am.* 2.19.57; *Ars. am.* 2.553f; Parmenio, *Anth. Pal.* 11.4; Quint. *Inst.* 5.10.47; Mart. 2.47; Plut. *Mor.* 759F–60B; Apul. *Apol.* 75, 98; Vett. Val. p. 61.23f Kr.; Aristaenet. 1.13; *Anth. Lat.* 127, cf. 322; *Syntipas* p. 36f J. Cf. Lucil. 1223 (F.Münzer, *RE* 3, 2563); Tac. *Ann.* 6.45.3.

[97] Just. *Apol.* 1.27.4.

[98] Salv. *Gub. Dei* 7.103.

[99] August. *C. Faust.* 32.4. Wives who secretly engaged in prostitution: for example Apul. *Met.* 9.26; Synes. *Aeg.* 1.17 (112CD).

[100] Schneider, *Mer.* 1023; see also Plaut. *Merc.* 97–102; Hor. *Carm.* 3.7.9–22; Plut. *Ant.* 9.8. Regarding *hetairai* as gifts, see Aeschin. 1.75f.

[101] Artem. 1.78 p. 73 H; see also Firm. Mat. *Math.* 7.25.9. One finds references to free-moving prostitutes in Chrys. *Fem. reg.* 1 and Moschus, *Prat.* 186.

[102] Schneider, *Mer.* 1024.

[103] Schneider, *Het.* 1342.

[104] See [Dem.] 59.26, 28, 108, *RAC* 3, 1173. Even two at one time (Lys. fr. 8 Th.; [Dem.] 59.29, 46f; Plaut. *Asin.* 915–19; *Truc.* 958–63; Ter. *Eun.* 1072–83; Plut. *Mor.* 759F; see also Mart. 10.81; Nicarch. *Anth. Pal.* 11.328; Ath. 13.594BC; M. Bieber, *The Sculpture of the Hellenistic Age* (New York 1955) Fig. 654). Competition between father and son for the same *hetaira* (Amos 2.7; cf. *RAC* 3, 1162) is despicable (Bas. *Ep.* 160.3).

a free *hetaira*, with one whose freedom one had purchased or with one who had been reserved through an agent. One could then leave her where she was, lodge her in separate lodgings or with a friend.[105] She could only be housed in one's own home if one was not married, unless one was like Alcibiades and did not fear creating grounds for divorce.[106] A permanent relationship, which is depicted in New Comedy as the reward for good *hetairai*,[107] could lead if not to marriage, then at least to the status of *pallakê*, concubine.[108] There are numerous documented examples of such long-term relationships with men of intellect, among them philosophers,[109] and also with rulers, beginning with Sardanapalus.[110] Naturally some men would take a prostitute temporarily into their apartments,[111] not into their bedrooms, but rather into a hidden corner.[112] It was common for women of widely differing social standing to follow behind a column of soldiers and they were not always rejected by the person in command.[113] Scipio had difficulty cleaning out the military camp in front of Numantia.[114] Roman governors and other politicians were often criticized for their

[105] [Dem.] 59.22. Men. *Epitr.* 528f Körte.

[106] L. A. Post *TAPA* 71(1940) 425. Hyp. Ath. 13.590CD. In *Isae.* 6.21 a husband owns a brothel and moves into it himself. See also Plat. *Resp.* 8.574BC; Chrys. *Virg.* 55.

[107] Post (1940) 445–51; M. Neumann, *Die poetische Gerechtigkeit in der neuen Komödie*, Diss. Mainz (1958) 21–7, 100–11. Regarding the *hetairai* that are mentioned in Philemon, see C. A. Dietze, *De Philemone comico*, Diss. Göttingen (1901) 24–37.

[108] See *RAC* 3, 1173, and M. de Vries, *Pallake* (Amsterdam 1927); Post (1940) 444–6. The transition is fluid; see for example Plut. *Crass.* 32.3–5.

[109] These people are particularly criticized for having contact with prostitutes (Eratosth. Ath. 13.587F–8A), not only Aristippus (Ath. 12.544B, see also Aristipp. fr. 57–66, 78, 121, 123, 183 B.D. p. 82f Maneb.; *RAC* 3, 1183, 1202) and Epicurus (Cleomed. 2.1.92; Epiph. *Exp. fid.* 9.48; see also *RAC* 3, 1183) and the Epicureans (Epicur. fr. 237, Plut. *Mor.* 1086E; Metrodorus, Diog. Laert. 10.7), but also Socrates (see also Lucian, *Salt.* 25; *RAC* 3, 1183, 1202) and Aristotle (Gerhard, *Phoinix* 150). Julian. *Or.* 6.201D–2A glosses over Diogenes' relations with prostitutes. See L. Radermacher, *SÖAW* 202.1 (1924) 29–39, *RAC* 3, 1186f, 1202. Alcidamas wrote a eulogy concerning Nais (J. Krischan, *RE* 16,1586f). Cf. Ath. 7.279E, 13.590C–3F, 594D, 596F–7A, 607A–F, Dion. Hal. *Lys.* 3.

[110] See for example Machon, Ath. 13.583AB; Polyb. 14.11.2–5; Diod. Sic. 17.108.5f; Plut. *Mor.* 753 D–F, Ath. 13.576D–7A, 577C–8B, 586CD, 589D–90A, 593A–F, 594D–6B, 607F–8A, *RAC* 3, 1176, 1202. Antiochos Hierax fled out of prison with the aid of a *hetaira* with whom he had previously had a relationship (Just. *Epit.* 27.3.11); regarding a prostitute who was concerned about Roman prisoners, see Livy, 26.33.7f (cf. *RAC* 3, 1175). Cf. Phylarchus fr. 30 J. Commodus loved to see Marcia painted as an amazon and was therefore called Amazonius (*Hist. Aug. Comm.* 11.9). See Diyll. fr. 4 J. = Ath. 13.593EF; Didymus = Diog. Laert. 5.76. *Hetairai* are part of the household of a tyrant, according to Pl. *Resp.* 8.568E.

[111] Chrys. *Hom. in Hebr.* 14.4. Cf. *RAC* 3, 1161.

[112] August. *Serm.* 161.2.

[113] Ar. *Ach.* 551; Lys. fr. 8 Th.; Xen. *Anab.* 4.3.19, 30 (?); 5.4.33; Theopomp. fr. 213 J.; Alex. Sam. fr. 1 J. = Ath. 13.572F–3A; Cic. *Cat.* 2.23f; Val. Max. 7.3.7; Curt. 6.6.8–10, cf. 6.2.1; Plin. *HN* 3.103; Plut. *Ag. et Cleom.* 33 (12). 4; *Ant.* 18.4; Polyaen. 4.2.3; Cass. Dio 59.21.2; Ath. 13.572EF, 576DE; *Hist. Aug. Pesc.* 3.10. See also Dio Chrys. 5.25.

[114] F. Münzer, *RE* 4,1455. See also Quint. *Decl.* 3.12.

dubious entourage.[115] Jerome was still familiar with the scandalous affair of L. Quinctius Flamininus.[116] The different situations among prostitutes often converged with each other: Tibullus's Delia sometimes appears in the hands of a man, other times subjected to the power of a madam, and at other times in the care of an older woman. The Christian women, professed widows and virgins, who lived with men often acquired the reputation of being prostitutes.[117]

## 3 CAREERS AND ORIGINS OF PROSTITUTES

The career of a prostitute sometimes began very early.[118] Frequently young girls exchanged their real names[119] for assumed names.[120] But such names only occasionally betrayed the girls' true occupation and if these names did so, the name was either a flattering one[121] or a pejorative nickname[122] that was imposed by men. In other instances the names did not apply to real people but were inventions of a humorist. On the whole these names were appropriate, but certainly not without ambiguity,[123] and one must be careful not to assume that the Tryphaena who is referred to in Paul's *Epistle to the Romans* 16:12 was necessarily a *hetaira*.[124] In the event that a prostitute married, she could reverse this naming process.[125]

---

[115] C. Gracchus, Gell. 15.12.3. So, for example Verres' Chelidon and Tertia, Cethegus' Praecia, Pompeius' Flora; in addition, Cic. *Mil.* 55; *Att.* 10.10.5; Prop. 2. 16; Cass. Dio 45.26, 2, 28.2.

[116] Cic. *Sen.* 42; Livy 39.42f; Val. Max. 2.9.2; Sen. *Controv.* 9.2; Plut. *Cato mai.* 17; Jer. *In Mt.* 2.14. Perhaps this was actually a male *scortum* [prostitute] (M. Gelzer, *RE* 22,127).

[117] Chrys. *Fem. reg.* 3.5.

[118] [Dem.] 59.22; Heraclit. *Ep.* 7.5; *Nov.* 14.

[119] Regarding the names of prostitutes, see P. Legrand, *REG* 20 (1907) 184 n. 2; Navarre 1833f; Schneider, *Het.* 1334, 1336, 1338f, 1358–60, 1362–71; see also F. Bechtel, *Die attischen Frauennamen* (Göttingen 1902); G. Fridberg, *Die Schmeichelworte der antiken Literatur*, Diss. Rostock 1912; K. Gatzert, *De nova comoedia quaestiones onomatologicae*, Diss. Gießen (1913) 30–41, 59–61; A. Hug, *RE* 3 A, 1824; L. Radermacher, *Mythos und Sage²* (Vienna 1943) 344 n. 208; J. Colin, *RBPh* 33 (1955) 853–76. Regarding the names in Lucian's *Dial. meret.* that are taken from comedies, see C. Wendel, *JKPh* Suppl. 26 (1901) 39–41 n. 84. Eucharion, see P. Schmitz, *Gymnasium* 59 (1952) 216–23. Lampadion, see W. Süss, *RhM* 97 (1954) 294. Philemation, see B. Marzullo, *SIFC* 27–8 (1956) 266. Regarding prostitutes without fathers' names, see A. Calderini, *Aegyptus* 33 (1953) 364.

[120] Plaut. *Poen.* 1139f; Ath. 13.576D; L.A. Post, *AJPh* 74 (1953) 108f.

[121] Ov. *Ars am.* 2.657–62. See also note 395.

[122] So for example the *Palaioporne* of an artistic troop that was visiting in Dura-Europos.

[123] For example Aphrodite (C. Sittl, *Die Gebärden der Griechen und Römer* [Leipzig 1890] 183; E. Maass, *NJb* 27 [1911] 467). *Aphroditaridion*: Plat. Com. fr. 48A Edm.

[124] A. Cabaniss, *CPh* 49 (1954) 98. On the basis of the names, G. Roux, *BCH* 79 (1955) 374f, identifies a *hetaira* in Cyparissia. But one must be careful (A. Wilhelm, *JÖA* 25 [1929] 59–65; K. Latte, *Gnomon* 23 [1951] 255).

[125] Aristaenet. 1.19.

The legal situation for prostitutes varied considerably.[126] In a brothel one would normally find female slaves,[127] but there were also free prostitutes who were there under contract. Women in both categories could only attain their freedom if they satisfied the demands of the pimp or the person who was entitled to force them into this employment.[128] Naturally there were instances in which a prostitute simply ran away.[129] Those who moved about outside a brothel were usually either prostitutes who had been let free or else ones who had been born free. Generally speaking, prostitutes were drawn from the lower social classes, as the Church Fathers emphasized.[130] It was often financial need that drove them to prostitution or to working in a brothel,[131] but the seductive example that a Neaera offered for the daughters of poor people was generally looked down upon.[132] The Church Fathers sometimes recognized the economic motives behind prostitution and shifted the responsibility for this phenomenon to the world of men.[133] But not all writers accepted this excuse.[134] John Chrysostom did not find this explanation satisfactory, pointing out that opportunities to work existed. Citing *Jeremiah* 3:3 he maintained that women became prostitutes because they had no shame.[135] In fact some women followed the principle: better to be rich in a dishonorable way rather than virtuous and poor.[136] The fear of hard work, such as spinning or weaving, and the temptation of a much easier way of life only made the pathway toward prostitution that much more attractive and made it possible for mothers to demand immediate obedience from their daughters,[137] or for young women of

---

[126] Hauschild, 53–67; L. A. Post (1940) 442, 446f; Hauschild, *AJPh* 74 (1953) 108f; F. O. Copley, *Exclusus Amator* (Madison WI 1956) 36f; [Andoc.] 4.14; Calpurnius Flaccus 5.

[127] Schneider, *Mer.* 1024; G. Kleinfeller, *RE* 12, 1942.

[128] Hdt. 2.135; Men. *Epit.* 319–24, 340–3, 360–5, 372f, 381–4; Plaut. *Cas.* 82–6; *Priap.* 40; Sen. *Controv.* 10.4.11; Dio Chrys. 7.133; Plut. *Mor.* 64F; *Phoc.* 38.3f; Ulpian, *Dig.* 3.2.4.2; *Nov.* 14 (39); Schol. Ar. *Vesp.* 1353; *RAC* 3, 1171. Regarding the novella motif, *ibid.* 1209–11.

[129] Dessau, *ILS* 9455.

[130] Chrys. *Thdr.* 1.13; *Hom. in Mt.* 68 (69).4; *Hom. in Rom.* 27.3; 30.4; Bas. Sel. *PG* 85.488C. Noble lineage, for example Ath. 13.596EF.

[131] Timocles fr. 23; Ter. *Haut.* 446f; Quint. *Decl.* 3.16; Ath. 13.583E; Firm. Mat. *Math.* 3.6.22; 6.30.16; Aristaenet. 1.19; Procop. *Aed.* 1.9.3, 6; Georg. Pachym. *Decl.* 10; cf. Men. fr. 783, 810 Kö. Post (1940) 442, 446f, 448f.

[132] [Dem.] 59.133.

[133] Lactant. *Div. inst.* 5.8.7; *Cod. Theod.* 15.8.2; Proc. G. *Anast.* 13; Jo. Mosch. *Prat.* 136, 186, 207; *V. Marciani* 19.

[134] Philo, *Spec. leg.* 1.103, 280.

[135] Chrys. *Hom. in Hebr.* 15.3 (see also *Hom. in Mt.* 75 [76].5).

[136] Ter. *An.* 797f. On the contrary, a prostitute became a weaver, even though she had wealthy admirers (Anon. *Anth. Pal.* 6.283).

[137] Strabo 8.378 (Herod. fr. 69 Cr.); Ter. *An.* 69–79, 797f; cf. Plaut. *Asin.* 504–44; *Cist.* 40–50; Antip. Sid. *Anth. Pal.* 6.47; Nicarch. (?) *ibid.* 6.285; Lucian, *Dial. meret.* 3.3, 6; Anon. *Anth. Pal.* 6.48, 284.

weak disposition to believe the promises of pimps,[138] often to their bitter disappointment. Naturally lasciviousness always played a role,[139] and during the time of the Caesars sexual perversity developed to the point that women of high social standing and means registered themselves as prostitutes[140] or gave full vent to their impulses in brothels and elsewhere.[141] Clement of Alexandria maintained that sexual permissiveness led down the path to the brothel.[142]

One often reads about prostitutes who became the possessions of pimps against their will.[143] Not only did slave owners sell their female slaves into prostitution, parents used to sell their daughters[144] or rent them;[145] church sources insist that this happened.[146] John Chrysostom writes about women of nobility or high social standing who through some circumstance found themselves in unclean houses.[147] Young girls who had been captured through war[148] or by robbers or pirates[149] could find themselves in the same situation. Lepers in particular became subject to the power of pimps,[150] which gave Christian writers an excuse for describing dark possibilities for incest.[151] The discovery and freeing of such unfortunates, which resulted in heavy punishment for the pimp,[152] became standard topics in Attic and Roman comedies and in novels.[153] Occasionally one finds the tracks of people who trafficked in young girls.[154] Banishment to a brothel was sometimes a form of punishment for female slaves and for concubines whom one wished

---

[138] *Nov.* 14 (39); Trull. *cn.* 86.

[139] *PGrenf.* 1.53; Firm. Mat. *Math.* 6.31.91. Compare the phenomenon of the protected young girl who suddenly appears as a *leôphoros* ["people-heaver" prostitute] (cf. P. Maas, *Acme* 8 [1955] 113f), in Anac. fr. 60 in Gentili's interpretation p. 179–96 (see *RAC* 3, 1169f). Elegeis-Pero: Lycophr. 1385–7 with Schol.

[140] Suet. *Tib.* 35.2.

[141] Tac. *Ann.* 15.37; Juv. 6.115–32; Suet. *Calig.* 41. 1; Paul. *Dig.* 23.2.47; Cass. Dio 60.31.1; cf. 59.28.9; 62.15.2–6; *Hist. Aug. Comm.* 2.8.

[142] Clem. Al. *Strom.* 3.28.1.

[143] Sen. *Controv.* 10.4.11; Basil. *In princ. prov.* 9; *Hom. in Ps.* 32.5; see also *Hom. in Ps.* 7 5.

[144] Quint. *Inst.* 7.1.55.

[145] BGU 1024 p. 7, 8–18, 26f, p. 8, 11–21. Cf. Varro, *Sat. Men.* 235; Sen. *Ep.* 101.15.

[146] Just. *Apol.* 1.27; Elvira, *Cn.* 12; Chrys. *Hom. in 1 Cor.* 18.2; Jo. Mal. *Chron.* 440.15–21; *Chron. Pasch.* 550.1–4; *Virt. Andr.* 26 (R. A. Lipsius, *Die apokryphen Apostelgeschichten* 1 [Braunschweig 1886] 560). Compare the conditions among the Babylonians, Lydians and Egyptians: Hdt. 1.94,196; 2.121, 126; *Dissoi logoi* 2.16.

[147] Chrys. *Thdr.* 1.13.

[148] POxy. 1241 III 9–12; Sen. *Dial.* 2.6.5; Dio Chrys. 7.133; *Cod. Iust.* 8.50.7; Cypr. *Ep.* 62.2; Lactant. *Div. inst.* 4.21.4. L. Bieler, *C&M* 11 [1950] 98.

[149] Plaut. *Curc.* 644–52; *Pers.* 134–4 etc.; *Rud.* 39–41, 1105; Sen. *Controv.* 1.2; Apul. *Met.* 7.9; *Hist. Apoll. Tyr. passim.*

[150] W. Kroll, *RE* 11, 471; Plaut. *Cist.*; Ter. *Haut.* 639–43.

[151] *RAC* 3, 1198.

[152] Din. 1.23 and elsewhere.

[153] *RAC* 3, 1174f; see also Hauschild, 53–67; M. Neumann, *Die poetische Gerechtigkeit in der neuen Komödie*, Diss. Mainz (1958) 15–19, 100–11.

[154] IG 14, 2000; Clem. Al. *Paed.* 3.22.1. See note 34.

to be rid of.[155] Free concubines who had been rejected sank back into their old status as *hetairai*.[156] Such women were placed not only in an uncertain economic situation but also in a socially less respectable one, as is shown by the practice in some regions of requiring that women who had committed adultery be placed in the same status as prostitutes, as penance. In Cyprus such women were shaved and forced to become prostitutes;[157] in Lepreon they were punished with *atimia* [loss of civil status] and were assimilated into the class of prostitutes by being put on display in the market in transparent clothing, without undergarments, for eleven days.[158] According to other sources, unfaithful wives in Locris and Syracuse were also punished by being treated as whores.[159] Theodosius ended the practice of sending such women to brothels.[160]

The only example in Roman times of preliminaries to a death sentence is the rape of Sejanus's daughter by the executioner in AD 31,[161] allegedly because it was believed that virgins could not be subjected to the death penalty.[162] Forced sexual activity and, in particular, banishment to a brothel, were used by the criminal prosecution system or the *coercitio* [punitive power] of magistrates not as possible long-term punishments, but rather as a means to delay the execution of Christians, especially virgins. This elicited indignation among the faithful, but heathen judges did not always regard this punishment as an intensification of the sentence; rather, they sometimes seem to have hoped to gain something by this form of delay.[163]

---

[155] Antiph.1.14; *Virt. Andr.* 26. Cf. Xen. Eph. 5.5.

[156] Men. *Sam.* 175–82.

[157] Dio Chrys. 64.3.

[158] Heraclid. Pont. *De reb. publ.* 14; Arist. fr. 611.42 (379.17 Rose).

[159] Diod. Sic. 12.21.1f; Phylarch. fr. 45 J.: Lécrivain, 189. See also *Syntipas* p. 111 J.

[160] Socr. *HE* 5.18; Thphn. *Chron., PG* 108. 209.

[161] Tac. *Ann.* 5.9; Suet. *Tib.* 61.5; Cass. Dio 8.11.5. One should also consider the fate of the wife and the daughters of Dionysius II (Clearch. fr. 47 W = Ath. 12.541DE; Strabo 6.260; Plut. *Mor.* 821D; *Tim.* 13.10; Aelian, *VH* 6.12, 9.8). After Agrippa's death the masses brought the statues of his daughters into the brothels and had their pleasure with them there (Jos. *AJ* 19.9.1).

[162] F. Augar, *Die Frau im römischen Christenprocess* (Leipzig 1905) 77, 81f .

[163] Augar; Tert. *Apol.* 50; *Pud.* 1; Hipp. *Dan.* 4.51; Pall. *H. Laus.* 148f (65 B. Georg. Mon. *Chron.* p. 479f); Cypr. *Mort.* 15; Euseb. *Hist. eccl.* 6.5 (cf. Pall. 3); 8.12.3f; 8.14.14–16; Mart. *Pal.* 5.7.8. The statements in some of the lives of the saints are reliable: Sabina, the sister of Pionius, under Decius in Smyrna; Irene 304 in Thessalonica; Theodora, probably during her last persecution in Alexandreia (according to Ambros. *Virg.* 2.22–33 in Antiocheia). Post-Eusebian accounts are generally unreliable ([Bas.] *Virg.* 52; Ambros. *Virg.* 3.38 (cf. *Exh. virg.* 82); 3.32–4 (cf. *Ep.* 37.38); *Laps. Virg.* 11; Chrys. *Pan. Bern., Pan. Pelag. Ant.*). The Acts of Peter, Andrew, Paul and the Dionysia are unhistorical, as is the *Pass. Theod. Ancyr. et 7 virg.*; the martyrologies are totally unreliable (Lucia, Agnes, Antonina, Serapia). Cf. Beda, *Hymn.* 7.

## 4 ECONOMIC SITUATION OF PROSTITUTES

Normally prostitutes accepted wages for their services,[164] but there were also some who offered themselves without remuneration *palam* [publicly], that is *sine dilectu* [without discrimination].[165] The amount of money they were paid varied considerably[166] and differed from place to place.[167] The peripatetic Lycon is supposed to have known the prices of all the courtesans of Athens.[168] In a brothel[169] the fee that was to be paid in advance[170] (Eupolis fr. 48 jokingly refers to it as *ellimenion* [harbor dues]) was usually not very high, and even other girls of the common variety did not cost very much. Frequently, and especially where the issue is the simplest form of love,[171] the

[164] *RAC* 3, 1154–6. F. Wilhelm, *RhM* 59 (1904) 282–5; F. Leo, *Plautinische Forschungen*[2] 149f. Regarding the texts: *RAC* 3, 1165–7, cf. also Thgn. 861 (?); Simon. fr. 157 = *Anth. Pal.* 5.158; Plat. *Resp.* 4.420A; Aeschin. 1.75; Men. fr. 588 Kö.; Machon, Ath. 13.579A; Dioscurides, *Anth. Pal.* 6.290; Plaut. *Bacch.* 26–30, 376, 465f, 737f, 742f; *Curc.* 508; *Epid.* 220; *Men.* 193, 343, 377, 384–6; *Merc.* 30, 40–60; *Poen.* 108, 327f, 345f; *Trin.* 412; *Truc.* 13–17 etc.; Ter. *Eun.* 927–9; *Haut.* 223–9, 381–91, 443–66; Turpil. 42; Antip. Sid. *Anth. Pal.* 7.218.7, 13f; Antip. Thess. *ibid.* 5.29f; Marc. Arg. *ibid.* 5.15; Hor. *Carm.* 2.8.22; *Epist.* 1.14.33; Tib. 2.3.49–60, 4.13–44; Prop. 2.16, 24.9–15, 3.13; 4.5; Ov. *Ars am.* 2.626; *Rem. am.* 321f; *Pont.* 2.3.20; *Her.* 15.63–6; *Priapea*, 40; Sen. *Controv.* 1.2.21; Stat. *Silv.* 1.6.67; Parmenio, *Anth. Pal.* 5.33; Maecius, *ibid.* 5.113; Pers. 5.163–6; Quint. *Decl.* 1.6 (8.29 L.) 344; 356; Mart. 5.42.5; 9.4; 12.55; Plut. *Demetr.* 27.12–14 (see also J. Leipoldt, in S. Morenz (ed.), *Aus Antike und Orient. Festschrift W. Schubart zum 75. Geburtstag* [Leipzig 1950] 57f); *Mor.* 5B; Juv. 3.132–4; Lucian, *Dial. meret.* 1.2; *Tim.* 23; Artem. 3.23; Harp. s. v. *pôlôsi*; Ael. *VH* 12.1; fr. 12; Alciphr. 1.6.2f; 1.21.1, 3; 2.31.2; 3.5.2; 3.14.1f; 4.9.1f; 4.15; 4.17.5; Ath. 13.571D, 584E, 585A, 588EF; Cass. Dio 45.28.4; Paul. Fest. p. 76.5 M.; Pythag. *Ep.* 5.3, 6; Firm. Mat. *Math.* 4.13.4; 6.30.16, 31, 79, 91; 8.23.3; Synes. *Aeg.* 1.17; Ach. Tat. 8.16.1; Xen. Eph. 5.7.3; Lib. *Comp.* 5.6; Aristaenet. 1.23; 2.1; Maced. *Anth. Pal.* 5.239; Agath. *ibid.* 5.301.1f; *Anth. Plan.* 80; Pall. *Anth. Pal.* 10.48; Anon. *Anth. Pal.* 5.1, 100; 6.283; 9.621f; *Cod. Iust.* 8.50.7; *Anth. Lat.* 826; *Philogelus* 151; [Acro] Hor. *Sat.* 1.2.61; *Ars P.* 238; Porph. Hor. *Carm.* 1.25 pr.; Don. Ter. *Andr.* 72; *Eun.* 585, 748; *De com.* 8.6 (71.2 Kaib.); Schol. Lucian *Iupp. trag.* 48; Isid. *Or.* 10.182; 18.42.2; *Diff.* 1.263; *Suda* s. v. *misthôma*. For Solon, see below note 702. Dowry as a form of prostitution: Mart. 9.80; cf. 10.16 (15). See also Jer. *Ep.* 54.15. Regarding the phylax vases, E. Wüst, *RE* 20, 300 nr. 59 (L. M. Catteruccia, *Pitture vascolari italiote di soggetto teatrale comico* [Rome 1951] 55 nr. 50) depicts an applicant with his purse of money in front of a woman playing a lyre (not likely Alcaeus in front of Sappho, as R. Zahn, *Antike* 7 [1931] 90–3, believed).

[165] Ulpian, *Dig.* 23.2.43 pr. 1–3. See also *RAC* 3, 1156; C. Castello, *In tema di matrimonio e concubinato nel mondo romano* (Milan 1940) 122–4. This was the case with old prostitutes (Mart. 7.75; Nicarch. *Anth. Pal.* 11.73). In individual instances a loving *hetaira* could decline the business proposition, as did Horace's Cinara (Hor. *Epist.* 1.14.33) or as did Lais with Diogenes (*RAC* 3, 1186f; on the contrary Agath. *Anth. Pal.* 5.301.19f). Cf. Plaut. *Poen.* 866–8. Regarding Ulpian *Dig.* 12.5.4.3 see G. Sciascia, *Varietà giuridiche* (Milan 1956) 19.

[166] Eur. fr. 675 N.[2]; Antig. Car. Ath. 12.547D.

[167] Corinth was particularly expensive (Ar. *Plut.* 149–52 with Schol., Strabo 8.378; regarding the proverb *ou pantos es Korinthon esth' ho plous* [the voyage to Corinth isn't for everyone], M. Goebel, *Ethnica*, Diss. Berlin [1915] 36f); for Egypt, see Bringmann 120f. The numerical values that are provided for different times tell their own story about a differing real value.

[168] Antig. Car. Ath. 12.547D.

[169] Cass. Dio 77.16.5.

[170] Juv. 6.125.

[171] *RAC* 3, 1180–2.

cheap price of prostitutes is emphasized.[172] The exact price or else the rounded off price was one *obolos*,[173] occasionally even one *khalkous*.[174] In Cyzicus it was one *kollybos*[175] and Hesychius even knows about a *triantos pornê* [whore who costs a third of an *as*]. In Italy one *as*[176] or two[177] were sufficient, and there was even an abusive word *quadrantaria* [one quarter of an *as*; two-bit whore].[178] The fee increased to two,[179] three,[180] and four *oboloi*[181] and even one[182] or two drachmas.[183] In Athens this amount was officially established as the maximum,[184] but the regulations may have varied and in any case they were not enforced.[185] We hear about fees of four[186] or even five drachmas, which is still not a large amount,[187] and the fee could increase, based on the status of the establishment or of the *hetaira*, to ten drachmas[188] and in Italy to one[189] or even two denarii.[190] Twelve drachmas were a large amount,[191] but the price could increase to the dizzying heights of *megalomisthoi* [the highly paid], to the extent that such numbers can even be taken literally.[192]

[172] Eub. fr. 67.7; Theopomp. fr. 253J.; Hor. *Sat.* 1.2.121f; Prop. 2.23.17f; *Priapea* 34; Phil. *Anth. Pal.* 9.416.5; Dio Chrys. 7.140; Juv. 6.125; Artem. 1.78 (p. 72 H.); Ath. 13.568DE, 595C.

[173] Philem. fr. 4; Antisthenes in Diog. Laert. 6.4; Cercid. fr. 2b, 15D.

[174] *Anon. in turpil.* 41 D.; cf. *khalkiditis* [penny whore]: *Com. Adesp.* 1352; *Suda*, and Eust. 1329.35f., 1921.61; *hê epi khalkôi* [the girl for a copper coin]: L. Radermacher, *RhM* 88 (1939) 188f, cf. Cillactor, *Anth. Pal.* 5.29; Gerhard, *Phoinix* 169f, 288.

[175] Eup. fr. 233.

[176] Petron. 8.4; Mart. 1.103.10; Juv. 6. 125; *Anth. Lat.* 794.46. RAC 3, 1203.

[177] Mart. 2.53.7; *CIL* 4.8185, 8394, 8465, 8511.

[178] Caelius in Quint. *Inst.* 8.6.53; cf. Cic. *Cael.* 62. On the contrary, see J. Colin, *RBPh* 33 (1955) 860f.

[179] Bass. *Anth. Pal.* 5.125; *diobolaris* [for two obols]: Plaut. *Cist.* 407; *Poen.* 270, cf. *TLL.* s. v.

[180] Epicr. fr. 2–3. 18; Antiphan. fr. 300; Plaut. *Poen.* 868; Procop. *Arc.* 17.5.

[181] Aristaenet. 2.16.

[182] Ar. *Thesm.* 1195; Antip. Thess. *Anth. Pal.* 5.109; Plut. *Mor.* 759E.

[183] Ath. 13.596F with Kaibel's annotations; J. Colin, *RFIC* NS 29 (1951) 124; *RBPh* 33 (1955) 858f.

[184] See notes 692f.

[185] Hyp. 3.3; cf. Post (1940) 448 n. 67.

[186] Theopomp. Com. fr. 21; Epicr. fr. 2–3.18.

[187] Phld. *Anth. Pal.* 5.125.

[188] Men. *Sam.* 175–82; Lucian, *Dial. meret.* 8.2f., 11.1.

[189] Kroll, 161, with note 84; Schneider, *Mer.* 1025. Compare the price at Palmyra, *ibid.* 1022. *CIL* 4.8160, 8187 (?), 8197 (?), 8224, 8357 (?).

[190] Mart. 9.32.

[191] Men. *Epitr.* 10–15, 220 (261 Kö.).

[192] Aeschin. 1.75; Dem. in Gell. 1.8; Crates fr. 13 D.; Men. *Kol.* 114–16 J.; Lynceus, Ath. 13.584C; Macho, Ath. 13.581A–582A, 583BC; Lucian, *Dial. meret.* 6.1f; 7.3; 11.3; 14.4; Ath. 13.569A, 570B. Roman instances: Catull. 41; Mart. 2.63; 3.54; 9.4; a special case: Suet. *Calig.* 41.1. Devirginating was particularly expensive (Epicr. fr. 9; Lucian, *Dial. meret.* 6.1.2; cf. Sen. *Controv.* 1.2.2, 12), after which the fee dropped (*Hist. Ap. Tyr.* 33; Modern Greek version, v. 545–53, 723–6); people strove for a "new one" (Sen. *Controv.* 1.2.10), particularly for young prostitutes (Men. *Kol.* fr. 4 Kö., cf. Ar. fr. 140E.; *Com. Adesp.* fr. 766, see below note 203). Offering more: *RAC* 3, 1165; see also Plaut. *Truc.* 81; Alciphr. 1.6.3; *Hist. Ap. Tyr.* 33 (modern Greek version, v. 538f, 720); *Anth. Lat.* 794; Chrys. *Opp. vit. mon.* 2.10. See also the motif of considering the possibilities: L. Radermacher, *SAWW* 201, 1 (1924) 39. A *hetaira* between two

The rent for a female lover for a specific period of time could in some cases be quite high.[193] Naturally there was a contract[194] and one could even secure ahead of time the right to a woman's services.[195] The passing of a soldier's prostitute from one person to another was also regulated.[196] As far as the price is concerned, a pimp working at a market or elsewhere[197] usually received less than he initially asked for, but for various reasons, different amounts could be charged for the same girl, even within a short space of time.[198] Not infrequently an amount of between 20 minas and one talent[199] was mentioned—these were clearly sentimental values[200]—sometimes more,[201] but also sometimes less.[202] Young girls were particularly expensive.[203] Long-term relationships were usually quite expensive,[204] because the mistress expected not only love and good treatment but also presents. These consisted not only of clothing or jewelry, but also of rent and furnishings for an apartment, male and female servants, as well as victuals;[205] in short, all the things that the pimp would otherwise supply.[206] Such presents, which became the property of the recipient,[207] were in fact the only form of reimbursement in the case of more refined relationships and were all the more exquisite because they were not expressly demanded.[208] Phryne received the famous statue of Eros from Praxiteles,[209] but in general the

old ones on the phylax vase in Wüst, *RE* 20, 298 no. 40 (Catteruccia 45f no. 40). Regarding *hetairai* underbidding each other, see Ath. 13.588E.

[193] Men. *Kol.* 114–16; Plaut. *Asin.* 89, 229f., 746–809; *Bacch.* 29f; 42–7, 1097f; *Poen.* 1280, 1353, 1359; *Truc.* 31; Lucian, *Dial. meret.* 8.3; 9.3f; 15.2; *Hist. Ap. Tyr.* 40; see also Lucian, *Philops.* 15. Schneider, *Het.* 1340.

[194] Plaut. *Asin.* (above note 193); Lucian, *Dial. meret.* 15.2; Poll. 8.140.

[195] Plaut. *Pseud.* 351–3.

[196] K. Sudhoff, *Ärztliches aus griechischen Papyrusurkunden: Bausteine zu einer medizinischen Kulturgeschichte des Hellenismus* (Leipzig 1909) 106–8; Bringmann, 121 n. 133.

[197] Plaut. *Curc.* 343f., 491f., 528–30, 535f; *Poen.* 339–42; Procop. *Aed.* 1.9.4.

[198] Mart. 10.75; cf. 6.66.

[199] [Dem.] 59.29, 30–2; Plaut. *Asin.* 915f; *Bacch.* 706, 882; *Curc.* 63–70, 343f. etc.; *Epid.* 52, 296 etc.; *Merc.* 429–40; *Most.* 297–300 etc.; *Pers.* 662–70; *Pseud.* 51–9, 111–18 etc.; *Rud.* 45, 1406; Ter. *Ad.* 191, 223; *Haut.* 600–12; *Phorm.* 557 etc.

[200] M. Delcourt, *AC* 17 (1948) 123–32.

[201] Plaut. *Asin.* 193.

[202] Plaut. *Pers.* 36; *Poen.* 897f; *Truc.* 530–44; cf. Mart. 6.66.

[203] Apul. *Met.* 7.9; *Nov.* 14 (39); see above note 192.

[204] Plaut. *Bacch.* 29f, 42–7, 1097f; *Poen.* 713–16, 1280, 1353, 1359; *Truc.* 22–84, 543f.

[205] [Dem.] 59.35; Men. fr. 224, 314f, 329, cf. 318; Hedyl. *Anth. Pal.* 6. 292; Plaut. *Cist.* 312–14, 319, 477, 487; Men. 130–5 etc.; *Pseud.* 172–229; *Truc.* 33, 52–6, 445, 543f., 652–62; Lygdamus, [Tib.] 3.1.7f; Ov. *Ars am.* 1.417f; 2.261–72; 3.461–6, 531; Mart. 10.29; 11.27, 29.49 (50); 12.55, 65, 79; Lucian, *Dial. meret.* 14, cf. 7.1; Alciphr. 1.6.2f; 4.11.4; Ath. 13.594BC; Aristaenet. 2.19; Anon. *Anth. Pal.* 6.283; *Anth. Lat.* 794; *RAC* 3, 1165–7.

[206] Plaut. *Pseud.* 182, 343.

[207] Ulpian, *Dig.* 12.5.4.3; see Plaut. *Mil.* 1099f., 1126, 1147f., 1204f., 1302–4; Castello (note 165) 124f.

[208] *RAC* 3, 1166.

[209] Ath. 13.59AB and elsewhere, see A. E. Raubitschek, *RE* 20, 899f. According to Alciphr. 4.3.5, in the court case involving Phryne, the issue revolved around material demands.

ideal reimbursements could not be adequately valued.[210] Complaints about high costs[211] were frequently justified, even if these complaints were tendentious. When Sappho expresses scorn at the love affairs of her brother, she was thinking of his expenditures.[212] Some *hetairai* were in fact able to become well-off and even rich[213] and could afford to erect imposing votive monuments[214] or afford a splendid gravestone.[215] Some of these women may have exchanged expensive gifts among each other.[216] Pimps, on the other hand, complained, with varying degrees of justification,[217] and some of them were ruined financially by their own women.[218]

In Christian literature one also finds frequent derogatory references concerning payments or gifts to prostitutes.[219] The topic of these expenses continued, and one also encounters rich prostitutes who, upon their conversion, divested themselves of their treasures.[220] The expenses related to having a mistress, particularly if the money had to be borrowed, could lead to one's downfall and could not be disguised as gifts to the poor. God demands less from those who follow the pathway to true generosity than prostitutes do.[221] Similarly, the amount paid to a prostitute was also reduced when it was desired to show how low the financial benefit of sin was.[222] The Egyptian Maria is described as being so desirous of men that she would offer herself free to anyone.[223] When Abraham underwent his conversion, he received a *nomisma*, a coin, and accommodation.[224] Didymus received three *nomismata* for his act of conversion as well as two more for the whole night.[225] As Prudentius sees it, Ariadne was paid by being transported into the stars.[226] In Bulla, prostitutes could be bought at the weekly market;[227] we learn that Simon's Helena cost

[210] *RAC* 3, 1165; *Anacreont.* 29.6.

[211] See also Aeschin. 1.42; Antiphan. fr. 26. 11; Men. fr. 185 Kö.; Metrod. *Epist.* in C. Diano, *Epicuri Ethica* (Florence 1946) 140 no. 48; Crates A20; Phld. *Rht.* 1.236.21 Sudh.; Quint. *Decl.* 1.6; Plut. *Mor.* 706B; Alciphr. 2.32.1; 3.5.2; 3.14.1f; Ath. 13.588CE, 590CD, 591CD, 592F-3A; Lib. *Comp.* 5.6; *Anacreont.* 29; Heraclit. *Incred.* 2.8.14. Regarding the comparison between Scylla and others, see also E. Riess, *CW* 37 (1943–4) 178f. Cf. Dio Chrys. 6.16–20.

[212] Hdt. 2.135; Ath. 13.596BC; *POxy.* 1800 I 7–13 (Sapph. fr. 202 L.-P.).

[213] Hdt. 2.126, 135; Amphis fr. 23; Timocl. fr. 23; Noss. *Anth. Pal.* 9.332; Prop. 2.6.6; Plin. *HN* 36.82; Claud. 18.90f; Ath. 13.591D; Agath. *Anth. Pal.* 6.74; Anon. *Anth. Pal.* 11.416; *Gnom. hom.* 178 Elt.; *RAC* 3, 1175f. A prostitute who wastes herself and her money, Heraclit. *Incred.* 1.

[214] *RAC* 3, 1175f; Polemo, Ath. 13.574CD; Phryne, see Raubitschek, *RE* 20, 898–903. The consecration inscription on the roasting spit of Rhodopis in Delphi (Hdt. 2.135) appears to have been identified by N. Mastro-Kostas (*BCH* 78 [1954] 133, 444; *JHS* 74 [1954] 158; *REG* 68 [1955] 229). Regarding Rhodopis, see B. van de Walle, *AC* 3 (1934) 303–12.

[215] Cic. *Dom.* 111f. Cf. Ath. 13.573AB, 594E–5C.

[216] P. Schmitz, *Gymnasium* 59 (1952) 216–23.

[217] Diph. fr. 87; Herod. 2.4; Plaut. *Pseud.* 133–229.

1000 denarii.²²⁸ Theodora spent five pieces of gold on her great act of rescuing someone.²²⁹

The economic situation of the servants of free love varied considerably. The exclusive *hetairai* from Greece and the libertines from Rome cannot be compared using the yardstick of the "prostitute,"²³⁰ and even among the lower classes there were different gradations of prostitutes, down to the truly common ones, as they are described by Plautus (*Poen.* 265–70). The upper-class paramours, even some of the women who worked in brothels, had female servants, such as Milphidippa, Sophoclidisca, or Astaphion,²³¹ who were often a danger to men.²³² These paramours also had male servants,²³³ in particular young boys and *exoleti* [those worn out by debauchery],²³⁴ but also eunuchs²³⁵ and dwarfs.²³⁶ Even in Christian literature one encounters such *hetairai*, in particular actresses, who had servants.²³⁷ These women had beautiful houses with corresponding

²¹⁸ Palaeph. 6. For this whole topic, see also those who explain *Anth. Pal.* 5.124f; Schneider, *Het.* 1340f., 1344f., 1345–7; Della Corte, *Case ed abitanti* ²389; J. Colin, *RBPh* 33 (1955) 858–61.

²¹⁹ *Ev. Naz.* 18: A. Resch, *Agrapha—TU* NF 15, 3–4 (1906) 219 (G. Hennecke, W. Schneemelcher, *Neutestamentliche Apokryphen* 1 [Tübingen 1959] 97); Tert. *Pall.* 4; *De spect.* 17; Arn. 2.42; 6.12; Ephr. *Admon. et paen.* 9 (1, 292 Lamy); Zeno Ver. 1. 4. 4; Iuvencus 3.706; Jer. *In Isa.* 5.23.17; 16.57.9f; 17.61.8f; August. *Faust.* 22.61; Gr. Nyss. *V. Greg. Thaum.*, PG 46. 904; Gr. Naz. *Carm.* 1.2.10.860, 33.28; Chrys. *Ebr.* 1; *Hom. ad Ant.*14.4; *Hom. in Rom.* 24.4; *Hom. in 2 Cor.* 13.3; 19.3; *Hom. in Hebr.* 15.3; Bas. Sel. *V. Thecl.*, PG 85.524. See also *RAC* 3, 1189, 1192, 1203, 1210.

²²⁰ *Act. Petr. Verc.* 30 (245 Hennecke): Pelag. *Epist. ad Demetr.* 14 (PL 30. 29); Chrys. *Hom. in Eph.* 20.8; *Pass. Afrae* 2.

²²¹ Chrys. *Oppugn.* 2.10; *Hom. Suppl.* 4; *Hom. in Jo.* 42 (41). 4; 79 (78). 4f; *Hom. in 2 Cor.* 13.3; cf. *Van. glor.* 12.

²²² Clem. Al. *Paed.* 3.22.1; Gr. Naz. *Carm.* 1.2.29.24f. Scornfully, Niceph. Greg. *Hist. Byz.* 32.37. *RAC* 3, 1203.

²²³ Sophr. H. *V. Mar. Aeg.* 18–22.

²²⁴ Sym. Metaphr. *V. Abr.* 21–7.

²²⁵ Hipp. fr., Bd. 1.2.273–7 B.–Ach.

²²⁶ Prudent. *C. Symm.* 1.143f.

²²⁷ August. *Serm.* Denis 17. 7 (87f Morin); cf. *RAC* 3, 1178. "Market" was *porneia* among the heathen: Athenag. *Leg.* 34.

²²⁸ Tert. *An.* 34.5.

²²⁹ A. Nagl, *RE* 5A, 1784.

²³⁰ See W. Kroll on Catull. 41.2; Copley, *Exclusus amator* 51; Ov. *Ars am.* 3.613–16. Regarding the difference between *hetaira* and *pornê*, see *RAC* 3, 1154, cf. 1181f.

²³¹ Plaut. *Mil.*, *Pers.*, *Truc.*

²³² Pherecr. fr. 70; Xen. *Mem.* 3.11.4; [Dem.] 59.35, 42, 46, 120–5; Plaut. *Asin.* 183f, 804; *Poen.* 221–3; Ter. *Haut.* 451f; *Hec.* 773, 793; Ov. *Am.* 2.8, cf. 2.7; *Ars am.* 1.375; 3.665; Lucian, *Dial. meret.* 6.2, 10; Poll. 4.154; Alciphr. 4.8.1; 9.1; 11.4; 13.17; Ath. 13.582B, cf. DE; Aristaenet. 1.4. See note 205.

²³³Plaut. *Asin.* 184, 237; *Poen.* 224, 866–8; Prop. 2.22.39, 49f; Lucian, *Dial. meret.* 10.

²³⁴ᵛTib. 2.3.55f.

²³⁵ Ter. *Eun.* 165–9, 470–9 etc.; Alciphr. 4.11.4.

²³⁶ R. Herbig, in R. Lullies (ed.), *Neue Beiträge zur klassischen Altertumswissenschaft. Festschrift zum 60. Geburtstag von B. Schweitzer* (Stuttgart 1954) 271.

²³⁷ *Vit. Pelag.* 2.7.11; see also Chrys. *Fem. reg.* 5.

furnishings,[238] sometimes shared by two people,[239] and this was where they could host their lovers for banquets. Christian writers also describe scenes of exquisite furnishings[240] and perfumes,[241] when they wish to achieve a special effect. In Roman comedies the life of a *hetaira* frequently takes on the character of life in a common brothel.[242] Sometimes the houses of pleasure are depicted in a more elegant style[243] and they contain an exclusive section[244] whose female occupants could be punished by being banished to a lower-class section.[245] In these finer sections there could be regular activities of bathing, eating, and drinking[246] that could easily be viewed as similar to the activities in a tavern.[247] Sometimes there are people who keep watch or else function as servants: an old hag who serves as a doorkeeper,[248] a *lenonis minister* [pimp's servant],[249] or a *villicus puellarum* [overseer of girls].[250] Pictures on the wall usually denote more exclusive furnishings;[251] scribblings could almost always be found on walls,[252] especially on doors.[253] Even a cell[254] can be decorated.[255] A good place to sleep was always a recommendation,[256] for in the typical *oikêmata* [brothels]—whether they functioned by themselves or were part of larger operations[257]— the comfort level was not usually very high, even if a mattress was laid

[238] Xen. *Mem.* 3.11.4; Polyb. 14.11.3; Plaut. *Bacch.* 373; Schneider, *Het.* 1351.
[239] Plaut. *Bacch.*; cf. Anaxil. fr. 22.13f (Schiassi 234); Jos. *AJ* 8.27 (according to 3 *Reg.* 3.17).
[240] *V. Abr.* 25.
[241] Chrys. *Fem. reg.* 1. Cf. *Prov.* 7.
[242] Ed. Fränkel, *Plautinisches im Plautus* (Berlin 1922) 147f, 151f; Hauschild 67.
[243] Suet. *Calig.* 41. 1.
[244] Diph. fr. 43.38–40.
[245] *Pergula*: Plaut. *Pseud.* 178, 214, 229. Cf. V. Spinazzola, *Pompei* (Rome 1953) 615 n. 88.
[246] Plaut. *Bacch.* 743; *Pers.* 568; *Poen.* 695–703, 713–16, 835–8, 867; Bas. *Renunt.* 5; *V. Abr.* 24f. Pictures from Pompeii, for example Sogliano 641; see Della Corte, *Neapolis* 2 (1914) 326; cf. Della Corte, *Case ed abitanti*² 142.
[247] It even seems to be the case that such houses could serve as overnight accommodation for visitors (Eup. fr. 344; Plaut. *Poen.* 174–80, 600–3, 656–63).
[248] Plaut. *Curc.* 76–161.
[249] *Hist. Aug. Comm.* 2.9.
[250] *Hist. Ap. Tyr.* 33, 35, 36, 46 (modern Greek version, v. 543 and elsewhere).
[251] Plaut. *Asin.* 763f; Ter. *Eun.* 583–91; cf. Prop. 2.6.27–34; Schneider, *Het.* 1351. Image of Priapus, H. Herter, *De Priapo* (Giessen 1932) 226f, 255f. Pictures that could be opened up, W. Helbig, *Wandgemälde der vom Vesuv vershütteten Städte Campaniens* (Leipzig 1868) 1506.
[252] Catull. 37.9f.
[253] Plaut. *Merc.* 409; Prop. 1.16.9f. Ov. *Am.* 3.1.53f.
[254] *Anth. Lat.* 128; Schol. Hor. *Sat.* 2.7.51; Schol. Juv. 6.123; Ambros. *In Psa.* 118, 1.12.2; Apophth. *Patr. Serap.* 1.
[255] *Hist. Ap. Tyr.* 33.
[256] Antip. Thess. *Anth. Pal.* 5.109; Anon. *Anth. Pal.* 9.259; IG 14, 2135; cf. Archipp. fr. 45A; Titinius 74f.
[257] Cass. Dio 59.28.9; 62.15.2–6; therefore very often *hai ep' oikêmatos* [the girls in the brothel], *ibid.* 60.31.1f; Hld. 7.10. See above, note 60.

on a stone bed,[258] as one can observe in Pompeii.[259] All too frequently one hears about small, dark, narrow, dirty, poorly ventilated rooms that are filled with smoke or soot from a lamp.[260] The descriptions provided by pagan writers correspond to those provided by church writers.[261]

Some prostitutes almost starved[262] and earned the epithet *athlios*, "wretched," a word that could also take on a moral tone,[263] or even *trisathlios*, "thrice wretched."[264] Pimps promised women a good life but frequently did not keep their word.[265] More exclusive *hetairai* were able to attach themselves to wealthier men,[266] in particular traders and merchant seamen as well as the sons of wealthy fathers,[267] as is also attested by Christian writers.[268] Officers could be dangerous rivals, but they often lost their opportunities because of their crudeness, vanity, boastfulness, or failure to pay promptly.[269] When the price for the services of a prostitute is lower, one finds a colourful mixture of customers, a *sordida iniuriosaque turba* [dirty and harmful crowd];[270] pedlars and farmers, seamen and fishermen, soldiers and gladiators, slaves and former slaves come and go.[271]

---

[258] Juv. 6.117.

[259] Schneider, *Mer.* 1023; Navarre 1836; Kroll 160f; Kleberg, *Hôtels* 113.

[260] Hdt. 2.121.5; Antisth. Ath. 5.220D; Hor. *Sat.* 1.2.30; 2.7.48; *Priapea* 14.10; Sen. *Controv.* 1.2.21; Petron. 7.5; Man. 6.143; Mart. 4.4.9; 12.61.8; Dio Chrys. 7.133; Juv. 6.131f, 11.172f; Apul. *Met.* 7.10; *De dog. Plat.* 1.13. In the case of Plaut. *Poen.* 835, it appears to me that *tenebrae* [dark places] and *latebrae* [hiding places] both mean something different (contrary to Fränkel, *Plautinisches* 151), for the beautiful house of Bacchides is a *latebrosus locus* [place full of hideouts] (Plaut. *Bacch.* 56, 430); *occulti loci* [secret places], Plaut. *Curc.* 507. Regarding the association with filth, see *RAC* 3, 1179, 1193;. J.-G. Préaux, *RBPh* 33 (1955) 558–60; Sen. *Ep.* 59.9; Dio Chrys. 4.114; Chrys. *Hom. in* 1 *Cor.* 5; *Hom. in* 1 *Tim.* 2.3; *syphorbia*, "whorehouse": Diosc. *Anth. Pal.* 11.363.5; cf. Plut. *Mor.* 1094A.

[261] Tert. *Pall.* 4; *De spect.* 17; Zeno Ver. 1.4.4; Jer. *In Isa.* 16.57.9; *In Ez.* 5.16.23–6; Chrys. *Hom. in Mt.* 28 (29).4; *Hom. in Jo.* 79 (78).4; Prudent. *C. Symm.* 2.836.

[262] Ter. *Eun.* 934–40; Sulpicia, [Tib.] 3.16.3f; Mart. 1.92.6; 3.82.2f; 4.4.9; Jo. Mal. *Chron.* 18 (440, 14—441, 7).

[263] Julian. *Or.* 6.203C; Anon. *Anth. Pal.* 15.19.

[264] Men. *Peric.* 150; cf. *Com. Adesp.* 120 K.

[265] Nov. 14 (39); Jo. Mal. *Chron.* 13 [345, 20f Bonn.] and later texts.

[266] Anon. *Anth. Pal.* 6.283. See note 211.

[267] Simon. *Epigr.* 157, *Anth. Pal.* 5.158; Metag. fr. 4 = Aristag. fr. 2; Anaxil. fr. 22.19; Plaut. *Asin.* 68–72; Strabo 8.378; 12.559; Lucian, *Dial. meret.* 4, 7, 9, 12, 14; Ath. 13.587A; Ach. Tat. 8.16.1.

[268] *RAC* 3, 1192.

[269] Phoenicid. fr. 4.4–10; Hipparch. Com. fr. 1 K; Philem. fr. 16; Men. *Kol.* fr. 2, 4, J. Kö.; Macho, Ath. 13.579A–D; Aristodem. *ibid.* 13.585A; Plaut. *Mil. passim*; *Poen.* 470–95; Ter. *Eun.* 391–453; Prop. 4.5.49; Ov. *Am.* 3.8; Strabo 12.559; Lucian, *Dial. meret.* 1, 13, 15; Alciphr. 2.34; 3.22; Philostr. *Ep.* 23; F. Wilhelm, *RhM* 57 (1902) 608; 59 (1904) 284; Wehrli 101–13. Regarding the physician as lover, see Phoenicid. fr. 4.10–15.

[270] Sen. *Controv.* 1.2.8.

[271] Plaut. *Poen.* 830–4; Hor. *Epod.* 17.20; Prop. 4.5.50–2; Sen. *Controv.* 1.2.8, 10; Col. 1.8.2; Lucian, *Dial. meret.* 14, 15; Alciphr. 1.6; Philostr. *Ep.* 38; Schneider, *Mer.* 1025. *Mastigiai* [whips] even in the case of finer *hetairai*, Ath. 13.585A–C.

Prostitutes have always been criticized for not being selective.[272] Christian writers in particular accused them of accepting the lowest and the basest of men as customers, but rejecting a noble man if he did not have money.[273] In church writings one finds instances of liberators who liked to disguise themselves as slaves, animal fighters, gladiators, and even soldiers.[274]

## 5 THE BROTHELS AND PLACES OF ACTIVITY

The places in which prostitutes were lodged tended to be secluded.[275] They would often situate themselves on the outer side of city walls[276] or in the archways of a circus, theater, stadium, or public bath, or at least close to one of these buildings.[277] Complaints were often made that harmless visitors to such buildings had to pass by the prostitutes.[278] The houses of prostitution were concentrated in sections of the city with bad reputations; understandably these were often in the vicinity of harbours[279] or at city gates.[280] But such houses were also sometimes found in more distinguished areas: in the marketplace[281] or near to temples or government buildings.[282] Justinian's *Novella* 14 mentions prostitutes in Constantinople who were not afraid to be near churches or palaces.[283]

Thus the whole city was full of temptations,[284] because prostitutes

---

[272] *RAC* 3, 1167, 1192. In this connection Archil. fr. 15D, Ath. 13.594CD (*Pasiphilê*); Hermipp. fr. 10 K.; Posidipp. fr. 17, *Anth. Pal.* 12.131; Phld. *Anth. Pal.* 12.173; Philo, *Spec. leg.* 3.51; Phil. Thess. *Anth. Pal.* 9.416; Cass. Dio 62.15.2–6; Heraclit. *Incred.* 25. See note 329.

[273] Chrys. *Hom. in 1 Cor.* 33.2; *Hom. in 1 Thess.* 5.4; *Hom. in Hebr.* 15.3. *RAC* 3, 1199.

[274] Euseb. *Hist. eccl.* 6.5; Chrys. *Thdr.* 1.13; *Hom. in Hebr.* 15.3; Ambros. *Virg.* 2.28–33; *V. Abr.* 21–7.

[275] Petron. 7.2, 8.3; Cypr. *Spect.* 6; Prudent. *Perist.* 14.39, 49; Evagr. *H. E.* 3.39.

[276] *Submoenianae* [low-lifes of a certain region of Rome]: Mart. 1.34.6; 3.82.2; 11.61.2; 12.32.22; Tert. *Pudic.* 4. Rahab at the city wall: Jos. *AJ* 5.7, 15 according to Jos. 2.

[277] Lucil. 1034; Hor. *Sat.* 1.6.113; *Priapea* 27.1; Juv. 3.65 (cf. Schol. on 6.116); *Hist. Aug. Hel.* 26.3, 32.9; *Anth. Lat.* 190.7; Arnob. 7.33; Jer. *In Isa.* 1.2.7; *Cod. Theod.* 15.7.12; cf. Suet. *Ner.* 27.2. Jordan, *Topogr.* 2. 69f; Jordan-Huelsen 1. 2. 236f n. 43; Schneider, *Mer.* 1023. E. V. Marmorale, *Pertinenze e impertinenze* 1 (Naples 1960) 194–203.

[278] Cypr. *Spect.* 5. Christian women who had been convicted of prostitution could easily be subjected to execution (Augar, 77f).

[279] Poll. 9.34; Schol. Ar. *Pax* 165; cf. Rufin. *Anth. Pal.* 5.43.

[280] Ar. *Eq.* 1398–1400; *Com. Adesp.* 805; *V. Ephr.* 4 (*PL* 73.322) with Metaphr. and Gr. Nyss.; *CIL* 4.8356. Official demands that these be placed in front of the gates are cited by Julian. *Or.* 6.186D–7A. A section of a city on Samos devoted to pleasure, the counterpart to *Agkôn glykys* [Sweet Nook] in Sardis, Clearch. fr. 44, Ath. 12.540F-41A.

[281] Mac. Aeg. *PG* 34.221; cf. *Prov.* 7.

[282] Dio Chrys. 7.133, cf. 139. *Palatium*, Suet. *Calig.* 41.1; Dio Cass. 59.28.9; 60.31.1f, cf. 79.13.3; *Hist. Aug. Carin.* 16.7.

[283] A brothel always remained a *locus inhonestus* [dishonorable place], to which opposing parties did not need to be directed by a judge (Ulpian, *Dig.* 4.8.21.11).

[284] Xen. *Mem.* 2.2.4; Lucian, *Nigr.* 16.

moved around everywhere,[285] even in sedan chairs.[286] This was particularly true of the lowest class of prostitutes, the *khamaitypai* [earth beaters], who were willing to make do with any location.[287] Even burial chambers served as places for a rendezvous, even if they could not offer long-term accommodation.[288] Prostitutes could be found on all streets and alleys, even on the Via Sacra,[289] and as a result, one category of prostitutes carried the designation *spodêsilaurai* [street walkers]. Intersections where there was much activity[290] and bridges[291] were particularly convenient. Christian and pagan source material support each other on this point.[292] Naturally prostitutes made the marketplaces unsafe; pagan[293] and Christian writers also agree on this.[294] Wherever the upper classes could be found, the classes of lower virtue could also be found.[295] Even in temples, whose inner chambers were not sacrosanct,[296] one could encounter prostitutes,[297] particularly the temples dedicated to Aphrodite[298] and, in Rome, those dedicated to *Isiaca lena* [Isis the procuress].[299] Prostitutes used to appear here particularly on festival days; Christian sources report that Julian the Apostate moved moved through all the streets of Antiocheia—probably on the occasion of the Aphrodisia festival —together with *effeminati* and whores, surrounded by male and

---

[285] Tert. *Pall.* 4.

[286] Bas. *Renunt.* 5. Cf. Theogn. 581f; Anac. (note 139); Phrynich. fr. 33 K.; Callim. *Epigr.* 38.

[287] Eur. fr. 676 N.² Noteworthy: Plat. *Resp.* 3.390C; Sen. *Ben.* 6.32.1.

[288] Mart. 1.34.8, cf. 3.93.15; Juv. 6.365; W. Crönert, *RhM* 64 (1909) 447f.

[289] Prop. 2.23.15; Mart. 2.63.2.

[290] Xen. *Mem.* 2.2.4; *Com. Adesp.* fr. 25a Demiańczuk; Catull. 58; Hor. *Carm.* 1.25; Prop. 2.22.3, 23.15; 4.7.19; Mart. 2.63.2; Artem. 1.56 (54, 24f H.); Agath. *Anth. Pal.* 5.301.1; cf. Ar. *Eccl.* 693; Dio Chrys. 32.32.

[291] *Gephyris* [prostitute]: see the dictionaries; cf. Artem. 4.66.

[292] Clem. Al. *Paed.* 3.21.2; Origen, *C. Cels.* 3.53; Ambros. *Cain et Abel* 1.4.14; Gr. Naz. *Or.* 8.10; Amph. *In mul. pecc.* 5; Chrys. *Stat.* 15.1; *Hom. in Is.* 6 = 1 1.2; Salv. *Gub. Dei* 7.72–4; Bas. Sel. *V. Thecl.*, PG 85.524; Jo. Mosch. *Prat.* 186. At the corners, Ioh. Eph. *v. ss. orient.* 52 (*PO* 19, 167 Brooks).

[293] Cerc. fr. 2 b.13D.; Plaut. *Truc.* 66–73; Philo, *Spec. leg.* 3.51; Diog. *Ep.* 28.4; Harp. s. v. *pôlôsi*; Hsch. s. v. *ekasôreuon* (according to Kukules 137 n. 2).

[294] Amph. *In mul. pecc.* 5; Chrys. *Stat.* 15.1; *Hom. in Mt.* 73 (74). 3; *Hom. in Act.* 31.2; Procl. PG 61.731, 734.

[295] Porticus of Pompeius, Mart. 11.47.3. Cf. note 311.

[296] Tert. *Apol.* 15.7; Alciphr. 4.1.

[297] Turpil. 72–6; Prop. 2.19.9f; Juv. 9.24; Manetho 5.318f; cf. 2 *Macc.* 6. 4; *RAC* 3, 1202, 1203f.

[298] Ath. 13.581A. See also Wilamowitz, *Glaube der Hellenen* 1, 97 n. 1. *Kyllou Pêra*: Ar. fr. 273; *RAC* 3, 1177f, 1202. Aphrodite's *pornika mystêria* [whorish mysteries]: Gr. Naz. *Or.* 39.4; she herself as a *pornê*: *RAC* 3, 1202f; Gr. Naz. *Or.* 5.32; Lactant. *Div. inst.* 5.10.15. Sacrifices and prayers to Aphrodite as well as oaths sworn in her name: Men. *Epitr.* 263 (304); Noss. *Anth. Pal.* 9. 605; Posidipp. 17, *Anth. Pal.* 12.131; Secundus, *Anth. Pal.* 9.260; Callim. *Epigr.* 38. Death in the sacred precincts of Aphrodite, Ath. 13.589B. Euhemerus (fr. 25J) introduced Aphrodite as the inventor of prostitution.

[299] Juv. 6.489; [Acro] Hor. *Carm.* 2.7.48.

female pimps who laughed and told dirty jokes.[300] Some of the well-known areas of prostitution in Athens were Peiraieus,[301] Diomeia,[302] Sciron, and Ceramicus.[303] The same applies to the Leocoreion[304] and the Heroon of Calamites near the old market;[305] the deserted area near the Pnyx offered places where all kinds of dubious characters could hide out.[306] In Rome the Subura was regarded as disreputable[307] as was the *vicus Tuscus*[308] and the Caelian hill,[309] not to mention Baiae, the *deversorium vitiorum* [resort of vices];[310] there were enough other places for a rendezvous.[311] Fine young women walking to and from their music instruction offered other opportunities for contact[312] as did the appropriate festivals[313] and the mixed baths.[314]

The accounts of the activities of prostitutes as recorded by church sources harmonize with the information in other sources. Some prostitutes were not even afraid to appear in the crowds at noon[315] but these women mostly appeared at night,[316] when proper women were no longer to be seen.[317] According to a legal notice, the *prostibula* [prostitutes] were available day and night.[318] We know, however, that Roman brothels did not open until the ninth hour.[319] In the case of *prostibula* and *prosedae* [common prostitutes] it was characteris-

---

[300] Chrys. *Pan. Bab.* 14.

[301] Ar. *Pax* 165; Theopomp. fr. 290 J., Alciphr. 1.6.2.

[302] Eup. fr. 235 K.

[303] Lucian, *Dial. meret.* 4.2f, 10.4; Alciphr. 2.22.2; 3.5.1, 12.3, 28.3; Hsch. s. v. *Kerameikos*; cf. Alex. fr. 203; Schol. Plat. *Parm.* 127C, Schol. Ar. *Eq.* 772.

[304] Alciphr. 3.2.1; Thphyl. *Ep.* 12.

[305] Dem. 18.129 with Schol.; Apollon. V. *Aeschin.* 2.

[306] Aeschin. 1.81–5.

[307] Hor. *Epod.* 5.58; Prop. 4.7.15; *Priapea* 40; Livy, 3.13.2; Pers. 5.32f; Mart. 2.17.1; 6.66.2; 11.61.3, 78.11.

[308] Tusca of Laberius etc., [Acro] Hor. *Sat.* 2.3.228.

[309] C. Huelsen, *RE* 3, 1275.

[310] Prop. 1.11; Sen. *Ep.* 51.

[311] Catull. 55; Prop. 2.19.9, 22.4–12; 4.8.75–8; Ov. *Am.* 3.2; *Ars am.* 1.67–100, 487–504; 3.387–96, 633–40; *Rem. am.* 487f, 627–30; Juv. 11.202. Regarding the Marsyas statue, see Sen. *Ben.* 6.32.1; Plin. *HN* 21.8f; I. Hilberg, *WS* 25 (1903) 156–8. Approaching, for example Catull. 55.11f; Antiphan. or Phld. *Anth. Pal.* 5.307; *Anth. Lat.* 728f.

[312] Ter. *Phorm.* 80–8, 144; cf. Plaut. *Rud.* 42f; Ambros. *Ep.* 1.2 (*PL* 17. 813).

[313] *RAC* 3, 1177f, 1203. See especially Herod. 1.56f; Men. fr. 382 Kö. = Plaut *Cist.* 89–93; Stat. *Silv.* 1.6.67; Lucian, *Dial. meret.* 11.2. Pimps occasionally travelled to more distant *panegyreis* [public festivals] with their entourage (Dio Chrys. 77.4). Regarding Jewish festivals, see note 544.

[314] Amm. Marc. 28.4.9; Anon. *Anth. Pal.* 9.621f; cf. Suet. *Dom.* 22; Jer. *Ep.* 117.7.

[315] Aristaenet. 1.4; see also Lys. 10.19 (?); *Priapea* 19; Mart. 9. 32.

[316] Prop. 4.7.39f; Jer. *In Ier.* 1.3.2; Chrys. *Hom. in Jo.* 79 (78).4; Theogn. 861 4 (?).

[317] Phylarch. fr. 45 J.; Diod. Sic. 12.21.1; cf. Phintys, Stob. 4.23.61.

[318] Non. 423.10–16M, 684.10–16L. Cf. Ar. *Vesp.* 500–2.

[319] Pers. 1.133 with Schol; Schol. Juv. 6.116; hence the designation *nonariae* [nine c'clock girls]. Cf. Plut. *Mor.* 759EF, F. Bücheler, *Kleine Schriften* 3.219.

tic for the prostitutes to stand[320] or sit[321] in front of their cells[322] or their doors[323] or at the doorways to houses for rent.[324] They could also appear at windows,[325] perhaps even on rooftops. The designation of these women as *hai epi (s)tegous* [the girls in the house], among others, is common in secular[326] and Christian texts,[327] although the *(s)tegos* [house] in this phrase can refer either to a brothel or to a cell.[328] Prostitutes did not seem to be embarrassed about their activities,[329] although some tended to be secretive.[330] From their locations they would entice passersby,[331] in the event that their victims were not brought to them[332] or even subjected to violence.[333] The scene as depicted by Ar. *Eccl.* 877–1111 is a characteristic one, although the women are not actually prostitutes. The unfortunate prostitutes recognize the abstainer through his eyes and they turn away from him.[334]

Houses of prostitution were also designated by signs,[335] perhaps

---

[320] *(Pro)estêkenai* [to stand in front], thus *hai proistamenai* or *proestôsai* [the girls who stand in front], for example Din. 1.23; Chrys. *Fem. reg.* 1.3; *Hom. in Rom.* 17.4; *Hom. in Eph.* 15.3; *Hom. in Hebr.* 15.3; *(pro)stare* [to stand in front], compare for example Sen. *Ben.* 1.9.3. Schneider, *Mer.* 1024.

[321] *Kathêsthai ep' oikêmatos* [to sit at a brothel] and other similar terms. See also Harp. s. v. *pôlôsi*; Ov. *Pont.* 2.3.20; Isid. *Or.* 10.229; Schol. Juv. 3.136; Tert. *Cult. fem.* 2.12.

[322] Petron. 8.4 and elsewhere.

[323] Plaut. *Cist.* 331; Cass. Dio 79.13.3; cf. Ath. 12.586A. Similarly Mac. Aeg. *Hom.* 17.10; Chrys. *Fem. reg.* 1.3; *Hom. in Hebr.* 15. 3; Proc. G. Anast. 13.

[324] Jer. *In Isa.* 16.57.9.

[325] Mart. 11.61; Ambros. *Cain et Abel* 1.4.14; V. *Ephr.*, *PL* 73.222 with Metaph. and Gr. Nyss.; Jer. *In Isa.* 7.12.15ff; K. Sudhoff, *Ärztliches* (Leipzig 1909) 108f. Cf. *Prov.* 7; Ar. *Eccl.* 877–1111.

[326] Zeno fr. 246 Arn.; *Anon. iamb. in turpil.* 40D; Diosc. *Anth. Pal.* 11.363.4; Jos. *AJ* 19. 9. 1; Manetho 2.430; 6.143, 533; Lucian, *Bis acc.* 31; Poll. 7.201; Vett. Val. 2.38 (121, 32 Kr.); *Orac. Sib.* 5.388; Xen. Eph. 5.7.1; Synes. *Provid.* 1.17; *Cat. Cod. Astr.* 8.4.169.7; Hsch. s. v. *stegitis*.

[327] Clem. Al. *Paed.* 3.21.2; *Strom.* 3.28.1, cf. Thdt. *Haer.* 1.6; Iren. 1.23.2; Euseb. *Hist. eccl.* 2.13; Epiph. *Haer.* 66.2.4; Gr. Naz. *Carm.* 1.2.10.860; 1.2.25.494; Chrys. *Pan. Bab.* 14; *Thdr.* 1.13; *Fem. reg.* 1, cf. 3; *Hom. in Mt.* 30 (31). 6; *Hom. in Rom.* 17.4; Isid. Pel. *Ep.* 1.464; Bas. Sel. *V. Thecl.*, *PG* 85.488; Eust. *Il.* 741.28.

[328] Thus Casaubon on Suet. *Calig.* 57.2. Chrys. *Van. glor.* 2 says *pro tou tegous* [in front of the house].

[329] Dio Chrys. 7.139. Regarding their indiscriminate actions, see note 272f.

[330] Firm. Mat. *Math.* 7.25.7, 9; Mich. Psell. *Ep.* 97 K.-Dr. Cf. note 491, Chrys. *Fem. reg.* 1.

[331] Plut. *Mor.* 759EF; *CIL* 4.2013; Chyrs. *Fem. reg.* 1.3.9. Isid. Pel. *Ep.* 5.319; Jo. D. *Parall.* 11. *RAC* 3, 1200. A naked old woman standing invitingly in front of a door, on a phylax vase (C. Drago, *Iapigia* N. S. 7 [1936] 390f; Catteruccia 72 nr. e; G. Alessio, *SIFC* 24 [1950] 124) derives her name from *cunnus* [vagina].

[332] Xenarch. fr. 4; Petron. 8.4; cf. Isid. *Or.* 18.42.2; Theophr. *Char.* 28.3.

[333] Sudhoff, *Ärztliches* (Leipzig 1909) 108f; Schneider, *Het.* 1345.

[334] Pall *V. Chrys.* 5. The *pornotrophoi* [brothel keepers] are, according to Pall. 5, not as bad as the seducers, because they only bring the "disease" to those who wish to have it. For Christianity the decisive factor is naturally the immoral desire. One enters the brothel with the awakening of desire, and evil thoughts transform one's heart into a brothel (Ambros. *In Psa.* 1181.12). Cf. *RAC* 3, 1185, 1197; Ambros. *Paen.* 1.68; Chrys. *Ebr.* 5.

[335] Tert. *Pud.* 1.

even by pictorial images.[336] When such houses were opened, they were adorned with a wreath.[337] Above each cell there was an *elogium* [inscription][338] with the name and the price.[339] The entrance to the houses tended to be partly concealed,[340] but practically open.[341] The building also had a lockable door on which the visitor was to knock.[342] From the women who were inside one learns that they could bolt the door.[343] In spite of all of this it was necessary for the prostitutes to have a form of courier service.[344] Harbours were carefully watched[345] and free prostitutes could send their assistants.[346] To the extent that these people were not pimps, they served as messengers and they were frequently flattered.[347] They would look after the transmitting of messages and the presentation of gifts.[348] Naturally the prostitutes could also secretly give their customers something themselves[349] or present them with an apple as a sign of affection.[350] Markings on the walls and other similar customs sometimes played a role in the evolution of a love relationship.[351] One clever means of attracting a customer, which was known to Clement of Alexandria,[352] was the inscription *akolouthei*, "follow," on the sole of a shoe, which could be pressed into the ground.[353]

[336] Schneider, *Mer.* 1024f; but see above, note 74. Specific signs used to attract someone, Jer. *In Ez.* 5.16.23–6. Inscriptions that point out the way, *CIL* 4, 1751, 8356.

[337] Tert. *Apol.* 35.4; *Cor. mil.* 13; *Ad uxor.* 2.6.

[338] Tert. *De spect.* 17.

[339] Sen. *Controv.* 1.2.1, 5, 7; Petron. 7.3; Mart. 11.45.1; Juv. 6.123 with Schol.; *Vit. Ap. Tyr.* 33 (modern Greek version, v. 545–8, 555, 722–6). If necessary, there was also the term *occupata* [engaged] (Plaut. *Asin.* 760; correctly in Becker-Rein, 3.64).

[340] Schneider, *Mer.* 1024; Sen. *Q. Nat.* 1.16.6. Zeugma in Byzantium, see *Patria Const.* 2.65. Cf. C. Weyman, *Beiträge zur Geschichte der christlich-lateinischen Poesie* (Munich 1926) 85–7.

[341] Dio Chrys. 7.140.

[342] Claudian. 1.93; Ambr. *In Psa.* 118 1.12. Cf. note 319.

[343] Ov. *Am.* 3.14.9f; Mart. 1.34.5f; 11.45; *Hist. Apoll. Tyr.* 34; cf. Aeschin. 1.74; Mart. 7.62; Diog. Laert. 2.105. Regarding the practice of locking the farthermost rooms in an inn, *V. Abr.* 25.

[344] Petron. 6.4–8.4; see also Suet. *Calig.* 41.1.

[345] Plaut. *Men.* 338–43; *Poen.* 619–83.

[346] Plaut. *Men.* 338f.

[347] Examples: Plaut. *Asin.* 183–5; cf. *Men.* 541–4; Ter. *Haut.* 297–301; Tib. 1.2.95f; Ov. *Am.* 1.8.87–90, 11. 12; 2.2.3; *Ars am.* 1.351–96; 2.251–60; 3.619–30, 649f, 665f; *Rem. am.* 637–42; Lucian, *Dial. meret.* 10, 14.3; Alciphr. 4.8.1; Aristaenet. 1.4.22; 2.19. Chrys. *Hom. in Jo.* 79 (78).5.

[348] Plaut. *Asin.* 761–7, 803–5; Catull. 32; Prop. 2.20.33; 3.23; Ov. *Am.* 2.19.41; 3.1.55f; 14.31; *Ars am.* 1.383, 437–86; 3.469–98; Petron. fr. 30.14; 33; Alciphr. 4.10.2; Ath. 13.585DE.

[349] Naev. 79.

[350] Ar. *Nub.* 997; Lucian, *Dial. meret.* 12.1; Aristaenet. 1.25.

[351] Lucian, *Dial. meret.* 4.2f, 10.4; see also the numerous inscriptions in Pompeii. Regarding poems that were attached to doors, see Ov. *Am.* 3.1.53f; regarding epigrams addressed to a beloved, see Hor. *Carm.* 1.16.

[352] Clem. Al. *Paed.* 2.116.1.

[353] Navarre fig. 4068; G. Lumbroso, *BSSA* 17 (1919) 165f. The lover whistles to his beloved, Aristaenet. 2.4; *Apophth. Patr. Ioh. Col.* 16. Regarding other secret signals, see Aristaenet. 1.4; W. Crönert-R. Wünsch, *RhM* 64 (1909) 441.

## 6 THE PHYSICAL APPEARANCE OF PROSTITUTES

Everywhere that prostitutes presented themselves, they were recognizable as *makhlades*, "lewd," because of their overall appearance and actions,[354] especially their obtrusive clothing and jewelry.[355] Even secular moralists denounced this style of dress in women, claiming that they would become *hetairikon ti*, "a little whorish."[356] Christian writers in particular forbad every form of excessive adornment among women, especially women of the church, claiming that it was suggestive of a prostitute.[357] In reality, the differences in appearance were not so great. Tertullian[358] mentions that the tendency of many Roman women to neglect their feminine appearance in public was criticized by A. Caecina Severus in the Senate and was regarded by the augur Cn. Cornelius Lentulus as *stuprum* [lewd behaviour] and threatened with punishment. However charming a courtesan might be in her outward appearance, she is still ugly, according to John Chrysostom, and her soul does not correspond to her outward appearance.[359] When the Midianites employed the seductive powers of their daughters, in order to gain control over the Israelites, the cunning seductresses were told that they did not need to fear the criticism of *hetairêsis* [prostitution] and *moikheia*, as Philo describes this event (*Fort.* 35–41), because within their innermost being they would still remain virgins. But in the course of engaging in these activities they discovered their true identity. The description of the prostitutes was also transferred to symbolic figures such as Hedone

[354] Aeschrio fr. 6.6D.; Philo, *Op. mund.* 166; Marc. Arg. *Anth. Pal.* 5.104.1; Manetho 4.357f; Artem. 4.11; Clem. Al. *Paed.* 3.21.5; Claudian. *Anth. Pal.* 9.139.1; Agath. *Anth. Pal.* 5.301.2; id. *Anth. Plan.* 80; Pall. *Anth. Pal.* 10.56.12; Gr. Naz. *Carm.* 1.2.29.264.

[355] E. Burck, *WS* 69 (1956) 274; see Xen. *Mem.* 3.11.4; [Dem.] 59.35, 46; Plaut. *Cist.* 55, 113–15, 306, 477, 487; *Curc.* 344, 435, 488; *Ep.* 222–5; *Men.* 103–5, 166–73, 531–8; *Mil.* 1099f, 1126f, 1147f, 1204f, 1302–4; *Most.* 166–73, 248f, 282–94; *Pseud.* 182; *Truc.* 270–3, 287–94, 318; Ter. *Haut.* 778, 854–6, 891–3; Catull. 69.3f; Diod. Sic. 2.23.1; Ov. *Ars am.* 3.101–92; Philo, *Prov. in Euseb. Praep. evang.* 8.14.31; Plut. *Mor.* 133B; Lucian, *Dial. meret.* 6.2, 7.2; *Hist. conscr.* 8; *Dom.* 7, cf. note 39f; Xen. Eph. 5.7.1; Alciphr. 1.6.3; 4.9.1f; Aristaenet. 1.4; *Gnom. hom.* 178 Elt.

[356] Sen. *Q. Nat.* 7.31.2; Plut. *Mor.* 142BC; Lucian, *Tox.* 13; *Ver. hist.* 2.46; Auson. *Epigr.* 104 (434 P.); cf. Aristaenet. 1.19. A *philêdonos* [lover of pleasure] makes his wife *hetairikê kai akolastos* [whorish and wanton] (Plut. *Mor.* 140C); cf. *RAC* 3, 1172.

[357] Clem. Al. *Paed.* 3.5.4; 3.7.2; 3.11.2; 3.13.1f; 3.67.1; 3.68f; Tert. *Cult. fem.* 1.4, 6; 2.9, 12; Cypr. *Hab. virg.* 12, cf. 13–17; Arnob. 4.16; Ambros. *In Psa.* 1184.4; Jer. *Ep.* 22.3.5; Chrys. *Fem. reg.* 1.3.5; *Ill. Cat.* 1.37; *Hom. in Mt.* 30 (31).6; *Hom. in 1 Cor.* 18.3; *Hom. in Col.* 10.5; *Hom. in 1 Tim.* 8.2f; *Ep. ad Ol.* 2.9; *Const. App.* 1.8; *Comm. Instr.* 2.18.22. Cf. Is. 3.16–26. *RAC* 3, 1197.

[358] Tert. *Pall.* 4, cf. *Apol.* 6.3; *Cult. fem.* 2.12; J. Geffcken, *Kynika* (Heidelberg 1909) 74, 119f.

[359] Chrys. *Hom. in Jo.* 27 (26).3; *Hom. in 1 Cor.* 18. 3. Regarding the Midianites, see Chrys. *Hom. ad Ant.* 14.4; *In Kal.* 6.

and Apate, by secular,[360] Jewish,[361] and Christian[362] writers alike, and applied by them to false religions[363] or the Old Law[364] and naturally to the Great Whore described in the Book of Revelation.[365] There are also references to speech that is embellished by make-up or like a prostitute.[366] One can easily imagine that young boys who dressed like prostitutes were disapproved of.[367]

Beauty is one of the important attributes of the ideal image of a courtesan but it is not important for a married woman.[368] Only occasionally and much later does one find references to female beauty on gravestones.[369] Beauty functions as *empnous porneusis* [the breath of harlotry][370] through the eye, which is regarded as the path of love[371] by both pagan[372] and Christian writers.[373] They felt that it was not the act of seeing, but rather the desire that is aroused through seeing, which is to be viewed as sin.[374] According to Synesius, Archilochus fr. 25 had already described the charms of a woman in terms of a *hetaira*.[375] Since that time secular[376] writers have emphasized the

[360] Sen. *Dial.* 7.7.3; Dio Chrys. 4.111–15; Ceb. 6.9; Lucian, *Bis acc.* 20. Regarding Circe as a prostitute, see Heraclit. *Incred.* 16; Pall. *Anth. Pal.* 10.50. Cf. Prodic., Xen. *Mem.* 2.1.22.

[361] Philo, *Op. mund.* 166.

[362] Zeno Ver. 1. 4. 3; Ambros. *Cain et Abel* 1.4.14; *In Psa.* 118 4.4; Zeno Ver. 1.12.5.

[363] Anast. S. Hex. 12 p. 1072C; see the passages regarding intellectual *porneia* at *RAC* 3, 1188; there could be any number more.

[364] Petr. Chrys. 115.516A.

[365] *Apoc.* 17.1f (Cypr. *Hab. virg.* 12 etc.).

[366] Tac. *Dial.* 26.1; Jer. *In Gal.* 3 prol. (*PL* 26. 427); Sid. Apoll. *Epist.* 3.13.11.

[367] Zeno fr. 246 (1, 58 Arn.); Lucian, *Gall.* 19; see also Strato, *Anth. Pal.* 12.192; Clem. Al. *Paed.* 3.15.3, cf. 3.16.1, 18.1; *RAC* s. v. *Effeminatus*.

[368] Eur. *Andr.* 207f.

[369] G. Fohlen, *LEC* 22 (1954) 145f.

[370] Secund. *Sent.* 14 (1.514 Mull.).

[371] E. Rohde, *Roman*² (Leipzig 1900) 158f; M. B. Ogle, *AJPh* 34 (1913) 125–52; F. J. Dölger, *Antike & Christentum* 3 (1932) 139 n. 19.

[372] Hdt. 5.18.4; *Com. Adesp.* fr. 388K.; Ter. *Phorm.* 1053; Varro, *Sat. Men.* 176; Prop. 2.32.1f; Quint. *Decl.* 1.6; Plut. *Alex.* 21; Ath. 13.608A; Nonn. 15.240; 42.42; Musaeus 94f; Aristaenet. 1.1 etc.; cf. Lécrivain 184, 186.

[373] *RAC* 3, 1200; Ambros. *Paen.* 1.73; Gr. Naz. *Or.* 24. 9; *Carm.* 2.2.8.111–13; Isid. *Sent.* 2.39.8; *Synon.* 2.16 etc.

[374] Ambros. *Paen.* 1. 67–73. See also note 334.

[375] Synes. *Calv.* 75BC. See V. de Falco, *PP* 1 (1946) 352 n. 1; B. Marzullo, *RhM* 100 (1957) 68–72.

[376] Hdt. 2.135; [Dem.] 59.39; Hyp. fr. 13J.; Anaxandr. fr. 9; Theophil. fr. 12; Men. *Epitr.* 462 (503); fr. 185 Kö; Theophr. fr. 147, Ath. 10.435A: Diog., Diog. Laert. 6.61 and Stob. 4.21a.15; Crates Com. fr. 27; Macho Ath. 13.578CD; Noss. *Anth. Pal.* 9.605; Plaut. *Asin.* 675; *Men.* 189; *Merc.* 13, 101; *Mil.* 782–804, 870–3; *Poen.* 1174–85; *Rud.* 51f and elsewhere; Ter. *Haut.* 523; Hegesand. Ath. 4.167E; Antip. Sid. *Anth. Pal.* 7.218; Varro, *Sat. Men.* 432; Hor. *Carm.* 2.8; Philo, *Spec. leg.* 3.51; Quint. *Inst.* 2.15.9; *Decl.* 15.5; Plut. *Mor.* 128D, 133B, 768A. *Luc.* 6.2f; Dio Chrys. 4.114; Artem. 4.83 (251 H.); Philostr. *Ep.* 20, 38, 47 etc.; Alciphr. 4.11.1; fr. 5; Ath. 13.576D, F, 588DE, 589B, 590EF, 592B, 594B, 596D–E; Ael. *VH* 12.1, 52, Xen. Eph. 5.7.2f; Heliod. 7.10; Firm. Math. *Math.* 6.31.90; Donat. Ter. *Andr.* 119; Lib. *Decl.* 38.45; Synes. *Ep.* 110 and elsewhere; Maxim. 5.15, 23–30; Aristaenet. 1.12, 17, 19, 25; *Anacreont.* 16; Paul. Sil. *Anth. Pal.* 6. 71; Anon. *Anth. Pal.* 7.221; Heraclit. *Incred.* 1.2.14; *IG* 14, 2135. Regarding the *kallipygoi* [beautifully bummed], see G. A. Gerhard, *Phoinix* 218–20; *WS* 37

physical beauty of prostitutes; it also plays a role in the arsenal of motives that Christian writers drew on, particularly in those situations where women tried to woo someone by selling their beauty or used it to ensnare their victims.[377] There were virtual beauty championships among these women.[378] Prostitutes also served frequently as models for artists,[379] according to Lais[380] and Phryne.[381]

Not without some exceptions,[382] prostitutes also confirm the old lesson that even the greatest degree of physical attractiveness wanes over time;[383] this is emphasized by Christian writers too.[384] Old coquettes such as Phryne, who in her later years tried to charge more for the dregs than for the wine,[385] found that they had to use considerable adornment,[386] but usually in vain: the price that they could command dropped,[387] they were subject to ridicule, and they were abandoned.[388] Even Lais, who used to be unsurpassable,[389] was

---

(1915) 1–6; B. Warnecke, *RE* 4A, 2237; T. Dohrn, *MDAI* 2 (1949) 82. In general see K. Jax, *Die weibliche Schönheit in der griechischen Dichtung* (Innsbruck 1933); *id.*, *Der Frauentypus der römischen Dichtung* (Innsbruck 1938); Neumann, *Poetische Gerechtigkeit* 103f, 179.

[377] Tert. *Cult. fem.* 2.12; Cypr. *Hab. virg.* 12; Ephr. *Admon. et paen.* 9 (1.292 Lamy); Epiph. *Anac.* 66.2.4; Bas. *Renunt.* 5; Gr. Naz. *Carm.* 1.2.29.23f; Ambros. *Paen.* 1.68; Aug. *Lib. arb.* 2.138; Nemes. *Nat. hom.* 30; Chrys. *Fr. in Jer.* 4; *Van. glor.* 2; *Apophth. Patr. Ioh. Cell.* 1; Bas. Sel. *V. Thecl.*, *PG* 85.524; *V. Pelag.* 3.

[378] Lucian, *Dial. meret.* 3.2; Alciphr. 4.14 (see T. Kock, *Hermes* 21 [1886] 406–9; P. Legrand, *Daos: tableau de la comédie grecque pendant la période dite nouvelle, komoidia nea* [Lyon 1910] 113 n. 4; G. A. Gerhard, *WS* 37 [1915] 1–6; L. Castiglioni, in *Mélanges offerts à M. Octave Navarre par ses élèves et ses amis* [Toulouse 1935] 57–61); Rufin. *Anth. Pal.* 5.34f, cf. 36; cf. Plin. *HN* 10.172; Ath. 13.609E-10B. Illustration: M. Rostovtzeff, *The Social and Economic History of the Hellenistic World* 1 (Oxford 1941) plate 34.2.

[379] Xen. *Mem.* 3.11.1f. Plut. *Pomp.* 2.8. *RAC* 3, 1203. Arnob. 6.13. According to T. Kock, the Venus Callipygos of Naples is a *hetaira*.

[380] Ath. 13.588DE, cf. Aristaenet. 1.1.

[381] A. E. Raubitschek, *RE* 20, 898–903. Regarding Phryne and her defender, see G. Hafner, *JDAI* 70 (1955) 112.

[382] Asclep. *Anth. Pal.* 7.217; Antip. Sid. *Anth. Pal.*, 6.47; Ov. *Ars am.* 2.663–702; Philostr. *Ep.* 51; cf. Paul. Sil. *Anth. Pal.* 5.258; Agath. *Anth. Pal.* 5.281.

[383] Philetaer. fr 9; Anaxil. fr. 22; Timocl. fr. 25; Ter. *Haut.* 381–91; Papin. epigr. p. 42 Mor. (E. Vetter, *RhM* 101 [1958] 304f); Prop. 2.18.19f; 3.25; 4.5.59–62; Ov. *Am.* 1.8.49–53; *Ars am.* 3. 59–82; *Fast.* 5.353f; Lucill. *Anth. Pal.* 11.256; Philostr. *Ep.* 51; Alciphr. 4.7.8; Auson. *Epigr.* 13 [34]; Aristaenet. 2.1; Rufin. *Anth. Pal.* 5.20. Cf. R. Pack, *AJPh* 76 (1955) 98.

[384] Tert. *Cult. fem.* 2.6; Amph. *Mul. pecc.* 5; *Cod. Theod.* 15.7.8.

[385] Plut. *Mor.* 125B.

[386] Tib. 1.8.41–6; Lucian, *Dial. meret.* 11.3f; Philostr. *Ep.* 40; Claudian. *Anth. Pal.* 9.139; S. Lieberman, *Greek in Jewish Palestine* (New York 1942) 44–7.

[387] Mart. 7.75; 10.75; Nicarch. *Anth. Pal.* 11.73.

[388] Philetaer. fr. 9; Antiphan. fr. 26.12–15; Plaut. *Most.* 196, 199–202, 216f; Ter. *Haut.* 388–91; Afran. 378–82; Herodic. Ath. 13.586A; Hor. *Carm.* 1.25; 3.15; 4.13; Tib. 1.6.77–84; Prop. 3.25.11–18; Ov. *Ars am.* 3.65–80; *Priapea* 57; Mart. 6.40; 9.37; 10.90; Lucian, *Anth. Pal.* 11.408; Amm. Marc. 28.4.9; Maced. *Anth. Pal.* 5.270; Myrin. *ibid.* 11.67. Cf. F. Wilhelm, *Philologus* 60 (1901) 585f; F. J. Brecht, *ibid.* Suppl. 22. 2 (1930) 62–6; F. Wehrli, *Motivstudien* (Zürich 1936) 25f; Theogn. 861–4 (?).

[389] Mart. 10.68; 11.104; Plut. *Mor.* 759EF, 1039A; cf. G. Luck, *Philologus* 100 (1965) 273f; Alciphr. p. 156 Schepers; Georg. Pachym. *Decl.* 9 (178); 10 (189, 205B.).

unable to command any attention in her old age.[390] Some women abandon prostitution in time;[391] at least this was what they should do if they want to marry.[392]

Naturally there are also ugly and ordinary prostitutes,[393] who would not even appeal to the rabble.[394] But a man who is in love does not see the blemishes of the one whom he adores, or else is attracted by them.[395] An ugly prostitute only seems to be pretty as long as one is in love with her.[396] A young girl's appeal lies in her natural charms,[397] but sometimes it is necessary to employ some of the general skills of make-up, or to cover up or correct specific blemishes and to emphasize certain attractive features.[398] The Church Fathers write about means that female suitors use to make up for those instances where true beauty is lacking.[399] Horace, on the other hand, feels that simple prostitutes should present themselves as they are.[400] However much prostitutes of the lowest classes may seem to have neglected their appearance,[401] many of these women placed great value on a carefully groomed look, even if this did not correspond to their daily form of existence,[402] and they placed great emphasis on their baths.[403] A careful young woman made sure, as Adelphasium did,[404] that the money that she spent on cosmetics did not exceed her financial means. Even the Church Fathers note that prostitutes who

---

[390] Pl. Jun. *Anth. Pal.* 6.1 (Auson. *Epigr.* 65 P.); Epicr. fr. 2–3; Secundus, *Anth. Pal.* 9.260; Claud. 18.90–7; Jul. *Anth. Pal.* 6.18–20; Myrin. *Anth. Pal.* 11.67.

[391] *RAC* 3, 1174. Cf. also Philet. *Anth. Pal.* 6.210; Philo, *Spec. leg.* 1.282; Anon. *Anth. Pal.* 6.283. Regarding precautionary measures for old age, see Ter. *Haut.* 389–91.

[392] Hor. *Carm.* 3.15.

[393] Plaut. *Cist.* 405–8; Catull. 6; *Anth. Lat.* 361f; *Philogelos* 151. Caricatures, W. Binsfeld, *Grylloi*, Diss. Köln (1956) 19, 23, 38. See also Ar. *Eccl.* 877–1111; Ov. *Am.* 1.14; Nicarch. *Anth. Pal.* 11. 328; Chrys. *Vid.* 6.

[394] Chrys. *Thdr.* 1.13.

[395] Hor. *Sat.* 1.3.38–40; cf. Pl. *Resp.* 5.474D–5A, 485BC; Theoc. 10.26f; Ov. *Rem.* 315–40; Aristaenet. 1.18; F. Wilhelm, *RhM* 77 (1928) 402. See note 121.

[396] Chrys. *Hom. in Act.* 28. 3.

[397] Plaut. *Most.* 168–294; Tib. 1.8.9–16; Prop. 1.2; 3.14; *Anth. Lat.* 458; Clem. Al. *Paed.* 3.67.1; K. Flower Smith, *AJPh* 34 (1913) 62–73.

[398] Alex. fr. 98; Ter. *Eun.* 313–17; Ov. *Ars am.* 1.523; 3.199–278; Philo, *Fort.* 39; Euseb. *Praep. evang.* 8.14.31; Ath.13.568A–E; Heliod. 7.10; *Anth. Lat.* 130; cf. Plut. *Mor.* 752C; Achmet, *On.* p. 225, 2f Dr.; Schneider, *Het.* 1352. A *hetaira* who was highly made up had the nickname *Proskênion* [stage scenery] (Ath. 13.587B).

[399] Cypr. *Hab. virg.* 12; Chrys. *Hom. in Mt.* 70 (71). 4; *Hom. in Hebr.* 15. 3; Nil. *Exerc.* 67.

[400] Hor. *Sat.* 1.2.83–85, 101–3.

[401] Antiphan. fr. 26.4; Plaut. *Nerv.* fr. 100; Ath. 13.586A. Cf. note 260.

[402] Ter. *Eun.* 934–40.

[403] Pherecr. fr. 69; Antiphan. fr. 106, 148; Plaut. *Bacch.* 105; *Most.* 157–71; *Poen.* 210–51; *Truc.* 198, 322–30, 378–81; Lucil. 264–6; Lucill. *Anth. Pal.* 11.256; Lucian, *Dial. meret.* 6.4; Anon. *Anth. Pal.* 9.621, cf. 622. A fountain where *hetairai* bathe is disgusting in the opinion of Jos. *AJ* 8.417 (K. H. Rengstorf, *Theologisches Wörterbuch zum Neuen Testament* 6, 588). See also *POxy.* 840.34–41. Regarding grooming scenes, see Schneider, *Het.* 1353.

[404] Plaut. *Poen.* 283–8, 297–307.

wish to be able to charge a high fee[405] have to spend considerable time on their grooming,[406] because they need clothing and jewelry as they do *lenones et prostitutores* [pimps and procurers].[407] They spend much time washing, rubbing, oiling, and beautifying their skin,[408] but deep inside they are full of scorpions, capable of any kind of evil,[409] and no match whatsoever for the attractiveness of a woman of honour.[410]

Make-up was a substantial feature of the life of a prostitute, although make-up was not the exclusive preserve of such women.[411] Christian writers regarded make-up, along with other resources of beauty,[412] as characteristic of paramours[413] who adorned themselves with artificial substances and all the essences of color merchants,[414] and these writers forbad all proper women and especially single women who were devoted to Christian service the use of these adornments.[415] Make-up had the disadvantage that it was not resistant to tears[416] and tended to fall off in the summer.[417] A Phryne did not need these resources[418] and this *adulterina fallacia* [adulterous deception][419] did not benefit an ugly peasant woman very much.[420] Perfumes were regarded with suspicion by both pagan[421] and Christian writers;[422] they were also used as part of room decorations, as is shown in *Prov.*

---

[405] Chrys. *Hom. in Rom.* 24. 4.

[406] Clem. Al. *Paed.* 3.7.2; Tert. *Adv. Valent.* 4; Meth. *Res.* 1.28.1; Chrys. *Subintr.* 11; *Hom. in 1 Cor.* 18.3; Isid. Pel. *Ep.* 5.319; V. *Pelag.* 2.

[407] Tert. *Cult. fem.* 2.9.

[408] *POxy.* 840.35–41.

[409] Clem. Al. *Paed.* 3.5.3; Ambros. *Bon. mort.* 9.40.

[410] Eust. *Hex.* 3.8.

[411] Plaut. *Most.* 258–64; *Truc.* 290–4; Antiphil. *Anth. Pal.* 9.415.6; Lucil. 265; Prop. 3.24.8; *Priapea* 50; Euseb. *Praep. evang.* 8.14.31; Sen. *Dial.* 7.7.7; Mart. 1.72; Lucian, *Hist. conscr.* 8; *Bis acc.* 31; Philostr. *Ep.* 22; Alciphr. 4.6.4, 12.2; Ath. 13.557F; Claudian. *Anth. Pal.* 9.139; Aristaenet. 1.25; Rufin. *Anth. Pal.* 5.18; Achmet, *On.* p. 225, 2f Dr.; cf. Sen. *Dial.* 12.16.4.

[412] Chrys. *Hom. in Mt.* 31 (32).6.

[413] Tert. *Cult. fem.* 2.12; Ast. Soph. *Ps.* 4.19; Arn. 4.16; Zeno Ver. 1.4.3; Ambros. *Cain et Abel* 1.4.14; *In Psa.* 118 4.4; Jer. *Ep.* 54.7; Bas. *Contub.* 6; Gr. Naz. *Or.* 8.10; *Carm.* 1.2.29.23–8, 261f; Amph. *Mul. pecc.* 4f; Chrys. *David* 3.1; *Hom. in Mt.* 70 (71). 4; *Hom. in Jo.* 18 (17). 4; *Hom. in Hebr.* 15. 3; *Fr. in Jer.* 4; *Vid.* 6; [Chrys.], *PG* 59.592; cf. 61.746f; 62.742; Procl. *PG* 61.727, 734; Petr. Chrys. p. 115.

[414] Ast. Am. *Hom.* 3.

[415] Chrys. *Hom. in 1 Tim.* 8.2f.

[416] Jer. *Ep.* 54.7; Gr. Naz. *Or.* 8.10; *Carm.* 2.1.29.25–8.

[417] Eub. fr. 98; Mart. 2.41.11f.

[418] Gal. *Libr. protr.* 10.

[419] August. *Ep.* 245.1; cf. Cypr. *Hab. virg.* 15.

[420] Chrys. *Hom. in Hebr.* 15.3.

[421] Antiphan. fr. 106, 148; Posidipp. fr. 6 Sch.: Ath. 13.596CD; Plaut. *Most.* 272–8; *Truc.* 288f; Antip. Sid. *Anth. Pal.* 7.218; Mel. *Anth. Pal.* 5.174; Sen. *Dial.* 7.7.3; Alciphr. 4.9.2; Aristaenet. 1.4; *Anacreont.* 16.9; *IG* 14.2135 (Kaibel, *Epigr. Gr.* 610, *GVI* 112a).

[422] Clem. Al. *Paed.* 2.68.4; 3.7.2; Ath. *Gent.* 5; Jer. *In Isa.* 16.57.9; Chrys. *Fem. reg.* 1; *Van. glor.* 2; *Hom. in Rom.* 30.4; *Hom. in 1 Thess.* 4.4; *Hom. in 1 Tim.* 8.2f; Prudent. *Ham.* 312–15; V. *Pelag.* 2.

7. The *plaggonion* [a kind of ointment] was named after a *hetaira*. Conversely the *schoeniculae* [perfumed whores] were named for poor-quality ointments.⁴²³ Hair was usually carefully cut⁴²⁴ and sometimes colored⁴²⁵ or replaced by a wig.⁴²⁶ The *cinerarius* [hair-curler] was described as *doulos hetairas*, the *hetaira*'s slave.⁴²⁷ Naturally the artistry of a hairstylist was regarded as undesirable in the teachings of the church.⁴²⁸ Prostitutes paid great attention to their clothing and their jewelry. If these were not the gifts of a pimp,⁴²⁹ then they were usually presents from a lover. If one reads that the residents of a brothel stood there *gymnai* [naked] or *nudae* [unclothed],⁴³⁰ then one can assume that they were either wearing a very light garment⁴³¹ or that their upper bodies were unclothed.⁴³² Otherwise the clothing of a prostitute conformed to the prevailing fashion and a toiletry item taken from the wife of an unfaithful husband could be welcomed by a *hetaira*.⁴³³ All too frequently, however, prostitutes were distinguishable by their striking or luxuriant appearance.⁴³⁴ Their clothing was distinctive because it was shorter⁴³⁵ and more colourful.⁴³⁶ It was sometimes thinner or almost transparent and suited to fine *tarantinidia*

⁴²³ Navarre 1835 n. 8.

⁴²⁴ Posidipp. fr.6 Sch. (A. Wilhelm, *WS* 64 [1949] 150–2; F. Scheidweiler, *RhM* 101 [1958] 92–5). Macho, Ath. 13.579D; Plaut. *Most.* 254f; *Truc.* 287f; Poll. 4.153; Lucian, *Dial. meret.* 11.3; 12.5; *Bis acc.* 31; Claudian. *Anth. Pal.* 9.139; Aristaenet. 1.19, 25; [Arist.] *Phgn.* 1.258.2–4; Delling, 103f; the *lampadion* [topknot] hair styles of *hetairai*: J. Colin, *RBPh* 33 (1955) 867.

⁴²⁵ Prop. 2.18.23f and elsewhere.

⁴²⁶ Bas. *Contub.* 6; *galerus flavus* [blonde wig]: Juv. 6.120 with Schol.

⁴²⁷ *Gloss. Lat.* 2.100.45.

⁴²⁸ Clem. Al. *Paed.* 3.11.2, 62.3, 63.2; Cypr. *Hab. virg.* 12; Bas. *Contub.* 6; Amph. *Mul. pecc.* 5; Const. *Ap.* 1.8; Chrys. *Van. glor.* 2; *Hom. in Jo.* 18 (17). 4; *Hom. in 1 Tim.* 8.2, 3; [Chrys.] *PG* 59.756; 61.746f; Procl. *PG* 61.710, 734; Jer. *Ep.* 117.7; Pall. *V. Chrys.* 8.

⁴²⁹ Sen. *Controv.* 1.2.7.

⁴³⁰ Eub. fr. 67.4–6; Philem. fr. 4.10; Hor. *Sat.* 2.7.48; Juv. 11.172; Tac. *Ann.* 15.37; Cass. Dio 79.13.3; [Cypr.] *Spect.* 5; Arn. 6.12.

⁴³¹ Petron. 55.6.15f; Antiphil. *Anth. Pal.* 9.415.5f; cf. Sen. *Controv.* 1.2.7.

⁴³² Xenarch. fr. 4; Lucil. 859f; Juv. 6.122. Cf. Schneider, *Het.* 1352; Schneider, *Mer.* 1024. The images on vases show *hetairai* in widely different settings and sometimes totally naked, as are the female tricksters.

⁴³³ Plaut. *Asin.* 884–9, 929–32, 939; *Men.* 130–5, 166–73, 531–8 etc.

⁴³⁴ Schneider, *Het.* 1354. Cf. Philo, *Fort.* 39; Plut. *Ant.* 18.4; Lucian, *Am.* 38–42, 44; Ath. 13.587B; Aristaenet. 1.19; *Etym. Magn.* s. v. *pygostolos*; Chrys. *Ep. ad Ol.* 2.9.

⁴³⁵ Afran. 133f; Varro, Non. p. 541.7–10; cf. Juv. 8.162.

⁴³⁶ Ar. *Thesm.* 98–138; *Eccl.* 879; Phylarch. fr. 45: Ath. 12.521B; Plaut. *Truc.* 271; Antip. Sid. *Anth. Pal.* 7.218.1; Lucil. 71; Tib. 2.3.57f, 4.28; Sen. *Q. Nat.* 7.31.2; Dio Chrys. 4.96; Artem. 2.3 (88 H.); Lucian, *Hist. conscr.* 8; Pythag. *Ep.* 11.1; Donat. *Com.* 8.6 (71.2 Kaib.); Anon. *Anth. Pal.* 6.284; *IG* 14.2135. Eratosthenes (Strabo 1, p. 15; Diog. Laert. 4.52 among others) stated that Bion had applied *anthina* [colored dresses] to philosophy, clearly those of the *hetairai* (Rohde, *Roman*³ 268 n; W. Capelle, *RhM* 101 [1958] 25 n. 86; for a different point of view see A. Alföldi, in K. Weitzmann (ed.), *Late Classical and Mediaeval Studies in honor of Albert Mathias Friend, Jr.* [Princeton 1955] 24).

[light wraps] and *Coae vestes* [Coan clothing].[437] Extravagant prostitutes tried to make an impression with masculine styles of dress.[438] Christian writers often emphasized the tendency of *hetairai* to be concerned about their clothing[439] and to prefer soft, light,[440] silken,[441] colorful[442] and even golden[443] clothing. Headscarves, especially if they were colorful, were regarded everywhere as characteristic of a prostitute.[444] Christian writers held the same opinion about splendid shoes.[445] Prostitutes avoided wearing veils, or else used them for special forms of coquetry.[446] A veil was not exactly obligatory for decent women, but according to Paul (*1 Cor.* 11:3–16) it was required of all Christian women.[447]

Chrysippus claims that at first, prostitutes only plied their trade outside of cities, wearing masks but later doing without them, and that they eventually moved into cities on a daily basis, but this is only asserted by him and it is unlikely.[448] There is no evidence that in Athens *anthina* [colored dresses] were required of prostitutes.[449] On the other hand one finds Greek laws that forbid married women from wearing certain kinds of clothing and ornaments but do not forbid courtesans from doing so.[450] In Rome, prostitutes wore a short tunic without *instita* [border][451] and a dark toga, similar to what a man would wear,[452] but

---

[437] Hor. *Carm.* 4.13.13; *Sat.* 1.2.101f; Tib. 2.3.53f, 4.29f; Marc. Arg. *Anth. Pal.* 5.103; Lucian, *Dial. meret.* 7.2; Philostr. *Ep.* 22; Alciphr. 4.9.2; Ath. 4.129A; Pythag. *Ep.* 11.1; Aristaenet. 1.25; *Anacreont.* 16.31f; Lyd. *Mag.* 3.64f; Schol. Juv. 2.66. Regarding Prop. 4.5.55–7, see G. Jachmann, in *Studi in onore di U. E. Paoli* (Florence 1955) 414–21.

[438] Asclep. *Anth. Pal.* 12.161; Juv. 1.62; *Exomis*: Ar. fr. 8.

[439] Tert. *Cult. fem.* 2.9; Cypr. *Hab. virg.* 12; Ambros. *Cain et Abel* 1.4.14; Bas. *Is.* 123; Chrys. *Fem reg.* 1; *David* 3.1; *Hom. in Jo.* 27 (26). 3; *Hom. in 1 Tim.* 2.3; *Hom. in Hebr.* 28.5; Jer. *Ep.* 117.7.

[440] Jer. *Virg. Mar.* 20; Chrys. *Van. glor.* 2.

[441] Tert. *Pall.* 4; Mac. Aeg. *Hom.* 17.9; Chrys. *Inscr. alt.* 1; Salv. *Ad eccl.* 4.33.

[442] Clem. Al. *Paed.* 2.105.2; 3.10.3; cf. 2.44.5; Bas. *Contub.* 6.

[443] Chrys. *Theatr.* 2; *Van. glor.* 2; *Hom. in Mt.* 68 (69).4; *Hom. in Rom.* 31.4; *Hom. in 1 Tim.* 2.3.

[444] Lucil. 71; *Copa* 1; Mart. 2.36; Juv. 3.66; Plut. *Mor.* 154B; Poll. 4.151, 154; Alciphr. 1.6.3; Schol. Dan. Serv. *Aen.* 4.216; 9.613; Clem. Al. *Paed.* 3.11.2; Jer. *Ep.* 54.7, cf. 38.4.

[445] Tert. *Pall.* 4; Jer. *Ep.* 54.7, 117.1; Chrys. *Hom. in 1 Tim.* 8.2f; cf. Const. *Ap.* 1.8; Ephr. *Pecc.* 3, 4, 6, 15; cf. Pers. 5.169; S. G. Korres, *Platôn* 4.2 (1952) 327f.

[446] Lucil. 71; Prop. 2.23.13; Aristaenet. 1.19; 2.18; Clem. Al. *Paed.* 3.11; Chrys. *Theatr.* 2; *Hom. in Mt.* 37 (38).6.

[447] Delling, 98f; S. Lösch, *ThQ* 127 (1947) 216–61.

[448] Chrysipp. 3.196 Arn. (Origen, *C. Cels.* 4.63).

[449] In Phot. and *Suda* s. v. *hetairôn anthinôn*, *nomos* probably means only convention.

[450] Syracuse: Phylarch. fr. 45 J.; Epizeph. Locri: the so-called law of Zaleucus: Diod. Sic. 12.21.1; Sparta: Clem. Al. *Paed.* 2.10.2. See Hermann-Blümner, 189 n. 4; Schneider, *Het.* 1353f; Navarre 1831f.

[451] Cic. *Phil.* 2.44; Tib. 1.6.68; Ov. *Ars am.* 1.32; 2.600; *Fast.* 4.134; *Tr.* 2.248; *Pont.* 3.3.52.

[452] Hor. *Sat.* 1.2.63, 82 with Schol.; Sulpicia, Tib. 3.16.3; Mart. 2.39; 6.64.4; 10.52; Juv. 2.65–70; 3.135.

they did not wear a *vitta*, a braid.[453] Thus they could be distinguished from an older married woman.[454] This *meretricia vestis* [prostitutes' clothing][455] was not always worn, however, even if it was officially prescribed, so that neither of these categories of clothing served as a norm.[456] In AD 394 Theodosius forbad prostitutes and actresses from wearing the clothing of nuns and deaconesses, for such women frequently wore this kind of clothing as a form of disguise on the kalends and other festivals, to avoid attracting attention.[457] Jewelry is not always shown on pictures, but it was part of the normal attire of high-class *hetairai* and it must have been more noticeable on such women than others, because it was supposed to be very expensive.[458] Thus honorable women in Syracuse, Epizephyrian Locri, and Sparta were forbidden from wearing gold jewelry, on the basis of the rules mentioned above. On the other hand one hears about a contradictory regulation: *hetaira ei phoreiê, dêmosia estô* [if a prostitute wears it, she must be public property/common].[459] The Church Fathers also maintained that substantial amounts of jewelry, pearls and other precious stones, arm bands and neck bands, and rings on fingers were the standard attractions of *hetairai*, particularly those associated with the theater,[460] and that such splendor evoked the envy of the poorer members of theater audiences[461] and did not correspond to the inner qualities of the women who wore such things.[462] Women who had converted to Christianity divested themselves of their valuable jewelry.[463]

[453] Tib. 1.6.67f; Ov. *Ars am.* 1.31; 3.483; *Rem. am.* 386; *Fast.* 4.134; *Tr.* 2.247; *Pont.* 3.3.51f; Serv. *Aen.* 7.403.

[454] Plaut. *Mil.* 791–3, 872, 897–9.

[455] Ulpian, *Dig.* 47.10.15.15.

[456] Afran. 133f; cf. Varro, *Sat. Men.* 302; Tert. *Apol.* 6.3; *Cult. fem.* 2.12; *Pall.* 4.

[457] *Cod. Theod.* 15.7.12. Cf. A. Müller, *NJb* 23 (1909) 54.

[458] See also Men. fr. 224, 314f, 329, cf. 318 Kö.; Antip. Sid. *Anth. Pal.* 7.21.1; Philo, *Fort.* 39; Hor. *Carm.* 4.13.14; *Epist.* 1.17.55; Tib. 2.4.27; Ceb. 9, cf. 20; Dio Chrys. 4.144; Poll. 4.153; Lucian, *Bis acc.* 31; *Hist. conscr.* 8; Philostr. *Ep.* 22; Alciphr. 1.6.3; 4.11.4; Ath. 13.587B; Claudian. *Anth. Pal.* 9.139; Aristaenet. 1.4, 19, 25; Agath. *Anth. Pal.* 6.74; *Anth. Lat.* 794; Schneider, *Het.* 1353f. Mart. 5.11 ridicules someone because of a ring on a finger, each of whose ten stones supposedly bore the likeness of a lover (R. Durand, *Latomus* 5 [1946] 259–61). Cf. W. Ludwig, *Philologus* 103 (1959) 10–12; see note 205 above.

[459] If one were to place the emphasis on *dêmosia* [in the sense of public rather than common] in this phrase, this would result in an interpretation that is legally unfounded, in which the *hetaira* would become a public slave (Hermog. p. 41, 16–20; imitated in Latin with *corona* [crown], Cic. *Inv. rhet.* 2.118). Theon *Prog.* 13 (129, 17–22 Sp.) translates as *therapaina* [servant]. Georg. Pachym. *Decl.* 10 (186–207 B.) argues for a milder interpretation, positing an imaginary female client and arguing that it would be impossible to remove the rights of a citizen.

[460] Tert. *Pall.* 4; Cypr. *Hab. virg.* 12: Mac. Aeg. *Hom.* 17.9; Gr. Naz. *Or.* 8.10; Chrys. *Van. glor.* 2.4; *Hom. in Rom.* 31.4; *Hom. in 1 Cor.* 23.6; *Hom. in 1 Tim.* 8.2f; *Hom. in Hebr.* 28.5; Procl. *PG* 61.734; *V. Pelag.* 2, 8, 10, 11. The jewelry of prostitutes is particularly disgusting material to be used for pictures of gods (Arn. 6.14).

[461] Chrys. *Hom. in 1 Cor.* 23.5 extr.

[462] Mac. Aeg. *Hom.* 17.9.

[463] Ephr. *Pecc.* 3, 4, 6.

## 7 ARTES MERETRICIAE

More than anything else prostitutes needed skill for their trade, the *artes meretriciae* [tricks of the prostitute].[464] Socrates discusses this occupation as matter-of-factly as anyone else in his dialog with Theodote but at the same time he takes on the role of *praeceptor amoris* [instructor of love].[465] The *mastropos* with whom he compares himself[466] also instructs his pupils how they in turn can arouse pleasure.[467] Admittedly, the instruction that a pimp, a female procurer of the normal type, a similar kind of mother, or an experienced *hetaira*[468] gives to a beginner is somewhat coarser.[469] The words that a poor lover has to hear are of a similar type.[470] A coquette is disposed of even more viciously.[471] The Church Fathers write often about the arts that coquettes use and they warn married women against using them. Some married women even behave in church in a manner suggestive of a prostitute.[472] Even the canonesses speak, laugh, and carry or behave themselves more freely than prostitutes do, and to the extent that they arouse visitors by this behavior, these women become morally, though not physically, impure.[473] Prostitutes have at their disposal a *tekhnê* [craft] of shamelessness,[474] whose individual aspects are frequently itemized by John Chrysostom.[475] These passages are strongly influenced by *Isaiah* 3:16–26, as is the passage in Philo (*Fort.* 40), but there are also elements of such descriptions in pagan literature,[476] as well as frequent individual examples. Writers emphasize the sumptuousness in the overall appearance of these women,[477] their facial expressions,

[464] See for example Tull. Gem. *Anth. Pal.* 6.260; Quint. *Decl.* 3.3; Aur. Vict. *Caes. epit.* 17.5.
[465] Xen. *Mem.* 3.11.
[466] *RAC* 3, 1183.
[467] Xen. *Symp.* 4.56–64.
[468] A sister: Aristaenet. 1.14.
[469] Alexis fr. 98; Plaut. *Bacch.* 163–5; *Cist.* 95–7; *Most.* 188–292; *Truc.* 169f; Ter. *Hec.* 58–75; Tib. 1.4, cf. 1.5.48; Prop. 4.5 (see G. Luck, *Hermes* 81 [1955] 428–38); Ov. *Am.* 1.8; 3.5.39f; Nicarch. *Anth. Pal.* 5.39; Lucian, *Dial. meret.* 6; Synes. *Ep.* 3. Cf. P. Legrand, *REG* 20 (1907) 198–207; Leo, *Plaut. Forsch.*² 146–8; A. L. Wheeler, *CPh* 5 (1910) 28–40; 6 (1911) 56–77; E. Paludan, *C&M* 4 (1941) 211f.
[470] Plaut. *Asin.* 153–242.
[471] Strato, *Anth. Pal.* 12.7.4; *Anth. Lat.* 190. Regarding the *meretrix mala* [wicked prostitute], see G. E. Duckworth, *The Nature of Roman Comedy* (Princeton 1952) 258–61; M. Neumann, *Die poetische Gerechtigkeit in der neuen Komödie*, Diss. Mainz (1958) 131–6. Regarding Terence see I. Lana, *RFIC* 75 (1947) 60–80.
[472] Chrys. *Hom. in Mt.* 73.3.
[473] Chrys. *Fem. reg.* 1.3.
[474] Gr. Naz. *Carm.* 1.2.25, 490–6; Jer. *Ep.* 117.7; August. *Serm.* Denis 17.8 (88 Morin).
[475] See especially *Theatr.* 2; *David* 3.1.2; *Hom. in Mt.* 17.3; 68 (69).4; *Hom. in Jo.* 18 (17).4; *Hom. in 1 Tim.* 8.2f; in addition, see Clem. Al. *Paed.* 2.98.1; Bas. *Is.* 123; Procl. *PG* 61.730.
[476] Maced. *Anth. Pal.* 5.244; Aristaenet. 1.19.
[477] Cypr. *Hab. virg.* 12; Chrys. *Theatr.* 2; *Hom. in Rom.* 30.4; cf. Eur. *Cycl.* 499–502; *tryphas*: *RAC* 3, 1188.

their gestures,[478] in particular the manner in which they play with their eyes,[479] the manner in which they carry themselves and the way that they walk,[480] their broken voices[481] and the special sounds that they make,[482] their impudent and persistent laughing and giggling, their provocative smiling,[483] their tears,[484] but more than anything, their whole *pornikos logos* [whorish discourse][485] with its coarse jokes.[486] In first place among their arts of seduction are flattering words,[487] but one also reads about their aloofness, their coyness and their haughty manner.[488] Impudence is the most recurring characteristic among those who practice this profession,[489] but a higher-class *hetaira* is reserved, and she smiles rather than laughs.[490] But no matter how careful she is, John Chrysostom observes,[491] she will be discovered on the Day of Judgment.

These combined skills were not always sufficient.[492] When the

[478] Ephr. *Admon.* 9 (1.292L.); Jer. *Ep.* 77.4; Chrys. *Hom. in Is.* 6.1 1.2; cf. Maced. *Anth. Pal.* 5.244.

[479] Ambros. *Cain et Abel* 1.4.14; Bas. *Is.* 123; Gr. Naz. *Or.* 8.10; Amph. *Mul. pecc.* 5; Chrys. *Fem. reg.* 1.3; *Theatr.* 2; *David* 3.2; *Stat.* 14.4; *Hom. in Is.* 3.8; *Hom. in Mt.*, *Hom. in Jo.*, *Hom. in 1 Tim.* (note 475); *Ep. ad Ol.* 2.9; Procl. *PG* 61.730; Petr. Chrys. p. 115; cf. Philo *Fort.* 40; Philetaer. fr. 5; Philostr. *Ep.* 38; Aristaenet. 1.19; Claudian. *Anth. Pal.* 9.139.

[480] Clem. Al. *Paed.* 2.98.1; 3.69.2f; Ambros. *Cain et Abel* 1.4.14; Bas. *Is.* 123; Gr. Naz. *Carm.* 1.2.29.263f; Amph. *Mul. pecc.* 5; Chrys. *Fem. reg.* 1.3; *Theatr.*, *David*, *Stat.*, *Hom. in Mt.*, *Hom. in 1 Tim.*, *Ep. ad Ol.* (note 479); *Subintr.* 11; *Hom. in Rom.* 30.4; Procl., Petr. Chrys., Philo (note 479); Cic. *Cael.* 49; Dio Chrys. 5.25; Philostr. Ep. 38.; Aristaenet. 1.19.

[481] Chrys. *David*, *Hom. in Mt.*, *Hom. in 1 Tim.*, *Ep. ad Ol.* (note 479); cf. Dio Chrys. 33.60.

[482] Clem. Al. *Paed.* 3.29.2f; Ath. *H. Ar.* 57; cf. Dio Chrys. 33.36,60; Maced. *Anth. Pal.* 5.244.

[483] Bas. *Is.* 123; Gr. Naz. *Carm.* 1.2.29.263f; Ast. Am. *Hom.* 3; Chrys. *Fem. reg.* 1; *Hom. in Mt.* 6.7; *Hom. in Hebr.* 28.5; cf. Mart. 2.41; Dio Chrys. 4.114; Aristaenet. 1.19; Maced. *Anth. Pal.* 5.244 and below, note 552.

[484] Amph. *Mul. pecc.* 5.

[485] Strato, *Anth. Pal.* 12.7.3.

[486] There was a virtual brothel language (Cleom. p. 166.7f; cf. Schol. Dan. *Aen.* 4.23; Donat. Ter. *Eun.* 796).

[487] Ephr. *Admon.* 9 (1.292L.); Ambros. *Bon. mort.* 9.40; *In Psa.* 118 5.30.3f; *Fug. saec.* 1.3; [Chrys.] *Phar. et mer.* 3; cf. Men. *Epit.* fr. 7, fr. 185 Kö.; Plaut. *Asin.* 222f; *Bacch.* 50; *Cas.* 585f; *Most.* 221; *Truc.* 28, 162, 318, 572f; Turp. 186; Phld. *Anth. Pal.* 7.222 (?); Ov. *Am.* 1.8.103f; 15.18; Sen. *Controv.* 1.2.5, 12; Quint. *Decl.* 14.5, 15.5; Mart. 10.68; Plut. *Mor.* 46A, 62D; Apul. *Apol.* 98; Lucian, *Rh. Pr.* 12; Ael. *VH* 12.1; Maximian. 5.5–12; Anon. *Anth. Pal.* 7.221; *Anth. Lat.* 323, 826; Eugr. Ter. *Hec.* 1.1.6. Naturally the lover also flatters (Pl. *Com.* fr. 3 Dem. = 48A Edm.; Licinius Imbrex fr.).

[488] *RAC* 3, 1168; Gr. Nyss. *V. Gr. Thaum.*, *PG* 46.904; Chrys. *Hom. in Mt.* 6.7; *Hom. in Jo.* 79 (78).4f; *Hom. in Rom.* 30.4; *Hom. in Eph.* 7.3; cf. *RAC* 3, 1168; see also Pl. Jun. *Anth. Pal.* 6.1.1; Antip. Sid. *Anth. Pal.* 7.218; Heraclit. *All.* 5 (Anacr. fr. 88D. = 78G.); Plut. *Luc.* 6.2f; *Mor.* 706B; Alciphr. 3.5.2, 14.1; Ach. Tat. 6.20.2; Heliod. 7.10; Myrin. *Anth. Pal.* 11.67; Anon., *Anth. Pal.*, 6.283. Pall., *Anth. Pal.* 10.87, 96 writes about the prostitute-like moodiness of *Tykhê*, "Fate."

[489] *RAC* 3, 1192; Clem. Al. *Paed.* 3.11.2; Ath. *Ar.* 3.1; Zeno Ver. 1.4.3; Jer. *Ep.* 147.8; Chrys. *Fem. reg.* 3; cf. *RAC* 3, 1167f; in this connection, see Men. *Sam.* 124–33; fr. 185 Kö.; Timae. fr. 122; Philo, *Spec. leg.* 3.51; Plut. *Mor.* 528E; Dio Chrys. 4.111; Poll. 6.127; Philostr. *Ep.* 38; Heliod. 7.10; Julian. *Or.* 7.210D.

[490] Ov. *Ars am.* 3.279–90; Lucian, *Dial. meret.* 6.3.

[491] Chrys. *Hom. in 1 Tim.* 8.2; cf. *Van. glor.* 2. See note 330.

[492] Maced. *Anth. Pal.* 5.244.

demands were greater, it was very important that the prostitute be clever and intelligent.[493] The elegant lover demanded not only skills in dancing and in the arts, but also education.[494] It was only in this way that the *hetairai* in Athens were able to provide what married women lacked in intellect. The intellectual discourse gave rise to a literary genre.[495] Lais was able to demonstrate that she was equal to Euripides in dialectic skills,[496] and some prostitutes were actually students of philosophy.[497] Among the Church Fathers this phenomenon reflects itself in complaints about the clever teasing and lewd remarks of the prostitutes[498] as well as about their songs,[499] which carried through from the stage and the brothels onto the street;[500] songs that come from the devil.[501] Even at its best times, one should not overestimate the general intellectual level in Athens;[502] at the other extreme, there were a not insignificant number of *fatuae ac stupidae* [foolish and stupid women] that could be found everywhere.[503]

In contrast to the *pezai* [foot soldiers], who had no special abilities,[504] some prostitutes were specifically trained, notably as *mousourgoi* [musicians].[505] In this capacity they were hired for symposia and parades, or else they rented themselves out for these occasions, if they were self-employed prostitutes. The instruction that they had

[493] Antiphan. fr. 212; Anaxil. fr. 21; Ter. *Haut.* 522; Ath. 13.576D, 577DE, 585B; Heliod. 7.10.

[494] Schneider, *Het.* 1335f, 1357f; Schneider, *Mer.* 1022. Glycera was educated by Menander: Alciphr. 4.19.19f.

[495] Machon *et al.*; especially Ath. 13.577D–88A; Gerhard, *Phoinix* 250.

[496] Ath. 13.582CD.

[497] *RAC* 3, 1183, 1202. Ath. 13.596E; Alciphr. 4.7.5. U. von Wilamowitz-Moellendorff (*Hellenistische Dichtung in der Zeit des Kallimachos* [Berlin 1924 ]1.135) disputes the claim that Nossis was a *hetaira*, as does G. Carugno, *GIF* 10 (1957) 332–4. Philaenis is made to challenge the charge in Anon. *Anth. Pal.* 7.345. See also Diosc. *Anth. Pal.* 7.351.

[498] Clem. Al. *Paed.* 2.98.1; Ambros. *In Psa.* 118 5.30, 3f; *Fug. Saec.* 1.3; Bas. Renunt. 5; Amph. *Mul. pecc.* 5; Chrys. Van. glor. 78; *Fem. reg.* 1; *Theatr.* 2; David 3.2; *Hom. ad Ant.* 14.4; 15.1; *Hom. in Mt.* 37 (38).5; *Hom. in Jo.* 1.4; 60 (59). 5; *Hom. in 2 Cor.* 6.4; *Hom. in Eph.* 17.3; *Hom. in 1 Thess.* 5.4; *Hom. in Hebr.* 28.5; Sophr. H. V. *Mar. Aeg.* 20; cf. Philo, *Spec. leg.* 3.51; *Fort.* 40; Juv. 11.172f; Lyd. *Mag.* 3.59; Aristaenet. 1.19. Stories: Lucian, *Am.* 37.

[499] Cypr. *Hab. virg.* 11; Eust. *Hex.* 4.1; Bas. *Ebr.* 1.8; *Hex.* 4.1; Chrys. *Forn. ux.* 1f; *Theatr.* 2; *David* 3.1, 2; *Diab.* 3.1; *Hom. in Mt.* 2.5; 37 (38).5; 68 (69).4; *Hom. in 1 Thess.* 5.4; August. *In Psa.* 136.9; sirens: *RAC* 3, 1203. Cf. Ar. *Ran.* 1301; Lucian, *Bis acc.* 31; *Teretismata* [humming, prattle] of the *hetairai* still found in a glossator in approx. 1300 (P. Maas, *ByzZ* 38 [1938] 63).

[500] Chrys. *Stat.* 15.1.

[501] Ast. Soph. *Ps.* 24.13; Georg. Cedr. 2.333.21f Bonn.

[502] Cf. Jacobs, 311–15. Schneider, *Het.* 1357; Navarre, 1824, 1828; Hauck-Schulz, 583.

[503] [Placid.], F. Buecheler, *RhM* 33 (1878) 309f; W. M. Lindsay, *CQ* 23 (1929) 31f; Ribbeck, *SRPF* 2³ p. 131.

[504] Eup. fr. 169; Pl. Com. fr. 155; Arist. in Phot. s. v. *pezas moskhous*; Theopomp. fr. 213J.; Procop. *Arc.* 9.11.

[505] Schneider, *Het.* 1341f; F. Studniczka, *JDAI* 38–9 (1923–4) 89–95; A. Calderini, *SIFC* 27–8 (1956) 67.

undergone paid off.[506] They often performed as flautists, harpists, or singers, sometimes accompanying themselves,[507] other times accompanied by someone else. [508] One can see from depictions on vases and from the writings of this period that these musicians offered services other than just their musical skills.[509] There were also *tympanistriai* [drummers],[510] *kymbalistriai* [cymbalists], [511] *sambykistriai* [guitarists],[512] and *krotalistriai* [castanet players].[513] This last category illustrates the transition to the dancers,[514] who were very widely present.[515] A specific category of them was the Gaditanae,[516] as well as the *collegium* [guild] of the Syrian Ambubaiae.[517] The female traveling entertainers belong in this group as well.[518]

None of these elements normally attracted very much attention:

[506] Plaut. *Rud.* 42f, see also F. Marx *ad loc.*; Ter. *Phorm.* 80–8. Cf. Cic. in Quint. *Inst.* 6.3.51.

[507] Anon. *Anth. Pal.* 7.221; *Hist. Ap. Tyr.* 36, 40f (modern Greek edition, v. 594–606, 662–76, 747–56). Cf. Theophr. *Char.* 19.10 (cf. 11.7, 20.10).

[508] Alciphr. 4.13.11.

[509] Simon. *Anth. Pal.* 5.158; Hippoc. *Nat. puer.* 13 (7.490–2 L.); Lys. 4.7; Ar. *Ach.* 551; *Nub.* 996; *Vesp.* 1331–81; *Ran.* 513–20, 543–5; Archipp. fr. 27; Aristag. fr. 2 = Metag. fr. 4; Ath. 5.220E; Isoc. 7.48; Aeschin. 1.42; Hyp. fr. 168 Bl. = 142 J.; Antiphan. fr. 127, 225, 236; Eub. fr. 84; Theophil. fr. 12; Theopomp. fr. 49, 114, 213; Men. *Epitr.* fr. 1 (p. 9 Kö.) and elsewhere; fr. 699; Lync. and Hippoloch. Ath. 4.128B, 129A; Pers. Ath. 13.607DE; Leon, *Anth. Pal.* 5.205; Macho, Ath. 13.577E, 579E; *Com. Adesp.* fr. 25. 34, 25a Dem.; Polemo, fr. 3P; Plaut. *Aul.* 280f; *Epid.* 47f, 218, 475–525; *Most.* 934, 959–61, 971f; *Pseud.* 482, 528; *Stich.* 380f; Ter. *Ad.* 388 and elsewhere; *Phorm.* 109 and elsewhere; Polyb. 14.11.4; Ptol. Megal. fr. 4J.; Lucil. 1193; Mel. *Anth. Pal.* 5.174; Sall. *Cat.* 25.2; Hor. *Carm.* 1.17; 2.11.21–4; 3.15.14; *Epist.* 1.14.25; Autom. *Anth. Pal.* 5.128; Strabo 2.3.4 p. 99; Plin. *HN* 34.63; Manetho 5.142f, 236; Nicarch. (?) *Anth. Pal.* 6.285; Dio Chrys. 32.50; 70.9; Plut. *Crass.* 32.3; *Demetr.* 27.9; *Tim.* 14.3; *Mor.* 753D, cf. 150D; Polyaen. 5.2.13; Lucian, *Am.* 10; *Sat.* 4; *Dial. meret.* 12.1, 14. 4, 15; Aristid. 50.56 (250f K.); Alciphr. 1.15.3f, 21f; 2.14; 2.31.1; 3.19.8f; 3.29.2; 4.11.8; 4.13.11; 4.16.2, 6; Ath. 1.6F -7A; 13.576F, 577BC, E, 591F, 597A, 605B; Diog. Laert. 7.13; Anon. *Anth. Pal.* 7.221; Lib. *Or.* 1.22; Synes. *Dion* 1 p. 36; Heraclit. *Incred.* 14; Maximian. 4; 5.17f; Agath. *Anth. Plan.* 80; Thphyl. *Ep.* 12; phlylax vase, see note 164; Schneider, *Het.* 1341f; G. Zuntz, *Gnomon* 30 (1958) 20. G. Wille, *Die Bedeutung der Musik im Leben der Römer*, Diss. Tübingen (1951) 314–21. Pictures, see L. Stephani, *Compte-rendu Comm. imp. Arch.* 1868, 92–8; 1869, 219–32; G. Rodenwaldt, *AA* 1932, 12–19; E. Simon, *Die Geburt der Aphrodite* (Berlin 1959) 20–6, 55, 65, 93, 97, 100. Caricatures: *Ancient Corinth* 15. 2 (1952) 153 no. 8, plate 32. Consider also the female singer *Khelidonis* [Swallow], *GVI* 2008.

[510] Hor. *Carm.* 3.15.10; Plut. *Mor.* 753D.

[511] Alciphr. 1.15.4.

[512] Hippoloch. Ath. 4.129A; Plaut. *Stich.* 381; Plut. *Ant.* 9.

[513] Mel. *Anth. Pal.* 5.174; *Copa* 1–4; Thyill. *Anth. Pal.* 7.223; Rufin. *Anth. Pal.* 5.18; Claudian. *Anth. Pal.* 9.139; Maced. *Anth. Pal.*, 5.270; Navarre, 1836 fig. 4965, 4971.

[514] Cf. *Priapea* 27.

[515] Crates Com. fr. 27; Ar. *Ach.* 1093; *Nub.* 996; *Thesm.* 1172–1201; *Ran.* 513–20, 543–5; Aristag. fr. 2; Antiphan. fr. 127; Theopomp. fr. 49, 114J; Pers. Ath. 13.607CD; *Priapea* 19; Plut. *Mor.* 753D; Lucian, *Am.* 10; Alciphr. 4.13.12; 4.16.6. Cf. E. Roos, *Die tragische Orchestik im Zerrbild der altattischen Komödie* (Stockholm 1951).

[516] O. Jahn, *SBLeipz* 1851, 168f. See also *PGrenf.* 1.53.28; Stat. *Silv.* 1.6.71.

[517] A. Mau, *RE* s. v.

[518] Matron, Ath. 4.137C. Cf. E. Wüst, *RE* 15, 1737; H. Blümner, *Fahrendes Volk im Altertum* (*SBA* 1918, 6).

the music of *hetairai* did not enjoy a high reputation.[519] Dio Chrysostom demands of a leader that he should forbid women from performing lascivious dances and dance gestures that are suggestive of a prostitute.[520] Even in Byzantine times, most of the female artists who did not excel in their categories were regarded as prostitutes,[521] and their reputation within specifically Christian writings is not much better.[522]

Female musicians and dancers also entered the service of Mimus and placed themselves in association with actresses, whose *munus turpe* [foul job] also had a dubious reputation,[523] in spite of the fame of the old modesty of the *scaenici* [actors] that is noted by Cicero (*Off.* 1.129). It is very unlikely that women of dubious virtue actually appeared on the stage more or less undressed at appropriate moments in Athenian theater performances.[524] Actresses in late antiquity frequently had to act out scenes of marital infidelity, but probably not in the very realistic manner that Heliogabalus is said to have demanded.[525] In some plays women who were essentially prostitutes appeared on the stage, for example in Laberius' *Hetairai* and later on in a fragment of a play, preserved on papyrus, in which a woman, clearly of dubious reputation, appears on the stage accompanied by a lawyer, in order to press a legal claim.[526] When necessary, an actress appeared on the stage accompanied by supporting actresses, supernumeraries, female singers, or female musicians.[527] Female mime artists wore clothing that corresponded to their roles, sometimes quite magnificent clothing. In Rome it was customary for these artists to wear a *recinium* (which was later referred to as a *mafurtium* or a *maforte*), a shawl which could be used for many purposes. In real life, however, this garment went out of style at the beginning of the period

[519] Phld. *Mus.* p. 79 K. = 168 Kr. (Diog. Bab. 76 Arn.). Cf. Pl. Com. fr. 69.12K.; Clem. Al. *Paed.* 2.44.5. Regarding *Ithyphallos* as the song of a *hetaira*, see H. Herter, *De dis Atticis Priapi similibus*, Diss. Bonn (1926) 49.

[520] Dio Chrys. *Or.* 2.56. Regarding Plato's view, see *RAC* 3, 1183. According to Plut. *Mor.* 150D, there were no female flute players among the Scythians.

[521] Procop. *Arc.* 17.34, cf. 9.12; Niceph. Greg. *Hist.* 1.477.8.

[522] *Ev. Naz.* 14: A. Resch, *Agrapha* (1906) 219 (this strict denial stands, in spite of J. Jeremias, *Unbekannte Jesusworte* [Zürich 1951] 46, which would be dubious for the true Jesus); Arn. 2.42; Bas. *Hom. in Ps.* 1.6; Gr. Nyss. *Paup.*, PG 46. 468; Ast. Am. *Hom. adv. ka.* 4; Chrys. *Forn.* 2; *Hom. in Col.* 12.4; cf. *Hom. in Rom.* 30.4; August. *Serm.* 153.6; Jer. *In Isa.* 7.23.15–18. *Pornika skhêmata* [whorish gestures] of dancing women: Bas. *Ebr.* 8.

[523] *Cod. Theod.* 15.7.4. Cf. A. Müller, *Njb* 23 (1909) 51–4.

[524] K. v. Holzinger, *SAWW* 208, 5 (1928) 37–54. For a differing opinion, see W. Süss, *RhM* 97 (1954) 128f.

[525] *Hist. Aug. Hel.* 25.4. Cf. Augar, 75f n. 1.

[526] *PLond.* 1984, see A.Körte, *APF* 6 (1913) 1–8; Crusius, *Herondas*[5] (1914) 117–21; H. Wiemken, *Der griechische Mimus*, Diss. Göttingen (1951) 92–104.

[527] Wiemken, 148–50.

of the emperors.[528] On the occasion of the Floralia, the female stage persons had to undress, upon the command of the audience,[529] unless these roles were played by actual prostitutes, as Lactantius seems to suggest.[530] The younger Cato, it was believed, did not take pleasure in such activities.[531] In general, actresses were expected to wear an apron on the stage.[532] A career on the stage brought an actress many male admirers and sometimes led to marriage.[533]

Outstanding female mime players acquired the status of artists and had connections to high-ranking people.[534] In general, however, actresses received little attention[535] and were often equated with prostitutes.[536] The reputation of all traveling actors was as poor in Roman Egypt[537] as everywhere else. In the middle of the third century AD a large group of players gave guest performances for the amusement of a garrison at Dura-Europos, a group that included many Syrian women of low social background who clearly also served as prostitutes.[538] There are records of a musician and dancer who supported a theater troupe in Caesarea that consisted of prostitutes.[539] Even military troops were never without their female mime artists.[540] Procopius gives a picture of the impoverished life of the young Theodora:[541] she performed in a theater that was called *Pornai* [whores].[542]

---

[528] Wüst, *RE* 15, 1747; Wiemken, 176f. The *cento* [patchwork] is not worn by all mime artistis, but only by the *stupidus* (comical character); this is not totally clear in G. Widengren, *Orientalia Suecana* 2 (1953) 43–7, 106f; *pancarpipanniraphia* "garment of a harlequin" (Tert. *Adv. Valent.* 12 ): see G. Pfligersdorffer, in R. Muth and J. Knobloch, eds, *Natalicium Carolo Jax septuagenario a. D. VII kal. Dec. MCMLV oblatum I* (Innsbruck 1955) 219f.

[529] G. Wissowa, *RE* 6, 2751f; Wüst, *RE* 15, 1747; Phld. *Anth. Pal.* 5.131.

[530] Lactant. *Div. inst.* 1.20.10 (cf. Schol. Juv. 6.250); cf. H. Reich, *Der Mimus* 1 (Berlin 1903) 171–3.

[531] Sen. *Ep.* 97.8; Val. Max. 2.10.8.

[532] Procop. *Arc.* 9.20.

[533] Aristaenet. 1.19.

[534] Wüst, *RE* 15, 1742f, 1748–50, 1753, 1757. Thus a *deiktêrias* [mime] becomes a royal *hetaira* (Polyb. 14.11.4).

[535] Wüst, 1737, 1755.

[536] Polyb. 14.11.4; Cic. *Verr.* 2.3.83 (cf. F. Münzer, *RE* 5A, 822); Cic. *Phil.* 13.24; Q. Cic. *Comment. pet.* 8; Hor. *Sat.* 1.258f; Ael. fr. 123; *Hist. Aug. Tyr. Trig.* 9.1; Serv. Verg. *Ecl.* 10.6; Synes. *Ep.* 110; Aristaenet. 1.24; Procop. *Arc.* 1.11, 17.34f; Cassiod. *Var.* 7.10.3; Wüst, 1747, 1755f, 1759f. Regarding the muses as prostitutes of the stage, see Boeth. *Consol.* 1 pr. 1 p. 3. For a defense of the art of the theater, see *RAC* 3, 1182. Cf. M. Aur. *Med.* 5.28.4.

[537] P. Collart, *RPh* 70 (1944) 144. Cf. W. L. Westermann, *JEA* 18 (1932) 16–27.

[538] Thus a *paleopornê* [old whore]. See *Excavations at Dura-Europos 1935–6* (1944) 203–65.

[539] S. Lieberman, *Greek in Jewish Palestine* (New York 1942) 31–3; *Excavations at Dura-Europos* 263.

[540] Wüst, 1758.

[541] Procop. *Arc.* 9.8–29. Cf. A. Nagl, *RE* 5A, 1776f, 1787f; B. Rubin, *RE* 23, 540–2.

[542] *Nov.* 105 (81).1. Isid. *Or.* 18.42.2 (cf. *Gloss. Lat.* 2.586.55) even claims that the theaters were called *prostibula* [brothels]. Dio Cass. 62.15.2–6 describes one of the boisterous folk festivals organized by Tigellinus during the reign of Nero.

If we turn to Christian writings, we find that theater and circus performances are viewed at the outset in an unfavorable light and it is not surprising that actresses, infamous as they are,[543] are referred to as whores.[544] They are examples of a frivolous lifestyle[545] and the theater is a *pudoris publici lupanarium* [brothel of public disgrace] or a *porneias gymnasion* [gymnasium of whoredom][546] in which the devils rejoice.[547] In fact, female dancers were the sensation of daily conversation[548] and their performances were supposed to be not only a source of enjoyment for the city but also an honor for the ruler.[549] The recurring depictions of mistresses and adultery—according to Ps.-Cyprian massively recurring[550]—were seen as reprehensible.[551] The speeches and songs that were reminiscent of prostitutes, the continuous laughing,[552] and even the dances on stage, were seen as offensive.[553] Classical antiquity is fortunate that its background music has not been preserved.[554] During the reign of Constantine, the Patriarch Theophylactus sought to incorporate into the church liturgy the dances and secular melodies that were borrowed from the crossroads and the whorehouses.[555] Elsewhere the Sicilian conquerors in Thessalonica interrupted church ceremonies with the songs of prostitutes.[556]

The Church Fathers were particularly displeased about the presentation of naked or very thinly clad women on the stage,[557] or

[543] Cf. Chrys. *Hom. in Act.* 31.4.

[544] Ast. Am. *Hom.* 4; Chrys. *Van. glor.* 8, 12; *Hom. in Gen.* 6.2; *Hom. in Mt.* 1.7; 6.7f; 7.6f; 10.5; 37 (38).6f; 67 (68).3; 68 (69).4; *Hom. in Jo.* 1.4; *Hom. in 1 Cor.* 12.5; 23.6; *Hom. in 2 Cor.* 6.4; *Hom. in Col.* 12.4; Jer. *Ep.* 58.4; August. *De civ. D.* 6.7 extr.; *V. Pelag.* 2; *Cod. Theod.* 15.7.8; Niceph. *V. Andr.* 20–2; Leont. N. *V. Sym.* 6.43. Cf. *RAC* 3, 1196f, 1199. According to Chrys. *Jud.* 1.2, 3, 7, weak persons and prostitutes assemble on Jewish festivals in synagogues, as if they were on the stage. Thus the synagogue becomes a *porneion* (see M. Simon, *Verus Israel* [Paris 1948] 257, 260).

[545] Chrys. *Hom. in Mt.* 10.5; 37 (38). 6; *Hom. in Hebr.* 15.3.

[546] Cypr. *Spect.* 6; Chrys. *Hom. in Act.* 42.4.

[547] Cypr. *Spect.* 4; Chrys. *Hom. in Mt.* 1.7; 6.7; 37 (38). 6; August. *Serm.* 198.3; see Caill. 2.19.7.

[548] Chrys. *Hom. in Rom.* 16: 3 1.

[549] Chrys. *Hom. in 1 Cor.* 12.5.

[550] [Cypr.] *Spect.* 6.

[551] Tatian. 22; Chrys. *Poenit.* 1; *Hom. in Jo.* 1.4; Salv. *Gub. Dei* 6.19; BKV: Armen. Väter 2.188. Venus is depicted *per affectus omnes meretriciae vilitatis* [through all the dispositions of chippy cheapness] (Arn. 4.35). Regarding the enticement of comedies, see Lactant. *Div. inst.* 6.20.27 (cf. Ov. *Rem. am.* 751–6).

[552] Isid. Pel. *Ep.* 5.185.

[553] Ambros. *Paen.* 2.42f; Gr. Naz. *Carm.* 2.2.8.102; Dio Chrys. *Or.* 2.56. Traveling entertainers also sang erotic songs (Chrys. *Hom. in 1 Thess.* 11.3).

[554] One can consider the Locrian songs (O. Crusius, *Herondas*[5] [1914] 128; *Carm. Pop.* 43D; K. Ziegler, *RhM* 82 [1933] 50–3) and the song of Marisa (Crusius 129; *RAC* 3, 1173; very boldly discussed by H. W. Garrod, *CR* 37 [1923] 161f; cf. G. Carugno, *GIF* 10 [1957] 328).

[555] Georg. Cedr. 2.333 Bonn.

[556] Nicet. Chon. Andronic. Comn. 1.9 (398 Bonn).

[557] Chrys. *Van. glor.* 78; *Hom. in Mt.* 6.8; *Hom. in 1 Thess.* 5.4; Procl. PG 61.729. Floralia: Arn. 7.33; *RAC* 3, 1199.

swimming in a pool of water on the stage.[558] They were true instruments of entrapment from the devil.[559] John Chrysostom was willing to grant these women some degree of modesty, but he questions the male members of the audience and wonders how their wives will feel when the men return home after a performance.[560] The theater, like the circus, only appears to be a place of enjoyable entertainment. In reality, it is a bitter form of entertainment, if one falls in love with a dancer.[561] The prostitutes use their voice, glance, posture, and way of walking as means of conquest,[562] and frequently enough they achieve their goal.[563] The danger is even greater because one does not go to such places of entertainment purely by chance, but rather with the specific intention of watching these women.[564] Simply the decision to go to the theater makes one impure and certainly transforms one into a cause of stumbling for others.[565] The image of a prostitute pursues a male theatergoer through to his dreams and he becomes her slave.[566] The plays are not simply *hypokrisis* [acting]; they tempt one to imitate what one sees,[567] and there is nothing more indecent or impudent than an eye that has watched such scenes.[568] The public also bears a measure of the blame for this moral decline.[569]

According to one view of life, a mistress is a requirement for a man's happiness—a departure from earlier times[570]—just as an unrestrained indulgence is necessary for the enjoyment of leisure.[571] Thus,

---

[558] G. Traversari, *Dioniso* NS 13 (1950) 18–35; 15 (1952) 302–11, assumes that for the purposes of a performance there were pools of water in the orchestra and that later the whole orchestra could be transformed into a giant pool of water; he claims to recognize a "Thetimimos" as he calls it in Chrys. *Hom. in Mt.* 7, but this could also simply be a choreographic device as is the case in Mart. *Spect.* 26 (contribution by A. v. Gerkan). See also E. Mehl, *Antike Schwimmkunst* (Munich 1927) 83f, 87, 104, 121; L. Robert, *REG* 49 (1936) 13 n. 6. Regarding love as a result of gazing at a young girl swimming, see S. Trenkner, *The Greek Novella in the Classical Period* (Cambridge 1958) 110 n. 7

[559] Chrys. *Hom. in Mt.* 7.6f; *Hom. in Jo.* 60 (59).5.

[560] Chrys. *Hom. in Mt.* 6.8, cf. *Hom. in Act.* 42.4.

[561] Chrys. *Hom. in Mt.* 68.3.

[562] Ast. Soph. *Ps.* 29.2; Chrys. *Hom. in Mt.* 68.4; *Hom. in Jo.* 60 (59). 5; *Hom. in 1 Thess.* 5.4; *Hom. in Hebr.* 28.5.

[563] Chrys. *Hom. in Mt.* 37.6f; *Hom. in Act.* 42.4; BKV: Armen. Väter 2. 189f.

[564] Chrys. *Theatr.* 2; *Hom. in Gen.* 1 6.2.

[565] Chrys. *Theatr.* 2; *Hom. in Mt.* 7.6; Salv. *Gub. Dei* 6.18f.

[566] Chrys. *Hom. in 1 Thess.* 5.4; *Hom. in Mt.* 6.8.

[567] Cypr. *Don.* 8, Chrys. *Hom. ad Ant.* 15.4.

[568] Chrys. *Hom. in Mt.* 6.8.

[569] Chrys. *Hom. in Mt.* 37 (38). 7; Salv. *Gub. Dei* 6.3f.

[570] Plaut. *Bacch.* 428–30.

[571] *RAC* 3, 1164f. Further, Ar. *Ach.* 1198f; Pl. *Resp.* 4.420A, 9.573D, 574BC; *Phdr.* 240B; Theophr. *Char.* 17.3; Men. *Epitr.* 461–3 (502–4); Ter. *Haut.* 109; Ov. *Rem. am.* 135–50; Sen. *Ben.* 1.9.4; *Dial.* 2.6.7; 10.16.4; *Ep.* 59.17, 114.25, 120.21, 122.14, 123.10; Juv. 9.128; Plut. *Otho* 2.2; *Mor.* 73B, 97C, 128D; Tac. *Ann.* 14.20; Alciphr. 2.14; Julian. *Dig.* 41.4.8; Poll. 3.117; *Hist. Aug. Tyr. Trig.* 9.1; Them. *Or.* 20 p. 238B; Anacreont. 55.3; *PSI* 352; cf. F. Leo, *Senecae tragoediae* 1. 174–6; I. Borzsák, *AAntHung* 4 (1956) 211–19. Christian material: *RAC* 3, 1200; *Ev.*

where it is possible, *hetairai* are intent on enjoyments,[572] at the least eating and drinking,[573] and they make great demands in their enjoyments, as Neaera did.[574] On the other hand, roses and wine are not appropriate for an old woman.[575] No matter how comfortable they were,[576] *hetairai* used to maintain the pretence of domestic virtures, and would arrange for their guests to surprise them at spinning, for example.[577] Sometimes they really were dependent on secondary sources of income.[578]

Excursions to the countryside were among the pleasures that *hetairai* enjoyed, and these were usually combined with offerings and subsequent luxurious meals. Sometimes there were more extended sojourns in the country,[579] even excursions on the water,[580] and, in particular, symposia.[581] Occasionally the women were alone in such activities but usually they were accompanied by men. They would meet in the women's houses,[582] in the house of the pimp,[583] in their lover's apartment,[584] or in some other location.[585] In any event, these women were a regular feature of a banquet, even if they were not appreciated by everyone.[586] From Hellenistic times on, other women were not excluded from such events.[587] In the case of weddings, one can seldom

---

*Naz.* 18 (see note 219); Ign. *Ant.* 11; [Cypr.] *Dupl. mart.* 36; Jer. *In Isa.* 2.3.3; *In Os.* 1.4.10–12; August. *In Ps.* 70.1.9; *Serm.* 142.2; Pall. *V. Chrys.* 20 p. 139 C.-N.; see above note 70. According to Prudent. *C. Symm.* 1.104–10, Priapus was a human *scortator* [fornicator]. In the writings of Georg. Pachym. *Decl.* 11 (207–29B), a father who had killed his son for leading a riotous life (*pornos* [fornicator] in the active sense) defends himself. If "Houris" pertain to the hopes of the soldiers for the afterlife, as is argued by Reinach, *Rép. rel.* 2.52.6; 2.72.2, they have lost the specific aspect that pertains to a *hetaira*.

[572] Phld. *Anth. Pal.* 7.222 (?); Nicarch. *Anth. Pal.* 6.285.

[573] Plaut. *Truc.* 155; Lucil. 861f; Varro, *Sat. Men.* 136; Alciphr. 3.2.

[574] [Dem.] 59.29, 36; Plaut. *Cist.* 50; *Pseud.* 182–4, 221f; *Truc.* 155; Ter. *Haut.* 225f, 248, 451–4; Lucian, *Dial. meret.* 7.2.

[575] Hor. *Carm.* 3.15.14–16.

[576] Epicr. fr. 2–3; Plaut. *Cist.* 379f.

[577] G. Rodenwaldt, *AA* (1932) 7–21; R. Herbig, in R. Lullies (ed.), *Neue Beiträge zur klassischen Altertumswissenschaft. Festschrift zum 60. Geburtstag von Bernhard Schweitzer* (Stuttgart 1954) 270f.

[578] Sulpicia, Tib. 3.16.3f. Cf. Strabo 8.378 (Herod. fr. 69 Cr.).

[579] Titin. fr. 2–3; Aristaenet. 1.3.

[580] Alciphr. 1.15; Schneider, *Het.* 1350.

[581] Schneider, *Het.* 1347–50.

[582] Pherecr. fr. 67–70; Crobyl. fr. 5; Alex. fr. 2 (for a contrary viewpoint, see W. G. Arnott, *RhM* 102 [1959] 256 n. 12); Macho, Ath. 13.579E–80A; Lync. Ath. 584D; Plaut. *Bacch.* 47–9, 79–84, 88, 94–100, 139–44, 716–25 etc.; *Men.* 353–6; Ath. 13.585D; Turpil. 185–8 (?); Lucian, *Dial. meret.* 5; Alciphr. 4.14. Parasites of *hetairai*, for example Ath. 13.591DE; Heraclit. *Incred.* 2.

[583] Plaut. *Poen.* 615–18; Sen. *Controv.* 1.2.10; Harp. = Suid. s. v. *matrylleion*.

[584] Men. fr. 452 Kö. etc. Cf. Alciphr. 3. 2.

[585] Men. *Epitr.* 19f (528f Kö.); Plut. *Ant.* 9; cf. Lucian, *Dial. meret.* 7.1.

[586] *RAC* 3, 1183, 1186.

[587] S. Lieberman, *Greek in Jewish Palestine* (New York 1942) 47–50; J. Carcopino, *Das Alltagsleben im alten Rom* (1950) 411, 418; K. Latte, *Gnomon* 23 (1951) 255.

confirm the presence of the demi-monde.[588] Wine was one of the things that a *hetaira* could expect from her lover.[589] A man would bring his mistress with him to a symposium, or else a female musician or a dancer whom he had hired.[590] Some women forced themselves into such events, so as not to go hungry.[591] Sometimes, at an appropriate moment, a pimp would introduce young women whose services had not been engaged.[592] Courtesans were responsible for the presentations of music and dancing and they carried out other activities, such as applying ointment to the feet of the banquet guests or washing their feet,[593] or else serving the beverages.[594] These women would also lie about at the tables and take part in the general entertainment, such as playing dice or other pastimes,[595] notably *kottabos*,[596] where the prize consisted of a young woman or a young boy.[597] They also participated in *kômoi*, "revels,"[598] and these would sometimes lead to the

[588] Anon. *Anth. Pal.* 15.19.

[589] Vase: *RAC* 3, 1165.

[590] Ath. 12.526BC.

[591] Men. *Sam.* 175–82.

[592] Men. fr. 471 Kö.; cf. Nicostr. Com. fr. 25; Marc. Arg. *Anth. Pal.* 7.403.1f. Regarding *hetairai* who were requested by the participants, see Xen. *Hell.* 5.4.5f. In addition to the countless depictions on vases there are also many literary sources that document the presence of *hetairai* at banquets, for example Ar. *Ach.* 1091, 1093; *Ran.* 513–16, 519f, 543–5; Pl. Com. fr. 178; Theopomp. Com. fr. 32; Lys. fr. 112; Pl. *Symp.* 212CD; Ctes. Ath. 12.530D; Xen. *Mem.* 1.5.4; Isae. 3.14; [Dem.] 59.24f, 28, 33f, 48; Theopomp. fr. 114J.; Eub. fr. 75–9; Epicr. fr. 2f; Men. *Sam.* 175–82; fr. 452 Kö.; Asclep. *Anth. Pal.* 5.184; *PSI* 352; Lyc. Ath. 13.555A; Polyb. 14.11.2; Plaut. *Asin.* 810f; *Bacch.* 47–9, 79–84 etc.; *Capt.* 69–76; *Men.* 124, 170–5, 207–25 etc.; *Most.* 294f; *Poen.* 615–18; *Pseud.* 948, 1259–78; *Truc.* 127f, 279, 359–67; Ter. *Ad.* 964f; Turpil. 185–8; Laber. 80; Mel. *Anth. Pal.* 5.136, 174; Varro, *Sat. Men.* 136; Cic. *Cat.* 2.10; *Fam.* 9.26.2; *Sen.* 42 (Livy 39.42f; Val. Max. 2.9.2; Sen. *Controv.* 9.2); Catull. 13.27; Thyill. *Anth. Pal.* 7.223; Phld. *Anth. Pal.* 11.34f; Hor. *Carm.* 1.6.17, 19; 2.11.21–4; 3.14; 4.11, 13.4–8; *Epist.* 1.7.28; Tib. 1.9.59–64; Prop. 2.9.21; 2.15.42; 2.16.5; 2.30.13; 2.33.25; 2.34.57; 3.10.25; 4.8.29f and elsewhere; Ov. *Ars am.* 1.229–52, 565–630; 3.749–68; Quint. *Decl.* 15.6; Nicarch. (?) *Anth. Pal.* 6.285; Mart. 3.82.11; 5.78.26–8; 8.51.23–6; Juv. 9.128; 11.162–71; Plut. *Ant.* 9; *Mor.* 140AB (cf. Hdt. 5.18f), 463A, 644C; Suet. *Ner.* 27.2; Gell. *NA* 1.11.7; Lucian, *Dial. meret.* 1.1; 3; 6.2f; 12.1; 15; Alciphr. 3.29.2; Ath. 10.437E; 13.586F, 588CD; *Hist. Aug. Gall.* 17.7; Aelian, *VH* 12.1; *Anacreont.* 12, 32; Maced. *Anth. Pal.* 11.39; Anon. *Anth. Pal.* 7.221. Cf. Mart. 1.71; Schneider, *Het.* 1347–50.

[593] Ath. 12.553A–E; 13.583F.

[594] Alex. fr. 59: Ath. 3.125F.

[595] Ar. *Plut.* 243; Aeschin. 1.42, 53, 59, 75f; Diph. fr. 73; Men. *Epitr.* 383f (424f); Plaut. *Asin.* 779f, 904–6; *Bacch.* 71; *Most.* 309; Prop. 2.33.26; Ov. *Ars am.* 2.203–8; 3.353–80; Philostr. *VA* 1.13 (7). Playing chip with the inscription *lupa* [she-wolf, prostitute]: *CIL* 11.6728 n. 23. Regarding the guessing of riddles, see Diph. fr. 50.

[596] Bacchyl. fr. 17 Sn.; Pl. Com. fr. 46–8; Synes. *Dion* 1 p. 36 A. Regarding vases, see Schneider, *RE* 11, 1528–41.

[597] P. Mingazzini, *AA* (1950–1) 35–47. Similarly with dice games: Plut. *Mor.* 273A; *Anth. Lat.* 323.

[598] Eur. *Cyc.* 495–502; Pl. *Tht.* 173D; [Dem.] 59.33f; Nicarch. *Anth. Pal.* 6.285; Pomp. *Anth. Pat.* 7.219.5; Plut. *Mor.* 596D; Philostr. *Ep.* 47; Paul. Sil. *Anth. Pal.* 5.281, 6.71. The *hetaireioi kômoi* [whorish revels] at Myrin. *Anth. Pal.* 6.254 could be the same as those of the old *cinaedus* [pathic] and persons like him (G. Luck, *Gnomon* 30 [1958] 274).

woman's door.[599] High-class *hetairai* were very attentive to their manners, especially at meals,[600] and made sure that they kept a cool head while drinking wine.[601] There was a *nomos syssitikos* [law on banquets] from Gnathaena.[602] Careless *hetairai* allowed themselves to become intoxicated[603] and in comedies, especially Middle Comedy, one finds the figure of an older *hetaira* who is addicted to alcohol.[604]

It has long been known that wine and gluttony[605] encourage love, and an early inscription in a vessel from Pithecusae bears testimony to this.[606] Thus banquets often took on an erotic aspect and sometimes descended into debauchery.[607] Men and women would engage in risqué dances[608] and prostitutes would sing questionable songs, which they always held in readiness.[609] They would happily exchange their clothing with that of the men.[610] On other occasions they were

[599] Isae. 3.13f; Plaut. *Merc.* 408–11, 418; *Pers.* 568–73; Hor. *Carm.* 3.7.29–32; Lucian, *Bis acc.* 31; Philostr. *Ep.* 47 (?); Alciphr. 4.10.1 (the opposite, 4.14.7); Ath. 13.574DE, 585A; Aristaenet. 2.19. Cf. G. L. Hendrickson, *CPh* 20 (1925) 289–308; K. Baus, *Der Kranz in Antike und Christentum* (Diss. Bonn 1940) 78. The *komoi* of Phryne (Spengel, *Rhet.*² = Cornut. p. 42 Gr.) and Lais (Philostr. *Ep.* 47). The *comissatio* [revel] before the night signified a great *dedecus* [outrage] (Hor. *Sat.* 1.4.51f).

[600] Eub. fr. 42; Lucian, *Dial. meret.* 6.3.

[601] Plaut. *Truc.* 854f.

[602] Ath. 13.585B.

[603] [Dem.] 59.33; Plin. *HN* 34.63; Lucian, *Dial. meret.* 3, 6.3; cf. Plaut. *Asin.* 771–3.

[604] Cratin. fr. 273; Pherecr. fr. 70; Epicr. fr. 2–3; Alex. fr. 223; Axionic. fr. 1; Men. *Sam.* 175–82; Plaut. *Cist.* 149; Ter. *Haut.* 457–9; Thyill. *Anth. Pal.* 7.233; Hor. *Carm.* 3.15.16; 4.13.4f; Sen. *Dial.* 7.7.3; Nicarch. *Anth. Pal.* 11.73; Ath. 13.587B; Aristaenet. 1.18; *Anth. Lat.* 363; cf. W. Süss, *De personarum antiquae comoediae Atticae usu atque origine*, Diss. Gießen (1905) 127–30; Süss, *RhM* 97 (1954) 311; Legrand, *REG* 21 (1908) 42 n. 1; Hauschild 16 n. 36.

[605] Hopfner, *RE* Suppl. 7, 53f.

[606] G. Buchner—C. F. Russo, *RAL* 8, 10 (1955) 215–34; W. Marg, in *Navicula Chiloniensis: Studia philologa Felici Jacoby professori Chiloniensi emerito octogenario oblata* (Leiden 1956) 29 n. 1; D. L. Page, *CR* NS 6 (1956) 95–7; K. Marót, *AAntHung* 6 (1958) 11f. In general see Leo, *Plautinische Forschungen*² 156 n. 1; Herter, *De Priapo* 63f; R. B. Onians, *The Origins of European Thought about the Body, the Mind, the Soul, Time, and Fate*² (Cambridge 1954) 218f; Neumann, *Poetische Gerechtigkeit* 129f; T. Hopfner, *Das Sexualleben der Griechen und Römer von den Anfängen bis ins 6. Jahrhundert nach Christus* (Prague 1938) 296–304; E. v. Leutsch on Apostol. 4, 58; *RAC* 3, 1184.

[607] Ar. *Ach.* 1147–9, 1199–1201, 1220f; Mel. *Anth. Pal.* 5.174; Quint. *Inst.* 1.2.8; Procop. *Arc.* 9.16; cf. Cass. Dio 62.15.2–6; Webster, *Art and Literature* (see note 83) 105f. *Paroinia hetairikê* [drunken wantonness] means the abuse of a young boy during a banquet, Diod. Sic. 16.93.7. (Justin. 9.6.6 is to be similarly understood.) The "sale" of prostitutes: Persaeus, Ath. 13.607DE; cf. Hdt. 1.196; Plaut. *Men.* 1160 (regarding the auctioning of young girls, J. Dietz, *Rheinwestf. Ztschr. Volksk.* 3 [1956] 94–9). A young girl looks for companionship at a symposium (Lygd. [Tib.] 3.6.59–61), another one steals away (Hor. *Epist.* 1.7.28).

[608] Plaut. *Pseud.* 1272–80; Sen. *Controv.* 9.2.8; Lucian, *Dial. meret.* 3, 15.2, *Hist. Aug. Comm.* 11.3.

[609] Quint. *Inst.* 1.2.8.

[610] Sen. *Controv.* 1.2.10; Philostr. *Imag.* 1.2 (A. Lesky, *Hermes* 75 [1940] 43); Ath. 13.607F. Cf. A. Greifenhagen, *Eine attische schwarzfigurige Vasengattung und die Darstellung des Kosmos im VI. Jahrhundert*, Diss. Königsberg (1929) 45f; Herter, *Vom dionysischen Tanz zum komischen Spiel: die Anfänge der attischen Komödie* (Iserlohn 1947) 8; A. Rumpf, in G. Mylonas (ed.), *Studies presented to David Moore Robinson on his seventieth Birthday* (St. Louis 1953) 2.88f, T. B. L. Webster, *WS* 69 (1956) 113f.

very lightly clad[611] and on Attic vases they are frequently depicted without clothes.[612] They are also noticeable because of their unrestrained manners.[613] It is debatable, however, how much these depictions corresponded to reality.[614]

If one examines the Christian side of things, one also finds female dancers and female musicians and even prostitutes who are present at banquets.[615] Conversely, there were allegedly male dancers who came into the sections of towns or cities where *hetairai* lived.[616] These women are part of the luxury of merciless rich men who could not claim to be magnanimous.[617] The people who arranged these relationships are despicable.[618] According to John Chrysostom, the characteristics of a decadent life included visits to brothels, playing dice, and *kômoi*.[619] He was particularly displeased about the light clothing that the young girls would wear,[620] their suggestive songs,[621] their voluptuous dance movements,[622] and their off-color jokes.[623] All of these things could have a negative influence on persons of both sexes.[624] In 787 the Council of Nicaea forbad banquets where satanic songs were sung and whore-like dances were performed.[625]

He finds it outrageous that indecent words and songs were even heard at Christian weddings[626] and that prostitutes performed there as dancers.[627] In the tone of the Mysteries Chrysostom calls out: *mystêrion teleitai mega. Exô hai pornai, exô hoi bebêloi* [A great mystery is brought to fulfilment. Outside, whores! Outside, uninitiated!].[628] The

---

[611] Ath. 4.129A.

[612] P. Jacobsthal, *Göttinger Vasen nebst einer Abhandlung Symposiaká* (Berlin 1912) 37; Rumpf, *JDAI* 65–6 (1950–1) 172f; Larisa 2. 162 n. 5; Greifenhagen (see note 610), 63f.

[613] R. Herbig, in R. Lullies (ed.), *Neue Beiträge zur klassischen Altertumswissenschaft. Festschrift zum 60. Geburtstag von Bernhard Schweitzer* (Stuttgart 1954) 267–70.

[614] Schneider, *Het.* 1348. Cf. Schneider, *Het.* 1349–51; Curt. 5.1. 38; Ath. 13.548B.

[615] Arn. 2.41; Gr. Naz. *Carm.* 2.1.88.91f; Gr. Nyss. *Paup.*, PG 46.468; Jer. *Ep.* 117.7; Chrys. *Hom in I Cor.* 7: 2; *Hom. in Ps.* 41.2; *Hom. in Rom.* 24.3; *Hom. in Eph.* 17.3, 19.3; *Hom. in I Tim.* 3.3; [Chrys.] *Poenit.* 3.

[616] Chrys. *Hom. in Rom.* 4.4.

[617] [Chrys.] *Poenit.* 3; *Hom. in Act.* 48.3.

[618] Gr. Naz. *Carm.* 2.1.88.91–6; Chrys. *Hom. in Mt.* 48 (49).6.

[619] Chrys. *Stag.* 2.1; cf. *Hom. in Mt.* 59.7; the Sicilian conquerors aroused bitterness in Thessalonica because of their high life with prostitutes (Nicet. Chon. Andronic. Comm. 1.9 [398 Bonn]).

[620] Jer. *Virg. Mar.* 20; Gr. Naz. *Carm.* 2.1.88.91–6.

[621] Bas. *Hom.* 14.1, 8; cf. Chrys. *Hom. in Rom.* 24.3. Cf. note 609.

[622] Bas. *Hom.* 14.8, Chrys. *Hom. in Mt.* 48.3, 5f, cf. *Hom. in I Cor.* 12.6.

[623] Chrys. *Hom. in Mt.* 48.5f.

[624] Bas. *Hom.* 14.8; Chrys. *Hom. in Mt.* 48 (49).5, cf. 3; *Hom. in I Cor.* 12.5f.

[625] Nicaea, *cn.* 22.

[626] Chrys. *Hom. in I Cor.* 7: 2 1–3; *Hom. in Ps.* 41. 2; *Hom. in I Cor.* 12.5f.

[627] Chrys. *Hom. in I Cor.* 7: 2 2f; *Hom. in Col.* 12.4; cf. *Hom. in I Cor.* 12.6.

[628] Chrys. *Hom. in Col.* 12.5. Cf. Dölger, *AChr* 4 (1934) 249f.

Church Fathers knew very well that wine can induce excitement[629] and they regarded gluttony as a cause of immoral behavior.[630] In such circumstances male participants at a symposium are, at the very least, engaging mentally in illicit love[631] and women who dance at weddings are regarded as more dishonorable than prostitutes.[632] Clerics must not watch the questionable presentations at such events.[633]

Drunkenness leads beyond love to excessive pride.[634] Thus one finds arrogance at symposia, directed for example toward a parasite,[635] as well as sneering remarks and scornful songs.[636] Sometimes there was direct conflict. If someone took a *hetaira* aside who was supposed to be there for the general entertainment, this could cause dissatisfaction.[637] A prostitute who had been brought to such an event was supposed to keep her eyes solely on her male companion,[638] but unlike the married women and concubines, *hetairai* were sought after by others, and they in turn could engage in coquettish behavior[639] and make secret arrangements.[640] On many different occasions there were scenes of jealousy and fights, even in brothels, and these could become violent and even fatal.[641] Rivals would sometimes break in on festive occasions.[642] According to John Chrysostom, no matter how attractive prostitutes may look during a banquet,[643] they do not bring any true joy. They only incite wild passion that can turn a house into a brothel[644] or else they arouse desires that cannot be satisfied, and soon the drinking companions become angry or worked up, and they get up to leave.[645] According to Basil of Caesarea, even one coquette

[629] Tert. *De spect.* 10; Origen, *Comm. Ser.* 44 *in Mt.*; Chrys. *Hom. in Rom.* 24.3f and elsewhere. Cf. *Apoc.* 17.2. Cf. T. Klauser, *JbAC* 1 (1958) 25.

[630] Clem. Al. *Paed.* 3.21.4; Tert. *Jejun.* 1 and elsewhere.

[631] Bas. *Hom.* 14.8; cf. Chrys. *Hom. in 1 Cor.* 12. 5f; cf. Ambr. *Virg.* 3.13.

[632] Chrys. *Hom. in 1 Cor.* 12.6.

[633] Trull. *cn.* 24.

[634] Aesop., Phot. in. V. Grumel, in *Mélanges H. Grégoire* 3 (Brussels 1951) 129–32.

[635] Alciphr. 3.12.3.

[636] Alciphr. 4.6.3.

[637] Ar. *Vesp.* 1331–81; cf. A. Wilhelm, *AAWW* (1937) 90.

[638] Plaut. *Asin.* 768–80; *Mil.* 652; Lucian, *Dial. meret.* 3.2, 6.3, 15.2. Regarding rivalries, see *RAC* 3, 1172.

[639] Naev. 75–9; Prop. 2.33.34; Sen. *Ben.* 1.14.4 etc.

[640] Tib. 1.2.21f, 1.6.17–20, 25–8; Prop. 3.8.25f; Ov. *Am.* 1.4, 3.11.23f; *Ars am.* 1.565–630; Lygd., [Tib.] 3. 6.11f. Regarding rules, see F. Wilhelm, *RhM* 57 (1902) 604–8.

[641] Ar. *Vesp.* 1254; Lys. 3.43; 4 *passim* (especially 9); Isae. 3.13; Aeschin. 1.65 (?); Dem. 54.14; Theophr. *Char.* 27.9; Lyc. Ath. 13.555A; Lync. Ath. 13.584C; Ter. *Eun.* 422–33; Cic. *De or.* 2.240; Phld. *Mus.* p. 82 K. = 174 Kr.; Hor. *Carm.* 3.14.26; Tib. 1.1.74; Prop. 1.16.5, 2.5.21–6, 19.5; Ov. *Ars am.* 3.71; *Rem. am.* 31; Sen. *Dial.* 5.34.3; Quint. *Decl.* 14.12, 15. 2, 4, 6, 7; Max. Tyr. 35.6; Lucian, *Dial. meret.* 3.2; *Nigr.* 22; Cass. Dio 62.15.6; Lib. *Comp.* 5.5, 7; Aristaenet. 2.19.

[642] Lucian, *Dial. meret.* 15.

[643] Chrys. *Hom. in Col.* 1.5.

[644] Chrys. *Hom. in 1 Cor.* 12.5f, possibly also *Hom. in Hebr.* 14.4.

[645] Chrys. *Hom. in Col.* 1.5.

can play men off against each other and inflame them all.[646] Thus, Chrysostom warns about arguments among male rivals, which can lead to threats against a lover, mistreatment, wounds, and even death.[647]

In other respects, prostitutes were constantly subjected to quarrels and more or less harmless types of scorn.[648] Having one's clothes torn apart by a lover was the least that a prostitute had to deal with.[649] Sometimes these women heard sarcastic or threatening words at the doors of their houses.[650] Disappointed men poured out their full anger in their acts of submission.[651] From the transcript of a court case from AD 185–6 one learns that someone was sentenced to death for killing a public whore "for the sake of the honor of the city."[652] Another man is reported to have blinded a prostitute and then claimed that it was incompatible with his honor to become her guide.[653] From other sources one learns that prostitutes were subjected to all forms of unreasonable demands.[654] When John Chrysostom mentions[655] that greedy men allow themselves to be subjected to more than a prostitute would have to endure in the theater and elsewhere, this may apply to more than just sexual activities.[656] Naturally prostitutes ridiculed one another.[657]

Men certainly had occasion enough to complain about the scorn that they received from their lovers,[658] for these women tried to enslave their men, whereas a proper wife always treats her husband with great respect.[659] Not only did prostitutes always insist on having their way,[660] they would also spit on their lovers, beat them, or ridi-

---

[646] Bas. *Hom. in Ps.* 1.6.

[647] Chrys. *Oppugn.* 2.10; *Theatr.* 2; *Hom. in Mt.* 68 (69).4; *Hom. in Jo.* 79 (78).4f; *Hom. in 1 Cor.* 37.2; *Hom. in Eph.* 7.3; *Hom. in Phil.* 14.2; August. *Conf.* 3.1. For a different opinion, see Clem. Rom. *Rec.* 2.23.

[648] Ar. *Eq.* 1400, 1403; Herod. 2.65–71; Tib. 1.6.73f; Ov. *Am.* 1.7; *Ars am.* 2.169–76; 3.565–71; Lucian, *Dial. meret.* 8.15; Paul. Sil. *Anth. Pal.* 5.247; Agath. *Anth. Pal.* 5.217; F. Wilhelm, *RhM* 57 (1902) 599–602. Cf. Ephr. *Admon. et paen.* 9 (1, 292L).

[649] Hor. *Carm.* 1.17 and elsewhere.

[650] Aristod. *Ath.* 13.585A; Donat. *Ter. Ad.* 783; G. L. Hendrickson, *CPh* 20 (1925) 299. Cf. Diog. Laert. 6.90.

[651] *IG* 3.3 App. 102b (A. Wilhelm, *SO* 27 [1949] 39).

[652] *BGU* 1024, p. 6–8.

[653] Quint. *Decl.* 297. Cf. Hor. *Sat.* 2.3.277; Suet. *Calig.* 33.

[654] Quint. *Decl.* 14.7; cf. 3.6.

[655] Chrys. *Hom. in Hebr.* 15.3; on the other hand, see *Oppugn.* 3.8.

[656] Arn. 2.42; Jer. *Ep.* 77.3; Isid. *Or.* 18.42.2. A prostitute in the hand of a *mastropos* [pimp] behaves in accordance with her customers (Chrys. *Hom. in Mt.* 71 [72].3). Regarding submissiveness, see *RAC* 3, 1167. Regarding Naev. com. 90f, see M. Zicàri, *Philologus* 102 (1958) 154.

[657] Orig. *C. Cels.* 3.52. See also *RAC* 3, 1172.

[658] *RAC* 3, 1168, 1172. In addition, Sen. *Ep.* 22.10, Ath. 13.588E.

[659] Chrys. *Fem. reg.* 6, *Hom. in Mt.* 6.8, *Hom. in Jo.* 79 (78).4f, *Hom. in 1 Cor.* 19.5, *Vid.* 6, Procl. *PG* 61.709f.

[660] August. *Serm.* 161.10, cf. Plut. *Mor.* 192E, 808E.

cule them, and in doing so made themselves even more enticing.[661] Delay serves to heighten desire[662] and a man's anger at a lover who is dominating or unfaithful is quickly pacified.[663] These abused men stand in front of their lovers' doors, day and night,[664] they cry and complain, they subject themselves to unworthy directives, and they endure all forms of insults and even part with their possessions.[665] If men do not pay enough, they certainly fall into disrepute.[666] Some men are not only locked out, but even thrown out.[667] In any case, a man brings scorn and shame on himself and becomes the object of ridicule, if he allows his sense of reason to be overpowered by his desire.[668] The love of a female dancer is much worse than a thousand military expeditions and a thousand journeys, according to John Chrysostom.[669]

The magic of love that prostitutes (or their pimps) practiced could sometimes become dangerous.[670] John Chrysostom writes about these kinds of practices: songs, potions, and similar things, but also conjuring up demons and communicating with the dead, and even attempts to poison a wife who was deceived or even the lover himself.[671] There was always the world of the *pharmakeutria* [sorceress] and Canidia.[672] An actress who had ensnared a prince was believed to have used magical powers.[673] Such women also knew about contraceptive devices, abortions, and the disposal of children.[674] The Church Fathers knew about these matters, but John

---

[661] Chrys. *Forn.* 5, *Hom. in Jo.* 79 (78).4f, *Hom. in Rom.* 27.3, cf. Sen. *Q. Nat.* 4 *praef.* 6.

[662] Ambros. *In Ps.* 118 11.3.3, *RAC* 3, 1167f; cf. Men. *Dys.* 62f.

[663] Chrys. *Hom. in Jo.* 79 (78).4, cf. Plut. *Mor.* 61A–C.

[664] For the water vessel from Aderno in Leningrad (*RAC* 3, 1168), see F. Messerschmidt, *MDAI (R)* 47 (1932) 126–8. Regarding Copley's book about the *paraclausithyron* [appeal by a locked-out lover], see G. Luck, *Gnomon* 29 (1957) 338–42. Cf. passages such as Men. fr. 185 Kö, Plut. *Mor.* 753AB, Paul. Sil. *Anth. Pal.* 6.71, Anon. *Anth. Pal.* 9.621.6, 12.90 and elsewhere.

[665] Ambros. *In Ps.* 118 11.3.3, Chrys. *Hom. in Jo.* 79 (78).5; *Hom. in 1 Cor.* 37.2, *Hom. in Eph.* 7.3, *Hom. in Phil.* 14.2.

[666] Chrys. *Oppugn.* 2.10, *Hom. ad Ant.* 14.4.

[667] Asclep. or Hedyl. *Anth. Pal.* 5.160, cf. Rufin. *Anth. Pal.* 5.65, Niceph. *V. Andr.* 22.

[668] Chrys. *Forn.* 5, *Hom. ad Ant.* 14.4, *Hom. in Mt.* 68 (69).4, *Hom. in Jo.* 79 (78).4f, *Hom. in 1 Cor.* 37.2, Isid. *Or.* 18.42.2, cf. *RAC* 3, 1193, Heraclit. *Incred.* 16.

[669] Chrys. *Hom. in Mt.* 68 (69).3, cf. Aug. *En. Ps.* 136.9. Regarding moral decline, see Pall. *V. Chrys.* 20 (133C.–N.), *Acta Thomae* 12.

[670] Isae. 6.21, Livy 39.11.2, Quint. *Decl.* 14, 15, cf. 385, Mart. 9.29.9f, Plut. *Mor.* 752C, Lucian, *Am.* 43, *Dial. meret.* 1.2, 4, 8.3, Alciphr. 4.10.4f; cf. F. Wilhelm, *RhM* 57 (1902) 606–8, Legrand, *REG* 21 (1908) 58–60, Copley, *Excl. amator* 164 n. 16.

[671] Chrys. *Forn. ux.* 5 (=*Ecl. de mul. et pulchr.* 14), *Virg.* 52, *Hom. in Mt.* 67 (68).3, *Hom. in Rom.* 24.4.

[672] B. Wyss, *SchweizArchVolksk* 47 (1951) 264f.

[673] Chrys. *Hom. in Mt.* 67 (68).3.

[674] Hippocr. *Nat. puer.* 13 (7.490–2L), *Carn.* 19 (8.610L), cf. J. Ilberg, *ARW* 13 (1910) 12f, Plaut. *Truc.* 201f, Lucr. 4.1268–77, Ov. *Am.* 2.13f, Aristaenet. 1.19, Isid. Pel. 4.129, Procop. *Arc.* 9.19, 10.3, 17.16, Thphyl. *Ep.* 30 (772H), Eust. *Od.* 2.131, Achmet, *On.* p. 93 Dr.

Chrysostom always made the man responsible for them.[675] Diseases that affected a prostitute or her lover are only occasionally mentioned.[676] It is not necessary to delve into the intimate sphere of *pornikê askhêmosynê* [whorish wantonness],[677] for these matters are not dealt with by Christian writers. There is, however, a rather extended description of the activities of Maria of Egypt,[678] as well as some occasional, vivid expressions.[679]

## 8  THE LEGAL STATUS OF PROSTITUTES

In conclusion, if one examines the legal status of prostitutes one can explain it in terms of the general attitude toward sexuality in antiquity: prostitution was subject to very little restriction by the state and there was no public administration of it.[680] *Moikheia* was regarded as an offence, but *porneia* did not cause any legal offence. One could say that the state and social customs probably encouraged prostitution more than they inhibited it.[681] Even occasional protests had little impact, for example the peroration of Dio Chrys. 7.133–42, who called for legal action against brothels because they did nothing to diminish promiscuity but rather made it worse, and caused it to progress from public *moikheia*, that is, *porneia* to private (and finally to pederasty). The state seems to have denied *hetairai* the legal status of persons, in contrast to performers in mimes.[682] Throughout Greece they (or their pimps) were subject to taxes,[683] specifically in Athens[684]

---

[675] Clem. Al. *Paed.* 2.96.1, Gr. Nyss. *Fat.*, PG 45.157, Chrys. *Hom. in Rom.* 24.4, August. *Serm.* 10.5, Ancyra *cn.* 21. Cf. *RAC* 3, 1192.

[676] Hippolyt. fr., vol. 1.2.273–7B.-A., Chrys. *Hom. in Phil.* 14.2, Philost. *H.E.* 3.12, Pall. *H. Laus.* 26 (32) and 65 (149) (=Georg. Mon. 2.479.22). The detrimental aspects of lust: *RAC* 3, 1184, 1195, Plat. *Resp.* 3.404D. Even if the later *Morbus Gallicus* was a form of syphilis, it has not been proved that syphilis existed in antiquity (W. Katner, *DeutschMedJourn* 6 [1955] 286–8, J. Wiesner, *Jahrbuch der Albertus-Universität zu Königsberg* 9 [1959] 74–6, cf. A. D. Nock, *Gnomon* 24 [1952] 162 n. 1, M. Della Corte, *Case ed abitanti di Pompei*² 389f, Schneider, *Mer.* 1026 as opposed to Schneider, *Het.* 1361).

[677] Hsch. s. v. *kinda*, Schol. Pl. *Grg.* 494E, *pornika bakkheumata* [whorish revelries]: Gr. Naz. *Carm.* 2.2.8.102, cf. Dio Chrys. 4.112.

[678] Sophr. H. *V. Mar. Aeg.* 20.

[679] Jer. *Ep.* 22.6 based on *Ez.* 16.25. *Hetairika philêmata*, Clem. Al. *Paed.* 2.98.1 (cf. Sen. *Ep.* 75.3, Plut. *Mor.* 61B, Jo. Lyd. *Mag.* 3.65 and elsewhere). The *katapygones* [buggers] in inscriptions on Greek vases appear in a particularly disrespectful new formation *Anthylê katapygaina* [Anthyle the bitch] (M. J. Milne and D. v. Bothmer, *Hesperia* 22 (1953) 215–24, Ed. Fraenkel, *Glotta* 34 [1955] 42–5, J. and L. Robert, *REG* 68 [1955] 201, 71 [1958] 294).

[680] Cic. *Inv. Rhet.* 2.118.

[681] Hermann-Blümer, 256.

[682] P. Mingazzini, *Athenaeum* NS 25 (1947) 163. There was no collegium of *hetairai* on Paros (Poland, *Vereinswesen* 191).

[683] Diod. Sic. 12.21.1.

[684] Aeschin. 1.119f, Poll. 7.202. Cf. A. Boeckh, *Die Staatshaushaltung der Athener*, ed. M. Frankel (Berlin 1886) 1.404f.

and on Cos.[685] In Rome, Caligula introduced such a tax,[686] apparently for the whole Roman empire,[687] and one finds similar taxes in Egypt[688] and in the Chersonese.[689] Alexander Severus did not permit prostitutes to enter the *sacrum aerarium* [public treasury] but used their tax revenue for the repair of the theater, the circus, the amphitheater, and the stadium.[690] Caligula linked the amount of the monthly payment to the earnings of a concubine,[691] and a similar practice may have been followed in Greece. There must have been some form of regulated earnings, for there is documentation that in Athens this was the task of the *agoranomoi* [market supervisors];[692] Aristotle's mention of a parallel, the regulations governing female musicians,[693] appears to confirm[694] this fact rather than contradict it.[695] In practice, neither prostitutes, pimps, nor female musicians followed the established rules.[696] There was, however, a certain control over the earnings of prostitutes through the tax officials,[697] for in Rome there was a requirement that prostitutes register with the aediles.[698] A few forms from Egypt have been preserved that permitted prostitutes to ply their trade on specific days.[699] In this respect this occupation seems to have been somewhat recognized.

Naturally a prostitute could not accuse a person of *moikheia*[700] or of rape.[701] According to Solon, such a woman could not claim to have

---

[685] T. Reinach, *REG* 5 (1892) 100–2. It is clear from Polyaen. 5.2.13 that this form of taxation was quite usual. He states that Dionysius II arranged for the Syracusan *hetairai* to be registered, but not to be taxed.

[686] Suet. *Calig.* 40.

[68] [7]Justin. *Apol.* 1.27.

[688] U. Wilcken, *Griechische ostraka aus Aegypten und Nubien* (Leipzig 1899) 1.217–19, K. Sudhoff, *Ärztliches* 105f, S. L. Wallace, *Taxation in Egypt from Augustus to Diocletian* (Princeton 1938) 193, 209–11, 300, Bringmann, 120, F. W. v. Bissing, *RM* 92 (1944) 376, A. Calderini, *Aegyptus* 33 (1953) 364.

[689] Cagnat, *IGRom.* 1.860.

[690] *Hist. Aug. Alex. Sev.* 24.3.

[691] Similar to the taxation levels in Palmyra, 137 A.D. *OGI* 2.629.73–6, H. Dessau, *Hermes* 19 (1884) 517f.

[692] Suda s. v. *diagramma*. Cf. D. M. Robinson, *AJA* 37 (1933) 602–4.

[693] Arist. *Ath. Pol.* 50.2. On the other hand, in Corinth, Dionysius II used the office of the *astynomoi* (cf. *Com. adesp.* fr. 25b Dem.) to complain to the aediles regarding the pimps (Justin. 21.5.7). Cf. Navarre, 1833 n. 12.

[694] Navarre, 1833.

[695] Schneider, *Het.* 1361.

[696] Hyp. 3.3, see Post (1940) 448 n. 67.

[697] *Pernotelônia* [prostitute tax]: (Philonid. fr. 5 Kock).

[698] Tac. *Ann.* 2.85, cf. Mommsen, *StrR* 159.2, Navarre, 1838.34f. Similarly in Syracuse (see note 685) and possibly in Corinth (see note 693).

[699] Bringmann, 120, G. Plaumann, *APF* 6 (1913) 219f, no. 5.

[700] *RAC* 3, 1155, B. Biondi, in *Conferenze augustee nel bimillenario della nascità* (Milan 1939) 228.

[701] Plut. *Sol.* 23.1

been abducted,[702] and Ulpian was of the opinion that no one could be accused of *furtum* [theft] if, in the course of abducting or concealing a prostitute for his own enjoyment, or of breaking into her house, he also made it possible for thieves to break in.[703] A number of exceptional regulations, such as one that forbad persons from adopting the name of a festival,[704] were apparently not followed and the attempts by the authorities to uphold morals seem not to have been successful.[705] A law that is mentioned by Harpocration was probably effective only for a short time.[706]

One of the most significant factors about prostitutes in Greece was that they had no social standing,[707] even if they were not detested as much as pimps were.[708] Their children were viewed as a disgrace to their fathers[709] and the children themselves were neglected and legally disadvantaged.[710] Solon did not want any children who were born of prostitutes.[711] The old motif, that the children of the gods came from extramarital relationships,[712] was sometimes applied to relationships with paramours.[713] Prostitutes were also disgraced in Rome,[714] and

---

[702] Plut. *Sol.* 23.1. A special case is described by Dem. 21.36–40, *RAC* 3, 1171f. R. Flacelière (*RPh* 75 [1949] 126f) interprets *pôlountai* in Solon's laws in the sense of *polobuntai* [they go about], as does Plut. *Sol.*, Lys. 10.19 and [Dem.] 59.67, whereas Did. fr. 24k (315 Schm.) interprets this passage as "they sold themselves," even though one would expect to see *pôlousin heautas*. Abduction (*RAC* 3, 1163, 1171) by a third party: Men. *Dys.* 58–63.

[703] Ulpian, *Dig.* 47.2.39, contrary to Paul. *Sent.* 2.31.12.

[704] Polemo fr. 3P.

[705] The Areopagus: see Hegesand, *FHG* 4.415. Cf. W. G. Becker, *Platons Gesetze und das griechische Familienrecht: eine rechtsvergleichende Untersuchung* (Munich 1932) 19, 92 n. 1.

[706] Harp. p. 141.11–4B, E. Bayer, *Demetrios Phalereus, der Athener* (Stuttgart 1942) 60.

[707] *RAC* 3, 1170, 1179, 1193. Chrys. *Reg.* 3, *Hom. in Mt.* 70 (71).4, Georg. Pachym. *Decl.* 10 *passim*.

[708] Ulpian, *Dig.* 23.2.43.6.

[709] Aeschin. 2.177, Men. *Epit.* 428f (469f), Plut. *Mor.* 1127C, Chrys. *Hom. in Rom.* 24.3, Is. Pel. 4.129.

[710] *RAC* 3, 1161f, 1173, 1185, 1212. Cf. Aeschin. *Ep.* 7.3, Callim. fr. 527 Pf., Dioscur. *Anth. Pal.* 11.363, Philostr. *VA* 5.32 (190K), Lucian, *Iupp. trag.* 52, Diog. Laert. 2.81, 6.62, Is. Pel. 4.129, Ennod. *Carm.* 2.24. Numerous instances can be found: Ath. 13.576C, 577A–C, 578A, 589C, 591F–592A, 592E, Diog. Laert. 4.46. According to Hermog. P. 40.18fR, neither the son of a *hetaira* nor the son of a *pornos* is permitted to speak publicly (cf. *Proleg.* p. 220.4–6R). In Georg. Pachym. (*Decl.* 9.159–86B) a person protests against both charges (here *pornos* in the active sense). Regarding the *nothoi* [bastards], or *spurii* [illegitimates] in general, see E. Weiss, *RE* 3A, 1889–91, K. Latte, *RE* 17, 1066–74, Post (1940) 444–50. According to *Ev. Thom. log.* 105, the legitimate son will one day be called the "son of a whore."

[711] Thphl. *Ant. Autol.* 3.6. For instances in the Old Testament, see Jeptha (*Jud.* 11:2, e.g. Cypr. Gall. *Jud.* 417–20) and David (1 *Kings* 20:30. e.g. Chrys. *Hom. in 1 Cor.* 33.2). Clem. Al. *Protr.* 25.1. Regarding the tradition about Jesus, see Tert. *De spect.* 30.

[712] Eur. *Bacch.* 26–31, 245 and elsewhere.

[713] Marcion, Cypr. *Ep.* 74.8; Fulg. *De aetat.* 11 (167.20–24H). "Women who live canonically" do not differ from prostitutes when they give birth (Pall. *V. Chrys.* 12). On the other hand, many prostitutes who gave birth to children try to create the impression that they are childless (Chrys. *Fem. reg.* 3).

[714] *RAC* 3, 1190. Regarding personnel who served in taverns, see Kleberg, *Hôtels* 81f.

they retained this status even when they give up their profession,[715] unless they married.[716] As was the case in Greece, prostitutes in Rome could not only become concubines,[717] but under certain social circumstances could get married.[718] The *lex Julia* or *Papia Poppaea* decreed that senators, the sons of senators, and all free-born men were forbidden from marrying prostitutes.[719] According to Constantine, senators from the status of *clarissimi* and above could not marry a *scaenica vel scaenicae filia, tabernaria vel tabernarii filia* [actress or actress' daughter, shopkeeper or shopkeeper's daughter], or a *lenonis filia* [pimp's daughter].[720] The daughter of a senator who became a prostitute or an actress was no longer subject to the restrictions of her social status and was free to marry a freedman.[721]

The *lex Julia de vi* did not allow prostitutes to serve as witnesses.[722] From the time of Domitian on, they were not permitted to use a sedan chair or to receive inheritances or legacies.[723] A magistrate could have prostitutes driven away by his lictors[724] and was not permitted to be seen at a brothel carrying his *fasces* [badge of office].[725] During the time of Caracalla, a young knight who paid the fees for a brothel using a coin that contained the likeness of the emperor was subject to death.[726] In Persia, a coward had to walk around the market for a whole day, carrying a naked prostitute on his shoulders.[727]

Procuring was strongly opposed. In Athens, Solon had forbidden the practice of leading daughters or sisters who were still unmarried

---

[715] Ulpian, *Dig.* 23.2.43.

[716] Ulpian, *Dig.* 48.5.14.2.

[717] *RAC* 3, 1173. Marcian. *Dig.* 25.7.3, cf. Modestin. *Dig.* 23.2.24, Castello (note 165) 120–2. Cf. Aelian, *VH* 12.52. To retain numerous concubines is ultimately the same as to engage in whoring (Justinian, *Nov.* 18 [42].5, 89 [111].12.5).

[718] *RAC* 3, 1161, 1173, 1191, 1211. Aristaenet. 1.19, possibly also Leon. Tar. *Anth. Pal.* 6.211, Hsch. s.v. *thyrsos* (cf. Archipp. fr. 27). Becoming engaged: Caecil. *Hymnis*. Constellation for the marriage of a prostitute, e.g. *Cat. Cod. Astr.* 2.166.27–9, childlessness as a result, *ibid.* 8.4.130.17f. Clerics forbidden from doing this, *Cn. apost.* 18.

[719] Ulpian, *Tit.* 13.1, 16.2, cf. *Dig.* 23.2.43, 44 pr., Modestin. *Dig.* 23.2.24. P. Jörs, in Jörs *et al.* eds, *Festschrift Theodor Mommsen zum fünfzigjährigen Doctorjubiläum* (Marburg 1893) 21, 24, W. Kunkel, ed., *Römisches Privatrecht, auf Grund des Werkes von Paul Jörs*[3] (Berlin 1949) 275f, S. Solazzi, *BIDR* 46 (1939) 51–3, Biondi (note 700) 221, 235.

[720] *Cod. Iust.* 5.27.1. Cf. Lex Julia, *Dig.* 23.2.44.

[721] Paul. *Dig.* 23.2.47. Solazzi, 49–51.

[722] Callistr. *Dig.* 22.5.3.5. Cf. Suet. *Claud.* 15.4.

[723] Suet. *Dom.* 8.3, cf. Tryphon. *Dig.* 29.1.41.1, Paul. *Dig.* 37.12.3 pr. (Castello 125), Papin. *Dig.* 34.9.14, Caracalla, *Cod. Iust.* 5.16.2, cf. 6.46.3, P. M. Meyer, *Der römische Konkubinat nach den Rechtsquellen und den Inschriften* (Leipzig 1895) 97–100. Earlier, see Quint. *Inst.* 8.5.17, 19, Plut. *Mor.* 273B. See also Jer. *Ep.* 52.6: *scorta hereditates capiunt* [prostitutes get inheritances].

[724] Sen. *Controv.* 9.2.2, 21, cf. 1.2.7.

[725] Sen. *Controv.* 9.2.17, cf. Gell. 4.14.

[726] Cass. Dio 77.16.5.

[727] Plut. *Artax.* 14.

into prostitution[728] and anyone who forced a free woman into a brothel was subject to the death penalty.[729] One reads in the *History of Apollonius* that a procurer was burned for doing this and that his possessions, as well as the young women and their supervisor, were awarded to the woman who brought the lawsuit. This woman set the other young women free.[730] Since a prostitute did not lose her status as a citizen, it was very embarrassing for the man who had caused her *hybris doulikê* [slavish indignity] if she was restored to her former legal status.[731] In Rome,[732] Hadrian forbad the sale, without cause, of female slaves to procurers.[733] If they were sold to someone on condition that they not be forced into prostitution, they became free, though they might be encouraged into sexual deviance, for example in an inn.[734]

If prostitutes were registered with the aediles they were removed from the protection of the *lex Julia*, which forbad adultery and *stuprum* [illicit sexual intercourse] but not prostitution. It was customary to pretend that pimping had taken place, in order to circumvent the punishment that was due to someone who encouraged adultery.[735] Because even women of high social standing were not afraid to register,[736] in AD 19 the Senate forbad members of the equestrian order (either hereditary or through marriage) and therefore *a priori* the members of the senatorial classes from engaging in prostitution. In Julian's writings one finds frequent mention of measures to clean out brothels and small stores from central parts of cities (*Or.* 6.186D-7A). We know that the emperor Tacitus tried similar measures but that he was unable to sustain them for long.[737] It is claimed that Pythagoras tried to stop the practice of extramarital relationships among the Crotoniates.[738] Cleomenes drowned the most infamous free-born prostitutes in Methymna.[739]

---

[728] Plut. *Sol.* 23. R. Flacelière, *RPh* 75 (1949) 127 n. 4, connects *mê* [not] to *parthenon* [unmarried girl].

[729] Din. 1.23, Lipsius 2.435 n. 58.

[730] *Hist. Apoll. Tyr.* 46 (modern Greek version, v. 781-3).

[731] Ter. *Eun.* 943-61, *Cod. Iust.* 8.50.7. Unclear: *PSI* 1055a. According to Georg. Pachym. (*Decl.* 10 *passim*) there was no loss of citizenship rights.

[732] Mommsen, *StrR* 699-701.

[733] *Hist. Aug. Hadr.* 18.8. Further Ulpian, *Dig.* 1.12.1.8 (B. Biondi, *Il diritto romano cristiano* [Milan 1952] 2.275f).

[734] Alex. Sev. *Cod. Iust.* 4.56, cf. Pompon. *Dig.* 21.2.34, Ulpian *Dig.* 2.4.10.1, Paul. *Dig.* 18.1.56, 7.9, 40.8.7, Papin. *Dig.* 40.8.6, *Cod. Iust.* 7.6.1.4. For more details, see W. W. Buckland, *The Roman law of slavery: the condition of the slave in private law from Augustus to Justinian* (Cambridge 1908) 70f, 603f, Biondi, *Il diritto romano cristiano* 2.277-9, G. Sciascia, *Varietà giuridiche: scritti brasiliani di diritto romano e moderno* (Milan 1956) 103-9.

[735] Papin. *Dig.* 48.5.11 (10).

[736] Suet. *Tib.* 35.2.

[737] *Hist. Aug. Tac.* 10.2.

[738] Iambl. *VP* 132.

[739] Theopomp. fr. 227J.

## 9 MEASURES THAT WERE ADOPTED BY THE CHRISTIAN CHURCH

Generally speaking, prostitutes enjoyed little legal protection, especially in foreign countries.[740] In the Christian period numerous measures were introduced to protect those who had been forced into prostitution. According to a decree of Constantius, Christian prostitutes could only be bought and freed by Christians.[741] Beginning with the time of Theodosius II and Valentinian, attempts were made to ensure that young women who had been forced into prostitution by their fathers or by their masters (or else brought into the world of the theater), and who were now no longer subject to the person who had sold them,[742] could be freed by secular authorities or by the bishop. The procurer lost any right to the young girls' property.[743] Justinian continued and expanded upon earlier ordinances (*Nov.* 14 (39)) and forbad all forms of procurement; any tolerance of prostitution by a landlord was subject to severe punishment, in Constantinople and its surroundings as well as in the whole empire. Young women were not allowed to be enticed into gainful prostitution by cunning, by promises, or by contracts (even if they were offered citizenship). The *cn.* 86 of Trullanum[744] threatened excommunication to anyone who endangered the souls of prostitutes by forcing them into prostitution and keeping them there. A cleric who did this was threatened with degradation. According to the prevailing interpretation and prevailing practice, neither the ordinances of Justinian nor the legal canon dealt with women who voluntarily went into prostitution, because of personal inclination or because of poverty. Balsamon dealt with every aspect of prostitution. A dishonorable daughter was subject to punishment for her disobedience to her father.[745] Elvira *cn.* 12 frowned upon pimping for one's own mother. Generally speaking, the frequently criticized problem prevailed[746] that no heathen law forbad brothels or sexual offences, and as a result the clergy had ample room for activity.[747]

---

[740] Firm. Mat. *Math.* 6.31.90.

[741] *Cod. Theod.* 15.8.1. Cf. Ambros. *Off.* 2.15.70.

[742] Chrys. *Hom. in* 1 *Cor.* 18.2.

[743] *Cod. Theod.* 15.8.2, *Nov. Theod.* 18, *Cod. Iust.* 1.4.12, 14, 33; 5.4.29, 6.4.4.2; 7.6.1.4; 11.41.6f, Buckland, *Roman law of slavery*, 603. Cf. *Cod. Iust.* 8.50.7 (Biondi, *Il diritto romano cristiano* 2.276, A. Piganiol, *Romanitas* 1 [1958] 17). Regarding Ulpian, *Dig.* 13.7.24.3, see Biondi, *Il diritto romano cristiano* 2.278f.

[744] Bals., Zonar., Arist., *PG* 137.804–8.

[745] Chrys. *Prod.* 1.

[746] Jer. *Ep.* 77.3, August. *De civ. D.* 14.18, *Serm.* 153.6, Chrys. *Hom in* 1 *Cor.* 12.4, Salv. *Gub. Dei* 7.99.

Fundamentally only *moikheia* was and remained an *adikêma* [intentional wrong]. *Porneia* was regarded as a *hamartêma* [fault], which was despised but was not subject to a specific law.[748]

The amount of prostitution tax which a pimp was required to pay[749] was defined on an ongoing basis by the guidelines of the *Collatio* [Collection].[750] Under Constantine this led to such a crisis that some fathers were obliged to prostitute their daughters, because of a lack of money.[751] This *Collatio*, which was later called *khrysargyron* [tribute of gold and silver], was discontinued under Theodosius and Valentinian,[752] was reinstituted under Leon, and was removed by Anastasius in AD 500.[753] Prostitutes continued to be dishonorable. Constantine had demanded this tax only from female innkeepers who maintained an honourable establishment, but not from the women who worked for these innkeepers. The latter were held in such low esteem that they were not expected to obey any laws.[754] Ambrose (*In Psa.* 118 8.19.3) appears to refer to the fact that these women were not permitted to serve as witnesses; they were kept away from *loci honesti* [honorable places].[755] Theodosius forbad the practice of raping unfaithful wives in brothels and publicizing their punishment with the ringing of bells.[756]

Constantine created a general *porneion* [brothel] in the so-called Zeugma of Constantinople, and he forbad everything more than that, as well as public appearances by prostitutes outside of Constantinople.[757] However, the institute of Theophilus was later turned into an inn. Theodosius the Great made the former temple of Aphrodite into a station for coaches and arranged for buildings to be constructed where poor prostitutes could be housed for free.[758] Either because of or in spite of their reputation,[759] Theodora closed the houses of enjoyment in Constantinople and placed more than 500 prostitutes in the monastery of repentance, not entirely to their

---

[747] The case of the *politikê* who was sent to a large oasis (*PGrenf* 2.73.9) is contentious (and hardly plausible, according to W. Croenert, in *Raccolta di scritti in onore de Giacomo Lumbroso, 1844–1925* [Milan 1925] 514–28).
[748] Dio Chrys. 14.14, Joh. Sard. *In Aphth.* p. 91–2, cf. 93R.
[749] Tert. *Fug. in pers.* 13.
[750] O. Seeck, *RE* 4,370–6.
[751] Zos. 2.38.
[752] *Nov. Theod.* 18 pr.
[753] Evagr. *HE* 3.39, Proc. G. *Anast.* 13, Georg. Cedr. hist. 1. 626f Bonn.
[754] *Cod. Iust.* 9.9.28 (29).
[755] *Cod. Theod.* 15.7.12.
[756] Thphn. Chron. *PG* 108.209, Socr. *HE* 5.18.
[757] *Patr. Const.* 2.65 (185–7 Pr.).
[758] Jo. Mal. 13 p. 345.19–21 Bonn.
[759] Joh. Eph. *V. ss. or.* 12 (PO 17 1.167).

pleasure.[760] A parallel in Egyptian history can be found in the removal of pubs and open houses by Baibar, the Sultan of the Mamelukes, in AD 1266.[761] As a very old man Justinian neglected the army and allowed money to be spent on mistresses and other things.[762] In the African kingdom the Vandals proceeded energetically with the punishment and the forcible marrying off of prostitutes.[763] The laws of the Visigoths also provided for severe punishment for pimps and prostitutes.[764] Salvian (*Gub. Dei* 7.24f ) observed that fornication was frowned upon by the Goths but was regarded by Romans as a virtue. Bardesanes claimed that there were no prostitutes among the Seres[765] and the Brahmans are said to have differed from other Indians for the same reason.[766] In general it must be noted that everywhere where social conditions favored the existence of prostitution, moral sanctions against it and measures by the authorities to combat it were successful only to a limited degree.

---

[760] Procop. *Aed.* 1.9.1–10, *Arc.* 17.5f, Jo. Mal. 18 p. 440.14–441.7 Bonn. Cf. A. Nagl, *RE* 5A, 1783f, B. Rubin, *RE* 23, 550, N. B. Tomadakis *EEAth* 2.4 (1953–4) 168–74.

[761] Applause in the Arabic shadow theater: see P. Kahle, *WissAnnalen* 3 (1954) 756–9.

[762] Agath. 5.14 (307.17–21 Bonn).

[763] Salv. *Gub. Dei* 7.89–108.

[764] *Lex Visigoth.* 3.4.17 (157 Zeumer).

[765] Eus. *P.E.* 6.10.12, [Clem.] *Recogn.* 9.19, *Caesar. Dial.* 2.109, Phrantz. 32.49 p. 218 and other later examples.

[766] Eus. *P.E.* 6.10.14. *Hetairizesthai* [to be a prostitute] of many women with one man in Britannia is mentioned by *Caesar. Dial.* 2.109 and Georg. Ham., Cramer, *Anecd. Ox.* 4.237.10. According to a Christian source, there was severe punishment among the Tartars for forms of love that were not permitted, see H. Dörrie, *GGN* (1956) 6.191.

# 5 Classical Greek Attitudes to Sexual Behaviour

## K. J. DOVER[†]

## 1 WORDS AND ASSUMPTIONS

The Greeks regarded sexual enjoyment as the area of life in which the goddess Aphrodite was interested, as Ares was interested in war and other deities in other activities. Sexual intercourse was *aphrodisia*, "the things of Aphrodite." Sexual desire could be denoted by general words for "desire," but the obsessive desire for a particular person was *eros*, "love" in the sense which it has in our expressions "be in love with …" (*eran*) and "fall in love with …" (*erasthenai*). Eros, like all powerful emotional forces, but more consistently than most, was personified and deified; treated by some early poets as a cosmic force older than Aphrodite, occasionally (though not often) alleged to be her son, he was most commonly thought of as her minister or agent, to the extent that she could, when she wished (as in Euripides' *Hippolytus*), cause X to fall in love with Y.

At some time in the latter part of the fifth century Prodicus defined eros as "desire doubled"; eros doubled, he said, was madness.[1] Both philosophical and unphilosophical Greeks treated sexual desire as a response to the stimulus of visual beauty, which is reasonable enough; rather more surprisingly, they also treated eros as a strong response to great visual beauty, a response which may be intensified by admirable or lovable qualities in the desired person but is not in the first instance evoked by those qualities. Plato finds it philosophically necessary in *Phaedrus* and *Symposium* to treat eros as a response to beauty; but even Plato shows his awareness elsewhere (*Rep.* 474DE) that superior visual stimuli from Z do not necessarily make X fall out of love with Y.[2]

---

[†] Originally published in *Arethusa*, 6 (1973), 59–73.
[1] Prodicus fr. B7 (Diels-Kranz).
[2] See for more detailed discussion my article, "Aristophanes' Speech in Plato's *Symposium*," *Journal of Hellenic Studies* lvi (1966), 41ff., especially 48f.

Eros generates *philia*, "love"; the same word can denote milder degrees of affection, just as "my *philoi*" can mean my friends or my inner-most family circle, according to context. For the important question "Do you love me?" the verb used is *philein*, whether the question is put by a youth to a girl as their kissing becomes more passionate[3] or by a father to his son as an anxious preliminary to a test of filial obedience.[4]

## 2 INHIBITION

Our own culture has its myths about the remote past, and one myth that dies hard is that the "invention" of sexual guilt, shame and fear by the Christians destroyed a golden age of free, fearless, pagan sexuality. That most pagans were in many ways less inhibited than most Christians is undeniable. Not only had they a goddess specially concerned with sexual pleasure; their other deities were portrayed in legend as enjoying fornication, adultery and sodomy. A pillar surmounted by the head of Hermes and adorned with an erect penis stood at every Athenian front door; great models of the erect penis were borne in procession at festivals of Dionysus, and it too was personified as the tirelessly lascivious Phales.[5] The vase-painters often depicted sexual intercourse, sometimes masturbation (male or female) and fellatio, and in respect of any kind of sexual behaviour Aristophanic comedy appears to have had total license of word and act. A century ago there was a tendency to explain Aristophanic obscenity by positing a kind of dispensation for festive occasions which were once fertility-rituals, but this has no relevance to the vase-painters, nor, indeed, to the iambic poets of the archaic period, Archilochus and Hipponax, in whom no vestige of inhibition is apparent.

There is, however, another side of the coin. Sexual intercourse was not permitted in the temples or sanctuaries of deities (not even of deities whose sexual enthusiasm was conspicuous in mythology), and regulations prescribing chastity or formal purification after intercourse played a part in many Greek cults. Homeric epic, for all its unquestioning acceptance of fornication as one of the good things of life, is circumspect in vocabulary, and more than once denotes the male genitals by *aidos*, "shame," "disgrace." Serious poetry in the early classical poetry was often direct in what it said, but preserved a certain level of dignity in the ways of saying it; even when Pindar

---

[3] Xenophon, *Symposium* 9.6.
[4] Aristophanes, *Clouds*, 82.
[5] Aristophanes, *Acharnians* 259–279.

states the parentage of Castor in terms of Tyndareus' ejaculation into Leda, his style has the highest poetic credentials.[6] Poets (notably Homer) sometimes describe interesting and agreeable activities— cooking, mixing wine, stabbing an enemy through a chink in his armour—in meticulous detail, but nowhere is there a comparable description of the mechanisms of sexual activity. Prose literature, even on medical subjects, is euphemistic ("be with ..." is a common way of saying "have sexual intercourse with ..."), and can degenerate into coyness, as when "we all know what" is substituted for "the genitals" in a list of the bodily organs which convey pleasurable sensations.[7] The fourth-century orators show some skill in insinuating allegations of sexual misconduct and simultaneously suggesting that both the speaker's sense of propriety and the jury's would be outraged by a plain statement of the facts; when a coarse word is unavoidable, they make a show of reluctance to utter it.[8] By the late fourth century, the obscene words which had been so lavishly used by Aristophanes and his contemporaries had been almost entirely excluded from comedy; Aristotle, commenting on this, calls the old style *aiskhrologia*, "speaking what is shameful (disgraceful, ugly)."[9]

Linguistic inhibition, then, was observably strengthened in the course of the classical period; and at least in some art-forms, inhibition extended also to content. These are data which do not fit the popular concept of a guilt-free or shame-free sexual morality, and require explanation. Why so many human cultures use derogatory words as synonyms of "sexual" and reproach sexual prowess while praising prowess in (e.g.) swimming and riding, is a question which would take us to a remote level of speculation. Why the Greeks did so is a question which can at least be related intelligibly to the structure of Greek society and to Greek moral schemata which have no special bearing on sex.

## 3 SEGREGATION AND ADULTERY

As far as was practicable (cf. §7), Greek girls were segregated from boys and brought up at home in ignorance of the world outside the home; one speaker in court seeks to impress the jury with the respectability of his family by saying that his sister and nieces are "so well brought up that they are embarrassed in the presence even of a

[6] Pindar, *Nemean Odes* 10.80–82.
[7] Xenophon, *Hiero* 1.4.
[8] E.g. Aeschines i 52.
[9] Aristotle, *Nicomachean Ethics* 1128ᵃ 22–25.

man who is a member of the family".[10] Married young, perhaps at fourteen[11] (and perhaps to a man twenty years or more her senior), a girl exchanged confinement in her father's house for confinement in her husband's. When he was invited out, his children might be invited with him, but not his wife;[12] and when he had friends in, she did not join the company. Shopping seems to have been a man's job, to judge from references in comedy,[13] and slaves could be sent on other errands outside the house. Upholders of the proprieties pronounced the front door to be the boundaries of a good woman's territory.[14]

Consider now the situation of an adolescent boy growing up in such a society. Every obstacle is put in the way of his speaking to the girl next door; it may not be easy for him even to get a glimpse of her. Festivals, sacrifices and funerals, for which women and girls did come out in public, provided the occasion for seeing and being seen. They could hardly afford more than that, for there were too many people about, but from such an occasion (both in real life and in fiction) an intrigue could be set on foot, with a female slave of respectable age as the indispensable go-between.[15]

In a society which practices segregation of the sexes, it is likely that boys and girls should devote a good deal of time and ingenuity to defeating society, and many slaves may have co-operated with enthusiasm. But Greek laws were not lenient towards adultery, and *moikheia*, for which we have no suitable translation except "adultery," denoted not only the seduction of another man's wife, but also the seduction of his widowed mother, unmarried daughter, sister, niece, or any other woman whose legal guardian he was.[16] The adulterer could be prosecuted by the offended father, husband or guardian; alternatively, if caught in the act, he could be killed, maltreated, or imprisoned by force until he purchased his freedom by paying heavy compensation. A certain tendency to regard women as irresponsible and ever ready to yield to sexual temptation (see §5) relieved a cuckolded husband of a sense of shame or inadequacy and made him willing to seek the co-operation of his friends in apprehending an adulterer,[17] just as he

---

[10] Lysias iii 6.

[11] E.g. Xenophon, *Oeconomicus* 7.5.

[12] Isaeus iii 14 (general statement); Aristophanes, *Birds* 130–132 bears it out.

[13] E.g. Aristophanes, *Ecclesiazusae* 818–822, *Wasps* 788–790.

[14] E.g. Menander fr. 592, Euripides fr. 521.

[15] E.g. Lysias i 8 (an adulterer's designs on a married woman), Theocritus 2.70–103.

[16] The law is cited and discussed by Demosthenes xxiii 53–55. Cf. A.R.W. Harrison, *The Law of Athens*, i (Oxford, 1968), 32–38.

[17] The speaker of Lysias i regards his wife and children as "shamed" by the adulterer but himself as "wronged." However, an alternative view seems to be expressed in Callias fr. 1, "Profit is better than shame; off with the adulterer to the inner room!"

would seek their co-operation to defend himself against fraud, encroachment, breach of contract, or any other threat to his property. The adulterer was open to reproach in the same way, and to the same extent, as any other violator of the laws protecting the individual citizen against arbitrary treatment by other citizens. To seduce a woman of citizen status was more culpable than to rape her, not only because rape was presumed to be unpremeditated but because seduction involved the capture of her affection and loyalty;[18] it was the degree of offence against the man to whom she belonged, not her own feelings, which mattered.

It naturally follows from the state of the law and from the attitudes and values implied by segregation that an adolescent boy who showed an exceptional enthusiasm for the opposite sex could be regarded as a potential adulterer and his propensity discouraged just as one would discourage theft, lies and trickery, while an adolescent boy who blushed at the mere idea of proximity to a woman was praised as *sophron*, "right-minded," i.e. unlikely to do anything without reflecting first whether it might incur punishment, disapproval, dishonour or other undesirable consequences.

## 4 COMMERCIAL SEX

Greek society was a slave-owning society, and a female slave was not in a position to refuse the sexual demands of her owner or of anyone else to whom he granted the temporary use of her. Large cities, notably Athens, also had a big population of resident aliens, and these included women who made a living as prostitutes, on short-term relations with a succession of clients, or as *hetairai*, who endeavoured to establish long-term relations with wealthy and agreeable men. Both aliens and citizens could own brothels and stock them with slave-prostitutes. Slave-girls and alien girls who took part in men's parties as dancers or musicians could also be mauled and importuned in a manner which might cost a man his life if he attempted it with a woman of citizen status. In an instructive scene at the close of Aristophanes' *Thesmophoriazusae* (1160–1231) Euripides, disguised as an old woman, distracts the attention of a policeman with the help of a pretty dancing-girl; for a drachma, the policeman is allowed to have intercourse with the girl, but it is the "old woman," not the girl, who strikes the bargain, exactly as if it were a matter of paying rent for use of an inanimate object.

[18] Lysias i 32f.

It was therefore easy enough to purchase sexual satisfaction, and the richer a man was the better provision he could make for himself. But money spent on sex was money not spent on other things, and there seems to have been substantial agreement on what were proper or improper items of expenditure. Throughout the work of the Attic orators, who offer us by far the best evidence on the moral standards which it was prudent to uphold in addressing large juries composed of ordinary citizens, it is regarded as virtuous to impoverish oneself by gifts and loans to friends in misfortune (for their daughters' dowries, their fathers' funerals, and the like), by ransoming Athenian citizens taken prisoner in war, and by paying out more than the required minimum in the performance of public duties (the upkeep of a warship, for example, or the dressing and training of a chorus at a festival). This kind of expenditure was boasted about and treated as a claim on the gratitude of the community.[19] On the other hand, to "devour an inheritance" by expenditure on one's own consumption was treated as disgraceful.[20] Hence gluttony, drunkenness and purchased sexual relations were classified together as "shameful pleasures"; Demosthenes[21] castigates one of his fellow-ambassadors for "going round buying prostitutes and fish" with the money he had corruptly received. When a young man fell in love, he might well fall in love with a hetaira or a slave, since his chances of falling in love with a girl of citizen status were so restricted, and to secure the object of his love he would need to purchase or ransom her. A close association between eros and extravagance therefore tends to be assumed, especially in comedy; a character in Menander[22] says, "No one is so parsimonious as not to make some sacrifice of his property to Eros." More than three centuries earlier, Archilochus[23] put the matter in characteristically violent form when he spoke of wealth accumulated by long labour "pouring down into a whore's guts." A fourth-century litigant[24] venomously asserts that his adversary, whose tastes were predominantly homosexual, has "buggered away all his estate."

We have here another reason for the discouragement and disapproval of sexual enthusiasm in the adolescent; it was seen as presenting a threat that the family's wealth would be dissipated in ways other

---

[19] E.g. Lysias xix 9f., "My father, throughout his life, spent more on the city than on himself and his family...."

[20] E.g. Aeschines i 42, on Timarchus' "devouring of his considerable estate ... because he is a slave to the most shameful pleasures."

[21] Demosthenes xix 229.

[22] Menander fr. 198.

[23] Archilochus fr. 118 (Tarditi) = 142 *(Bergk).

[24] Isaeus x 25.

than those which earned honour and respect from the community. The idea that one has a right to spend one's own money as one wishes (or a right to do anything which detracts from one's health and physical fitness) is not Greek, and would have seemed absurd to a Greek. He had only the rights which the law of his city explicitly gave him; no right was inalienable, and no claim superior to the city's.

## 5  RESISTANCE

Living in a fragmented and predatory world, the inhabitants of a Greek city-state, who could never afford to take the survival of their community completely for granted, attached great importance to the qualities required of a soldier: not only to strength and speed, in which men are normally superior to women, but also to the endurance of hunger, thirst, pain, fatigue, discomfort and disagreeably hot or cold weather. The ability to resist and master the body's demands for nourishment and rest was normally regarded as belonging to the same moral category as the ability to resist sexual desire. Xenophon describes the chastity of King Agesilaus together with his physical toughness,[25] and elsewhere[26] summarises "lack of self-control" as the inability to hold out against "hunger, thirst, sexual desire and long hours without sleep." The reasons for this association are manifold: the treatment of sex—a treatment virtually inevitable in a slave-owning society—as a commodity, and therefore as something which the toughest and most frugal men will be able to cut down to a minimum; the need for a soldier to resist the blandishments of comfort (for if he does not resist, the enemy who does will win), to sacrifice himself as an individual entirely, to accept pain and death as the price to be paid for the attainment of a goal which is not easily quantified, the honour of victory; and the inveterate Greek tendency to conceive of strong desires and emotional states as forces which assail the soul from the outside. To resist is manly and "free"; to be distracted by immediate pleasure from the pursuit of honour through toil and suffering is to be a "slave" to the forces which "defeat" and "worst" one's own personality.

Here is a third reason for praise of chastity in the young, the encouragement of the capacity to resist, to go without, to become the sort of man on whom the community depends for its defence. If the segregation and legal and administrative subordination of women received their original impetus from the fragmentation of the

---

[25]  Xenophon, *Agesilaus* 5.
[26]  Xenophon, *Memorabilia* iv 5.9.

early Greek world into small, continuously warring states, they also gave an impetus to the formation of certain beliefs about women which served as a rationalization of segregation and no doubt affected behaviour to the extent that people tend to behave in the ways expected of them. Just as it was thought masculine to resist and endure, it was thought femine to yield to fear, desire and impulse. "Now you must be a *man*," says Demeas to himself as he tries to make up his mind to get rid of his concubine.[27] "Forget your desire, fall out of love." Women in comedy are notoriously unable to keep off the bottle, and in tragedy women are regarded as naturally more prone than men to panic, uncontrollable grief, jealousy and spite. It seems to have been believed not only that women enjoyed sexual intercourse more intensely than men,[28] but also that experience of intercourse put the woman more under the man's power than it put him under hers,[29] and that if not segregated and guarded women would be insatiably promiscuous.

## 6   HOMOSEXUALITY

It was taken for granted in the Classical period that a man was sexually attracted by a good-looking younger male,[30] and no Greek who said that he was "in love" would have taken it amiss if his hearers assumed without further enquiry that he was in love with a boy and that he desired more than anything to ejaculate in or on the boy's body. I put the matter in these coarse and clinical terms to preclude any misapprehension arising from modern application of the expression "Platonic love" or from Greek euphemism (see below). Xenophon[31] portrays the Syracusan tyrant Hiero as declaring that he wants from the youth Dailochus, with whom he is in love, "what, perhaps, the nature of man compels us to want from the beautiful." Aphrodite, despite her femininity, is not hostile to homosexual desire, and homosexual intercourse is denoted by the same term, *aphrodisia*, as heterosexual intercourse.[32] Vase-painting was noticeably affected by the homosexual ethos; painters sometimes depicted a naked woman with a male waist and hips, as if a woman's body was nothing but a young

---

[27] Menander, *Samia* (Austin) 349f.
[28] Hesiod fr. 275 (Merkelbach and West).
[29] Cf. Euripides, *Troades* 665 f., *Medea* 569–575, fr. 323.
[30] I have discussed the evidence more fully in "Eros and Nomos," *Bulletin of the Institute of Classical Studies* x (1964), 31–42.
[31] Xenophon, *Hiero* 1.33.
[32] E.g. Xenophon, *Oeconomicus* 12.14, *Symposium* 8.21.

man's body plus breasts and minus external genitals,[33] and in many of their pictures of heterosexual intercourse from the rear position the penis appears (whatever the painter's intention) to be penetrating the anus, not the vagina.[34]

Why homosexuality—or, to speak more precisely, "pseudo-homosexuality,"[35] since the Greeks saw nothing surprising in the co-existence of desire for boys and desire for girls in the same person—obtained so firm and widespread a hold on Greek society, is a difficult and speculative question.[36] Segregation alone cannot be the answer, for comparable segregation has failed to engender a comparable degree of homosexuality in other cultures. Why the Greeks of the Classical period accepted homosexual desire as natural and normal is a much easier question: they did so because previous generations had accepted it, and segregation of the sexes in adolescence fortified and sustained the acceptance and the practice.

Money may have enabled the adolescent boy to have plenty of sexual intercourse with girls of alien or servile status, but it could not give him the satisfaction which can be pursued by his counterpart in a society which does not own slaves: the satisfaction of being wel-comed *for his own sake* by a sexual partner of equal status. This is what the Greek boy was offered by homosexual relations. He was probably accustomed (as often happens with boys who do not have the company of girls) to a good deal of homosexual play at the time of puberty, and he never heard from his elders the suggestion that one was destined to become *either* "a homosexual" *or* "a heterosexual."[37] As he grew older, he could seek among his juniors a partner of citizen status, who could certainly not be forced and who might be totally resistant to even the most disguised kind of purchase. If he was to succeed in seducing this boy (or if later, as a mature man, he was to seduce a youth), he could do so only by *earning* hero-worship.[38]

This is why, when Greek writers "idealize" eros and treat the phys-ical act as the "lowest" ingredient in a rich and complex relationship

[33] E.g. J. D. Beazley, *Greek Vases in Poland* (Oxford, 1928), pl. 19.1, *Corpus Vasorum Antiquorum*, Italy VIII, III Ic. 1.38.

[34] E.g. B. Graef and E. Langlotz, *Die antiken Vasen von der Akropolis zu Athen* 1 (Berlin, 1925), pl. 85 (no. 1639), 90 (no. 1913).

[35] Cf. G. Devereux, "Greek Pseudo-Homosexuality and the 'Greek Miracle,'" *Symbolae Osloenses* xlii (1967), 69–92.

[36] The Greeks never suggested that it originated among "decadent Asiatics"; Herodotus i 135 regards the Persians as having learned pederasty from the Greeks.

[37] That is not to say that no one was exclusively or predominantly homosexual; Pausanias and Agathon maintained a relationship that sounds rather like a homosexual "marriage" (Plato, *Symposium* 193B).

[38] E.g. [Xenophon], *Cynegeticus* 12.20 on the efforts of the lover to excel when the eyes of his boy are on him.

which comprises mutual devotion, reciprocal sacrifice, emulation, and the awakening of sensibility, imagination and intellect, they look not to what most of us understand by sexual love but to the desire of an older for a younger male and the admiration felt by the younger for the older. It is noticeable also that in art and literature inhibitions operate in much the same way as in the romantic treatment of heterosexual love in our own tradition. When physical gratification is directly referred to, the younger partner is said to "grant favours" or "render services"; but a great deal is written about homosexual eros from which the innocent reader would not easily gather that any physical contact at all was involved. Aeschines, who follows Aeschylus and Classical sentiment generally in treating the relation between Achilles and Patroclus in the *Iliad* as homoerotic, commends Homer for leaving it to "the educated among his hearers" to perceive the nature of the relation from the extravagant grief expressed by Achilles at the death of Patroclus.[39] The vase-painters very frequently depict the giving of presents by men to boys and the "courting" of boys (a mild term for an approach which includes putting a hand on the boy's genitals), but their pursuit of the subject to the stage of erection, let alone penetration, in a variety of positions, is commonplace.[40]

We also observe in the field of homosexual relations the operation of the "dual standard of morality" which so often characterizes societies in which segregation of the sexes is minimal.[41] If a Greek admitted that he was in love with a boy, he could expect sympathy and encouragement from his friends, and if it was known that he had attained his goal, envy and admiration. The boy, on the other hand, was praised if he retained his chastity, and he could expect strong disapproval if he was thought in any way to have taken the initiative in attracting a lover. The probable implication is that neither partner would actually say anything about the physical aspect of their relationship to anyone else,[42] nor would they expect any question about it to be put to them or any allusion to it made in their presence.

## 7  CLASS AND STATUS

Once we have accepted the universality of homosexual relations in Greek society as a fact, it surprises us to learn that if a man had at

[39] Aeschines i 142.

[40] *Corpus Vasorum Antiquorum*, Italy III, III He 50.13 (two youths), Italy XL, III I 3.2 (group of youths); H. Licht, *Sittengeschichte Griechenlands*, iii (Dresden and Zürich, 1928), figg. 192, 199 (boys).

[41] See especially Plato, *Symposium* 182A–183D.

[42] No doubt an ungentlemanly lover would boast of success, as suggested by Plato, *Phaedrus* 232A.

any time in his life prostituted himself to another man for money he was debarred from exercising his political rights.[43] If he was an alien, he had no political rights to exercise, and was in no way penalized for living as a male prostitute, so long as he paid the prostitution tax levied upon males and females alike.[44] It was therefore not the physical act *per se* which incurred penalty, but the incorporation of the act in a certain deliberately chosen role which could only be fully defined with reference to the nationality and status of the participants.

This datum illustrates an attitude which was fundamental to Greek society. They tended to believe that one's moral character is formed in the main by the circumstances in which one lives: the wealthy man is tempted to arrogance and oppression, the poor man to robbery and fraud, the slave to cowardice and petty greed. A citizen compelled by great and sudden economic misfortune to do work of a kind normally done by slaves was shamed because his assumption of a role which so closely resembled a slave's role altered his relationship to his fellow-citizens.[45] Since prostitutes were usually slaves or aliens, to play the role of a prostitute was, as it were, to remove oneself from the citizen-body, and the formal exclusion of a male prostitute from the rights of a citizen was a penalty for disloyalty to the community in his choice of role.

Prostitution is not easily defined—submission in gratitude for gifts, services or help is not so different in kind from submission in return for an agreed fee[46]—nor was it easily proved in a Greek city, unless people were willing (as they were not)[47] to come forward and testify that they had helped to cause a citizen's son to incur the penalty of disenfranchisement. A boy involved in a homosexual relationship absolutely untainted by mercenary considerations could still be called a prostitute by his family's enemies, just as the term can be recklessly applied today by unfriendly neighbours or indignant parents to a girl who sleeps with a lover. He could also be called effeminate; not always rightly, since athletic success seems to have been a powerful stimulus to his potential lovers, but it is possible (and the visual arts do not help us much here) that positively feminine characteristics in the appearance, movements and manner of boys and youths played a larger part in the ordinary run of homosexual activity than the idealization and

---

[43] Aeschines i *passim*.

[44] Aeschines i 119 f.

[45] Cf. the embarrassment of the speaker of Demosthenes lvii 44f. on the "servile and humble" function to which his mother had been compelled by poverty (she was a wet-nurse).

[46] Cf. Aristophanes, *Wealth* (= "*Plutus*") 153–159.

[47] Cf. Aeschines i 45 f., on the difficulty of getting Timarchus' lover (or client) Misgolas to give evidence.

romanticisation of the subject in literature indicates. There were certainly circumstances in which homosexuality could be treated as a substitute for heterosexuality; a comic poet[48] says of the Greeks who besieged Troy for ten years, "they never saw a hetaira ... and ended up with arseholes wider than the gates of Troy." The homosexual courting scene which becomes so common in vase-paintings of the sixth century B.C.—the man touching the face and genitals of the boy, the boy indignantly grasping the man's wrists to push them away—first appears in the seventh century as a youth courting a woman.[49] A sixth-century vase in which all of a group of men except one are penetrating women shows the odd man out grasping his erect penis and approaching, with a gesture of entreaty, a youth—who starts to run away.[50] In so far as the "passive partner" in a homosexual act takes on himself the role of a woman, he was open to the suspicion, like the male prostitute, that he abjured his prescribed role as a future soldier and defender of the community.

The comic poets, like the orators, ridicule individuals for effeminacy, for participation in homosexual activity, or for both together; at the same time, the sturdy, wilful, roguish characters whom we meet in Aristophanes are not averse to handling and penetrating good-looking boys when the opportunity presents itself,[51] as a supplement to their busy and enjoyable heterosexual programmes. They represent a social class which, though in the main solidly prosperous, is below the level of most of the people we meet in reading Plato, and there is one obvious factor which we should expect to determine different sexual attitudes in different classes. The thorough-going segregation of women of citizen status was possible only in households which owned enough slaves and could afford to confine its womenfolk to a leisure enlivened only by the exercise of domestic crafts such as weaving and spinning. This degree of segregation was simply not possible in poorer families; the women who sold bread and vegetables in the market—Athenian women,[52] not resident aliens—were not segregated, and there must have been plenty of women in the demes of the Attic countryside who took a hand in work on the land and drove animals to market. No doubt convention required that they should protect each other's virtue by staying in pairs or groups as much as they could, but clearly the generalizations which I

---

[48] Eubulus, fr. 120.
[49] K. Schefold, *Myth and Legend in Early Greek Art* (English tr. London, 1966), pl. 27b.
[50] *Corpus Vasorum Antiquorum*, Germany XXXI, III Hd 143f.
[51] Aristophanes, *Birds* 136–143, *Knights* 1384–1387, *Wasps* 578.
[52] The bread-woman of Aristophanes, *Wasps* 1388–1414, is plainly of citizen status.

formulated in § 3 on the subject of segregation and the obstacles to love-affairs between citizens' sons and citizens' daughters lose their validity as one goes down the social scale. Where there are love-affairs, both boys and girls can have decided views—not enforceable *de jure*, but very important *de facto*—on whom they wish to marry. The girl in Aristophanes' *Ecclesiazusae* who waits impatiently for her young man's arrival while her mother is out may be much nearer the norm of Athenian life than those cloistered ladies who were "embarrassed by the presence even of a male relative." It would not be discordant with modern experience to believe that speakers in an Athenian law-court professed, and were careful to attribute to the jury, standards of propriety higher than the average member of the jury actually set himself.

## 8 PHILOSOPHERS AND OTHERS

Much Classical Greek philosophy is characterized by contempt for sexual intercourse, which the author of the Seventh Letter of Plato,[53] offended at the traditional association of sex with a deity, calls "the slavish and ugly pleasure wrongly called *aphrodisios*." Xenophon's Socrates, although disposed to think it a gift of beneficent providence that humans, unlike other mammals, can enjoy sex all the year round,[54] is wary of troubling the soul over what he regards as the minimum needs of the body.[55] Virtue reproached Vice, in Prodicus' allegory of the choice of Herakles,[56] for "forcing sexual activity before [a man] has a need of it." Antisthenes boasted[57] of having intercourse only with the most readily available woman (and the least desired by other men) "when my body needs it." One logical outcome of this attitude to sex is exemplified by Diogenes the Cynic, who was alleged to have masturbated in public when his penis erected itself,[58] as if he were scratching a mosquito-bite.[59] Another outcome was the doctrine (influential in Christianity, but not of Christian origin)[60] that a wise and virtuous man will not have intercourse except for the

---

[53] 335B; whether the author is Plato or not, does not matter in the present context.

[54] Xenophon, *Memorabilia* i 4.12.

[55] Ibid., i 3.14.

[56] Ibid., ii 1.30.

[57] Xenophon, *Symposium* 4.38.

[58] Plutarch, *De Stoicorum Repugnantiis* 1044B.

[59] Socrates was said to have compared Critias' eros for Euthydemus to the desire of a pig to rub its itching back against a rock (Xenophon, *Memorabilia* i 2.30). Democritus fr. B 127 (Diels-Kranz) is evidence for high valuation of scratching rather than low valuation of sex.

[60] Musonius Rufus (p. 63.17 ff., Hense) can hardly be supposed to exhibit Christian influence.

purpose of procreating legitimate offspring, a doctrine which necessarily proscribes much heterosexual and all homosexual activity.

Although philosophical preoccupation with the contrast between "body" and "soul" had much to do with these developments, we can discern, as the ground from which these philosophical plants sprouted, Greek admiration for invulnerability, hostility towards the diversion of resources to the pursuit of pleasure, and disbelief in the possibility that dissimilar ways of feeling and behaving can be synthesised in the same person without detracting from his attainment of the virtues expected of a selfless defender of his city. It is also clear that the refusal of Greek law and society to treat a woman as a responsible person, while on the one hand it encouraged a complacent acceptance of prostitution and concubinage, on the other hand led to the classification of sexual activity as a male indulgence which could be reduced to a minimum by those who were not self-indulgent.[61]

Comedy presents a different picture. The speech put into the mouth of Aristophanes in Plato's *Symposium* differs from the speeches of the other characters in that work by treating eros as the individual's passionate search for the "other half" of himself (or of herself). This view of eros is firmly rejected by Plato,[62] who presumably chose Aristophanes as its proponent because it seemed to him the view which one would expect of a comic poet; and it may have seemed so to him because comedy looked at sexual behaviour through the eyes of the lower middle class (cf. § 7). Certainly in comedy of the late fourth century we find much which accords with Plato's Aristophanes, notably the remorse of a sensitive young man who realizes that he has adopted a "dual standard" in condemning his wife and excusing himself.[63] But we have to consider also Aristophanes' *Lysistrata*, produced in 411. There is much fantasy and inconsequentiality in the play, more, indeed, than is commonly observed—and the fact that citizens denied intercourse by their wives are apparently unable to turn their attention to slaves, prostitutes or boys, or even to masturbation,[64] may be no more than inconsequentiality; Aristophanic comedy easily ignores all those

[61] Modern Christian critics of the "permissive society" sometimes speak as if they really believed (and maybe they do) that an extra-marital sexual relationship with a person of the opposite sex is the same sort of experience as sinking one's teeth into a tender steak.

[62] Plato, *Symposium* 205DE, 212C, *Laws* 731D–732B.

[63] Charisius in Menander, *Epitrepontes* 588–612 (Körte).

[64] However inadequate a substitute for sexual intercourse masturbation may be, it is Aristophanes himself, by representing the Athenians and Spartans as creeping around in an unremitting state of erection, who forces us to ask, "Why don't they masturbate?" Cf. also Eubulus fr. 120 on the Greeks at Troy: "they masturbated for ten years…"

aspects of reality which would be inconvenient for the development of the comic plot. Yet when every allowance is made for that important comic convention, the central idea of the play, that a sex-strike by citizens' wives against their husbands can be imagined as having so devastating an effect, implies that the marital relationship was much more important in people's actual lives than we would have inferred simply from our knowledge of the law and our acquaintance with litigation about property and inheritance; more important, too, than could ever be inferred from a comprehensive survey of the varieties of sexual experience and attitude which were possible for the Greeks.

PART II

# Foucault and After: The Construction of Ancient Gender and Sexuality

# 6  The Social Body and the Sexual Body[†]

## DAVID HALPERIN

Plato's testimony and Caelius Aurelianus's testimony [not reprinted here] combine to make a basic conceptual and historical point. Homosexuality presupposes sexuality, and sexuality itself (as I shall argue in a moment) is a modern invention. Homosexuality presupposes sexuality because the very concept of homosexuality implies that there is a specifically sexual dimension to the human personality, a characterological seat within the individual of sexual acts, desires, and pleasures—a determinate source from which all sexual expression proceeds. Whether or not such a distinct and unified psychophysical entity actually exists, homosexuality (like heterosexuality, in this respect) necessarily assumes that it does: it posits sexuality as a constitutive principle of the self. Sexuality in this sense is not a purely descriptive term, a neutral representation of some objective state of affairs. Rather, it serves to interpret and to organize human experience, and it performs quite a lot of conceptual work.

First of all, sexuality defines itself as a separate, sexual domain within the larger field of man's psychophysical nature. Second, sexuality effects the conceptual demarcation and isolation of that domain from other areas of personal and social life that have traditionally cut across it, such as carnality, venery, libertinism, virility, passion, amorousness, eroticism, intimacy, love, affection, appetite, and desire—to name but a few of the older claimants to territories more recently staked out by sexuality. Finally, sexuality generates sexual identity: it endows each of us with an individual sexual nature, with a personal essence defined (at least in part) in specifically sexual terms.[1] Now sexual identity, so conceived, is not to be

---

[†] Originally published in *One Hundred Years of Homosexuality and Other Essays on Greek Love* (New York and London 1990), 24–38.
[1] See Jeffrey Weeks, "Questions of Identity," in Caplan, 31–51.

confused with gender identity or gender role: indeed, one of the chief conceptual functions of sexuality is to distinguish, once and for all, sexual identity from matters of gender—to decouple, as it were, *kinds* of sexual predilection from *degrees* of masculinity and femininity. That is precisely what makes sexuality alien to the spirit of ancient Mediterranean cultures. For as the example of Caelius Aurelianus makes plain, ancient sexual typologies generally derived their criteria for categorizing people not from sex but from gender: they tended to construe sexual desire as normative or deviant according to whether it impelled social actors to conform to or to violate their conventionally defined gender roles.[2]

Sexuality, then, is not, as it often pretends to be, a universal feature of human life in every society. For as the word is used today (outside the life sciences, at least)[3] sexuality does not refer to some positive physical property—such as the property of being anatomically sexed—that exists independently of culture; it does not rightly denote some common aspect or attribute of bodies. Unlike sex, which is a natural fact, sexuality is a cultural production:[4] it represents the *appropriation* of the human body and of its erogenous zones by an ideological discourse. Far from reflecting a purely natural and uninterpreted recognition of some familiar facts about us, sexuality represents a peculiar turn in conceptualizing, experiencing, and institutionalizing human nature, a turn that (along with many other developments) marks the transition to modernity in northern and western Europe. As Robert Padgug, in a classic essay on sexuality in history, puts it,

> what we consider "sexuality" was, in the pre-bourgeois world, a group of acts and institutions not necessarily linked to one another, or, if they were linked, combined in ways very different from our own. Intercourse, kinship, and the family, and gender, did not form anything like a "field" of sexuality. Rather, each group of sexual acts was connected directly or indirectly—that is, formed part of—institutions and thought patterns which we tend to view as

---

[2] Gleason trenchantly analyzes many other examples of this outlook, which even today remains largely unchanged in Mediterranean cultures: see Gilmore (1987), esp. 10–12.

[3] For some definitions of sex and sexuality as biological concepts, see Lynn Margulis, Dorion Sagan, and Lorraine Olendzenski, "What is Sex?" in *The Origin and Evolution of Sex*, ed. H. O. Halvorson and Alberto Monroy (New York, 1985), 69–85.

[4] For a similar insistence on the distinction between sex and sexuality, see Davidson (1987–8), 23–25; Henderson (1988), 1250. Because so much of my argument derives from Foucault, I should point out that Foucault himself decisively abandoned the distinction between sex and sexuality, as I have drawn it. Not only is Foucault's final conception of "sex" much less positivistic (he categorically denies that "sex" is a biological fact), but his own understanding of the distinction between "sex" and "sexuality" reverses the sequence postulated here: "sexuality," on his view, arises in the eighteenth century and eventually produces "sex," as an idea internal to its own apparatus, only in the nineteenth century. See Foucault (1978), 152–57; (1980b), 190, 210–11.

political, economic, or social in nature, and the connections cut across our idea of sexuality as a thing, detachable from other things, and as a separate sphere of private existence.[5]

Where there is no such conception of sexuality, there can be no conception of either homo- or heterosexuality—no notion that human beings are individuated at the level of their sexuality, that they differ from one another in their sexuality or belong to different types of being by virtue of their sexuality.[6]

The invention of homosexuality (and, ultimately, of heterosexuality) had therefore to await, in the first place, the eighteenth-century discovery and definition of sexuality as the total ensemble of physiological and psychological mechanisms governing the individual's genital functions and the concomitant identification of that ensemble with a specially developed part of the brain and nervous system; it had also to await, in the second place, the nineteenth-century interpretation of sexuality as a singular "instinct" or "drive," a force that shapes our conscious life according to its own unassailable logic and thereby determines, at least in part, the character and personality of each one of us.[7] Sexuality, on this latter interpretation, turns out to be something more than an endogenous principle of motivation outwardly expressed by the performance of sexual acts; it is a mute power subtly and deviously at work throughout a wide range of human behaviors, attitudes, tastes, choices, gestures, styles, pursuits, judgments, and utterances. Sexuality is thus the inmost part of an individual human nature. It is the feature of a person that takes longest to get to know well, and knowing it renders transparent and intelligible to the knower the person to whom it belongs. Sexuality

---

[5] Padgug, 16. Compare duBois (1984); Moodie, 228: "We tend to think of sexuality as a psychological unity. Different aspects of the self such as 'desire', 'moral ideals', 'proper conduct', 'gender attitudes', 'personal relationships', 'mental images', and 'physical sensations' tend to be tied together by us to form a particular sexual character. With the self thus sexually defined, homosexuality and heterosexuality ... are seen as specific personality types."

[6] Padgug, 8, analyzes the connection between the modern interpretation of sexuality as an autonomous domain and the modern construction of sexual identities thus: "the most commonly held twentieth-century assumptions about sexuality imply that it is a separate category of existence (like 'the economy,' or 'the state,' other supposedly independent spheres of reality), almost identical with the sphere of private life. Such a view necessitates the location of sexuality within the individual as a fixed essence, leading to a classic division of individual and society and to a variety of psychological determinisms, and, often enough, to a full-blown biological determinism as well. These in turn involve the enshrinement of contemporary sexual categories as universal, static, and permanent, suitable for the analysis of all human beings and all societies."

[7] See Féray, 247–51; Laqueur; Davidson (1986/7), 258–62; also, Weeks (1980), 13 (paraphrasing Foucault): "our culture has developed a notion of sexuality linked to reproduction and genitality and to 'deviations' from these. ...." The biological conceptualization of "sexuality" as an instinct is neatly disposed of by Tripp, 10–21.

holds the key to unlocking the deepest mysteries of the human personality: it lies at the center of the hermeneutics of the self.[8]

Before the scientific construction of "sexuality" as a supposedly positive, distinct, and constitutive feature of individual human beings—an autonomous system within the physiological and psychological economy of the human organism—certain kinds of sexual *acts* could be individually evaluated and categorized, and so could certain sexual tastes or inclinations, but there was no conceptual apparatus available for identifying a person's fixed and determinate sexual *orientation*, much less for assessing and classifying it.[9] That human beings differ, often markedly, from one another in their sexual tastes in a great variety of ways (of which sexual object-choice—the liking for a sexual partner of a specific sex—is only one, and not necessarily the most significant one) is an unexceptionable and, indeed, an ancient observation;[10] but it is not immediately evident that differences in sexual

---

[8] See Foucault (1978), 68–69; (1980a), vii–xi; (1985), 35–52.

[9] See Foucault (1978), 43: "As defined by the ancient civil or canonical codes, sodomy was a category of forbidden acts; their perpetrator was nothing more than the juridical subject of them. The nineteenth-century homosexual became a personage, a past, a case history, and a childhood, in addition to being a type of life, a life form, and a morphology, with an indiscreet anatomy and possibly a mysterious physiology. Nothing that went into his total composition was unaffected by his sexuality. It was everywhere present in him: at the root of all his actions because it was their insidious and indefinitely active principle; written immodestly on his face and body because it was a secret that always gave itself away. It was consubstantial with him, less as a habitual sin than as a singular nature." Cf. Trumbach, 9; Weeks (1977), 12; Richard Sennett, *The Fall of Public Man* (New York, 1977), 6–8; Padgug, 13–14; Féray, 246–47; Schnapp (1981), 116 (speaking of Attic vase-paintings): "One does not paint acts that characterize persons so much as behaviors that distinguish groups"; Payer [(1984)], 40–44, esp. 40–41: "there is no word in general usage in the penitentials for homosexuality as a category. ... Furthermore, the distinction between homosexual acts and people who might be called homosexuals does not seem to be operative in these manuals. ..." (also, 14–15, 140–53); Bynum (1986), 406; Petersen [(1986)].
In this light, the significance of Westphal's famous article [(1870)] is clear: the crucial and decisive break with tradition comes when Westphal defines "contrary sexual feeling" not in terms of its outward manifestations but in terms of its inward dynamics, its distinctive *orientation* of the inner life of the individual. Apologizing in a note for the necessity of coining a new formula, Westphal explains, "I have chosen the designation 'contrary sexual feeling' at the suggestion of an esteemed colleague, distinguished in the field of philology and classical studies, inasmuch as we were unable to succeed in constructing shorter and more apt correlatives. The phrase is intended to express the fact that 'contrary sexual feeling' does not always coincidentally concern the sexual drive as such but simply *the feeling of being alienated, with one's entire inner being, from one's own sex*—a less developed stage, as it were, of the pathological phenomenon" (p. 107n.; my emphasis: I wish to thank Linda Frisch and Ira Levine for assisting me with the translation of this passage; a nearly identical version has now been provided by Herzer [(1985)], 18). See Davidson (1987–8), 21–22, who identifies a "psychiatric style of reasoning that begins, roughly speaking, in the second half of the nineteenth century, a period during which rules for the production of true discourses about sexuality change radically. Sexual identity ... is now a matter of impulses, tastes, aptitudes, satisfactions, and psychic traits."

[10] For attestations to the strength of individual preferences (even to the point of exclusivity) on the part of Greek males for a sexual partner of one sex rather than another, see, e.g., Theognis, 1367–68; Euripides, *Cyclops* 583–84; Xenophon, *Anabasis* 7.4.7–8; Aeschines,

preference are by their very nature more revealing about the temperament of individual human beings, more significant determinants of personal identity, than, for example, differences in dietary preference.[11] And yet, it would never occur to us to refer a person's dietary object-choice to some innate, characterological disposition or to see in his or her strongly expressed and even unvarying preference for the white meat of chicken the symptom of a profound psychophysical orientation, leading us to identify him or her in contexts quite removed from that of the eating of food as, say (to continue the practice of combining Greek and Latin roots), a "pectoriphage" or a "stethovore"; nor would we be likely to inquire further, making nicer discriminations according to whether an individual's predilection for chicken breasts expressed itself in a tendency to eat them quickly or slowly, seldom or often, alone or in company, under normal circumstances or only in periods of great stress, with a guilty or a clear conscience, beginning in earliest childhood or originating with a gastronomic trauma suffered in adolescence. If such questions did occur to us, moreover, I very much doubt whether we would turn to the academic disciplines of anatomy, neurology, clinical psychology, genetics, or sociobiology in the hope of obtaining a clear causal solution to them. That is because (1) we regard the liking for certain foods as a matter of taste; (2) we currently lack a theory of taste; and (3) in the absence of a theory we do not normally subject our behavior to intense, scientific or aetiological, scrutiny.[12]

In the same way, it never occurred to pre-modern cultures to ascribe a person's sexual tastes to some positive, structural, or constitutive feature of his or her personality.[13] Just as we tend to assume that

1.41, 195; the *Life of Zeno* by Antigonus of Carystus, cited by Athenaeus, 13.563e; the fragment of Seleucus quoted by Athenaeus, 15.697de (= Powell, 176); an anonymous dramatic fragment cited by Plutarch, *Moralia* 766f–767a (= Nauck, 906, #355; Kock, III, 467, #360); Athenaeus, 12.540e, 13.601e and ff.; Achilles Tatius, 2.35.2–3; pseudo-Lucian, *Erôtes* 9–10; Firmicus Maternus, *Mathesis* 7.15.1–2; and a number of epigrams, by various hands, contained in the *Palatine Anthology*; 5.19, 65, 116, 208, 277, 278; 11.216; 12.7, 17, 41, 87, 145, 192, 198, and *passim*. See, generally, Dover (1978), 62–63; Boswell (1982–3), 98–101; Winkler (1989a); and, for a list of passages, Claude Courouve, *Tableau synoptique de références à l'amour masculin: Auteurs grecs et latins* (Paris: author, 1986).

[11] Foucault (1985), 10, 51–52, remarks that it would be interesting to determine exactly when in the evolving course of Western cultural history sex became more morally problematic than eating; see, also, Foucault (1983), 229; (1986), 143. For a criticism of Foucault's answer to that question, see "Two Views of Greek Love," [Halperin (1990), 54–71].

[12] Hilary Putnam, *Reason, Truth and History* (Cambridge, 1981), 150–55, in the course of analyzing the various criteria by which we judge matters of taste to be "subjective," implies that we are right to consider sexual preferences more thoroughly constitutive of the human personality than dietary preferences, but his argument remains circumscribed, as Putnam himself emphasizes, by highly culture-specific assumptions about sex, food, and personhood.

[13] Hence, some students of classical Greek medicine prefer to speak of the authors of the gynaecological treatises in the Hippocratic corpus as concerned exclusively with human "genitality" rather than "sexuality": see, for example, Manuli (1980), 394; (1983), 152; Rousselle (1980), 1092. For similar arguments about Renaissance painting, to the effect that it is con-

human beings are not individuated at the level of dietary preference
and that we all, despite many pronounced and frankly acknowledged
differences from one another in dietary habits, share the same fundamental set of alimentary appetites, and hence the same "dieticity"
or "edility," so most pre-modern and non-Western cultures, despite
an awareness of the range of possible variations in human sexual
behavior, refuse to individuate human beings at the level of sexual
preference and assume, instead, that we all share the same fundamental set of sexual appetites, the same "sexuality." For most of the
world's inhabitants, in other words, "sexuality" is no more a fact of
life than "dieticity." Far from being a necessary or intrinsic con-
stituent of the eternal grammar of human subjectivity, "sexuality"
seems to be one of those cultural fictions which in every society give
human beings access to themselves as meaningful actors in their
world, and which are thereby objectivated.[14]

cerned (*pace* Leo Steinberg, *The Sexuality of Christ in Renaissance Art and Modern Oblivion*
[New York, 1983]) not with Jesus's sexuality but with his genitality, see Bynum (1986), 405–10;
Davidson (1987–8), 25–32.

[14] In order to avoid misunderstanding, let me emphasize that I am not saying it would be
outlandish to categorize people according to dietary preference; I do not believe my analogy
between dietary and sexual object-choice shows that distinctions based on object-choice are
absurd and that we should place no more credence in sexual categories than in dietary ones.
On the contrary, it is easy to enumerate forms of dietary behavior whose subjects we tend to
classify as specific types of human beings; there are many conditions under which we refer a
person's dietary behavior, even today, to some constitutive feature of his or her personality: if,
for example, I eat so little as virtually to starve myself, I am identified as an "anorectic," which
is to say that I become a particular *species* of person, characterologically different from other
people, with a peculiar case history, presumed psychology, and so forth—just as if I have sex
"too much" or "too often," I am regarded as "sexually compulsive" or, even, as "*a* sexual compulsive," yet another species of humankind. Whereas some aspects of one's dietary patterns
(e.g., preference for white meat) are considered unremarkable, and are therefore not marked,
others *are* marked, just as only some aspects of sexual behavior (e.g., homosexual object-
choice) are marked, whereas others (e.g., preference for persons with blue eyes) remain
unmarked. (I wish to thank George Chauncey for supplying me with this formulation of the
issue.) Moreover, a growing mass of historical data suggests that dietary categories have
indeed provided, in certain times and places, a viable basis on which to construct typologies
of human beings: see Bynum (1987), and for an example from relatively recent history of the
possible linkage between sexual and dietary morality, see Stephen Nissenbaum, *Sex, Diet, and
Debility in Jacksonian America: Sylvester Graham and Health Reform*, Contributions in
Medical History, 4 (Westport, CT: Greenwood Press, 1980).

My argument, then, is simply this: (1) there seems to be no way of proving that sexual preferences are more *fundamental* features of the human personality than dietary preferences; (2)
dietary preferences don't, for the most part, determine our personal identities nowadays; (3)
therefore, sexual preferences should not be thought of as intrinsic constituents of the personality; rather, sexual categories based on preference should be considered culturally contingent. Now contingency is not the same thing as absurdity. To be sure, so long as one's
notions of "truth" are connected—as Western notions have tended to be, since the
Renaissance—to notions of "nature" and "necessity," to what is naturally and necessarily and
always the case (whether human beings recognize it to be the case or not), there may be some
difficulty establishing that a traditional way of looking at things is grounded in culture rather
than in nature without *also* seeming to imply that it is false. But I am not claiming that it is

To say that sexual categories and identities are objectivated fictions is not to say that they are false or unreal, merely that they are not positive, natural, or essential features of the world, outside of history and culture. Homosexuals and heterosexuals do exist, after all, at least nowadays; they actually desire what they do: they are not deluded participants in some cultural charade, or victims of "false consciousness." Moreover, the modern term "homosexual" does indeed refer to any person, whether ancient or modern, who seeks sexual contact with another person of the same sex; it is not, strictly speaking, incorrect to predicate that term of some classical Greeks.[15] But the issue before us is not captured by the problematics of reference: it cannot be innocently reformulated as the issue of whether or not we can accurately apply our concept of homosexuality to the ancients—whether or not, that is, we can discover in the historical record of classical antiquity evidence of behaviors or psychologies that are amenable to classification in our own terms (obviously, we can, given the supposedly descriptive, trans-historical nature of those terms); the issue isn't even whether or not the ancients were able to express within the terms provided by their own conceptual schemes an experience of something approximating to homosexuality as we understand it today.[16] The real issue confronting any cultural historian of antiquity, and any critic of contemporary culture, is, first of all, how to recover the terms in which the experiences of individuals belonging to past societies were actually constituted and, second, how to measure and assess the differences between those terms and the ones we currently employ. For, as this very controversy over the scope and applicability of sexual categories illustrates, concepts in the human sciences—unlike in this respect, perhaps,

false to categorize people according to sexual object-choice, merely that it is not natural or necessary to do so; such classifications are, instead, just as contingent, arbitrary, and conventional as are classifications of people according to dietary object-choice. Both schemes are possible; neither is inevitable. To maintain that something isn't a fact, in short, is not to maintain that it's a lie. We are concerned here neither with truths nor falsehoods but with representations, and our willingness to accept or believe in representations generally has to do more with their representational power than with their truth.

[15] I accept, in this sense, the point insisted upon by K. J. Dover: "The fact that the object of homosexual desire in the Greek world was almost always, like Ganymede, adolescent does not justify … [the] denial that [paederasty] is homosexuality. Homosexuality is a genus definable by the sex of the person participating (in reality or in fantasy) in action leading towards genital orgasm, and the predilections of a given society at a given time constitute one or more species of the genus" (*Journal of Hellenic Studies*, 104 [1984], 240).

[16] Thus, Boswell (1982–3), 99n., argues that the term "paederast," at least as it is applied to Gnathon by Longus in *Daphnis and Chloe* 4.11, is "obviously a conventional term for 'homosexual,'" and he would presumably place a similar construction on *paiderastês* and *philerastês* in the myth of Plato's Aristophanes, dismissing my interpretation as a terminological quibble or as a misguided attempt to reify lexical entities into categories of experience.

concepts in the natural sciences (such as gravity)—do not merely describe reality but, at least partly, constitute it.[17] What this implies about the issue before us may sound paradoxical but it is, I believe, profound—or, at least, worth pondering: although there have been, in many different times and places (including classical Greece), persons who sought sexual contact with other persons of the same sex as themselves, it is only within the last hundred years or so that such persons (or some portion of them, at any rate) have been homosexuals.

Instead of attempting to trace the history of "homosexuality" as if it were a *thing*, therefore, we might more profitably analyze how the significance of same-sex sexual contacts has been variously constructed over time by members of human living-groups. Such an analysis will probably lead us (and we must be prepared for this) into a plurality of only partly overlapping social and conceptual territories, a series of cultural formations that shift as their constituents change, combine in different sequences, or compose new patterns. The sort of history that will result from this procedure will no longer be gay history as John Boswell tends to conceptualize it (i.e., as the history of gay people), but it will not fail to be gay history in a different, and perhaps more relevant, sense: for it will be history written from the perspective of contemporary gay interests—just as feminist history is not, properly speaking, the history of women but history that reflects the concerns of contemporary feminism.[18] In the following paragraphs I shall attempt to exemplify the approach I am advocating by drawing, in very crude outline, a picture of the cultural formation underlying the classical Athenian institution of paederasty, a picture whose details will have to be filled in at some later point if this aspect of ancient Greek social relations is ever to be understood historically.[19]

Let me begin by observing that the attitudes and behaviors publicly displayed by the citizens of Athens (to whom the surviving evidence for the classical period effectively restricts our power to generalize) tend to portray sex not as a collective enterprise in which two or more

[17] For a philosophical defense and qualification of this claim (and of other, similarly "constructionist," claims), see Ian Hacking, "Making Up People," in Heller, Sosna, and Wellbery [(1986)], 222–36, 347–48.
[18] See Joan Kelly, "The Social Relation of the Sexes: Methodological Implications of Woman's History," in *Women, History, and Theory: The Essays of Joan Kelly* (Chicago, 1984), 1–18.
[19] See, now Winkler (1989a). See, generally, Henderson (1988)—the single best, most comprehensive and reliable introduction to Greek sexual *mores* for non-specialists.

persons jointly engage but rather as an action performed by one person upon another.[20] I hasten to emphasize that this formulation does not purport to describe positively what the experience of sex was "really" like for all members of Athenian society but to indicate how sex is *represented* by those utterances and actions of free adult males that were intended to be overheard and witnessed by other free adult males.[21] Sex, as it is constituted by this public, masculine discourse, is either act or impact (according to one's point of view): it is not knit up in a web of mutuality, not something one invariably has *with* someone. Even the verb *aphrodisiazein*, meaning "to have sex" or "to take active sexual pleasure," is carefully differentiated into an active and a passive form; the active form occurs, tellingly, in a late antique list (that we nonetheless have good reason to consider representative for ancient Mediterranean culture, rather than eccentric to it)[22] of acts that "do not regard one's neighbors but only the subjects themselves and are not done in regard to or through others: namely, speaking, singing, dancing, fist-fighting, competing, hanging oneself, dying, being crucified, diving, finding a treasure, having sex, vomiting, moving one's bowels, sleeping, laughing, crying, talking to the gods, and the like."[23] As John J. Winkler, in a commentary on this passage, observes, "It is not that second parties are not present at some of these events (speaking, boxing, competing, having sex, being crucified, flattering one's favorite divinity), but that their successful achievement does not depend on the cooperation, much less the benefit, of a second party."[24]

Not only is sex in classical Athens not intrinsically relational or collaborative in character; it is, further, a deeply polarizing experience: it effectively divides, classifies, and distributes its participants into distinct and radically opposed categories. Sex possesses this valence, apparently, because it is conceived to center essentially on, and to define itself around, an asymmetrical gesture, that of the penetration of the body of one person by the body—and, specifically, by

[20] See, generally, Dover (1978), 16, 84–106; Foucault (1985), 46–47.

[21] On the characteristic failure of "culturally dominant ideologies" actually to dominate all sectors of a society, and for a demonstration of their greater pertinence to the dominant than to the dominated classes, see Nicholas Abercrombie, Stephen Hill, and Bryan S. Turner, *The Dominant Ideology Thesis* (London, 1980), esp. 70–127. For the documentation of a particular instance, see R. M. Smith, "Marriage Processes in the English Past: some Continuities," in *The World We have Gained: Histories of Population and Social structure*, ed. Lloyd Bonfield, Richard M. Smith, and Keith Wrightson (Oxford, 1986), 43–99, esp. 46–47.

[22] See Winkler (1989b).

[23] Artemidorus, *Oneirocritica* 1.2 (pp. 8.21–9.4 pack).

[24] Winkler (1989b).

the phallus[25]—of another. Sex is not only polarizing, however; it is also hierarchical. For the insertive partner is construed as a sexual agent, whose phallic penetration of another person's body expresses sexual "activity," whereas the receptive partner is construed as a sexual patient, whose submission to phallic penetration expresses sexual "passivity." Sexual "activity," moreover, is thematized as domination: the relation between the "active" and the "passive" sexual partner is thought of as the same kind of relation as that obtaining between social superior and social inferior.[26] "Active" and "passive" sexual roles are therefore necessarily isomorphic with superordinate and subordinate social status; hence, an adult, male citizen of Athens can have legitimate sexual relations only with statutory minors (his inferiors not in age but in social and political status): the proper targets of his sexual desire include, specifically, women, boys, foreigners, and slaves—all of them persons who do not enjoy the same legal and political rights and privileges that he does.[27] Furthermore, what a citizen does in bed reflects the differential in status that distinguishes him from his sexual partner: the citizen's superior prestige and authority express themselves in his sexual precedence—in his power to initiate a sexual act, his right to obtain pleasure from it, and his assumption of an insertive rather than a receptive sexual role. (Even if a sexual act does not involve physical penetration, it still remains hierarchically polarized by the distribution of phallic pleasure: the partner whose pleasure is promoted is considered "active," while the partner who puts his or her body *at the*

[25] I say "phallus" rather than "penis" because (1) what qualifies as a phallus in this discursive system does not always turn out to be a penis (see note 44, below) and (2) even when phallus and penis have the same extension, or reference, they still do not have the same intension, or meaning: "Phallus" betokens not a specific item of the male anatomy *simpliciter* but that same item *taken under the description* of a cultural signifier; (3) hence, the meaning of "phallus" is ultimately determined by its function in the larger socio-sexual discourse: i.e., it is that which penetrates, that which enables its possessor to play an "active" sexual role, and so forth: see Rubin (1975), 190–92.

[26] Foucault (1985), 215, puts it very well: "sexual relations—always conceived in terms of the model act of penetration, assuming a polarity that opposed activity and passivity—were seen as being of the same type as the relationship between a superior and a subordinate, an individual who dominates and one who is dominated, one who commands and one who complies, one who vanquishes and one who is vanquished."

[27] In order to avoid misunderstanding, I should emphasize that by calling all persons belonging to these four groups "statutory minors," I do not wish either to suggest that they enjoyed the *same* status as one another or to obscure the many differences in status that could obtain between members of a single group—e.g., between a wife and a courtesan—differences that may not have been perfectly isomorphic with the legitimate modes of their sexual use. Nonetheless, what is striking about Athenian social usage is the tendency to collapse such distinctions as did indeed obtian between different categories of social subordinates and to create a single oppostions between them all, *en masse*, and the class of adult male citizens: on this point, see Golden (1985), 101 and 102, n. 38.

*service* of another's pleasure is deemed "passive"—read "pene-trated," in the culture's unselfconscious ideological shorthand.) What Paul Veyne has said about the Romans can apply equally well to the classical Athenians: they were indeed puritans when it came to sex, but (unlike modern bourgeois Westerners) they were not puritans about conjugality and reproduction; rather, like many Mediterranean peoples, they were puritans about virility.[28]

When the sexual system of the classical Athenians is described in that fashion, as though it constituted a separate sphere of life governed by its own internal laws, it appears merely exotic or bizarre, one of the many curiosities recorded in the annals of ethnography. But if, instead of treating Athenian sexual attitudes and practices as expressions of ancient Greek "sexuality" (conceived, in modern terms, as an autonomous domain), we situate them in the larger social context in which they were embedded, they will at once disclose their systematic coherence. For the "sexuality" of the classical Athenians, far from being independent and detached from "politics" (as we conceive sexuality to be), was constituted by the very principles on which Athenian public life was organized. In fact, the correspondences in classical Athens between sexual norms and social practices were so strict that an inquiry into Athenian "sexuality" *per se* would be non-sensical: such an inquiry could only obscure the phenomenon it was intended to elucidate, for by isolating sexual norms from social practices it would conceal the sole context in which the sexual protocols of the classical Athenians make any sense—namely, the structure of the Athenian polity.

In classical Athens a relatively small group made up of the adult male citizens held a virtual monopoly of social power and constituted a clearly defined élite within the political and social life of the city-state. The extraordinary polarization of sexual roles in classical Athens merely reflects the marked division in the Athenian polity between this socially superordinate group, composed of citizens, and various subordinate groups (all lacking full civil rights, though not all equally subordinate), composed respectively of women, foreigners, slaves, and children (the latter three groups comprising persons of both sexes). Sex between members of the superordinate group was

[28] Veyne (1978), 55, and (1985). Cf. Alan Dundes, Jerry W. Leach, and Bora Özkök, "The Strategy of Turkish Boys' Verbal Dueling Rhymes," *Journal of American Folklore*, 83 (1970), 325–49, supplemented and qualified by Mark Glazer, "On Verbal Dueling Among Turkish Boys," *Journal of American Folklore*, 89 (1976), 87–89; J. M. Carrier, "Mexican Male Bisexuality," in Klein and Wolf [(1985)], 75–85; De Martino and Schmitt, esp. 3–22; Michael Herzfeld, *The Poetics of Manhood: Contest and Identity in a Cretan Mountain Village* (Princeton, 1985); now, Gilmore (1987).

virtually inconceivable, whereas sex between a member of the super-ordinate group and a member of any one of the subordinate groups mirrored in the minute details of its hierarchical arrangement, as we have seen, the relation of structured inequality that governed the lovers' wider social interaction.[29]

Sex in classical Athens, then, was not a simply a collaboration in some private quest for mutual pleasure that absorbed or obscured, if only temporarily, the social identities of its participants. On the contrary, sex was a manifestation of personal status, a declaration of social identity; sexual behavior did not so much express inward dispositions or inclinations (although, of course, it did also do that) as it served to position social actors in the places assigned to them, by virtue of their political standing, in the hierarchical structure of the Athenian polity. Far from being interpreted as an expression of commonality, as a sign of some shared sexual status or identity, sex between social superior and social inferior was a miniature drama of polarization which served to measure and to define the social distance between them. To assimilate both the senior and the junior partner in a paederastic relationship to the same "(homo)sexuality," for example, would have struck a classical Athenian as no less bizarre than to classify a burglar as an "active criminal," his victim as a "passive criminal," and the two of them alike as partners in crime:[30] burglary—like sex, as the Greeks understood it—is, after all, a "non-relational" act. Each act of sex in classical Athens was no doubt an expression of real, personal desire on the part of the sexual actors involved, but their very desires had already been shaped by the shared cultural definition of sex as an activity that generally occurred only between a citizen and a non-citizen, between a person invested with full civil status and a statutory minor.

The social articulation of sexual desire in classical Athens fur-

---

[29] This account of the principles that structured sexual and social roles in classical Athens does not capture, of course, what the *sensation* of being in love was like: I am interested here not in erotic phenomenology but in the social articulation of sexual categories and in the public meanings attached to sex. Hence, my discussion of the male citizen's social and sexual precedence is not intended either to convey what an erotic relation felt like to him or to obscure the extent to which he may have experienced being in love as a *loss* of mastery—as "enslavement" to his beloved or to his own desire. Such feelings on a lover's part were evidently conventional (see Dover [1974], 208; Golden [1984], 313–16; Foucault [1985], 65–70) and possibly even cherished (see Xenophon, *Symposium* 4.14 and *Oeconomicus* 7.42). Indeed, the citizen-lover could afford to luxuriate in his sense of helplessness or erotic dependency precisely because his self-abandonment was at some level a chosen strategy and, in any case, his actual position of social preëminence was not in jeopardy.

[30] I have borrowed this analogy form Arno Schmitt, who uses it to convey what the modern sexual categories would look like form a traditional Islamic perspective: see De Martino and Schmitt, 19.

nishes a telling illustration of the interdependence in culture of social practices and subjective experiences. It thereby casts a strong and revealing light on the ideological dimension—the purely conventional and arbitrary character—of our own conceptions of sex and sexuality. The Greek record suggests that sexual choices do not always express the agent's individual essence or reveal the profound orientation of the inner life of a person, independent of social and political life. Quite the contrary: the sexual identities of the classical Athenians—their experiences of themselves as sexual actors and as desiring human beings—seem to have been inseparable from, if not determined by, their social identities, their public standing.[31] If the Greeks thought sex was "non-relational" in character, for example, that is because sex was so closely tied to differentials in the personal status of the sexual actors rather than to the expressive capacities of individual human subjects. Thus, the classical Greek record strongly supports the conclusion drawn (from a quite different body of evidence) by the French anthropologist Maurice Godelier: "it is not sexuality which haunts society, but society which haunts the body's sexuality."[32]

Even the relevant features of a sexual object in classical Athens were not so much determined by a physical typology of sexes as by the social articulation of power.[33] Sexual partners came in two significantly different kinds—not male and female but "active" and "passive," dominant and submissive.[34] That is why the currently fashionable distinction between homosexuality and heterosexuality (and, similarly, between "homosexuals" and "heterosexuals" as individual types) had no meaning for the classical Athenians: there were not, so far as they knew, two different kinds of "sexuality," two differently structured psychosexual states or modes of affective orientation, corresponding to the sameness or difference of the anatomical sexes of the persons engaged in a sexual act; there was, rather, but a single form of sexual experience which all free adult males shared[35]—making due allowance for variations in individual tastes, as one might make for individual

---

[31] See Dover (1978), 84; Henderson (1988), 1251: "Social status defined one's sexual identity and determined the proper sexual behavior that one was allowed."

[32] Godelier (1981), 17.

[33] On this general theme, see Golden (1985). For some comparative material, see Adam (1985), 22; De Martino and Schmitt, 3–22; Gill Shepherd, "Rank, Gender, and Homosexuality: Mombasa as a Key to Understanding Sexual Options," in Caplan, 240–70.

[34] The same point is made, in the course of an otherwise unenlightening (from the specialist's point of view) survey of Greek social relations, by Bernard I. Murstein, *Love, Sex, and Marriage through the Ages* (New York, 1974), 58.

[35] So Padgug, 3–4; Sartre, 12–14.

palates. This "universal" form of sexual experience could be looked at differently, to be sure, according to whether one viewed it from the perspective of the "active" or the "passive" sexual partner, but its essential nature did not change with such shifts in point of view.

In the Third Dithyramb by the classical poet Bacchylides, the Athenian hero Theseus, voyaging to Crete among the seven youths and seven maidens destined for the Minotaur and defending one of the maidens from the advances of the libidinous Cretan commander, warns him vehemently against molesting *any one* of the Athenian youths (*tin' êitheôn*: 43) — that is, any girl *or boy*. Conversely, the antiquarian *littérateur* Athenaeus, writing six or seven hundred years later, is amazed that Polycrates, the tyrant of Samos in the sixth century BC, did not send for any boys *or women* along with the other luxury articles he imported to Samos for his personal use during his reign, "despite his passion for relations with males" (12.540c–e).[36] Now *both* the notion that an act of heterosexual aggression in itself makes the aggressor suspect of homosexual tendencies *and* the mirror-opposite notion that a person with marked homosexual tendencies is bound to hanker after heterosexual contacts are nonsensical to us, associating as we do sexual object-choice with a determinate kind of "sexuality," a fixed sexual nature, but it would be a monumental task indeed to enumerate all the ancient documents in which the alternative "boy or woman" occurs with perfect nonchalance in an erotic context, as if the two were functionally interchangeable.[37]

A testimony to the imaginable extent of male indifference to the sex of sexual objects,[38] one that may be particularly startling to modern eyes, can be found in a marriage-contract from Hellenistic Egypt, dating to 92 BC. This not untypical document stipulates that "it shall not be lawful for Philiscus [the prospective husband] to bring home another wife in addition to Apollonia or to have a concubine *or boy-lover*. ..."[39]

---

[36] See Padgug, 3, who mistakenly ascribes Athenaeus's comment to Alexis of Samos (see *FGrHist* 539, fr. 2).

[37] See Dover (1978), 63–67, for an extensive, but admittedly partial, list. For some Roman examples, see Richardson [(1984)], 111. For ritual regulations, see Parker [(1983)], 94; Cole (1991).

[38] I wish to emphasize that I am *not* claiming that all Greek men felt such indifference: on the contrary, plenty of ancient evidence testifies to the strength of individual preferences for a sexual object of one sex rather than another (see note 10). But many ancient documents bear witness to a certain constitutional reluctance on the part of the Greeks to predict, in any given instance, the sex of another man's beloved merely on the basis of that man's past sexual behavior or previous pattern of sexual object-choice.

[39] *P. Tebtunis* I 104, translated by A. S. Hunt and C. C. Edgar, in *Women's Life in Greece and Rome*, ed. Mary Lefkowitz and Maureen B. Fant (Baltimore, 1982), 59–60; another translation is provided, along with a helpful discussion of the document and its typicality, by Pomeroy [(1984)], 87–89.

The possibility that one's husband might decide at some point during one's marriage to set up another household with his boyfriend evidently figured among the various potential domestic disasters that a prudent fiancée would be sure to anticipate and to indemnify herself against. A somewhat similar expectation is articulated in an entirely different context by Dio Chrysostom, a moralizing Greek orator from the late first century AD. In a speech denouncing the corrupt morals of city life, Dio asserts that even respectable women are so easy to seduce nowadays that men will soon tire of them and will turn their attention to boys instead—just as addicts progress inexorably from wine to hard drugs (7.150–152). According to Dio, then, paederasty is not simply a *pis aller*; it is not "caused," as many modern historians of the ancient Mediterranean appear to believe, by the supposed seclusion of women, by the practice (it was more likely an ideal) of locking them away in the inner rooms of their fathers' or husbands' houses and thereby preventing them from serving as sexual targets for adult men. In Dio's fantasy, at least, paederasty springs not from the insufficient but from the superabundant supply of sexually available women; the easier it is to have sex with women, on his view, the less desirable sex with women becomes, and the more likely men are to seek sexual pleasure with boys. Scholars sometimes describe the cultural formation underlying this apparent refusal by Greek males to discriminate categorically among sexual objects on the basis of anatomical sex as a bisexuality of penetration[40] or—even more intriguingly—as a heterosexuality indifferent to its object,[41,42] but I think it would be advisable not to speak of it as a sexuality at all but to describe it, rather, as

---

[40] "Une bisexualté de sabrage": Veyne (1978), 50–55; cf. the critique by MacMullen [(1983)], 491–97. Other scholars who describe the ancient behavioral phenomenon as "bisexuality" include Brisson; Schnapp (1981), 116–17; Kelsen, 40–41; Lawrence Stone, "Sex in the West," *The New Republic* (July 8, 1985), 25–37, esp. 30–32 (with doubts). *Contra*, Padgug, 13: "to speak, as is common, of the Greeks, as 'bisexual' is illegitimate as well, since that merely adds a new, intermediate category, whereas it was precisely the categories themselves which had no meaning in antiquity."

[41] Cf. Robinson, 162: "the reason why a heterosexual majority might have looked with a tolerant eye on 'active' homosexual practice among the minority, and even in some measure within their own group [!], ... is predictably a sexist one: to the heterosexual majority, to whom (in a man's universe) the 'good' woman is *kata physin* [i.e., naturally] passive, obedient, and submissive, the 'role' of the 'active' homosexual will be tolerable precisely because his goings-on can, without too much difficulty, be equated with the 'role' of the male *heterosexual*, i.e., to dominate and subdue; what the two have in common is greater than what divides them." But this seems to me to beg the very question that the distinction between heterosexuality and homosexuality is supposedly designed to solve.

[42] This is not so paradoxical as it may at first appear. Whether the object of a free adult male's desire turns out to be a woman, a boy, a foreigner, or a slave, it remains from his point of view "hetero"—in the sense of "different" or "other": it always belongs to a different social category or status.

a more generalized ethos of penetration and domination,[43] a socio-sexual discourse structured by the presence or absence of its central term: the phallus.[44]

If that discourse does not seem to have looked to gender for a criterion by means of which to differentiate permissible from impermissible sexual objects (but to have featured, instead, a gender-blind distinction between dominant and submissive persons), we should not therefore conclude that gender was unimplicated in the socio-sexual system of the ancient Greeks. Gender did indeed figure in that system—not at the level at which sexual *objects* were categorized,[45] to be sure, but at the level at which sexual *subjects* were constituted.[46] Let us not forget, after all, that the kind of desire described by Greek sources as failing to discriminate between male and female objects was itself *gendered* as a specifically *male* desire. Now, to define the scope of sexual object-choice *for men* in terms independent of gender is almost certainly to construct different subjectivities for men and for women, to do so specifically in terms of gender, and thus to define male and female desire asymmetrically. For women and boys will

[43] An excellent analysis of the contemporary Mediterranean version of this ethos has been provided by Gilmore (1987), 8–16.

[44] By "phallus" I mean a culturally constructed signifier of social power: for the terminology, see note 25, above. I call Greek sexual discourse phallic because (1) sexual contacts are polarized around phallic action—i.e., they are defined by who has the phallus and by what is done with it; (2) sexual pleasures other than phallic pleasures do not count in categorizing sexual contacts; (3) in order for a contact to qualify as sexual, one—and no more than one—of the two partners is required to have a phallus (boys are treated in paederastic contexts as essentially un-phallused [see Martial, 11.22; but cf. *Palatine Anthology* 12.3, 7, 197, 207, 216, 222, 242] and tend to be assimilated to women; in the case of sex between women, one partner—the "tribad"—is assumed to possess a phallus-equivalent [an over-developed clitoris] and to penetrate the other: sources for the ancient conceptualization of the tribad—no complete modern study of this fascinating and longlived fictional type, which survived into the early decades of the twentieth century, is known to me—have been assembled by Friedrich Karl Forberg, *Manual of Classical Erotology*, trans, Julian Smithson [Manchester, 1884; repr. New York, 1966], II, 108–67; Brandt [(1932)], 316–28; Gaston Vorberg, *Glossarium eroticum* [Hanau, 1965], 654–55; Werner A. Krenkel, "Masturbation in der Antike," *Wissenschaftliche Zeitschrift der Wilhelm-Pieck-Universität Rostock*, 28 [1979], 159–78, esp. 171; see, now, Judith P. Hallett, "Female Homoeroticism and the Denial of Roman Reality in Latin Literature," *Yale Journal of Criticism*, 3.1 [1989], 209–27).

[45] Even at this level, however, gender had an impact: it can be felt in the male liking for some physical characteristics of boys which Greek culture associated with women (e.g., smooth and hairless skin [for details, see "The Democratic Body," [Halperin (1990), 88–112]]); the courtesan Glycera went so far as to claim, according to Clearchus, that "boys are attractive for as long as they resemble a woman" (Athenaeus, 13.605d). Dover (1978), 68–81, however, argues convincingly that in a number of other departments besides hair and skin boyish good looks, as Greek males defined them, included features that qualified as specifically "masculine" by contemporary standards.

[46] I owe this insight to the acute criticisms of an earlier version of the present essay by Sylvia Yanagisako, "Sex and Gender: You Can't Have One Without the Other," Paper presented at the first annual meeting of the Society for Cultural Anthropology, Washington, D.C. (20 May 1988).

qualify as equally appropriate sexual targets for adult men only so long as they remain relatively stationary targets (so to speak), only so long as they are content to surrender the erotic initiative to men and to await the results of male deliberation. A *sexual* ethos of phallic penetration and domination, in which the gender of the object does not determine male sexual object-choice, requires the differential *gendering* of both desire and power: if women and boys had the kind of wide-ranging, object-directed desires that men have, and if they had the social authority to act on those desires, they would be more likely to frustrate or to interfere with men's sexual choices.

Desire appears to have been gendered in precisely this way in classical Athens. Neither boys nor women were thought to possess the sort of desires that would impel them to become autonomous sexual actors in their relations with men, constantly scanning the erotic horizon for attractive candidates uniquely adapted to their personal requirements. On the contrary: both women and boys, in different ways and for different reasons, were considered sexually inert. Boys did not (supposedly) experience any erotic desire at all for adult men,[47] whereas women's desire was not directed in the first instance to individual male objects: it did not present itself as a longing for one or another man in particular but as an undifferentiated appetite for sexual pleasure; it arose, in other words, out of a more diffuse and generalized somatic need, determined by the physiological economy of the female body, and even then it was fundamentally reactive in character—it appeared in response to a specific male stimulus (whereupon, of course, it immediately became insatiable) and it could be aroused, allegedly, by anyone (even a woman)[48] with the proper phallic equipment.[49] As Andromache remarks, with pardonable skepticism, in Euripides's *Trojan Women*,

[47] Halperin (1986), 63–66; also [...] section 6 of "Why is Diotima a Woman?" [Halperin (1990), 113–51].

[48] See Lucian, *Dialogues of the Courtesans* 5. On "tribads," see my discussion of Caelius Aurelianus [not reprinted here] as well as note 44, above.

[49] I must point out, once again, that I am speaking about Greek canons of sexual propriety, not about the actual phenomenology of sexual life in ancient Greece. It would be easy to come up with many counter-examples to the generalizations I am making here in order to show, for instance, that women sometimes were considered capable of pursuing men. Thus, in Euripides's *Hippolytus*, Phaedra becomes erotically obsessed by one man in particular without having ever received much direct encouragement from him; her example, however, far from refuting the picture I have drawn, might actually corroborate it, if we remember that it was precisely by portraying such instances of female "shamelessness" that Euripides earned his ancient reputation for misogyny. His portrait of Phaedra was interpreted by his contemporaries, in other words, not as realism but as slander. Hanson notes, further, that if Phaedra had followed her Nurse's advice and consulted a male doctor (295–96), he would most likely have prescribed phallic penetration (real or simulated) to ease her hysterical symptoms.

"They say that one night in bed dissolves a woman's hostility to sexual union with a man" (665–66).[50]

The *sexual* system of classical Athens, which defined the scope of sexual object-choice for adult men in terms independent of gender, was therefore logically inseparable from the *gender* system of classical Athens, which distributed to men and to women different kinds of desires, constructing male desire as wide-ranging, acquisitive, and object-directed, while constructing female desire (in opposition to it) as objectless, passive, and entirely determined by the female body's need for regular phallic irrigation.[51] Instead of associating different sorts of sexual object-choice with different *kinds* of "sexuality," as we do, the classical Greeks assigned different forms of desire to different genders. The relation between sex and gender in classical Athens, then, was perhaps just as strict as it is in modern bourgeois Europe and America, but it was elaborated according to a strategy radically different from that governing the relation of sex and gender under the current régime of "sexuality."

For those inhabitants of the ancient world about whom it is possible to generalize, "sexuality" obviously did not hold the key to the secrets of the human personality.[52] The measure of a free male in Greek society was most often taken not by scrutinizing his sexual constitution but by observing how he fared when tested against other free males in public competition. War (and other agonistic contests), not love, served to reveal the inner man, the stuff a free Greek male was made of.[53] A striking example of this emphasis on public life as the primary locus of signification can be found in the work of Artemidorus, a master dream-analyst who lived and wrote in the second century of our era but whose basic approach to the interpretation of dreams does not differ—in this respect, at least—from attitudes current in the classical period.[54] Artemidorus saw public life, not erotic life, as the principal tenor of dreams. Even sexual dreams,

---

[50] See Dover (1974), 101–02.

[51] See Halperin (1985), 164–66, and section 7 of "Why is Diotima a Woman?" [Halperin (1990), 113–51]; [Dean-Jones (1992)].

[52] In fact, the very concept of and set of practices centering on "the human personality"— the physical and social sciences of the blank individual—belong to a much later era and bespeak the modern social and economic conditions (urban, capitalist, bureaucratic) that accompanied their rise.

[53] I am indebted for this observation to professor Peter M. Smith of the University of North Carolina at Chapel Hill, who notes that Sappho and Plato are the chief exceptions to this general rule. See, further, Paul A. Rahe, "The Primacy of Politics in Classical Greece," *American Historical Review*, 89 (1984), 265–93, who makes a similar point in the course of an otherwise schematic and idealized portrayal of the political culture of classical Greece.

[54] Compare, e.g., Herodotus, 6.107.

in Artemidorus's system, are seldom *really* about sex: rather, they are about the rise and fall of the dreamer's public fortunes, the vicissitudes of his domestic economy.[55] If a man dreams of having sex with his mother, for example, his dream signifies to Artemidorus nothing in particular about the dreamer's own sexual psychology, his fantasy life, or the history of his relations with his parents; it's a very common dream, and so it's a bit tricky to interpret precisely, but basically it's a lucky dream: it may signify—depending on the family's circumstances at the time, the postures of the partners in the dream, and the mode of penetration—that the dreamer will be successful in politics ("success in politics" meaning, evidently, the power to screw one's country), that he will go into exile or return from exile, that he will win his law-suit, obtain a rich harvest from his lands, or change professions, among many other things (1.79). Artemidorus's system of dream interpretation resembles the indigenous dream-lore of certain Amazonian tribes who, despite their quite different socio-sexual systems, share with the ancients a belief in the predictive value of dreams. Like Artemidorus, these Amazonian peoples reverse what modern bourgeois Westerners take to be the natural flow of signification in dreams (from images of public and social events to private and sexual meanings): in both Kagwahiv and Mehinaku culture, for example, dreaming about the female genitals portends a wound (and so a man who has such a dream is especially careful when he handles axes or other sharp implements the next day); dreamt wounds do not symbolize the female genitals.[56] Both these ancient and modern dream-interpreters, then, are innocent of "sexuality": what is fundamental to their experience of sex is not anything *we* would regard as

[55] S.R.F. Price, "The Future of Dreams: From Freud to Artemidorus," *Past and Present*, 113 (November 1986), 3–37, abridged in Halperin, Winkler, and Zeitlin; see, also, Foucault (1986), 3–36, esp. 26–34.

[56] See Waud H. Kracke, "Dreaming in Kagwahiv: Dream Beliefs and Their Psychic Uses in an Amazonian Indian Culture," *The Psychoanalytic Study of Society*, 8 (1979), 119–71, esp. 130–32, 163 (on the predictive value of dreams) and 130–31, 142–45, 163–64, 168 (on the reversal of the Freudian direction of signification—which Kracke takes to be a culturally constituted defense mechanism and which he accordingly undervalues); Thomas Gregor, "'Far, Far Away My Shadow Wandered …': The Dream Symbolism and Dream Theories of the Mehinaku Indians of Brazil," *American Ethnologist*, 8 (1981), 709–20, esp. 712–13 (on predictive value) and 714 (on the reversal of signification), largely recapitulated in Gregor, 152–61, esp. 153. Cf. Foucault (1986), 35–36: "The movement of analysis and the procedures of valuation do not go from the act to a domain such as sexuality or the flesh, a domain whose divine, civil, or natural laws would delineate the permitted forms; they go from the subject as a sexual actor to the other areas of life in which he pursues his [familial, social and economic] activity. And it is in the relationship between these different forms of activity that the principles of evaluation of a sexual behavior are essentially, but not exclusively, situated."

essentially sexual;[57] it is something essentially outward, public, and social. Instead of viewing public and political life as a dramatization of individual sexual psychology, as we often tend to do, they see sexual behavior as an expression of political and social relations.[58] "Sexuality," for cultures not shaped by some very recent European and American bourgeois developments, is not a cause but an effect. The social body precedes the sexual body.

[57] Note that even the human genitals themselves do not necessarily figure as sexual signifiers in all cultural or representational contexts: for example, Bynum (1986) argues, in considerable detail, that there is "reason to think that medieval people saw Christ's penis not primarily as a sexual organ but as the object of circumcision and therefore as the wounded, bleeding flesh with which it was associated in painting and in text" (p. 407).

[58] duBois (1984), 47–48; Edmunds, 81–84.

# 7 *Law, Society and Homosexuality in Classical Athens*†

## DAVID COHEN

Recent scholarship has succeeded in greatly advancing our understanding of "Greek homosexuality". Kenneth Dover and Michel Foucault have argued that the modern dichotomization of sexuality as heterosexuality/homosexuality does not apply to the ancient world, and they have shown how distinctions between active and passive roles in male sexuality defined the contours of the permissible and impermissible in pederastic courtship and other forms of homoerotic behaviour. Among the Greeks, we are told, active homosexuality was regarded as perfectly natural (sexual desire was not distinguished according to its object). There was, however, a prohibition against males of any age adopting a submissive role that was unworthy of a free citizen.[1]

Some Athenians in the classical period may well have thought that some men by nature liked boys, others women, still others both. But it does not follow that the categories of sexual roles associated with the dichotomy of homosexual/heterosexual were entirely absent.

†Originally published in *Past and Present*, 117 (1987), 3–21.
I would like to thank Sir Moses Finley and John Crook, David Daube, Peter Garnsey, A. A. Long, Laurent Mayali and Gregory Vlastos for reading this article in draft and giving me the benefit of their comments and criticisms.

[1] K. Dover, *Greek Homosexuality* (New York, 1985), pp. 60–8, 81–109; and see M. Foucault, *L'usage des plaisirs* (Paris, 1984), pp. 47–62. Most recently a considerable literature purports to trace the origins of pederasty in the ritualized process by which adolescents make the passage to full manhood and membership in the community: see A. Brelich, *Paides e Parthenoi* (Rome, 1969); W. Le Barre, *Muelos* (New York, 1984); H. Patzer, *Die griechische Knabenliebe* (Wiesbaden, 1982); B. Sergent, *La homosexualité dans la mythologie grecque* (Paris, 1984); and P. Vidal-Naquet, *Le chasseur noir* (Paris, 1981). For the best and most recent anthropological studies of initiation and sexuality, see G. Herdt (ed.), *Rituals of Manhood* (Berkeley, 1982); and G. Herdt (ed.), *Ritualized Homosexuality in Melanesia* (Berkeley, 1984). These two volumes replace the earlier studies which are usually relied upon by classicists for comparative purposes.

Further, though the delineation of active and passive roles was certainly important, it was by no means the only determinant of social norms related to sexual roles and homoerotic behaviour. Indeed an exploration of Greek homosexuality ought to begin by insisting very strongly on the profundity of the conflicts which permeated Athenian values and practices in this area.

I shall argue that current interpretations do not do justice to the complexity of these social patterns, and that Athenian homoeroticism must be understood in the context of a theory of social practice which emphasizes the centrality of cultural contradiction and ambivalence.

From the classical studies of Malinowski among the Trobrianders to the more recent work of scholars like Bailey and Barrett, there is a strain of anthropological theory which identifies contradiction as a central feature of cultural systems. Malinowski spoke of the conflict between cultural ideals and social practices, Bailey of the contradiction between, in his terms, normative and pragmatic values.[2] Whichever terminology one adopts, the point is that the historian should not always attempt to explain away every contradiction or ambiguity as if socio-historical explanation were a puzzle which admits of a univocal solution. ...

The Athenians themselves were not unaware of these ambiguities and contradictions. To begin with: according to Xenophon, Greeks were well aware that laws and customs regarding pederasty varied widely between different states. Some prohibited it outright, others explicitly permitted it.[3] In the *Symposium* Plato put into the mouth of Pausanias an encomium of love which explicitly addresses the conflicts within Athenian norms and customs pertaining to pederasty.[4] Whereas for the rest of Greece these laws and customs are clear and well defined, explains Pausanias, those of Sparta are "poikilos"— intricate, complicated, subtle. He comments that Athenian legislation in this area is admirable, but difficult to understand; the difficulty consists in the simultaneous approbation and censure which social norms and legal rules attach to the pursuit of a pederastic courtship.

Whatever its philosophical or other merits, Pausanias' famous

---

[2] B. Malinowski, *The Sexual Life of Savages* (New York, 1929), pp. 565–72; F. G. Bailey, *Stratagems and Spoils* (New York, 1969), pp. 125 ff.; and see generally S. Barrett, *The Rebirth of Anthropological Theory* (Toronto, 1984), *passim*, who discusses Bailey and Malinowski in some detail and offers his own theory of contradiction. For an attempt to give contradiction a central role in a general theory of social practice, see A. Giddens, *Central Problems in Social Theory* (Berkeley, 1979), pp. 131–64.

[3] Xenophon, *Lac. Constitution*, 2.12–13; Xenophon, *Symposium*, 8.34–5.

[4] Plato, *Symposium*, 182a ff.

explanation—that society only condemns the unchaste love of Aphrodite Pandemus while justly praising the noble (that is, uncon-summated) love of Uranian Aphrodite—does not dispel the contra-diction which it has correctly identified. Part of the difficulty is that Pausanias' speech conflates at least two distinct categories of norms and institutions. For although he repeatedly uses words like "nomos" (law, custom), it is often not clear whether he is referring to law, or to custom in the sense of social practice. It may be appropriate, then, to start by examining Athenian legislation on this subject, and then move to a comparison of the legal norms with social codes and prac-tices.

The legal provisions regulating various forms of homoerotic behaviour may be grouped in three categories: laws relating to pros-titution; laws relating to education and courtship; and, finally, general provisions concerning sexual assault. These are only catego-ries of convenience, however, and there can be considerable overlap between them. The laws concerning male prostitution may be consid-ered first. One statute partially disenfranchised any Athenian citizen who prostituted himself, whether as a boy or as an adult; he lost his right to address the Assembly and to participate in other important areas of civic life.[5] Secondly, if a boy was hired out for sexual services by his father, brother, uncle or guardian, they were subject to a public action, as was the man who hired him.[6] Thirdly, a general statute pro-hibited procuring and applied to any free-born child or woman.[7] Finally, Aeschines several times suggests that the man who hired an Athenian male for sexual services was likewise liable to severe penal-ties but it is not clear whether he is referring to the second statute described above, which pertains to boys, or to a separate one. Moreover many of the passages suggest that he may be extending his description of the law for particular rhetorical purposes.[8]

The second category of laws pertained to education and set out a series of detailed prohibitions designed, among other things, to protect schoolboys from the erotic attentions of older males. These laws reg-ulated all the contacts which boys had with adult males during the period at school, and provided for the appointment of public officials to ensure that proper order was maintained. According to Aeschines, the law forbade the schools to open before sunrise or stay open after

---

[5] Aristotle, *Ath. Pol.*, 18.2; Demosthenes, 19, 200, 257; Aeschines, 1, 3, 13–14, 18–19, 29; Aristophanes, *Knights*, 880 ff.
[6] Aeschines, 1, 13–14.
[7] *Ibid.*, 1, 14; and cf. Aristotle, *Ethics*, 1131a 7.
[8] Aeschines, 1, 11, 45, 72, 90, 163.

dark, and strictly regulated who might enter and under what circumstances.[9] Finally, another law prohibited slaves from courting free
boys.[10]

The third kind of statutory prohibition is rather more problematical than the first two and has received scant attention in regard to
regulation of homoerotic conduct. Here I refer to the law of hubris
(outrage or abuse). Current scholarship on pederasty commonly
asserts that there was no law prohibiting an Athenian male from con-
summating a sexual relationship with a free boy without using force
or payment.[11] This point is usually adduced as the cornerstone of the
standard interpretation. This interpretation ignores, however, a series
of questions concerning the legal context of pederastic sexuality
which, to my knowledge, has never been asked. Did Athenian law
acknowledge an age of consent in its conceptualization of sexual
assault and seduction? If the consent of the boy was not a bar to prosecution, did *any* consummated sexual relationship with a boy fulfil
the required elements of the offence? Did Athenian law have some
notion equivalent to statutory rape in modern legal systems, where
consent is *the* crucial issue in the definition of rape offences?[12] An
affirmative answer to any of these questions would require one to
reassess the standard view that the active role in pederastic relations
was absolutely free from any taint of disapprobation.

First of all, it must be emphasized that the noun "hubris" and the
verb "hubrizein" have a strong sexual connotation. Many authors,
for example, refer to captive women and children being taken off to
suffer hubris.[13] Scholars usually do not refer to hubris in connection
with pederasty because they believe hubris to require violent insult or
outrage, as in rape.[14] According to Aristotle, however, hubris is actually any behaviour which dishonours and shames the victim for the

---

[9] *Ibid.*, 1, 9–14.

[10] Perhaps the "laws" referred to by Pausanias also regulated courtship. There is, however,
a great deal of ambiguity in the text. Plato repeatedly uses the vocabulary of statutes and legislation, but at many points he is clearly referring to societal attitudes and customs.

[11] See Dover, *Greek Homosexuality*, pp. 64ff., 88 ff.; Foucault, *Usage des plaisirs*, p. 238.

[12] See, for example, *People v. Hernandez* (1964), 61 C. 2d 529, 339 P. 2d 673. In the traditional statutory formulations, consent negates a required element of the offence (see *Regina
v. Morgan*, House of Lords (1976), A.C. 182) or operates as an affirmative defence. An allegation that the victim consented to intercourse is, however, irrelevant in a prosecution for statutory rape where the age of the victim obviates any enquiry into his/her state of mind. For
German law on this point, see [*Strafgesetzbuch*], 180. For hints of Athenian attitudes, see
Aeschines, 1, 139–40.

[13] See, for example, Thucydides, 8.74; Plato, *Laws*, 874c; Herodotus, 3.80, 4.114; Aristotle,
*Rhetoric*, 1373a 35; Demosthenes, 19, 309.

[14] See, for example, D. MacDowell's superficial treatment in *The Law of Classical Athens*
(London, 1978), pp. 129–32; and Dover, *Greek Homosexuality*, pp. 34–9.

pleasure or gratification of the offender.[15] It is in this connection that the orator Aeschines introduced the law of hubris into the catalogue of statutes which he enumerated as regulating pederasty in Athens in the fourth century BC. In fact when he first refers to the law of hubris he characterizes it as the statute which includes all such conduct in one summary prohibition: "If anyone commits hubris against a child or man or woman or anyone free or slave …".[16]

Sexual relations with children, particularly for pay, dishonours them, and under this statute such shame and dishonour for the gratification of the offender constituted hubris. Given the strong sexual connotations of the words "hubris" and "hubrizein" in ordinary language, Aeschines' argument seems perfectly reasonable, particularly in the case of minors, whose consent may have been felt to be irrelevant. In fact numerous passages from Greek orators indicate that using a male in a passive sexual role dishonours him and thus qualifies as hubris. In the case of adults, voluntary consent may undercut the attribution of blame to the offender, and indeed such men who consent are often described as committing hubris against themselves by their submission.[17] But in the case of a boy, such consent might have been regarded as irrelevant, and thus the attribution of wrongdoing adheres to the man who dishonours the boy, whether through rape or seduction. As in the modern law of statutory rape, the consent of a boy younger than a certain age would not negate the charge of hubris.

Aristotle, in his description of shameful actions which cause dishonour to those who suffer them, gives as his example providing sexual services with one's body, and adds that such shameful actions involve submitting to hubris.[18] In Demosthenes and Lysias, seduction and

[15] Aristotle, *Rhetoric*, 1378b.

[16] Aeschines, 1, 15.

[17] *Ibid.*, 1, 29, 40, 116. On the humiliation of submission to homosexual intercourse, see Bailey, *Stratagems and Spoils*, p. 123, who sets out the pattern as follows: "The males of one troop sort themselves out into patterns of dominance and subordination. If annoyed by a challenge—perhaps inadvertent—from an inferior, the dominant male will stare fixedly at him; the inferior should then look away. If he does not the dominant male will move as if to charge; the weaker baboon should then cringe down to the ground … failing that there will be a charge and a chase … The weaker baboon may still save itself being bitten by turning its back, presenting its hindquarters and allowing itself to be mounted, just as a female is mounted in copulation". A. Dundes and A. Falassi in *La terra in piazza* (Berkeley, 1975) describe the way that such a pattern plays itself out in the rivalry of gangs of young men during the Pallio in Siena: "Typically, the rival group is demeaned through its having to submit to symbolic anal intercourse. One must keep in mind that in terms of metaphor there is no disgrace in being the active aggressor in the alleged homosexual attack. It is only the recipient of the phallic thrust who is shamed" (pp. 188–9). For similar associations in the biblical context, see D. G. Bailey, *Homosexuality and the Western Christian Tradition* (London, 1975), pp. 32–4.

[18] Aristotle, *Ethics*, 1148b 29.

adultery involving free women are characterized as hubris (once again, consent is irrelevant), and Aristotle applies the same standard to boys when he says that some males enjoy homosexual intercourse because they were subjected to hubris as boys.[19] Demosthenes, in *Against Androtion*, applies precisely the same judgement as Aeschines, arguing that the man who prostitutes himself must submit to hubris.[20] Finally, Xenophon says that using men as women constitutes hubris.[21] In short, Aeschines' characterization of the law of hubris as potentially providing penalties for certain homoerotic relations is not inconsistent with a good deal of other evidence. There is no way of knowing, however, if, or how often, the law was actually applied in this way.

After this brief survey of the wide range of legislation pertaining to homoerotic behaviour, it is easy to understand why Plato made Pausanias characterize Athenian law as many-hued, intricate and difficult to understand in contrast with the laws of other Greek cities, which either prohibited or permitted pederasty in a straightforward way. Now if legal norms are one reflection or embodiment of the values, attitudes and ideology of a society (or parts of a society), what do these Athenian laws reveal about the values and beliefs of the social order which they defined and regulated? Scholars have not addressed this question, despite its crucial importance in unravelling the way in which homoeroticism was regarded at Athens.

The set of legal norms embodied in these statutes reflects a social order which encompassed a profound ambivalence and anxiety in regard to male-male sexuality; a social order which recognized the existence and persistence of such behaviour, but was deeply concerned about the dangers which it represented. The chief of these dangers was the corruption of the future of the polis, represented by the male children of citizen families. Boys who, under certain circumstances, participated in sexual intercourse with men were believed to have acted for gain and to have adopted a submissive role which disqualified them as potential citizens.[22] Likewise, adult citizens who prostituted them-

---

[19] Demosthenes, 23, 56; Lysias, 1, 4, 16, 25; Aristotle, *Ethics*, 1148b 29.
[20] Demosthenes, 22, 58.
[21] Xenophon, *Memorabilia*, 2.1.30.
[22] See, for example, Xenophon, *Symposium*, 8.34 ff. This point marks the great difference which separates Athens from other cultures where homosexual intercourse is a mandatory part of initiation of young males. Although some scholars (for example, J. Bremmer, "An Enigmatic Indo-European Rite: Paederasty", *Arethusa*, xiii (1980), pp. 279–98; Sergent, *Homosexualité dans la mythologie grecque, passim*) wish to trace Athenian pederasty back to such a process of initiation, the whole point is that at Athens the public submission to such intercourse as required of Melanesian initiates would result in disenfranchisement. On the variety of Melanesian rituals and attitudes, see Herdt (ed.), *Ritualized Homosexuality in Melanesia, passim*.

selves were subject to the same civic disabilities and opprobium. These laws represented one of the severest sanctions which such a society could impose, and they reflect the level of concern for the preservation of the citizen body. Passages in Aristophanes refer to the possibilities for extortion and political advantage which such laws created, and of which Aeschines' prosecution of Timarchus was an actual example. In order to ensure that those who, in the words of Aeschines, were "hunters of young men" did not deplete the supply of new citizens, a group of laws aimed at deterring others from leading boys or young men into disenfranchisement: hence the various statutes regarding procuring, prostitution, regulation of schools, etc. Clearly, such laws imply severe censure both of the boy or young man who allowed himself to be led astray and of those who did the leading, whether by means of financial incentives or otherwise.[23]

In short, the range, variety and overlapping of the Athenian statutes seem to reflect a society which was attempting over a period of time to cope with persistent patterns of behaviour which were felt to jeopardize the well-being of the city. The mechanisms of the public law were deployed to deter and punish such conduct and to protect free boys.

Protection from their fathers or relatives who might hire them out, protection from their schoolmasters, protection from seducers, protection from themselves: such legislation reflects strong underlying tensions about homoerotic behaviour. The law may reflect such underlying conflicts, but (and this is particularly the case in the sexual sphere) is always an inadequate mechanism by which to resolve them. Hence it is not surprising that one knows of so few cases in which this impressive panoply of statutes was actually applied. Some of the reasons for this seeming disjunction between the normative potential which the law represented and the actual will to apply it may emerge from an examination of the cultural ideals, norms and practices which, together with the law, ordered the social fabric.

Turning to the social norms which formed the basis for societal evaluation of homoerotic practices, it is not surprising that the normative poles are honour and shame. As Pausanias puts it in the *Symposium*, the erastes (the wooing, pursuing lover) gains honour by his success and is humiliated by defeat in his pursuit.[24] Likewise, the

---

[23] G. Koch-Harnack's discussion of courtship gifts reveals the way in which the giving of animals and money seems to be portrayed as interchangeable in Attic vase-painting. She emphasizes the reciprocal nature of the transaction which is implied in the portrayal of such "gifts": G. Koch-Harnack, *Knabenliebe und Tiergeschenke* (Berlin, 1983), pp. 77–9, 93–4. See also Aristophanes, *Birds*, 704 ff.

[24] Plato, *Symposium*, 182e.

victory of the erastes means the defeat of the eromenos (the pursued beloved), for "it is shameful to gratify an erastes".[25] As Gouldner put it, honour is a zero-sum game;[26] the increase of one man's honour is at the expense of another's. That honour and shame defined the normative boundaries of homoeroticism (and sexuality in general) is implicit, and often explicit, in all our sources from Plato, Aristotle and Xenophon to the orators and drama.[27] Though it is well known that they were dominant values in Greek society, some of the consequences which arose through their operation according to a zero-sum rule in the area of homoeroticism deserve elaboration. Having set out some of the general principles of the sexual code of honour and shame, one will be better able to examine some of the divergent attitudes and practices in Athenian homosexuality. [...]

Now one obvious way in which a man may demonstrate his virility in an agonistic society like this is in competition for the favours of women. There is one hitch here, however: success in this competition is purchased at the price of dishonour for the man who has failed to protect the woman whose favours have been received. Honour is a zero-sum game. Thus, since sexual conquest serves as a demonstration of masculinity, the adulterer or seducer gains in stature, but at the expense of others; the husband becomes the *cabron*, the cuckold. [...]

In Athens agonistic sexuality could scarcely manifest itself in competition for women, for a variety of reasons. First, courtship of unmarried women was non-existent, and clandestine courtship was hardly practicable since girls were married very young to prevent just such "accidents" and were zealously guarded during the brief period between pubescence and marriage.[28] One does hear of adulterous conquest, but, as Lysias' oration *On the Murder of Eratosthenes* shows, this could be dangerous since the adulterer caught in the act could be killed with impunity. There also seems to have been rivalry for hetaerae and boy prostitutes, but great honour could hardly be gained here since slaves and prostitutes were automatically in a submissive and inferior position anyway, at the economic disposal of all who could pay.[29]

---

[25] *Ibid.*, 182a, 183c–d.

[26] A. Gouldner, *Enter Plato* (New York, 1965), p. 49.

[27] Aristotle, *Rhetoric*, 1370b, 1378b, 1383b–4b; Aristotle, *Politics*, 1311b; Plato, *Symposium*, 182, 217; Plato, *Phaedrus*, 251; Xenophon, *Agesilaus*, 5.7; Xenophon, *Symposium*, 4.52 ff., 7.9 ff., 8.23–35; Xenophon, *Memorabilia*, 1.2.29, 1.3.11; Lysias, 3, *passim*; Demosthenes, *Erotic Essay*, 1, 3, 5, 6, 17, 19–20; Aristophanes, *Clouds* 1085; Aristophanes, *Knights*, 880 ff.

[28] This is the typical traditional Mediterranean pattern. See, for example, V. Maher, *Women and Property in Morocco* (Cambridge, 1974), p. 150.

[29] See Lysias, 3, *passim*; Xenophon, *Hiero*, 1. 27 ff.

Sexual competition for honour, then, had largely to be directed towards boys (particularly since chasing after prostitutes was in itself judged as shameful according to conventional norms). This fact established the basic dynamic of pederastic courtship, a dynamic which necessarily threatened to put the boy eromenos in the role of a woman; pursued rather than pursuing, defensive rather than aggressive, submissive rather than dominant, mounted rather than mounting. The way in which this dynamic turned pederastic courtship into an *agon* for honour, in which the erastes sought to gain honour by making the boy a woman and the eromenos to do the same by showing himself to be a man, must now be addressed. First, however, some preliminary remarks on gender and sexual roles may be appropriate.

What does it mean "to make a boy a woman"? It is necessary to distinguish two related aspects of this claim. The first concerns the sexual act itself and the way in which the roles of the two participants are seen, while the second involves the larger social context of courtship and the role patterns associated with it. Although it has become quite fashionable to deny that the Greeks thought homosexuality to be unnatural and that modern categories of homosexuality/heterosexuality can be applied to classical Greece, one should not make such assertions too facilely. Sexual roles in both of the senses distinguished above were defined in terms of a male/female dichotomy and judged by norms that were felt by some to be at once social and natural.

To begin with the first sense of "making a boy a woman", there is ample evidence to show that the Levitical formulation "to lie with mankind as with womankind" represents a way of categorizing homosexual intercourse that was not unknown in Athens.[30] Indeed Xenophon refers to the hubristic practice of "using men as women", and Plato argues that the man who adopts the passive role in homosexual intercourse can be rebuked as the impersonator of the female, a situation which is "against nature".[31] Such usage was not confined to philosophical circles, for Aeschines, for example, uses the same formulation.[32] In a lengthy passage in the *Laws*, Plato several times makes an analogy to nature and the mating patterns of animals.[33] He argues that as it is natural for a male and female to mate, and natural

---

[30] Lev. 20:13. See Herdt (ed.), *Ritualized Homosexuality in Melanesia*, pp. 118, 220, for descriptions of the way in which the younger partner is seen as taking the woman's role.

[31] Xenophon, *Memorabilia*, 2.1.31; Plato, *Laws*, 836e, 841d.

[32] Aeschines, 1, 185.

[33] Plato, *Laws*, 836–41.

that male animals do not seek other males, so it is unnatural when men do not follow their example.[34] It should be emphasized that Plato does not merely characterize *passive* behaviour as unnatural for men, but rather sexual relations between men *per se*, although the passive role is seen as more shameful.[35] Such judgements are clearly based upon an implicit sexual norm of male-female intercourse, and they put the passive man or boy into the submissive role which is, according to nature, that of the female.

This characterization also represents the view of Aristotle, a view which is the basis for the analysis of procreation in his treatise on the *Generation of Animals*. What underlies that entire work is the same analogy that Plato uses in the *Laws*: in their procreative capacities human beings are like animals and it is natural for male to mate with female. These latter categories are defined not only in terms of physiological differentiation, but also with reference to the principle which underlies them. Thus Aristotle says that after castration a male organism changes to become very much like the female [...] In the Greek context, eunuchs were commonly judged in this light; and boys, regarded as being incapable of emitting semen or performing intercourse, were not truly male.[36] At the more general level, Aristotle goes on to characterize the underlying principles of masculinity and femininity as based upon the dichotomy of active and passive sexual roles, and this characterization enables one to distinguish two levels of his analysis of what is natural in sexual relations.

In the first instance, it is natural that the physiological male should mate with the physiological female. This is natural both in the sense that it represents the basic reproductive pattern of living organisms and also because nature has developed our sexual organs towards the fulfilment of this procreative purpose. The second level concerns the roles which are adopted within the procreative act, based upon the principles of activity and passivity. At the level of physiology, the infertile male is likened to a woman[37] because he lacks the capacity

---

[34] *Ibid.*, 836c.

[35] See also Plato, *Symposium*, 152a, where the opinion of some is said to be that all male-male sexual relations are shameful; and Aristotle, *Ethics*, 1148b 24 ff.

[36] Aristotle, *Generation of Animals*, 728a; Aristotle, *Problems*, 879a. This view of the boy is widespread: see Herdt (ed.), *Ritualized Homosexuality in Melanesia, passim* and, in particular, p. 220: "Male cults have been known in Melanesia for a long time, and I think they share a common, basic, and underlying theme. To put it as simply and colloquially as possible, it is this: 'Girls *will* be women' but 'boys *will not* necessarily be men'. One may indeed say that 'male' and 'female' are opposed to each other as 'nurture' to 'nature' and thus the cultural necessity for promoting masculinity, of finishing through ritual an 'unfinished, possibly ambiguous biological entity.'"

[37] Aristotle, *Generation of Animals*, 728a.

to produce semen, the active ingredient required for procreation.[38] At the level of sexual role behaviour, the man who adopts a submissive, passive role is unmanly, woman-like and he therefore dishonours and shames himself. Since a boy also cannot produce semen, physiologically speaking he is not yet a man.[39] Further, when he lends himself to sexual intercourse with a man it *necessarily* places him in the role of the female, the object to which desire is directed. Yet because he is not female, in the normal case he will experience no pleasure in the act,[40] and hence must be providing services with his body for gain, which dishonours and shames him, placing him in a submissive role which is against nature.[41] On the other hand, if he does experience pleasure this is seen, at least in one text, as due to a physiological disorder, and hence unnatural in another sense.[42]

What this brief survey of views reveals is that, despite the variations as to details, for those who took procreation as their starting-point the "natural" pattern which provided the norm for sexual activity was the mating of male with female. Males who pursued other males were a category defined in relation to a heterosexual norm.[43] Whereas males who submitted to other males were regarded as disgraced, the way in which the former category was judged was more controversial. But the force which the procreative heterosexual norm had for them too is perhaps most vividly seen in a text which seeks to honour such behaviour: Aristophanes' famous encomium of love in Plato's *Symposium*.

Aristophanes here presents heterosexuality and homosexuality as categories which are indeed both defined by nature, but in order to justify the positive evaluation which he attaches to the latter, he must create a fantastic new natural order, ignoring the real one with its implicit valuation of heterosexuality. Hence the famous creation myth, which is elaborated so as to reach the conclusion that the homoerotic man is not shameless, as opinion holds, but rather more virile.[44] The need to present a new creation myth, a new model of nature, testifies eloquently to the power of the norm felt to be implicit within the traditional view.

Aristophanes' speech is interesting in yet a further respect. When he descends from the level of myth he comments that the homoerotic

---

[38] *Ibid.*, 728–9.
[39] *Ibid.*, 728a.
[40] Xenophon, *Symposium*, 8.22.
[41] Aristotle, *Rhetoric*, 1384a; Aeschines, 1, 185.
[42] [Aristotle], *Problems*, 879b ff.
[43] See Xenophon, *Anabasis*, 4.7, where such a disposition is described as a *tropos*.
[44] Plato, *Symposium*, 191d–2a.

man is by nature not inclined to marry, but is compelled to do so by law and custom.[45] This follows on the statement that "Some regard them all as shameless". This passage demonstrates the social force that such normative judgements could have and bears further witness to the ambivalence in Athens concerning the kinds of sexual behaviour considered natural, shameful or honourable.[46] It also raises the question of the second of the two senses in which a boy can be made into a woman, the socio-sexual sense as opposed to the physiological. For Aristophanes reveals that, for this society, law, custom and opinion dictated that the natural role of every man was to be a husband and father. Heterosexuality is institutionalized as the foundation of the most basic social unit, the family.[47] This fact is perhaps most forcefully expressed in Aristotle's *Oeconomica*, where the opening passages repeatedly emphasize that it is according to nature that a man and a woman join together to form a family.[48] From the differentiated economic tasks and spheres which are sexually appropriate to husband and wife devolve the social roles which make up the patterns of community and family life.[49] It is in this broader context that the homoerotic valuation of boys became problematic, for while they were in the process of being educated to be citizens and warriors, they were also subjected to patterns of courtship and norms of behaviour which assimilated them to women. [...]

Given this ambivalent view of the sexual identity of boys, it is not surprising that in Attic vase-painting courtship of boys and courtship of women were depicted in an almost identical manner. Apart from one major difference (the depiction of the sexual consummation of courtship), the stages, gestures, rituals and gifts of courtship were much the same whether the object was a boy or a woman.[50] It seems that a sort of displaced courtship leading to a sort of displaced marriage is the appropriate context in which to understand the assimilation of the boy to a woman, both in terms of his sexual identity, his

[45] *Ibid.*, 192b.

[46] *Ibid.*, 192a–b, reads, in a way, like a plea for greater understanding; not Plato's own plea, but his representation of one contemporary position on homoeroticism.

[47] It is relevant here that when sexuality is viewed from the starting-point of the ideology of the family, the perspective, though not necessarily monogamous, seems inevitably heterosexual. Hence the famous tripartite division of the Demosthenic *Against Neaera*, 122: "Mistresses we keep for pleasure, concubines for the daily care of our persons, but wives to bear us legitimate children and guard our households". One might object that boys are only not mentioned out of a sense of shame, but doesn't that just reinforce the point?

[48] Aristotle, *Oeconomica*, 1343a–4a.

[49] See also Xenophon's *Oeconomica*.

[50] Dover, *Greek Homosexuality*, pp. 81 ff.; Koch-Harnack, *Knabenliebe und Tiergeschenke*, pp. 59–82; Foucault, *Usage des plaisirs*, pp. 244–7.

role in courtship and, in a mixed way, his social role in general. An example may help to clarify this notion of displaced courtship and marriage.

In an unjustly neglected article entitled "Sexual Inversion among the Azande", Evans-Pritchard describes the case of a warrior society in which the age of marriage for men is quite late, as at Athens, from the late twenties to the thirties.[51] Since girls were betrothed very young, the only way in which young men could obtain heterosexual satisfaction was through adultery. But that was what Evans-Pritchard terms "a very dangerous solution to a young man's problem", since husbands often tortured and mutilated adulterers taken in the act.[52] The solution to this dilemma was, according to Azande informants, for young men to marry boys when they went into the king's service as warriors. Not marry in the legal sense, but rather to court a boy who would then move into the warriors' house with his lover. The pair often referred to each other as "husband" and "wife", with the man helping to educated the boy and the boy providing sexual and other services. When the period of military duty was over the warrior would end the relationship, return to his village and marry. The boy would, in his turn, become a warrior and repeat the process in the "male" role. After the termination of this relationship and marriage, sexual activity was purely heterosexual. Significantly, all the Azande informants insisted that intercourse with the boys was only intercrural; they all expressed disgust at the suggestion of anal penetration.[53]

This account suggests a number of interesting parallels with the situation at Athens. There, too, late marriage for men, the early marriage of closely guarded adolescent girls and the dangers of adultery combined to make boys an attractive alternative—but with a difference. Athenian men who pursued boys were not merely seeking immediate sexual gratification (nor in all likelihood were their Azande counterparts) since, as Xenophon put it, in this slave society cheap sexual fulfilment was available at every corner.[54] Devereux has remarked that courtship behaviour is almost universal because it seems to fulfil a deep human need,[55] and in Athens courtship and the erotic relationship which it aims at was only possible with boys. When the boy was seen as having become a man physiologically—

[51] E. E. Evans-Pritchard, "Sexual Inversion among the Azande", *American Anthropologist*, lxxii (1970), pp. 1428–35.
[52] *Ibid.*, p. 1429.
[53] *Ibid.*, p. 1430.
[54] Xenophon, *Memorabilia*, 2.2.4.
[55] G. Devereux, "Greek Pseudo-Homosexuality and the 'Greek Miracle'", *Symbolae Osloenses*, xlii (1968), p. 82.

after the growth of his first beard—he was no longer an appropriate object for pursuit; his ambiguously defined androgynous sexuality had become definitively male.[56] Once again the heterosexual norm was the standard by which roles and behaviour were judged.

Thus the Athenian boy seems to have found himself in a situation which, like the Athenian code of conduct itself, is aptly described by Pausanias' term "poikilos"—intricate, many-hued, ambiguous. While he was being educated to be a warrior and a citizen the Athenian boy was also, in many ways, cast into a feminine social role, as the vase-paintings depicting courtship imply.[57] Thus the ideal boy was supposed to be modest and chaste, avoid contact with adult males who were not relatives or close friends of the family, keep his eyes lowered and blush when made the object of attention, etc.[58] Their families protected them from male attention as if they were daughters, but since they could not be confined to the house like a daughter, a paidagogus watched over them:

> Yet we find in practice that if a father discovers that someone has fallen in love with his son, he puts the boy in the charge of an attendant, with strict injunctions not to let him have anything to do with his lover. And if the boy's little friends see anything of that kind going on you may be sure they'll call him names, while their elders will neither stop their being rude nor tell them they are talking nonsense.[59]

Thus the sexual purity of the boy was protected by the family under the same code of honour and shame as that which applied to women, but for boys sexual purity was defined as not assuming the woman's role in sexual intercourse. Moreover the politics of sexual reputation applied to boys just as to women. As Aristotle puts it, some men prefer to shroud in silence their dishonour from the hubris done to their wives or daughters *or sons* rather than accept the publicity and humiliation of a lawsuit. The reputation of a boy was determined by the inferences drawn from his public behaviour with men. Just as in a modern Mediterranean village (or in classical Athens) a girl who lingers at the fountain or takes longer than necessary to return from the fields compromises her honour and becomes the object of gossip

[56] Note that it was also thought to be shameful for men past a certain age to be interested in boys: Lysias, 3, 1; Aeschines, 1, 11.

[57] Again it must be underscored that Athens is different from societies where, as in parts of Melanesia, sexual relations between boys and men are a necessary part of initiation. The services that the boy is expected to provide in parts of Melanesia are clearly viewed as shameful according to Athenian norms.

[58] See, for example, Plato, *Lysis* and *Charmides*.

[59] Plato, *Symposium*, 183c-d; see also Plato, *Phaedrus*, 240; Xenophon, *Memorabilia*, 1.5.2; Xenophon, *Symposium*, 4.52 ff., 8.19; Aeschines, 1, 187; Aristophanes, *Birds*, 137 ff.; Aristotle, *Ethics*, 1119b 14.

and slander,[60] so a boy who was seen at the house of a man or seen alone with a man in a deserted place (particularly after dark) was compromised and might become the object of blackmail.[61]

Hence courtship was an elaborate and public game of honour, a zero-sum game in which the erastes won honour by conquering, the boy by attracting much attention but not submitting.[62] The erastes was shamed by his failure to conquer, the boy by his submission, all of this behaviour being judged by the community through its manifestations in the public arena of reputation, honour and shame. [...]

In Athens an ideal solution was offered to the dilemma of the zero-sum game of honour, an ideal indicated by the descriptions of chaste courtship in the *Phaedrus, Symposium* and other texts. According to this ideal, an equilibrium was reached whereby the erastes and eromenos could both maintain their honour. The erastes was granted "favours" by his eromenos, but the eromenos stopped short of granting (or appearing to grant) favours which would dishonour him (that is, as Dover and Foucault argue, the eromenos only allowed intercrural intercourse and never anal penetration).[63] These texts reveal that some Athenians, at least, felt able to resolve to their own satisfaction the contradictions implicit in their sexual code by means of this sort of ideal equilibrium. But others viewed this solution as hollow, raising again Malinowski's problem of distinguishing cultural ideals from actual social practices. For there may be disagreement within a culture as to what is practice, what is ideal, and how each is to be valued. Wilamowitz-Moellendorf referred to Pausanias' speech as the "Ehrenkodex der athenischen Knabenliebe", but Victor Ehrenberg has aptly commented that "There is little in common between the blushing boys of Plato's dialogues, and the world of unnatural lust which the comedians depict".[64]

---

[60] See, for example, A. Fuller, *Buarij* (Cambridge, Mass., 1961), p. 47; F. G. Bailey, *Gifts and Poison: The Politics of Reputation* (New York, 1971), *passim*: Campbell, *Honour, Family and Patronage*, pp. 86, 190–201.

[61] See Aeschines, 1, 42, 51, 60, 75–6, 90; Aristophanes, *Clouds*, 995 ff.; Aristophanes, *Knights*, 880; Lysias, 14, 25; Plato, *Symposium*, 217c; Plato, *Phaedrus*, 232a–b, 234a–b; Plato, *Charmides* 155a; Aristotle, *Rhetoric*, 1384b f.

[62] For the honour which a boy receives by being admired and sought after for his beauty, see the well-known discussions in Plato, *Charmides, Lysis* and *Symposium*.

[63] See, for example, Koch-Harnack, *Knabenliebe und Tiergeschenke*, pp. 62–3. The politics of reputation as outlined above exist in a state of tension *vis-à-vis* this ideal. Reputation is based upon inferences from *public* behaviour and hence not upon such fine distinctions as intercrural versus anal intercourse, distinctions beyond the realm of possible public knowledge. Dover and others do not take this fact sufficiently into account. See the sources cited in n. 60 and also J. du Boulay, "Lies, Mockery and Family Integrity", in J. Peristiany (ed.), *Mediterranean Family Structures* (Cambridge, 1976), pp. 389–406.

[64] U. von Wilamowitz-Moellendorf, *Platon*, 2 vols. (Berlin, 1920), i, p. 365; V. Ehrenberg, *The People of Aristophanes* (New York, 1962), p. 100.

Aristophanes in *Clouds* depicts the way in which such cultural
ideals of chaste and virile youth are projected into the past to create
a false history which is nothing more than ideology.[65] Indeed he
appears to have been acutely aware of the problem of the contrast
between ideal and practice, for in a number of passages he attempts
to expose the hypocrisy of the pederastic ideal by contrasting it with
stark reality (a view of reality strongly supported by Attic vase-
painting). In *Birds* and *Wealth* he refers to the general courtship practice of giving gifts of animals to the eromenos and he seems to suggest
that it is pure hypocrisy to regard it as distinguishable from the prostitution forbidden by the law:

> And they say that boys do the same, not for their lovers but for gold. Not
> those of good family, but the prostitutes. The well-bred ones don't ask for
> money. What then? A good horse or hunting dogs. Being ashamed to ask for
> money they disguise their vice with a name.[66]

What, then, is one to conclude about a culture whose laws
expressed a deep-rooted anxiety about pederasty while not altogether
forbidding it?[67] A culture in which attitudes and values ranged from
the differing modes of approbation represented in Plato's *Symposium*
to the stark realism of Aristophanes and the judgement of Aristotle
that homosexuality is a diseased or morbid state acquired by habit
and comparable to biting fingernails or habitually eating earth or
ashes?[68] A culture is not a homogeneous unity; there was no one
"Athenian attitude" towards homoeroticism. The widely differing
attitudes and conflicting norms and practices which have been discussed above represent the disagreements, contradictions and anxie-
ties which make up the patterned chaos of a complex culture. They
should not be rationalized away. To make them over into a neatly
coherent and internally consistent system would only serve to diminish our understanding of the "many-hued" nature of Athenian
homosexuality.

[65] Aristophanes, *Clouds*, 961 ff.
[66] Aristophanes, *Plutus*, 153–9, and cf. *Birds*, 704 f., and *Frogs*, 147.
[67] Cf. Plato, *Symposium*, 182 ff., and Xenophon, *Symposium*, 8.35.
[68] Aristotle, *Ethics*, 1148b.

# 8 Pandora Unbound: A Feminist Critique of Foucault's History of Sexuality[†]

## LIN FOXHALL

It is rare that we who study past societies can claim any analytical advantage over colleagues who work in the present. But however much we do not and cannot know about a culture long dead, we have a panoramic view of social landscapes which those caught in the on-going flow of the same present as the people they study can never catch.

The influence of Foucault's writings on sexuality, especially *The History of Sexuality* (1978–86), on subsequent studies of sexuality, gender and the discourses of power and oppression has been profound. In particular, Foucault has revolutionized the study of the social history of classical antiquity, where, with fifth–fourth century BC Athens, he ultimately decided to begin his investigations. Foucault's intellectual framework is a maze in which a large amount of recent work on gender in classical antiquity is trapped. But every maze has a way out. Here I will argue that there are considerable difficulties with Foucault's historical construction and contextualization of the discourses of sexuality and the implications of these discourses for both past societies and our own. This is not to say his contribution has been negligible; far from it. Foucault provides an analytical framework which can be expanded to explore the implications of sex and gender in the whole of social life.

Foucault fashioned his analytical "techniques" over a lifetime of archaeology, genealogy and ethics. This is grossly oversimplified, but archaeology (to maintain the metaphor) consists less of the systematic excavation of discourses than of remote sensing: of inferring the

[†]Originally published in A. Cornwall and N. Lindisfarne (eds), *Dislocating Masculinity: Comparative Ethnographies* (London and New York, 1994), 133–46.

meanings of hidden landscapes of the mind by the lumps and bumps
on the textual surface. Genealogy is the progenesis of power in discourse: the uncomfortable kindred relation between claims to
authority and the use of power. Ethics first emerges in Volume 2 of
*The History of Sexuality*; its development as an analytical technique
seems to be entangled with the major change in scope and design of
his project. Ethics is best summed up by Foucault's own phrase,
"*rapport à soi*"; that is, the relationship of the self to itself and the
concomitant creation of moral systems. All these techniques have
opened new directions in historical and cultural analysis. But the
weakness of archaeology and genealogy is that in both Foucault's
usage and other senses of the terms they are modes of enquiry
founded in a past which has only a tenuous sense of the breadth and
complexity of *their* present. Ethics, in contrast, collapses in on itself.
The revelation that there is a reflexive dimension to morality is an
immensely valuable insight. But the exercise falters in the absence of
the protean "others" which are part of the self's reflexive definition.
Foucault produces a sophisticated history of ideas but ignores the
complex ethnographic settings of these ideas. In the case of classical
Greece (as laid out in *The History of Sexuality*, Volume 2) it is especially crucial that the reflexive self has been limited to an idealized
male self—a limitation totally unjustified by the historical evidence.
This kind of masculinist reflexivity underwrites and absorbs the masculine ideologies of the past as part of the process of living out those
of the present.

The dimension of enquiry I add to redress the balance could be
called ethnography; that is, a consideration of the synchronic, simultaneous, changing contexts in which conflicting (often incompatible)
discourses operate. Here I re-evaluate sexuality as a part of personal
and political identity through the social acts of constructing gender,
whose meanings change with context. Being a man or being a
woman, male or female, boy or girl does not always mean the same
thing.

Not that the Greek sources give us much positive assistance in such
an exercise. For specific reasons, all sorts of text from classical Greece
are largely the products of a dominant masculine ideology. One can
hardly blame Foucault for taking them literally. So do virtually all
other scholars. I have tried to circumvent this problem by searching
for the meanings of actions as well as ideologies, without delegating
preferential constitutive status to either.

I have also tried to avoid a mistake made by Foucault and others in
working with Greek material—that of construing the part for the

whole. Even for ethnographers (in both a metaphorical and a practical sense) working in contemporary societies, not all contexts are accessible or are equally accessible. For ancient Greece only a limited number of contexts can be explored. Precisely because of the nature and context of the production of virtually all our sources, the touchstone of understanding is always the free, adult, male citizen. Hence discourses on power, love and life itself frequently take on the form of hierarchical definitions of "otherness" in polar opposition to the pivotal pillar of society: the adult, free, male citizen. This illusion, partly a consequence of the production of the sources themselves, blurs our vision of the intricate detail of lived reality, if we allow ourselves to be swallowed up in it (Foxhall [1995]).

The "other" of man is not only woman, but also slave, child, old man, god, beast and barbarian. But what is the "other" of woman? For Foucault, she has no "other"; only male selves are admissible in his analysis, and he never questions whether women complied with this negation of female selves. It is indeed harder to perceive woman as a first element from the texts alone. So, for example, women are never the starting point or focal person for defining an *ankhisteia*— which is the formally structured bilateral kindred that children of first cousins used to determine inheritance and funerary obligations. In anthropological terms a woman can never formally be "ego", because "significant" kinship networks were seen to link men. None the less, women were essential for connecting the *ankhisteia* together. Indeed, it could not work without them and frequently female links were chosen as a means of emphasizing relationships between men who had no male link. Moreover, there were alternative social and kinship structures, which operated in particular contexts. These were just as real in people's lives as those governed by the ideology of the adult male citizen. What is interesting is that they are not openly expressed in the texts. But if we start instead from the viewpoint that a number of significant aspects of social life were governed by feminine ideologies, an entirely new set of contemporary and simultaneous contexts is opened up in an ethnographic way.[1]

There are three aspects of life in which male and female discourses are at cross-purposes, to the point that they are sometimes mutually unintelligible. One is the relationship to time and hence to monumentality. Another is the constitution and political construction of

---

[1] I do not use the unmodified terms "man" and "woman" in an essentialist way. I refer specifically to persons of the citizen category. Of these, the best-documented group are the wealthy elite of Athens; their behaviour was not necessarily typical of less well-off citizens of their own or other cities.

households, and the relation of individuals to them. The third is the area problematized (but not so contextualized) by Foucault: the development and construction of sexuality *vis-à-vis* social and political relationships.

## TIME AND MONUMENTALITY

Women and men experience time in different ways. I think this is probably true in many societies, but it is certainly demonstrable for classical Greece. There are two areas where gender-specific relationships to time are most obvious. One is the different ways men and women pass through life stages; the second is the way individuals access the past and the future (which are different pasts and futures for men and women) beyond their own life spans.

One can still read that Greek women were considered to be permanent children (Sealey 1990: 40–2; Foucault comes close to arguing this). This is surely incorrect. Xenophon in the *Oikonomikos* portrays a newly married woman as an adult (albeit a young adult), who is taking on adult responsibilities with her marriage: women are realized, children are potential. Of course adulthood did not mean the same thing for women as for men. But it would seem that in general girls were felt to reach adulthood sooner than boys (cf. Aristotle, *de gen. an.* 775a.5ff—females take longer to generate in the womb, but grow up faster; female diseases work on different time spans from male diseases). Girls might be "finished off" after marriage under the tutelage of a mother-in-law (e.g. Lysias 1), but they were fully adult when the babies started to arrive, within a few years of their marriage shortly after puberty (12–14 or so, so they were "adult" by the time they were 15 or 16). Boys slid more gradually into adulthood over a longer period of time, through a process which began at around age 17 or 18 (cf. Vidal-Naquet 1981). They might not reach full adulthood until around 30, and few Athenian men married much younger than this. Similarly at the other end of life, women frequently remained powerful and active in their world of the household longer than men remained powerful and active in the world of the city. Men faded out of politics when they were no longer militarily active, but women's influence over their younger kin increased as they grew older. The corollary of these differences in life cycle must be that the meaning of being a man or being a woman itself changed in relation to the other over time.

Individuals' contact with the past and the future is similarly gender specific, and related to gender-specific life cycles. Women projected themselves into the future directly via their children and grandchildren, especially their sons (Hunter 1989). In most of the contexts of everyday life, classical Greeks rarely had much concern for a past or future reaching out more than three generations (Foxhall 1995). So, for example, the *ankhisteia* comprised the group of people who shared an ancestor three generations back; concomitantly one planted olives for one's grandchildren and great-grandchildren. Indeed much of a household's social and economic activity was for the sake of its children; that is, its own immediate future. Because of the special role of women's relationships in directing and managing households, much of the practical direction of life on this three-generation time scale was in women's hands. I shall return to this point, though it is worth noting that in a Greek context household management means much more than simply doing the housework, since a family's economic enterprises (including factories and farms) were conceptually contained within the household—no notion of independent, corporate, economic institutions existed (see Foxhall 1989).

Men were dependent on women for access to the three-generation time scale which framed most of everyday life (some of the later discussion about sexuality returns to this theme). But the formal network of kinship was appropriated by men. This was the *ankhisteia* (mentioned earlier), which was most often invoked when kinship affairs became public matters (as in funerals, or in the marriage of brotherless, fatherless girls, which could become a state problem). Men also appropriated a larger-scale past and future, which existed in a rather undifferentiated way beyond the three-generation limit, and excluded women from it. The way in which this kind of time was used I have called monumentality (see Foxhall [1995]). This notion of monumentality is explicit throughout Greek literature, art and inscriptions. It becomes entwined with a complex rhetoric about fame, glory, reputation and memory. For example, the (male) historical/journalistic writer Thucydides describes *his* account of the Peloponnesian Wars as *ktema eis aei*, "a possession for eternity". Many other examples of male monumentality could be cited, in forms varying from the Parthenon to individuals' grave stelae or vases inscribed with graffiti. Virtually all of the literary and epigraphical sources for ancient Greece emanate from this context of male monumentality, generated by men in their relatively short period of full, powerful adulthood. More specifically, they are the artefacts produced by the purveyors of a (perhaps "the") "hegemonic masculinity" which attempts to dominate, subordinate and feminize the rest, and their production is an intrinsic part of this process of domination (see Cornwall and Lindisfarne [1994]).

Similarly with access to the past, because men married older than women and older men married much younger women, children were likely to have contact for longer with a grandmother than with a grandfather. Thus part of classical Greek socialization processes would have been learning about the short-term past from women in the household.[2] The past and the future (on this roughly three-generation scale) were thus more accessible to women than to men, and it may be partly because of this that women had special roles in marking the passage of time in human lives—in *rites de passage*, notably weddings and funerals and most obviously in childbirth.

These contested discourses, the problematizations of gender and time, also reverberate in the relationship between the ritual and the agricultural calenders of ancient Athens. There were three major festivals of Demeter and Kore, which related directly to crucial periods in the growth of cereals, the main food staple, and to a lesser extent grapes. The Thesmophoria was celebrated in late October over five days just before the start of the sowing period, which was also the busiest period of the year for agricultural work. The festival excluded men (virtually no Athenian festivals excluded women), and during this period women took over the city, held sacrifices, fasted, and performed magic to infuse the seed corn with fertility. The Haloa, a rowdy women's festival (again excluding men) celebrated at the end of December in honour of Demeter and Kore and Dionysos, marked the end of the autumn agricultural work (sowing and vine pruning). The third festival of this type was the Skira in June, which was tied to the ritual plastering of threshing floors towards the end of the harvest.

Significantly, in all of these festivals women displayed their sexuality to, among and with each other in the absence of men— Aristophanes depicts "homosexual" as well as heterosexual desires and behaviour between women in these gatherings, and this is supported by the anxiety with which other sources document these festivals. It is also significant that immediately after the Thesmophoria and shortly before the Skira there were festivals to Apollo which were centred on the phratries (patrilateral clans) and thus celebrated the principles of male descent. The Apatouria (immediately after the Thesmophoria in early November) also celebrated the moment at which youths were becoming men (beautifully analysed by Vidal-Naquet 1981). The Thargelion came in mid-May, just before the

---

[2] Contact with the past via older men may have been largely outside the household, in a context that pulled young men away from it, as is described below with respect to sexuality.

cereal harvest. Though it included a sacrifice to Demeter Chloe (Green Demeter), the victim was a ram—one of the very few occasions when a goddess received a male animal. Perhaps most important in relation to the Thesmophoria were Haloa and Skira (the women's festivals to Demeter and Kore): all of the agricultural tasks at the heart of the rituals were men's jobs.

Over and over, women's ritual activity was essential for men's work to be effective. That ritual activity consisted in large part of women constituting their sexuality. The core of Greek social continuity was symbolized by Demeter and Kore—the relationship of mother and daughter. This became symbolically tied up with the continuity of the physical body through the social activities of food consumption and production: Demeter was the *kourotrophos*, the nursemaid, of humanity (this was one of her cult titles). In contrast, the celebration of the generations of men in festivals to Apollo complemented, or perhaps resisted, the centrality of continuity and kindred through female links which excluded men. Demeter and Kore—lines of mothers and daughters spanning generations of men—thus provided alternative kinship structures to the male-dominated *ankhisteia* (three-generation kindred) and phratry (patrilateral clan). Women might almost be said to control time in some contexts, but hegemonic masculinity wrested the control of one kind of eternity from them. Monumentality in the public sphere, the struggle to achieve glory, fame and remembrance, largely excluded women.

## THE CONSTITUTION AND POLITICAL CONSTRUCTION OF HOUSEHOLDS

Even for Aristotle (*Politics* 1), the fundamental sociopolitical unit of Greek city-states was the household (*oikos*), not the individual. The household was not simply "the private sphere" to which women's activities were relegated, leaving it as "other" to the public, political world of male citizens (usually defined as more important by modern academics). "Public" and "private" were interleaved in a complex way, and were not always hierarchized with the "public" holding sway over the "private". Depending on the context, the household was itself a public entity, with political significance. The adult male in his prime[3] held a privileged position *vis-à-vis* the household in that as *kyrios* (literally "master", head of household), he could move freely

---

[3] Sometimes more than one adult male resided in a household, but this could cause trouble, as I discuss later. Long adolescence usually prevented more than one household head.

between the contexts in which the household behaved as the private sphere and those in which it became a public entity (Foxhall 1989).[4] Much of the power of the *kyrios* derived from his ability to transcend contexts and to mediate in this way.

In spatial terms, it has been observed that in Greek town planning, household space (houses and fields) dominated over public space (Jameson 1990a, 1990b). And houses themselves contained space which was, at different times, sometimes defined as "private" and sometimes as "public", though on the whole exclusively male activities were marginalized within Greek houses. It was the aggregate of household decisions which formed the economy of Greek city-states, since economic enterprises largely existed and were managed within the structure of households. Similarly, it was households that were represented by individuals in the assembly, the law courts and the agora, as well as at the Thesmophoria. And households could not be constituted without their women; indeed women might be said to have constituted the household more fundamentally than the men who spoke for it. "Plato is wrong to argue that women and men can do the same work on the analogy of animals", says Aristotle. "Animals don't have households to run" (*Politics* 2). Interestingly, Aristotle's objection to Plato here is not that women are physically or even mentally *inferior* to men (though he certainly implies this elsewhere) or that they do not have the capacity to do men's work, but that culture is "biologically" intrinsic to humans as it is not to other animals, and people "naturally" live in households in societies (so "humans are political animals", *Politics* 1). Hence the nature of man is culture, and without woman that culture is impossible.

It was households which reproduced the political institutions of a city, for descent was one of the most crucial tenets of citizenship in all Greek city-states (though its precise significance varied). Citizens emerged from households and claimed their right of citizenship by virtue of the place they held in a household. Obviously women were essential to physical reproduction. And clearly men attempted to appropriate social reproduction, especially its public and political aspects, by monopolizing civic life. But I would argue women were central to other, equally important aspects of social reproduction, because of their special relationship to time. *Oikoi* (households) did not stretch themselves into the past and the future in simple linear

---

4 Like many words in ancient Greek, *kyrios* is protean and context-specific. It also refers to a man who acted for a woman in a public capacity in contexts from which women were excluded. Although it is often translated as "guardian", no fixed relation to the woman is implied and the relationship was negotiable—see Foxhall (1996) and Hunter (1989).

continuity. Rather, when property and social roles passed from one generation to the next, *oikoi re-created* themselves, rather than continuing indefinitely. This is reflected in the naming system: people died in the household in which people named after them (their grandchildren) were the next step in the re-creation process (Foxhall 1989). *Oikoi* were then really re-created every *other* generation. But because women's life cycles were "out of synch" with men's, they married earlier, they were "adult" for longer and they had a different relationship with the past and future of lived life; so it was that women were most likely to be the ones bridging the two generations it took to re-create the household. In other words, men lived within one generation while women's lives spanned over two formal generations of men. This also reinforced the special relationship already noted between women and *rites de passage*, and their relation to time. In a sense this relation of women to time might be said to be at the heart of the social reproduction of the household. And, as I shall discuss in more detail below when I come to sexuality, men's institutions of male social reproduction could be seen as an alternative discourse to those of the household in its communal setting, which centred on women.

Women (as constituents of households) penetrated even apparently exclusively male, "public" arenas. In Athens and Corinth and other Greek cities the earliest public buildings in the agora (datable to the seventh and sixth century BC) were not law courts or council chambers or stoas, they were fountain houses. And women used fountain houses. These were areas of female public space in zones of male activity. Here women met, talked (away from men), and filled their jugs with the water necessary to keep their households operating. Tyrants like Peisistratos in sixth-century BC Athens rated the building and upkeep of fountain houses high among their most important public works, essential to the identification of themselves with the community of the *polis* and hence to their maintenence of power. To what end? That women could keep the households of the city running and reproducing.

Foucault has construed the household as a male-dominated institution whose bars between itself and the outside world confined women's lives, including (perhaps especially) their sexuality and its expression. But the bars separating off households were different ones for women and for men. Men traversed them, but the only unproblematic way in which they could do so was as *kyrioi*—heads of household. But while men usually lived out their lives in one household, women lived in two: their natal and their marital

households.[5] This left open an avenue with the potential for some
autonomy which many women seem to have traversed with alacrity
(for example, Demosthenes' mother; see Hunter 1989). Women
became related (in terms of kinship) to their husbands, their
mothers-in-law, and their marital households through their children,
while they also maintained their relations of kinship and affect with
their parents and siblings from their natal household, especially with
female kin. Women's networks of alliances, then, ranged quite widely
beyond the confines of their own households. Men could suppress
these bonds so long as they were formed so that women remained
nested in their "proper" place within the *ankhisteia*. From here,
women's bonds strengthened the household unit against threatening
competition from other households outside. Women kept to their
place, and that place upheld men's individuality.

But women were not always passive and families and households
were not always ideally configured. Women could and apparently
often did form relationships with other kin, especially female kin,
with slaves (especially female slaves) and with children, which contra-
vened the interests of men and their positions of authority *vis-à-vis*
their household. Men's control over women's relationships and bonds
was in fact often tenuous. This is perhaps what spawned the male fantasies of women conspiring against men which are prominent in
comedy (Menander, *Samia*; Aristophanes, *Clouds, Ekklesiazusai,
Thesmophoriazusai, Lysistrata*), tragedy (*Medea, Agamemnon,
Antigone, Bacchai*) and law-court speeches (Lysias 1; Antiphon 1;
Demosthenes 41; cf. Foxhall 1996). In most of these examples,
women are perceived and portrayed as acting against the autonomy
and the interests of an individual man (or men) via relationships and
bonds over which the man is not fully in control. Male individuality
appears as a discourse incompatible with the bonds and relationships, generated by women, which ran so much of men's everyday
lives through household structures.

For men, kinship within and beyond the household was an important tool for maintaining their political and economic status and
autonomy. The interesting thing is that though women's manipulation of kinship ought to have been subject to male authority according to the dominant masculinist ideology, patently it often was not.

---

[5] This, at least, is the ideal. In practice, the man who married an *epikleros* (a fatherless,
brotherless girl) and/or was adopted by another household did not live out this ideal, and may
have had a different relationship to the women of his household.

## SEXUALITY, SOCIALIZATION AND POWER

Greek male ideologies of sexuality have a lot to do with notions of control, autonomy and individuality, as Foucault has quite rightly argued. A very important source of men's power and authority as heads of households was that (ideally, at least) they could control the sexual activities of other household members (including animals and slaves), but that they themselves were autonomous and no one else could dictate their sexual activities. But reality, however hard to get at, is usually more complicated than ideology. And this ideology works only as long as women are assumed to be passive and boys obedient. I shall consider women's sexuality first, then boys'.

That women's sexuality was not passive is clear from the sources. Sexual offences by men involving women (rape, adultery, seduction, even sexual insults) were offences against men's *authority* over their households and against their *power* to control the sexual activities of household members, as Foucault argues. So, for example, in a lawcourt speech, a man arguing that he had caught the man he killed in bed with his wife says: "he committed adultery with my wife, and he violated me inside my very own house" (Lysias 1.29). *Moikheia* (usually translated "adultery", but probably really sex with a woman in someone else's charge) was committed with the wife, and this was *hybris* against the husband (see Cohen 1991; Cantarella 1991; Foxhall 1991).

But *moikheia* was not legally worse than rape nor were legal penalties in Athens more severe, as Foucault (and others) have maintained. The situation is more complicated and more interesting. Rape was not isolated as an offence, nor was it specifically construed as a crime against women. Generally it came under the category of *hybris*, "assault", in legal terms. Hence boys and men, as well as women, could be victims of what we call "rape". Moreover, *moikheia* and rape were legally not very clearly distinguished, and the punishments were the same most of the time (Harris 1990). The reason for this was almost certainly that from the point of view of the laws the victim of both crimes was not the person attacked but the man in whose house she dwelt. But when we turn to the moral assessment of rape and *moikheia* (at least in terms of male ideologies), a different picture emerges. Women (like boys) who were objects of rape were pitied (Cole 1984: 111–13) and gratuitous violence against free women was despised. Women could be moral, if not legal, victims.

But in *moikheia* both parties were considered despicable (for different reasons). This difference in moral attitude between *moikheia* and rape has as much to do with the reality of women's behaviour as with ideologies of male superiority. In *moikheia* it was less easy to maintain the ideology that women had no well-defined sexuality of their own but were merely the passive vehicles of men. *Moikheia*, at least in the few cases where we have some details, implied a longer-term, larger-scale relationship, with a more active role played by women (and female networks). For example, in the case I have just cited, the wife was said to have been close to (and attended a major religious festival with) the mother of the murdered adulterer, while a slave girl acted as go-between for the lovers. The husband claimed he was finally informed about what was going on by a disgruntled ex-lover (female) of the adulterer. And perhaps most significantly, all the trouble with the wife started (so the husband says) when his mother (who lived with the couple) died. A woman with a lover (*moikhos*) has taken control of her own sexuality, and has taken that control away from the man who purports to dictate her sexual activity (cf. the women in *Lysistrata* who swear to have sex with neither *moikhos* nor husband). A woman with female lovers takes her sexuality away from men altogether. The paucity of references (though there are a few) to female homosexuality may represent the threat it posed to male individuality and autonomy, and its removal from male spheres of activity and knowledge.

Foucault argued that adultery depended on the behaviour of only one marital partner: the woman. In fact, it seems to have depended more on whether the existence of a wife's lovers were acknowledged by her husband. There was an uncomfortable subtext for the man whose authority and power was penetrated by a *moikhos*. A public accusation of *moikheia* must have elicited the communal question of whether the control exerted by the accuser was ineffectual. A man those wife took a *moikhos* was a cuckold. Was the accuser, then, considered to be as much at fault in a social sense as the accused might have been at fault legally? It is hard to know the answer to this. But this aspect of *moikheia* allows for a slightly different interpretation of the interesting penalty problematically referred to by Demosthenes (59. 66–7) and Aristotle (*Ath. Pol.* 51.2), permitting the wronged husband to attack the guilty *moikhos* and "to use him however he wished without a knife". Was this a chance for a cuckolded husband publicly to re-exert his sexual authority and his autonomy via his own physical strength and personal courage, as well as having the more obvious aim of taking revenge for the *hybris* committed against him? The unflattering implication that a man might not be looking after his authority very well, the potential messiness of divorce, and, in perhaps a number of cases, status differences between the offended party and the *moikhos* all provide reasons why real cases involving *moikheia* are thinly represented in our sources. This is certainly implied in Aiskhines 1.107, where he suggests that the cuckolded husbands of Andros would not be willing to expose themselves to testify to Timarkhos' iniquities with their wives. Whether or not this is a spurious excuse on Aeschines' part to account for lack of witnesses, it was meant to sound plausible to jurors. It is probably significant that the one victim of *moikheia* of whom we can be certain, Euphiletos (Lysias 1), had to choose between representing himself as a cuckold and the possibility of execution for murder. Again this disjuncture of incompatible discourses made room for women to wrest some autonomy from men.

But male sexuality, especially the emergence of male sexuality from boyhood, was also problematic in relation to notions of adult male control and autonomy. By Foucault and some of his commentators (e.g. Poster 1986: 213; Seidler 1987; Winkler 1990) this was considered the central problematic of Greek sexuality. What he did not consider was the connections between the emergence of male sexuality, the tension it created between the development of a male, autonomous individual from childhood, and the relationship to household bonds and structures of this new person (with a new notion of self) who came out of the chrysalis of a very long male "adolescence". We can still, with Foucault, avoid the long line of psychoanalytic explanations of the development of male sexuality from Freud to Chodorow, for the issue is not the separation of the male child from his mother but the life cycle of socialization which excluded fathers (by the self-separation of a boy from the household) as it came to include mothers.

The creation of female sexual identity took place within the household (indeed within two households: marital and natal). But the creation of male sexual identity happened out of reach of the household, in the gymnasium and in other public places, at a time when a boy or a young man was still part of a household which he did not "control" (that is, he was not the head who spoke for it and represented it). This is at the heart of the problematic nature of male erotic and "romantic" love which Foucault persuasively identified. The whole process of the emergence of male sexuality happened over a long time, starting before puberty and culminating in marriage around age 30. The emergence of female sexuality was much faster, and seems to have taken only the couple of years around puberty (though it probably continued to develop within marriage).

Although boys were ideally not supposed to take pleasure from their passive role in sex, they are sometimes shown with erections during the sex act. Further, among the numerous depictions of sex between males in Athenian vase painting, a large minority do not show the canonical *erastes/eromenos* (lover/beloved—older/younger male) relationship, but men or boys who are closer in age. Moreover, boys and adolescents are frequently shown having sex with girls and women. This shows up the cracks in the dominant masculine ideology of the *erastes/eromenos*, so prominent in the literary sources. Though boys were subordinate in certain circumstances to older men (who might also often have been of higher status),[6] they were neither entirely passive nor fully feminized. Boys and women shared some traits in masculine perceptions, but they were inherently different. Overly feminine boys were disdained, and a boy was beautiful specifically because he manifested the acme of masculinity, just as a girl or woman was beautiful through her femininity.

The development of adult male sexuality pulled a boy away from his household (as it took place outside it), most especially away from the authority of its head (usually his father). The conflicts between sons entering adulthood and fathers losing control are highlighted in Attic comedy, a literary genre which by its nature frequently homes in on the critical structural tensions of Greek social and political life (Aristophanes, *Clouds, Wasps*). A father's authority became weaker as his son's sexual identity (and with it autonomy and individuality) grew stronger over time. Foucault's paradox of the *eromenos* (the beloved) who evades his father to submit to a lover (*erastes*), and who must submit without being seen to do so too easily or dishonourably, is not, as Poster argues, simply the problematization of the sexual passivity of free boys and thus the implication of unfree status. Status was relative and so boys submitted to men. It is in fact also another paradox: submission to unrelated male lovers from other households weakened the ties of authority to a boy's own father (who resisted the infringement of his authority). Yet this was essential to the development of a young man's own sexual identity, autonomy, and his ability to become the head of a household of his own and a political person in his own right.

Adolescence presented similar tensions, though in a different sociopolitical context, to the association of "ritualized" homosexuality with entry into adulthood which Herdt (1987) has identified among the Sambia in New Guinea. This process of developing auton-

---

[6] Frequently the man or men who were a boy's lovers became his political and economic patrons when he grew up.

omy was complete or near completion when the son married and became an autonomous head of his own household. And the ramification, the really crucial paradox which Foucault did not take on board, is that this culmination, which put the newly matured son almost out of reach of *paternal* authority, brought him back into the *maternal* fold. When he married, the network of female bonds of his household and that of his mother (and other female relatives) took responsibility for socializing his wife into her new household, and ultimately his children as well (as in Lysias 1, the adultery case mentioned above). His mother's authority might be enhanced at this time relative to his father's.

In summary, the gymnasium, like other institutions of male social reproduction, pulled young men away from the dominion of their households, thus encouraging their development as sexual and political individuals. The irony is that the end of that process brought a new kind of tie to the household, which was rooted primarily in female links. It is significant that it is these masculine institutions of social reproduction which are monumentalized and celebrated in art and in literature, to the near-exclusion of female roles in social reproduction.

## CONCLUSIONS

Seidler (1987) has argued on rather different grounds from me that Foucault's attempt to analyse discourses of sexuality fails because it is divorced from structures of gender. Gender was probably the most important organizing principle for Greek society, both on the level of everyday life and on the level of metaphor. It is clear that the complexities of gender were the template for expressions of power. I have tried to show that most aspects of life in classical Greece consisted of complex discourses and "conversations". Though the dominant masculinist ideology of the elite, citizen, adult male shouts loudest, this voice never quite overwhelms the others, though it certainly configures their speech. No voice can shout continually, and when the dominant one pauses for breath, the others are ready to fill the gap in their own way, even if they can never permanently win. It is my task as a feminist scholar to listen for the other voices and report what I hear.

Foucault's arguments and methodologies in *The History of Sexuality* are significantly flawed. One aim of this revised account of Greek "sexuality" has been to make manifest these problems, by examining the intricacies of gendered roles in areas of Greek life that went beyond "sexuality" in a narrow sense and yet were intimately entwined with it. The wider context of the household in its temporal, spatial and political setting provided the context in which sexuality was expressed and developed. Foucault illegitimately removed masculine sexuality from that context.

The most fundamental problem remains: that the nature of the historical sources and the contexts of their production and survival emanate from, and indeed celebrate, only a very small slice of male life and power. The contexts of the production of these texts happen to be the ones that our culture privileges: I am not sure this was so in ancient Greece, and there is enough evidence of other discourses to problematize Foucault's privileging of these. Is it possible that Foucault's intellectual methodology itself, in isolating the discourse as the object of analysis and interpretation, succeeds in decontextualizing discourses from their social setting precisely because alternative discourses are not always mutually audible or intelligible? In refusing to hear alternative discourses he has deprived Greek women of their selves, he has left them passive and compliant in the face of male ideologies of oppression, and he has robbed them of their recourses to autonomy. I would not argue that women in classical Greece were not oppressed, but I would maintain that they resisted suppression. The dominant masculinist ideologies which ruled political life and serve as the context for the creation of most of the surviving source material never completely drowned out the other voices in the Greek conversations we can still hear.

# 9 The Cultural Construct of the Female Body in Classical Greek Science[†]

## LESLEY DEAN-JONES

In most cultures an individual is ascribed to one sex or another at birth on the evidence of external genitalia, and this categorization is taken to predict his or her physical and mental development and capabilities, which in turn support the differentiation between the sexes in the home, the workplace, religion, the law—even in hairstyles and dress. There is an obvious correlation between genitalia and an individual's role in the propagation of the species, but no culture considers this difference in external genitalia in and of itself sufficient to justify the complete separation of male and female roles in society. Rather, cultures support this division by claiming that there are other, less apparent physical, mental, and emotional traits which naturally differentiate the sexes. The traits that a culture decides are typical of a male or a female form the construct of that sex in that society. These stereotypes are often contradicted by individuals. Taking our own culture as an example, a woman can be more muscular or more aggressive than many men, a man can be smaller and more gentle than many women. However, these challenges to the cultural constructs of male and female are neutralized by claiming that they are exceptions to a natural law.[1] The belief in a natural law of

[†]Originally published in S. B. Pomeroy (ed.), *Women's History and Ancient History* (Chapel Hill and London 1991), 111–37.
A few frequently cited texts from the Hippocratic Corpus are abbreviated as follows: *On Generation (Gen.); Diseases of Women (DW); On the Nature of the Child (NC); Nature of Women (NW).* Parallel references with Hippocratic citations are to *Œuvres complètes d'Hippocrate*, ed. Emile Littré, 10 vols. (Paris, 1839–61; reprinted Amsterdam: A.M. Hakkert, 1961–62). Unless otherwise noted, other abbreviations conform to those used in *L'année philologique* and the second edition of the *Oxford Classical Dictionary.*
[1] During the nineteenth century many people still believed intelligence to be an exclusively male attribute. In 1879 the French scholar Le Bon (whose work on crowd psychology is still widely respected) stated, "Without doubt there exist some distinguished women, very

the disjunction of the sexes can find its initial expression in mythology or religion, as in the derivation of Eve from Adam's rib. And although, as a society develops, this mythological expression can appear allegorical at best, the deeply implanted cultural belief that men and women are radically different can condition the interpretation of empirical evidence so that science, in its turn, supports the belief that perceived differences between men and women are a result of biology rather than social conditioning.[2]

In ancient Greece the polarization of sexual roles was far more marked than in our own society, and consequently there was a stronger need to sever the male from the female. This disjunction was expressed in Greek myth by the separate origins of the sexes. In *Works and Days* (60–95) and *Theogony* (570–616) Hesiod portrays man as already existing when woman, a later manufactured product of the gods, was given to him.[3] But after the beginnings of natural philosophy in Ionia in the sixth century BC mythology was no longer universally accepted as giving a true explanation of the world; as in our own society, science assumed the task of bolstering the traditional dichotomy between male and female.[4] However, although the Greeks could observe the difference in external genitalia and typical secondary sexual characteristics, they did not dissect the human body and so had only the vaguest understanding of the internal reproductive organs; nor, obviously, could they have any knowledge of genet-

superior to the average man, but they are as exceptional as the birth of any monstrosity, as, for example, of a gorilla with two heads." He believed that recent work in craniometry, demonstrating that the average woman had a smaller head and therefore a smaller brain than the average man, proved scientifically that she was also less intelligent. He failed to take into account the fact that the average woman is smaller than the average man overall, and that large men with large heads were not always more intelligent than smaller representatives of the male sex. See Stephen Jay Gould, "Women's Brains," in *The Panda's Thumb: More Reflections in Natural History* (New York: W. W. Norton, 1982), 152–59.

[2] Hence the misinterpretation of the data on XYY males which led to the supposed discovery of a gene for aggression on the Y chromosome; see Stephen Jay Gould, *The Mismeasure of Man* (New York: W.W. Norton, 1981), 143–45; Anne Fausto-Sterling, *Myths of Gender* (New York: Basic Books, 1985), 150–53. I do not wish to argue that it has been scientifically proven that all supposed male and female behavioral patterns are socially rather than biologically conditioned, or that there can be no biologically determined differences between men and women apart from their reproductive roles. However, I do believe that thus far all attempts at accounting biologically for supposed male-female dichotomies have proved, at best, inconclusive.

[3] For a discussion of the mythological separation of the sexes see Jean-Pierre Vernant, "Hestia-Hermes: The Religious Expression of Space and Movement in Ancient Greece," in *Myth and Thought among the Greeks* (London: Routledge & Kegan Paul, 1983), 127–75; Nicole Loraux, *Les enfants d'Athéna: idées athéniennes sur la citoyenneté et la division des sexes* (Paris: F. Maspero, 1981), 75–117; Helen King, "From Parthenos to Gyne: The Dynamics of Category" (Ph.D. dissertation, University of London 1985), 15–27.

[4] Though it should be clearly understood that "science" has a more assured institutionalized position in our society than it did in the ancient world.

ics or endocrinology. The strict biological polarization of the sexes was thus even more dependent on external sexual characteristics than our own society. But because, as today, many bodies would have been annoyingly recalcitrant in conforming to the culturally determined sexual norm, the archetype of the male or female body could not be substantiated by referring simply to the actual bodies that men and women possessed. The cultural paradigm of masculinity and femininity had to be supported by demonstrating that typical male or female observable characteristics (both genitalia and the less constant differences of body shape and behavior) were evidence of a more perfectly male or female invisible nature (*physis*). Once the cultural archetype was shown to be grounded in nature, a man or woman who deviated from this norm could be viewed as aberrant–lacking in something essentially masculine or feminine—rather than as a challenge to what it was to be male or female, and the traditional polarization of the sexual roles could claim a scientific foundation.

The sexual roles in ancient Greece were complementary; men were thought to be best suited to dealing with matters outside the home, the *polis*, and women with the concerns of the household, the *oikos*. The female role in managing the *oikos* was recognized as important, and a woman could gain satisfaction and respect from performing her tasks well; but she was nevertheless considered inferior and subordinate to her husband.[5] She was barred from the male sphere by her inability to perform certain mental and physical tasks. On the other hand, although a man could not bear or nurse a child, he was not thought incapable of performing female tasks in the same way; the management of a household was considered beneath rather than beyond him.[6] Hesiod's account of the first woman as a gift (albeit

---

[5] This view of woman's position relative to man's is that of elite males, the authors of the overwhelming majority of our sources from ancient Greece. The extent to which women concurred in this opinion is an extremely complex question which will not be discussed in this essay but of which the reader should be aware.

[6] Ischomachus in Xenophon's *Oeconomicus* (7.22–30) states that a man is fitted for the outdoors whereas a woman is suited to the interior of the house and, in addition, that it is more honorable for them both to remain in their natural spheres. However, a woman's physical limitations (as described by Ischomachus) play a greater part in restricting her sphere of influence than do a man's. The indoor tasks were allotted to her because she was less capable of physical endurance than a man. The only positive attribute she has over a man is her greater affection for the newborn. It might seem as if Xenophon wishes to argue that her fearfulness makes her a better protector of the household stores than a man, but all he actually says is that this is not a disadvantage (*ou kakion esti*). The male's greater amount of courage would not disqualify him from protecting the stores. In fact, Ischomachus is so well informed on how to run a household that it is he who undertakes the training of his own wife in these matters. Various scholars have noted how improbable this was; the girl would normally have received such instruction from her mother before she married. See Sheila Murnaghan, "How a Woman Can Be More Like a Man: The Dialogue between Ischomachus and His Wife in Xenophon's

malicious) of the gods to men reflects this cultural construct of woman as secondary and subordinate to man. In the same way, scientific theories attempted to justify not only the polarization of the sexes but also the subordination of the female to the male. This essay demonstrates how Greek scientific theories of female anatomy and physiology were conditioned by cultural assumptions of female nature: specifically, how Greek scientists used menstruation, breasts, womb, and lack of body hair to define female physical nature as fundamentally different from and inferior to the physical nature of the male, and how, on occasion, their assumptions led them to misinterpret or overlook data which could have challenged their theories.[7]

Little explicit reference is made to female anatomy or physiology in the majority of Greek literature, but there are two sources which discuss these matters in great detail. The first of these is the gynecology of the Hippocratic Corpus, a collection of theoretical and therapeutical treatises written between the last quarter of the fifth and the middle of the fourth century BC.[8] The treatises were written by several different authors, and although they are on the whole consistent with each other, there are occasions where differences of opinion are evident (as on the origin of menstrual blood, discussed below). I draw attention to these differences where it is necessary, but for most purposes here I refer to a general "Hippocratic" model of the female, because the Hippocratic theories have a great deal more in common with each other than they do with the second source with which I want to compare them. This second source is the biology of Aristotle (primarily *History of Animals, Parts of Animals, Generation of Animals*), written around the third quarter of the fourth century BC. Some of the later Hippocratic authors may have still been writing when Aristotle began to compile his biology, but even if all the gyne-

*Oeconomicus,*" *Helios* 15 (1988): 9–22, for an explanation of the strategy of the dialogue. Nevertheless Xenophon, although male, believed he knew how to run a well-ordered household and did not think it unsuitable to portray his hero Ischomachus as displaying the same knowledge. It was simply unseemly that men should actually engage in such activities, not impossible.

[7] I do not consider this to have been a conscious manipulation or falsification of data to maintain the status quo; rather, the theories were the result of a good-faith effort by intelligent men to explain what they considered to be the facts of the world. I suspect that the vast majority of Greek women, raised under the same cultural conditioning, concurred in these beliefs, though they may have drawn somewhat different implications from them. Ann Ellis Hanson, "Continuity and Change: Three Case Studies in Hippocratic Gynecological Therapy and Theory," [in *Women's History and Ancient History*, ed. S.B. Pomeroy (Chapel Hill and London, 1991), 73–110], demonstrates how cultural preconceptions caused ancient physicians to overlook the role of uterine contractions and to assert that it was healthier for a woman to be pregnant with a boy than with a girl.

[8] See Hanson, "Continuity and Change," for a fuller description of the composition of the Hippocratic gynecological treatises.

cological treatises had been completed before Aristotle began his researches, there is no indication that there was any revolution in medical theory during the fourth century. Thus the theory and practice of Hippocratic gynecology was in all probability still flourishing when Aristotle wrote.[9] Therefore, although the Hippocratic gynecological theories were produced slightly earlier than Aristotle's biology, they functioned in the same culture.

The Hippocratic theory is the product of different physicians in different generations concerned, primarily, with pathology. Aristotle, on the other hand, was a single philosopher of nature, interested more in normative physiology and in developing a thoroughgoing theory of the female which could explain the similarities as well as the differences between the male and the female, between the human and other animals. This is not to say that the Hippocratics would have come up with the Aristotelian theory had they attempted to systematize, but it explains in some measure why Aristotle rejected many Hippocratic ideas.[10] Still, although the Hippocratics and Aristotle constructed different models of the female body and observed or overlooked different pieces of evidence in support of their theories, their constructs were similar in that both were shaped by their cultural assumption that the female body was inherently inferior to that of the male.

Both the Hippocratics and Aristotle argued that despite the difference in external genitalia which developed in the fetus, the fundamental differentiation between the sexes which occurred at conception did not become apparent until puberty.[11] The Hippocratic treatises rarely characterize prepubescent children by sex, and a similar homology underlies Aristotle's statement that a woman's body is like a boy's.[12] According to Aristotle, at puberty a man's body changes more drastically than a woman's; until then the two sexes are very similar. Once

---

[9] Aristotle takes issue with theories that are espoused in those treatises; e.g., the theory of pangenesis as described in *Gen.* 8 = 7:480–82 is criticized in *GA* 712b12–24a14.

[10] The significance of Hippocratic clinical practice and Aristotelian teleology is addressed more fully in Lesley Ann Jones, "Morbidity and Vitality: The Interpretation of Menstrual Blood in Greek Science" (Ph.D. dissertation, Stanford University, 1987).

[11] *Gen.* 2 = 7:472–74. At *GA* 737b11 Aristotle says that conception is not complete until the fetus is differentiated as either male or female. *GA* 716a27–31 locates this differentiation in the specifically male and female parts rather than in the body as a whole. *GA* 765a35–766b10 says that male and female each have their own instrument (*organon*), which Nature gives to each simultaneously with its secretions and abilities. These secretions and abilities are related to their instruments in the same way as the ability to see is related to the eye. An animal cannot see without an eye, and an "eye" that cannot see is an eye in name only. Obviously, newborn boys and girls, although differentiated in genitalia, do not have generative abilities and secretions. They possess both the tools and their powers potentially. The receptacles and residues are not fully developed until puberty (*GA* 728b22–32).

[12] *GA* 728a17.

puberty is passed, however, the female body is marked as differing in many aspects from the male. The two most striking observable developments in the female body at puberty—menstruation and breasts—are explained by both the Hippocratics and Aristotle as the manifestation of the hitherto concealed female nature which made it difficult for women to perform in the male sphere.

*Diseases of Women* 1.1 (= 8:2) attributes menstruation to the very nature of a woman's flesh, which at puberty becomes loose and spongy, causing her body to soak up excess blood from her stomach (where it has been converted from the food she has consumed). The author uses an analogy to explain the difference between female and male flesh. If wool and cloth of equal weight are stretched above water and left for two days and nights, at the end of this period the wool will have become much heavier than the cloth. It soaks up more moisture because it is more porous (*araia*).[13] So it is with men and women. A woman's spongy, porous flesh is like wool (*eirion*) and soaks up more moisture from her belly than a man's from his.

If a man should have any excess moisture in his body after exercise, it is absorbed by his glands, which are especially constructed for this purpose. The author of *Glands* 1 (= 8:556) describes their nature as spongy, porous, and plump (*spongōdēs araiai kai piones*), language very similar to that which is used in *Diseases of Women* to describe the female body in general. Later in the same chapter the author likens the texture of glands to *eirion*, wool, and emphasizes how much they differ from the rest of the body in this: "and there is no flesh like it in the rest of the body, nor anything like it at all in the body."[14] In chapter 16 (= 8:572), however, he says: "The nature of glands in women is porous, *just like the rest of the body.*"[15] The body of a mature woman was one big gland and therefore similar to that flesh in a male body which functioned only after a man had evacuated or used up most of his excess fluid through vigorous activity. The implication is that a truly feminine woman would be incapable of developing the sort of flesh that would

[13] Ann Ellis Hanson, "The Medical Writer's Woman," in *Before Sexuality*, ed. David Halperin, John Winkler, and Froma Zeitlin (Princeton: Princeton University Press, 1990), 309–38, has detailed how fleeces were used in this way to locate underground water sources in Mother Earth.

[14] The Greek reads: *kai estin oute sarkia ikela tōi allōi sōmati, oute, allo ti omoin tōi sōmati.* Unless otherwise stated, translations throughout this essay are my own.

[15] The Greek reads: *tēisi men gynaixin araiē te hē physis kata tōn adenōn, hōsper to allo sōma.* Where Littré simply suppresses a *kai* that appears in the manuscripts before *kata*, Robert Joly, *Hippocrate* (Paris: Les Belles Lettres, 1978), 13:121, adopts Zwinger's emendation to *karta.* This could be interpreted as an even stronger statement, that a woman's glands were very porous, even more porous than a man's glands, just as the rest of her body was more porous than a man's body.

enable her to perform the same tasks as a man, despite the fact that many female slaves worked very strenuously and must have developed leaner and more muscular bodies than some men.

The breasts were regarded as glands, and the difference in the size of male and female breasts was used as another indication of the extent to which a woman's body is looser than a man's. In both sexes they swell at puberty, but the treatise says that breasts become prominent (*diairontai*) only in those who make milk,[16] because man's firm flesh prevents the spongy parts of his body from swelling too far. Even where the bodies of both sexes are constructed to soak up moisture, women soak up more. *Epidemics* 2.6.19 (= 5:136) states that a large vein runs to each breast and that these are the seat of the greatest part of consciousness. From this the author draws the conclusion that if a person is about to be mad, blood collects in the breasts. That women would always be more susceptible to having more blood in their breasts than men, would give a "scientific" basis to the belief that women were always closer to the irrational than men.[17]

Here we see how the biological facts of menstruation and breasts were used to create a biological construct which upheld society's characterization of a woman's body as inherently inferior to that of a man. Underlying the Hippocratic characterization of male and female flesh is a value judgment: firm and compact is good/loose and spongy is bad. This is clear from the fact that a contributory reason for a man's flesh remaining compact was his more excellent mode of life. He was thought to work much harder than a woman and thereby to use up all his nourishment in building a stronger body. A woman soaks up moisture through inactivity; a man does not, because labor strengthens his body.[18] *Regimen* 1.34 (= 6:512) says that women are

---

[16] It is perhaps surprising that in *Prorrhetic* 2 = 9:54, when listing factors which predict good childbearing capacity, the Hippocratics give a positive endorsement to large breasts, for as Jeffrey Henderson remarks in *The Maculate Muse* (New Haven: Yale University Press, 1975), 148–49, "firmness and thus youthfulness is the usual attribute" desired of breasts in a *parthenos* [unmarried girl]. The Hippocratics, on this occasion, did not ratify the culture's ideal female body type (for a lover at least) as the most fertile. It may be relevant that the gradual movement away from assimilation of the proportions of female statues to male— documented by Eleanor Guralnick, "Proportions of Korai," *AJA* 85 (1981): 269–80—began in Ionia, the geographical origin of Hippocratic medicine. However, even the more feminine shapes of the Classical period retained small breasts, and Soranus at *Gyn.* 2.84 advises swaddling an infant girl tightly around the chest, but letting the bandages loose around the buttocks, as this is a more becoming shape.

[17] See Ruth Padel, "Women: Model for Possession by Greek Daemons," in *Images of Women in Antiquity*, ed. Averil Cameron and Amélie Kuhrt (Detroit: Wayne State University Press, 1983), 3–19.

[18] DW 1.1 = 8:14, *dia tecn argiēn*; Glands 16 = 8:572, *ho ponos kratynei autou to sōma*. Hesiod (*Theog.* 592–99) and Semonides (*On Women*; only the bee-woman actually works) also characterize the typical female life-style as slothful.

colder and moister than men in part because they use a more frivolous (*rhaithymoterēisi*) regimen. *Diseases* 4.45 (= 7:568) states that if
a person remains at rest and does no work (which, to the Greek mind,
would be to follow a more typically feminine way of life), the body of
that person contains illness (*kakon*), even if the person is not immediately aware of it because the body is otherwise so healthy. Less
work, therefore, does not simply result in a different type of body;
characterizing the result of idleness as *kakon* shows that the change
was looked upon as a deterioration. This could lead one to ask
whether, on this theory, a woman could change her body type and
cease to menstruate if she led a strenuous life. But although various
means are suggested for reducing the menstruation of women who
menstruate too abundantly (for example, by curtailing food intake,
and by bleeding at the breasts), no Hippocratic author recommends
that an overmenstruating woman should work harder or increase her
exercise, and nowhere in the Hippocratic Corpus is there a suggestion
that a woman could overcome her inherently inferior *physis* to the
extent that she could cease to menstruate altogether.[19] In fact,
however, if, as now seems to be the case, regularly monthly periods
among women are a phenomenon of better nutrition in the postin-
dustrial age,[20] it seems likely that women of that time would have
menstruated less than the Hippocratics expected rather than more.
Nevertheless, despite the frequency of menstrual cycles which must
have lasted longer than the canonical month, the Hippocratics
assumed that an absence of menses for longer than a month meant
that the blood was trapped in a woman's body, not that there was no
excess blood to be evacuated.[21]

By the second century AD, when, perhaps partly as a result of dissection, partly under the influence of Aristotelian theories, male and
female bodies were treated as members of the same species partaking
in basically the same *physis*, Soranus expressed the opinion that
excessively active women did cease to menstruate.[22] [...] Because the
Hippocratics believed that the difference between men and women
was to be explained primarily by biology rather than by their socially
allotted ways of life, they did not believe the female could ever assim-

---

[19] Curtailing food intake, bleeding at the breasts: *DW* 1.5 = 8:28; *Aphorisms* 5.50 = 4:550.
*DW* 1.11 = 8:44 advises a woman who is too moist because of phlegm (not menses) to exercise (*gymnazesthai*) frequently.
[20] Cf. Doreen Asso, *The Real Menstrual Cycle* (Chichester: John Wiley & Sons, 1983), 17,
90, 148.
[21] For a more detailed discussion of this issue cf. Lesley Dean-Jones, "Menstrual Bleeding
according to the Hippocratics and Aristotle," *TAPhA* 119 (1989): 179–94.
[22] *Gyn.* 1.22–23.

ilate to the male in this way or, thus, could ever expect to live more like a man. The converse, however, seemed quite possible. The description of Scythian men in *Airs, Waters, Places* 20–22 (= 2:72–82) shows that if a man pursues a sedentary lifestyle, his body becomes loose, flabby, and moist (though he does not begin to menstruate) and therefore more like a woman's. The Scythians who developed this condition were able to follow a female life-style (apart from bearing children), because this always lay within the capabilities of every man, though it was usually avoided. [...]

The models of female physiology developed by the Hippocratics and Aristotle were in large measure attempts to explain menstruation. The relative status of male and female in Greek society meant that although the female body was acknowledged to be necessary and its differences from the male valuable for society as a whole (a woman was most precious to society in her reproductive years, when her body was thought to diverge most widely from the male's), science used menstruation to construct a female body inherently weak and capable of exerting influence on her emotions and intellect, thereby buttressing her subordinate and restricted position in society. For the Hippocratics the weakness of a woman's body (her porous flesh) caused menstruation; for Aristotle menstruation caused her physical weakness.

In the Hippocratic theory, the release of excess matter in menstrual blood once a month prevented a woman's body from becoming diseased. Even if menstrual fluid had no role to play in childbearing, a woman would have had to produce it as it was only thus that she could approach the male ideal of health. For Aristotle, on the other hand, the production of menstrual blood for the sake of generation was what forced women away from the ideal of male health. He attributes a woman's paleness and deficiency of physique to her heavy menstrual flow.[23] Moreover, at *Generation of Animals* 728b10–15 he comments on the abundance of menstrual fluid in women in comparison not only with men's seminal fluid but also with other female animals.[24] Consequently, whereas Aristotle considers the male of almost every species as physically superior to the female, the ascendancy in humans is more marked.

Let us now consider how the "scientific" accounts of the external indication of the female gender (menses and breasts) were related to theories of the internal organ of the womb. [...]

[23] *GA* 727a22–25.
[24] Here Aristotle appears to be confusing the menstrual discharge of primates with the estrus discharge of all other mammals.

*On the Nature of the Child* 15 (= 7:492–94) says that the drawing
of the blood from the woman's body into her womb happens all at
once each month when she is not pregnant; perhaps this is an attempt
to account for some of the symptoms that some women report before
menstruation each month, which have been termed "premenstrual
syndrome." Once the womb has collected the blood, it discharges it
through the vagina—if its mouth is open and it is correctly aligned.
The passage may be blocked, particularly in young girls, for whom
the best way to remove the impediment is to be married as soon as
possible.[25] Lack of sexual intercourse can cause the womb of a
woman who has already been deflowered to close over again; hence
the impediment seems to be regarded as a constriction of the *stoma*,
which could be relaxed and prized apart by the warmth and friction
of intercourse.[26] The Hippocratics believed that an imperforate membrane could stretch across the vagina, but they viewed this as an
unusual pathological symptom, not as a natural hymen common to
all women.[27]

The womb could become misaligned with the vagina by tipping
slightly in one direction or the other or by moving to a different position in the body altogether. The concept of "the wandering womb"
has its most famous statement in Plato's *Timaeus* (91b–d), where the
womb is portrayed as an animal travelling round the body of a
woman seeking satisfaction in sexual intercourse and pregnancy. The
Hippocratics never describe the womb explicitly as an individual
animal wandering at will within the body of a woman.[28] Their explanation of its movements throughout a woman's body is that if it is
not anchored in place by pregnancy or kept moist by intercourse, it
becomes dry and is attracted to the moister organs of the heart, the
liver, the brain, and sometimes to the bladder and the rectum (it is
especially easy for it to move if the stomach has emptied itself more

[25] *Diseases of Young Girls* = 8:468–70.

[26] DW 1.2 = 8:16.

[27] DW 1.20 = 8:58–60. At GA 773a15–29 Aristotle mentions a pathological condition in
which the *os uteri* grows together and has to be surgically separated. His coalescing of the
vagina and the urethra (see below) would have prevented him from positing an imperforate
membrane across the passage itself. See Giulia Sissa, "Une virginité sans hymen: le corps
féminin en Grèce ancienne," *Annales ESC* 39 (1984): 1131–32. Hanson, "Medical Writer's
Woman," argues against this interpretation.

[28] But see Paula Manuli, "Fisiologia e patologia del femminile negli scritti Ippocratici del-
l'antica ginecologia greca," in *Hippocratica, actes du colloque hippocratique de Paris* (4–9
septembre 1978), ed. M. D. Grmek (Paris: Editions du CNRS, 1980), 393–408, and "Donne
mascoline, femmine sterili, vergini perpetua: la ginecologia greca tra Ippocrate e Sorano," in
*Madre Materia*, ed. Silvia Campese, Paola Manuli, and Giulia Sissa (Torino: Boringhieri,
1983), 149–204. For more details of uterine displacement see Hanson, "Continuity and
Change."

than usual and so does not get in the way).[29] Young girls, widows, and other women who are not having regular sexual intercourse are prone to this displacement of the womb.[30] The wombs of older women are lighter, not only because they have their wombs moistened less by sexual intercourse and pregnancy but also because after a certain point they cease to produce menstrual fluid.[31] A womb which was full of menstrual blood or a fetus was not quite as peripatetic as an empty womb.

The womb could prolapse completely and issue from the vulva as a result of intercourse too soon after childbirth or a difficult birth.[32] A prolapsed uterus is recognized as a medical condition today, and it has been suggested that it was this which gave rise to the belief that the womb could wander in other directions. However, the prolapse of the uterus is simply a falling downward of the organ through the vagina; it can, and does, occur in spite of the tendons that usually hold it in place. This could in and of itself have suggested that the female body was possessed of an ambulatory womb and convenient upward and downward thoroughfares. Much more significant is Hanson's remark that as men's bodies held no uterus, the human body had no special place for it to reside, so of course it wandered.[33] However, even this is not sufficient to explain the tenacity of the concept in the Greek imagination.[34] That "rational medicine" did not reject such a strange idea out of hand suggests that it fulfilled an important role in characterizing the female sex.

One of the main explanatory values of the wandering womb was to account for the suffocating sensation (*pnix*) some women

[29] *DW* 2.124 = 8:266–68 (heart); 2.127 = 8:272–74 (liver); 2.123 = 8:266 (brain); 2.137 = 8:308–10 (bladder and rectum); 1.2, 1.7 = 8:14, 32 (empty stomach). However, as Hanson, "Continuity and Change," points out, mechanical reasons could also cause displacement, and sometimes the womb could move because it became too wet.

[30] *DW* 1.7 = 8:32.

[31] *DW* 2.137 = 8:310.

[32] *NW* 4, 5 = 7:316, 318. These chapters suggest as treatment for this condition that a woman be strapped upside down on a ladder, bounced up and down a few times, and left overnight. Succussion on a ladder was also practiced on male patients in *Joints* 42 (= 4:182–84; cf. Hanson, "Continuity and Change"), but this does not seem so bizarre nowadays, when people buy special boots for hanging upside down to cure backache. Indeed the effects of gravity probably brought about some short-term relief for a prolapse, and many women may have sanctioned the treatment. It is also possible that many women claimed to be cured to avoid any similar solicitous intervention in their welfare.

[33] Hanson, "Continuity and Change."

[34] After the dissection of human bodies at Alexandria in the third and second centuries BC, Greek physicians had a much clearer idea of female reproductive organs and knew that they were held in place by tendons and connected to other organs in the abdomen. Even so, in the second century AD Soranus (*Gyn.* 1.8), Galen (*Diss. Ut.* 4), and Aretaeus (6.10) described the uterus as being very loosely moored and capable of causing severe discomfort by displacement in all directions.

experienced in the chest and for various other pains dispersed throughout the body. Aline Rousselle has argued that it was women themselves who attributed various subjective physical experiences to the movement of the womb and that male Hippocratic doctors merely adopted their explanation.[35] There is no evidence for a divergent oral tradition among women on this matter, but even if women did "volunteer" such observations, they were putting them in a framework which already constructed their bodies as inferior and in need of external control. The odor therapies which the Hippocratics seem to have taken over from folk medicine presuppose an irrational womb moving about the body at whim.[36] In their explanations of womb movements the Hippocratics were rationalizing the theories, not of women themselves, but of a culture which needed to promote, and yet at the same time wished to maintain control over, women's power of procreation.

The wandering womb, while providing a convenient explanation for various illnesses in a woman's body, simultaneously deprived a woman of independent control over her own sexuality.[37] Manuli has demonstrated that even within their rationalization the Hippocratics retain the model of the womb as a separate animal within the woman which, without the intervention of a man (husband or doctor), is in danger of subjugating the woman's own life force (*psychē*) if it does not have its own wants satisfied. Its preferred destinations (heart, liver, brain) were all thought to be possible seats of the *psychē* and the method the Hippocratics suggest for drawing the womb back to its proper position is to administer foul-smelling substances to the nostrils while the woman is sitting on a bowl filled with sweet perfumes, simultaneously repelling the womb from one end of the body and attracting it to the other.[38] Manuli points out that employing perfumes in attracting the womb parallels the use of incense in invoking a god, an entity with a very definite mind of its own which is not easy for even a man to control.

King, however, asserts that the idea of the womb as an independent animal is not present in the Hippocratic texts and would not suggest itself if we were not reading back from the *Timaeus*. In citing the principles of attraction of the dry to the moist, she says, the Hippocratics

---

[35] "Observation féminine et idéologie masculine: le corps de la femme d'après les médecins grecs," *Annales ESC* 35 (1980): 1089–1115; *Porneia: de la maîtrise du corps à la privation sensorielle, IIe–IVe siècles de l'ère chrétienne* (Paris: Presses Universitaires de France, 1983).

[36] On odor therapies see below, and Hanson, "Continuity and Change."

[37] See Bennet Simon, *Mind and Madness in Ancient Greece* (Ithaca: Cornell University Press, 1978), 238–68.

[38] NW 3, 14 = 7:314, 332. Cf. Manuli, "Fisiologia e patologia" and "Donne mascoline."

give a completely mechanical explanation of the movement of the womb, which does not necessitate attributing to it any desires of its own.[39] This is true so far as the displacement of the womb is concerned, but even so we have to ask why the Hippocratics expended so much effort explicating a traditional belief which seems to us to have such little basis in reality. Just as the treatise *On the Sacred Disease* pours ridicule on traditional explanations of the causes of epilepsy, so it lay within the purview of the gynecological writers to dissent from the common opinion that the womb was mobile, using as evidence the anatomy revealed in female sacrificial animals. As it is, although the Hippocratics may have attempted to deny that the womb had any desires by explaining its movements away from its normal position as a function of the attraction of the dry to the moist, the use of foul and sweet-smelling substances to draw it back contradicts the idea that their system was totally mechanical. The belief in the efficacy of this therapy derived from some prerational theory of womb movements and depended upon an assumption that the womb enjoyed the sense of smell in some way.[40] The Hippocratics might have denied this had it been put to them in so many words, but that they still prescribed such a treatment is an indication of the strength of the cultural construct of the female body binding their "scientific" theory.

As Aristotle denied that the womb was active in even so minor a role as drawing the blood to itself, he was hardly likely to allow it any capacity for desire or decision making. Moreover, as he did not regard the human female as quite so anomalous in comparison with the female gender of other species or the other gender of the human species, he asserted that the womb was held in place just like the wombs of other animals and like the seminal passages in the male.[41] Nevertheless, even he thought that when the womb was empty it could be pushed upwards and cause a stifling sensation.[42]

Surprisingly, at *History of Animals* 582b22–26 Aristotle explains a prolapsed womb as a result of lack of sexual intercourse: it descends and will not return to its proper position until it has

[39] King, "Parthenos," 115. But see now her "Once upon a Text: The Hippocratic Origins of Hysteria," in *Hysteria Beyond Freud*, ed. S. L. Gilman *et al.* (Berkeley and Los Angeles: University of California Press, 1993), 3–90.

[40] Soranus (*Gyn.* 3.29) denies that this treatment has any efficacy, but he indicates that some of his contemporaries were still using it on the theory that "the uterus fleeing the first-mentioned [evil] odors, but pursuing the last-mentioned [fragrant], might move from the upper to the lower parts"; trans. Oswei Temkin, *Soranus' Gynecology* (Baltimore: The Johns Hopkins University Press, 1956), 152.

[41] *GA* 720a12–14.

[42] *GA* 719a21–22.

conceived.[43] No rationale is offered for this, and it is hard to imagine a physical explanation that could justify weighing down with a fetus a uterus that was already protruding beyond the vulva. A prolapsed uterus is one of the rare female conditions for which the Hippocratics recommend abstinence from intercourse.[44] Aristotle may have been more rigorously "scientific" in observing anatomical and physiological phenomena, but to some extent (perhaps because he never had to translate his theories into therapy) he was more bound by his cultural assumptions than the Hippocratic doctors.

King has provided a solution to the mystery of how the womb was ever thought to pass through the diaphragm. The nostrils and the vagina of a woman were thought to be connected by one long hollow tube giving the womb free passage from the top to the bottom of the body. Hence a favored method for deciding whether a woman could conceive was to sit her over something strong-smelling (garlic was a standard ingredient for these recipes) and see if it could be smelled through her mouth. If it could, all was well; if not, her tube was blocked and steps had to be taken to unblock it before she could conceive.[45] These steps often included pessaries made from such ingredients as cuttlefish eggs and dung beetles. The model of a tube connecting the mouth to the vagina perhaps explains why the gynecology includes a specific cure for bad breath in women.[46] This involves taking the head of a hare and three mice or rats (two having had all their innards removed apart from their brains and liver), mixing these up with various other ingredients, and smearing them on a woman's gums for a period of days. One would imagine that however rancid a woman's breath was naturally, it would smell sweet in comparison to the cure![47]

Aristotle mentions using pessaries to test if a woman could conceive.[48] He agrees that if the pessaries cannot be smelled through the

---

[43] This echoes the description of the wandering womb in the *Timaeus*, where it issues forth looking for sexual fulfillment if a woman does not have intercourse.

[44] See Hanson, "Continuity and Change."

[45] *DW* 2.146 = 8:322; *NW* 96 = 7:412–14; *Aphorisms* 5.59 = 4:554. See King, "Once upon a Text."

[46] *DW* 2.185 = 8:366.

[47] There is no specific cure for halitosis in a male in the Hippocratic Corpus, but the *Philogelos* (a collection of jokes put together in the second century AD but containing some jokes dating from much earlier) has a section of twelve jokes on smelly-mouths (*ozostomoi*), in one of which (235) the patient complains to his doctor that his uvula (*staphylē*) has "gone down" (*katebē*). The doctor recoils from his examination and says, "No, your anus has come up." This suggests a connection between mouth and anus in men paralleling that between mouth and vagina in women.

[48] *GA* 747a7–23. He does not identify the passage in which they should be inserted, merely that the smell should penetrate "from below upward" (*katōthen anō*).

mouth, it shows that the passages in the body have closed over. However, the connection he posits between the genital area and the breath is not quite as simplistic as the Hippocratic tube. He believed that the seminal secretion originates in the area of the diaphragm, and just as this passes down to genitalia, any movement set up in that area passes back to the chest, such that it is from here that the scent becomes perceptible on the breath. The seminal discharge could also pass up the body to the eyes, the most "seminal" part of the head;[49] hence another check on whether all the passages in the body were open as they should be was to rub pigments on the eyes and see if they colored the saliva. The Hippocratics also mention this test, but without any indication of how it would indicate a woman's ability to conceive.[50] Unless they too thought that the eyes were full of seminal fluid, demonstrating a sympathy between mouth and eyes would do nothing to prove that the passages to and from the womb were clear.

The Hippocratics frequently refer to the human womb in the plural, and Aristotle explicitly says that it is double.[51] This presents no problem in Aristotle's physiology, but it is a little difficult to reconcile a double womb with *On Ancient Medicine's* picture of the womb as a broad, shallow cupping instrument. If we do try to conceive of the two models in conjunction, we should picture the body of the receptacle as divided into two longitudinal compartments. The occasional birth of twins probably confirmed this belief. The misapprehension could also have arisen from the observation of other mammalian uteri, particularly that of the pig, which is divided. The Hippocratics showed no hesitation in transferring their knowledge of animal anatomy to the human female where they had no strong cultural counter-assumption of a woman's body to prevent them. When such a counter-assumption did exist, as in the belief that a woman possessed a wandering womb (which ran counter to the observation that other mammalian wombs were held in place by tendons), they did not use animal anatomy to construct a woman's internal space. Ironically their conception of woman led them to assimilate her anatomy to other female animals where it differed (in the double womb) and to differentiate it where it shared a common feature (the tendons holding the womb in place).

From the internal reproductive organs we can now move on to a

---

[49] Thus if a person overindulged in sexual intercourse, the first part of his body to show it would be the eyes, which become hollow and sunken. Note that Aristotle is concerned with the movement of seminal fluids around the body, not with the movement of organs.

[50] NW 99 = 7:416.

[51] GA 716b32–33.

consideration of one particular part of the external female genitalia: the vagina.

Because they were compiling a pathology rather than a physiology, the Hippocratics did not describe in detail every part of the female anatomy of which they were aware. They generally refer to the genitalia by the commonplace plural form *ta aidoia* and use the singular *to aidoion* to refer to the vagina when describing treatment for the womb. They explicitly differentiate this from the urethra in *Airs, Waters, Places* 9 (= 2:40–42) and often advise inserting pessaries into the vagina without any directions for steps to avoid obstructing the flow of urine, which again suggests that they viewed the vagina solely as the passage to the womb and completely separate from the urethra.

Although he was interested in physiology per se and particularly in noting the differences between male and female, Aristotle failed to make the distinction between the vagina and the urethra. This was a direct result of one of the founding principles of his biology: that the female is a less perfect representative of the human form than the male. The same principle led him to make other erroneous claims. [. . .]

At another point, on the principle that men are naturally superior to women, Aristotle claims that men have more teeth,[52] which he associates with a longer life-span (perhaps because this allows men to masticate more and therefore digest their food better). Here again, we know that men and women have exactly the same number of teeth, at least to start with. Aristotle's statement that other animals have not yet been examined (*epi de allōn ou tetheōrētai pō*) suggests that he considered some sort of survey to have been held on this topic, and it is conceivable that, by sheer coincidence, in all the mouths he examined men had lost fewer teeth than women.[53] In this case Aristotle's presupposition of female inferiority would have led him to a wrong inference from correctly observed empirical phenomena. [. . .]

Finally, I would like to discuss one of the secondary sexual characteristics in the light of the "scientific" theories on the more fundamental issues of gender.

The seemingly most superficial of physical differences between

---

[52] *HA* 501b20–24.

[53] It may not have been so much a coincidence if men had a consistently superior diet and women had lost more teeth due to calcium deficiency in pregnancy. This would also account for Aristotle's observation that women were more knock-kneed than men (*HA* 538b10). In addition Aristotle may have been comparing young wives whose wisdom teeth had not yet come through with older husbands whose had.

men and women, that men are on the whole hairier, is credited to a man's greater volume and agitation of semen by the author of *On the Nature of the Child* 20 (= 7:506–10). Hair, he claims, needs moisture (primarily semen) to grow, and the reason humans have so much on their heads is because that is where the semen is stored and where the epidermis is most porous. Secondary body hair first makes its appearance at puberty, around the genital area as a direct result of the agitation of semen in the body and of the flesh in this area becoming more porous. Thus women have some semen, but not as much as males, nor does it become agitated in women throughout the whole body, so that the genital area is the only place secondary body hair grows. On the other hand, during intercourse the agitated semen of a man has to pass from his brain through the length of his body. Hair grows on his chin and chest because he is normally facing downward and these project beyond the straight course of the semen and so act as reservoirs which have to be filled up before the semen can continue on its journey.[54] The same theory is used to explain why men become bald and women do not. The semen in the brain, in becoming agitated, heats up the phlegm which burns through the roots of the hair on the head. The theory is consistent within itself and with the observed physical differences between men and women. It is predicated upon the assumption that men derive greater pleasure from intercourse (a view not held universally in the ancient world) and that they normally face downward during the act of intercourse—though the theory can obviously accommodate men with hairy backs too.

Aristotle thought hair grew when moisture was able to seep through the skin and then evaporated, leaving an earthy precipitate behind. Humans diverted a greater amount of their nourishment to producing a greater volume of seminal residue in accordance with their size than did other animals; hence there was not as much nourishment left over to be diverted into hair, nor was human flesh as loose-textured.[55] People had most hair on their heads because the brain was the moistest part of the body and the sutures in the skull would allow the fluid to seep through.[56] Pubic hair grew when the seminal fluids began to be produced, because the flesh was less firm in the genital area.[57] At *Generation of Animals* 782b18, Aristotle states that it is because the brain is fluid and cold that it causes most

[54] Cf. Pseudo-Aristotle *Prob.* 10.24, 10.53.
[55] GA 728b19–23.
[56] PA 658b2–6.
[57] GA 728b26–27.

hair growth.[58] From these considerations the adult man would seem to be the most fluid, cold, and loose-textured member of the human race. However, Aristotle attributes the hairier appearance of the adult male in comparison with other humans to the fact that women, children, and eunuchs are unable to concoct semen, which men can do because of their heat. He does not explain further, but it would seem that he imagines the semen in a man's body coming near the surface at times and being encouraged to evaporate by the man's heat, whereas a woman's unused fluid residue would remain as blood in the interior of her cold body. Men go bald at the front of their heads because this is where semen is stored. Hair begins to drop out after sexual activity begins, because the emission of semen results in a deficiency of hot fluid.[59] One might well ask why women, children, and eunuchs do not begin to go bald much sooner than men, as they are presumably always deficient in hot fluid. Aristotle has difficulty in attaining consistency in his theory of hair growth because adult men produce more but also lose more, and he wants both to be indications of male superiority.

To summarize: The sexual differentia of menstruation, breasts, and womb are all accounted for in Hippocratic theory by the nature of female flesh. They are utilized in procreation, but they are the result of a difference between men and women which does not have sexual generation as its prime purpose. For this purpose men possess a penis and both women and men produce seed; as a man produces more and it becomes more agitated, he produces more hair. Thus in Hippocratic theory there are two fundamental causes for the observable differences in male and female physiology, and it is the differences between male and female flesh rather than those between reproductive fluids which dictate a woman's incapacity to perform in a man's world.[60] Aristotle's theory is more economical in that it ties all differences to a man's naturally greater heat, which allows him to concoct nourishment to a greater degree for the purposes of sexual reproduction.

Because of this one small difference Aristotle considered women to be less "other" and more like men than the Hippocratics, but he could only maintain this general theory while adhering to the principle of

---

[58] And at *GA* 783a23–27 he says that sea urchins produce long spines because they are too cold to concoct nourishment and have to use up the residue.

[59] *GA* 783b18–784a12.

[60] The Hippocratic theories viewed the male and female contributions to conception as more nearly equal than Aristotle did; thus they could not hang male-female differences from this hook.

male superiority in every feature at the loss of some consistency (as in hair growth) and the neglect of some observable anatomical realities (as in the distinction of the urethra and the vagina). Because they thought woman was a completely different creature and not simply a substandard man, the Hippocratics did not have to look for a correspondence between all male and female body parts. They felt woman was inferior, of course, but her "otherness" allowed her body to be defined more by its own parameters. However, because they thought a woman was so different, these parameters sometimes spread a little too widely (as in the case of spongy flesh and the wandering womb).

Whether Greek scientists focused their construct of the female body on assimilation to the male or on divergence, however hard they tried to take the empirical evidence into account and to bring rational argument to bear on the "facts," the culture's unwavering belief in female inferiority constrained their theories.

# *10* *Gender and Rhetoric: Producing Manhood in the Schools*[†]

## AMY RICHLIN

"An orator is, son Marcus, a good man skilled at speaking." This famous line contains worlds of gendered cultural experience in each word. The orator is male, not female; father teaches son; the orator conforms to moral norms; he is trained; he speaks—in public, in a certain way. Yet the orator's gender was a crux of Roman culture and still demands study.

## STATE OF THE QUESTION

The question of the relation of gender to rhetoric could not well have been considered before the Roman gender system itself came to be examined, and indeed seems not to have arisen.[1] Recent years have seen a surge of relevant research.[2] Most of this work, as well as my own, shows the influence of the Berkeley New Historicists, treating the rhetorical schools and performance halls as a locus of gender construction, a place where manhood is contested, defended, defined, and indeed produced.[3] Related approaches deal with Rome in the context of cultural studies, wherein ideological apparatus, of which rhetoric is surely one, are analysed as parts of an organic culture.[4]

---

[†] Originally published in W. J. Dominik (ed.), *Roman Eloquence* (London and New York 1997), 90–110.

[1] No mention of the subject appears in the lengthy bibliography compiled by Sussman 1984.

[2] For recent work on gender and Roman rhetoric, see Corbeill 1990; Santoro L'hoir 1992; Richlin 1992e; Gleason 1995; Richlin 1995: 204–5; Corbeill 1996; Gunderson 1996; Richlin 1996; Richlin ([1997a]); Gunderson [1998].

[3] For a brief early discussion of sexuality and rhetorical style, see Richlin 1992b: 92–3. On the New Historicists see Veeser 1989. On cultural studies see Grossberg *et al.* 1992.

[4] Bloomer 1995; Bloomer [1997].

This work, however, depends on a critical tradition allied to, but often divergent from, feminist theory.[5] Manhood and male sexuality have tended to take centre stage here, as, for example, in Stephen Greenblatt's influential work, or in the way John Winkler looked toward Michael Herzfeld's *Poetics of Manhood*.[6] The overwhelmingly male nature of ancient rhetoric naturally has promoted a similarly male focus in current work on gender and rhetoric, with a few exceptions.[7] It has at least been possible to study ways in which the female persona was used within the rhetorical schools, as if women were good "to think with"—much like the "elegiac women" described by Maria Wyke, textual figures doing generic work.[8] In the case of the *scholae* [schools], the female can be seen to serve important social functions as well.[9] But real women are few and far between in rhetoric, so this chapter is regrettably lopsided.

A full study of the issue would have to consider the nature of the forum as gendered space; the socialization of Roman citizen boys into manhood through the study of rhetoric; the rhetorical handbooks as guides to gender construction; the subject matter of the extant rhetorical exercises; the analogy between gender and geography in the Atticist–Asianist debate; the relation between Greeks, Romans, and others in the rhetorical schools; the contrast between Greek ideas of the meaning of rhetoric and Roman ideas; and the ways in which womanhood is constructed in Roman culture through exclusion from rhetoric. This essay will focus mainly on gender construction in the rhetorical schools, spotlighting the elder Seneca.

## THEORETICAL BASIS

### Gender and public space

Feminist theorists in architecture and geography have emphasized this axiom: "Throughout history and across cultures, architectural and geographic spatial arrangements have reinforced status differences between women and men."[10] These theorists have not dealt

---

[5] On the relations and divergences between the New Historicism and feminist theory on the body, see Richlin (1997c).

[6] Greenblatt 1980; Herzfeld 1985; Winkler 1990.

[7] For consideration of women's participation in Roman oratory, see Hallett 1989b: 62, 66; Richlin 1992e.

[8] Wyke 1987; Wyke 1995.

[9] For ventriloquism of the female in rhetoric, see Santoro L'hoir 1992: 29–46; Bloomer 1995; Richlin 1996.

[10] Spain 1992: 3. For feminist theory on space, see also Women and Geography Study Group 1984; Ardener 1993; Rose 1993.

with pre-industrial Europe, but the ancient Mediterranean constitutes a prime example; the spaces of the forum and the *scholae* themselves separated male from female.

## Gender construction

Judith Butler analyses gender as "performative—that is, constituting
the identity it is purported to be".[11] Current analysts of the masculine postulate that masculinity is particularly problematic, "a precarious or artificial state that boys must win against powerful odds", and
have often turned to the Mediterranean for examples.[12] This
approach seems eminently applicable to the world of the forum,
where the concern of the oratorical theorists with the precariousness
of virility verges on the obsessive.[13]

Similarly, Wayne Koestenbaum traces connections between the
singer's throat and the homosexual's body in opera. He notes: "As
long as there have been trained voices, there have been effeminate
voices—tainted by affectation or "false" production. The ancients
concurred in condemning such emissions."[14] The conflict between
female voice and male body problematizes the gender of orators as
well as singers.

## Orientalism

Finally, the Atticist–Asianist controversy forms part of the Roman
attitude toward the East, so essential to Roman ideas of self/Other.
Edward Said's definition of Orientalism as discourse helps to locate
this debate over proper oratorical style in the context of Rome's relation to its empire and to other cultures.[15]

## THE GENDERED FORUM AND THE *TIROCINIUM FORI*

During the late republic and early empire, the Roman forum was a
major site for the establishment of the cultural meaning of gender.
The forum was ringed by buildings in which the (male) business of

---

[11] Butler 1990: 25.
[12] Gilmore 1990: 11; cf. Brandes 1981; Herzfeld 1985; Winkler 1990; Gleason 1995.
[13] For performative gender, compare work by Latinists on masculinity in Roman literary
texts: Fitzgerald 1988; Fitzgerald 1992; Skinner 1993; Fitzgerald 1995: 34–58; Oliensis [1997].
[14] See Koestenbaum 1991; the cited passage is found on p. 218.
[15] Said 1979; pp. 55–8 deal with Greek and Roman orientalizing.

running the Roman state was carried on; voting, political speeches, the censors' assessment of senators and knights, and jury trials were held in the middle.[16] Women's important business was carried on elsewhere, their girlhood togas dedicated at the temple of Fortuna Virgo in the *forum Boarium*, next to the temple of Mater Matuta; important women's cults were located outside of the *forum Romanum*, with the unsurprising exception of the temple of Vesta.[17] But freeborn Roman boys, each year on the day of the Liberalia (March 17), were brought by their fathers to the forum, clad for the first time in the *toga virilis* [toga of adult males], in a *rite de passage* that may have included a physical inspection of the boy's genitalia; the day, then, links the male body with place, dress and male bonding.[18]

Indeed, apprenticeship to a great orator was an important factor in this Roman *rite de passage*. It was known as the *tirocinium fori* ("recruitment to the forum"); it paralleled the *tirocinium militiae* [military apprenticeship] of a young officer (Tac. *Dial.* 34).[19] Cicero's remarks on the adolescence of Caelius (*Cael.* 6–15) demonstrate how the boy's sexual attractiveness to older men structured this transition to the forum. Apprenticeship included chaperonage (9):

> As soon as [his father] gave him his *toga virilis* ... he was immediately handed over by his father to me; no one saw this Marcus Caelius in that flower of his youth unless with his father or me or when he was being instructed in the most honourable arts in the most chaste (*castissima*) home of Marcus Crassus.

The adolescent Caelius is passed from man to man in a way reminiscent of the "traffic in women": from his father to Cicero to his teacher Crassus.

Whatever the process was really like, we have some attestations that it was charged with emotions and sentiments similar to those we attach to boarding school or summer camp, and that it involved a strong hierarchical bonding between seniors and juniors. Both Cicero (*Amic.* 1–2; cf. *Brut.* 304–12) and Tacitus (*Dial.* 2) write fondly of the days when they were sitting at the feet of their beloved mentors. This was a time of pride for young men; the younger Seneca writes to his

---

[16] On activities in the forum, see Stambaugh 1988: 112–19; Zanker 1990: 79–82; Moore 1991. On the gender significance of the shape of the forum of Augustus, see Kellum [this volume].

[17] On Roman women's religion see Richlin ([1997b]); on the androgyny of the Vestals, see Beard 1980.

[18] On the Liberalia see Richlin 1993: 545–8. On Roman (unlike Greek) rhetorical education as "responsible for a whole cadre of young men", see Gleason 1995: 121.

[19] See Bonner 1977: 84–5 with bibliography.

friend (*Ep.* 4.2): "Of course you cherish in your memory the joy you felt when you put aside your *praetexta* [boys' toga] and took up the *toga virilis* and were led to the forum."

Nothing resembling this process happened to a young woman, and our scanty evidence suggests that a woman orator was an anomaly.[20] Despite Cicero's praise of distinguished ladies who trained their sons to speak well (*Brut.* 210–11, cf. Quint. *Inst.* 1.1.6), the only list of women speakers is three names long and is presented less than enthusiastically: "We ought not to keep silent even about those women whom the condition of their nature and the robe of decorum were not able to constrain into silence in the forum and the courts' (Val. Max. 5.3 *pr.*). Amaesia Sentia (5.3.1) is presented favourably, but Valerius says she won the nickname "Androgyne" for her efforts; the speech of Gaia Afrania (5.3.2) is described as "barking"; only Hortensia, daughter of the great Hortensius, wins undiluted praise (5.3.3). Justinian's *Digest* says flatly (3.1.1.5): "It is prohibited to women to plead on behalf of others. And indeed there is reason for the prohibition: lest women mix themselves up in other people's cases, going against the chastity that befits their gender, and lest women perform the duties proper to men." So speech is proper to manhood, but chastity seems to call for silence—a dilemma, in fact, for men.

## STYLE AND GENDER IN PUBLIC PERFORMANCE

Considering how the forum served as the locus of the boy's transition to manhood, it is not surprising that the content of Roman oratory includes a consistent strain of invective in which rival orators impugn each other's masculinity.[21] But these gender terms were also applied by Roman theorists to literary style itself. The logical link seems to be the principle *talis oratio qualis vita* (Sen. *Ep.* 114.1): a man's style indicates his morals, and his morals will affect the way he speaks.

Seneca's 114th epistle instances several kinds of undesirable personal/literary style, but harps on effeminacy.[22] Sometimes style is too inflated, sometimes *infracta et in morem cantici ducta* ("broken and drawn out in the fashion of singing", 114.1). On the connotations of *infracta* ("broken"), we may compare Seneca's association elsewhere (*De Vita Beata* 13.4): *enervis, fractus, degenerans viro, perventurus in*

---

[20] Richlin 1992d; cf. Bonner 1977: 135–6 on coeducation in secondary schools; Hallett 1989b. On voice training for women as a health measure, see Gleason 1995: 94–8.

[21] For overview and discussion see Richlin 1992b: 83–104, 278–84. For a parallel discussion of rhetoric and gender slippage, see Gleason 1995: 71–3, 75, 98–102.

[22] For previous discussions of this letter, see Richlin 1992b: 4–5; Gleason 1995: 113.

*turpia* ("emasculated, broken, degenerating from what a man is, on the way to disgusting things"). The terms *fractus* ("broken") and *enervis* ("emasculated"; literally, "sinewless") recur in this kind of critique and normally connote a lapse in masculinity.[23] Seneca even rejects what he calls an "immodest" (*inverecunde*) use of metaphor (114.1), exemplifying the Roman perception of even prose rhythm and rhetorical *figurae* [figures] as subject to the rules governing sexual behaviour (cf. 114.16 on unchaste *sententiae* [sentences]). The *actio* ("movement") of each person is similar to his speech (114.2); thus the *lascivia* ("sexiness") of public oratory is proof of *luxuria* ("a degenerate lifestyle"). Seneca uses Maecenas as his case in point, reproaching him for a style in line with his effeminate affect (cf. *Ep.* 19.9, where Seneca describes Maecenas as "castrated"). His speech is *soluta* ("loose"), as he himself is *discinctus* ("unbelted").[24] The epistle closes with an elaborate portrait of the affect of the effeminate man—his haircut, the way he shaves, the colours he wears, his see-through toga, the way he is willing to do anything to be conspicuous—and concludes, "Such is the *oratio* of Maecenas and all others who err not by accident but knowingly and willingly" (114.21).

Seneca's own father's collection of remembered speeches and anecdotes, a memoir as well as a handbook, shows how gender and style served as signs in the rhetorical *scholae* of the early empire. This book was written by the elder Seneca for his sons and expressly dedicated to them, again marking the importance of the training of sons by fathers. Seneca invokes at the outset Cato's definition of an orator; like Seneca, his model addressed his definition of an orator to his son and wrote a book on rhetoric dedicated to that son.[25] Cicero wrote the *Partitiones Oratoriae* for his son Marcus, and the book is actually framed as a sort of dialogue, or catechism, the characters being "Cicero" (that is, Cicero's son Marcus) and "Father" (that is, Cicero). Seneca's three sons appear occasionally as the intended audience throughout his book; for example, at the end of *Suasoriae* 2.23, Seneca remarks that the style of Arellius Fuscus "will offend you when you get to my age; meanwhile I don't doubt that the very *vitia* that will offend you now delight you". This goes along with an idea voiced by Cicero that the Asianist style is both more appropriate to

---

[23] On the sexual connotations of *fractus* and its compounds in the context of rhetoric, see Gleason 1995: 112; for other stereotypical adjectives used to connote effeminacy, see Richlin 1992b: 258 n. 3; Edwards 1993: 63–97, esp. 68–9; Gleason 1995: 67–70. On the vocabulary of Roman male gender variance, see ch. 4 of Williams [1999].

[24] For the connection of *discinctus* with effeminacy, see Richlin 1992b: 92, 280; Edwards 1993: 90; Corbeill 1996: 160 n. 81.

[25] Bonner 1977: 10–14.

young men than to mature men and more admired by young men than
by old men (*Brut*. 325–7).

The elder Seneca depicts declamations in the *scholae* staged as
verbal duels among the participants, exchanges of witty criticisms,
establishing and contesting a hierarchy—often gendered, as in one
story about Iunius Gallio (*Suas*. 3.6–7):[26]

> I remember [Iunius Gallio and I] came together from hearing Nicetes to
> Messalla's house. Nicetes had pleased the Greeks mightily by his rush [of lan-
> guage]. Messalla asked Gallio how he'd liked Nicetes. Gallio said: "She's full
> of the god." [Seneca says this is a Vergilian tag.] Whenever he had heard one
> of those declaimers whom the men of the *scholae* call "the hot ones", he used
> to say at once, "She's full of the god." Messalla himself, whenever he met
> [Gallio] fresh from hearing a new speaker, always used to greet him with the
> words, "Well, was she full of the god?" And so this became such a habit with
> Gallio that it used to fall from his lips involuntarily. Once in the presence of
> the emperor, when mention had been made of the talents of Haterius, falling
> into his usual form, he said, "She's another man who's full of the god." When
> the emperor wanted to know what this was supposed to mean, he explained
> the line of Vergil and how this once had escaped him in front of Messalla and
> always seemed to pop out after that. Tiberius himself, being of the school of
> Theodorus, used to dislike the style of Nicetes; and so he was delighted by
> Gallio's story.

The story points to several features of the game as played in the
*scholae*. First, a speaker's style is rejected by labelling him as a woman.
The style of the original target, Nicetes, is associated with Greek
declaimers in particular and said to be characterized by *impetus*, a
flood or rush of words. So the bad style is feminine, foreign, and overly
effusive. Second, the people involved range from Ovid's friends and
patron to Augustus; this august circle is following, like sports fans,
questions of style among declaimers ranging from the Greek Nicetes
to the consular Haterius. Moreover, these fans are also players:
Tiberius' team affiliation is noted here; Messalla appears repeatedly
in Seneca, sometimes as a noted declaimer himself (*Controv*. 3 *pr*. 14),
occasionally insulting another declaimer.

Another story shows how such insults were wielded during the
actual declaiming of speeches in the *scholae* (Sen. *Suas*. 7.12):

> This *suasoria* [persuasive speech] [Should Cicero burn his writings to get
> Antony to spare his life?] was declaimed in the *schola* of the rhetor Cestius
> Pius by Surdinus. He was a young man of talent, by whom Greek plays were
> elegantly translated into Latin. He used to make sweet (*dulces*) *sententiae*,
> but often they were too sweet (*praedulces*) and broken (*infractas*). In this *sua-*

---

[26] On the agonistic structure of Greek declamation in the second century CE, see Gleason
1995: 72–3, 122–6.

*soria*, when he had closed out his previous pretty thoughts with an oath [a common ornament of declamations], he added the words, "So may I read you" (*ita te legam*). Cestius, the most witty of men, pretended he hadn't heard him so that he could insult this elegant young man as if he were unchaste (*impudens*), and said, "What did you say? What? "So may I ream you?" (*ita te fruar*, literally 'so may I enjoy you')."

For us, it is easier to see the mechanics of the situation than to understand Cestius' joke. The young man speaks, the master-declaimer interrupts, and gives his interruption a form that enables him to (verbally) penetrate the young man. It is harder to see what exactly it was that set him off. According to Seneca, Surdinus' style of speech was to make *infractas sententias*. I would assume it was not *ita te legam* that bothered Cestius but the unspecified list of *belli sensus* ("pretty thoughts") that preceded it.

The style wars came to play an important role in the history of Latin literature. One of the chief offenders, according to Seneca, was Arellius Fuscus, Ovid's teacher. Here Seneca deplores how Arellius trained the young philosopher Fabianus (*Controv. 2 pr. 1*):

> Arellius Fuscus' *explicatio* was splendid, indeed, but laborious and convoluted; his ornament (*cultus*) was too far-fetched; the arrangement of his words more effeminate (*mollior*) than could be tolerated (*pati*) by a mind preparing itself according to such sacred and staunch precepts; the overall effect of his oratory was its unevenness, since it was at one point slender (*exilis*), at another wandering and overflowing with excessive licence (*licentia*): his premises, his arguments, his narratives were spoken drily (*aride*), but in his descriptions, all the words were given their freedom (*libertas*), breaking the rules, as long as they sounded brilliant; there was nothing keen, nothing solid, nothing shaggy; his oratory was splendid, and more sexy (*lasciva*) than happy.

The problem seems to consist largely in the relation between Arellius' style and poetry, a relation both literary and social (cf. *Suas.* 3.5); and poetry is connected with what is *mollior* ("more effeminate"), what is out of control, and what is *lasciva* ("sexy").

Yet, as Seneca makes clear, Arellius was highly thought of: "No one was thought to have been a more elegant (*cultius*) speaker" (*Suas.* 4.5); his speeches are met with cheering (*Suas.* 4.4). Indeed, Seneca himself had a high opinion of Arellius and not only quotes him extensively but puts him among his top four orators (*Controv. 10 pr. 13*); Arellius' "too cultivated and broken word-order" (*nimius cultus et fracta compositio, Suas.* 2.23) is evidently not just for young men. Seneca claims to have included *Suasoria* 2 just so his sons can know "how brilliantly (*nitide*) Fuscus spoke—or how licentiously (*licenter*)" (2.10), leaving it to them to judge. And then, giving an extraordinary and charming insight into the world of the forum, he says, "I remember that, when I was a young man, nothing was so familiar as these *explicationes* [interpretations] of Fuscus; we all used to sing (*cantabat*) them, each with a different lilt of the voice, each to his own tune." "Singing" speeches was a highly charged practice and Seneca hardly advocates it; still, there he and his friends were, warbling away at Fuscus' well-known words, which they all knew by heart.

The danger to young men of experimenting with extreme style is the theme of Seneca's account of the boy orator Alfius Flavus, who peaked too young, declaiming while still wearing the *toga praetexta*. This poor boy's "natural force" was "emasculated (*enervata*) by poetry" (*Controv.* 1.1.22). How did poetry spoil Alfius Flavus, we wonder, and what poetry was it? We find out in the *controversia* [subject for legal argument] about the father who gave his son poison because he had gone mad and was chewing on his own body (*Controv.* 3.7):

> Alfius Flavus made this epigram: "He was his own nourishment and his own ruin." Cestius attacked him for speaking corruptly (*corrupte*): "It is clear", he said, "that you have read the poets carefully; for this is an idea of that man who filled this age not just with arts but with *sententiae* that are amorous. For Ovid...."

And he goes on to quote Ovid's lines on Erysichthon. Seneca has plenty to say elsewhere about Ovid's style and its faults; here Ovid is responsible for leading young Alfius astray. His very way of turning a phrase is said to be erotic (*amatoria*), just like his subject matter. The adjective *corruptus* is often used in Seneca to deplore style (e.g., *Suas.* 1.12, 1.13) or to label anything he finds in bad taste. The story of Alfius Flavus points to a feeling that oratory is contaminated by influence from a certain kind of poetry—a kind of poetry that itself represents a falling-off from a manly style.

A correlative critique from within the world of poetry is presented in the first satire of Persius.[27] The relationship between the audience and the speaker's words is depicted by Persius as a sexual one (1.19–21):

> Then you may see, neither with right morals nor calm voice,
> the big Tituses tremble, when poetry enters
> their groins, and they are scratched where it's inmost by a quavering verse.

The poet likewise is effeminate, as evinced not only by his clothing but by his manner of speech and by the content and style of what he says (1.32–35):

---

[27] Richlin 1992b: 186–7 with further bibliography.

> Here some man, wearing a lavender cloak about his shoulders,
> speaking some rancid drop from his stammering nose –
> Phyllises, Hypsipyles, and something weepy from the bards –
> he squeezes it out and trips his words under his tender palate.

And Persius implicitly compares the manly style he claims for himself with the unmanly style he deplores. He puts this in physical terms (1.103–5):

> Would these things happen if any vein of our paternal balls
> lived on in us? Groinless (*delumbe*), on the tip of saliva,
> this swims on their lips, and "Maenad" and "Attis" are all wet.

Content (Greek, orgiastic, female, transsexual), style (Greek vocabulary, line structure, *enargeia* [clarity], artistic syntax), and the feminized physical body of both speaker and audience unite to form what the manly satirist rejects. Ironically, the critic himself provides a flamboyant example of what he is criticizing; it would be hard to find a more artificial poet than Persius.

It is likewise ironic that the younger Seneca produced such a lengthy sermon on the corrupt style, since he himself was reproached as an outstanding case of it by Quintilian (*Inst.* 10.1.125–31). Quintilian says that, much as he admires Seneca's style, he had occasion to criticize it (10.1.125–6, 127)

> when I was trying to recall [my students] from a corrupt style of speech, broken by all vices (*corruptum et omnibus vitiis fractum dicendi genus*), to a more severe standard. Then, however, [Seneca] was practically the only [author] in the hands of young men. ... But he pleased [them] precisely for his vices....

If only Seneca had had more self-control, Quintilian concludes, he might have enjoyed the "approval of the learned rather than the love of boys (*puerorum amore*)" (10.1.130).

This modelling, as has been seen, is not peculiar to Seneca and his fans: style is seen above all as something that is passed on from older men to younger men. Seneca's sons like Arellius Fuscus; Alfius Flavus likes Ovid; teachers train students or ridicule them; young men have fun imitating noted speakers. Young men are said to have a weakness for the ornate style sometimes castigated as effeminate. Oratory, then, not only manifests gender attributes in itself but is a medium whereby older men seduce younger men—though in the word, not in the flesh.

To sum up: the forum was a place for activities that defined Roman male citizens; young men came there to begin their lives as adults and were there trained by older men. This was a time when their sexual identity was felt to be in jeopardy and, perhaps for this reason, to them is attributed a predilection for a style felt to be effeminate. The "effeminate" style was so called by Roman rhetoricians for multiple reasons: they related it to the putatively effeminate body of the speaker; they found it even in phrasing, syntax and use of rhetorical figures. Orators used imputations of effeminacy to attack each other's style in a world in which men's reputations were on the line while they vied with each other in public performance. That the performative aspect of their world was a source of concern to them is amply attested by the next group of sources.

## ACTING AND *ACTIO*

If one major source of anxiety about style was the danger of effeminacy, another—and related—source was the danger of resembling an actor. The sexuality of actors was itself suspect and actors (partly on that account) suffered a diminished civil status as *infames* [those in disgrace]—much like men marked as *molles* [effeminate].[28] William Fitzgerald has suggested that poetry, as a public performance, might have been seen as itself akin to acting, hence tending to cast a shadow on the sexual integrity of poets.[29] Certainly this was the case for oratory; the handbooks are full of insistent disclaimers explaining how orators, though as talented as actors, though very like actors, are really not like actors at all.

The problem was not only that orators, like actors, performed in public. The problem was that orators used their bodies in performance in ways that resembled what actors did on stage. They used their voices for effect, and sometimes this reached the point that critics described as "singing" or "chanting". They used their voices to impersonate different kinds of people, including women. And they moved their bodies. The effects to be achieved by various hand and arm gestures, arrangements of the toga, eye movements, and so on constitute the branch of oratory called *pronuntiatio* ("delivery"), or *actio* ("movement"); Quintilian devotes a whole section of the *Institutio Oratoria* to it (11.3), which he begins by stating *actio* to be preeminently the most important branch of oratory, appealing to authorities including Demosthenes and Cicero. Students who read the Catilinarians today rarely even hear of *actio*, and it is startling to

---

[28] On these terms and the ideas behind them, see Bonner 1949: 20–2; Dupont 1985: 95–110; Edwards 1993: 98–136; Richlin 1993: 554–61; Edwards [1997].
[29] Fitzgerald 1992: 420–1.

realize that a Roman orator must have looked more like a hula dancer than like a television anchorman. And that is just what bothered the Roman critics—that oratory should be assimilated to dancing. So it is the orator as singer and dancer who runs the risk of looking like an actor, since actors sang and danced; moreover, this dancing was regarded as morally suspect *per se* (e.g., Macrob. *Sat.* 3.14.4–8, where Scipio watches the dancing school).[30] Acting and dancing were both closely associated in Roman thought with effeminacy and sexual penetrability; hence the oratorical style that employed flowing *actio* was associated with the "effeminate" verbal style discussed above.

The conflation of ideas about oratory, sexuality, acting and dancing is easy to find in sources from the period. The earliest extant Roman rhetorical handbook, the *Rhetorica ad Herennium* (early first century BCE), discusses *pronuntiatio* with special attention to voice (3.19–28).[31] Considering the sexual overtones of *mollitudo* [effeminacy], it is striking that the *auctor* [author] gives this name to one aspect of voice control; at the same time, the name is a good indicator of the hazards that await an orator who misuses his voice.

Such pitfalls for the oratorical vocalist and performer suggest this warning (*Rhet. Her.* 3.22): "Sharp exclamation wounds the voice; it also wounds the listener, for it has something about it that is ungentlemanly (*inliberale*) and more suited to womanish clamours (*muliebrem … vociferationem*) than to manly dignity (*virilem dignitatem*) in speaking." Several sections (3.23–5) are devoted to *mollitudo*; the *auctor* observes that the speaker should use the "full throat" (*plenis faucibus*), yet "in such a way that we should not cross from oratorical practice to that of tragedy" (3.24). Finally, in the two sections he devotes to body movement, he argues that the purpose of gestures and facial expression is to make the argument "more probable"; therefore (3.26): "It is fitting that chastity (*pudorem*) and briskness (*acrimoniam*) should be on your face, and that in your gesture should be neither conspicuous charm (*venustatem*) nor anything disgusting (*turpitudinem*), lest we seem to be either actors (*histriones*) or construction workers (*operarii*)."

Comments on the theatre by other writers explain what underlies these caveats. Columella, who wrote on the quintessentially Roman and manly art of agriculture in the mid-first century CE, begins his book with a classic *locus de saeculo* [rhetorical commonplace about

---

[30] Richlin 1992b: 92, 98, 101, 284; Gleason 1995: 106, 113–21; see also Edwards [1997].
[31] Also discussed in Gleason 1995: 104–5.

contemporary life] that includes the following comment on the theatre (1 *pr.* 15): "Astonished, we marvel at the gestures of effeminates (*effeminatorum*), that, by womanish movement, they counterfeit a sex denied to men by nature, and deceive the eyes of the spectators." But both dancing and the theatre were extremely popular in Roman culture, and even that hero of Roman conservatism, Scipio Aemilianus, "moved that triumphal and military body of his to a rhythmical beat" (Sen. *Tranq.* 17.4).

If Scipio was a manly dancer, this oxymoronic state seems to have been the precarious goal of the Roman orator. Quintilian's treatment of *actio* ("movement") is full of cautions about lapses in masculinity. Effeminate *actio* repels him (*Inst.* 4.2.39): "They bend their voices and incline their necks and flail their arms against their sides and act sexy (*lasciviunt*) in their whole style of subject matter, words and composition; finally, what is like a monstrosity (*monstro*), the *actio* pleases, while the case is not intelligible." In an extended passage (2.5.10–12), he complains that "corrupt and vice-filled ways of speaking" (*corruptas et vitiosas orationes*) find popular favour out of the moral degradation of their audience; they are full of what is "improper, obscure, swollen, vulgar, dirty, sexy, effeminate" (*impropria, obscura, tumida, humilis, sordida, lasciva, effeminata*). And they are praised precisely because they are "perverse" (*prava*). Instead of speech that is "straight" (*rectus*) and "natural" (*secundum naturam*), people like what is "bent" (*deflexa*). He concludes with a lengthy analogy between the taste for such speech and the admiration for bodies that are "twisted" (*distortis*) and "monstrous" (*prodigiosis*)—even those that have been "depilated and smoothed", adorned with curled hair and cosmetics, rather than deriving their beauty from "uncorrupted nature" (*incorrupta natura*). "The result is that it seems that beauty of the body comes from bad morals." The bad body, in Quintilian's book, is that elsewhere associated with the *cinaedus* [pathic];[32] bad speech is *effeminata*, good speech is "straight" and natural, tallying with the common assertion that the actions of the *cinaedus* are "against nature". The effeminate body stands both by metonymy and synecdoche for the kind of speech that Quintilian rejects; bad speech is both like such bodies and produced by such bodies.

This critique is applied specifically to the voice.[33] "The transition from boyhood to adolescence" is precisely the time at which the voice

---

[32] On this word see Richlin 1993.
[33] On the voice and voice training see Edwards 1993: 86; Gleason 1995: 82–102, esp. 82–3.

is in most danger, for physiological reasons: "not because of [the body's] heat, but rather because of its *humor* [moisture], with which that time of life is swollen" (*Inst.* 11.3.28). That is, the voice is vulnerable to bad oratorical practice at just the age when the young man is most susceptible to penetration. A healthy voice is neither too rough nor too feeble (11.3.32); the extremes are expressed by strings of adjectives, constituting a spectrum of masculinity, although the voice itself is feminine, posing a problematical androgyny. It won't do to be too rough—we might think of the Stoic/pathics targeted by satire;[34] nor yet too smooth, explicitly effeminate. But the voice has to be both firm and sweet, great and pure.

Other aspects of *actio* also come in for regulation. It is important to be careful about your eye movements; your eyes should not be "sexy (*lascivi*) and mobile, swimming and suffused with a certain kind of pleasure, or giving sidelong glances (*limi*) and, if I might say, venereal (*venerei*), or asking or promising anything" (*Inst.* 11.3.76; cf. Cic. *Orat.* 60). In a discussion of *vitia* in hand gestures, Quintilian quotes Cicero, who rules out "cleverness of the fingers" but approves of a "manly bending of the sides" (*Inst.* 11.3.122, cf. Cic. *Orat.* 59). The speaker even has to be careful about where he walks: approaching the opponents' bench is "not quite chaste" (*parum verecundum, Inst.* 11.3.133). The arrangement of the toga is an art in itself (11.3.137): it should be "shining and manly" (*splendidus et virilis*); the toga should come just below the knees in front and to the mid-knee in back "because a longer length belongs to women and a shorter to centurions" (11.3.138). Among other possible flaws, throwing the fold from the bottom over the right shoulder would be "loose and prissy" (*solutum ac delicatum*, 11.3.146).

Moreover, *actio* should not smack of acting or dancing. Quintilian insists that the orator's vocal training is not the same as that of singing-teachers (*phonasci*), though they have much in common; orators need (11.3.19): "firmness of the body, lest our voice be attenuated to the thinness of eunuchs and women and sick people; this is achieved by walking, applying body lotion (*unctio*), abstinence from sex, and the easy digestion of food—that is, frugality." For Quintilian, the orator's training should be rough and tough, as opposed to the coddling a singer might give his voice (11.3.23–4): "For we do not need so much a soft (*molli*) and tender (*tenera*) voice as we do a strong and durable one." We have to speak "roughly" (*aspere*); so "let us not soften (*molliamus*) our voice by pampering

---

[34] See Richlin 1992b: 138–9.

(*deliciis*) ... but let it be made firm by practice". Likewise, our movements should not look like dancing (11.3.128): "Most of all should be avoided *mollis actio*, such as Cicero says was exhibited by a man named Titius, so that even a certain kind of dance was called 'the Titius'."

The need to divide the orator from the actor shows up repeatedly in the oratorical handbooks. Cicero, in the *Orator*, calls for *actio* that is "not tragic (*tragica*) nor of the stage (*scaenae*), but by a moderate movement of the body and face still expresses much" (86). The elder Seneca says of Cassius Severus (*Controv.* 3 *pr.* 3) that his "pronunciation is that which an actor might produce, but still not that which could seem to belong to an actor". A fine distinction. Yet Seneca puts into Cassius' own mouth a speech on oratory in which he draws on his own *morbus* [sickness]—his theatre craze—to use the actors Pylades and Bathyllus as instances to illustrate a point (*Controv.* 3 *pr.* 10).

Quintilian emphasizes that too close an imitation of the comic actors will corrupt the youthful student (*Inst.* 1.11.2–3):

> Indeed, not every gesture (*gestus*) and movement is to be sought from the comedians. For although the orator ought to use both of these up to a certain point, still he will be very different from an actor; nor will he be excessive in his facial expression or his hand [gestures] or his body movements.

And again, arguing that orators need not study all the nuances of *gestus* (11.3.181–4), he suggests that *actio* "should be moderated, lest, while we strive for the elegance of an actor, we lose the *auctoritas* [authority] of a good and serious man"—a telling opposition (for further remarks on acting and oratory, see 1.12.14; 11.3.103,123, 125).

One of the causes of the problem was the fact that orators had to impersonate various characters in the course of making speeches. Quintilian lists "children, women, foreigners (*populorum*), and even inanimate things" as posing challenges to the orator's skill (11.1.42). The failure to observe the correct tone is especially a problem in the *scholae* because "many emotions are acted out (*finguntur*) in the *schola*, which we undergo not as advocates, but as victims' (*non ut advocati sed ut passi subimus*, 11.1.55)—might we here posit that the lawyer stood to the client as active sexuality stood to passive? That what "unmanned" the orator was too close an identification with the experience of the contesting parties? But here Quintilian is advocating a scrupulous adherence to the tone necessitated by the plot of the *controversia*: weep, be emotional, and do it consistently. Yet, paradoxically, what he rejects here is precisely the kind of style associated with acting and effeminacy elsewhere (11.1.56): *cantare, quod vitium pervasit, aut lascivire* ("singing/chanting, a vice that has become pervasive, or sexy style").

A singing or chanting intonation is mentioned repeatedly as a vice plaguing the practice of oratory. It shows up as early as Cicero's *Orator ad M. Brutum* in a passage in which he discusses earlier Greek practices (57):[35]

> There is, however, even in speaking a certain rather muffled (*obscurior*) singing tone (*cantus*), not that peroration of the rhetors out of Phrygia and Caria that is almost an aria, but that which Demosthenes and Aeschines mean when one charges the other with modulations of the voice (*vocis flexiones*)....

As we have seen, the elder Seneca talks of himself and his friends, in his younger days, singing the purple passages from Arellius Fuscus. Seneca likewise calls Vibius Gallus crazy for his habit of singing out cues that he is about to begin a descriptive passage (*Controv.* 2.1.26): "When he was about to describe love, he would say, almost like someone singing, "I want to describe love", just as if he were saying, 'I want to have an orgy (*bacchari*)'." Quintilian suggests that singing may be taken up as the refuge of a weak voice; such a speaker may ease his "weary throat and side by an ugly aria (*deformi cantico*)" (*Inst.* 11.3.13). He introduces an extended discussion of the vice of chanting by a list of other faults that includes spitting on bystanders and hawking up phlegm, continuing (11.3.57–60):

> But any one of these vices would I prefer to the one that now is so belaboured in all court cases and in the *scholae*—that of chanting; I don't know whether it is more useless or more disgusting (*foedius*). For what is less fitting for an orator than a stagy modulation, not infrequently approaching the licence of drunks or carousers? (57) What indeed is more contrary to moving the feelings than ... to loosen the very holiness of the forum by the licence of the Lycians and Carians? ... (58) But if it is to be generally accepted, there is no reason why we shouldn't help out that vocal modulation with lyres and flutes —no, by God, with cymbals, which are closer to this ugliness. ... (59) And there are some who are led by this pleasure of hearing everywhere what might soothe their ears, in accord with the other vices of their lives (60).

Here Quintilian brings together many elements of the critique of gender in style. Singing is repellent, ugly, in the sense that it is morally repugnant and like the improper body; it is associated with the stage or with drunks, recalling the younger Seneca's description of Maecenas' verbal style; it is associated with *licentia* [wantonness], the

---

[35] On singing see Bonner 1949: 21–2, 59; Gleason 1995: 93–4, 108, 112, 117–18.

opposite of the desired control of the body; it threatens to dissolve, to loosen, the forum, which is called "holy", and opposed to the licence here attributed to Asia Minor (Quintilian seems to have the passage from Cicero's *Orator* in mind); it is associated first with the musical accompaniment of the stage and, climactically, with the cymbals of the eunuch priests of Cybele—an association both with Asia and with effeminacy. Finally, Quintilian hints that those who like this style have problems with vice in their own lives.

To sum up: the orator's training involved a surprising amount of physical work. The formalized list of appropriate gestures in *Institutio* 11.3 must have involved substantial practice for novices. The orator's vocal range was close enough to a singer's to necessitate training with a voice coach. But always, in these endeavours, the orator risked running to various extremes, among which effeminacy always looms large. The problem above all was how to avoid looking like a dancer and sounding like a singer, dubious statuses that themselves carried the stigma of effeminacy. But the beleaguered orator had even more to worry about; in Quintilian's tirade on singing, we see the traces of a further aspect of gender trouble in oratorical style: the threat to the virile forum from the effeminate East.[36]

## THE ATTICIST–ASIANIST CONTROVERSY

The debate over oratorical style known as the split between Atticists and Asianists is well known and is discussed in detail by modern analysts.[37] But the Roman ambivalence over an art so markedly Eastern in origin was often expressed in terms of gender. The Orient, in Roman thought, was associated with luxury and a concomitant deviant sexuality—effeminacy, even self-castration.[38] Thus it was logical for a style of speech that came from the East to be labelled as effeminate. The problem was, if you wanted to be an orator, you had to submit to an Eastern regimen—Greek, if not absolutely Asiatic. A solution was to divide the East into less-East and more-East and to identify oneself with the lesser of the two evils. Hence the "Atticists",

[36] For a later version of this critique by a Greek writer (without the ethnic angle), see Lucian *Nigr.* 11 (actors who speak *gunaikôdes*, "effeminately"); *Demon.* 12 (Demonax mocks Favorinus' prose rhythm as *agennês*, "low-born", and *gunaikeion*, "womanish"); and the extended description of an effeminate, chanting orator at *Rhêtorôn Didaskalos* 11–12, 15, 19. These and related texts are discussed in detail by Gleason 1995: 126–30, 132–8.

[37] On Asianists and Atticists see Leeman 1963: 136–67. Gleason 1995: 107–8 de-emphasizes the issue.

[38] On gender and the East see Griffin 1976; Balsdon 1979: 60–3, 225–30; Edwards 1993: 92–7; Skinner 1993; and for modern Orientalizing, Said 1979: 190.

who spoke of their style as more manly, claimed that it derived from the writers of Athens; the term "Asianist" was applied to writing associated with the rhetorical schools of Asia Minor. "Asianist" was generally a term of abuse, and it is hard to find an instance of someone claiming to be one, though it is not hard to find denunciations of the Atticists.

Quintilian discusses the difference between Atticists and Asianists at some length (*Inst*. 12.10.12–26) and gives an account of the origins of the two schools (12.10.16–17). In antiquity, he says, the Attic was good, the Asianist bad. The Attic speakers were *pressi* ("concise") and *integri* ("whole"), while the Asianists were *inflati* ("inflated") and *inanes* ("empty"); the former had nothing extra, the latter were lacking in both judgement and moderation. Some say, he continues, that this happened because Greek spread from Greece to Asia Minor and the Asianists tried their strength at eloquence when they were not yet skilled in speaking Greek; so they expressed ideas by circumlocutions because they did not know the right words; and then they kept up the habit. Quintilian, however, thinks that the difference is an ethnic one and stems both from the orators and their audience (12.10.17): "The Attici, refined and discriminating, tolerated nothing empty or gushing (*redundans*); but the Asiatic race (*gens*), somehow more swollen (*tumidior*) and boastful (*iactantior*), was inflated with a more vainglory of speaking." The Asiatics are thus branded both as upstarts on the rhetorical scene and as inherently, even physically, less capable of excellence.

These ethnic adjectives show up associated with gender adjectives in descriptions of the battle between Cicero and his Atticist opponents. Tacitus, in the *Dialogus*, preserves an interchange between Cicero, Calvus, and Brutus (18.4–5):

> It is established that not even Cicero was without his detractors, to whom he seemed inflated and swollen (*inflatus et tumens*), not concise (*pressus*) enough, but jumping over the limits (*supra modum exultans*), overflowing (*superfluens*) and not Attic enough. In particular you have read the letters sent by Calvus and Brutus to Cicero, from which it is easy to gather that Calvus seemed to Cicero bloodless and worn (*attritum*) while Brutus seemed idle (*otiosus*) and disjointed. In return, Cicero indeed got bad reviews from Calvus as loose (*solutum*) and sinewless (*enervem*) and from Brutus, if I may use his own words, as "broken and loinless" (*fractum atque elumbem*).

Compare Quintilian's report of the attack on Cicero (*Inst*. 12.10.12):

> But even people of his own times dared to attack him as too swollen (*tumidiorem*), Asianist, gushing (*redundantem*), too repetitive, sometimes frigid in

his humour, and in his composition broken (*fractum*), jumping-over (*exsul-tantem*), and almost—which could not be farther from the truth—softer than a man (*viro molliorem*).

The list of adjectives associated with effeminacy is a familiar one, but thought-provoking in its connection with the East. We move from the familiar *mollis* ("soft") to the explicit and physiological *elumbis* ("loin-less") and *enervis* ("sinewless"/"emasculated"), to a group of adjectives evoking space and substance: *inflatus* ("inflated"), *tumens, tumidus* ("swollen"), *exultans* ("jumping-over"), *redundans* ("gushing"), *super-fluens* ("overflowing"), *solutus* ("loose"), *fractus* ("broken"). These adjectives, also familiar from Seneca *Epistulae* 114 (and cf. *Rhet. Her.* 4.16), are located in the body of the orator as well as in his speech, and in addition suggest a quality he may be passing on to the world around him; compare what Quintilian said about "loosening the holiness of the forum" by importing style from Lycia and Caria (*Inst.* 11.3.58). This fear of flowing, loosening, leaping the boundaries, breaking up, per-vades Roman imagery of the city, state and empire.[39] In contrast, the Attici are *pressi* ("concise") and *integri* ("whole").

Yet the heroes of Roman oratory are not Brutus and Calvus but Cicero and Hortensius. Despite the problematic aspects of the Asianist style, the experts agree that it is more beautiful, more noble, and more effective than the arid wastes of the Atticists.


## CONCLUSIONS

Although the feminine plays a major part in the world of the forum, real women themselves are almost entirely absent. The players in these all-male games seem to need the feminine both for their own enjoyment and in order to insult each other, but an actual female body does not belong in the forum. Indeed, the charming minutes of the elder Seneca's men's club convey no sense of lack; women are else-where, maybe in the women's club, but who cares?[40]

---

[39] On the use of the image of fluid body boundaries to express anxiety over the body politic, see Joshel 1992.

[40] Sections of this chapter were delivered at a session on "Configurations of Gender in Roman Literature" held on 29 December 1992 at the 123rd Meeting of the American Philological Association in New Orleans, USA. I thank the panel organizer, Micaela Janan, and my fellow panellists—William Fitzgerald, Holt Parker, Ellen Oliensis and Marilyn Skinner—for helpful discussion.

# 11 *Representations of Male-to-Female Lovemaking*†

## J. R. CLARKE

What kind of paintings of lovemaking did the elite class enjoy? Fortunately there exist fresco paintings from this period to help us answer this question. Equally fortunate is the unusual circumstance that the literature of the period brings us several references on owning and looking at the explicit paintings of sexual intercourse. In one letter to Augustus from exile on the Black Sea, Ovid uses the word *tabella* to denote a small picture with illustrations of sexual positions. The words *concubitus varii* (various forms of copulation) and *figurae veneris* (sexual positions) leave no doubt about the subject matter of this painting. The setting he creates is one of a fine picture gallery hung with masterpieces from the Greek classical and Hellenistic periods:

> Surely in your houses, just as figures of great men of old shine—painted by some artist's hand—so somewhere a small picture depicts the various forms of copulation and the sexual positions. Telamonian Ajax sulks in rage, barbarian Medea glares infanticide, but there's Venus as well—wringing her dripping hair dry with her hands—and barely covered by the waters that bore her.[1]

Ovid's comments clearly indicate that for the upper class it is the norm, not the exception, to own and display little paintings that showed couples illustrating a variety of sexual positions. It seems that

---

†Originally published in *Looking at Lovemaking: Constructions of Sexuality in Roman Art 100 BC–AD 250* (Berkeley and Los Angeles, 1998), 91–118.
[1]  scilicet in domibus vestris [nostris] ut prisca virorum
artificis fulgent corpora picta manu
sic quae concubitus varios venerisque figuras
exprimat, et aliquo parva tabella loco.
· utque sedet vultu fassus Telamonius iram,
inque oculis facinus barbara mater habet
sic madidos siccat digitis Venus uda capillos
et modo maternis tecta videtur aquis.

Ovid *Tristia* 2.521–528; my translation in text.

such pictures belonged in the proper elite citizen's art collection; they fit his image as a connoisseur of Greek art. [...]

## REPRESENTATIONS OF MALE-FEMALE INTERCOURSE: THE FARNESINA PAINTINGS

Although none of these panel pictures remains, we do have painted depictions of them in frescoes from a villa in the heart of Rome itself, dated with certainty to the early years of Augustus' reign. This is the Villa of the Farnesina, so called because in 1879 workers discovered it while cutting through the garden of the Renaissance villa to construct the Lungotevere Farnesina, a broad avenue that today runs along the right bank of the Tiber. [...] Some scholars believe that the villa belonged to Augustus' own daughter Julia, married to his right-hand man, Agrippa.[2] The decorations date to around 20 BC.

Painted representations of panel paintings are the building blocks of the rich decoration of the three cubicula [bedrooms] that survived. Six of these panel paintings represent couples engaged in lovemaking. But before examining these paintings in detail, we need to consider the possible uses of the rooms where they appear; we also need to understand how these representations of paintings fit into the all-over decorative schemes that the artist designed for these rooms.

The Roman house, particularly that of an elite citizen, was anything but a private retreat from the public world of business. Because the owner had to conduct daily business in the house, it probably had no rooms that we today would consider "private." In the mornings the ritual of *salutatio* [greeting, ceremonial visit] brought all the paterfamilias' clients into the front part of the house surrounding the atrium. At other times the rooms of the house arranged around the enclosed garden or peristyle would find use as reception spaces for the owner's peers, and on many occasions he could have an intimate business discussion in a cubiculum.[3] It was the status of the individ-

---

[2] Hendrik G. Beyen ("Les *domini* de la Villa de la Farnesine," *Studia varia Carolo Guilielmo Vollgraff a disciplulis oblata* [Amsterdam, 1948], 3–21) attributes the villa to Agrippa and Julia, followed by Peter von Blanckenhagen and Christine Alexander (*The Paintings from Boscotrecase*, Römische Mitteilungen, Supplement 6 [1962]: 60), but Frédéric Bastet and Mariette de Vos (*Proposta per una classificazione del terzo stile pompeiano*, Archeologische Studiën van het Nederlands Instituut te Rome, 4 [The Hague, 1979], 8–9) question the date of the closely related Villa of Agrippa at Boscotrecase, and Robert B. Lloyd ("The Aqua Virgo, Euripus, and Pons Agrippa," *American Journal of Archaeology* 83 [1979]: 193–204) attributes the Villa under the Farnesina to A. Crispinus Caepio.

[3] Andrew Wallace-Hadrill, *Houses and Society in Pompeii and Herculaneum* (Princeton, 1994) 17, 58; Andrew M. Riggsby, "'Public' and 'Private' in Roman Culture: The Case of the Cubiculum," *Journal of Roman Archaeology* 10 (1997): 1–20.

*Figure 11.1* Male-female couple on bed attended by three servants, Rome, Villa under the Farnesina, cubiculum B, left wall, attic zone, to left of central aedicula [niche framed by a pair of columns and topped with a pediment] (ca. 19 BC). Rome, National Museum of the Terme, inv. 1128. Photo Deutsches Archäologisches Institut, Rome, inst. neg. 77–1305.

ual who entered the Roman house that determined her or his access to its rooms. Living barriers, in the from of household slaves, controlled access. In fact, Romans often named slaves in reference to the room where they served. The *cubicularius* was a servant who oversaw all the functions of the cubiculum, from the business tête à tête to lovemaking and sleeping. He guarded the cubiculum as well, sleeping at its entrance on a mat.[4] [...]

Two pinakes [panel paintings, often with wooden shutters] of the original four remain in cubiculum B. The one on the left wall (Fig. 11.1), presents five figures in all: the couple on the bed and three female servants. The woman sits on the bed with her back to the viewer, her head turned in profile to her lover. She wears a pink chiton

[4] Mikhail Rostowzew, "A cubiculo, cubicularius," *Pauly-Wissowa*, vol. 4, cols. 1734–1737; see also Sandra Joshel, *Work, Identity, and Legal Status at Rome: A Study of the Occupational Inscriptions* (Norman, Okla., 1992), passim.

tied at the waist and has a yellow cloak draped over her midsection and legs. Her hair is pulled back and gathered in a bun at the nape of her neck. The man sits, pressing close to her as he turns to look in her eyes. His head is profile and he is nude. The woman leans back on the blue cushion behind her back, while he sits upright, his hand on the bed near the woman's knee. Behind the bed and to the right the artist depicted two servant girls, one in profile and the other in three-quarters view. Like the girl at the extreme left of the picture, they do not look at the couple. Perhaps they are crossing the back of the room, having just arranged the white covers on the bed. Their small size in relation to the couple on the bed signals to the viewer that they are servant girls, rather than grown women. Whereas these two mark the back spatial plane of the picture, the girl on the left marks the foremost plane. The artist positioned the table holding the basin very close to the lower edge of the picture, and the girl stands right behind it, in frontal view with head turned slightly to her right. [...]

These compositional and pictorial effects comment on the tranquil, unaggressive sexual dalliance that is unfolding. The position of the woman's body tells the viewer that she is contemplating the pleasure of making love with the man, but without haste. The man's fervent gaze, his body language, and the fact that he is nude at least to the buttocks all suggest that he may be a bit impatient; yet finally he, too, seems ready to take his time. The water will be poured, the other two servants will perhaps leave, and love will take its course. [. . .]

Excavators were able to retrieve only half of this cubiculum's right wall, and only two-thirds of the pinax in the attic story survives. This pinax, opposite the one just described, presents a moment of greater passion (Fig. 11.2). Although the woman is fully and even voluminously clothed, she dangles her feet off the edge of the bed with jaunty abandon as she turns to kiss the man. Like the man in the pinax opposite, he is nude to the waist, but here he needs to lean forward only very slightly to return the woman's kiss. His hair seems disheveled, but paint loss makes it unclear whether we see his hair or a leafy crown. [...]

Cubiculum D, although a wider space than B, otherwise is its mirror reversal in the villa's plan. [...] The picture to the left of the aedicula on the right wall seems to depict a serious moment between the couple on the bed (Fig. 11.3). Not only is the woman fully clothed from head to foot while the man is nude to the waist, but this time the woman wears a veil. The artist further heightened the contrast between the two in their poses: his legs (under the covers) stretch out the length of the bed, and he leans his left elbow on the cushions while

*Figure 11.2* Male-female couple on bed, Rome, Villa under the Farnesina, cubiculum B, right wall, attic zone, to left of central aedicula (ca. 19 BC). Rome, National Museum of the Terme, inv. 1127. Photo Deutsches Archäologisches Institut, Rome, inst. neg. 77–1263.

attempting to place his hand on the woman's thigh. She sits upright, her head bowed demurely while she grasps the man's forearm to keep it from resting on her thigh. In the background a boy stands, expressionless, an object (perhaps a shield) between him and the man's foot.

Similarities of the woman's dress and pose to the figure of the bride in the painting known as the Aldobrandini Wedding[5] cause Andreae to see this picture as a young married couple on their wedding night.[6] [...]

If this painting from cubiculum D represents a woman—whether a bride or not—as modest and resisting, the painting that formed its pendant, to the right of the central aedicula, constructs the woman as unrestrained and aggressive [...] The artist stretched out her body on the bed and presented her nude to the waist as she reaches her arm around the man's neck to pull his head toward her. It seems that she

[5] Bartolomeo Nogara, *Le Nozze Aldobrandine* (Milan, 1907), 1–25; Nogara cites dating by August Mau to the early Augustan period; Frank G.J.M. Müller, *The Aldobrandini Wedding* (Amsterdam, 1994).

[6] Bernard Andreae, "Stuckreliefs und Fresken der Farnesina," in Wolfgang Helbig, *Führer durch den offentlichen Sammlungen Roms*, ed. Hermione Speier, 4th ed. (Tübingen, 1969), 3:448.

*Figure 11.3* Male-female couple on bed attended by a servant, Rome, Villa under the Farnesina, cubiculum D, right wall, attic zone, to left of central aedicula (ca. 19 BC). Rome, National Museum of the Terme, inv. 1188. Photo Deutsches Archäologisches Institut, Rome, inst. neg. 77–1295.

wants to kiss him, but her mouth is at the bridge of his nose. The man, nude also to the waist, has his right arm around the woman's neck and shoulder; his fingers are just visible on her left shoulder. His right hand makes an ambiguous gesture: whether he has just disrobed the woman or is about to touch her breast is difficult to say. The artist created a contrast between the woman's expressive gesture and the man's wooden posture. The eye follows the sweep of her body from the toes that rest on the bed, through her voluminous yellow robe to her gesture of reaching around the man's neck. He seems disengaged, or perhaps stunned by the woman's passion.

Because the woman appears unrestrained, Andreae construes her as a hetaira, or prostitute. He rules out the possibility that the woman could be the chaste bride turned by passion into an eager sex partner. Why did the artist put these two representations of sex—one chaste and tentative, the other passionate and explicit—in juxtaposition? If the one woman is an elite bride, the sexual roles that her society constructed for her included sex with only one man (her husband) for the purpose of producing legitimate heirs. The prostitute's role is that of the sex worker: a slave or a freedwoman, bought or hired to provide sexual recreation for male clients of various classes. Yet prostitutes do not wear such voluminous clothing, nor do they wear the veil. By law they wore togas or were dressed for quick sex under the arches of the city (Martial mentions the arches); Catullus 55.11–12 has them wearing clothing that allows them to "flash" potential clients. Many Roman texts recognize the wife's erotic interest in her husband.[7] And in the Farnesina cubiculum it seems certain that Roman matrons would have looked at these paintings, perhaps recognizing themselves there as young brides. The woman of the left-hand painting must be a reluctant bride (a type attested both by the Aldobrandini Wedding and in literary sources) and the right-hand painting must represent a bride inflamed by passion.

An unusual feature of the right-hand painting that features the passionate woman is the nude boy servant gazing directly out at the viewer. The artist of cubiculum B took pains to keep the servants busy with their own work, unaware of either the couple on the bed or the viewer. Here in cubiculum D the boy is obviously ministering to the couple—he has poured the water into the large gilded basin and holds a wine vessel—yet seems to be aware of the viewer's gaze at him and the couple. This device of having a figure within the pictorial space look out to address the viewer [...] appears with greater frequency in the latter half of the first century. Here the figure seems designed to heighten the viewer's awareness that he or she is a voyeur, looking in on the couple's sexual intimacies. The servant belongs there, his gaze seems to say, but you, the viewer, do not. Behind the bed to the left are traces of another figure who, like all the others in the Farnesina paintings, goes about his business without paying attention to either his owners or the viewer. At the top of the picture the artist represented a white curtain, knotted in the center and swagged to right and left.

If the painting is a vignette of the wedding night, as I believe it is, it is a narrative of the modest bride becoming the immodest lover—perhaps fulfilling a ribald male fantasy. In this reading the slave who looks directly out at the viewer fills the role of bringing the viewer in on the joke [...] What is more, the artist of these two juxtaposed paintings also created a deliberate contrast between two kinds of lovemaking scene [...].

On the opposite wall—to the left of someone entering cubiculum D—only one erotic picture remains (Fig. 11.4). Although it is directly

---

[7] Catullus 61.169–171; Propertius 4.3.29–30, 55–56; Martial 10.35, 38. I thank Andrew Riggsby for these references.

*Figure 11.4* Male-female couple on bed attended by three servants, Rome, Villa under the Farnesina, cubiculum D, left wall, attic zone, to right of central aedicula (ca. 19 BC). Rome, National Museum of the Terme, inv. 1187. Photo Alinari/Art Resource, New York.

opposite the chastest of these paintings, it is as passionate as the painting just considered. The couple is about to kiss: this time the artist aligned both their gazes and their faces to leave no doubt. The woman raises her right arm over her head, in a variation of the gesture of erotic repose [...]. Her arms frame her own head while her fingers rest on the top of the man's head. Her face is in three-quarters' view, as is her body, clothed in a chiton that billows at her knees. The man, his face and torso in profile, is nude to the waist. He rests his fingers loosely on the woman's left arm above the elbow.

This, too, is a bedchamber full of busy servants. A small girl at the lower right bends deeply to loosen the woman's sandals. Behind the bed are two servants. A small boy dressed in a tunic is touching a vessel as he turns to an adult woman servant who carries a wine vessel while moving toward him. Like all the other servant figures—with the exception of the nude boy looking out at the viewer in the painting on the opposite wall—they busy themselves with their duties and ignore the lovemaking couple. [...]

The Farnesina lovemaking paintings raise several important questions for the cultural construction of sexuality in the early Augustan period. Consideration of Ovid's *parva tabella* at least partially answers the most important question: why the patron would want erotic paintings represented in his or her bedchambers along with other nonsexual subjects. Such paintings belonged with the decoration of a stylish room. We are left with the question of the Roman viewer's relation to such pictures. Did the viewer see him- or herself in their scenarios? Or did the subject matter of the paintings belong in the world of art, not in that of the viewer's experience? Given their context, we must assume that these were not paintings meant to represent scenes from the viewer's life. They certainly were not illustrations of the sexual positions that Ovid discusses, for they are about the preliminaries to lovemaking, not about actual copulation. Given the emphasis on the *style* of representation in all the paintings in these rooms, content must be a secondary consideration. The erotic pictures stand out as much for their bold use of color and their illusionism as they do for their representation of sexual dalliance [...]. Furthermore, it is hard to make a case for the subject matter being a commentary upon what went on in the bedchamber when mythological paintings or landscape paintings are the really large ones that take pride of place in the central aediculae. The very eclecticism of subject matter and style that characterizes the cubicula's decoration constitutes their primary meaning for the ancient Roman viewer, who would identify with the connoisseur of the treasures of Greek art in appreciating the enormous temporal and iconographic leaps between one picture and another. If there is a cultural construction of attitudes toward sex between men and women in the pictures, it is one of sophisticated appreciation—of their rich setting (signaled by the appointments of the chamber and the numerous servants) and of the unhurried pace of the couple's lovemaking. These are not images that "document" in any sense the acts of lovemaking that might take place in these rooms. Their role is decorative, not instructive or documentary.

Finally, what was the culture of the men who painted these pictures? On a column in cubiculum D is a graffito, *Seleukos epoiei* (Seleukos made this), causing Bianchi Bandinelli to attribute the work to an artist from Asia Minor.[8] Others consider it a product of artists from Asia Minor or Alexandria. Bragantini and de Vos point out that the Farnesina decorations take part in a repertoire of late Hellenistic painting that finds workshops of equally high levels in

[8] Ranuccio Bianchi–Bandinelli, *Rome: The Center of Power*, trans. Peter Green (New York, 1970), 121, followed by Paolo Moreno, "Seleukos 3°," *Enciclopedia dell'arte antica*, 7:175.

the area around Naples.[9] [...] Artists from centers around the entire eastern Mediterranean, including Athens, Pergamon, Ephesos, and Alexandria, had access to models in high art with representations of lovemaking. So too did the artists within the workshops who, in creating decorations in painting and stucco like those of the Farnesina, were able to revisit the entire history of Greek and Hellenistic art.

## MALE-TO-FEMALE LOVEMAKING IN MASS-PRODUCED ARRETINE WARE

If the refined paintings of the Farnesina give a full context for the uses of paintings of male-to-female [sex] in the picture galleries of the elite, the mass-produced Arretine ceramics of the Augustan and early Julio-Claudian period show how analogous images of lovemaking found their way to poorer consumers. [...] One figural type within Arretine ceramic production put male-male and male-female copulation on an equal footing [...]. The two or possibly three variants on this type show the couple on a bed, the man tenderly embracing the boy while preparing to enter him. [...] Rather than an isolated phenomenon peculiar to Arretine ware alone, this representation embraced the high art models of much more expensive products like silver vessels and even super-expensive cut cameo glass. We must reconstruct a similar model for the male-to-female lovemaking representations on Arretine vessels.

Brendel emphasizes that the artists of the Arretine ceramics placed the lovemaking couples in settings that correspond to the symposium or banquet compositions in Greek red-figured painted vases; their fastidious formal design is an effort to recapture the Greek past through a romantic, neoclassicizing lens: "For once, a group of Roman artists tried to raise the social standing of erotic representations; and their way of accomplishing this was to recall the Greek paragons. In this somewhat esoteric undertaking the ease and naturalness of the prototypes went by the boards, to be replaced by a new and impeccable formal elegance."[10]

With the Farnesina paintings as a context (Brendel omits these from his brief discussion), it becomes clear that the Arretine representations of male-female lovemaking range from the elegant amorous dalliance of the Farnesina panels to the explicit insertion of

---

[9] [Irene Bragantini and Mariette de Vos, *Le decorazioni della villa romana della Farnesina*, vol. 2, part 1 of *Museo Nazionale Romano: Le pitture* (Rome, 1982), 22–23.]
[10] Brendel [1977], "Erotic Art," 58–59.

the penis into the vagina [...]. Their variety indicates that artists wished to present buyers with a choice—or that buyers demanded a choice of representations of male-female lovemaking.

## FROM AMOROUS DALLIANCE TO SEXUAL PENETRATION: CONTRAST OR CONTINUUM?

The scenes on the Arretine ware go far beyond the passionate gestures of the couples in the Farnesina paintings when they show actual inter-course. Arranging them in a hierarchy of increasing explicitness brings me to another important question: did the Roman buyer rank the images by degrees of explicitness? If I accept a late twentieth-century construction of sexual representation that differentiates between soft porn and hard-core porn, did the ancient viewer do so? Educated Romans certainly believed in different levels of verbal obscenity [...]. Yet the Arretine ceramics were, first and foremost, decorated vessels that were mass-produced and in the hands of people, both women and men, of less than elite status. To divide up the Arretine representations in explicitness of sexual penetration is probably anachronistic. Rather than a contrast between suggestive-ness and explicitness, I believe that the Roman viewer would see all these acts of lovemaking as part of a continuum. These were the blessings of Venus, the joys of sexual passion and release.

In purely artistic terms, however, arranging these images of sex allows us to examine the choices artists made in composing a scene and arranging the figures. What emerges—from our far from exhaus-tive treatment—is the artists' careful manipulation of stock figural groups to create variations in the emotional and physical relations of the couples. In this way they gave viewers variety in the illustration of sexual positions and in the range of emotional responses from the partners. Comparison of two bowl fragments, formerly in the Warren collection and now in Boston, clarifies this point. In one (inv. Res. 08.33g, which I call "Warren g") the man reclines to the viewer's right, supporting himself on his heavily draped left forearm (Fig. 11.5). In the other ("Warren h") it is the woman who reclines, entirely nude and supporting herself with her left elbow and forearm resting on the bed's headboard [...].[11] At first glance, we might imagine that the artist simply switched the figures' positions, having the woman sit on the man in one and having the man kneeling between the woman's

[11] The old inventory number of "Warren h" is Boston Museum of Fine Arts, Res 08.33h; the new inventory number is Res 08.3314.

*Figure 11.5* Male-female couple, Arretine bowl fragment, Warren g (30 BC–AD 30).
Courtesy, Museum of Fine Arts, Boston. Reproduced with permission. © 2000
Museum of Fine Arts, Boston. All Rights Reserved.

parted legs in the other. But consideration of each figure's body language reveals expressions of different states of mind, and perhaps different emotions. The artist emphasized the relaxed pose of the
reclining man in Warren g in much the same way as he expresses the
woman's relaxation in Warren h. Yet in Warren g the artist represented the man's head in profile, so that he does not engage the
woman's glance. His bodily repose and avoidance of the woman's
gaze become signs of mental reverie and detachment [...]

The reclining woman on Warren h, the other hand, wraps her left
leg around her partner's knees while turning her torso in three quarters, so that while her upper body is in repose, her lower body actively
seeks what is happening. The artist also created a dialogue between
the reclining woman and the kneeling man in Warren h by emphasizing the twist of the man's torso—turned in nearly frontal view in
contrast to his profile head. The man is directing his gaze at the beautiful woman's face even as he enters her. He seems about to speak.
Another kind of balance between activity and repose appears in his
hand: his right on his hip communicates the tension of his upright
body and perhaps the act of entering the woman while his left drapes

*Figure 11.6* Male-female couple on bed, Arretine bowl fragment, Warren d¹ (30 BC–AD 30). Courtesy, Museum of Fine Arts, Boston. Reproduced with permission. © 2000 Museum of Fine Arts, Boston. All Rights Reserved.

loosely on the woman's right thigh as she rests her raised leg on his left shoulder.

In Warren g the woman kneels very deeply, suggesting that the man has already inserted his penis in her vagina, and she leans backward perhaps playfully. Again it seems that counterbalancing both the physical positions and the emotional states of the couple is uppermost in the artist's mind. Both lean back, away from the point of genital contact, but he seems as distant from the sexual act as she seems to be engaged.

The artist's cunning use of variation within the very same composition is the foremost quality emerging from close comparison of two other fragments that originally decorated the same vase (Fig. 11.6, inv. Res. 08.33d, here "Warren d¹" and Fig. 11.7, here "Warren d²"). In both the woman reclines to the viewer's right, raising her left leg sharply while the man presses into her from the right. His right leg extends out along the bed and his chest and head near the woman's. Once again, from this general scheme the artist built very different physical and psychological nuances. In Warren d¹ he turned the woman's head and breasts toward the viewer. Her left shoulder and

*Figure* 11.7  Male-female couple on bed, Arretine bowl fragment, Warren d²
(30 BC–AD 30). Courtesy, Museum of Fine Arts, Boston. Reproduced with
permission. © 2000 Museum of Fine Arts, Boston. All Rights Reserved.

upper arm are hidden in drapery while she limply raises her forearm
and hand, bent at the wrist, from the cushions it rests on. Her right
arm, in low relief, seems to reach for the man's penis. The man in
Warren d¹ is farther from the act of penetration than the man in
Warren d², he is also physically farther from the woman, since he
grasps her left shin as he nears her. By contrast, the man in Warren d²
is much closer to the woman. He grasps her upper thigh just below
the buttocks. If the woman's pose in Warren d¹, head slightly inclined,
hand dangling, suggests detachment, that of the woman in Warren d²
suggests engagement. The artist turned her body so that the viewer
sees her shoulders and back; she turns her head toward the man and
lowers it slightly in what seems to be her aggressive grasp of the man's
torso with her outstretched left arm. He, in turn, pushes into her, his
head very close to hers. Her hair is in disarray, having fallen from its
bun into massy locks upon her neck and shoulder.
    Would the ancient Roman viewer find some sort of message in

these two variations of pose? Seeing the two images as pendants, a viewer might notice the contrasts between the two couples, especially in the different levels of engagement in the two women. Or perhaps the viewer was meant to see a kind of narrative, to read a progression in the couple's contact. Both representations illustrate essentially the same position yet one seems to show the initial stages, the other deep engagement. Supporting both the pendant and the narrative readings of this vessel are the enormous differences between the gestures of the two women: one detached and the other engaged; one in self-absorbed reverie, the other focused on the sexual union. [...]

If there is a common thread in these representations of sexual coupling on the Arretine vessels, it is the balance of opposites. It is an equilibrium won through many different means, from the composition of individual bodies to the juxtaposition of scenes. In the few examples we consider the artist took care to counterbalance the tense limb with the languid one, torsion with uprightness, a dreaming countenance with an alert one. This visual balance informs the relation of the couples—one body to the other, one couple to another. He is relaxed, she strains; she holds back, he presses forward. Within the context of their place in the overall composition of each vessel, each pair of lovemakers counterbalances another. At times, as in two Boston fragments, the variations are slight and suggest successive moments in the lovemaking of a single couple. At other times, as in the alternating images of boy-man and man-woman, the balance is between different positions and the man's use of sexual partners of different sex.

These various aspects of balance account for the "almost dignified" air that Zanker [1990] finds in the Arretine representations. The ideal body types, Polykleitan for the men and Pheidian for the woman, carried the educated Roman viewer right back to the Parthenon frieze and canonical sculptural types of the 440s BC. Seen in the context of the other subjects of Arretine vases, such as divinities, dancers, myths, and the hunt, the vessels with lovemaking belong to a real or imagined culture of Hellenistic luxury interpreted in Augustan neoclassical terms. Absent are the gladiatorial combats and caricatured figures that come to crowd the medallions of later terra-cotta vessels—the so-called *terra sigillata* produced in Gaul and Germany. The artists who made the Arretine vessels with scenes of lovemaking on them were looking to models in high art close to the Farnesina paintings; their products share with those paintings a construction of sexuality characterized by a fundamental unity of style and intent in all its variety—from dalliance to frank penetration: all stages belong within the same sphere of sexual pleasure.

The answer to our question—whether the different degrees of explicitness of the representations on Arretine ware corresponded to socially constructed boundaries or taboos about what was "permissible" and what was "taboo" in Augustan society—is that the visual evidence argues strongly for there being no significant difference for the ancient viewer. The vessels construct human lovemaking as a gift of the goddess of love. Venus brings carnal pleasure in love, and all stages of lovemaking are pleasurable. This essentially positive conception of all manner of lovemaking extended to elite society. If the male-female lovemaking paintings in the Farnesina show slightly more restraint than the imagery of the Arretine vessels, it is clear that they express a similar embrace of sexual pleasure. [...]

One question, however, suggests another: who is the person receiving the pleasure? Can we identify these representations as strictly phallic constructions, a one-way experience for the insertive male—or are there indications that the object of that insertion, the penetrated woman or boy, also finds pleasure in looking at these scenes of lovemaking?

We have already reviewed what texts say. Written by male elites or men working for them, they celebrate the pleasures of phallic, penetrative sex, that is, of inserting the penis into the vagina or anus of the beautiful beloved.[12] We cannot argue for the equal status of the receptive partner in any of these acts as pictured in Arretine ware. The women in these scenes are dignified and perfectly coiffed, and the Roman viewer could see them as he or she wished. The Roman man could see in the women either a beautiful wife or servant; the Roman woman could read them in the same way. Most noteworthy, particularly if we compare the Arretine images with those of the late Hellenistic period, is that the Arretine stands out by its emphasis on signs of subjectivity in the penetrated partner.

An example from the same medium but dated to the late Hellenistic period helps clarify this difference. The terra-cotta fragment in Berlin (Fig. 11.8) presents a couple on a bed with vessels from the symposium beneath the bed [...]. The woman reclines on her side while parting her legs to reveal her vagina. The man presses energetically against her body while grasping her upper right thigh with his arm. She crooks her arm around his head to crush his face into hers. Probably the artist who carried out this terra-cotta lacked talent for nuance. Yet central to the image, even imagining a much more refined and skilled execution, is the representation of the woman as orifice

---

[12] The [suggested] female authorship of the sex manuals is highly dubious [...].

*Figure 11.8* Male-female couple on bed, fragment of terra-cotta vessel (2d–1st c.
BC). Berlin, Antikensammlung, inv. V.I. 4991. Photo courtesy Antikensammlung,
Staatliche Museen zu Berlin, Preussischer Kulturbesitz.

to be opened, to be viewed, and to be penetrated by the strong male.
The woman's surrender follows from this phallic model of male as
penetrator—and also from the fact that the artist represented an
advanced stage of the lovemaking process. How far this is from the
counterpoised figures on the Arretine vessel, especially the woman's
relaxed pose as she, too, raises her right leg high in the air. Would a
Roman woman looking at the Arretine cup see her own subjectivity
reflected there? Could she identify—not with the status of the prostitute but with her relaxed attitude—with the woman at the moment
when the man *looks* at her?

What of the subjective experience of the penetrated boy as represented in Arretine vessels? Here we are on shakier ground for [...] the
penetrated male had to be of inferior status to the man who penetrated him. How do we understand the feelings of the penetrated

male, if he was the ancient Roman looking at Arretine (or other) images of male-male lovemaking? Would he be a former slave, now a freedman of some means, who could look back at himself as a boy performing a duty that was expected of him in no uncertain terms?[13] Or simply a freedman or a foreigner, that is, a man of any class but that of freeborn? The central aspect that makes the Arretine representations different from late Hellenistic ones is the tenderness of the male-male couple's contact. [...] The Arretine scene of male-male lovemaking emphasizes not the boy's buttocks and the man's assault on his anus but the kiss—and it seems the boy's tender willingness to make love in this manner [...]. Although we could attribute this condition to the adaptation of an existing male-female type, the artist had a choice that would include the less romantic representations of the late Hellenistic period. If these Augustan-period images spoke to a man who liked to be penetrated or had been penetrated as a boy—and there would be many such viewers—it is clear that they underscored the romantic and pleasurable aspects of that union. [...]

Artists in the Roman world rarely invented a new representation without stimulus from the patrons who paid them. It follows that the depiction of varying, but always tender, physical and emotional relations in the Arretine vessels must be an artistic response to new social attitudes toward sex on the part of some Romans. The audience for these new artistic representations of sexuality belonged to a variety of classes and included both men and women. Whether, when looking at such images, they saw themselves or some aspect of their sexual fantasies is a moot point. One thing is certain: looking at new images of lovemaking brought them pleasure.

---

[13] The situation described in Petronius *Satyricon* 63, 69, 75; see in general J. Kolendo, "L'esclavage et la vie sexuelle des hommes libres à Rome," *Index* 10 (1981): 288–297.

# PART III

# *What if There Were No Foucault? Separate Spheres Revisited*

# 12  Women's Life in Oriental Seclusion? On the History and Use of a Topos[†]

## B. WAGNER-HASEL
### translated by Reyes Bertolín-Cebrián

### 1 THE DISCOURSE ABOUT WOMEN'S PLACE

The most recent statements about research on women in ancient studies give the impression that a new chapter has been opened in historiography, a chapter entitled "The History of Women: Neglected So Far". A glance at the general handbooks of ancient history, even a glance at some recent studies of social history in antiquity, seems to confirm the impression that women have been neglected. Often we encounter only the male actors of history: politicians, heroes, warriors, farmers, and sometimes also the male victims—the slaves, the persecuted, the defeated. The impression, however, is misleading. The discourse about women's place is older than the silence in some works suggests. This statement is valid not only for ancient evidence, especially Greek, but also for historical research over the last 200 years, which has produced a noteworthy number of studies about the life of women in antiquity.

"Greek thought on the problem of the division of the sexes evolved." This is a challenging assertion published in a work in 1984. The author, Pauline Schmitt-Pantel (1992: 79), reminds us that the theoretical reflections on the state by Aristotle or Plato (contrary to those of their modern colleagues) ended up making reference to the relation between the sexes. She also notes that Greek cosmogonies were even earlier structured by the contrast of male and female. Although this ancient discourse was primarily directed by men, it is

[†] Originally published as "Frauenleben in orientalischer Abgeschlossenheit? Zur Geschichte und Nutzanwendung eines Topos," *Die altsprachliche Unterricht*, 32.2 (1989), 18–29.

highly questionable to derive from this the hypothesis that women have generally been inferior in respect to men since antiquity. I would like to challenge this assumption through a topos which has determined the image of women's life more than any other.

## 2  A TOPOS IN MODERN TIMES

The topos is the assumption that women in Ancient Greece, but especially in Athens, lived in Oriental seclusion. The question of the separation of women from the public sphere and the amount of freedom of movement within it will be treated in this conceptual frame, which has given rise to an almost 200-year-old controversy. The debate is in my opinion not only an attempt to reconstruct past conditions of life, but also at the same time a discourse about the place of women in modern bourgeois society. This starts with the Enlightenment and continues until our day. It is based in its main features on a supposed East/West dichotomy projected back into antiquity. I will point here to the problematic origins of this contradiction, but I cannot follow them up in detail. The preoccupation with gender relations started early in ancient studies and has continued for the last 200 years. Beside the thesis on Oriental seclusion, I want to place the thesis of the disjuncture between the actual living conditions of women and their valuation from antiquity until today.

First, however, I would like to explain this disjuncture as a product of the conceptualization of women's place in modern bourgeois society. This process started at the end of the eighteenth century as a result of structural changes in the relation between the private and the public. I will proceed in two steps: first I will briefly set out the history and function of this topos and present some typical positions. Secondly, I will confront these modern judgments with some selected texts from antiquity. It is not my intention to contradict or verify the thesis of Oriental seclusion with an analysis based on sources, because in my opinion this thesis does not present an adequate question or hypothesis for understanding the circumstances of women's life in antiquity. It is important, in my view, to ask the basic question: which are the categories for comprehending and evaluating women's lives? I look for these categories in the exact terms used to describe the place of men and women by ancient witnesses. Finally I end with some very preliminary thoughts about the applicability of modern categories such as private and public to ancient society.

When Greece became the destination of scholars who no longer wanted just to study the extant ancient texts, but wanted to capture *in situ* the "sublime Greek *Geist*," it was under Turkish dominion. It was a part of that East which in the tradition of modernity was conceived as the opposite of European culture. But the reconquest of Greece for the West was near. Since the Enlightenment, European ideas of republican freedom had been based on ancient models. In the new nations of the nineteenth and twentieth centuries there was a striving for this freedom, and the lines of the tradition from ancient to modern times were drawn in new ways. The Greek liberation fighters received support from Central Europe, where there were aspirations to a democracy comparable to the ancient model. The same scholars who created the theoretical grounds for the interpretation of modern and ancient democracy, and who saw their models in Attic *stratêgoi* such as Pericles or Roman senators like Cicero, banished or abandoned the female half of the ancient culture they admired to the East. The technical term for this allocation of place is "Oriental seclusion," often characterized with an "almost."

At the beginning of the twentieth century, Charles A. Savage in a work about the Athenian family expressed a deep surprise about the discrepancy between Attic grandeur and the life of women in "almost Oriental seclusion."[1] In the opinion of Johann Leipoldt (1954: 24ff) the woman in classical Greece lived "totally or almost as in a harem." Gustave Glotz says it more mildly: "without being cloistered according to Oriental custom, she lived an isolated life."[2] The destiny of the women in Athens especially, in scholarly opinion until today, was social immobility: "bound and banished to the house, she should only seldom leave it, usually only with the husband's permission and in the company of female slaves"—that is the assumption of a nineteenth-century handbook about private life in antiquity.[3] Modern studies of women, represented by Sarah B. Pomeroy, offer an image not far from jail: "free women were usually held so separated that no man except a very close relative could see them."[4]

In search of the origin of the idea, I found the *History of the Female Gender (Geschichte des weiblichen Geschlechts)* in four volumes by Christoph Meiners, whose first volume appeared in Hannover in 1788. The "tenured teacher of wisdom," as he calls himself, supposes here that already in the time of Homer, the Greeks "secluded their wives and maidens in the manner of Oriental countries." In addition, Solon's laws, according to Meiners, proclaim

[1] C. A. Savage, "The Athenian Family" (Diss. Johns Hopkins, Baltimore 1907) 23.
[2] G. Glotz, *Histoire grecque* 2 (Paris 1983) 576.
[3] A. Bauer, *Die griechische Privataltertümer* (Munich 1893) 150.
[4] S. B. Pomeroy, *Goddesses, Whores, Wives and Slaves* (New York 1975) 121.

"either the Oriental character of the lawgiver or the Oriental depravity and tendencies of the women of Athens." Shortly afterwards, in 1790, Carl Gotthold Lenz revised this position for early Greece, and since then the conception has been imposed that women in the times of Homer indeed could live a free life, but "Athenian women, in contrast," as a French scholar of the mid-nineteenth century states, "had a hidden life, hidden in the retreat of the women's quarters."[5]

This allocation of place also aroused contradiction. Only a few years after women in Europe were granted the right to vote, the British ancient historian A. W. Gomme demanded a new assessment of the situation of women in Athens and pointed especially to the evidence of tragedy. He thought he could infer clear traces of an important freedom of movement of Athenian women from the evidence of the tragedians of the fifth century BC. He comes to the conclusion that "in Attic tragedy women come and go from their homes at will and play an important and public part."[6] Since the publication of Gomme's article other studies with similar arguments have appeared. Wolfgang Schuller uses the evidence of comedy for his argument against seclusion. Schuller writes:

> The two owners of the food stands in the *Frogs* are a *finale furioso* of the parade of market women, whom even the god Dionysus fears. Both of them are Athenians, for they direct their demands to the Athenian politicians Cleon and Hyperbolus (*Frogs* 576–9):
>
> Woman 1: "I'd like to get a reaping-hook and cut out that gullet you devoured my tripe with."
> Woman 2: "But I'll go to Cleon: he'll summons you and wind it out of you today, he will."

He concludes:

> It is very clear. These fine specimens of women were not little souls jealously guarded in a seraglio and shy in front of men. They stood with wide open legs, highly aggressive with their words, in the middle of the Athenian agora and contradict with their mere existence the opinion that "Athenian women" had to live a shy life behind window bars.

The seclusion of Greek women within the constraints of the women's quarters and their subsequent "scholarly liberation" follows a clear logic. It is connected to the modern relation of "public" and "private," as it developed after the Enlightenment.

---

[5] C. G. Lenz, *Geschichte der Weiber im heroischen Zeitalter* (Hannover 1790) 13ff; Lallier, *De la condition de la femme dans la famille athénienne au Ve et au IVe siècle* (Paris 1875) 12.
[6] A. W. Gomme, "The position of women in Athens in the fifth and fourth century," *CPh* 20 (1925) 10.

Meiners imagines seclusion in the house, that is a separation of the women from "public life," at a time when there was a division of life in his contemporary society. On the one hand, members of the bourgeois "privateness," who make up the "public," constitute a public attitude or opinion to be contrasted to the ruling public power. On the other hand, the family, which was until then the central element of the bourgeois "privateness," suffers a marginalization as a result of the separation of livelihood and family life. The development of gender-role stereotypes corresponds to the attribution of genders to spaces. The public space is occupied by men, the private by women. The female space appears as a place of virtue, the male as a sphere of rationality and energetic action. In Meiners again we find this perspective oriented toward "morality," whose positive dimension I do not want to demean. The seclusion of women coincides for him with a lack of good manners and education (1. 330, 314f.). Solon's laws show "the Oriental depravity of women":

> Solon forbade not only the mostly artificial, barbarian outbreaks of female sorrow, but also the frequent visits to tombs and monuments of strangers, because this visiting of tombs in Athens, like in the East, was an excuse and opportunity for punishable liaisons or debauchery. (1. 323)

He conceives the Trojan War, which represents for him a battle for an "aging adulterous woman," as the expression of a lack of feeling for decorum (1. 319). Ancient conditions do not appear equal to those of the times of the author (a critic of the seclusion thesis suspects this to be the origin of this conception), but they correspond to and contradict them at the same time: Greek women are banished to the house on the grounds of propriety, because these women lack the virtue of bourgeois women due to their Eastern character (1. 119, 314f.). It is noticeable that criticism of Meiners' position, which starts early, makes reference precisely to this moral assessment. It tries to show that the prose writers of the classical period give testimony of "genuine female truthfulness" and "the great intimacy of married life." It is also noticeable that with Gomme the question of freedom of movement gains importance.

This discourse moves along with a relativization of the "Oriental" origin of the custom of seclusion. For instance, a Swiss scholar of the mid-nineteenth century, Hermann Koechly, recognizes the custom of seclusion first among the Ionians.[7] Others consider it a new development after the Persian wars. The metaphor of the East is appropriate

---

[7] H. Koechly, *Über Sappho mit Rücksicht auf die gesellschaftliche Stellung der Frauen bei den Griechen* (Zürich 1859) 159.

for the denotation of what is not common to one's own culture and for giving to it the seal of foreignness. Consequently, it is rejected by those who are not willing to recognize foreignness. The change of perspective, toward freedom of movement, runs parallel with the process of female emancipation—their introduction into the realms of men, the loss of the family's power of integration. This process of emancipation is not mirrored in attitudes. According to Gomme, the attribution of the woman to the house remains a continuum in human history: "when Theognis said, 'I hate a woman who gads about and neglects her home', I think, he expressed a sentiment common to most people of all ages." In this way, the British scholar ends his argument against the seclusion thesis. The woman, freed from the harem, leaves the house physically; morally, however, she is still detained in it.

Women win actual participation in the men's sphere only at the price of the accusation of immorality. This impression appears also in Schuller. He remarks on the intrigues of the Hellenistic queens, which do not differ from those of men: "should there be a correlation in the sense that extraordinary political activity on the part of women is purchased by extraordinary criminality?" (96).

## 3 WOMEN'S PLACES — MEN'S PLACES

Do all discourses about antiquity find their solution in the contemporary understanding of women's place? I think not. I do not want to accuse the authors quoted here of not having reconstructed the past, but instead of only bringing the present to light. However, I think it is necessary to reflect about the categories with which anyone approaches an ancient subject and to be conscious of the structural difference between antiquity and modern times. The presence of a special space for women only, the *gynaikônitis*, their association with the house, the separation of genders—all this need not mean exclusion or subordination. The only exclusion is the result of what has to be overcome in today's perspective: it is the establishment of men's spheres—the result of a history writing directed toward heroes, questions of power, the institutionalizing of forms of government—which opens up the perception of women's spaces or shifts them to the margins.

I want to propose the perspective of "genus." I mean by this simply to expand the historical perception of the structural category of gender. In this case, it is to inquire into not the physical but the structural presence of women, to inquire into the interrelation or separation in space occupied according to gender. In my opinion, the way forward can only lead through the mediation of the terms which the Greeks themselves used to describe women's place. In Aristophanes' *Thesmophoriazusae*, we encounter the obscure manifestation of the harem, the *gynaikônitis*. It is a place determined for women, watched by big Molossian dogs, a jail. The women consider themselves bereft of access to provisions, they have lost to men their power to have the key, as the complaint of this Athenian woman expresses (*Thes.* 414–28):

> Then because of this man they now throw seals and bars on the women's quarters to guard us and they raise Molossian dogs to scare off our lovers. That's forgivable. But what was previously ours to manage and to select and take—flour, oil, wine—we can't any more. For the men carry the keys concealed, nasty Spartan things with three teeth. Before now we could get a three-obol ring made to open the door. But now this household slave Euripides has taught them to fasten worm-eaten seals to their clothes.

The scandal here is based on the reversal of an evident distribution of competence between women and men: the men have the key, not the women any more. The humor, as in other Aristophanic comedies, lies in role reversal. In the *Thesmophoriazusae*, it is insinuated that men are the rulers of the house, while at the day of the Thesmophoria festival the women have their own assembly in the manner of men. They rule the place of men, the *polis* [city–state]. They play "assembly," display themselves as orators, elect presiding officers, choose guardians of public order. Even more clear is the reversal in *Lysistrata*, in which war is defined as "women's task" and to men is attributed the work of women, wool spinning. The women abandon the house, silence their sexuality, and occupy the Acropolis, where they take over the *polis'* finances and make the business of war impossible for men. Through reversal of women's and men's roles in the comedies of Aristophanes the proper distribution of competence between genders is visible: war is men's work, weaving and spinning is women's work. The first means responsibility for the needs of the *polis*, the second for those of the house. The *oikos* [household] is female, the *polis* is male space.

Now let us have a look at the description of distribution of competence between genders in Xenophon, *Oeconomicus*, which appeared some decades after the performance of Aristophanes' comedies. Here it is not the term *oikos* that characterizes the area of competence of the women, but the house, *stegos*, literally "the roof." A roof is necessary for the provisions, for the upbringing of the children. The woman is guardian of both, her duties are the *endon erga*, inside work: the care of newborn children, preparation of food from

the products of the fields, but especially the production of clothes
from wool. Men's duties are outside work, *ta exô erga*: to sow, to
plant, to harvest (*Oeconomicus* 7.20–23). Under the roof, however,
there are objects that both men and women use. These are the objects
through which the inhabitants of the house as a community of consumers are recognized: shoes, clothing, blankets, utensils, all of them
united metaphorically as in the harmony of a dramatic chorus
(Xenophon, *Oeconomicus* 8.18–20).

> It has already been said how good is to keep one's stock of utensils in order,
> and how easy to find a place in the house which suits each set. And how good
> it looks whenever the footwear of whatever kind is set out in order, how good
> to see cloaks of whatever kind set out separately, or bedding, or cooking pots,
> or table ware.... And everything else, I imagine, seems more beautiful when
> it is set out in order. For each set looks like a chorus of tools, and what is
> between them looks good, clear of everything. In the same way a circular
> chorus is not only a beautiful sight in itself but the space it surrounds is beau-
> tiful and clean.

Xenophon uses a metaphor which we would not associate with the
sphere of the house, but with the *polis*, *khoros*—the chorus, i.e. the
dance surface, the place and the occurrence of musical and dramatic
performances in the heart of the *polis*, in the theater, in the agora. In
the chorus song, the participants (women as well as men) move in a
rhythmically organized dance to the *aulos* [a wind instrument] and
the strings around a chorus leader. Movement and song do not occur
separately, but in relation to each other. The common action, the
togetherness, the interdependence of human beings in the space of
the *polis* are transferred by Xenophon to the household objects,
which concern both female and male activity.

In the account of the instruction of Ischomachus's young wife, the
order of things, which is necessary for the success of the house
economy (*Oeconomicus* 3.2–3), occupies a central place. The presentation does not reveal a hierarchy of gender (*Oeconomicus* 9.6–8):

> And when we had gone through these things, we began to separate the furni-
> ture by tribe. We began first (he said) by gathering together what we use for
> sacrifices and then we selected women's festival finery and men's clothing for
> festivals and for war, and bedding for women's quarters and for men's, and
> female and male footwear. There was another tribe of weapons, others of
> tools for spinning, baking and cooking, and others of the equipment used for
> washing, kneading, meals. All these we divided into things we need every day
> and things for a feast.

Ischomachus names first the instruments for the sacrifices to the gods,
then he continues with clothing and blankets, as well as tools and

instruments for daily use. The separation he makes is between cult and daily use, between female and male use. The clothing is divided into the festival attire of the women and the clothing of men (separated according to occasion: festival or war), as well as the blankets, shoes of the female and male members of the house, and the tools: men's weapons, and tools for spinning wool, for the preparation of food, for the meal, and bathing. Male and female objects appear in relation to each other, as the work of the couple, which Xenophon calls *zeugos*—a yoke that pulls together a cart: the household, the common *oikos*. *Oikos* is here—the order of things makes it clear— both male and female space. Not the household in general but only a portion of it, the roof and what it covers, the inside of the house, is the special sphere of the woman and under her responsibility. As much as we find a term from the sphere of the *polis* applied to the order of the house, so also we observe, contrariwise, how terms from living together enter into the world of the *polis*.

This is united to women's stepping out into what was previously the sphere of men, the *polis*. In the *agora*, the proper assembly space of men, there were since Hellenistic times numerous statues commemorating women who are referred to as benefactors. They participated in the construction of public buildings, public banquets, etc. They even to some extent assumed public offices, which during classical times were open only to men. As the relations of *polis* and house are represented at those times, in this same way there is also an intersection of both spheres. Male and female benefactors are described as fathers and mothers of the *polis*. The *polis* is subsumed under family designations. *Oikos* and *polis* now form a new family, are both male and female space.

The ascription to the *polis* of terms from domestic life during the Hellenistic period is contrasted with the lack of differentiation of these spheres in Homeric times. The house of Alcinous, called not *oikos* but *dôma*, hosts the common meals of the leaders of the Phaeacians as much as the collective of working women, *dmôai gynaikes*, the women belonging to the house. The common meal is the fellowship of the warriors. The women, who according to Lenz (27) compose their "own, very simple society," go afterwards to their work at the spinning stool, spindle and grindstone (*Odyssey* 7.95–111):

> Inside, chairs leaned against the walls here and there, from the threshold right through to the inner room, and fine well-spun covers had been thrown over them, women's work. There the leaders of the Phaeacians sat, drinking and eating, for they had plenty. Golden youths on well-made bases stood by

holding blazing torches in their hands, lighting up the night all through the house for the banqueters. And he had fifty female domestics about the house, some grinding yellow grain with a mill, others weaving webs and turning the distaff as they sat, moving like leaves of the tall poplar, and the flowing olive oil dripped from the close-woven linen. As the Phaeacians know better than all men how to drive a swift ship over the sea, so too the women are experts at the loom. For to them Athena gave the gifts of knowing how to do very beautiful work and of good sense.

Here again, we encounter the relation of objects. The products of the women's work, their weaving, lie on the seats of the male group. They will be given to the guest Odysseus, with whose eyes the poet allows us to look at the interior of the house. Arete, lady of the house, whose agreement is necessary to accept a guest, is asked by Alcinous to present Odysseus with a gift of clothing, but she also gives at her own initiative. She participates in the specific form of power in Homeric times, *timê*, which includes the right to demand presents and labor. She can claim the textiles of the working women, who are not slaves (as mentioned some lines earlier). This power of disposal makes her —as well as other Homeric women—attractive to men in a special way. They cannot invite any quests without access to the textiles, cannot form friendships or gain allies for their war enterprises.

## 4  PUBLIC SPACE — PRIVATE SPACE

Not separation but relation is noticeable. Men's and women's spheres appear separated, but not just in relation to only one place: *dôma, oikos, gynaikônitis, stegos, polis*—all of them are female places, conceived partially exclusively, but partially together with men.

Which of these places is to be defined as public? Which as private? I add some remarks from a study by Jürgen Habermas:[8]

> In German, the noun "public" (*Öffentlichkeit*) was derived from the older adjective "public" (*öffentlich*) during the eighteenth century in analogy to *publicité* and *publicity* (12).... In England, there was talk about "public" only from the mid-seventeenth century; before that "world" or "mankind" was in place. Also in French "*le public*" appears to denote that which in the eighteenth century, according to Grimm's dictionary, was called in German "*Publikum*" and spread from Berlin to all Germany. Until then the word used was "readership" or "world." (36 f.)

Habermas later analyses the genesis of the bourgeois public (*Öffentlichkeit*) from the sphere of private people gathered to be the

---

[8] *Strukturwandel der Öffentlichkeit. Untersuchungen zu eines Kategorie der bürgerlichen Gesellschaft* (Berlin 1968).

public (*Publikum*). But this historical approach does not prevent him from believing that the terms private/public were already Greek categories.

> In the cultured Greek city-state the *oikos,* which is to be owned by each person individually (*idia*), is set apart. The public life, *bios politikos*, occurs in the market place. The citizen's participation in public life depends on his private autonomy as master of his house. Under the umbrella of his power the reproduction of life takes place: as well as the work of the slaves and the service of the women, birth and death occur. The power of necessity and impermanence remains hidden in the shade of the private sphere. In front of it there is the public sphere, which in the understanding the Greeks was the province of freedom and continuity. (13)

Note: 200 years ago, the power of necessity and impermanence (if this metaphor is even adequate to the house) was hidden in the shade of the private sphere. But in the imagination of the sociologist Habermas this step appears to have occurred more than 2,000 years ago among the Greeks. If we consider this, the sphere of women seems less impermanent, that of men less eternal and constant. In the epic, the work of the women grants men the glory which protects them from forgetfulness, as much as in Hellenistic times the statues of the female benefactors have brought them to our historical consciousness. Habermas' work does not give any criteria to decide the question of which of the spaces where women act are private or public.

As much as it is clear that with the origin of the *polis* a proper sphere of the political constitutes itself beside the house, it is less clear for me that through it the house, the *oikos,* is relegated to the private. The gender-specific attribution of space which was presented here is mostly a distribution of roles. This distribution introduces the house as a place for agricultural and handicraft (textile) production. This function is excluded in the modern definition of "private." Above all, the use of "public" and "political" as synonyms seems to me increasingly questionable: with this use other forms of "public" disappear (e.g. the whole field of cult practices) and each form of women's fellowship receives the stamp of "private" under the primacy of politics as the activity of men. However, how important the cult sphere is for the understanding of the Greeks is shown in the high rank that the cultic objects occupy in Xenophon's description. Objects for sacrifices to the gods are in the first place. It is necessary then to ask if in antiquity there were not other oppositions besides "private" and "public," such as "individual use" and "communal use," as we can see in the opposition "*idios*"/"*dêmosios*." We can also suspect their presence in the extant complaints about the burden of liturgies and their final transformation into a benefaction, which breaks with the priority of communal use. These contradictions are not dissolved in a male–female opposition. Rather, as the examples of the women benefactors indicate, they show women in places, such as the *agora* of men, where they were not suspected because of the dichotomy "private"/"public."

In order to completely understand the place of women, a new perspective on history is needed.

# *13  The Attitudes of the* Polis *to Childbirth: Putting Women into the Grid*†

## NANCY DEMAND

I would rather stand three times in the front of battle than bear one child.

Euripides, *Medea* 250–51 (trans. Rex Warner)

One of the messages of the Thesmophoria was that the continuity of the *polis* depended upon the cycle of female life: after risking death in childbirth themselves, women must soon give up their daughters to a similar fate. If childbirth was a mortal peril, [. . .] it was a peril that women had to undergo so that the community might live on. Was Medea's complaint not then justified? Is it not reasonable to assume that the *polis* honored women's contribution equally with that of men who risked their lives in battle?

In fact, modern scholars have enthusiastically embraced Medea's words as evidence that the Greeks did regard death in childbirth as heroic and the equivalent of male death in battle.[1] Supporting evidence has been found in Plutarch's statement (as emended) that the Spartans allowed the name of the deceased to be inscribed on tombstones only for men who had died in battle and women who had died in childbirth.[2]

---

† Originally published in *Birth, Death, and Motherhood in Classical Greece* (Baltimore and London 1994), 121–30.

[1] Michon 1905, 198; Riemann 1940; Loraux 1981; Vernant 1980–1, 404; Keuls 1985, 138; and Vedder 1988, 190, 182. Vedder expressed it in its most extreme form when she claimed that the group of tombstones portraying labor scenes discussed in this chapter provided a "direkt" analogy with memorials for men who had died in battle, and that both the warriors and the women were similarly portrayed as "in Aktion."

[2] Plut. *Lyc.* 27.2–3 (as emended by Latte). The case for the emendation is made by Wallace 1970; one good manuscript reads των ἱερων [holding a sacred office], and Wallace argued that this reading is confirmed by the text of Herodotus 9.85 before the mistaken emendation of *that* text changed ιρέας [priests] to ἰρένας [eirens; a Spartan term]. Despite the difficulty in attributing to scribal error the shift from τῶν ἱερῶν to ἐν λέχῳ [in childbirth], MacDowell 1986, 120–22, accepts the emendation because it "gives precisely the sense required" by "the Spartan principle that a man's aim in life is to be a good soldier and a woman's to be the mother of good soldiers." But the argument is circular: if the text depends upon the principle, it cannot be used in support of the principle.

Although the emendation is rather daring [. . .], appropriately inscribed tombstones have been found in Laconia that appear to support it.[3] Moreover, other funerary monuments have also been adduced as evidence. These consist of a group of Attic and atticizing monuments portraying women in labor.[4] Supporters of the equation argue that these were the memorials of women who died in childbirth and that they parallel tombstones honoring men who died in battle,[5] thus they are offered as evidence that both types of death were equally honored.

Aside from these tombstones depicting labor scenes, the case for this interpretation is by no means a compelling one. Euripides' Medea says nothing about anyone actually granting childbearing women honor equal to that accorded to warriors; on the contrary, her point is that they do not. And she is not alone. Female characters in the comedies of Aristophanes similarly complain about the lack of appreciation for their contribution of sons to the *polis*.[6] The evidence of Plutarch is also less than conclusive, depending upon a radical textual emendation that is supported by Laconian—but not necessarily Spartan—tombstones. And even if the stones are accepted as evidence for Sparta, the idiosyncrasies of the Spartan life-style cast doubt upon an extension of the equation to other Greek *poleis*. As Loraux stated, in Athens, at least on the civic level at which the Spartan practice operated, "the Spartan parallel between war and reproduction (dead *en polemoi* [in war]/dead *lecho* [in childbirth]) would be unthinkable."[7] But Loraux also argued that the parallel did exist in Athens on the *private* level, calling upon the evidence of the scenes portraying women in labor and those commemorating warriors fallen in battle on Attic funerary monuments.[8] Given the weakness in the other evidence offered in support of this piece of received opinion, we thus need to look more closely at these funerary monuments.

---

[3] *IG* v 1, 713–14, 1128, 1277, in childbirth; 701–10, 918, 1124, 1125, in battle.

[4] Wolters in Wolters and Friederichs 1885, no. 1042, first identified the scene on the stele of Malthake (no. 8 in this chapter) as labor, citing the epigram of Neotima (*Anth. Pal.* 7.730 [. . .]); Wolters 1892 discussed other members of the group and called attention to the loosened clothing as a sign of childbirth (see my n. 10); see also Michon 1905; Riemann 1940; Loraux 1981, with emphasis on private memorials; Vedder 1988 gives a full discussion and bibliography of the group; see also Vedder 1989, a special study of the stele in the Sackler Museum, Harvard University.

[5] Michon 1905, 198 first suggested the equation of death in childbirth with death in battle; see my n. 1.

[6] Ar. *Lys.* 651; *Thesm.* 832–47.

[7] Loraux 1986, 24.

[8] Loraux 1981. Loraux also added as evidence an epitaph (Peek 1955, no. 548 [IG II/III[2] 11907], dated after 350) that applies the term *iphthime*, which she translates as "courageuse," to a woman named Kratista who died in childbirth. But the term *iphthime* is Homeric, and the Homeric evidence does not support the translation "courageous" when the epithet is applied to a woman. Homer applies the adjective to women in seven passages. Two of these

The scenes appear on two types of monument, stelai [gravestones] and lekythoi [oil flasks] (a vase type rendered in stone).⁹ They depict a seated woman who is visibly distressed or collapsing, usually with hair and clothing loosened. She is physically supported by a woman who stands behind her. In some scenes a third female figure approaches her to offer assistance; in others another figure, male or female, stands nearby in an attitude of mourning. This type scene was identified as a representation of labor by Wolters in 1885; he relied upon the woman's sinking posture and, more specifically, her loosened hair and clothing, which serve as signs of childbirth in ancient texts.¹⁰ Most scholars have agreed with this identification,¹¹ and it seems to be confirmed both by those few examples that are graphic in their physical depiction of pregnancy, and by the appearance of a woman in the "sinking posture" on a fifth-century votive relief in New York, where the childbirth context is made explicit by the presence of a swaddled infant [. . .].¹² Since Wolters' identification, other stones have been added to the group. In 1905, Michon suggested the parallel with warrior monuments; Loraux took up the idea in 1981, and, in 1988, when the German scholar Ursula Vedder published the labor scenes as a group, she adopted this interpretation of them as portrayals of heroic female deaths.¹³

In the following descriptive summary of the monuments I omit

use the epithet in contexts that offer no suggestion as to its exact meaning: *Od.* 12.452, of Queen Arete of the Phaeacians; *Od.* 15.364, of Ktimene, Penelope's youngest child. In three passages the context is one of traditional female behavior: *Il.* 5.415, of Aigialeia in mourning; *Od.* 16.332, of Penelope when she must be informed of her son's safety lest she be frightened and cry; and *Od.* 23.92, of Penelope when she is admonished by her son. *Od.* 10.106 applies the term to a giant Laestrygonian woman; a translation of "stalwart" or even "huge" is appropriate, but would not justify using the same translation for a normal-sized woman. Finally, the adjective is applied to the wife of Sthenelos in connection with her illustrious descent; it is true that she is also described as giving birth at seven months, but in this she is portrayed as the passive victim of Hera, and the epithet is not applied to her behavior during the delivery. The epithet is also applied to cattle at *Il.* 23.260 (and similarly four times in the Homeric *Hymn to Hermes*: 94, 302, 394, 402). It is justified in this epitaph only because the usage is a special case, a pun on Kratista's name (Loraux calls it a "nom prédestiné).

⁹ Although the iconography of white-ground lekythoi used as funerary offerings is often considered in conjunction with grave reliefs, no labor or childbirth scenes appear on them; see Kurtz and Boardman 1971, 102–5; Shapiro 1991, 653–55.

¹⁰ Wolters in Wolters and Friederichs 1895 and Wolters 1892; loosened clothing: the epithet λυσίζωνος [belt-looser] was applied to childbirth divinities: Theoc. 17.60; Pind. *Ol.* 6.39; for references to later literature, see Aubert 1989, 444 and n. 48, 449 and n. 59. Vedder (1988) suggested that the major iconographical clue was an accentuation of the belly by the arrangement of the clothing.

¹¹ An exception was Brückner 1888; see Michon 1905. Vedder (1988) briefly discusses the history of the debate, which now seems resolved in favor of the identification.

¹² New York, Metropolitan Museum of Art MMA 24.97.92 [. . .] Another portrayal of this posture in a clear context of childbirth is provided by an Eretrian pyxis that depicts Leto in labor; see Speier 1932, 83 and pl. 28; Pingiatoglou 1981, 20–22, pl. 8.

¹³ Vedder 1988, 1989.

fragmentary and damaged pieces and consider only those stones that show the relationship between the various figures in the scene:[14]

1 The lekythos for Theophante in Athens, dated circa 340–330 [. . .][15] A female figure sits with hair and clothing loosened and stares downward into space; her arms are limp. A man standing to the right supports her left hand and raises his right hand to his head. On the left a female figure supports her with a hand under her arm.

2 The lekythos for Pheidestrate and Mnesagora in the National Archaeological Museum in Athens, dated circa 370/360 [. . .].[16] The names stand over the figures. The seated woman, labeled Pheidestrate, stares off into space. She is supported at the waist by a short female figure on the right. A third female figure, labeled Mnesagora, stands to the left and places her hand to her bowed head.

Both these scenes portray a seated woman with supporting and mourning figures. The other scenes include an additional, active helping figure:

3 A lekythos for Killaron in the Louvre, dated circa 370/360 [. . .].[17] A woman with loosened hair and clothing sits on a chair staring into space; her arms hang inertly. She is supported on the right by a less than full-sized female figure, while another female figure standing to the left reaches out to touch her and supports her right arm with her right hand.

4 A stele at Harvard in the Sackler Museum, dated circa 340 [. . .].[18] The seated woman is supported by a smaller figure on the right. She clasps the hand of a man standing before her, to

---

[14] Omitting Istanbul, Archaeological Museum 572 (Vedder 1988 pl. 24, no. 1), only the woman's head and upper torso are preserved; Thasos, Archaeological Museum 1172 (Vedder 1988, pl. 24, no. 2), a three-quarter life-sized scene reconstructed from a number of fragments in accordance with the type scenes on intact pieces—Devambez (1955) questioned the funerary context, arguing that the scene was part of a choregic monument depicting Phaedra; and a badly damaged stele in Messembria, Mihailov 1970, 290, no. 330 bis, and pls. 167, 168. Pingiatoglou (1981, 87, n. 237) added two unpublished fragments of stelai in the Paros Museum, nos. 983 and 370; of the first, she says only that it is somewhat similar to the Rhodes stele and slightly different from the stele of Malthake, omitting to specify even the number of figures in the scene; she gives no description at all of the second and no illustration of either. Her principle of selection is also unclear: she includes two Roman pieces in the group, the relief from Ostia, Ostia Museum 5204, post-Flavian; and the Basil relief of the second century AD, Phillips 1973, pl. 3.

[15] Athens, National Archaeological Museum NM 1055: Vedder 1988, pl. 21. 2, Conze 1893–1922, no. 309, pl. 75.

[16] Athens, National Archaeological Museum NM 1077: Conze 1893–1922, no. 308, pl. 74; Schmaltz 1970, 132, no. A140.

[17] Paris, Louvre MND 726: Vedder 1988, pl. 21.1; Michon 1905, 190–99, pl. 13.

[18] Cambridge, Mass., Arthur M. Sackler Museum 1905.8: Chase 1924, 103; Vedder 1989.

whom she looks; his left hand is held palm up near her face. An inscription suggests that he is her father; however, this male figure has been reworked; originally the figure was a female.[19] A third female figure, only partially preserved, stands behind the reworked figure. This stone could function as a bridge between the first two, which portray only supporting and mourning figures, and the others in the group that include an active helping figure: in its original form it depicted an active female helper, but in its later form this figure has been reworked to portray a typical farewell handshake gesture: now a man, the figure bids the woman goodbye rather than offering her assistance.

5 The grave stele for Plangon and Tolmides in Athens, circa 320s, found at Oropus in the border territory between Attica and Boeotia [. . .].[20] The seated woman is more obviously afflicted than the seated women in the other monuments: she is physically contorted and out of control, with her right leg awkwardly swung upward. She is supported by a slightly shorter woman on the right, and on the left another female figure moves toward her, supporting her right hand with her own right hand and holding out her left hand to her. A man (Tolmides) stands on the extreme left, holding his head in his hand.

6 The stele for Nikomeneia in the Kerameikos Museum, dated in the 320s [. . .].[21] A second name is incomplete; it could read either "Stephane" (female) or "of Stephanios" (male). The seated woman is supported by a female figure on the right, and her right arm rests on the shoulder of another female figure on the left, at whom she looks and who offers her something, possibly in a bowl.

7 A lekythos in Copenhagen, dated in the 320s [. . .].[22] The seated woman is supported on the right by a female figure who holds her left hand and in whose direction she looks. The woman's hair is not loosened. To the right another smaller female figure reaches out to touch the right hand of the seated woman with her right hand, thus covering her own face with her arm (a gesture of mourning or of helping?). In this case, it is the supporting figure on the right who seems to be the primary helper;

---

[19] Vedder 1989.

[20] Athens, National Archaeological Museum NM 749: Johansen 1951, 51, n. 26.

[21] Athens, Kerameikos Museum P290: Vedder 1988, pl. 22.2; Riemann 1940, 24–28, no. 25, pl. 1.6.

[22] Ny Carlsberg Glyptotek 226a: Vedder 1988, pl. 22.1; Schmaltz 1970, 137, no. A205.

she is larger than the figure on the left and more actively involved with the seated woman.

8 The stele for Malthake in the Piraeus Museum, dated circa 300 [. . .].[23] A woman is seated on a couch leaning on pillows; her hair is done neatly in braids; her left arm hangs down and her right is on the shoulder of the only other figure, a woman who stands behind the couch and touches the seated woman's chin with her right hand. The inscription reads, "Malthake: Magadidos, Chreste." Clairmont suggests that Malthake is not the woman on the couch but the standing figure, and that she was a midwife (midwives were often called "Chreste,"[24] and the name "Magadis" is foreign,[25] thus fitting the context of midwifery). If this is the case, Malthake is depicted in her lifetime activity, and the funerary relief belongs to a group of reliefs that portray professional activity rather than death in childbirth.[26]

9 One of two similar relief stelai in Alexandria, early Hellenistic [. . .].[27] The second stele is less well preserved. The seated woman is visibly pregnant and physically contorted. The supporting figure on the right is child-sized; a second female figure on the left holds out something in a bowl to the seated woman. A third-century painted limestone stele from Hadra in the vicinity of Alexandria, now in the Metropolitan Museum in New York, portrays a similar scene in a different medium.[28]

10 A stele from Rhodes, third century [. . .].[29] The woman sits on a couch staring into space. A small female figure on the right places her hand on the woman's shoulder, while a full-sized female figure on the left touches the head and arm of the seated woman.

In contrast to these labor scenes, another and more frequently found type scene appears to have been used to commemorate death

[23] Piraeus Museum 21: Conze 1893–1922, no. 155, pl. 46; Brückner 1888, 518, no. 5.
[24] On the use of this epithet, never applied to citizens and rarely to metics, see Nielsen et al. 1989, 419; they suggest that its use is a strong indication that the inscription commemorates a slave.
[25] First noted by Furtwangler, cited in Brückner 1888, 518.
[26] C. Clairmont, personal communication, August 1989.
[27] Alexandria: Vedder 1988, pl. 23.2; Pfuhl 1901, 268–70, no. 7, pl. 18.1 (no. 6 similar but older, less well preserved), Breccia 1922, 134, no. 83b (no. 82b is the older stele); Noshy 1937, 106.
[28] New York, Metropolitan Museum MMA 04.17.1: Merriam 1887; Brown 1957.
[29] Rhodes, Archaeological Museum 1470–3: Vedder 1988, pl. 25.1.

in childbirth: it depicts a seated woman with an attendant who holds an infant; in most cases the seated woman appears oblivious to the infant.[30] The late painted stele of Hediste in the Volos Museum, which is usually included in the labor group, perhaps better fits this second type, and its inscription offers a clue about the message intended by those who dedicated such memorials.[31] It is the best preserved of several in the museum that bear the same motif: the deceased woman lies prostrate on a bed; a man sits beside her with his head in his hands, and in the background a female figure appears in a doorway holding a swaddled infant. An epitaph conveys the sense of pathos considered appropriate to such a situation:

> The Fates spun on their spindles then for Hediste their painful thread, when the bride went to meet the pains of labor. Miserable one! She will not embrace her infant, or wet the lips of her baby with her breast, for one light [of day] looked down on both, and then Fortune coming to both alike carried the two away to one tomb.[32]

That not all scenes portraying a woman and an infant were intended to be seen as mother and child by those who chose them is, however, demonstrated by the well-known stele of Ampharete in the Kerameikos Museum.[33] On Ampharete's monument, an inscription identifies the "mother-child" pair as grandmother and grandchild. Unexpected iconographical traps thus may lie in wait, and cautious skepticism about the "obvious" meaning is always in order in interpreting the significance of scenes on tombstones. In order to use the labor scenes to reveal Greek attitudes about childbirth, we should try to eliminate modern assumptions and see the scenes as much as possible in terms of Greek iconographical conventions. In this we are following and extending the method adopted by Wolters in his original identification of them as labor scenes, in which he relied on motifs of loosening associated with childbirth in ancient texts. We need especially to look for similar recurrent themes that are significant in terms of otherwise-attested Greek values but that may have been overlooked in modern interpretation.[34]

The principal iconographical elements in the labor scenes appear to be posture (seated, standing, collapsing), relative size, type of

---

[30] E.g., Athens, National Archaeological Museum NM 819.

[31] Volos Museum, corridor A, 1: Arvanitopoulos 1928, 147–49 and pl. 1; 1909, 215–19; Brown 1974; first half of the second century.

[32] Peek 1955, 1606.

[33] Stele of Ampharete, Athens, Kerameikos Museum: Clairmont 1970, no. 23; *IG* II² 10650; see Schmaltz 1983, 119.

[34] Sourvinou-Inwood 1987a, 1987b, 1990.

clothing (typical of slaves or free persons), state of clothing and hair (loosened or normal), mode (active or passive), and activity (suffering, helping, supporting, mourning). Of these, the active-passive dichotomy especially deserves our attention because, although it was important in defining Greek gender roles,[35] it bears less significance in our value system and has received little attention in modern interpretations.

The Greek application of the active-passive pair to gender roles was somewhat more complex than this dichotomous expression suggests, however. While in general the Greeks allotted the active role to the male and the passive to the female,[36] the situation was not a straightforward association of active-male-good. The sphere of operation was also relevant: women could be active within the home, where the busy and competent household manager was valued, although she was barred from activity in the public sphere of the *polis*. Thus active-female-*oikos* [household] was viewed as desirable, but active-female-*polis* was firmly rejected.

Attic comedy provides still another dimension of value in the application of this dichotomy in its distinction between women according to age (or, rather, childbearing capacity). In comedy, it is *young* women in particular who are portrayed as passive, as "weak, prone to passion and standing in need of constant supervision . . . frivolous, naive and unreliable, unable to speak sensibly about any matter of interest to the city . . . their weapons are intrigue, guile and sexual manipulation."[37] In contrast, *older* women play an active role in comedy: it is they who serve as spokespersons, offer useful advice to the city, directly confront the men, and keep the younger women in line. Similarly, we have seen that in real life a degree of activity was tolerated for older women (especially mothers) who were past the age of childbearing: they were free to move about in public and could in some circumstances even confront men directly in the affairs of the *oikos*. Thus we have the value judgments that female-childbearing-active (outside the *oikos*) is bad, but female-postmenopausal-active (in the community) is at least acceptable in some cases. Because of such complexities, Greek values are better thought of as a multidimensional grid rather than as a simple dichotomy.

Viewing the labor scenes through our own perceptual screen, we

---

[35] Halperin 1990, 30–36; Mason 1984, 61, 1987.
[36] [Aristotle] *GA* 729a28–33, 729b13–15.
[37] Henderson 1987, 109.

see the pregnant woman as the focus of the scene because she is central both spatially and by virtue of being the center of attention, both important clues in our iconographical system. Another sign—size as an indicator of importance—is also caught by our perceptual net: we generally recognize that the smaller size of the second female helper signals her ancillary position (and possibly younger age), an interpretation that is confirmed in some cases by clothing that indicates servile status. But the active-passive dichotomy is not of great significance from our iconographical viewpoint, and therefore we fail to focus upon it as an important element in the scenes.

In Greek terms, however, the passivity of the seated figure is readily comprehensible. In the first place, she is young—still of childbearing age. Thus passivity is appropriate for her. Moreover, since, as we have seen, the Hippocratics viewed women's role in childbirth as passive,[38] in this way, too, passivity is appropriate for her. By failing to register this aspect of the scenes, we not only underestimate the importance of the seated woman's passivity, but we also fail to appreciate the significance of the central helping figure who provides the active focus on a number of the monuments.

We should now turn to the tombstones commemorating men who died in battle. If the Greeks did equate death in childbirth with death in battle, we should be able to see similar iconographical signs on monuments for both types of deaths.

Most warrior tombstones portray a standing male figure, often shown shaking hands with another figure in a typical funerary farewell scene.[39] The man is identifiable as a warrior by his clothing and war gear. In such quiet scenes, while the men are not shown in military action, they are portrayed as self-composed and in control of the situation, active in taking the first step toward the warfare that will lead to their deaths.[40] There is no hint of pathos either in the scenes themselves or in epitaphs. They offer a parallel with the swaddled-infant type scenes on women's monuments, but without the element of pathos that is central in the women's scenes, signaled by the epitaph for Hediste.

This difference becomes even more striking when we compare the

---

[38] See chapter 1 [of Demand 1994].

[39] On "quiet" warrior monuments, see Clairmont 1972, 52, 54.

[40] One anomalous scene, Leiden, National Museum of Antiquities RO 1 A5 (see Schmaltz 1970, A34) shows the warrior seated on a rock. A second man is holding out his hand in farewell, while the warrior raises his right hand to his helmet (perhaps to remove it, signifying that he is finished with war?), and rests his left hand on his shield. There is no indication that he is wounded, suffering, or in less than full control of himself.

iconographic elements in the labor scenes with those employed in the scenes of warriors portrayed in military action, of which there are about a dozen.[41] In these, male figures are shown charging into battle with shield and drawn sword,[42] or in actual battle and overcoming an enemy. The portrayal of battle scenes on these monuments is not gruesome in its realism, but idealized; only defeated enemies are depicted as wounded or dying, never the honored warrior himself.[43] Again, as in the case of the quiet warrior scenes, there is no hint of suffering or pathos.

As we have seen, in Greek terms, the active-passive dichotomy applied to people in their prime was a significant value indicator. Taking it into consideration allows us to see that, far from supporting the view that the classical Athenians accorded equal honor to death in childbirth and death in battle, the funerary monuments reflect and reinforce the role traditionally assigned to women of childbearing age in the grid of Greek values: as childbearers, they were passive while men were active; they could display patience and submission, but not an active courage to match that of the warrior.[44] They elicited pity, while warriors inspired admiration and emulation.[45]

This is not to deny that the Greeks saw a sort of similarity between these two types of deaths. But the funerary monuments locate this similarity in the Greek grid according to age and gender, making it iconographically clear that the women who are memorialized are passive and worthy of pity, whereas the men are active and heroic. The monuments thus register an important distinction between men and women who died "for the *polis*," rather than establishing an equivalence between the two. For the Greeks, the sexes were separate

[41] See Clairmont 1972; with list in n. 4. In general, also see Stupperich 1977; and Schweitzer 1941, 35–48.

[42] Aristonautes, Athens, National Archaeological Museum NM 738. The motif is more often found in Boeotia on painted stelai, for example, Mnason in the Thebes Museum; see Schweitzer 1941, 38 n. 4.

[43] Although wounded warriors are portrayed on Attic white-ground lekythoi, they are figures from myth, such as Sarpedon and Patroclus (see Schweitzer 1941, nn. 10, 11). Moreover, the function of these ceramic lekythoi was quite different from that of the stone grave monuments, whether these were in the form of stelai or lekythoi: the ceramic lekythoi were offerings to the dead, whereas the stone stelai and lekythoi were display markers for the grave; see Stupperich 1977, 182–83.

[44] The fate of the Amazons who fought against Athens provided a warning to women of the consequences of violating this dichotomy: their anonymous death "justly punishes them for usurping the name of warriors", Loraux 1986, 148

[45] Although by the fourth century, pity was becoming increasingly acceptable in memorials to the dead, this did not extend to monuments celebrating the civic contribution of the citizen soldier (Loraux 1986, 114–15), nor to the private monuments that made use of scenes from the public memorials (Clairmont 1970, 100–102; 1972, 55–58).

and unequal, and the funerary monuments faithfully express and communicate this by attributing to the one passivity and pathos, to the other, activity and glory.[46]

---

[46] The disparity between Greek attitudes toward death in childbirth and death in battle that is expressed in these monuments is confirmed by the difference in the public treatment of these two forms of death, a point I owe to Christoph Clairmont. For men who died in battle, fifth-century Athens developed a system of public honor to celebrate death in warfare, which included the *epitaphios* and the common public monument, or *polyandrion* (see Loraux 1986). This must have been very clearly felt in antiquity, as it usurped the traditional family role (and especially the role of women) in the honoring of the dead (see Shapiro 1991, 646). In contrast, no similar public honors were offered for victims of childbirth, whose deaths remained a private, family matter, just as their lives had been.

# 14 Archaeology and Gender Ideologies in Early Archaic Greece†

## IAN MORRIS

## INTRODUCTION

In this paper, I argue that we can only hope to write proper histories of Greek gender ideologies in the archaic period if we find ways to ground our arguments in the archaeological record. The greatest achievement of feminist historians in the 1970s was to force the profession to take gender seriously as an organizing principle in human history. Feminist modern historians have followed up this initial success by returning to the archives, generating the data that allow them to refine and to answer their questions. But that has not been an option for ancient historians. The only part of the data base likely to expand significantly is the archaeological record.

Gender relations seem less rigid in Homer than in Hesiod or Semonides, and historians commonly argue that boundaries hardened during the early archaic period. As one recent survey puts it, "The Archaic Age was a critical period for women . . . it was within the developing framework of the *polis* that the laws and customs were · established which were to determine the position of women for several centuries to come."[1] This model depends largely on drawing contrasts between Homer and later authors, and the source problems involved in this procedure are well known and acute.[2] Homer offers us one poet's vision of what the vanished heroic age ought to have been like; how does his picture compare to normative eighth-century ideas about gender relations? How much did such norms vary by

---

† Originally published in *TAPhA*, 129 (1999), 305–17.
[1] Blundell 1995: 65.
[2] I set out my views on interpreting archaic poetry in Morris 1999: 157–85.

location and class? How much does contrasting them with the radically different genres of lyric, elegiac, and iambic poetry tell us about changes through time? And where did Homer stand in the longer-term development of gender ideologies? Does he speak for a vanishing set of Dark Age attitudes, or for new ideas? Lacking a deeper historical context, we cannot make proper sense of the texts.

In this paper I suggest that archaeological data can provide such a context. I identify changes in the use of domestic space in the eighth century and suggest that the contrast between Homer and the later sources does indeed represent an important diachronic shift in gender ideologies in the central parts of Greece, around the shores of the Aegean Sea. Before 800 BCE, I suggest, attitudes toward gender were much more flexible than those which we see in archaic and classical literary sources; but, by 700, the outlines of the classical model were becoming visible.

The evidence currently available for archaic Greek houses is woefully inadequate, and my arguments here are necessarily tentative. Further, archaeologists of gender confront severe theoretical and methodological problems.[3] But, that said, the fact remains that the only way to put the literary evidence into a longer historical and a broader sociological context is by combining it with the material record. The specific arguments I offer here may not stand the test of time, but until historians begin formulating testable hypotheses we cannot expect archaeologists to seek out relevant data.

I begin by looking briefly at the evidence for household space in fifth-and fourth-century Athens and its relationships to gender ideologies; then, in section 2, I summarize some of the early archaic evidence. In the third section, I discuss my methods and assumptions before closing by drawing out some broader implications.

## 1 CLASSICAL HOUSEHOLD SPACE

As is well known, Lysias (1.9–10) and Xenophon (*Oec.* 9.5) tell us that parts of fourth-century Athenian houses were set aside as women's quarters (the *gynaikon* or *gynaikonitis*), functionally associated with cooking, weaving, and storage. Contemporary legal speeches reinforce this. Lysias (3.23) and Demosthenes (37.45–46) speak of an inner, most private, part of the house, which outsiders should not enter unbidden. In a pathbreaking paper, Susan Walker divided the plans of several Greek houses into male and female

---

[3] See Gero and Conkey 1991; Gilchrist 1994; Meskell 1999.

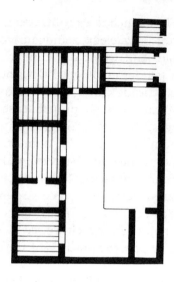

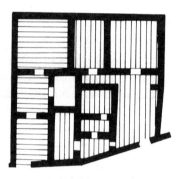

*Figure 14.1* Susan Walker's division of space in classical houses along gender lines.
Top: The Dema House, Attica. Bottom: A house from the North Slope of the
Areopagus, Athens. Vertical shading represents male space and horizontal shading
female space.

quarters to illustrate these principles (Fig. 14.1). However, as Michael
Jameson has shown, Walker's attempts to attribute gender to space
have little support in the published evidence, except in the case of the
men's dining room (*andron*). Jameson implied that archaeology
might therefore make us question the weight that literary sources
attach to gendered space, perhaps distinguishing between ideology
and behavioral realities.[4]

    [4] Walker 1983; Jameson 1990a, 1990b.

Lisa Nevett has offered a more nuanced argument.[5] She suggests that space was "asymmetrically gendered" in classical Greek houses. Houses normally had several rooms around a courtyard, entered from the street through a narrow door. Nevett identifies public areas firmly conceived as male space, while the rest of the house was an appropriate area for women, but barred to outsiders. Space was not rigidly divided into male and female, as Walker assumed, but into male and non-male; and space could be conceived as having varying amounts of maleness, lying along a gender spectrum rather than falling into two distinct categories. There is no reason to suggest that women only used certain parts of the house. Rather, the symbolism of domestic space marked the rear of the house as female, secret, and internal, accessible only through male space. It cut the family as a whole off from the broader polis, accessible only through a narrow door guarded by the *kyrios* [male head of the household]. As Lysias (1.4, 25, 36) and Demosthenes (18.132) make clear, crossing the threshold of the house without permission was an act of hubris, with all the associations that word carried. As in so many parts of the modern world, the symbolism of domestic space was a critical dimension of gender ideology in classical Athens. A true citizen was a man who ordered the space of his *oikos* [household] in proper measure.[6]

## 2  EARLY ARCHAIC HOUSES

But this attitude toward domestic space was hardly a new creation in fourth-century Athens. Hesiod already had similar ideas. He says in his description of winter that

> [Boreas] does not pierce the soft-skinned girl who stays
> Indoors at home with her mother, innocent
> Of golden Aphrodite's works. She bathes
> Her tender skin, anoints herself with oil,
> And going to an inner room at home,
> She takes a nap upon a winter's day, When, in his fireless house and dismal place
> The Boneless One is gnawing on his foot.[7]

Like the classical authors, Hesiod links space and gender, femininity and the inner rooms.

But before about 750 BCE this association between inner rooms and

---

[5] Nevett 1994, 1995, 1999.
[6] Cf. Cohen 1991: 73–76.
[7] Hes. *Op.* 519–25, trans. Wender.

femininity was not available in central Greece.[8] By 1100 BCE, Mycenaean multi-room houses[9] had disappeared from central Greece. Instead we find single-room apsidal and oval houses. At Asine, Tiryns, Argos, and Eretria, and further west at Nichoria, most activities—eating, sleeping, cooking, storage, stalling animals—went on either in an undivided main room or in the open air.[10]

After 750, however, rectilinear houses replaced these simple structures on some sites. At first, these were also single-roomed, or else megaron houses with a main room and a small porch. There had been ninth-century experiments with such houses at Thorikos and Smyrna, and at Miletus one rectilinear house was built early enough to burn down around 750. But generally rectilinear houses are a late eighth- and seventh-century fashion. At Pithekoussai and Miletus we even see people remodeling oval houses by just building corners onto them (Fig. 14.2).

By 700, the kind of courtyard houses that were normal in classical Greece were appearing. It was often a slow process, and at Miletus and Megara Hyblaea we see a gradual replacement of curvilinear houses across the seventh century. By 600, courtyard houses were normal everywhere. The best evidence comes from Zagora on Andros.[11]

Here we can identify one-room houses and megara built between 775 and 725. Some house-owners broke these into multi-room structures with functionally specific rooms after 725. For example, between 750 and 725, unit H24/25/32 was a simple megaron house (Fig. 14.3a). Sherds from the floors show that cooking, storage, eating, and drinking all went on in the one main room. By 725, though, the occupants had divided this room into three smaller rooms, H24, H25, H32. Judging from the finds, all three were used solely for storage. By 700, the south wall of the old porch was extended eight meters, and two new rooms, H40 and H41, built at its end (Fig. 14.3b). H40, with an unusually wide door, was probably an ante-room to H41, with a monumental stone hearth and many sherds from fine cups. The new house was reached from the courtyard now

---

[8] The evidence from Crete, western Greece, and Macedonia is different. I examine it, and explore the central Greek evidence in more detail, in Morris 1998: 16, 20–23, 27–29, 33–35, 40, 43, 46–47, 49, 55–56, 63–64.

[9] Hiesel 1990.

[10] Mazarakis Ainian 1997 and Lang 1995 provide excellent collections and discussions of the Dark Age and archaic finds respectively, with full references for the scattered excavation reports on the sites I mention in the text. The internal space of the tenth-century building at Lefkandi Toumba (Popham *et al.* 1993) is divided in more complex ways, but is open to numerous interpretations. I offer my own views in Morris 1999: 218–38.

[11] Cambitoglou *et al.* 1971, 1988.

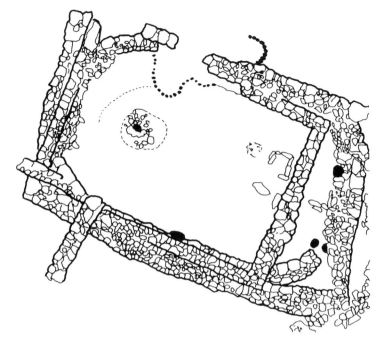

*Figure 14.2* Pithekoussai house, with oval and rectangular walls.

formed by the space between H32 and H40. Turning right, the visitor entered through the wide doorway into the public area of the house for feasting; turning left, into storerooms at the back. The house immediately to the south went through a similar transformation at just this time.

The rebuilding of Zagora between 725 and 700, and of most other Aegean communities over the next hundred years, constituted a revolution in domestic space. By the mid-seventh century, the experience of wandering through a Greek community–whether a little village like Koukounaries on Paros or a substantial town like Corinth–must already have been one of encountering high walls along the streets, pierced only by narrow doors letting on to secluded courtyards. Behind these walls, rooms were nestled in increasing levels of privacy. This was a total change from the open villages of the Dark Age. Within the space of a single lifetime, there had been a thoroughgoing transformation of what it meant to move through domestic space.

Attributing gender to excavated space is almost impossible, and I am not suggesting that men or women were restricted to particular parts of the house. Surely women often went into Zagora H40 and H41, and men into H24, H25, and H32. But I do want to suggest that

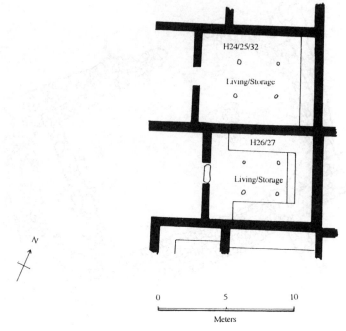

*Figure 14.3a* First phase at Zagora; house walls in black.

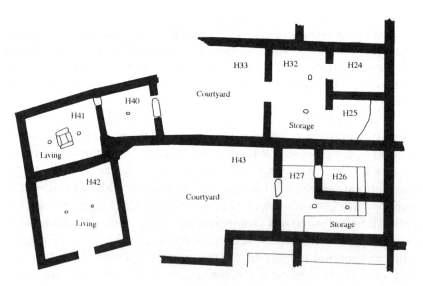

*Figure 14.3b* Second phase at Zagora; house walls in black.

the *ideas* about gendered space that we see in Hesiod and classical Athens began to take shape in the late eighth century. The courtyard houses we see at Zagora by 700 and Miletus by 600 cut the individual *oikos* off from other units. The *oikos* was accessible only through a narrow door, guarded by its male *kyrios*. Inside were his dependent women, children, relatives, and perhaps slaves, shielded from the world. The open, single-roomed houses of ninth-century Asine and early eighth-century Eretria did not work in this way.

## 3  INTERPRETATION

In section 2, I did no more than sketch in the crudest of strokes the outlines of the transformation of domestic space under way in the late eighth century. Rather than pile up examples, I want to turn now to discuss some of the assumptions that underlie this use of archaeological data. The most obvious of these is the fact that people *can* develop complex spatial symbolism without solid physical boundaries. The Brazilian Mehinaku are the best known case.[12] The appearance of archaeologically visible divisions does not *have* to mean anything of great significance; simply assuming that no boundaries mean fluid space and stone footings for walls mean structured space may be nothing more than the worst kind of positivism. Yet cross-cultural surveys do show regularly recurring correlations between rigid, hierarchical gender/age structures and firmly subdivided domestic space.[13] Comparative evidence can never prove a specific historical argument right or wrong, but it can show which way the burden of proof lies. In this case, we should *expect* these eighth-century changes in house forms to have been important.

Checklist approaches are of course open to many criticisms. Concrete ethnographic studies, like Henrietta Moore's of the symbolism of domestic space among the Kenyan Marakwet, or historical studies like Jane Adams' of farm houses in early twentieth-century Illinois,[14] always reveal more complexity. Meanings are open to debate, and individual actors simultaneously adapt the physical world to meet their desires and their desires to meet the constraints of the physical world. But certain recurrent themes recur in the mass of case studies, which suggests that there are three points we should bear in mind when looking at early archaic Greece.

---

[12] Gregor 1977.
[13] Kent 1990; Lawrence and Low 1990; Blanton 1994.
[14] Moore 1986; Adams 1993.

First, houses are expensive. When unknown residents of seventh-century Miletus rebuilt the oval structure now known as Südschnitt House A with corners, or another family remodeled a house excavated on the Kalabaktepe hill around a courtyard, they must have had good reasons to do so. Some archaeologists would dismiss changes in dress or burial customs as mere "fashion," too frivolous or too psychologically embedded for serious analysis. But recent work on such "fashions" in house design in the modern world suggests that only a cultural trend of the utmost importance will drive people to do something as expensive as rebuilding their homes.[15]

Second, a house is an emotional repository. In most documented settings, few things count for more than the layout of the home. A major change in house design like that around 700 may have been no small thing, if only we can read the historically specific symbolic language of space. Iron Age houses have been analyzed less often than graves or sanctuaries, but I submit that the eighth-century changes in house form were every bit as important as those better-known transformations in burial and the worship of the gods.[16]

Third, context. Without the kind of evidence ethnographers collect,[17] interpreting space is highly conjectural. But every case study shows that we can only interpret houses in the context of a broader symbolic system. In the late eighth century, we see that everything was in flux in central Greece. Recent studies of burial also point to hardening gender boundaries around 700, and I have argued that we can link together new forms of burial, worship, housing, art, writing, and travel as parts of the formation of and resistance to a new category of identity, the middling male citizen.[18] Male citizenship was as much about gender, cosmology, and ethnicity as about class and politics, and the huge overhaul of spatial categories between 750 and 650 was fundamental to it. The kinds of houses, sanctuaries, and cemeteries established by 650 remained normal in central Greece for the next millennium.

---

[15] Blier 1987; Blanton 1994: 79–113; Carsten and Hugh-Jones, eds., 1995.

[16] On burial, Morris 1987; Whitley 1991; on worship, Morgan 1990; de Polignac 1995.

[17] And even with it; the classic study of the meaning of domestic space, Bourdieu's interpretation of the Kabyle house (1970), is essentially unfalsifiable. As one biographer says, "it is not clear whether the symbolic edifice of binary oppositions exists in some sense in the culture and discourse of the Kabyle people, or whether it has simply been imposed by the anthropologist, who is thus its creator" (Jenkins 1992: 34–35).

[18] Houby-Nielsen 1992, 1995; Whitley, 1996; Morris 1999: 257–72; cf. Shanks 1999: 172–213.

## 4 CONCLUSION

I suggest that the great change in central Greek house design in the late eighth and seventh century reveals hardening gender ideologies. Before 750, it is not easy to see how the relationships between space and gender taken for granted by authors from Hesiod to Demosthenes would have worked in a world of one-roomed houses in very open settlements; by 600, the inward-turned courtyard house with functionally specific rooms was normal everywhere. I cannot prove that this was directly linked to more rigid gender distinctions. Eleventh- through ninth-century Greeks *may* have interpreted their simple, open houses in much the same ways as archaic and classical Greeks did the subdivided space of their courtyard houses. But, putting together the poetry and the transformation of house forms and activity areas between 750 and 600, the most economical theory is that gender ideologies did change in this period, in a general shift toward "middling" values. This, I submit, was (a) the most important moment in the evolution of gender ideologies in ancient Greece, and (b) part of a profound reorientation of every dimension of Greek society.

[. . .] My argument depends on what Anders Andrén calls the "method of correlation,"[19] looking for similarities between the structure of the material record and the verbal accounts that members of a past society gave of themselves. I have suggested, first of all, that the physical remains of classical Athenian houses and the writings of Athenian men about the gender implications of domestic space map onto each other closely, each helping to explain the other category of evidence. To borrow another of Andrén's terms, texts and artifacts provide "contemporary analogies" for each other.[20] I then showed that the kind of domestic space familiar in the fourth century began to appear around 700, and argued that the most plausible explanation of this phenomenon is that classical-type ideologies about gender also began to take shape around 700.

## WORKS CITED

Adams, J. 1993. "Resistance to 'Modernity': Southern Illinois Farm Women and the Cult of Domesticity." *American Ethnologist* 20: 89–113.
Andrén, A. 1998. *Between Artifacts and Texts: Historical Archaeology in Global Perspective*. Trans. A. Crozier. New York.

[19] Andrén 1998: 166.
[20] Andrén 1998: 156.

Blanton, R. E. 1994. *Houses and Households: A Comparative Study*. New York.

Blier, S. 1987. *The Anatomy of Architecture: Ontology and Metaphor in Batammaliba Architectural Expression*. Cambridge, UK.

Blundell, S. 1995. *Women in Ancient Greece*. Cambridge, MA.

Bourdieu, P. 1970. "The Kabyle House, or the World Reversed." *Social Science Information* 9: 151–70.

Carsten, J., and S. Hugh-Jones, eds. 1995. *About the House: Lévi-Strauss and Beyond*. Cambridge, UK.

Cambitoglou, A., J. J. Coulton, J. Birmingham, and J. R. Green. 1971. *Zagora* I. Sydney.

———. 1988. *Zagora* II. Athens.

Cohen, D. 1991. *Law, Sexuality, and Society: The Enforcement of Morals in Classical Athens*. Cambridge, UK.

de Polignac, F. 1995. *Cults, Territory, and the Origins of the Greek City-State*. Trans. J. Lloyd. Chicago.

Gero, J. M., and M. W. Conkey, eds. 1991. *Engendering Archaeology: Women and Prehistory*. Oxford.

Gilchrist, R. 1994. *Gender and Material Culture: The Archaeology of Religious Women*. London.

Gregor, T. 1977. *Mehinaku*. Chicago.

Hiesel, G. 1990. *Späthelladischer Hausarchitektur*. Mainz.

Houby-Nielsen, S. 1992. "Interaction Between Chieftains and Citizens?" *Acta Hyperborea* 4: 343–74.

———. 1995. "'Burial Language' in Archaic and Classical Kerameikos." *Proceedings of the Danish Institute at Athens* 1: 129–91.

Insoll, T. 1999. *The Archaeology of Islam*. Oxford.

Jameson, M. H. 1990a. "Domestic Space in the Greek City-State." In S. Kent, ed., *Domestic Architecture and the Use of Space*. Cambridge, UK. 92–113.

———. 1990b. "Private Space and the Greek City." In O. Murray and S. Price, eds., *The Greek City from Homer to Alexander*. Oxford. 171–95.

Jenkins, R. 1992. *Pierre Bourdieu*. London.

Kent, S. 1990. "A Cross-Cultural Study of Segmentation, Architecture, and the Use of Space." In S. Kent, ed., *Domestic Architecture and the Use of Space*. Cambridge, UK. 127–52.

Lang, F. 1995. *Archaische Siedlungsarchitektur*. Mainz.

Lawrence, D., and S. M. Low. 1990. "The Built Environment and Spatial Form." *Annual Review of Anthropology* 19: 453–505.

Mazarakis Ainian, A. 1997. *From Rulers' Dwellings to Temples: Architecture, Religion and Society in Early Iron Age Greece (1100–700 BCE)*. Studies in Mediterranean Archaeology 121. Jonsered.

Meskell, L. 1999. *An Archaeology of Social Life: Perspectives on Age, Sex and Class in Egyptian Society*. Oxford.

Moore, H. L. 1986. *Space, Text and Gender*, Cambridge, UK.

Morgan, C. 1990. *Athletes and Oracles: The Transformation of Olympia and Delphi in the Eighth Century* BCE. Cambridge, UK.

Morris, I. 1987. *Burial and Ancient Society: The Rise of the Greek City-State*. Cambridge, UK.

———. 1998. "Archaeology and Archaic Greek History." In N. Fisher and H. van Wees, eds., *Archaic Greece: New Approaches and New Evidence*. London. 1–91.

———. 1999. *Archaeology as Cultural History: Words and Things in Iron Age Greece*. Oxford.

Nevett, L. 1994. "Separation or Seclusion? Towards an Archaeological Approach to Investigating Women in the Greek Household in the Fifth to Third Centuries BCE." In M. Parker Pearson and C. Richards, eds., *Architecture and Order: Approaches to Social Space*. London. 98–112.

———. 1995. "Gender Relations in the Classical Greek Household: The Archaeological Evidence." *ABSA* 90: 363–81.

———. 1999. *House and Society in Ancient Greece*. Cambridge, UK.

Popham, M. R., P. G. Calligas, and L. H. Sackett. 1993. *Lefkandi* II.2. *The Protogeometric Building at Toumba: The Excavation, Architecture and Finds*. British School at Athens Supp. vol. 23 (Athens).

Shanks, M. 1999. *Art and the Early Greek State: An Interpretive Archaeology*. Cambridge, UK.

Walker, S. 1983. "Women and Housing in Classical Greece: The Archaeological Evidence." In A. Cameron and A. Kuhrt, eds., *Images of Women in Classical Antiquity*. London. 81–91.

Whitley, J. 1991. *Style and Society in Dark Age Greece: The Changing Face of a Pre-Literate Society, 1100–700 BCE*. Cambridge, UK.

———. 1996. "Gender and Hierarchy in Early Athens. The Strange Case of the Disappearance of the Rich Female Grave." *Métis* 11: 209–31.

# 15  Concealing/Revealing: Gender and the Play of Meaning in the Monuments of Augustan Rome†

## BARBARA KELLUM

The interrelatedness of gender and power is key to an understanding of the monuments of Augustan Rome. [. . .] Gender can be a useful category of analysis precisely because it tends to destabilize our understanding of the past.[1]

As I hope to demonstrate in examining the first of three structures that I will discuss, gender encodings, even at the most basic level of reading, are not transparent. The scene depicted on figure 15.1, one of a series of terracotta Campana plaques from the Temple of Apollo on the Palatine, has sometimes been identified as Apollo and Diana crowning a sacred pillar. The source of the identification is not diffi-cult to trace: Apollo is a god who sometimes wears the peplos and both he and his sister Diana were honored at the temple [. . .] Nonetheless, a consideration of hairstyle and costume and a recog-nition of the central device establishes that this is a *pas de deux* for two maidens, decorating an aniconic representation of Apollo Agyieus, a type of critical importance to Augustus and to the Palatine complex.[2] In context, the repeated plaques were self-consciously jux-taposed with their masculine counterparts, Apollo and Hercules, locked in contest over the Delphic tripod (figure 15.2).

Both sets, at the time the temple was dedicated in 28 BCE, must have looked to contemporary viewers simultaneously old and new. Terracotta revetments and sculpture typified the oldest temples in the

† Originally published in T. Habinek and A. Schiesaro (eds), *The Roman Cultural Revolution* (Cambridge 1997), 158–81.

[1]  Scott (1986).
[2]  Carettoni (1973): 78–80, & n.24; Strazzulla (1990): 22–9.

*Figure 15.1* Archaizing maidens crowning an aniconic representation of Apollo Agyieus, terra cotta Campana plaque from the Temple of Apollo on the Palatine, Rome.

city, and, from the second century BCE on, such ornament was supposedly disparaged by many Romans once they had laid eyes on the glistening marble temples of the Greek East.[3] The former antitheses were here combined, since the Temple of Apollo on the Palatine, although it alluded to Etruscan temples in its form, was one of the first built of solid marble, from the newly discovered Luna quarries.

[3] Livy 34.4.4; cf. Plin. *NH* 36.6–7.

*Figure 15.2* Apollo versus Hercules, terra cotta Campana plaque from the Temple of Apollo on the Palatine, Rome.

In motif, as in material, the two sets of plaques harkened back to "archaic" models. The "archaistic" maidens-composition was newly generated for the temple, but the Apollo *vs.* Hercules plaque was predicated on an earlier vase painting type. Significantly, it is not the popular "classical" vase painting composition—where Hercules has already shouldered the Delphic tripod which he is attempting to steal —that is chosen, but, instead, a rare "archaic" model which focuses on an earlier moment in the struggle, when Apollo and Hercules are ostensibly more evenly matched. Appearances, of course, can be deceiving, and, mythologically, the affirmation of Apollo's rightful possession of the tripod is a foregone conclusion, something that becomes the more important when it is recognized, as I first proposed in 1980, that what we are dealing with here is a thinly veiled allegory of the recent battle of Actium, cast in the form of a primordial contest between Apollo and Hercules, the divine progenitors of, respectively, Octavian and Antony.[4] The officially declared enemy, Cleopatra—pinioned between a male and a female sphinx, waving her sistrum as she does in Virgil's description of the battle of Actium[5] —appears here as the repeated sima decoration, literally enframing the whole.

The gendered discourse of the temple of Apollo on the Palatine extended to the porticus of the temple as well. Here, between columns of *giallo antico* marble—yellow marble spotched with blood red—statues of the fifty Danaids were on display.[6] These were not, *pace* Zanker, the Danaids as water carriers in the Underworld.[7] Rather, as both Propertius and Ovid make clear, this was the far rarer iconography of the wedding night itself, each Danaid with a dagger beneath her peplos—as is true of an example now in Basle—and Danaus, the *barbarus pater* [foreign father] standing with sword drawn.[8] Appropriately Greco-Egyptian, the Danaids were unequivocally linked to Cleopatra; yet, at the same time, the tale was undeniably one of cousins killing cousins, of fratricide and civil war. In the end, perhaps, it was the gender difference of the opponents that made the whole acceptable, an artful allusion to that which was ineffable —the undeclared civil war—and yet was to be avoided again at all costs. [ . . .]

The same significative play, in gendered terms, informs the other temple of Apollo in Augustan Rome, the Temple of Apollo Sosianus. Gaius Sosius, commander of the left wing of Antony's fleet at Actium, was a recipient of Augustus' clemency and was even one of the *quindecimviri sacris faciundis* at the Secular Games of 17 BCE.[9] Surely Sosius' lavish restoration of the temple of Apollo was a factor here; it is a *tour de force* performance honoring both Sosius and the new emperor simultaneously. The temple, the very place where Atia, Octavian/Augustus' mother, declared her son had been engendered

---

[4] Kellum (1981):200; (1985); Zanker (1983).
[5] Virg. *Aen*. 8.696.
[6] Prop. 2.31.
[7] Zanker (1983): 27–31.
[8] Prop. 2.31; Ovid *Trist*. 3.1.61–62; statue in Basle: Berger (1968), 65–7.
[9] Vell. 2.85.2, 2.86.2; *ILS* 5050, 1.150.

*Figure 15.3* Reconstruction of the Amazonomachy pedimental sculpture with
youthful hero crowned by hovering Victory and Hercules, Temple of Apollo
Sosianus, Rome.

by Apollo,[10] now took its restorer's name, but had as its dedication
day 23 September, the day of Augustus' birth.[11] Likewise, the pedimental sculptures representing an Amazonomachy may make reference to both (figure 15.3). On one level, it is a clear celebration of the
victory at Actium over the feminine forces of the East and, of course,
Cleopatra.[12] But, within this battle of the sexes, two male protago-
nists are juxtaposed: one is Hercules with his lion skin and the other
is a young man, perhaps Theseus. It is visually apparent that it is the
young man who is triumphant since it is he who wears the gilded
crown bestowed by Victory. Hercules, like all gods and heroes, had his
place in the Augustan dispensation; next door at the buildings of
Octavia, for example, a spectator would have seen Androbius' painting of Hercules Ascending to Heaven, received there by Apollo,[13] but
in the Actium-informed context of the temple pediment, it was surely
Antony, who had prided himself on his physical resemblance to
Hercules,[14] that would have come to the Augustan viewer's mind, just
as at the Temple of Apollo on the Palatine. It was precisely this kind
of identification, underscored by coinage imagery, that had wide currency in Rome, as the popular hue and cry surrounding Sextus
Pompey and the statue of Neptune at the Circensian Games of 40 BCE
attests.[15] If Hercules is associated with Antony, then the young victor
is Antony's fellow Roman and yet rival Octavian/Augustus, and, at
the same time, it is also Antony's lieutenant, Gaius Sosius, once triumphant himself over the forces of the East (*ex Iudaea* [from Judea]
34 BCE) and again in Augustan Rome as the dedicator of the Temple
of Apollo Sosianus. [. . .]

That this multiple level of reference could occur, that, as at the porticus of the Danaids, an aspect of contemporary history could be art-

[10] *Epigrammata Bobiensia* 39; Dio 45.1.2–3.
[11] Plin. *NH* 13.53; 36.28; *Fast. Urb. Arv. ad ix kal. Oct.*; *CIL* 12. pp. 215, 252, 339.
[12] LaRocca (1985), *passim*.
[13] Plin. *NH* 35.139.
[14] Plut. *Ant.* 4.1–2.
[15] Dio 48.31.5–6.

fully concealed and revealed at the same time, has everything to do with the fact that these monuments existed in a nexus of presuppositions about gender and power on the battlefield, in the bedroom, and in the law courts, that is historically specific and only tangentially related to our own. In order to explore this notion fully, I would like to focus now on a more detailed analysis of the Forum of Augustus with its Temple of Mars Ultor dedicated in 2 BCE (figure 15.4). Although usually presented as a staid monument of military history, filled with a didactic statuary program, and built by a leader who was by all accounts less than a virile super-hero, the Forum of Augustus was, I will argue, a sexually charged, gendered masculine environment.

The temple and the Forum functioned as the locus for the political and military rituals through which the masculine was defined.[16] Here young men came when they put aside the garb of childhood—the *toga praetexta* with its purple stripe and the *bulla*, a locket containing an apotropaic phallic amulet—to assume the all-white *toga virilis*, the garment of the Roman citizen.[17] [. . .] The "increase in the number of the people and of cases at law" was a primary impetus for the building of the Forum; here the *praetor urbanus* [city magistrate] and the emperors themselves set up their tribunals and public prosecutions and jury selection were held.[18] Here governors on their way to military provinces were to take their leave of the city, here the Senate was to debate declarations of war and claims for triumph, and here, after ritually entering the city and processing through it in his quadriga, the triumphator [one celebrating a triumph]—dressed in purple, wearing the *bulla* [permitted in adulthood to triumphators only], his face painted red like that of the statue of Jupiter Capitolinus—would arrive to dedicate his scepter and crown to Mars.[19]

Present were not just the heroes of the moment, but those of the past. The walls of the forum were literally lined with a vast statuary program of *summi viri* [distinguished men], great military and civic heroes of the Roman past trooped around a statue of Aeneas carrying his father Anchises and leading his son Iulus by the hand in the central niche of the northern hemicycle, and one of Romulus carrying the *spolia opima* [spoils offered by a Roman general who had slain an enemy leader in single combat] in the southern hemicycle.[20]

---

16  Suet. *Aug.* 29.1–2.
17  Macrob. *Sat.* 1.6.7f.; Dio 55.10.2; *NSc* 1933 464–5, Nr. 85.
18  Suet. *Aug.* 29.1–2; Pugliese-Carratelli (1948), tablet XIV, p.2; Suet. *Claud.* 33.1.
19  Serv. *Ecl.* 10.27; Serv. Dan. *Ecl.* 6.22; Suet. *Aug.* 29; Dio 55.10.1–5.
20  Ovid *Fast.* 5.563ff.

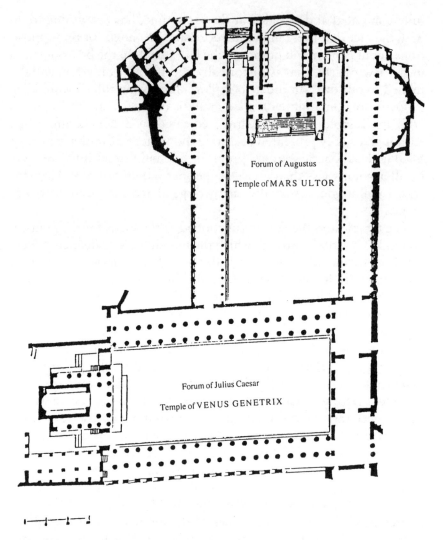

*Figure 15.4* Plan of the Forum of Augustus and the Forum of Julius Caesar, Rome.

[...] Set around them, ranged as if in a gigantic family atrium,[21] were all the leaders of the distant and more recent past, many of them familiar faces, copied from the statues that appeared on earlier familial monuments, gathered here as if by evocation. [...]

The statues must have been as close to living presences as were the public funeral parades of ancestors personified by individuals wearing the death-masks and regalia of those long dead.[22] [...]

[21] Cf. Plin. *NH* 35.6–7.
[22] Cf. Polybius 6.53.

Without question, the program set the standard by which all men were to be measured.²³

Strategically, the viewer gained access to the statues of the *summi viri* by passing beneath an attic level frieze of repeated Caryatid figures. [. . .] Within the masculine environment of the Forum of Augustus, the role of these repeated female figures was hardly a neutral one. Although our own Romantic notions of "the porch of the maidens" may obscure this for us, it is striking that Vitruvius, writing in the 20s BCE, read Caryatids in a very specific way. As an architect, he maintained that these "marble statues of robed women used as columns" had a history: after the Greeks destroyed Caryae, a city in the Peloponnese which had allied herself with the Persians, they led the matrons away into captivity, compelling them to retain their robes and matronly ornaments as permanent symbols of their shame.²⁴

In the Forum of Augustus—the very performance space for the triumph—the Caryatids' significance as captive women and the time-worn analogies between the penetration of a woman's body and the breeching of enemy fortresses were certainly primary.²⁵ The extent of Rome's domination was mapped in turn by the repeated shield devices that appeared between each pair of Caryatids—Zeus Ammon for the East and a Gaul with torque for the West. Suetonius tells us that Augustus forced certain barbarian chiefs to come to the temple of Mars Ultor itself in the Forum of Augustus to take an oath to keep the peace and "in some cases, indeed, he tried exacting a new kind of hostages, namely women, realizing that the barbarians disregarded pledges secured by males."²⁶ The connection between the actual women hostages and the Caryatids, as well as the linkage between women and subdued barbarians, were likely not lost on a Roman audience.

In functional terms, then, the Forum of Augustus was a sexually fraught theater for the engendering of the masculine. This is also, I believe, fundamental to the very structuring of the building itself. [. . .]

In plan, with its two bulging *exedrae* and projecting forecourt, the forum resembles nothing so much as the schema for the phallus represented on buildings throughout the Roman world [. . .] There are, of course later examples of phallic building plans like Ledoux's 1804

²³ Suet. *Aug.* 31.5.
²⁴ Vitr. 1.1.5.
²⁵ *Il.* 22.468–70, cf. *Il.* 16.100; *Od.* 13.388; Eur. *Hec.* 536–38, *Tr.* 308–13; Ovid *Am.* 1.9.15–20; Paul (1982) 144–55.
²⁶ Suet. *Aug.* 21.2.

plan for the Oikema, an institutionalized brothel. [. . .] Because to us, as to Ledoux's contemporaries, its form bespeaks its function, we recognize in it an example of *architecture parlante*. If the Forum of Augustus does not appear to speak to us in the same way, it is perhaps because our own concept of the phallus as signifier is as historically specific as that of ancient Rome.[27]

The sheer ubiquity of the phallus in that context, in scales ranging from the gigantic to the minuscule, is difficult for us to imagine. The erect phallus certainly served as the shop sign of the *lupinar* (brothel), but equally appeared on house walls, on baker's ovens, on paving stones, at the baths, at fortress gateways, and on objects ranging from *ex votos* to suggestively flaming lamps.[28] Projected in at least three dimensions, and hung with bells, the polyphallus became a whimsical doorbell (*tintinnabulum*). In daily speech too, the male organ was everywhere; Augustus' nickname for one of his favorite poets, the short-of-stature Horace, was *purissimus penis* (most immaculate penis).[29]

Key to an assessment of this seemingly overweening plethora of display is an understanding of the primary function of the phallus as signifier in context. Like the phallic amulet in the child's *bulla* or the phallic harness ornament on the prized horse, representations of the phallus offered protection from the evil eye. [. . .] The more prominent one was, the more exposed to the evil eye of gods and mortals alike. Thus, the triumphator, dressed as a god and a king, wore his *bulla* and had an additional phallus (*fascinum*) hung beneath his chariot.[30] Within this system, the moment of being the most powerful was also the moment of being the most vulnerable, a fact which was both acknowledged and deflected by the scurrilous insults hurled by the troops at the triumphator during the triumph.[31] In so doing the community simultaneously protected, humiliated, and exalted the leader, and often in explicitly sexual terms. At his triumph in 46 BCE, for example, Julius Caesar was hailed as vanquisher of the Gauls and at the same time ridiculed for having been vanquished—for having lost his virginity—to Nicomedes the king of Bithynia.[32]

This allusion to Caesar's taking the passive role in a homoerotic relationship indicates another important aspect of the Roman

[27] Compare Lacan (1977).
[28] On walls, the phallus could be vertically or laterally disposed: Ling (1990): 51–55. In general, Johns (1982):61–75; Grant (1975).
[29] Suet. *Vit. Hor.* See Adams (1982):9ff.
[30] Plin. *NH* 28.39.
[31] Livy 3.29.5; Dion. Hal. *Ant. Rom.* 7.72.11.
[32] Suet. *Iul.* 49.3; cf. Cic. frg. inc. 5 Watt.

concept of the phallus as signifier. In sexual, military, and judicial encounters, it was not the genitalia that mattered, but the role that one played. In fact, in anatomical terms, as the similarity of the schemata suggests, men and women were thought to have the same genitals, one on the outside of the body and one on the inside, with what we call the ovaries termed testicles.[33]

There was, of course, still a presenting and a receiving role, and it was the aggressor who attempted to wield the phallus. The inscribed lead sling bullets, hurled by both sides at the siege of Perusia in 41/40 BCE, illustrated this graphically. The technical name for sling bullet, *glans*, also meant tip of the penis, and not only did some bear representations of the phallus, but they were also aimed, by means of their inscriptions, at allocating their opponents the passive/receiving sexual role. Thus, a sling bullet intended for Antony's wife, Fulvia, was launched at her *landica* (clitoris), while another, decorated with a phallus and directed at her opponent, Octavian, targeted his anus.[34] [...]

But if this is the nature of the phallus as signifier in the Roman sphere, what evidence do we have to indicate that it should be associated with the Forum of Augustus or its plan? Certainly the apotropaic significance of the phallus in the very ceremonies celebrated in the Forum, especially the triumph, have already been demonstrated, and the literary plays on the immense size of the Forum are suggestive,[35] but it is in the realm of the joke and of popular art that the most intriguing traces of this association are to be found.

First, it must be said that the Forum of Augustus—much like Virgil's great epic the *Aeneid*, to judge by the graffiti—seems to have captured the imaginations of Romans from many walks of life, as it is freely quoted in many contexts throughout the Roman world. [...] The serious and the amusing, the commemorative and the commercial, the military and the amatory, the high and the low: all were inextricably interlinked.

This is equally the case for the one caricature that we know of the Forum of Augustus statue of *the* progenitors: Aeneas carrying his father Anchises and leading his son Iulus by the hand. In a painting from Pompeii, or possibly from Stabiae, Aeneas and little Iulus are tricked out with the universal lighting rod for the evil eye, the giant exposed phallus that formed a part of the costume of the mime;

[33] Galen *On the Seed* 2.1–2 (citing Herophilus, third cent. BCE); *On the Use of the Parts* 14.6; on the crucial shift in the late eighteenth century, Thomas Laqueur (1986): 2.
[34] Hallett (1977).
[35] Ovid *Fast.* 5.553.

Anchises carries not the household gods, but a dice box; and all the figures have canine features. [. . .] It has been fashionable of late to dismiss this as a simple example of anti-Augustanism,[36] but this is to miss both its wit and its wisdom. [. . .] The image not only plays on the weighty role of Aeneas—who is to sire the Alban kings leading to Romulus—and of little Iulus—who is to found the line of Julius Caesar and Augustus—but also by depicting the figures with the faces of dogs, generates a visual pun on *canis*, which means both "dog" and "you sing."[37] For any Latin speaker, it would have again been the first line of the *Aeneid* that would have come to mind: "I sing of arms and the man" (*arma virumque cano*). Finally, aged Anchises with his dice box is not just a slur on Augustus, who, like most Romans, was addicted to the game,[38] but a play on the universal name for the high roll, "the Venus,"[39] which the old man had certainly once thrown. Aeneas was, after all, the son of Venus and Anchises, as the inscription beneath his statue in the Forum of Augustus made clear and which the caricature both satirizes and affirms in terms of the phallus and the intermingling of the military and the amatory.

As Mikhail Bakhtin has said "The literary and artistic conscious-ness of the Romans could not imagine a serious form without its comic equivalent."[40] But this was operative both in official and in private spheres and brings us to the presence of Venus in the Forum of Augustus. Just as Aeneas, the son of Venus, and Romulus, the son of Mars, stood at the center of each of the Forum's *exedrae* [open recesses], so Venus, with her son Amor, stood next to Mars Ultor both on the temple pediment and in the cult statue grouping. It is well known that Venus was the one deity capable of disarming Mars,[41] as we see Amor helping her to do here, but mythologically Mars and Venus were not husband and wife, but notorious lovers (figure 15.5). Since the reign of Augustus is often typified by the restrictive legislation on marriage and adultery it produced, this cou-pling of Mars and Venus in the temple of Mars Ultor—even if dynastically justified—has often been thought to be strangely contradictory. It was certainly played on by Ovid,[42] who like Propertius and Tibullus, developed the theme of love as a kind of

---

[36] Zanker (1990):209.

[37] Varro *L.L.* 5.99; Ahl (1988): 41f.

[38] Suet. *Aug.* 71.2–4.

[39] Hor. *Carm.* 2.7.25; etc. The low roll was, of course the *canis*, so there is at least another level of play here.[...]

[40] Bakhtin (1981): 58.

[41] Lucr. 1.31f.

[42] Ovid *Trist.* 2.295f.

*Figure 15.5* Venus, Cupid, Mars, cult statue grouping from the Temple of Mars Ultor as reflected on Algiers relief (Divus Iulius on right).

warfare and every lover a soldier.[43] We tend to read these as personal criticisms of a strict moral regime rather than recognizing them as a part of the same system of ordering where the martial and the amatory were inherently a part of one another. [. . .]

Moreover, the relationship of Mars and Venus was inscribed on the city plan, since the phallic Forum of Augustus with its temple of Mars Ultor was juxtaposed with—perhaps literally wedded to—the Forum of Julius Caesar with its temple of Venus Genetrix (figure 15.4). [. . .]

As difficult as these connections may be for us to grasp, they were seemingly not lost on contemporaries. The one graffito we have preserved from the Forum of Augustus, scratched on the stylobate of the temple, depicts a violent sexual encounter.[44] Although not an uncommon theme in graffiti, in this context it might also be a comment on the multiply nuanced Forum and its maker.

[43] *Ars Am.* 2.233; *Am.* 1.9.1–2; etc.
[44] Kockel (1983): 447, plate 20.

Surrounded by Aeneas, Romulus and the *summi viri*, the
Caryatids, and the statues of Mars and Venus, the seminal point of
the Forum of Augustus, placed centrally within the projecting forecourt, was a statue of the emperor himself in a triumphal quadriga
and bearing for the first time the title *pater patriae* [father of the
fatherland].[45] Here, simultaneously risking envy and warding it off,
Augustus served as the formative point of mediation between his
divine ancestors Mars and Venus. Their divine child was Harmonia,
Augustus was the creator of the *pax Augusta* [Peace of Augustus].
Clearly the central role in the Forum belonged to Augustus. Here he
held sway over the heroes of the past [. . .]

The language of the courts was equally sexually laden. As every
visitor to the Forum of Augustus would have known, *testis* was the
word for witness as well as for testicle and was frequently punned
on.[46] Rhetorical styles too were assessed in metaphors of sexual
potency. [47] [. . .] This was the world of the Forum of Augustus, of the
Temple of Apollo on the Palatine, and the Temple of Apollo
Sosianus. What we see here depends on the interpretative lenses we
use. If gender as a category of analysis has transformative value, it is
precisely because in destabilizing the perception of this one aspect of
the past, it necessitates a re-examination of all the presuppositions
which underlie the traditional political history of the period. Since
the time of Edward Gibbon, it has been primarily Tacitus who has
informed history's vision, and, for Gibbon, it was Augustus with his
"mask of hypocrisy" that was to be seen, a specter made all the more
real by the great Tacitus of the twentieth century, Sir Ronald Syme in
his 1939 *The Roman Revolution*. In addition, although it is still too
seldom mentioned, we in the latter-day twentieth century still perceive Augustus through the filters of the excavations, reconstructions,
and image-making of Benito Mussolini.

The displays of Augustan Rome were not the simplistic equiv-
alences of a Mussolini. What may, from without, look, as Paul
Zanker has said, "unrelentingly didactic"[48] to us, was, from within
Augustan Rome, both multiplex and mimetic. [. . .]

This is not an ossified system, nor should we construe it as one. In
order to understand the visual language of Augustan Rome, it is necessary to understand the many dimensions of signification it encompassed on all social levels. Here the clever allusion, the simultaneous

---

[45] *Res Gest.* 35.
[46] *Priapea* 15.7.
[47] Quint. *Inst.* 12.1.22; 12.10.12; Tac. *Dial.* 18.
[48] Zanker [1990]:209.

concealing and revealing of art, the familiarity with figured speech were not simply the adversarial strategies of beleaguered writers,[49] but the cultural strategies of the entire population, emperor and freedperson alike.

The usefulness of gender as a category of analysis is in the potential it holds for questioning the fixity of binary absolutes, whether it is the supposed opposition between male and female, between official and private, between "high" and "low" art, or between the ribald and the serious. Viewing the monuments of Augustan Rome as culturally and historically specific constructions reveals the levels of play that can exist within gendered performance spaces.

[49] Ahl (1988):17f.

# 16 Satyrs in the Women's Quarters[†]

## FRANÇOIS LISSARRAGUE
### translated by Alison Waters

Attic pottery of the fifth century presents a picture of the *gynaeceum* [women's quarters] as a world where, amongst themselves, women were sometimes visited by Eros and Aphrodite. The space assigned to women is defined by certain objects, limited in number, whose symbolic value reveals the nature of this world at first glance: mirror and perfume vases for the toilette; distaff, wool basket, loom for weaving; less often musical instruments or playthings. But above all, just as much in marriage scenes as in scenes within the gynaeceum, this defined space is characterised by a proliferation of caskets, chests, boxes or baskets. These are not simply utilitarian objects, they are also figurative indications of a particular way of thinking with regard to women.

Certain myths give to these chests and baskets an essential role to play, which confirms their symbolic value. Rather than Pandora's box —for she didn't have one, according to the tradition (it was a jar that she was entrusted with)—there is the chest in which Danaë was enclosed with her son Perseus, or the basket in which Erichthonios was hidden, entrusted by Athena to the daughters of Cecrops, or even the casket from which Polynices took the necklace which would seduce Eriphyle.

Hiding, enclosing, storing away, hoarding treasure: all these actions make plain, by means of an image, the day-to-day activities of women, who in real life actually carried baskets as did the *kane-phoroi* [basket-bearers], or used chests, managing as they did the household goods of the *oikos* [household].

The opposite of what is seen here is to be found when we turn to

---

[†] Originally published as 'Satyres chez les femmes," in P. Veyne, F. Lissarrague, and F. Frontisi-Ducroux, *Les mystères du gynécée* (Paris 1998), 179–98.

*Figure 16.1*

the satyrs and observe as they interfere in this sphere of activity, handling the objects belonging to the world of women. We move from a world as desired to a world of playful mockery, and the shifts that result are revealing.

Thus on a cup decorated only on the central medallion (fig. 16.1), we see a satyr, urged on by curiosity, plunging up to the waist into an open coffer. As opposed to Danaë, whose head and shoulders emerge from the chest in which her father is to shut her, this satyr leaves only his posterior on view and thus resembles some of his fellow satyrs diving into a *pithos*, a wine jar, in which they are engulfed in their drunken stupor. The satyr's curiosity transgresses the limits by which Greek society is ordered; it pushes him into the women's area and he can't resist, plunging his head down into the women's coffer even to the point of losing his head.

There exist two significant variants on this motif. On a cup attributed to the Oedipus painter the exterior and interior scenes are complementary. The exterior represents, on one side, a scene in which armour is put on, on the other side a woman is seated spinning wool under the gaze of two companions; the painter thus places masculine and feminine in parallel. In the central medallion—between these two worlds—a satyr holds a casket, as if he were bringing to the women the object which characterises them.

This interpretation is made explicit on a *skyphos* [cup] from Havana. On one side, a woman standing between a chair and a wool-basket holds out her hand towards the figure which appears on the other side. If the vase is turned around, the surprise is that this is a satyr, bald, snub-nosed and with pointed ears, who holds out a casket to her. Yet there is nothing indecent here. The satyr is draped in a cloak, leaning on the staff that is commonly held by citizens, and has become what might be seen as a respectable member of society; the image plays on the model of the visit to the gynaeceum and of the gift offered in order to seduce, but the man is replaced by a satyr accompanied by the ironic inscription *kalos*, "beautiful". There is nothing in this scene reminiscent of maenads; the seats—chair and stool— clearly indicate a domestic interior space, into which the satyr intrudes, taking on the appearance here of a good respectable Athenian in his city clothes.

Within the repertoire of these same scenes there exists also a little series of images which tend towards playful humour, where satyrs appear in the space of the gynaeceum. Like all good jokes, the image provokes laughter only if it has the element of surprise, and so it doesn't want to be repeated until it is stale. But the device on which this visual joke depends is clear to see here.

On a *lekythos* [oil-flask] at Tübingen (fig. 16.2) a satyr is standing before a wool-basket from which he has pulled out a skein of thread; he holds this at arm's length, as if to assist with the wool working, a task that satyrs are famously incapable of, if one is to believe Hesiod, who calls them "good for nothing" (*amechanoergoi*). The elegance of this satyr is noteworthy; he is naked but his hair is held in a fillet and his genitals bound in spiral fashion. This is a long way from the ithyphallic indecency which sometimes makes satyrs look like donkeys or mules, as is seen on the François Vase. As they enter the gynaeceum the genitals of the satyrs are discreetly hidden, so that it is not that kind of joke, although that intention is not absent from some of the images.

On another *lekythos* (fig. 16.3), at present in Florida, a satyr stands behind an empty chair. Just this item of furniture alone, appearing on a *lekythos*, is almost sufficient to indicate the gynaeceum; the mirror held by the satyr belongs decidedly in this area, where the presence of the satyr is incongruous. This time his posture is indecent: leaning forward, hindquarters raised high, his lifted horse's tail reveals his genitals between his thighs—quite the opposite of what decency

*Figure 16.2*

requires of the Athenian youth. Nudity in itself does not shock, but making a show of the genitals is indecent, as Aristophanes reminds us. This pose is at odds with the gesture of the satyr, holding a mirror in his hand. An item of women's toilette, the instrument that reveals their beauty, the mirror is an exclusively feminine object. What is this satyr doing here? Does he contemplate his own improbable beauty, contravening the expected image? And would he become feminine himself as a result of this? Or else, appropriating a "normal" image, is he in the act of offering the mirror to a woman as a seductive gesture? Or perhaps he holds it out to a woman as a servant does to her mistress, thus taking on the role of a slave, which would better suit his beast-like nature?

This last suggestion seems to apply to another of these small

*Figure 16.3*

*lekythoi* (fig. 16.4), where a satyr helps a woman at her toilette. She is naked, standing, facing a crouching humanoid figure; slightly leaning forward, she supports herself with her hand on the head of the satyr. Within the scene a mirror is an indication of toilette and beauty. The satyr raises his right hand towards this woman's genitals, delicately plucking the pubic hair. He thus takes the role which is seen to be regularly taken by a woman in the brief series of depilation scenes taking place in the gynaeceum. On a *krater* [mixing bowl] of later date this place is occupied by Eros in person, who makes use of a lamp while performing the action. The presence of this winged youth makes explicit the erotic nature of this intimate part of the toilette, which, when it is carried out with the help of a satyr, takes on

*Figure 16.4*

at the very least a paradoxical and unexpected aspect. No man takes this role; it is reserved for servants, female companions or Eros himself. The satyr enters the gynaeceum, a place where men do not enter, to see there what men do not see.

However, in the small group of images suggesting the presence of a satyr in the gynaeceum there are two features worth noting. The satyr is never engaged in an explicit sexual act; rather he behaves like a servant or a spectator; he enjoys the spectacle of feminine beauty, just as do the men whose real gaze his imaginary one replaces. Equally, the presence of the satyr, companion of Dionysos, never means that the woman must be a maenad, constant companion of the satyrs: in fact, maenads are definitely not met with in the gynaeceum.

*Figure 16.5*

A *lekythos* attributed to the Satyriskos painter confirms this observation and points us towards a related theme, childhood. In fact here is a little satyr up in the air above a chair and a wool-basket, jumping towards a bigger satyr who holds his arms out to catch him. The little satyr has a beard but hasn't yet got his horse tail; he is to some extent incomplete, and can be thought of as a child—as his size suggests. He plays with an adult, jumping on the chair usually occupied by the woman spinning wool in the gynaeceum. In place of the mother-and-child group as seen for example on the *pyxis* [box-shaped vase] from Athens we find here two satyrs—father and son?—playing together.

Such an image is not isolated; it forms part of the group of satyrs in the gynaeceum, but also part of the baby satyrs group, only rarely found in the gynaeceum. Size is not the only sign by which these satyr children may be recognised: they are usually beardless. Thus (fig. 16.5) on the central medallion of a cup from the Berlin Museum, an adult satyr is crouching in a rocky landscape. He has put down his *thyrsos* [ivy-wreathed wand topped with a pine-cone], symbol of

*Figure 16.6*

Dionysos, and balances on the palm of his hand a small child who holds his hands out towards the other's beard. But this child, beardless and without tail, does have pointed ears; it is a little satyr who is playing with an adult, rather like the young satyr mentioned above.

Representations of beardless satyrs, adolescents or children, are not rare on Attic pottery; they start to appear from 490 BC and do not really develop until about 450. By then we begin to see interplay of the various stages of life in the satyr world: babies, young *paides* [children], adults and white-haired old men. What interests us here—with regard to our ongoing study of the gynaeceum—is both the relationship of mother and child, displaced by the father in the satyr world, and the role of children themselves in this area of playful humour.

The most ancient example known of a child satyr appears in a purely masculine context, with no woman or maenad present, on an amphora attributed to the Flying Angel painter (who takes his name in fact from the image which concerns us here): the satyr, with a wreath on his head, throws into the air at arm's length a young beardless satyr, who emerges from behind the other's shoulders. On the reverse side another satyr brandishes a huge phallos, with an eye incorporated in the glans. It is difficult not to see at least some visual parallel between the large phallos and the small satyr—we will return to that.

Thus the most ancient examples of child satyrs are found in an exclusively masculine context; no woman of any kind is present. We must wait at least a generation to find complete families, father, mother and child. A good example is provided by a *krater* from London, attributed to the Niobid painter (fig. 16.6). On one of the friezes of this complex vase there are, on the right, two satyrs each carrying a fellow satyr on his shoulders. Those being carried, with hands raised, appeal to the satyr on the extreme left of the scene. He is dressed in a cloak and leans on a stick, which gives him the air of a "citizen" satyr, like the one on the *skyphos* from Havana. He has a ball in his hand which he is about to throw to the satyrs riding on the others' shoulders. Between them stands a small beardless satyr, hoop in hand, and as well there is a maenad, clothed in animal skin and holding a *thyrsos*. We have here one of the very first examples known, around 460, of satyrs in a family group. But it is a very playful family, entirely taken up with their game of ball or hoop, yet in a very well-ordered way, it is true, and with the father looking altogether respectable as if by having the position of father he became to some extent a typical citizen.

On another *krater* attributed to the Villa Giulia painter, there is a whole family procession: not only the father, mother and child, but also the white-haired grandfather, who leads the line-up with the music of the *aulos* [a wind instrument]. The image plays not only with the different age groups but also with names, which it seems are not given at random. The flutist is named Marsyas, recalling the dare addressed to Apollo and the musical superiority of the satyr who could be reduced to silence only by the god's trickery. The myth is not illustrated here but simply called to mind by the name Marsyas, which has a particular association with flute music. The father, on the left, is named Soteles, which seems to be quite an ordinary name. The woman's name is Mainas, Maenad, one of the most obviously generic and explicit names, while the young satyr has the name Posthon, derived from the Greek *posthe*, which is a word for the male genitals. We can recognise in this name the inclination to call a child by some diminutive that is related to words for the genitals.* In a way the name given to the child satyr anticipates what he will become, once he has grown up. Furthermore this name recalls the parallel suggested between the young satyr and the phallos when describing the amphora decorated by the Flying Angel painter.

On a *krater* from Compiègne, the child satyr is learning to drink, served by Dionysos in person, who is seated before him offering him his *kantharos* [drinking cup]. Above the maenad on the right is the inscription "Ariadne", the female companion of Dionysos. The other maenad, on the left, holds a *thyrsos* and a hare, a pet animal, perhaps the young satyr's play-fellow; this maenad is named Tragodia, which

---

* (Translator's footnote: the suggestion is that this has been a habit with the French. The untranslatable examples "mon kiki", "mon zizi" and, from Rabelais, "ma couille" are given. But is this so with English speakers?)

refers to another aspect of the Dionysiac ritual, the drama and the performance of tragedies. The young satyr has the inscription Komos, a name used with reference to a crowd of drinkers and merrymakers as well as to comic actors. The "family group" is made up here of different figures: not father and mother, but the god and his companion, as well as a maenad figure; the inscriptions tend towards the dramatic aspects of the Dionysiac ritual.

On a jug unfortunately very fragmentary, two maenads frame an adult satyr who leans forward. The maenad on the right is called Tragodia as on the previous vase; the name of her companion is lost, but that of the satyr can still be read: "Kissos," Ivy. A fragment from the Leipzig Museum partly completes this image and shows that this adult leans towards a baby satyr who pulls at the adult's beard. Elsewhere an adult satyr offers a long cake to a young satyr stretched out on an animal skin. On this type of pot-bellied jug (*chous*) we find quite a number of child satyrs, and on an example from the museum at Eleusis, an interesting variant: two children playing at frightening each other with a satyr mask. The proliferation of child motifs on such vases is explained by their function. These jugs were used at the wine festival, the Anthesteria, during which children learnt to drink. They were offered these vases, often miniature ones, with iconography essentially that of children and their games, at times also of child satyrs.

None of these images is repeated. There is no set model; each item offers a new combination starting from a fixed number of components: the god himself, the play on names, the relationship set up between the figures by means of their gestures. But the most surprising thing is that this kind of family scene between satyrs is elsewhere extremely rare amongst Attic images. Father, mother and child scarcely appear, apart from on gravestones. On vases, the subject does not seem relevant, unless it is part of a mythical context. Thus we find Heracles facing Deianira and Hylas, who holds out his arms to his father. Again there is Eriphyle breast-feeding her child Alcmeon, watched by the father Amphiaraos; but this scene is far from idyllic. A cock-fight suggests a more violent sequel: the child, when adult, will kill his mother to avenge his father, she having caused his death.

Life amongst the satyrs seems more light-hearted, and the satyr child is no threat to his mother. As well as the examples where the adult satyr takes the part of father and plays with the little one, there are scenes where a maenad, too, carries the baby satyr in her arms. This image is seen on a *stamnos* [jar] from Warsaw, which provides a curious variant both among the series of vases known as Lenaean, by custom dedicated to the cult of the masked god Dionysos, and among the series where the child Dionysos is given to the maenads. Alongside the scenes with a child satyr, there exist in fact images where adult satyrs and maenads play with the child Dionysos, as on a *krater* previously in Rome—known by an old drawing—where a white-haired satyr balances on his foot a child who does not have pointed ears and can only be Dionysos himself. The time span and relative ages are confused in these images, where the god accords the baby Komos the same attention as he himself is accorded in other satyr scenes.

The feature most to be noted in this series is that the satyr-children hold out arms to their father and even play with him. Such behaviour, which seems to us ordinary and to be expected, is in fact exceptional in the Attic repertoire. Vase painters never show a male citizen playing with his child. That is the business of women, who are themselves fond of playing, and it belongs in the space reserved for them, the gynaeceum. Such scenes are found on *lekythoi, pyxides* or *hydriae* [water-jugs], which are women's vases. Baby satyrs, however, appear on amphorae, *krateres* and wine jugs, vases that belong at the table in the space occupied by men. When a satyr plays with a child, it is a sort of joke; he does not behave like the father of a family, imitating an idyllic model which does not exist; he plays because he is himself like a child, whatever his age.

A fragment of the *skyphos* cup confirms this analysis. Two satyrs draped in "citizen"-type cloaks, but sitting on the ground like children, are busy playing amongst themselves the game *morra*, which consists of both players holding up a number of fingers which the other has to guess. It seems that the Greeks played with one hand, whilst the other was kept still by means of a stick which the two players held, each at opposite ends. These two satyrs are playing under the gaze of a third who leans on a long cane. These games are the sort that women or children play. Once more, dress is not enough to make a citizen; the world of satyrs is a child-like world, a world of play which, in the name of light-hearted humour, confuses accepted ideas of the male citizen's adult and masculine identity.

## THE SATYR AS FEMALE

In this visual play, bringing into question as it does the relationship between accepted types or categories and differing ages, certain images which take these ideas even further bring us back to the image of women.

*Figure 16.7*

As far as I know there are two examples of female satyrs amongst the images on Attic vases. Not maenads, the usual feminine accompaniment of satyrs, who appear in countless examples, but actual women having become satyrs. The first example is found on a cup from the beginning of the fourth century, discovered at Corinth (fig. 16.7). On the medallion a woman with naked torso, her hair tied in a pony-tail, stands, probably in the midst of a dance, facing a bearded man seated with a *thyrsos* in his hand: very likely Dionysos himself. This woman wears a sort of satyr-like short lower garment, which has both phallos and horse-tail attached. This is a purely visual play, confusing the sexes and the established categories: a woman is dressed as a satyr, yet her feminine nature remains explicit. The usual distinctions—both that made between satyr and maenad and that between man and satyr—are here bypassed and done away with. Should this image be interpreted as some sort of ritual? Probably not. We can, however, be sure that it is an example of visual play whereby one of the most powerful oppositions in Greek culture, that between male and female, is thrown into confusion.

By depicting the upper body of this woman in such clear detail, and also the garment around her hips that makes the parody so plain to see, the painter reveals the scene as obviously artificial. We know, at least, that there were no female actors at this time, so it is difficult to connect this image to any dramatic context, and it would be best to regard it entirely as a form of Dionysiac dance.

The second example is fragmentary. However, a beardless seated figure of Dionysos can still be seen, and a woman dancing before him. Like the figure on the vase from Corinth, she has her hair drawn back, her upper body bare, and she wears the same sort of satyr-like garment. She dances amongst various seated figures. It is some kind of performance, but not what might properly be called a dramatic presentation.

In both these examples, the artificial nature of the scene is made plain by the fact that the woman in the satyr's outfit is otherwise naked. Nevertheless the "equipment" that she wears casts some doubt on her sex. In order to create more of an element of surprise and to confuse the observer, the vase painters seem to have wanted to play with the oppositions between male and female, human and animal, mortal and Dionysiac, by manipulating the characteristic signs that defined these categories.

We might go further, but must pass on to another kind of artefact. A small terracotta figurine at Munich represents a satyr standing still, holding a mask in his hand—a woman's mask. Is he an actor already wearing a satyr's mask but holding another, for another role? Or is he a "real" satyr preparing to change to the role of a woman in the mask-play that he is performing? The statuette is one of a kind. A figurine without any context, with no examples similar, we cannot classify it; but the craftsman who made it clearly sought to combine and confuse the three categories that concern us: man, satyr, woman.

This imagery, as we can see, scarcely relates in any real way to the "ups and downs of everyday life". We are in a world of playful humour as far as the satyrs are concerned, and in a world of wishful thinking with regard to the gynaeceum. The relationship between women and satyrs, as seen in these images, is more complex than might have been expected. The satyrs here do not play the exaggerated and highly sexual role which they are known to do elsewhere; instead they serve to call into question—by means of humour and parody—the major categories within Athenian culture: what constitutes adult, man and citizen.

One final image on a *hydria* from the beginning of the fourth century, to end with, shows a satyr as the companion in a women's game in the gynaeceum. On the right a woman sits on a chest, on the left a couple, woman and satyr, are playing *morra*, the game we saw the satyrs playing on the fragment of the *skyphos* cup. By thus playing the game of *morra* (also a game of chance?) against a woman, the satyr doubles his illusory role. Good child-like fellow that he is— rather like the eunuch in the harem—he mixes with the women, who are also fond of a game; he finds in the gynaeceum a harmless part to play, which removes all trace of his usual excessively male character. But at the same time as a sexual creature—more than merely mascu-line—he achieves what is not permitted to the ordinary man: to enter the gynaeceum, to observe it at close quarters, to cast upon the world of women a bold glance which, thanks to the vase paintings, we also share.

PART IV

# Outside the Game: Gods, Eunuchs and Cross-Dressing

# 17 A Feminist Boomerang: The Great Goddess of Greek Prehistory[†]

## LAUREN E. TALALAY

Although women's roles in prehistory have been the subject of debate for well over a century, interest in *gender ideology* has emerged in the archaeological literature only within the last decade.[1] While the ultimate contribution of this newly articulated perspective must await the test of time, it is clear that the burgeoning literature is challenging some of the central epistemological assumptions of modern archaeology and redefining approaches to the study of women in prehistory.[2]

Surprisingly, prehistoric figurines from the Mediterranean, many of which are female, have not been tossed headlong into this revisionist "malestrom". Rather, much of the recent work on these early representations either has revived the nineteenth-century notion that, in early societies, power was initially vested in women or has side-stepped the issue of gender and women altogether. A well-constructed approach to these figurines that incorporates feminist and/or gender ideologies and sound archaeological arguments has yet to be designed.

---

[†] Originally published in *Gender and History*, 6(1994), 165–83.

[1] For some of the earlier discussions see Johann J. Bachofen, *Das Mutterrecht* (Stuttgart, 1861); Friedrich Engels, *The Origin of the Family, Private Property, and the State* (1884; repr. Pathfinder Press, New York, 1972); Lewis Henry Morgan, *Ancient Society* (New York, 1877).

[2] Pioneering books on the topic include: Joan M. Gero and Margaret W. Conkey (eds) *Engendering Archaeology* (Basil Blackwell, Oxford, England, and Cambridge, Mass., 1991); M. di Leonardo (ed.) *Gender at the Crossroads of Knowledge* (University of California Press, Berkeley, 1991); Dale Walde and Noreen D. Willows (eds) *The Archaeology of Gender* (Archaeological Association, The University of Calgary, Calgary, 1991); Cheryl Claassen (ed.) *Exploring Gender through Archaeology* (Prehistory Press, Madison, 1992); Elisabeth A. Bacus, et al., *A Gendered Past* (University of Michigan Museum of Anthropology, Ann Arbor, 1993). These archaeological works owe a great debt to the earlier efforts of anthropologists, e.g., Michelle Z. Rosaldo and Louise Lamphere (eds) *Woman, Culture, and Society* (Stanford University Press, Stanford, 1974); Sherry B. Ortner and Harriet Whitehead (eds) *Sexual Meanings* (Cambridge University Press, Cambridge, 1981); Henrietta L. Moore, *Feminism and Anthropology* (University of Minnesota Press, Minneapolis, 1988).

Some well-known works, notably those of Gimbutas, argue that the abundance of female figurines in prehistoric contexts of Greece and south-eastern Europe reflects an early, pan-Mediterranean belief in a Great Mother Goddess, a matriarchal social structure, and a time when women ruled either supreme or at least in partnership with men.[3] These writings have found widespread popular support in the feminist literature (e.g., *The First Sex; The Chalice and the Blade; Motherself; The Myth of the Goddess*) and have been utilized to legitimate some feminists' goals.[4] The notion of a primordial matri-archy/Mother Goddess in Greece and south-eastern Europe is, however, based on several unwarranted assumptions. Although some Aegean prehistorians have persuasively rejected this popular hypoth-esis, they have failed to communicate effectively with those outside their own specialized field.[5] By default, both the public and scholars in disciplines other than archaeology believe that most Aegean archaeologists subscribe to the Goddess thesis.[6]

In order to begin redressing some of these problems and to under-stand better the interrelationships among gender studies, prehistoric figurines, and the Great Goddess theory, this article examines the interpretive history of Greek Neolithic figurines.[7] While other works have addressed such matters as the use, function, meaning, and/or style of these early images, few have seriously explored why, despite manifest lack of archaeological support, contemporary scholarship

[3] Marija A. Gimbutas, *The Gods and Goddesses of Old Europe* (Thames and Hudson, London, 1974), and Gimbutas, *The Language of the Goddess* (Harper and Row, San Francisco, 1989). In 1982 Gimbutas produced a revised edition of *The Gods and Goddesses of Old Europe* in which she changed the title of the book to *The Goddesses and Gods of Old Europe*, a revealing indication of her perspective. See also earlier works: Robert Briffault, *The Mothers: The matriarchal theory of social origins* (Macmillan, New York, 1931); Erich Neumann, *The Great Mother* (Pantheon Books, New York, 1955); Edwin O. James, *The Cult of the Mother-Goddess* (Praeger, New York, 1959).

[4] Elizabeth G. Gould, *The First Sex* (G. P. Putnam's Sons, New York, 1971), esp. pp. 73–85; Merlin Stone, *When God Was a Woman* (Harcourt Brace Jovanovich, New York, 1978), esp. pp. 19–29, 49–53; Riane Eisler, *The Chalice and the Blade* (Harper and Row, San Francisco, 1987), esp. pp. 7–28; Kathryn A. Rabuzzi, *Motherself* (Indiana University Press, Bloomington, 1988), esp. pp. 22–26; Anne Baring and Jules Cashford, *The Myth of the Goddess* (Viking, London, 1991), esp. pp. 46–105.

[5] Brian Hayden, "Old Europe: sacred matriarchy or complementary opposition?", in *Archaeology and Fertility Cult in the Ancient Mediterranean*, ed. Anthony Bonnano (B. R. Grüner Pub. Co., Amsterdam, 1986), pp. 17–30; see also the entries for Gimbutas in Bacus, *A Gendered Past*, pp. 62–64.

[6] Joseph Campbell, *The Masks of God* (Viking, New York, 1959), pp. 136–51, 401–34; James J. Preston (ed.) *Mother Worship* (The University of North Carolina Press, Chapel Hill, 1982), pp. 325–41.

[7] There is good archaeological evidence in Greece of human occupation well before the Neolithic. Small hunting and foraging bands traversed the countryside by at least 100,000 BCE, if not earlier. To date, however, no human images have been reported from these earlier periods.

and popular writing have continued to insist that Stone Age societies worshipped an all-powerful Goddess.[8] As this article argues, the Great Goddess proposal is deeply rooted in a nineteenth-century mentality which still shapes modern scholarship. An unsalutory alternative to androcentric interpretations, the Goddess thesis ultimately acts as a boomerang to the women's movement and the future of gender studies.

The archaeological focus of this paper is the Greek Neolithic, a stretch of prehistory spanning approximately three millennia from *c*.6,000 to 3,000 BCE. Our understanding of this long, complex, and changing period remains fragmentary. Traditionally, archaeologists have discussed discrete aspects of Neolithic Greece as defined by classes of finds (e.g., lithics, pottery, bones, figurines, etc.) or by individual sites. Recently, a more synthetic approach has restructured scholarly debate, spawning articles on social structure, trade networks, religion, and economy.[9] Despite these advances, publications focus on macro-scale systems and are largely "faceless", though not entirely "genderless".

[8] See Richard W. Hutchinson, "Cretan Neolithic figurines", *Jahrbuch für Prähistorische und Ethnographische Kunst*, 12 (1938), pp. 50–57; Alan J. B. Wace, "Prehistoric stone figurines from the mainland", *Hesperia* (1949, suppl. 8); Saul Weinberg, "Neolithic figurines and Aegean interrelations", *American Journal of Archaeology*, 55 (1951), pp. 121–33; Peter J. Ucko, *Anthropomorphic Figurines* (A. Szmidla, London, 1968); Giorgos Ch. Hourmouziadis, *I Anthropomorphi Idoloplastiki tis Neolithikis Thessalias* (Volos, 1973); Bradley Bartel, "Cultural associations and mechanisms of change in anthropomorphic figurines during the Neolithic in the eastern Mediterranean basin", *World Archaeology*, 13 (1981), pp. 73–85; William W. Phelps, "Prehistoric figurines from Corinth", *Hesperia*, 56 (1987), pp. 233–53; Lauren E. Talalay, "Body imagery of the ancient Aegean", *Archaeology*, 4 (1991), pp. 46–49; L. E. Talalay, *Deities, Dolls, and Devices: Neolithic figurines from Franchthi Cave, Greece* (Indiana University Press, Bloomington, 1993).

[9] There is extensive literature on the Greek Neolithic, though few attempts to synthesize the period as a whole; see, however, Jean-Paul Demoule and Catherine Perlès, "The Greek Neolithic: a new review", *Journal of World Prehistory*, 7 (1993), pp. 355–416; and the earlier, lavishly illustrated book, Demitrios Theochares, *Neolithic Greece* (The National Bank of Greece, Athens, 1973). Among the more recent works are: Tracey Cullen, "Social implications of ceramic style in the Neolithic Peloponnese", in *Ancient Technology to Modern Science*, ed. William D. Kingery (The American Ceramic Society, Columbus, Ohio, 1985), pp. 77–100; Paul Halstead, "Counting sheep in Neolithic and Bronze Age Greece", in *Pattern of the Past: Studies in honour of David Clarke*, ed. Ian Hodder, Glynn Issac and Norman Hammond (Cambridge University Press, Cambridge, 1981), pp. 307–39; Julie M. Hansen, *The Palaeoethnobotany of Franchthi Cave* (Indiana University Press, Bloomington, 1991); Thomas W. Jacobsen and Tracey Cullen, "A consideration of mortuary practices in Neolithic Greece: Burials from Franchthi Cave", in *Mortality and Immortality: The anthropology and archaeology of death*, ed. Sally C. Humphreys and Helen King (Academic Press, London, 1981), pp. 79–101; Catherine Perlès, "Systems of exchange and organization of production in Neolithic Greece", *Journal of Mediterranean Archaeology*, 5 (1992), pp. 115–64; Curtis N. Runnels and Tjeerd H. van Andel, "Trade and the origins of agriculture in the eastern Mediterranean", *Journal of Mediterranean Archaeology*, 1 (1988), pp. 83–109; Robin Torrence, *Production and Exchange of Stone Tools* (Cambridge University Press, Cambridge, 1986), esp. pp. 121–37; Karen D. Vitelli, *Franchthi Neolithic Pottery*, vol. 1 (Indiana University Press, Bloomington, 1993).

In general, the Greek Neolithic is associated with the introduction of small, sedentary villages where subsistence was based on cereal agriculture (mostly wheats and barleys), some collecting (shellfish, nuts, wild fruit) and animal husbandry (primarily sheep, goat, cattle, and pig). Individual households are likely to have formed the basic economic unit within each community, though an extensive network of exchange or trade facilitated the circulation of commodities and finished products, both utilitarian and prestige. Significant distances were covered by foot and/or boat, which no doubt encouraged the transmission of information and ideas as well as the flow of goods. The socio-economic bases and precise mechanisms of these networks remain a matter of debate.[10] Settlement patterns vary chronologically and geographically, encompassing both densely distributed villages occupied for many generations and dispersed communities, some inhabited only briefly. The overall picture, however, is one of a strongly socialized environment.[11] Smaller villages were likely to have been exogamous, with individuals seeking marriage partners from outside the confines of their settlements; such strategies would have ensured, among other things, the biological viability of small settlements. Larger communities may have practiced endogamy but also maintained contact with neighbouring and distant villages for a variety of social and economic reasons. The social organization of Neolithic Greece is usually labelled "egalitarian", traditionally defined as societies where political leadership is weak, ranking is absent or muted, and access to important resources by all members is undifferentiated.[12] Status in such communities was probably based on age, gender, sex, and no doubt on the (archaeologically unretrievable) force of one's personality. Very little archaeological evidence from Greece supports the existence of stratification or ranking, though inequalities of some kind are arguable at select sites.

It is during this time period, with its rich mosaic of small villages and complex network of trade, that people (men, women, and/or children?) began fashioning female, sexually ambiguous or possibly sexless figurines, and a few male images. To date, excavations and surface reconnaissance have yielded thousands of (mostly clay) images, the bulk of which derive from northern Greece. Richer and

---

[10] See Catherine Perlès, *From Stone Procurement to Neolithic Society in Greece* (Indiana University Press, Bloomington, 1989).

[11] Perlès, "Systems of exchange".

[12] Although many prehistorians find common neo-evolutionary labels devised by anthropologists, such as egalitarian, tribe, chiefdom, etc., inadequate, they remain a useful shorthand; for a recent review, see Christopher Boehm, "Egalitarian behavior and reverse dominance hierarchy", *Current Anthropology*, 34 (1993), pp. 227–59.

more varied collections have been unearthed in parts of south-eastern Europe, especially Yugoslavia and Bulgaria. Adopting a gendered approach to these collections raises basic questions that have implications for Aegean prehistory in general. Given the fragmentary nature of the data, is a gender-driven analysis of Neolithic figurines and Aegean prehistory viable? If possible, how can these images and other data enlighten us on social and gender differentiations in the Neolithic or on women as an analytic unit of Aegean prehistory? Finally, is a gender-conscious perspective doomed to be marginalized by the archaeological "establishment" as hopelessly conditioned by the ideological stance of feminist scholars? As a first step toward answering these questions, we need to explore the historiography of these early images from Greece.

The earliest discovery of Greek Neolithic figurines occurred nearly a century ago. On 26 March 1900, Sir Arthur Evans's excavations at the now famous site of Knossos exposed the first human image from Crete that could be securely assigned to the Neolithic.[13] Eventually, Knossos would yield more than one hundred such figurines of Neolithic date.[14] Concurrently, archaeological investigation on the mainland was unearthing additional examples, many of which were female; a large percentage, however, were sexually indeterminate and only a very few were clearly male (though several clay phalluses turned up in later excavations).[15]

Although surprisingly little ink was spilled over the meanings of these pieces, a general interpretive consensus was forged: the early human representations from the Greek Neolithic represented either unidentified deities or a Mother Goddess derived from Near Eastern prototypes. The well-documented evidence in the Near East for later goddesses such as Inanna, Ishtar, and Astarte had already conditioned Near Eastern archaeologists to label (almost indiscriminately) all prehistoric nude female images as emanations of the Great Goddess. Greek scholars echoed their Near Eastern counterparts, assuming that form followed function and that the Greek examples were part of a vast, pan-Mediterranean cult which combined ideals of motherhood and virginity.

Scholars such as Evans must have drawn upon equally if not more

[13] Ucko, *Anthropomorphic Figurines*, p. 274.
[14] Ucko, *Anthropomorphic Figurines*, p. 302.
[15] Alan J. B. Wace and Maurice S. Thompson, *Prehistoric Thessaly* (Cambridge University Press, Cambridge, 1912); Christos Tsountas, *Ai Proistorikai Akropoleis Diminiou kai Sesklou* (Sakellarios, Athens, 1908).

compelling data from Crete to support their interpretations. Evans was fully aware of the frequent depictions of Minoan women on seals and paintings. Often bare-breasted, richly clad, brandishing snakes or other attributes, and performing "rituals", these women were usually considered goddesses or priestesses. Since the Neolithic levels at Knossos lay directly under the Bronze Age strata, it was a logical jump to argue for cultural continuity: If the later Bronze Age figures were associated with emanations of a Great Goddess, why not trace their origins back to the millennia immediately preceding?

At least one article by a female anthropologist adopted a universal approach to these early female figurines. M. A. Murray, who examined several collections of European and Mediterranean images, suggested that cross-cultural regularities could be identified among so-called fertility figures. She divided these images into three separate types reflecting motherhood, female perfection, and female sexuality. The first type was worshipped by men, women, and children throughout time and across cultures; the second was associated solely with male veneration; and the third was the exclusive domain of women, used to stimulate their own sexual desires.[16]

Beginning in the 1930s, more critical and varied approaches to the interpretation of Greek (and south-east European) Neolithic figurines emerged in the literature. Rival proposals suggested that figurines may have functioned as: symbols of wealth and rank; amulets to ensure a successful birth; toys or dolls; and fetishes to satisfy the sexual desires of the male. Most discussions from the thirties through the sixties, however, were *non*interpretive, focused on isolating styles and types of Neolithic figurines and identifying the temporal and geographic implications of those types.[17] Woven into the text of those publications, though, were passing comments testifying to the growing number of archaeologists who believed that Neolithic figurines were used exclusively as fertility items. Even if not explicitly stated, the implication was that a Goddess cult of some kind existed in early Greece. [. . .]

In general, the religious significance of these images was taken as a given, as were the economic insecurity of the times and, on occasion, the matrilineal structure of Neolithic society. In fact, none of those assumptions holds up to close scrutiny.

In 1968 Peter J. Ucko published the first full-length monograph on

---

[16] M. A. Murray, "Female fertility figurines", *Journal of the Royal Anthropological Institute*, 64 (1934), pp. 93–100.

[17] Saul Weinberg, "Neolithic figurines and Aegean interrelations", *American Journal of Archaeology*, 55 (1951), pp. 121–33.

Aegean figurines, *Anthropomorphic Figurines in Predynastic Egypt and Neolithic Crete with Comparative Material from the Prehistoric Near East and Mainland Greece*. Ucko's book was a milestone in the field of figurine research. Although he did not address issues of gender, Ucko took a dramatically new approach to the interpretation of prehistoric figurines. Unconvinced by the Mother Goddess explanation, he proposed that the ancient images were not only multifunctional but may have served purposes comparable to those of similar objects observed in modern "ethnographic societies" studied by anthropologists during the last few centuries. Ethnographic analogues suggested to Ucko that the Neolithic figures possibly were used in curing rites, initiation ceremonies, marriage rituals, oral narratives, and the like. Although Ucko only devoted four pages to a critical review of the Mother Goddess interpretation, his book is remembered a quarter-century later for demonstrating the unsupportable nature of that paradigm vis-à-vis the current archaeological evidence. Among other factors, Ucko pointed out that the Mother Goddess interpretation did not account for the variety of figurines in the Neolithic (e.g. seated, standing, steatopygous, slim-limbed, naked, clothed, tattooed, unadorned, seemingly deformed, etc.), the existence of many sexless and a few male images, and the variability of the figures' archaeological contexts, which often appeared to include rubbish heaps.

Disappointingly, Ucko's call for alternative explanations and for more rigour in the field triggered only a trickle of responses. [. . .]

While the more "scientifically" oriented archaeologists became circumspect and cautious in their discussions of prehistoric figurines and fertility goddesses, the Mother Goddess notion, far from receding into the background, was infused with new life by the work of several writers, particularly Marija Gimbutas, and by the crescendo of voices within the women's movement. The papers from an international conference on this topic were published in *Archaeology and Fertility Cult in the Ancient Mediterranean*. Gimbutas's arguments, which are embraced by a large segment of the public as well as by scholars outside the field of archaeology, state that the "civilization of Old Europe" (i.e., Greece and south-eastern Europe) was initially dominated by an harmonious, pre-patriarchal society characterized by a Goddess-centered religion. The wealth of anthropomorphic figurines testify to a complex pantheon centered on the Great Goddess of Life, Death, and Regeneration and the deity's various epiphanies, which include, among others, a Snake, Bird, Pregnant Woman, and Frog Goddess as well as a Male enthroned God. In Gimbutas's own words, "the Goddess-centered art . . . reflects a social order in which women as heads of clans or queen-priestesses played a central role. . . . [R]epeated incursions by Kurgan people put an end to the Old European culture . . ., changing it from gylanic to androcratic and from matrilineal to patrilineal."[18] Her work implies that the world was transformed from an age of harmony and accord (gylanic) to one of warfare and endless strife (androcratic).[19] [. . .]

Central to these debates are unspoken and opposing views about the nature of symbols in preliterate societies. On the one hand, those who endorse the Mother Goddess notion gloss over the complexities of nonverbal symbols in nonliterate cultures such as Neolithic Greece. On the other hand, those who reject the thesis seem to assume that these early human images, like other visual symbols, were polysemic and multivalent expressions. The images embodied several layers of meaning and probably held different meanings for different segments of the prehistoric population (e.g., men, women, children). Surely, it takes a great leap of faith to equate *all* female figurines with a belief in a poorly defined Mother Goddess and then to presume that the central position of women in the religious sphere of any culture is a direct reflection of the social organization of that culture. Such a leap denies the intricate nature of both social and symbolic systems in antiquity.

The convoluted relationship between religious symbolism and everyday reality was recently highlighted in a collection of essays which explored Mother Goddesses and "mother worship" among modern groups cross-culturally. The general consensus of the authors was that religious symbolism is not epiphenomenal. It is impossible to predict the types of deities in a religious system from an analysis of a culture's social structure. Indeed, several of the essays demonstrated that the subordinate status of women in some groups was associated with an elevated status of females as defined in that culture's religious sphere.[20] This perspective is a cautionary tale for all archaeologists who would attempt to erect simple bridges between the possible social organization of a culture and its symbolic systems, let alone between its material culture and its ideology.

Despite valid objections to the Goddess/matriarchy thesis, at least as applied to Neolithic Greece, the notion has endured. Its popularity cannot be accounted for by compelling arguments or a gradual accumulation of supporting archaeological data over the decades.

---

[18] Gimbutas, *The Language of the Goddess*, pp. xv–xxi; p. xx.

[19] Joseph Campbell, "Foreword", in Gimbutas, *The Language of the Goddess*, p. xiv.

[20] J. J. Preston, *Mother Worship*, esp. pp. 327–28.

Rather, its persistence is embedded in larger social and intellectual trends, some of which can be traced back to the mid-nineteenth century and continue to have a profound effect on modern thinking.[21] Working almost unwittingly in concert with those forces is the more contemporary choir of some women's voices. Their refrain appears to miss the negative implications of the Mother Goddess proposal.

The Goddess thesis was initially argued not by archaeologists but by such luminaries as Johann Bachofen, Sir James G. Frazer, and Sigmund Freud. Bachofen's work, *Das Mutterrecht* (1861), was one of the first major studies to articulate the principles of a *gynecocracy*. Like other thinkers of his day, Bachofen was searching for a general theory of social development, a single view to explain the evolution of human cultures. A jurist and a classicist, Bachofen argued that human society had originally been communal, characterized by promiscuity and with no principles of kinship or property. Eventually, women in these early societies revolted, took power and established the *Motherright* stage, which hailed ties between mother and child as an overriding legal principle. Ultimately, this radical matriarchy was supplanted by a patriarchy.[22]

These beliefs found further support in Frazer's influential work, *The Golden Bough* (1890, 1907–1915), which also argued for a matriarchal stage in the Classical world antecedent to the Greek and Roman patriarchal systems. Hints of support or outright agreement appeared in such works as Engels's *The Origin of the Family, Private Property, and the State* (1884) and Freud's *Totem and Taboo* (1920). While none of these works discussed at length the prehistoric images of nude females from Greece and the Mediterranean, all of the books had palpable effects on scholarship in prehistoric archaeology. Modern archaeologists have not yet escaped the hold of these early paradigms.

On the surface, the survival of this nineteenth-century vision of a prehistoric matriarchy would appear as a boon to the women's movement, insofar as women can employ (pre)history to contest their less

---

[21] Post-modern critiques have challenged claims to standard canons of scientific rationality, stressing that interpreters are ineluctably biased by the larger social and intellectual forces of their times. For archaeological discussions of the matter; see: Michael Shanks and Christopher Tilley, *Social Theory and Archaeology* (University of New Mexico Press, Albuquerque, 1987), and Shanks and Tilley, *Re-constructing Archaeology* (Cambridge University Press, Cambridge, 1987). Many archaeologists object to the relativism of this postmodern stance; see Norman Yoffee and Andrew Sherratt (eds) *Archaeological Theory: Who sets the agenda?* (Cambridge University Press, Cambridge, 1993).

[22] Josine Blok and Peter Mason, *Sexual Asymmetry* (J. C. Gieben, Amsterdam, 1987) p. 29.

than satisfactory contemporary status. It is indeed seductive for certain schools of feminist theory to argue that a "Golden Age" existed where gender roles were more balanced and women were empowered, although such speculations never specify *exactly what kinds* of power women had or the precise nature of their social and political relationships with men or each other. On a deeper level, however, the Mother Goddess notion and the vision of a Golden Age are antagonistic both to the future of women's movements and to the development of new perspectives on Mediterranean prehistory. This view polarizes not only men against women, but women against women within the ranks of archaeology. Moreover, the thesis remains almost insultingly simplistic in portraying the complex and no doubt shifting gender roles that existed in antiquity. Finally, the stance smacks of a feminist essentialism which limits the way we might view the power of women in the future.

As an eminent female prehistorian has observed, the whole topic of gender relations has not been "taken seriously by Establishment (yes, undoubtedly male-dominated) archaeology".[23] This is particularly true of works that focus on the Mother Goddess. Popular writings on the topic as well as more scholarly texts are often criticised by Establishment archaeology as "unscientific" and marred by soft or sloppy scholarship. Among the mostly female scholars who seek to engender prehistory, a vocal group takes exception to the often unrigorous nature of discussions on ancient matriarchies and the role of prehistoric figurines in early societies.[24] In many ways, these polarities reflect larger antagonisms between "humanistically" and "scientifically" oriented archaeologists. While those two camps will no doubt continue to debate, there is no reason that questions about gender and female iconography in prehistoric contexts need be the source of such polarities. The issue of gender as a fundamental structuring element in society is relevant to archaeologists of varying theoretical concerns.

Equally troubling is the simplicity of the Great Goddess explanation as presented in the literature. Religious beliefs, social structures, and gender roles in prehistory were certainly not static. Nor were they monolithic or monothetic entities that now lend themselves to shallow summaries. Although it may be extremely difficult to document variation and change from the preliterate archaeological record,

---

[23] Ruth E. Tringham, "Households with faces: The challenge of gender in prehistoric architectural remains", in Gero and Conkey, *Engendering Archaeology*, p. 97.

[24] See the essays by Conkey and Gero, Tringham, Handsman, and Pollack in Gero and Conkey, *Engendering Archaeology*.

the assumption that women persisted in a fixed role for millennia denies the complex nature of real societies and discounts the evolutionary changes in these communities over the span of several thousand years. Ethnographic and anthropological research during the last few decades has underscored the great variability of women's roles in society. One of the key conclusions of that research is that the roles of women in any society cannot be decontextualized. Women's roles are socially constructed and intimately linked to the constraints of their particular culture.

Finally, and perhaps most significantly, the essentialism engendered by the Mother Goddess idea serves to isolate women as outside of history. Although proponents of this interpretation never specify whether the power of women in these early matriarchies was given, granted, or taken, they assume that the elevated status of women was ultimately due to their reproductive capabilities. In a fundamental sense, adherence to such an idea ultimately relegates females to "the purposive roles [of] birth and childrearing [which define] their sexuality only as an expression of the means to guarantee the survival of the group".[25] If women's reproductive capabilities are the source of their power, then women remain, to some extent, locked within an unchanging domestic sphere. As Wylie (and others) have observed, if "biology is destiny" where gender is concerned and women's roles are forever fixed, then women run the risk of being defined as irrelevant to the process of cultural change. Being static, women's roles can never account for developments in cultural systems.[26]

With such perspectives popular in the literature, women's hypothetical dominion in the past will continue to be viewed as *given* and not *earned*. Embedded in such views is the notion that unearned dominion was especially susceptible to control by others, particularly those in authority. Women may have been valued and to some extent empowered by their reproductive capabilities, but they were not necessarily in control of that power. Thus defined, women run the risk of being seen more as cultural *object* than cultural *agent* in both the past and the present.[27] Feminist archaeology seeks to shift that per-

[25] Russell G. Handsman, "Whose art was found at Lepenski Vir? Gender relations and power in prehistory", in Gero and Conkey, *Engendering Archaeology*, p. 334.

[26] Alison Wylie, "Why is there no archaeology of gender", in Gero and Conkey, *Engendering Archaeology*, p. 34.

[27] Margaret W. Conkey and Joan M. Gero "Tensions, pluralities, and engendering archaeology: An introduction to women and prehistory", in Gero and Conkey, *Engendering Archaeology*, pp. 3–30.

spective by identifying how and in what contexts women were active participants in society.[28]

[28] Kathleen M. Bolen, "Prehistoric construction of mothering", in Claassen, *Exploring Gender*, pp. 49–62.

I am very grateful to colleagues and friends who offered insightful comments and constructive criticisms on various drafts of this article, especially Tracey Cullen, Steve Bank, Kathryn Talalay, Sue Alcock, John Alden, John Cherry, Thelma Thomas, and the anonymous reviewers for *Gender & History*.

# 18 The Asexuality of Dionysus[†]

## MICHAEL JAMESON

In this essay I examine a phenomenon which has been remarked on before—it is so conspicuous that it could hardly be overlooked—but which has received less attention than one might expect. In essence it is this: Dionysus was, of all gods, the most closely associated with the phallus, the erect male member, at once the instrument and symbol of male sexuality. His myths and cults also refer to the liberation, if only temporary, of both women and men from social controls, including sexual controls, which in most cultures are among the most rigid. The god himself is represented to a surprising degree as detached and unconcerned with sex. There certainly are a number of exceptions, as is to be expected in a body of evidence that is spread over a millennium and comes from very diverse sources. I do not suggest, however, that these exceptions are insignificant; there is a persistent ambivalence about the god's involvement with sex.

One can refer to the god's detachment as "asexuality," as I have in the title of this essay. But one might also speak of his bisexuality, the coexistence of elements of *both* genders that may, in effect, cancel each other out, or even of his transcendence of sexuality.[1] There are frequent references to his effeminacy. Aeschylus in his lost play *Edoni* has that Pentheus-like figure Lycurgus ask, "Where does this woman-man come from?" and in his satyr play *Theori* the god himself protests the satyrs' calumny, that he is a cowardly woman-man who is

[†] Originally published in T. H. Carpenter and C. A. Faraone (eds), *Masks of Dionysus* (Ithaca, NY, and London 1993), 44–64.

[1] "Asexuality" is also used by Hoffman 1989, 105, and by Stephen Fineberg in an unpublished paper, "Dionysos in the New Democracy," which he has kindly let me see and which will be incorporated in a longer study, forthcoming. Both scholars were members of a National Endowment for the Humanities Seminar on Greek religion and society that I organized at Stanford University in the summer of 1983. I profited from the stimulating experience the seminar provided, not least from the contributions of Fineberg and Hoffman. "Bisexuality" is the term used by Deutsch 1969 and Zeitlin 1982, while Frontisi-Ducroux and Lissarrague 1990, 232 n. 109, speak of the "alternation . . . between hypervirility . . . and the transcendence of sex."

not counted as a male.[2] There is, indeed, "something feminine in his nature."[3] Is this paradox, the effeminate god of the phallus, the phallic god of women, illusory, trivial, or quite central to the conception of the god and the nature of his cults? The subject can be examined under, roughly, three headings—iconography, myth, and cult.

## ICONOGRAPHY

The contrast is between the environment of the god and the depiction of his person. It is largely in vase painting, which as usual is mostly Attic, that he and his company are to be found. These scenes have been studied intensively, and I draw only on the most generally accepted conclusions.[4] Dionysus' company consists of both females and males—nymphs and maenads (the former usually thought to give way to the latter in the course of the sixth century), and satyrs and sileni. When the god is alone with the females the sexuality is not overt but latent, if we grant that the swirling dances of young and lovely superhuman women have sexual overtones (fig. 18.1). When the satyrs too are in the scene they show by their arousal and their behavior that they are not indifferent to their companions (fig. 18.2). By the second quarter of the fifth century they are usually no longer shown with erections and are generally less enthusiastically indecent in their actions (fig. 18.3). Perhaps it is worth remarking on what we all take for granted—there are only *male* satyrs. Even a detumescent satyr next to a woman or a nymph embodies male sexuality.[5]

---

[2] Aeschylus *Edoni* frag. 61 (*TrGF* 3), quoted by Aristophanes *Women of the Thesmophoria* 136, and *Theori* (or *Isthmiastae*) frag. 78a (*TrGF* 3). Devereux 1973 took the word *khlounēs* in another fragment of the *Edoni*, frag. 62 (*TrGF* 3), to be a reference to Dionysus as a eunuch.

[3] Otto 1965, 175. Otto explores this aspect of the god at some length. He stresses Dionysus' love for women and theirs for him. He cites Philostratus *Imagines* 2.17 (p. 367, 1–7 Kayser 1870): the Bacchant, ignoring the drunken Silenus who reaches for her, desires (*erōsa*) the absent Dionysus and sees him before her eyes (Otto's free rendering [p. 177] is considerably more fervent and mystical). The relevance of this mutual eroticism for the Dionysus of earlier centuries is questionable, but it turns out that, in Otto's view, "true womanliness reveals itself in the slighter importance of sexual desire" when compared with men (p. 178). He sees the maternal, nursing role of Dionysus' women as more significant. The relationship of Dionysus and his mother is also important for the very different, psychoanalytic perspectives of Slater 1968 and Deutsch 1969.

[4] Cf. Rapp 1872; Lawler 1927; Edwards 1960; McNally 1978; Carpenter 1986; Schöne 1987. I omit the South Italian repertoire, in which I have the impression the languid, beardless Dionysus of the later Attic vases prevails.

[5] At the same time it is worth noting that only satyrs, not men (except in scenes of actual or anticipated intercourse), are shown with erections, a point Lin Foxhall has made to me. Truly human males, we are to understand, show self-control. The sexuality of satyrs, by contrast, does not need the presence of women for arousal (cf. Lissarrague 1990, a valuable study that, along with Frontisi-Ducroux and Lissarrague 1990, I was able to use only in the revision of this essay).

*Figure 18.1* Dionysus, holding a cantharus and vine branch, moves to the right among satyrs and nymphs. Two nymphs play krotala; one carries a bearded snake. Attic red-figure cup from the late sixth century. © British Museum

The god, meanwhile, is never shown in art as involved in the satyrs' sexual shenanigans. He may dance, he may drink, but he is never paired with or shown taking any interest in any of the female companions of his rout. He is not shown with an erection, but then gods almost never are, except for a single goat-headed Pan chasing a shepherd boy and the semi-iconic pillars of Hermes we call herms, which are shown with phalli at the right height in the archaic and early classical periods.[6] What has not been remarked, as far as I know, is that before the change to a preference for a beardless Dionysus, the god's member is rarely shown, even at rest, though examples can be found (fig. 18.4). In archaic art and for most of the fifth century Dionysus is a full-bearded, full-grown but youthful male, usually wearing an ankle-length chiton that covers his body completely, on top of which a himation or a deerskin or leopard skin may be draped. Even when he wears a shorter chiton his loins remain hidden.[7] The contrast is not

[6] Keuls's statement (1984, 291) that gods are never shown with an erection is too sweeping. The aesthetic preference for the small penis must also have been a factor (cf. Dover 1978, 125–27; Lissarrague 1990, 56). The large penis and thus the phallus were comic and grotesque, inappropriate for beautiful and powerful gods. Pan: bell krater by the Pan Painter in the Boston Museum of Fine Arts, 10.185; *ARV*[2] 550.1; Borgeaud 1988, pl. 4.

[7] On his dress, see Stone 1981, 313–16; Veneri 1986, 414–15; Miller 1989, 314–19; Frontisi-Ducroux and Lissarrague 1990, 230–31.

*Figure 18.2* A nymph resists the advances of two satyrs. The nymph, with a snake
wrapped around her left arm, swings a thyrsus with her right. One satyr also holds a
thyrsus, and both carry wineskins. Attic red-figure cup from the first quarter of the
fifth century. (Munich, Direktion der Staatlichen Antikensammlungen und
Glyptothek 2644, ARV² 461.37.)

only with the satyrs in these scenes but with the representation of
other male gods. Nudity is common both on vases and in sculpture,
for Zeus, Poseidon, and especially for the beardless Apollo.[8] The
display of their bodies is consistent with their ostentatious masculinity. Dionysus, to be sure, fights in the ranks of the Olympians against
Titans and Giants according to the mythographers and in some vase
painting.[9] But even though Dionysus, like all Greek gods, could be
violent and dangerous, one suspects that the more characteristic
images for the Greeks were the terrified Dionysus who takes refuge in
the bosom of Thetis (Homer *Iliad* 6.135–37) and the cowardly, if
comic, figure who "gilds" his elegant Ionic gown when confronted
with the Hound of Hell in Aristophanes' *Frogs* (479).

The dress itself is not a feminine garment. With jewelry in hair
worn long it is part of the old-fashioned style of aristocratic

[8] On the uses of nudity, see Bonfante 1989.
[9] Diodorus Siculus 3.74.6 and Apollodorus 1.6.2; for the scenes on vases see Lissarrague 1987.

*Figure 18.3* Dionysus, holding a cantharus and an ivy sprig, moves to the right, led by a satyr playing pipes. Three satyrs follow: one, infibulated, pesters a nymph; the last in the procession carries a pointed amphora on his shoulder and a drinking horn in his right hand. Attic red-figure cup from the first quarter of the fifth century. (Munich, Direktion der Staatlichen Antikensammlungen und Glyptothek 2647, *ARV²* 438.132.)

Athenians of the archaic period. Other sixth-century depictions of male gods show a similar if simpler costume. Dionysus, however, continues to wear it long after it has been abandoned by the others. The saffron-dyed robe (*krokōtos*) he is described as wearing in comedy has unmistakable feminine connotations.[10]

When the rendering of Dionysus changes from a bearded adult to a beardless youth in the later fifth century the god is shown wholly or partly naked, but, as if to compensate for the absence of the symbolism of dress, his whole image is now even less virile—a graceful, languid figure, a *pais kalos* [beautiful boy]. This too may be suggested in Euripides' depiction of Dionysus as the young stranger in the *Bacchae* (e.g., 451–60).[11] [. . .]

[10] Cf. Aristophanes *Frogs* 46; Cratinus frag. 40 (*PCG* 4); and Dodds 1944, on Euripides *Bacchae* 453–54.

[11] Evans 1988, 33 (and cf. 134), is convinced that Dionysus tries to seduce Pentheus in this scene and is angered by the king's rejection of him. The latter point is surely mistaken. The king's fate is sealed by his opposition to the new cult. The god only toys with him. But

*Figure 18.4* A drunken Dionysus, naked except for Thracian boots and a cloak over his left shoulder, holds a thyrsus and a cantharus as he moves to the right in a procession of nymphs and satyrs. The nymph Methyse with a lyre (barbiton) leads the procession. The satyr Oinobios helps the god and is followed by the nymph Chryseis playing pipes and the satyr Maleos with a cantharus and wineskin. Attic red-figure bell krater from the mid-fifth century. (New York, Metropolitan Museum of Art, Rogers Fund, 1907, 07.286.85, *ARV²* 632.3.)

## MYTH

Dionysus and Aphrodite seem a natural pair, representing as they do two of the great joys of life, the pleasures in particular of the symposium. Yet their contacts in mythical genealogy are minor. They are made a couple only for the parentage of the phallic god Priapus of Lampsacus and of the Charites at Orchomenus in Boeotia.[12] The

Dionysus' attractiveness as a love object is consistent with the later conception of him. The first, early appearance of the beardless Dionysus is not effeminate, as is shown by Carpenter in Carpenter and Fardane 1993 ("On the Beardless Dionysus," pp. 185–206). That is not the case when he reappears later in the century. (On this and other points I have profited from Carpenter's knowledgeable comments.)

[12] Priapus of Lampsacus: Pausanias 9.31.2; Charites at Orchomenus in Boeotia: Servius *Aeneid* 1.720; cf. also [Orpheus] *Hymns* 46.1–3 and 55.7, of the second century AD.

most vivid sexually charged conjoining is in Anacreon's appeal to assist him in a homosexual conquest. Dionysus is the "Lord, with whom Eros the subduer, the dark-eyed Nymphs and bright-faced Aphrodite play."[13] For women Aphrodite and Dionysus are contrasted: Pentheus charges the maenads with ranking Aphrodite before Dionysus, that is, it is for sex that they go to the mountains (Euripides *Bacchae* 225, though Dionysus himself has "the charm of Aphrodite in his eyes," 236). Is there a divergence between an Ionic and an Attic tradition, or between an archaic and a classical? Is Dionysus the patron only of male love? Whatever the case, the potentially powerful image of Dionysus as a force corresponding to Aphrodite was little used.

Dionysus' chief amorous attachment is to Ariadne, and while early versions of their relations may have followed the pattern of the god who loves and then is betrayed by a mortal (Homer *Odyssey* 11.324), the later archaic and classical versions have him rescuing her when she has been abandoned by Theseus.[14] In art they are shown as the embodiment of the happy married couple [. . .].[15] While this relationship is hardly asexual, its gentle eroticism is a far cry from the violent swirl of the world of maenads and satyrs. This conjugal aspect of the god [. . .] has a ritual correlate in the annual marriage of Dionysus with the *basilinna* (or *basilissa*), the wife of the Athenian archon known as the *basileus* (king), in the days of the festival of the Anthesteria. There were both open and secret phases. The *basilinna* was assisted by fourteen honored women (the *gerarai*) appointed by the *basileus*. The queen performed rites "not to be spoken of" and saw what no one else should see, very likely referring to the handling of representations of sexual parts. The open aspect of the ceremonies was her passage from the god's sanctuary "in the Marshes" to the *basileus*' headquarters, the Boukoleion, where the marriage took place ([Aristotle] *Constitution of the Athenians* 3.5). The questions of what actually happened and what it may have meant have occasioned a good deal of discussion. Did the archon's wife mate with a mortal man, her husband, or with the priest of Dionysus, perhaps masked and robed as Dionysus? Was the mating a symbolic ceremony, performed in the presence of an image of the god? Or was it

---

[13] Anacreon, *PMG* frag. 12 (= *PLG* frag. 2).

[14] Cf. Otto 1965, 185–86.

[15] *LIMC* s.v. "Dionysos" nos. 708–79 and the comments of Veneri 1986, 417–18. A red-figure pelike [jar] of the second quarter of the fourth century has a very sensuous scene of Ariadne and the beardless Dionysus on a bed (*LIMC* s.v. "Dionysos" no. 762). The figure of Eros joins in Dionysiac scenes in the later fifth century as Dionysus becomes a youth (Lissarrague 1990, 66).

purely the imagined consequence of public ceremonies such as the wedding procession, which may have used an impersonation of the god? A number of vases have been cited as evidence for the event, but their connection with this wedding is at best indirect.[16] It is easier to reject than to confirm speculations. Thus, although the Anthesteria had elements of an All Souls festival, when the spirits of the dead returned, the cheerful depictions of the marriage or parodies of it do not allow us to suppose that a dark and sinister side to this ceremony prevailed and that it was seen as the marriage of a woman with the god of the dead.[17]

The public part of the ritual imitates the bridal procession to the house of the groom, which marks the important social change whereby the woman moves from her paternal *oikos* [household] to establish a new *oikos* with her husband. In this rite, however, the move is from the temple to the headquarters of the *basileus* and not vice versa. The god is assimilated to the man. On the vases that have

---

[16] The relevant vases are conveniently discussed in Deubner 1932, 104–10; Bieber 1949 (though it is not clear that brides were initiated into Dionysiac mysteries); Simon 1963; Simon 1983, 96–98; cf. Keuls 1984, 293–94. Three types of vases have been thought to refer to this wedding. (1) Vases showing a woman, apparently a bride, being led by a satyr or in the company of Dionysus himself; on one the woman is identified as Ariadne, but a connection with Athens has been seen in the presence of an attendant satyr carrying a cantharus and a *khous* [pitcher], a reference to the Choes rite at the Anthesteria (Simon 1963, pl. 5, 1, fragment of a calyx krater in Tübingen, no. 5439, "Group of Polygnotos"). (2) Vases showing a tipsy Dionysus (bearded, full grown, and nude); on one he is accompanied by a satyr boy carrying a *khous* while a woman seated on a bed awaits within (Simon 1963, pl. 5, 3; Simon 1983, pl. 31, 1; Keuls 1984, pl. XX, 14; Keuls 1985, 374, fig. 307; calyx krater in the National Museum in Tarquinia, inv. no. RC 4197, "Group of Polygnotos," *ARV²* 1057.96). (3) On an oinochoe [wine-jug] in New York (Metropolitan Museum, 25.190) children seem to be preparing for Dionysus' wedding procession: the god is seated on a decorated two-wheeled cart (he is bearded and carries a cantharus), and a male is about to help a female climb up to join him (Deubner 1932, pl. 11, 2–4; Bieber 1949, pl. 5, 1A and 1B; Parke 1977, pl. 44; Keuls 1984, pl. XXI, 24; *LIMC* s.v. "Dionysos" no. 825).
 For group 1 it is not evident that the reference is to the *basilinna* rather than to Ariadne, but it is an attractive notion that the presence of a *khous* in the scene in which Ariadne is named serves to compare the Athenian rite at the Anthesteria with Ariadne's wedding to the god. (But it is questionable whether we are to think of Theseus' having to relinquish Ariadne to Dionysus as comparable to the *basileus* surrendering his wife to the god, as Simon 1983, 97, suggests. In the best-known version of the story Theseus abandons her.) Seaford 1984, 8, deduces from these vases that men masked and dressed as satyrs accompanied the *basilinna*. In group 2 we seem to have a "realistic" rendering of Dionysus coming home to a wife (but must it be a bride?) after carousing. An allusion to the Choes rite may be implied, but I do not see that we learn anything about the *basilinna*'s wedding. Is some theatrical scene the source? Example 3, the preparation for a procession, would seem to be the most obvious rendering of the wedding, with an imagined or mimed Dionysus, but the scene has been excluded by Rumpf and Simon (see Simon 1983, 98). In the actual procession it is probable that no one represented the god. [Aristotle] *Constitution of the Athenians* 3.5 says that "the *summeixis* with Dionysus takes place there [at the Boukoleion] and the marriage." *Summeixis* is "ceremonial meeting" not "mating" (so Wilhelm 1937; cf. Rhodes 1981, 104–5). This may suggest that they did not meet before.
[17] So, mistakenly, Daraki 1985, 80–81.

been connected with this wedding one sees the conjugal themes of the marriage of Dionysus and Ariadne but nothing overtly or symbolically sexual, even though actual weddings were not lacking in sexual allusions and symbolism (cf., for example, the end of Aristophanes' *Peace*). The secret rites in which the *basilinna* engages as priestess suggest the controlled, covert sexuality of citizen marriage. Much of what we know of this sacred marriage comes from an allegation that a woman who did not meet the requirements of citizenship and purity had served as *basilinna* ([Demosthenes] *Against Neaera* 73–75). It is a far cry from the exuberant phallicism of the Country and City Dionysia or the abandon of the maenads. The conjugal Dionysus' engagement in sex seems carefully edited—mythologically, a placid marriage with Ariadne; ritually, a blessing of the community's marriages through the annual assimilation of the marriage of the city's most ancient officer, the "king," to that of the god, Dionysus.[18]

What of Dionysus' extramarital adventures? The chorus of Sophocles' *Oedipus the King* (1105–9) wonders if the king may be one of the children presented to a surprised Dionysus by some nymph with whom he disports on Helicon. No asexuality there, but I recall no other such allusions in either literature or art, though no doubt they can be found. A favorite theme of both literature and art is the pursuit by a god of an object of his lust; it would not be surprising if Dionysus had been cast in this role. Only one vase painter seems to have tried to do so, on a single pot where the god and a youth chase each other around a neck amphora of ca. 470–460 BC.[19] The story in Clement of Alexandria (*Protrepticus* 2.30) that the use of phalli as monuments derives from Dionysus' promise to Prosymnos that he would offer himself for sex in return for directions to the entrance to

---

[18] From the extensive literature on the subject, note especially Deubner 1932, 100–110; Parke 1977, 110–13; Simon 1983, 96–97. Burkert 1983, 230–38, stresses restitution and fits this whole ritual into a context of the death, dispersion, reassembly, and revival of the god. He believes the god was represented by his mask fastened to a pillar and it was with this that the *basilinna* was thought to copulate. It is not clear that the mask and pillar have to do with this ceremony (most recently Simon 1983, 100–101, follows Frickenhaus 1912, in attributing all scenes with the mask and pillar to the Lenaia; Hamilton 1992 is skeptical of all identifications). I do not know that a woman who could be identified with the *basilinna* is ever shown alone with the mask and pillar. Hoffman 1989, 110, sees the whole ceremony as a social humiliation of the *basileus*, since he is cuckolded and his wife commits adultery. This is not possible. She *marries* the god in a public ceremony. Nothing in the references we have suggests any shame or humiliation.

[19] Cf. Kaempf-Dimitriadou 1979, pp. 12 and 80, no. 43, pl. 5, 3–4: a neck amphora by the Alkimachos Painter in Naples (inv. 3050); *ARV²* 529.13; 470–460 BC. The god, bearded, wearing a chiton, carrying a thyrsus in his right hand and a vine branch and cantharus in his left, strides forward on one side; on the other a youth walks away from him while looking back and stretching out his hand.

Hades makes use of the "pathic" rather than the lustful conception of the god.

## CULT

In art and in myth we have seen a god who is essentially detached from the erotic and passionate aspects of sex. In his cult, though there is much more than sex, the image of the phallus is central, however we may wish to explain it—as a celebration of the life force, as a charm for fertility, even as a symbol of life after death. (The apotropaic function of the phallus does not seem important in this cult.) Large and small renderings of the part were made especially for the Country Dionysia celebrated throughout Attica and were carried in public and private processions. For the City Dionysia the colonies of Athens were expected to bring phalli every year and no doubt to march with them in procession through the town and then to show them to the assembled Athenians and to the statue of the god in the theater of Dionysus.[20] Probably ceremonies of this sort were at one time quite widespread in Greece (cf. Plutarch *Moralia* 527e). Delos certainly went to great expense to build and decorate a polychrome phallus every year, and we have mentioned the processional carrying of a phallic image of the god on Lesbos. These were the most blatant and enthusiastic demonstrations of sexuality, however metaphorical or symbolic, to be found in the ancient world. A cigar may sometimes be only a cigar, as Freud warned, but a phallus, I submit, is always a phallus.[21]

These festivals are not said to have been restricted to men; Dikaiopolis in his private celebration of the Country Dionysia has his daughter carry the basket just ahead of the slave who carries the phallus, while his wife watches from the roof of the house (Aristophanes *Acharnians* 247–79). But we do not hear of Dionysiac rites open to public view in which women carried or manipulated phalli. Herodotus, who was convinced the Greeks took their cult of Dionysus, including the phallic procession, from the Egyptians, noted that the Egyptian celebration lacked dancing and the phallus itself, instead of which women carried wooden figures whose large genitals they raised and lowered by means of cords (Herodotus

---

[20] Cf. *IG* I³, no. 46 (~ *IG* I², no. 45), line 17.

[21] On the *phallephoria*, see Cole [1993] (I am grateful to the author for providing me with a copy of the article). On phallicism, see Herter 1938 and 1972; Jameson 1949. Czaja 1974 is a fascinating study of phallic stones in Japan on which are often represented couples who are symbolically copulating.

2.48–49.1). Although he did not point it out, we should add that, to the best of our knowledge, it was not women who carried the Greek counterpart, the phallus, in Dionysus' cult; it may be that he expected his readers to savor not only the bizarre puppets but the fact that women operated them.[22]

In the closed women's cults of Demeter we hear of the use of representations of female and male sexual parts. Not only men recognized the necessity for the continuing vigor of phalli if the society was to continue, and while most Greek texts on procreation offered a male version in which the male is the dominant factor, the communal cults of Demeter and Kore and the private worship of Adonis helped to right the balance and put the phallus in its place, so to speak.[23] The Demeter cults in particular link the symbolism of human sexual vigor and fertility with that of agriculture. Dionysus, however, is not demonstrably concerned with fertility, agricultural or human, except in Neoplatonic theory (where the phallus appears as symbol of procreative power) and perhaps by virtue of a place in a Demeter cult.[24] His festivals are agricultural only in their celebration of the vine. Aristophanes has Dikaiopolis, in the Dionysia "in the fields" (*kat' agrous*) that marks his joyful return to the countryside, give free rein to his erotic imagination, without a word on the god's help with his land and crops (*Acharnians* 247–79). At the risk of seeming pedantic,

[22] Women would seem to be brought into close association with the phallus in a Dionysiac context through the ceremonial surrounding a phallus placed in a *liknon*, a basket used for winnowing grain and for carrying an infant; a mask of Dionysus is also shown in the *liknon*. Cf. Kerényi 1976, 260–61 and passim; and Slater 1968, 214, who sees the disembodied phallus as significant for "the deprived and resentful Greek matron." But Nilsson 1952 argues that the representations of the *liknon* in ritual use are of Roman date, and denies that it was so used in earlier times. More significant may be the fact that what were evidently private rites, not conducted in public view, were not depicted earlier.

[23] Brumfield 1981; Zeitlin 1982; Winkler 1990, 188–209.

[24] Iamblichus (*De mysteriis* 1.11) interprets the phallus as symbol of procreative power. For Dionysus' place in the cult of Demeter, see the learned writer excerpted in the scholia to Lucian *Dialogi meretricii* 7 (= pp. 279–81 Rabe), who reports that the use of clay representations of male genitals in the festival of the Haloa was explained as "a token of human generation [literally *spora*, 'seeding'] since Dionysus gave us wine as a tonic drug that would promote intercourse" (Winkler 1990, 194). He then tells the story of the shepherds who killed Icarius under the influence of wine and attacked Dionysus. Afflicted apparently with satyriasis, they recovered only when they made dedications of clay phalli. "This festival is a memorial of their experience." Nonetheless it does not seem that the Haloa was a festival of Dionysus (Deubner 1932, 60–67; Brumfield 1981, 104–31). The story makes better sense as the *aition* [mythological origin] of the Country Dionysia, also held in the month Poseidon (but were clay phalloi dedicated then?). Winkler 1990, 195–96, sees men and women separately "conducting a memorial rite representing some themes of sex and gender." The scholar quoted in the scholion evidently saw a correspondence between male and female ritual use of genitalia. Dionysus had from an early date a place in the cults of Demeter that modern scholars have tended to slight. But this is the only suggestion we have that Dionysiac cult was concerned with the procreative aspects of sex. The Country Dionysia are often assumed to be directed at the fertility of the countryside, a notion that is even harder to pin down.

it is worth emphasizing that it is the broader symbolism of sexual ebullience and the new life of springtime that the god and his rites evoke. Sexuality here is much more than a sanitized convention or traditional magic for securing good crops.

The evidence of vase painting, while far from transparent, rather supports our contention that in the cults of Dionysus the phallus is left to men. A number of vases show a naked woman holding a gigantic phallus or a phallus bird or examining a container of phalli, all animated by an eye on the glans.[25] These women are no doubt hetairai like other naked women on vases, not citizen women, and the scenes do not refer to the community's cults, if they have any cult reference at all. There is a unique scene of a clothed woman sprinkling something on to a row of phalloid plants springing from the ground.[26] We are in the dark about all these scenes, as we are for so much of what went on in the world of Greek women, but perhaps with these scenes we are not missing a great deal. Male artists are saying something about women to a largely male audience, probably that women are wonderfully impressed with the phallus, which is what men like to believe (we may compare the confidence of ancient pornographers in the importance of the dildo).[27] In any case, nothing shown in these scenes points to Dionysus. As far as we can see, overt, exuberant phallicism had no part in the Dionysiac cults of women.

Dionysus was also celebrated privately by means of *kōmoi*, "routs" or "wild parties" at night, in the course of which wine flowed, social barriers were breached, and sexual indulgence was at least thought to occur.[28] One thinks of the Menandrian foundlings, the products of

[25] E.g., (1) amphora by the Flying Angel Painter in Paris (Petit Palais 307), *ARV²* 279.2; Keuls 1985, 84, fig. 77; (2) fragment of a cup in Berlin; Deubner 1932, pl. 3, fig. 2; (3) cup in the Villa Giulia, 50404, *ARV²* 1565.1; Deubner 1932, pl. 4, fig. 1; Keuls 1985, 85, fig. 78; (4) column krater by the Pan Painter in Berlin; Deubner 1932, pl. 4, fig. 2; (5) pelike in Syracuse (inv. 20065), *ARV²* 238.5; Keuls 1985, 84, fig. 76. Lissarrague 1990, 65–66, rightly concludes, after reviewing these scenes, that a woman associated with a phallus is not Dionysiac, and vice versa.

[26] Red-figure pelike in the British Museum (E 819) by the Washing Painter, *ARV²* 1137.25; Deubner 1932, 65–66 and pl. 3, figs. 1 and 3; Winkler 1990, frontispiece. The scene has been associated with the Haloa, a Demeter festival (so Deubner). Winkler 1990, 206, describes it as "humorous fantasy not necessarily associated directly with the Adonia . . . but, illustrating the same cultural equation," i.e., that women cultivate and bring to growth the fragile and short-lived vigor of men. I think, however, that Winkler was mistaken in supposing that the woman sprinkles water on the plants. The object she carries would not do for water, nor would such sprinkling induce growth. Something more fantastic may be involved—perhaps she scatters seeds, and instantly phalli spring up.

[27] Cf. Keuls 1985, 83.

[28] A number of illustrations (the so-called Anacreontic vases) and some literary evidence point to the wearing of women's clothes and jewelry at drinking parties. Frontisi-Ducroux and Lissarrague's article in 1990 (stressing the ambivalence of the self and the other which encompasses that of male and female) supersedes earlier studies, but cf. also De Vries 1973 and Slater 1978. Price 1990 came to my attention too late for use in this study. In the worship of Dionysus

behavior otherwise proscribed. Ostensibly, however, these were occasions for men only (with of course whatever noncitizen women were wanted), while the women of the community had their own rites for the god in which men had limited roles or were excluded.

Maenadism, the withdrawal by women from the community to the mountains to engage in nighttime celebrations, known primarily from literary and artistic depictions, has been much debated—how much is imaginary, mythical, or symbolic, and how much corresponds to real life?[29] Ancients and moderns have been at pains to assure us that the expeditions of the women were entirely chaste.[30] It would certainly be surprising if Greek men, in view of their tight control of their women, had allowed them to go to the mountains with the expectation of sexual adventures. And yet it is not without significance that women indulging in wine at night and freed, however briefly, of social constraints were imagined as engaged in sex, as Pentheus repeatedly implies in the *Bacchae*. The situation is by its nature sexually charged. We might say that the communal Dionysia on the one hand and the mountain pilgrimage of the women on the other each emphasizes an aspect of human sexuality, the phallic and the female, and the two are brought together in the imagery of the satyrs and maenads seen on Attic vases. The enigma is the central figure of such scenes, the god who is both male and female but isolated from the sexuality that flourishes all around him.

Dionysus, the phallic god par excellence, is also more closely associated with the rites of women than any other male figure. The reasons for this have received considerable attention in recent years.[31] The god has been seen as a liberating figure in whose worship women found a temporary escape from male domination. There were probably also nonmaenadic rites in which women played the only or the leading parts. But by their nature these were, like the women's rites for Demeter and Kore, secret and remain, therefore, obscure to us. We have seen an example in the sacred marriage of the Athenian *basilinna*. There were consequences for the structure of the god's cult. For him

through participation in the *kōmos* the worshipers, like the god, play with sexual boundaries. Other occasions for cross-dressing in Greece are in rites of initiation and marriage when identities are changed and alien identities are briefly tried out.

[29] See especially Henrichs 1978 and Bremmer 1984.

[30] E.g., Eur. *Bacch*. 314–20, but cf. *Ion* 545–55. Devereux 1973 has no doubt that sexual orgasm, lesbian or heterosexual, was characteristic of most Bacchants. Only the most accomplished women achieved a trance state without it. (His warning that we must not be misled by the obtuse messenger verges on the fallacy of Lady MacBeth's children.) Detienne 1989, 261, on the other hand, denies that the erotic was for the Greeks a means of leaving oneself and becoming one with the god.

[31] Cf. Kraemer 1979; Segal 1982, 159; Zeitlin 1982.

alone among male gods were there priestesses and numerous groups of women with various names (e.g., *gerarai* involved in the *basilinna*'s wedding).[32] An example from Attica is seen in the sacrificial calendar of the deme of Erchia in the second quarter of the fourth century BC. Dionysus and Semele received a billy goat and a nanny goat, respectively, on the sixteenth of the month Elaphebolion. The flesh of Semele's goat was handed over "to the women," while the skin of both animals belonged to the priestess.[33] In terms of social organization as well as cult participation we see a predominantly female side to Dionysus' worship, matching the predominantly male and phallic.

## CONCLUSIONS

Two cautions are in order before we offer some conclusions. Looking for a consistent whole in the figure of a Greek god and worrying about seeming contradictions are, of course, essentially modern, not ancient, concerns. Furthermore we are able to attempt a reconstruction only for archaic and classical Athens, where alone there may have occurred the particular convergence and balance we think we can see. Dionysiac symbolism makes great play with the male member, on the one hand, and with the concept of liberated women, on the other. Sex may be incidental and not central to the meaning of Dionysus' cult, though our review makes that hard to believe, even if we do not go so far as to say with Keuls that "Dionysiac cult [was] centered around male–female confrontation."[34] But, in any case, his cult lends itself to a powerful nexus of signs. Violence and aggression are portrayed for both male and female, and yet at the center of the commotion stands a figure that presents features of softness, gentleness, and quiet. For women, I suggest, this is especially important. Aggression, the use of the phallus as a weapon, waxes and wanes in the scenes on Attic pots, and corresponding changes have been seen in Athenian society.[35] But while a growing appreciation of conjugality and harmony between the sexes is shown in art, the hostile and aggressive side of male sexuality is not likely to have faded away.[36] While Dionysus presides over phallic cavortings, he remains detached sexually, except for his rescue

[32] Cf. Otto 1965, 175; Henrichs 1978.

[33] *LSS* nos. 18A, 44–51, 18Δ, 33–40; *SEG* 21, no. 541.

[34] Keuls 1984, 288.

[35] Cf. McNally 1978; Fineberg 1983.

[36] Cf. Sutton 1981, 107–8; Keuls 1985, 174–86; Kilmer 1990. Kilmer compares scenes of sexual violence on Attic red-figure vases with an arbitrary selection of sadomasochistic scenes in European and Japanese art of the recent past to conclude that the Attic examples are relatively innocuous. I do not see that any useful conclusions are to be expected from such methods.

of and marriage to Ariadne and his sanctification of the marriage of *basileus* and *basilinna*. The beardless youth of later classical art is still less a threatening and aggressive figure than his bearded predecessor.

To use what has become a cliché, Dionysus is a mediating figure between male and female, needed because the forces his cult releases arouse both men and women in ways that threaten order. The reasons for the development and persistent strength of his potentially explosive cult lie, no doubt, deep within the structure of Greek society, which contained both the psychological tensions of the nuclear family and the wider social and institutional stresses of the approved roles of women and men. Any particular instance of Dionysian activity is not likely to exhibit the full repertoire of elements that we attach to his cult, a construct that is in effect of our own making. Nor are release and resolution of the pressures his cult addresses always achieved, according to some neat, functional model. The most I have hoped to do in this essay is to examine some aspects of a varied and constantly changing pattern.[37]

Two images may provide us with an appropriate conclusion: one is that of the embodiment of the epicene style of modern pop culture, the male leader of the pop group, who for all the violence of music, gestures, and words is neither traditionally masculine nor yet effeminate. To the established order he may be a threat but not to the adoring young, especially the young women. There is a fascination but also a certain horror about such a figure, who cannot be placed and straddles or crosses boundaries. The other image is that of Dionysus in the *Bacchae*, who draws Pentheus over a boundary as the king is led to make himself into a *bakkhē*. In that play is there not some of this chilling fascination about Dionysus too, whose gender puzzles Pentheus and who moves quietly between the raucous worlds of the male and the female?

---

[37] No one has been more sensitive to the contradictions in the conception of the god than Slater 1968, 210–307. He noted "a quality of dissonance about the god" (211) and his "conglomerate and morphologically unstable character" (212). He also brought out that "even the boundaries between the sexes are to be dissolved." "This," he observed, "was perhaps one of the central psychological functions of the Dionysian cult—it provided the ultimate fantasy solution to the torment which sex antagonism occasioned in Greek life by eliminating the exaggerated differentiation imposed by culturally defined sex roles" (283–84). Segal 1982, 213, who cites this last passage, rightly notes that in the *Bacchae* sexual differentiation is reinforced rather than eliminated and that tragedy by its nature is not concerned with such resolution. Indeed, it could be said that cult and myth in other forms as well may provide opportunities for demonstration and exploration rather than resolution. And yet the recurrent theme of the unclassifiable god seems always to be available as a palliative. It should be added that Slater, who emphasizes the obscuring of boundaries between mother and child and the mother's ambivalence toward child and phallus (conceived of as an isolated object and depicted as the member of depersonalized, inhuman satyrs), sees no resolution of "the Greek cultural sickness" by this route.

# 19 "Vested Interests" in Plautus' Casina: Cross-Dressing in Roman Comedy†

## BARBARA GOLD

Cross-dressing is a focal point at which the concerns of many contemporary fields of inquiry converge: gender studies, performance theory, gay/lesbian/bisexual studies, psychoanalysis, linguistics, anthropology, film theory, theater history and criticism, and feminism. In recent years, there has been intense interest in this subject, which calls into question the absolute binarism of male and female and highlights the potential biological, cultural, and psychological instabilities in the construction of gender.[1] Countless stories and anecdotes told by those exploring this theatrical and extra-theatrical act reveal its richness, complexity, and importance. I start with two dressing stories, each of which questions gender as a stable term. My essay will be concerned with the issues that these stories raise: gender and cross-dressing; the ways in which Plautus' *Casina* explores and defines these areas of debate; and the ways in which Roman comedy defines the construction of gender in ways similar to Roman elegy.[2]

One: Two small children stand in a museum, staring at a painting of Adam and Eve. One says to the other: "Which is the man and which is the lady?" The other child answers, "I can't tell—they don't have any clothes on."[3]

Two: A "womanless" beauty pageant is held annually in North Carolina to raise money for the fire and rescue departments. According to an account of this pageant, J. W., the deputy sheriff, was dressed in a "saucy little tangerine number with spike heels"; Ken, a school principal dressed in a tutu, performed a "hairy-chested rendi-

---

† Originally published in *Helios*, 25 (1998), 17–29.
[1] See Epstein and Straub 1991b: 2.
[2] See also James' introduction and the essays of James and Janan in [James 1998].
[3] Shapiro 248.

tion of *Swan Lake*." The male observers reportedly reacted with wild enthusiasm. Even more revealing than the actual costumes and talent events was the naively metatheatrical discussion that surrounded the pageant (a discussion that engaged the topics of sexual identity and ideology only accidentally). One wife worried that her husband was "enjoying dressing up a little too much." A group of gospel singers refused to perform for the pageant again because they did not want to appear to be endorsing "homosexual activity." Jeff, a fireman and fabric inspector at a local textile mill, said: "You have to be *very* sure of your masculinity to get up there and do that."[4]

The first story is a powerful piece of evidence for the social constructionist view of gender. The sex of Adam and Eve is not, for these youthful observers, based on their genitalia. These children recognize that gender might have more to do with outward appearance than with biological bodies, that gender is socially constructed, not simply determined by biology. The "womanless" beauty pageant is just the opposite: a story about cross-dressing that seems to show the importance of biology in determining how men and women think, dress, and feel. The men involved, both as participants and spectators, engage in cross-dressing as a way to gauge their degree of masculinity (perhaps without realizing the potentially disturbing effects). Their wives are more concerned than the men are about the ambiguities attendant on these activities and the possibly destabilizing effects of this annual homosocial acting-out on their heterosexual male identities. The gospel singers are more aware than anyone that this

---

[4] *Wilmington (N.C.) Morning Star*, March 19, 1994. Cf. Irigaray 170–91 ("Women on the Market" or "Le marché des femmes,") esp. 170–72, where she discusses "the reign of hom(m)o-sexuality ("hom(m)o-sexualité")," an institution that uses women as a medium of exchange between men. This exchange ratifies the social bonds between men and thus carries a strong presumption of homosocial behavior, although not the actual practice of "hommo-sexuality." Irigaray says: "Reigning everywhere, although prohibited in practice, hom(m)o-sexuality is played out through the bodies of women, matter, or sign, and heterosexuality has been up to now just an alibi for the smooth workings of man's relationship with himself, of relations among men" (172).

There are countless other examples of such transvestive events. The Kate Kennedy pageant in St. Andrews, Scotland, is an all-male student festival reconstructing a piece of St. Andrews' history. Kate was reportedly the beautiful niece of a founder of St. Andrews University. Each year, an all-male contingent parades in costume, with Kate being acted by a male first-year student, a member of the elite Kate Kennedy club. The Mummer's Parade in Philadelphia, presented annually since 1901, features the spectacle of middle-aged men "prancing down Broad Street in spangles and feathered boas" (Epstein and Straub 1991b:1). Abissa, a celebration in Grand-Bassam, Ivory Coast, involves men dressed as full-breasted women and women dressed as men in neckties in a week-long celebration of loss of inhibition and revelation of truth (*New York Times*, November 3, 1995, A 4). We cannot, however, assume that all transvestive events serve the same cultural purpose. One common element in them, however, would seem to be the deep anxiety about human sexuality present cross-culturally, which is allowed to work itself out in a whole variety of different venues and circumstances. And, as we will see in Plautus' *Casina*, more than one goal can be accomplished in any one dramatic enactment of cross-dressing.

cross-dressing parade clearly calls socially-prescribed sexual identities into question.[5]

But the cross-dressing in this instance is not meant to destroy or
confuse gender roles; quite the contrary, in its mockery of women's
behavior and style, its intent seems to be to reconfirm both the traditional roles and attributes assigned to gender and, in the process,
men's confidence in their superior position and power. Like such
Greek rituals as the Bacchic rites, which allowed women in strictly
controlled circumstances to "play the other,"[6] or the male-to-female
cross-dressing rites in the Oschophoria, in which two noble youths
dressed in women's dress and carried grape clusters to the priestess of
Athena Skiras in Phaleron,[7] such boundary-crossing behavior serves
to reinforce traditional roles rather than to question them institution-
ally. In these transvestive rituals, where someone always must play the
role of the other in order to solidify the status and gender of the dominant male order, the Greeks used a controlled setting to try to ensure
the rebirth of the perfect male. When cross-dressing was deployed in
Greek initiation rituals, the effect was not meant to be seen as ambiguous, although the act itself indicated anxiety about those traditional
roles. The act was a means of conjuring away the fear of just how
unstable gender identities are.

The figure of Chalinus/Casina in Plautus' *Casina* reveals how practices such as drag and cross-dressing construct gender by undermin-
ing the notion of a coherently gendered self or of a stable identity that
precedes the expression of an interest or point of view.[8] Here we have
a male actor (playing the male slave Chalinus) dressing up as Casina,
the bride and a character after whom the play is named but who never
appears on-stage except as played by Chalinus. The Chalinus/Casina
figure interacts throughout with males and females in homosocial,
homoerotic, heterosocial, and heteroerotic ways, creating gender
slippage both within him/herself and between him/herself and the
other characters.

---

[5] On homosociality, see Irigaray 170–91; Sedgwick 1985: 1–15 *et passim*; Faderman (for
women) 145–77 *et passim*.

[6] For playing the other in Greek tragedy, a ritualized form, see Zeitlin 1996b: 341–74.

[7] For the Oschophoria, see Ferguson 36–41, Simon 90–91. See also on cross-dressing in
initiation rituals, Ackroyd 39–48, esp. 46; Rehm 13; Delcourt, chap. 1.

[8] Drag and cross-dressing are not and should not be seen as synonymous. Performers in
drag usually do not try to create an illusion or to make an attempt to mimic the behavior of
the other gender in order to convince the audience of their authenticity. Their gender-switch-
ing is made transparent, and they call attention to the disparity between their off-stage and
on-stage selves. Cross-dressers, especially if they practice cross-dressing for any sustained
period and try to pass, make an effort to fit into their new gender and not to call attention to
its performative aspects. See on this Bullough and Bullough, esp. 166–68, 226–52; Garber
90–91.

This cross-dressed Plautine character seems to question whether the terms *man* and *woman* can have any internal stability. The act of cross-dressing here, as elsewhere, represents genders as relational terms, social constructions that are created in the *practice* of relating to other people.[9] Gender theorists, like Judith Butler, focus on the *production* of the seemingly foundational categories of identity ("the binary of sex, gender, the body," *Gender Trouble* viii) rather than accepting these categories as natural and inevitable. Butler (viii–ix) designates these traditional categories of identity as *effects* of practices and discourses rather than *origins* of them. For Butler, gender is an "ontological regime" (viii).

As the character Casina reveals, gender is something that is performed, that is, a matter of style, more a mode of presentation than a preexisting core identity. [. . .] When Casina performs her gender through dress, movement, gesture, and voice, the play of gendered symbols on the body creates, at least for the moment, an illusion of interior reality. But these performative acts make clear that this identity is a fabricated unity and that the reality projected is an illusion. Cross-dressing parodies the notion of gender, creating a temporarily unified picture of *man* or *woman*, while at the same time revealing the imitative, contingent, and heterogeneous nature of gender.

Any theatrical performance questions the supposition that the semiotics of gender is natural. When we see, for example, a cross-dressed performer in plays and movies like *Casina, Tootsie, Morocco* (with Marlene Dietrich), or *Hairspray* and *Female Trouble* (with Divine), we are seeing three genders represented: male, female, and a continually changing third gender. In *Hairspray*, for example, Divine moves back and forth from a clearly male character (Arvin) to a cross-dressed character named Edna Turnblad. Divine's Edna is in the business of producing gender at every moment. She is a mother, a slovenly housewife who spends her days ironing and trying to keep her daughter from wasting her life dancing along to a television dance show; she has long hair and wears dresses; but her physique and her contralto voice call constant attention to her fluid gender. In such a production, there is no question of believing the illusion that this is a female character; every dramatic device is calculated to call our attention to the fact that this is a cross-dressed performer. Similarly in

---

[9] For discussions of the construction of gender, performance theory, and cross-dressing, see Butler 1990, esp. viii–ix, 128–41 and 1993, esp. 27–55, 93–119; Weston 1–21. See also on the social construction of gender, Foucault, Vol. 1; Halperin; Winkler. On the construction of sexuality, see Sedgwick 1985, esp. 1–20, and 1990, esp. 1–63.

the *Casina*, Plautus keeps us constantly aware that gender is being performed (by Chalinus/Casina and also by other characters).

As Marjorie Garber points out in *Vested Interests*, the cross-dresser is not a "third sex" or "third term," indeed, not *a* term or *a* sex at all, but rather a "space of possibility," which is defined only by what it does not do. This space of possibility does not belong to either of the two traditional genders.[10] In this sense, it is a mistake to be influenced by gender binarism into trying to assimilate this figure to one pole or the other and thus to erase it. Rather, we should treat this third figure as a "disruptive act of putting into question" (Garber 13), which interrupts the text, reconfigures other relationships, and complicates identities previously considered stable (as Chalinus/Casina does). The power of the cross-dresser lies in his or her blurred identity, in the very act of his/her cross-dressing, not in either of his/her gendered identities (Garber 6).

One of Plautus' aims in the *Casina* seems to be to parody the notion of a primary gender identity. There are in this play many possible layers of dissonance between gender and sex, sex and performance, and gender and performance.[11] Such a performance may point up the distinction between the anatomy of the performer (which itself is not a stable point of reference) and the gender that is being performed, or between the gender identity of the performer and the gender performance. Acts such as Chalinus'/Casina's cross-dressing can be a deliberate attempt to disconcert the audience by denaturalizing gender through strategic mimicry. These acts mock both the performative model of gender and the idea of a true gender identity.

In the Roman theater of Plautus, theatrical performances operated under particular cultural conditions. First, since all the roles were acted by men, every actor who played the part of a woman was already a cross-dresser. Therefore, a distinction must be made between non-illusionary and illusionary cross-dressers, those who call attention to their performance as women and those who do not. Second, every aspect of the ancient theater was dominated by males. All the actors were male, the normative part of the audience was male, and all the writers of drama were male. Women were all but effaced on the ancient stage by the men who appropriated their roles, clothing, and dramatic power but could reject the actual conditions

[10] Garber 9–13. Luce Irigaray's description of women as the "sex which is not one" similarly portrays women as an unrepresentable, undesignatable, multiple third term not belonging to either of the two traditionally-defined sexes (1985: 23–33).
[11] Butler 1990: 137.

of being a woman.[12] Femininity was for them a mask, which they could put on or take off. As Mary Russo says, "To put on femininity with a vengeance suggests the power of taking it off" (224). In many contemporary forms of experimental theater, the feminine spectacle is subjected to the male gaze,[13] but in the ancient theater, the audience knew that a male figure (man or boy) lurked beneath every alluring female character; thus the illusion of a consistent female character was never unbroken.

On Plautus' stage, then, there was never a sustained female figure to receive the gaze. Casina did not exist, even for a dramatic moment. To complicate matters further, the gender of the ancient male viewer was equally open to question. If we accept a Foucauldian—or even a modified Foucauldian—view, gender is socially constructed. Roman men could slip in and out of women's roles because their own sexuality and gender were fluid. Their masculinity was a function of their behavior in particular situations and with specific partners; it was not dissociable from their sexual preferences for active versus passive roles.[14] A male viewer then might have been seen as "masculine" if he was the active member of a male–male relationship or if he was part of a male–female relationship, but "feminine" (*mollis*) if he was a passive member of a male–male relationship (a *cinaedus*).

The posture of such a male viewer opposite the cross-dresser Chalinus in Plautus' *Casina*, then, would be complex. Casina/Chalinus is presented in a highly self-aware way as a fully overdetermined masculinized character (by the end at least) so that a Roman male viewer might vicariously interact with this character in one of several ways. This hypothetical viewer might participate with Casina's male side (Chalinus) in a homosocial bonding; might take a passive, cinaedic pose opposite the aggressive, male posturing of the Chalinus/Casina character; or might even for a time adopt the posture of the ideal Roman male opposite Casina, the speechless and demure bride. The slippage from one gender performance to another depends both on how the characters on-stage are represented and on the focalizing of the viewer him- or herself.[15]

The ontological and epistemological uncertainty engendered by

[12] See Dolan 7. On the implications of male actors playing female roles in the Greek theater, see Rabinowitz 1998.

[13] See Straub 143.

[14] For a discussion and modification of the Foucauldian position and an examination of the *cinaedus*, see Richlin 1993. For a pro-Foucauldian view, see Halperin and Winkler.

[15] See Bassi 3–22. She points out that "bodies viewed theatrically communicate ontological and epistemological uncertainty" (3). She discusses this in the context of the Greek theater, but this statement is equally applicable to Roman comedy.

theatrical bodies is increased by the further complicating factors of class and gender in the makeup of the audience as well as the characters on-stage. Slave males, who were always forced to take a passive role, would have reacted quite differently to the antics on-stage surrounding Chalinus, Olympio, and Lysidamus than would free males (who were not permitted to take the passive role if they wanted free status). Female viewers, who also took passive roles of varying degrees depending upon their class and status, would have had yet a different perspective on the dramatic action. Plautus brings the perspectives of these non-free, male groups to the forefront of our interpretation of the play when he highlights their interactions with the slave Chalinus as they make their own comedy out of both free and slave male sexual access to Casina.

In order to examine some of the possible effects of "Casina's" performance on the audience, in particular the predominantly and normatively Roman male audience, I would like to turn to the extraordinary transvestite wedding scene, which, when coupled with the homoeroticism among the three main male characters, makes the *Casina* unique in the Plautine corpus.[16] In the play, Lysidamus, the main character, a "bisexual" lecher, has conceived a plan to have sex with Casina, his ward who was adopted in childhood and raised as a daughter by Lysidamus and his wife Cleostrata. His plan is for his slave Olympio to marry Casina and become a surrogate for his master, who will then enjoy the *ius primae noctis*. Cleostrata, Lysidamus' wife, knows about the plan and proposes in turn that her slave Chalinus marry Casina. A lot-drawing is held (thus the name of Diphilus' original version, the *Klêroumenoi*), with much manoeuvering and abuse on each side. Olympio and his master Lysidamus win. Cleostrata and her maid Pardalisca then set out to humiliate Lysidamus. Pardalisca enacts a mock-tragic scene in which she describes the bride Casina in the house, mad and brandishing two knives meant for Lysidamus and Olympio. Lysidamus, both terrified and titillated, pursues his goal hungrily; the false marriage takes place with Chalinus dressed as the bride Casina. Olympio is beaten up by Casina/Chalinus, and Lysidamus claims to

---

[16] For an examination of such a combination of elements in Plautus or in his sources, see Cody. Atellan farce comes the closest to having the combination of transvestism, weddings, and homoeroticism, but there is no parallel for the character of Lysidamus, who is not effeminate but rather is both homo- and heteroerotic because of an excess of lust. There are, however, many examples of epicene creatures such as Casina throughout literature, from Aristophanes' *Thesmophoriazusae* to Ben Jonson's *Epicene*. Several interesting seventeenth-century pamphlets focus on masculinized females or feminized males. Three published in 1620 were entitled *Hic Mulier, or the Man-Woman*; *Haec Vir, or the Womanish Man*; and *Muld Sacke, or the Apologie of the Mulier*; for a discussion, see Wright 465–507.

Cleostrata (who is enjoying the spectacle) that he himself has lost his *pallium* (cloak) in the sexual violence of a Bacchic orgy.[17] The play ends with Lysidamus' repentance and Cleostrata's ungracious forgiveness. Only in the epilogue do we discover that Casina is indeed the freeborn daughter of the next-door neighbors and that she will be duly wedded to Euthynicus, the son of Lysidamus and Cleostrata. This detail, however, is not central to the plot of Plautus' play.

Casina is the main character, after whom the play is named, but, oddly, she never appears in the play in her own person. "She" is instead presented through the eyes and mouths of other characters in many guises, and her identity is entirely determined by them. Despite, or because of, her existential lack in the play, she casts a long shadow over virtually every scene, providing a convenient vehicle through which Plautus can negotiate the central issues in the play: border crossings, the paradoxes of gender identification, and the resistance of marginalized, hidden, and silent characters (women and slaves). Casina herself (if "self" can be used as an operative term here) is doubly marginalized and potentially transgressive, since both her sex (female) and her status (slave) ascribe to her the passivity and fluidity often predicated of women.[18]

Casina is made physically present by the dressing up of the actor who plays the slave Chalinus and then brings Casina to life through his performance of her. She is also present in the imagination of Lysidamus, who breathes life into his version of her with erotic imaginings and longings (II.3, II.7), and in Pardalisca's vivid description of the Casina within wielding knives and threatening death and destruction to her would-be husbands (III.5). In each reconfiguration, the gaze of the actor, and its verbal representation, are important, and each character breathes into Casina his or her own desires and fears. To the lusty old goat Lysidamus, an overdetermined male character who fears his wife and other potentially harmful women, Casina is erotic and desirable but also dangerous (II.3, 7). Through the language of Pardalisca, the wild panther-lady, feisty, rebellious, and on the unstable margins of her sex (female) and class (slave), Casina is

---

[17] Lysidamus' free status is properly observed; only Olympio, the slave, is beaten up by Casina/Chalinus. Physical attacks by slaves on free *senes* [old men] never occur in Roman drama. See Arnott, forthcoming. The reference here to the *Bacchae* has been taken as a topical reference to the *senatus consultum de Bacchanalibus*, which banned the worship of Bacchus in 186 BCE; if so, this would date the play and make it one of the last plays of Plautus, who died in 184 BCE. On this see MacCary 1975: 459–63; Hallett 1996: 410–11.

[18] See Sissa, who "shows how the Aristotelian discourse concerning the female body is conducted around a polarity of 'more' and 'less,' so that the female is conceptualized, not as different from the male, but as a diminution of the male form" (Arthur-Katz 172).

masculinized, aggressive, wonderfully dangerous and exotic (III.5). To Olympio, himself a slave but male and able to see only from an erotically-aroused male focal point, Casina is fearsome, inscrutable, incomprehensible, and an impossible hybrid of sexual characteristics (V.2). Chalinus is the most interesting focalizer, being himself male and a slave, but identified in the play solely with the women. He is or becomes Casina and so sees her from the inside, and he is the only male who knows the secret of Casina. Never was a character both more and less present than Casina; never was a character's gender so constructed.

Whereas many depictions of cross-dressing orchestrate the play of gendered symbols on the body's exterior to create the illusion of an interior reality, Plautus uses cross-dressing on the stage with quite a different purpose in mind. We know—as do all the characters in the play except Olympio, Alcesimus, and Lysidamus—that Casina is a male character playing a female, but at no point in the play are we ever allowed to feel comfortable with the identification of Casina's gender.[19] Chalinus plays her at first as demure, submissive, and cooperative—every Roman man's ideal bride—(IV.4), but the stage has already been set for her gender instability in scene III.5, where Pardalisca describes her as a fury rampaging with two swords within the house.[20]

Shortly after Casina's appearance as the demure bride, she stomps on Olympio's foot and elbows him in the chest; Olympio describes her here as an elephant (*luca bos*, 846) and a battering ram (*pectus mi icit non cubito, verum ariete*, 849). By the time Olympio tries to rape the bride, she has become, through his eyes, a hodge-podge of genitalia, something both confusing and tantalizing for Olympio. When he reaches under her dress, he discovers there an object that he cannot identify because he thinks that Casina is female (V.2). He is unable to identify "Casina's" penis because he is limited by his prior assump-

---

[19] Cf. the remark in the prologue (81–86) that Casina will not commit any *stuprum* ("lewd act") in this comedy, but once the play is done, she will be sexually available to anyone for a fee. Since the character Casina does not ever appear in the play and her double is played by a male actor, this opening joke must have been intended to signal the sexual availability of the male actor playing the role and to encourage among the male members of the audience (free and slave, active and passive) a lecherous male gaze mirroring the gazes of Lysidamus and Olympio.

[20] The metamorphosis of the demure, appealing bride into a shrewish, aggressive, or violent woman (or a man) is a popular theme in later literature and opera. Cf. Ben Jonson's *Epicene, or The Silent Woman* (where the "bride" turns out to be a boy) and Donizetti's *Don Pasquale* (where Norina/Sofronia first masquerades as a demure woman recently released from a nunnery, content with only her sewing, but then turns into a violent and unfaithful wife so that she might obtain a "divorce" from Pasquale [to whom she was never really married] and marry his nephew and heir, Ernesto).

tions about "Casina's" sex. He gropes for a simile to describe this foreign object: a sword hilt? (no, there is no sword, and it is not cold enough); a horseradish? a cucumber? (no, but something fully grown, 908–12).

Meanwhile, Olympio professes his profound embarrassment at his continuing inability to decipher this gender confusion: Pard.: "Then it's only fair you confess the whole thing. . . . What happened inside? What did Casina do? Was she obedient enough for you?" Ol.: "It's so embarrassing!" (*pudet dicere*, 897). Pard.: "Tell the whole thing in order, the way you started to." Ol.: "Oh, it's so embarrassing!" (*pudet hercle*, 900). Pard.: "What did you find?" Ol.: "Oh, the most enormous thing . . ." Pard.: "Do go on." Ol.: "But it's so embarrassing!" (*at pudet*, 911).[21]

The confusion of sexes is foregrounded throughout these tease scenes, in which both the audience and the characters are led on: the bridal gown, the demeanor, and the name identify Casina as a woman, but the rough behavior, the swords, the bearded lips (929), and the sword hilt-shaped genitalia all mark her as a man. Pardalisca, who is a partner to the joke from the start and orchestrates the wedding scene, sums up Olympio's and Lysidamus' gender troubles when she exclaims as the new bride enters: *iam oboluit Casinus procul* ("The scent of the male Casina has preceded him," 814).[22]

This gender switching reflects other confusions which we find in this play, a typical Plautine feature: role-doubling (Chalinus/Casina, Lysidamus/Olympio as the two bridegrooms, Olympio/ "Casina" as the objects of Lysidamus' desire[23]) and the hybrid Greek and Roman wedding.[24] Further underscoring the confusion of Casina's gender is the blurring of other categories besides gender: age, class and status, sexuality, animal/human, lover/beloved, inside/outside. So, for example, Lysidamus, the free aristocratic master of Olympio and Chalinus, becomes at various moments the slave of (or to) his slave Olympio (III.6), to his wife Cleostrata (V.3), and to love (III.6), and he refers to himself as a *liber* [free man] when his wife disappears inside, leaving him to romp at will with his *corculum* [darling] (835–37).

Another and visual manifestation of the instability of identities is the

---

[21] The translation used here is by Tatum [1983]. *Morigera*, the word used by Pardalisca in line 896 to describe Casina, is a standard term for a submissive wife, but it hardly suits Casina's behavior here. See MacCary and Willcock 199; Williams 19.

[22] The speaker here is unclear; it could be Chalinus himself. See the discussion in MacCary and Willcock 186–87.

[23] See on this Cody, esp. 455–56.

[24] See MacCary and Willcock 188; Williams 16–29.

use of costumes and props, signs that help not only to heighten the hilar-
ious confusions but also to mark transformations of characters as they
glide from one role and status to another. So, Lysidamus' cane, a marker
of his age and authority, becomes in turns a sword and a club (weapons
aimed both at himself and at others) and a phallus. When Lysidamus is
at his weakest and most vulnerable, he loses his staff (975), but, at the
end, when Cleostrata reluctantly reinstates him to his place of authority in the household, she orders Chalinus to return it (*redde huic scipio-
nem et pallium* [give this man back his cane and cloak], 1009).

Such blurring of identities, roles, and props is a common element
in Plautus' plays, but the crossed-dressed, same-sex wedding scene is
not. The standard Plautine upheavals here serve to highlight and con-
textualize the unusual confusion on which the entire plot hinges and
to focus our attention on the figure of Chalinus/Casina, the always
present but always absent eponymous character. Casina's identity,
however, is never for a moment in doubt to the audience or to the
"female" characters on stage—only to the obtuse male characters,
Olympio, Lysidamus, and Alcesimus. The women seem to be in
charge throughout. They engineer their own plot within the plot
(860–61), and they alone are aware of Casina's true identity. They hold
both genital and authorial power over the development of the play.

Unlike certain cross-dressers in other times and cultures who fully
take on another identity at least for the duration of a performance,
Chalinus and Plautus constantly remind us with self-conscious gestures, props, costumes, and language that this "she" (Casina) is a he.
Plautus does everything to make clear "Casina's" true dramatic identity. Chalinus/Casina never really become a specularized female body
for the audience as did, for example, Margaret Woffington, the famed
eighteenth-century cross-dresser.[25] Chalinus' appeal is to men, both
on- and off-stage. His main role on-stage is to create a homosocial
bond between the master and slave, Lysidamus and Olympio, by
acting the woman who is traded off between them.[26] Thus Lysidamus
calls Olympio *meus socius, compar, commaritus* ("my ally, my equal,
my fellow hubby bridegroom," 797).

[25] For a description of Woffington's effect on her audience, see Straub 144–45. She quotes
a page of Woffington's 1760 memoir, which reports: "Females were equally well pleased with
her acting as the Men were, but could not persuade themselves that it was a Woman that acted
the Character."

[26] See Rabinowitz 1993 for a discussion of this use of the female in Greek tragedy. See also
Irigaray 170–72. This trading of Chalinus/Casina between Olympio and Lysidamus nicely
illustrates Irigaray's definition of "hom(m)o-sexuality," but the situation in the *Casina* is
doubly complicated because the "woman" who is being traded here between men is really a
man himself.

But there is also an explicitly homoerotic relationship both between the fellow bridegrooms (II.8, III.6) and between Olympio and Chalinus/Casina (V.2), which is packaged for the pleasure of the audience in a much more alluring way than any of the female or pseudofemale characters are.[27] In these various roles, Chalinus/Casina would have reinforced the traditional and unambiguous ideal of the dominance of men over women and slaves. But more to the point, Chalinus/Casina, a hypermalleable character, would also have undercut this ideal by doubling the ontological uncertainty that is always already present in theatrical settings.

Chalinus/Casina was there to set the traditional male Roman viewer on edge, to manipulate his sexuality, and to offer a choice of sexual posture to the male viewer along the male–male or male–female continuum. This viewer might first have bonded with Lysidamus and Olympio, taking an aggressive male over female posture as Lysidamus and Olympio traded the female "prize," fought against the phalanx of women opposing them, and swelled with desire for Casina.[28] The viewer would also have had a choice of taking the role of the pederast or aggressive male partner, associating himself with Lysidamus trying to rape Olympio (II.8), or of pathic *cinaedus*, becoming one with Olympio in that same scene or with Casina/Chalinus when Olympio is trying to rape her/him (V.2).[29] His worst fears might have been realized if he found himself in the thoroughly emasculated position of Olympio in V.2 or Lysidamus (*passim*). In such a posture, the viewer has fallen: from the aggressive male in a male–female relationship to aggressive partner in a male–male relationship to pathic partner in a male–male relationship to the degraded position of woman in a male–female relationship.[30]

Thus, in the figure of Casina and in other ambiguous figures in the *Casina*,[31] Plautus calls attention to the conditional nature of virility. This kind of figure posed a potential threat to the dominant, public form of masculinity and featured the disturbing specter of a castrating female. Cleostrata and Chalinus use their respective attributes of

[27] For a complete analysis of the homosexual scenes in the *Casina*, see Cody.
[28] This bonding is already set up in the prologue; see note 19.
[29] For a discussion of sexuality in Roman literature, see Richlin 1992, esp. 220–26.
[30] One could argue that the position of pathic and woman are equally degraded. It is not clear whether male pederasts in Rome would have been considered as lesser than the active partner in a male–female relationship, but there is some evidence that aggressive male pederasts were despised. See Richlin 1992: 221.
[31] E.g., Cleostrata, who shifts back and forth from aggressive, dominant shrew to obedient wife. Her mythological comparanda, Juno, is a perfect analogue for Cleostrata (II.3, II.6), being both female goddess and subject to Jupiter's power but also frequently subversive, uncooperative, and aggressive towards her husband. As Anderson 180 remarks, Cleostrata is one of Plautus' "rogue-females."

anatomy and status to humiliate the dominant free male, Lysidamus. Lysidamus is reduced to slave-like status, both by his wife Cleostrata and by Cleostrata's slave Chalinus.

Both Chalinus, a slave, and Cleostrata, a woman, are given dramatic, and possibly even social, agency by the playwright, who allows them to intimidate and humiliate the free *senex* and to guide the action up until the very end.[32] The characters representing the most powerless groups (slaves and women) rule the action and are even granted authorial direction (see Myrrhina's comment in lines 860–61). On the other hand, at the very end of the play, the male prerogative of sexual and social domination seems to be reaffirmed. Cleostrata's revenge depends partly on a borrowed phallus.[33] Lysidamus abandons his pathic status, receives again his emblems of power (cloak and staff, 1009) and recovers his role of husband; he then reconciles with his wife, who undergoes a transition from *irata* [angry] to *lepidior* [more delightful] (1007–08).

Plautus' recuperative strategies seem here to allow him to resolve the situation at the end in favor of the normative heterosexual, male-dominant model. The cross-dresser's true dramatic nature is revealed, a heterosexual marriage is announced, slaves remain slaves, and free remain free. The "women" in the play, the only characters to understand the joke and the ones who claim to be masterminding the plot (V.1), also drop their cross-dressed roles and the audience comes to know them as the men they really are. The cross-dressing in the *Casina* seems to have been sanctioned play for men.[34] The audience would have seen that only the men cross-dressed and played the other. For women to take on male roles would have been too dangerous and unsettling, but men were able simultaneously to absorb and appropriate the powers ascribed to women, return to their normal place in society, and lose little or nothing of their masculinity in the process.[35] The adoption of female clothing, gestures, and voice—if indeed this happened—was "at once a revelation of weakness hidden in strength and a chance for strength to circumscribe the feminine contained within it."[36]

---

[32] See Hallett 1996: 423, who says that the older women in the *Casina*—Cleostrata, Myrrhina, and Pardalisca—are the most attractive, sympathetic, moral characters and assume Plautus' function of playmaker. She even suggests that Plautus might have acted the role of Cleostrata. See also Slater 126–45 and Hallett 1993: 24–26 for the suggestion that Plautus either closely identified with his character Pseudolus (Slater) or perhaps even acted the role (Hallett).

[33] See Annalisa Rei, "Gender, Status, and Comic Justice in the Comedies of Plautus," unpublished paper delivered at the American Philological Association, December, 1994.

[34] See Russo 216.

[35] On this see Loraux.

[36] Loraux 39.

But the Plautine resolution within the play itself is not where the story ends. The highlighting of strong, attractive, female characters throughout the play must give us pause, as should the assigning of authorial hegemony to these women. Plautus seems to be reassuring the free males in the audience that social and political control had been restored to Lysidamus while also reminding them that literary control of dramatic action can rest with individuals who represent the powerless groups (slaves, women, non-citizens).

Furthermore, the crepuscular effects of the play must have continued long after the play was over, after the performative acts on the stage had been viewed by, transmitted to, and absorbed by the spectators. The ontological and/or epistemological uncertainty,[37] which is generated by theatrical performance and which allowed the viewers to engage in role-switching throughout the play, was present both in the bodies on-stage and in the spectating bodies, and these spectating bodies would have left the theater full of the ambiguities that Plautus presents.

[. . .] Plautus' playing with gender, class, and other traditionally-established categories was quite possibly an attempt to disrupt and to question the formalized, hierarchical gender divisions that existed in Roman families,[38] to replace the plots of his Greek predecessors with his own scenes of "domestic anarchy,"[39] and to extend the performative ambiguities from on-stage to off-stage.[40]

---

[37] See Bassi 3.

[38] Bullough and Bullough point out that "as gender divisions became more formalized . . . gender impersonation became a staple of the stage" (226). This is applied here to the nineteenth century, but could equally well be said of Plautus' time.

[39] Anderson 180. See also Joyce Penniston, "*Occisissimus Sum Omnium Qui Vivont*: Death, Metatheatre, and Coherence in Plautus's *Casina*," unpublished paper delivered at the American Philological Association meeting, December, 1993. She maintains that Plautus eliminated the Greek recognition and betrothal scenes in his play and thus focuses on the ruin of Lysidamus, which becomes the play's climax. The relationship of Plautus' *Casina* to Diphilus' *Klêroumenoi* is far from certain. Plautus makes clear in the prologue that he has both used and reworked his model, but the details are unclear. Plautus says that he eliminated the role of the son (64–66), and he perhaps indicates other deletions in lines 1005–06. Various scholars have pointed to the inclusion of homoerotic and transvestite motifs, the episodic plot, and oddities in the prologue and epilogue as unusual or unique in Plautine comedy and have surmised a source in Greek comedy (e.g., Diphilus) or in native Italian drama (Atellan farce or Phlyakes). For discussions, see Ladewig 179–205, 537–40, who posits a mixture of Diphilus with other sources including Atellan farce; see also Cody, who has a good discussion of previous work and postulates (475–76) that Plautus took the transvestite ceremony from Diphilus but cut off the ending including the recognition scene and added other elements—obscenity, farce, homoeroticism—thus placing his emphasis on role-reversal and social upheaval rather than on romance and recognition. See too MacCary 1973; MacCary and Willcock 36–38 n. 2, 188; O'Bryhim; and Arnott, who adds Aristophanes as another possible influence on Plautus.

[40] For role-playing in real life, see Goffman.

I would like to thank Judith Hallett and Paul Allen Miller for their perceptive and helpful comments on this essay.

# WORKS CITED

Ackroyd, P. 1979. *Dressing Up: Transvestism and Drag. The History of an Obsession*. New York.

Anderson, W. S. 1995. "The Roman Transformation of Greek Domestic Comedy." *CW* 88: 171–80.

Arnott, W. G. forthcoming. "Love Scenes in Plautus." In *Scaenica Saravi-Varsoviensia. Beiträge zum Antiken Theater und seinem Nachleben*, ed. J. Axe and W. Görler. Warsaw.

Arthur-Katz, M. 1989. "Sexuality and the Body in Ancient Greece." *Metis* 4: 155–79.

Bassi, K. 1995. "Male Nudity and Disguise in the Discourse of Greek Histrionics." *Helios* 22: 3–22.

Bullough, V. L. and B. Bullough. 1993. *Cross Dressing, Sex, and Gender*. Philadelphia.

Butler, J. 1990. *Gender Trouble: Feminism and the Subversion of Identity*. New York.

———. 1993. *Bodies That Matter: On the Discursive Limits of "Sex"*. New York.

Cody, J. 1976. "The *Senex Amator* in Plautus' *Casina*." *Hermes* 104: 453–76.

Delcourt, M. 1958. *Hermaphrodite: mythes et rites de la bisexualité dans l'antiquité classique*. Paris.

Dolan, J. 1985. "Gender Impersonation Onstage: Destroying or Maintaining the Mirror of Gender Roles?" *Women and Performance* 2: 5–11.

Epstein, J. and K. Straub. 1991a. *Body Guards: The Cultural Politics of Gender Ambiguity*. New York.

———. 1991b. "Introduction: The Guarded Body." In Epstein and Straub 1991a, 1–28.

Faderman, Lillian. 1981. *Surpassing the Love of Men: Romantic Friendship and Love Between Women from the Renaissance to the Present*. New York.

Ferguson, W. S. 1938. "The Salaminioi of Heptaphyla and Sounion." *Hesperia* 7: 36–41.

Foucault, M. 1978. *The History of Sexuality*, Vol. 1: *An Introduction*. Trans. Robert Hurley. New York.

Garber, M. 1992. *Vested Interests: Cross-Dressing and Cultural Anxiety*. New York.

Goffman, E. 1959. *The Presentation of Self in Everyday Life*. Garden City, NY.

Hallett, J. P. 1993. "Plautine Ingredients in the Performance of the *Pseudolus*." *CW* 87: 21–26.

———. 1996. "The Political Backdrop of Plautus's *Casina*." In *Transitions to Empire: Essays in Greco-Roman History, 360–146 B.C.E. in Honor of E. Badian*, ed. Robert W. Wallace and Edward M. Harris. Norman. 409–38.

Halperin, D. M. 1990. *One Hundred Years of Homosexuality*. New York.

Irigaray, L. 1985. *This Sex which Is Not One*. Trans. Catherine Porter with Carolyn Burke. Ithaca. (Originally published as *Ce sexe qui n'en est pas un* [Paris, 1977].)

Ladewig, T. 1845. "Einleitungen und Anmerkungen zu Plautinischen Lustspielen." *RhM* 3: 179–205, 537–40.

Loraux, N. 1990. "Heracles: The Super-Male and the Feminine." In *Before Sexuality: The Construction of Erotic Experience in the Ancient Greek World*, ed. D. M. Halperin, J. J. Winkler, and F. I. Zeitlin. Princeton. 21–52.

MacCary, W. T. 1973. "The Comic Tradition and Comic Structure in Diphilos' *Kleroumenoi*." *Hermes* 101: 194–208.

———. 1975. "The *Bacchae* in Plautus' *Casina*." *Hermes* 103: 459–63.

MacCary, W. T. and M. M. Willcock. 1976. *Plautus*, Casina. Cambridge.

O'Bryhim, S. 1989. "The Originality of Plautus's *Casina*." *AJP* 110: 81–103.

Rabinowitz, N. S. 1993. *Anxiety Veiled: Euripides and the Traffic in Women*. Ithaca.

———. 1998. "Embodying Tragedy: The Sex of the Actor." *Intertexts* 2: 3–25.

Rehm, R. 1992. *Greek Tragic Theatre*, New York.

Richlin, A. 1992. *The Garden of Priapus: Sexuality and Aggression in Roman Humor*. Rev. ed. Oxford and New York.

———. 1993, "Not Before Homosexuality." *The Journal of the History of Sexuality* 3: 523–73.

Russo, M. 1986. "Female Grotesques: Carnival and Theory." In *Feminist Studies/Critical Studies*, ed. Teresa de Lauretis. Bloomington. 213–29.

Sedgwick, Eve Kosofsky. 1985. *Between Men: English Literature and Male Homosocial Desire*. New York.

———. 1990. *Epistemology of the Closet*. Berkeley.

Shapiro, J. 1991. "Transsexualism: Reflections on the Persistence of Gender and the Mutability of Sex." In Epstein and Straub 1991a, 248–79.

Simon, E. 1983. *Festivals of Attica: An Archaeological Commentary*. Madison.

Sissa, G. 1983. "Il corpo della donna: Lineamenti di una ginecologia filosofica." In *Madre materia: Sociologia e biologia della donna greca*, ed. S. Campese, P. Manuli, and G. Sissa. Turin. 81–145.

Slater, Niall. 1985. *Plautus in Performance: The Theatre of the Mind*. Princeton.

Straub, K. 1991. "The Guilty Pleasures of Female Theatrical Cross-Dressing and the Autobiography of Charlotte Charke." In Epstein and Straub 1991a, 142–66.

Tatum, J. 1983. *Plautus: The Darker Comedies*. Baltimore.

Weston, K. 1993. "Do Clothes Make the Woman? Gender, Performance Theory, and Lesbian Eroticism." *Genders* 17: 1–21.

Williams, G. W. 1958. "Some Aspects of Roman Marriage Ceremonies and Ideals." *JRS* 48: 16–29.

Winkler, J. J. 1990. *The Constraints of Desire: The Anthropology of Sex and Gender in Ancient Greece*. New York.

Wright, L. 1935. *Middle-Class Culture in Elizabethan England*. Chapel Hill.

Zeitlin, F. I., ed. 1996a. *Playing the Other: Gender and Society in Classical Greek Literature*. Chicago.

———. 1996b. "Playing the Other: Theater, Theatricality, and the Feminine in Greek Drama." In Zeitlin 1996a, 341–74.

# 20 The Hippocratic "Airs, Waters, Places" on Cross-Dressing Eunuchs: "Natural" yet also "Divine"[†]

## ELINOR LIEBER

In the ancient Greek world the medical practitioner was considered as a craftsman who worked for the good of the public (δημιουργός).[1] As such many were peripatetic: travelling to every part of this realm which, by the fifth century BC, extended from North Africa to the east of the Black Sea. In the Hippocratic Περὶ ἀέρων (PA)[2] the author lays down the principles whereby such a physician might obtain prior knowledge of the sickness endemic to any place. In this way he could familiarise himself with the prevailing situation as soon as possible after arrival (PA I–II).

To this end it was essential to determine the local customs (νόμοι) and way of life (δίαιτα) (including the dietary habits), as well as the many "natural" factors with which they were linked: particularly the climate and its seasonal changes (PA I–II). For, according to the author, these all affect the "seed" (γόνος) of each individual and hence the physical "form" (εἶδος) and the "nature" (φύσις) with which he is born

[†] Originally published in R. Wittern and P. Pellegrin (eds), *Hippokratische Medizin und antike Philosophie: Verhandlungen der VIII. Internationalen Hippokrates-Kolloquiums in Kloster Banz/Staffelstein vom 23. bis 28. September 1993* (Hildesheim 1993), 451–76.
I am indebted to Professor G. Strohmaier of the Berlin-Brandenburgische Akademie der Wissenschaften, Berlin, for allowing me to see and use part of his unpublished translation of Galen's *Commentary* on PA (for which I am thus unable to provide page references), and also for drawing my attention to G. Harig's outstanding medical commentary on PA. I must also thank Dr. Stephanie West, Hertford College, Oxford, for her valuable comments and advice.
  [1] This category excludes the "academic" physicians, see Aristotle, *Politics* 1282a 3–5. For the still earlier "healer", see Homer, *Odyssey* XVII 383ff.
  [2] E. Littré, *Oeuvres complètes d'Hippocrate*, 10 vols., (Paris 1839–1861) (= L.) II 1–93 L.; H. Diller ed. and tr., *Hippocratis De Aere Aquis Locis: Hippokrates Über die Umwelt*, CMG I 1, 2 (Berlin 1970) (= D.). The translations below are my own.

(PA XIII; XIX; XXIII: all *passim*), and their influence continues throughout life.[3]

Examples of such variables are systematically presented for different geographical regions. They are intended to serve as templates for the personal observations of the travelling physician and include many exceptional cases.[4] Among the "European" anomalies are various groups of "Scythian" nomads, living mainly on meat and on milk (PA XVIII: II 68–70 L. = 66, 14–16D.), who then roamed the North Pontic steppe, in what is now known as the southern Ukraine, the Crimea and the area north of the Caucasus Mountains (PA XVII–XXIII).

On the northern shores of the Black Sea the Greek colonists established a number of towns. They maintained good relations with the local inhabitants, not all of whom were nomadic. In referring to these peoples as "Scythians", both the Hippocratic author and Herodotus (I; IV and *passim*)[5] appear to consider them as members of a loose confederation of the different tribes or clans in the region. Their chiefs owed allegiance to a king, who probably belonged to that group of nomads which in Greek sources is called the "Royal Scythians". Around the end of the eighth century BC, these began to migrate to the west and settled in the North Pontic region.[6]

Little is known about the "Royal Scythians" although, according to Herodotus (IV 20), they were "the finest and most numerous of the Scythians, who consider all other Scythians to be their slaves". By his time they apparently dominated that part of the steppe which lay between the Rivers Don on the east and the Danube to the west: a treeless expanse of perennial grass, which extends eastwards as far as

---

[3] On this problem in general see F. Heinimann, *Nomos und Physis* (Basel 1965) *passim*.

[4] It has long been suggested that PA consists of two separate parts (I–XI and XII–XXIV) and that these may be by two different authors (see G. E. R. Lloyd, *Magic, Reason and Experience* (Cambridge 1979) 27 n. 92). Both considerations have been rejected by, for example, H. Grensemann: "Das 24. Kapital von *De aeribus, aquis, locis* und die Einheit der Schrift", *Hermes* 107 (1979) 423–441. The two-part theory is based mainly on the conclusion that the "second part . . . is scarcely medical at all, but rather ethnographical", see *Hippocrates*, I, tr. W. H. S. Jones (Loeb 1962) 66. Throughout my paper I attempt to refute this last view, but as the rest of the question is largely irrelevant to my theme, here PA will be considered as a unity.

[5] *Herodoti historiae* I (Books I–IV), ed. H. B. Rosén (Leipzig 1987).

[6] On the Scythians in general see *inter alia*: E. H. Minns, *Scythians and Greeks* (Cambridge 1913); M. Rostovtzeff, *Iranians and Greeks in South Russia* (Oxford 1922); B. N. Grakow, *Die Skythen* (Berlin 1980); R. Rolle, *Die Welt der Skythen* (Luzern 1980) = *The World of the Scyths*, tr. G. Walls, (London 1989) especially 11–18: a remarkable evocation of their natural environment—at least as one sees it today; K. Marčenko, Y. Vinogradov, "The Scythian period in the northern Black Sea region 750–250 BC", *Antiquity* 63 (1989) 803–813; J. Boardman *et al.* eds., "Assyrian and Babylonian Empires", *Cambridge Ancient History* 2nd. ed., III, 2, (Cambridge 1991) 560–590; *Ancient Civilizations from Scythia to Siberia* I, pt. 1 (1994) (entire issue).

Manchuria. Here the men roamed on horseback with their cattle, while the women and young boys travelled seated in wagons (PA XVIII: II 68 L. = 66, 10–11D.; XX: II 74L. = 70, 14–16D; Herodotus IV 46). In theory such territory was the perfect environment for the nomadic "Royal Scythians". In fact, as related by Herodotus and fleshed out by the author of PA, it brought a terrible disaster upon them.

This story, of great medical interest, is reported by Herodotus in connection with the Scythian campaign against Egypt in the seventh century BC (I 105; IV 67). It refers to the Ἐνάρεες [Enarees]: the name, he says, given by the "Scythians" themselves to those of their people who had become ἀνδρόγυνοι [androgynoi], or "man-women", on account of a θήλεια νοῦσος. They attributed this "mysterious complaint" to their goddess Aphrodite Ourania (IV 59) for, in the course of this campaign, certain "Scythians" had plundered her Temple at Ashkelon in "Syria". Yet the goddess had then taught them to divine. Their descendants continued to suffer from the infliction, and at the time of Herodotus travellers to "Scythia" could still observe their plight. The deity in question was probably Atargatis (Derceto), who was equated with Aphrodite by the Greeks, but if the story be otherwise correct, there must have been many such sufferers in the area, whose appearance was in some way distinctive.

While Herodotus admits that much of his knowledge of peoples and places was gained through informants alone, in some cases he appears to have so assiduously reworked their reports, that these tend to lose all credibility. Thus it has even been questioned whether he himself ever visited the Black Sea.[7] The story of the Enarees and above all, the association of their condition with the Temple of Aphrodite at Ashkelon, have particularly been met with misgivings and even with complete incredulity.[8] However, many of his brief references to the Enarees are corroborated by the far longer and more detailed account in PA (XVIII–XXII). In all aspects of his *Histories* Herodotus particularly stresses the social and cultural factors involved, and PA is unique among ancient medical works in being written essentially from the same point of view. Yet, as will be seen, the two reports are largely complementary and barely overlap. Moreover, the author of PA always refers to the sufferers as Ἀναριεῖs

---

[7] D. Fehling, *Herodotus and his "Sources"*, revised from the German (1971), tr. J. G. Howie, (Leeds 1989) *passim*; S. West, "Herodotus' portrait of Hecataeus", *JHS* 111 (1991) 144–160; O. K. Armayor, "Did Herodotus ever go to the Black Sea?", *Harv. Stud. Class. Phil.* 82 (1978) 45–62.

[8] Fehling (see note 7 above): 88–89.

[Anarieis].⁹ It thus seems unlikely that either author took his information on the "Scythian" disease from the other.¹⁰

As the Greeks held that the frontier between Europe and Asia lay just east of the Sea of Azov (Herodotus IV 45), the Hippocratic author considers that these particular "Scythians" lived so near to Asia that the climate of their area differed from that of the remainder of Europe. It resembled that of Asia with regard to its lack of variation: being excessively cold and damp throughout most of the year, with only a brief summer period (PA XIX). The present climate of this steppe could hardly be considered as uniform. It is typically "continental" in nature and while the winters are bitterly cold, the remaining four months are extremely hot and dry. However, it has recently been claimed, on scientific grounds, that between the ninth and fifth centuries BC the climate of Scythia was much colder and drier than has ever since been the case.¹¹

According to PA, due to the absence of seasonal variation the climate did not exert its normal effect on the "coagulation of the seed", as part of the process of gestation. Hence these nomads were all born very similar in "form": "the men like the men and the women like the women"¹² and, due to the constant cold and damp, even when they grew older they continued to resemble one another (PA XIX: II 72L. = 68, 9–20D. and II 73L. = 70, 1–3D; XXIII: II 82 and 84L. = 76, 5–17D.). This effect of the climate on their "nature" was aggravated by their habits and customs (νόμοι): above all by the sedentary life led by the women and the "abstention from fatigue" of both sexes (PA XIX: II 72L. = 68, 14–15D.; XXIII: II 84 and 86L. =76, 17–78, 8D.).

Hence, their flesh was hairless (ψιλή) and their bodies were gross and so flabby and "watery" that they appeared to lack joints (ἄναρθρα) (PA XIX: II 72L. =68, 15–19 D.). The men were thus too weak to use the bow or spear. To reduce this "moistness" and regain their strength, they were cauterised all over the body (PA XX: II 74L. = 70, 4–11D.). Moreover, although the "Scythians" in general were white-skinned, the complexion of these people was "ruddy" (πυρρός): which the author attributes to the effect of the cold rather than sun (PA XX: II 74L. = 70, 17–19D.).

The women, fat and lazy, suffered from scanty menses and other

⁹ This version will be used here, except where reference is made directly to the text of Herodotus.
¹⁰ Fehling (see note 7 above); 88–89, for example, considers that here PA was the source for Herodotus.
¹¹ Marčenko (see note 6 above).
¹² In view of the early (though gradual) onset of their sex-changes (see below), could the last phrase be a later, and incorrect, gloss on the one immediately preceding it?

gynaecological complaints. Neither sex was prolific and the men lacked libido. This is contrasted with the fertility of the slim and active slave-girls (PA XXI: II 76L. = 72. 8–9D.), who were generally from some different tribe. The author considers that these men could be neither prolific nor lustful on account of their general "nature", allied to their habit of riding. These were the προφάσιες, the "causes" of their sorry condition (PA XXI: II 74 and 76L. = 70, 20–24 and 72, 1 D.).

"Nay more", he continues. "most of the 'Scythians' come to be like eunuchs (εὐνουχίαι)". At first the men hardly notice their condition: attributing it to cold or fatigue. But once they grasp that they are totally impotent, they blame the goddess, put on women's clothes and, denying their manhood, "play the woman": acting and speaking like women. "Such men they call Anarieis" (PA XXII: II 77 and 79L. = 72, 10–12 and 74, 5–11D.). Yet, although they are said to be "like eunuchs", there is no mention of "surgical" castration.[13]

According to PA, this "disease" (πάθος, νοῦσος) (PA XXII *passim*) mainly attacked the "noblest" and "strongest", the horse-riders: terms which seem to denote the "Royal Scythians", as Aristotle confirms (*Nicomachean Ethics* VII 7, 6; 1150b 12–16). The poor, who did not ride, were little affected (PA XXII: II 80L. = 74, 12–14D.).

On account of their riding these nomads also suffered from κέδματα [kedmata],[14] accompanied by "pain in the hips" (ἰσχιάδες)

---

[13] Eunuchs have been reported at all times and places. Many were "surgically" castrated and then sold as slaves, and the mediaeval "castrati" served in the choirs. However, many eunuchs retain their external genital organs and their condition is then due to some hereditary or congenital anomaly, or an acquired, generalised disease. Among the latter, leprosy (Hansen's disease) has always been by far the most common: see E. Lieber, "Leprosy in the lands of the Bible and the demons Bes and Pazuzu. Pt. I. Ancient Egypt and the Bes-image", *Korot* 10 (1993–4) 25–43. This also deals with the antiquity of leprosy, as does M. D. Grmek, *Diseases in the Ancient Greek World*, tr. M. and L. Muellner (Johns Hopkins Press 1989) 152–176.—Today the term eunuch is applied to any man whose permanent sterility is accompanied by other specific, bodily changes, whether or not his external genital organs appear normal. "Surgical" castration refers to the physical *removal* of part or all of the external genital organs, on a voluntary or involuntary basis. As will be seen below, those who are voluntarily castrated are usually sterile already from some other cause.—In all cases the early changes include increasing adiposity, softness of the skin and loss of hair, except from the head. If the condition is initiated before puberty, the secondary sexual characteristics do not appear, so that the voice does not break and the beard does not grow. Eunuchs do not always lose their libido entirely, nor do they necessarily cross-dress (see below).

[14] A long study could (and should) be devoted to the meaning of the term *kedmata*, which is found mainly in PA and several other Hippocratic works, but only a few aspects can be considered here. In her edition of *Die hippokratische Schrift De Morbis I* (Olms, Hildesheim 1974) 192, n. 14 to 1, 3, R. Wittern perspicaciously leaves it untranslated, but quotes an ancient gloss, probably citing Erotian, to the effect that it refers to "some chronic disease condition around the joints and sometimes around the genitals". However, it is rendered as "engorgements des hanches" by Littré (II 79L.), and more recently as "swellings at the joints" ("Airs, Waters, Places", tr. W. H. S. Jones, *Hippocrates* I (Loeb) 127, 131; "Diseases I", tr. P. Potter, *Hippocrates* V (Loeb 1988) 105), or even "von rheumatischen Beschwerden" (Diller 73, 4; 75,

and "gout" and, in severe cases, by lameness and "dragging of the hips"[15] (PA XXII: II 78L. = 72, 18–20D. and II 80L. = 74, 28D.). For these particular complaints the sufferers were early on treated by intensive venesection, which was pursued until they became "sleepy": that is, until they became faint from loss of blood.[16] Sometimes this "cured" them, sometimes it did not, but in either case the author considers it to be the direct cause of their loss of fertility. While it is clear that he had never treated such patients himself, he opines that the "Scythians" cut the veins which run behind the ears and that such a procedure would have led to "destruction of the seed" (PA XXII: II 78L. = 72, 20–74, 4–5D.).[17] Hence, although Herodotus states that the "feminine disease" affected the "Scythians" till his day, he may here have been implicating the traditional use of venesection, rather than the effect of heredity. However, the author of PA hints at the possibility of a congenital factor, by his general reference to the effect of "disease" on the "seed" (PA XIX: II 72L. = 70, 2D.).[18] [. . .]

11): all of which may seem to be its sense from its *context* in PA, although there is nothing of this in the text. This also seems to be the consensus of various ancient comments on the question, mainly reported by Galen in his *Commentaries* on PA and on *Epidemics* V, 15, including those of Galen himself, although all are extremely ambiguous. In his *Commentary* on PA, Galen also suggests that *kedmata* may denote hard or soft swellings in the muscles around the hips. In other words, as used in PA the term seems to indicate some kind of "arthritis"; yet the latter is not specifically mentioned in any ancient definition. In fact, the two are listed as entirely separate entities in the Hippocratic *De morbis* 1, 3, although here the reference to *kedmata* might have been taken from PA.—On the other hand *kedmata* are interpreted as varicose veins (due to riding) in "Airs, Waters, Places", tr. J. Chadwick, W. N. Mann, in *Hippocratic Writings*, ed. G. E. R. Lloyd (Penguin Classics 1983) 165, 166, although this interpretation of the term in PA is not considered by any ancient commentator: some of whom must surely have been aware of this condition. However, the term is used by Aretaeus (*Acute Diseases* 2, 8) to denote some dilatation of vessels in the chest. In view of the other references to *kedmata* not associated with the joints, it seems to me that, when unqualified, as in PA, the term only indicates some form of "swellings", hard or soft, in any part of the body, including varicosities, enlarged glands or buboes, or swollen joints or muscles: as suggested by Liddell and Scott, *Greek–English Lexicon s. v.* Its exact meaning can then only be determined by the context, if at all.

   [15] Reading ἕλκονται, as in the Arabic translation of Galen's *Commentary* on PA. Most translators choose "ulcers of the hips" (ἑλκοῦνται) but, if due to riding, these would surely be more likely to have affected the buttocks.

   [16] Up till quite recent times fainting has served as the criterion when "intensive" venesection was prescribed as treatment for any disease.

   [17] Here PA seems to refer to one prominent Greek theory of the time, whereby the "seed" descended from the brain to the genital organs via the vessels behind the ears and then along the spine. See H. von Staden, *Herophilus: the Art of Medicine in Early Alexandria* (Cambridge 1989) 288–289. According to the Hippocratic Περὶ γονῆς, 2 (VII 472L.), this flow might be obstructed by scarring of the vessels resulting from the phlebotomy. As this suggestion refers specifically to "eunuchs" (in general), it may itself have been based on PA.

   [18] One cannot expect ancient authors to distinguish specifically between hereditary and congenital effects. In connection with this "feminine disease" Aristotle (*Nicomachean Ethics* 1150 b; VII, vii, 6) refers to the "Scythian" "softness" or "weakness of spirit" (μαλακία) as διὰ τὸ γένος. According to PA this formed part of their "nature" and appeared long before the subject was considered to require venesection.

The identity of the "feminine disease" [which is called "divine" in PA is disputed]. The very existence of the Anarieis or Enarees has never been satisfactorily established. While it is now generally agreed that they are one and the same, many commentators still refer only to the brief reports of Herodotus on the latter (I 105; IV 67), which have already been cited above.

Since there is no indisputable evidence that Herodotus had himself seen the Enarees, it has been suggested that he conjured up the idea of their existence from a report by some traveller to the Black Sea, perhaps himself from Asia Minor. On observing "a class of magicians dressed in female attire", the latter was reminded of the male votaries of certain Near Eastern "mother-goddesses", who also dressed as women: the self-castrating eunuchs of Cybele. The "legend" that the Temple of Aphrodite had been sacked by "Scythian" raiders then generated the story of her curse.[19]

Even those who consult the Hippocratic source still tend to centre the debate on its references to "transvestism"[20] and impotence, and ignore its clear depiction of the Anarieis as suffering from some chronic, generalised, physical disease,[21] of which these are only two signs. Moreover, since the Anarieis are said to have descendants, even the impotence is sometimes denied.[22] Hence, up till at least the first part of [the twentieth] century, this *nousos* or *pathos* was largely considered as a "vice", or as a sign of mental or moral degeneration.[23] However, with the appearance of the reports of the Jesup North Pacific Expedition,[24] which told of non-castrated male shamans in north-eastern Siberia, who dressed as women and sometimes divined, the idea came to prevail that the Anarieis were simply "Scythian" shamans.[25]

There is no doubt that at least up to the time of Herodotus, the

---

[19] W. R. Halliday, "A note on the θηλεα νουσος of the Skythians", [*ABSA*] 17 (1910–1911) 94–103. Much more recently, however, it has been suggested by Fehling (see note 7 above) 88–89, that Herodotus reworked the story from PA, with the aid of his own imagination.

[20] The term "transvestite" is widely applied, in a non-medical sense, to any form of cross-dressing although, strictly speaking, it denotes only a psychological anomaly in heterosexuals: a fetish for clothes of the opposite sex. See R. F. Docter, *Transvestites and Transsexuals* (N.Y., 1988) 5–6. It will be seen that it does not apply to the cross-dressing Anarieis.

[21] As, for example, by C. Triebel-Schubert, "Anthropologie und Norm: Der Skythenabschnitt in der hippokratischen Schrift 'Über die Umwelt'", *Medizin-historisches Journal* 25 (1990) 90–103.

[22] See K. Meuli, "Scythica", *Hermes* 70 (1935) 121–176 (see 129), referring to Herodotus I 105.

[23] See discussion by Littré, II xxxix–xlvii L.; Minns 46 (see note 6 above).

[24] Jesup N. Pacific Expedition. *Memoirs of the American Museum of Natural History* (Leyden/N.Y.), VI, W. Jochelson, "The Koryak", 2 pts. (1908), Pt. 1, 52–54; *Ibid.* VII; W. Bogoras, "The Chuckchee", 2 pts. (1904–1909) Pt. 2, 449–456; J. G. Frazer, *The Golden Bough*, 3rd. ed., Pt. IV, "Adonis, Attis, Osiris", 3rd. ed., 2 vols. (London 1914) II, note IV § 1, 253–264.

[25] See Halliday (see note 19 above) and particularly Meuli (see note 22 above). This complex question will be discussed at length in a sequel to the present paper: E. Lieber, "Herodotus and the Hippocratic 'Airs, Waters, Places' on 'Scythian' eunuchs and shamans":

"Scythians" were a powerful and all-conquering force; as manifested, for example, by the Biblical reference to their Asian campaign in the seventh century BC (Jeremiah L: 41–42). Thus scholars have found it hard to believe that "many" of the "Scythians" could have been squat, fat and lethargic, as reported in PA, let alone cross-dressing eunuchs suffering from some chronic disease. Recently it has even been maintained that, despite its "air of scholarly objectivity", the Hippocratic account of the "Scythians" is even less reliable than that of Herodotus, since its Greek author's "unappetizing portrayal of their stature, skin colour and other physical attributes was distorted by his alien sensitivities".[26] Yet, some of the magnificent artefacts found in the area, such as the Gaymanova bowl from the fourth century BC, represent "Scythian" nobles as squat, corpulent and perhaps also somewhat lethargic, although indeed neither eunuchoid nor sick. The above commentator has therefore suggested that such "portly" figures were simply misrepresented in PA as being so "bloated" and "sweaty" that one "could not tell where their joints were".[27]

On the other hand, Galen, in his *Commentary* on PA, unquestioningly accepts the disease of the Anarieis as a medical syndrome, although admitting that, despite his vast clinical experience, he had never seen the condition. He repudiates at length the theory expressed in PA that the eunuchism was caused by the practice of venesection behind the ears, but accepts that it could result from phlebotomy: due, however, to the quantity of blood lost by the "Scythians" by pursuing this treatment to excess.[28]

The idea that the impotence of the Anarieis could in any way have been due to venesection has rightly been rejected by a modern historian of medicine, who has suggested another "medical" cause, associated directly with their continuous riding. In his view it was the result of repeated injury to the testis, as hinted by the Hippocratic author when referring to the continual "jolting" they underwent on their horses (PA XXI: II 74 and 76L. = 70, 23–24D.).[29] However, it is

in preparation. It includes a consideration of certain communicable diseases which may not only lead to a state of cross-dressing eunuchism, but also predispose the sufferer to adopt the role of shaman. These conditions differ entirely from the non-communicable disease of the Anarieis, which is considered in detail below.

[26] Rolle, 1989 (see note 6 above) 54–55.

[27] Rolle, *ibid.*, 59. The bowl is illustrated on plate 7 following p. 64 (German edn. p. 66, above), with a detail on p. 59, fig. 33.

[28] See G. Strohmaier, "Hellenistische Wissenschaft im neugefundenen Galenkommentar zur hippokratischen Schrift 'Über die Umwelt'", *Verhandlungen des IV. Internationalen Galen-Symposiums*, Berlin 1989, ed. J. Kollesch, D. Nickel (Stuttgart 1993) 157–164.

[29] G. Harig, "Zur medizinischen Analyse der hippokratischen Schrift Περὶ ἀέρων ὑδάτων τόπων", *Schriftenreihe der Zeitschrift für die gesamte Innere Medizin* 15 (1961) 23–89 (see 74 and 79–80).

nowadays generally accepted that although trauma from continual riding might indeed diminish fertility, it could not damage a normal testis sufficiently to produce total impotence, let alone a condition of eunuchism.[30] Moreover, like most other theories on the subject, even this "medical" hypothesis ignores the fact that these are only the culmination of a long series of pathological manifestations described by the Hippocratic author.

Yet a century and a half ago Littré, who was himself a physician, proposed a very different "medical" solution. Considering the Enarees and the Anarieis as one, and rejecting the prevalent idea that their condition represented a "vice" (II xxxix–xlvii L.), he considered that they suffered from some hereditary, physical disease, of which impotence was a late manifestation. Hence those "predisposed" to the condition could still have fathered children at an earlier stage, before they became totally sterile (II xliii L.).

Although Littré did not name any specific disease, he suggests that the condition might still have prevailed in his time among the nomadic Nogay "Tatars" in the Caucasus (II 5–6L.). Travellers to the steppes of the Kuban near the Black Sea had reported the existence of cross-dressed eunuchs, whose condition had followed "serious illness" or had appeared in their old age. None of their reports alludes to any kind of "surgical" castration; nor to the possibility that these people were "shamans", but such eunuchs are identified with the sufferers from the "disease" described by Herodotus and in PA, and it is even suggested that they might have been descendants of the "Scythians".[31] Today the latter are thought to be the Ossetes, who now inhabit high valleys in the Caucasus.[32]

---

[30] See below [. . .]. My thanks for their advice on this matter are due to G. J. Fellows and C. W. Burke, consultants to the United Oxford Hospitals in urological surgery and endocrinology, respectively.

[31] See especially, J. Reineggs, *Allgemeine historisch-topographische Beschreibung des Kaukasus*, ed. F. E. Schröder, 2 pts. (St. Petersburg 1796–1797) Pt. I, 266–270. His report is commented upon and supplemented by J. von Klaproth, *Travels in the Caucasus and Georgia Performed in the Years 1807 and 1808*, trans. F. Shoberl (London 1814) 159–161. The latter questions whether these eunuchs actually cross-dressed. He also suggests that the "Mongolian" appearance of these "Tatars", unlike that of the Anarieis, might have been due to subsequent intermarriage of the "Scythians" with "Turkish" peoples.—Somewhat misleadingly, however, Littré (IV ix–xi L.) also claims as a similar condition an extraordinary outbreak of eunuchism in 1799 among the French troops in Egypt, as well as sporadically among the soldiers at home: all reported by Napoleon's chief military surgeon. In fact the latter attributes this condition to very severe alcoholism from the powerful local spirits, probably aggravated by toxic contaminants: and in this he is probably correct. See D. J. Larrey, *Mémoires de Chirurgie militaire, et campagnes* (Paris 1812), II 62–66. On the eunuchoid effects of alcoholism, see C. F. Gastineau, "Alcohol and the endocrine system", in *Metabolic Effects of Alcohol*, ed. P. Avogaro, C. R. Sirtoni, E. Tremoli (Elsevier 1979) 103–110.

[32] See Minns, p. 36; Rolle, 1989, p. 56 (for both see note 6 above).

So who then were the Anarieis? Were they a figment of Greek imagination, or self-castrated votaries of some religious sect, or even "Scythian" shamans? Or were they, as apparently assumed in the Greek texts, a group of "Scythian" eunuchs suffering from a specific disease? Can we surmise that the term θήλεα νοῦσος denotes merely a feminine "constitution" or "nature" and ignore the extraordinary description provided by PA? The fact that this records the progression of such cases, starting with their initiation in the "seed", is particularly significant, since nosology plays so little part in ancient medicine. In fact this account in PA is possibly the only complete clinical *history* of any disease to be found in the Hippocratic Corpus.[33]

No specific medical diagnosis has yet been proposed to account for the syndrome as a whole, as described in PA and briefly by Herodotus and Aristotle. To summarise their views: this condition was specific to a particular group of "Royal Scythian" nomads, in whom it was probably hereditary. Due to the climate and its effect on their "seed", the sufferers were "by nature" physically weak and lethargic. Their bodies were "watery", "showing no joints" (terms which seem to indicate a state of generalised oedema, probably due to heart failure[34]) and the flesh was hairless and soft. The "ruddy" colour of their skin is attributed to the cold, rather than the sun.[35] The women suffered from menstrual disturbances and were not very fertile. Due to their constant riding, the men developed "swellings" (*kedmata*) around the joints, particularly the hips, as well as "gout". While intensive venesection "cured" some of these manifestations, the fertility of the men continued to decline until "most" became eventually "like eunuchs". Once they realised that they were totally impotent, they considered that a deity was responsible for their plight and assumed the clothes and the habits of women, and as such they were known as Anarieis.

[33] Numerous brief references to individual disease-entities are of course found in other Hippocratic writings, as in the *Epidemics*, but such a rare longer account, as of "epilepsy" in [*De morbo sacro*], is neither comprehensive nor applies to that condition alone.

[34] According to Galen in his *Commentary* on PA, their joints were not visible because of the fatness and flabbiness of their bodies, arising from their moist and cold temperament. However, *cf.* PAXV: II60L. = 60, 15–16D., regarding quite a different people, the dwellers along the marshy River Phasis, in whom the joints are also not visible. This too seems to indicate cardiac oedema, although from a different cause: being here accompanied by jaundice, it would seem to result from chronic quartan malaria.

[35] Galen, in his *Commentary* on PA, claims that according to "Hippocrates", in the men (unlike the women) the loss of fertility was due not only to the softness and coldness of the abdomen, but to the coldness of the whole body; although the latter factor was omitted by the scribe. Galen thus considers the redness of the face as evidence of their general cold and moist "temperament" due, in its turn, to the climate, which caused the blood to collect in the extremities.

In the light of modern medicine it seems clear that these eunuchs were suffering from some chronic, physical disease, which certainly could not have been leprosy (see note 13 above). Although it struck its final blow later in life, it began to manifest itself early on and environmental factors influenced its development. This was obviously a peculiar affliction. In fact, eunuchism following a combination of signs such as described in PA seems to point to one condition alone: some endemic form of the syndrome now known as hereditary iron-overload or primary haemochromatosis.[36]

The term haemochromatosis covers a group of diseases with a common basis of "iron overload": a condition which was only identified at the end of the last century. Unless this occurs secondarily to another disease, such as thalassaemia or porphyria,[37] it is due to some genetic defect in the mechanism which controls iron absorption and storage. Depending on the defect, "overload" may occur with a normal dietary intake of iron, or only when excessive quantities of iron are present in the water or food. However, while the genetic anomaly may vary, the basic result in each case is the same: the excess iron cannot be excreted and gradually accumulates in various parts of the body. This may give rise to widespread damage, depending on the organs involved, thereby determining the clinical syndrome. It is probable that certain types of the latter have not yet been distinguished, but the known manifestations are certainly far more frequent and severe in men than in women.

The condition may first present in childhood or only later in life, but early signs are lethargy and loss of body hair. The joints are often affected, particularly those in the hands, the hips and the knees, with characteristic thickening of the soft tissues. The latter brings to mind Galen's suggestion, in his *Commentary* on PA, that the term *kedmata* in PA might indicate hard or soft "swellings" in the muscles around the hips. The main arthritic symptoms are stiffness and pain.[38] Pseudo-gout may also occur. Eventually the syndrome may

[36] On haemochromatosis see *Clinical Disorders of Iron Metabolism*, 2nd edn., ed. V. F. Fairbanks, J. L. Fahey, E. Beutler (N.Y./London 1971) especially 399ff.; *Copeman's Textbook of the Rheumatic Diseases*, 6th edn., ed. J. T. Scott, 2 vols. (Edinburgh 1986) II 938 and 952; M. J. Pippard, "Haemochromatosis", in *Oxford Textbook of Medicine*, 2nd. edn., ed. D. J. Weatherall, J. G. G. Ledingham, D. A. Warrell, 2 vols. (Oxford 1987) II 19.87–19.91; N. D. C. Finlayson, "Hereditary (primary) haemochromatosis", *British Medical Journal* 301 (1990) 350–351; B. R. Bacon, "Causes of iron overload", *New England Journal of Medicine* 326 (1992) 126–127.

[37] PA records no signs, such as blistering of the skin provoked by sunlight, to justify a "diagnosis" of porphyria cutanea tarda associated with haemochromatosis.

[38] See B. L. Hazleman, "Arthritis in haemochromatosis", in Weatherall (see note 36 above), 16.5.5. Note the arthritic fingers of the "portly" "Scythian" nobleman on the Gaymanova bowl (depicted in Rolle, see note 27 above).

culminate in testicular atrophy, loss of libido and total impotence, but cross-dressing does not seem to be reported in modern eunuchs of this kind. Chronic heart-failure, causing generalised oedema, often leads to death. Typical of the condition is a brownish pigmentation of the skin, which could correspond with the "ruddy" complexion of the "Royal Scythians". If this had indeed been caused by the cold, as suggested in PA, it would surely have affected the other nomads of the region, who, however, are described as "white-skinned". The only serious features of haemochromatosis not mentioned by the Hippocratic author are diabetes mellitus and cirrhosis of the liver; neither of which were then recognised as pathological entities. [. . .]

Moreover, intensive blood-letting is still the only known treatment for haemochromatosis in general and, when initiated early (as by the "Scythians"), it may prevent the onset of the potentially fatal manifestations in the liver and heart. However, as also mentioned in PA, it is only partly successful, and does not affect the sexual changes, once they have occurred.[39]

Yet, even though a genotype for haemochromatosis (particularly for the heterozygote condition) is today very common among white persons of European descent, the condition is often not diagnosed as such, but is labelled as "diabetes", or "arthritis".[40] Just as described in PA, the clinical picture depends not only on the specific genetic "predisposition" but also on its interaction with environmental factors. *Endemic* forms of the condition, proved to be associated with iron-overload, have so far been reported only from Ethiopia and from parts of Africa south of the Sahara. Here the genetic defect appears to differ from that found in white persons with the sporadic condition. In Ethiopia the condition affects those who live on a staple diet of grain rich in iron. Elsewhere in Africa it is attributed to an abnormally high intake from the iron pots used for brewing home-made

---

[39] W. H. Crosby, "A history of phlebotomy therapy for haemochromatosis", *American Journal of Medical Sciences* 301 (1991) 28–31.

[40] Thus it has been suggested that the condition known as Kashin-Beck or Urov disease, which has hitherto been considered as a form of endemic arthritis, is in fact a form of haemochromatosis. Little is known of this condition in the West, but it has long been highly prevalent along the Amur River, in Manchuria and Eastern Siberia, and probably elsewhere in China and the former USSR. It is probably associated with the presence of excess iron and other heavy metals in the water supply, although it has also been ascribed to fungal infestation of the grain. If a genetic defect is involved, it probably differs from those underlying other types of haemochromatosis. See W. G. Schipatschoff, "Die Kaschin-Beck Krankheit (Osteoarthritis endemica)", *Deutsches Archiv für klinische Medizin* 170 (1931) 133–145; K. Hiyeda, "The cause of Kashin-Beck's disease", *Japanese Journal of Medical Sciences*, Pt. V, Pathology, 4 (1939) 91–106; L. Sokoloff, "The history of Kashin-Beck disease", *New York State Journal of Medicine* (June, 1989) 343–351.

beer. Any sex-changes reported are mild, even though they may be aggravated by additional liver-damage due to chronic alcoholism.[41]

With regard to the nomadic "Scythians", whatever their genotype, there seems little doubt that their iron intake was exceptionally high. For during and after the time of Herodotus they inhabited areas which contain some of the richest iron deposits in the whole of the former USSR: itself the world's chief source of iron. This was particularly the case around Krivoy Rog, along the bend of the River Dnieper in the southern Ukraine; as well as in the Crimean Kerch Peninsula, in the Caucasus (including the Kuban where, as noted above, a condition similar to that affecting the Anarieis was reported two centuries ago) and in the Altai region of Central Asia. Here much of the iron lies near the surface and is leached out by the rivers in colloid suspension,[42] so that excessive quantities enter the food and the drinking water.

While PA does not specifically associate iron with the Scythian "constitution", it claims that in general iron-containing water is only less harmful for drinking than the stagnant water of marshes (PA II 30L. = 36, 26–27D.). Thus it might seem anomalous that Herodotus specifically notes that the water of the River Borysthenes (the Dnieper) was "most sweet to drink, flowing clear"; unlike the other rivers of "Scythia", which were "turbid" (IV 53). Yet, even in 1980, both parts of this statement apparently still remained valid[43]: for iron purifies the water and is used for the purpose today. In such areas the clinical picture may be affected by the presence of other heavy metals and trace elements, but relatively little is known of the influence of these on the body, whether alone or in conjunction with iron.

It must, however, be stressed once again that iron in the diet will produce adverse effects solely in those born with a particular genotype. If only the "Royal Scythians" were affected and since few of them could have been poor, the Hippocratic author might easily conclude that the condition attacked mainly the wealthy: those who rode (PA XXII). Yet it is more likely that the poor, who did not ride, mainly belonged to other clans, with quite a different genetic inheritance.

Even so, the expression of the inborn "nature" of the "Royal

[41] Fairbanks *et al.* (see note 36 above) 404–406; V. Gordeuk *et al.*, "Iron overload in Africa: Interaction between a gene and dietary iron content", *New England Journal of Medicine* 326 (1992) 95–100.

[42] *The Iron Ore Deposits of Europe*, ed. H. W. Walther, A. Zitzmann, 2 vols. (Hanover 1977), I, 356; *Reallexikon der Germanischen Altertumskunde* V, Lief, 5–6, ed. V. Grasshof, H. Seemann (Berlin 1984), *s.v.* "Dnjepr IV, Archäologisches" (R. Rolle) 515–523, especially Abb. 62, p. 516, and Abb. 66, p. 522.

[43] Grakow (see note 6 above) 11.

Scythians" would have been reinforced by environmental factors, to which they were continuously exposed by their nomadic way of life. Thus, their diet of meat and mare's milk (PA XVIII: II 68 and 70L. = 66, 14–16D.) provided a relatively low intake of phytates but an abundance of vitamin C: both of which facilitate the absorption of iron.[44] Moreover, alcohol greatly exacerbates the condition and the "Scythians" in general were notorious for their drunken behaviour (Herodotus VI 84).[45] Even though the alcohol content of fermented mare's milk is relatively low, it was drunk by these nomads in large quantities, while the rich also imported expensive Greek wine.

Yet, while the interaction of innate and environmental factors is considered by the author of PA as predisposing to the "disease" of the Anarieis, like the "Scythians" themselves he does not recognise the syndrome as a whole: not only because he lacked personal experience of the condition, but because of the absence of modern nosological concepts in ancient Greek medicine (as is still the case in most non-western cultures). Thus, prominent manifestations earlier in life, such as lethargy or skin pigmentation, which are now recognised as pro-dromal signs of the condition [. . .], are considered as signs of a par-ticular "nature". Even manifestations of incipient eunuchism, such as "hairlessness" with increasing adiposity, are also accepted in this way. Only the final transformation into "Anarieis" is regarded as a physi-cal "disease". [. . .]

It has been noted above that although secondary sex-changes com-monly occur in the various conditions now considered to be due to iron-overload, there are no modern reports of such severe eunuchism associated with cross-dressing as are described in PA and even in accounts by later travellers. These "historical" reports may reflect a type of genetic defect which affected the sex-hormones more severely than in present-day cases of "iron-overload". Moreover, while the womanish "nature" was genetically and hormonally influenced, this was not necessarily the case with the cross-dressing. As PA tells us (XXII: II 78L. = 74, 7–11D.), once the Anarieis realised that they were no longer "men", they felt obliged to adopt the role of women. This was possibly a socio-cultural act: perhaps they were even ritually instructed by the deity to acknowledge their devirilisation in this way.[46] [. . .]

If the descriptions of the Anarieis themselves, which seem so bizarre at first sight, in fact largely ring true, a case exists for reassess-

[44] Fairbanks *et al.* (see note 36 above) 83.
[45] See also Rolle (1989, see note 6 above) 93.
[46] See Frazer (see note 24 above) 255.

ing the rest of the story: the relationship of these unfortunates to some unspecified deity, as asserted in PA, and the association of their condition with the Temple of Aphrodite at Ashkelon, as Herodotus reports.[47]

Since the Anarieis and Enarees are apparently one, the goddess referred to in PA was the Aphrodite Ourania of Herodotus, or her equivalent in the "Scythian" pantheon.[48] Hence it might simply be concluded from our texts that these unfortunates logically considered the hereditary late onset of impotence as punishment for some sin against the goddess of love. This they then identified with the legendary plunder by their ancestors of the Temple of Aphrodite at Ashkelon.

Can we, however, so lightly dismiss the possibility that some genuine connection existed between the disease of the Anarieis and this temple, or even with the goddess herself? We do not know whether the desecration actually took place, but neither is there reason to doubt it.[49] Nor is it likely that these "Scythians" would have admitted to a crime of this kind, had it not formed a part of their tradition.

Before examining this matter any further, it is necessary to consider certain general questions of eunuchism. According to its modern definition (see note 13 above), both Anarieis and Enarees were eunuchs. Yet, as has been seen, PA describes them only as "like" eunuchs and Herodotus calls them *androgynoi*, a non-specific term which in this case clearly bears the same meaning, but elsewhere could refer, for example, to hermaphrodites.

While haemochromatosis was never an important cause of the condition, as noted above (note 13) most cases have probably always been due to generalised diseases such as leprosy, or else to congenital anomalies. In former times, however, as defined in Matthew XIX: 12,

---

[47] Dr. S. West, Hertford College, Oxford (personal communication), considers it unlikely that "Scythian" oral traditions would have preserved information, in a form recognisable by Greeks, of any such deed committed some two centuries earlier. This was, however, associated with the "feminine disease" which, as has been seen, was no ordinary illness, but a strange and terrible affliction—for a warrior tribe in particular—and which, even in the time of Herodotus, still continued to ravage these people.

[48] It has been suggested by [M. Pohlenz, *Hippokrates und die Begründung der Wissenschaftlichen Medizin* (Berlin 1938)] 45 that the claim in PA that the gods are pleased by the veneration of men (II 80L. = 74, 17ff.D.) may echo a similar declaration by Aphrodite in the Prologue to the *Hippolytus* of Euripides. Although, as earlier noted by U. von Wilamowitz-Moellendorff, in his edition *Euripides Hippolytus* (Berlin 1891) 187, note on 7–8, this may simply have been a well-known saying of the time, the association here with Aphrodite would corroborate the idea that she is the deity referred to in PA.

[49] As does Fehling (see note 7 above) 88–89, for example, who derides the report of Herodotus.

only those were termed eunuchs who had been "surgically" castrated in some way, or in whom the external genital organs were absent or grossly abnormal from birth. If the genitals were fully present and the condition was thus due to disease, like the Anarieis they were only "like eunuchs". Yet, apart from their genital organs, eunuchs of all types present a similar and very typical appearance (see Aristotle, *Generation of animals* 766a 25), depending mainly on the age of onset of their state. Thus, whatever the underlying cause, in areas where eunuchism is common it can easily be recognised by the public, so that Greek travellers to "Scythia" could have been able to identify the Enarees.

However, these two ancient categories evoked an ambivalent reaction in society and even different attitudes among the sufferers themselves. On account of their very disability, "true" eunuchs have always been employed to guard the women's quarters and this Greek appellation literally means "the keeper of the bed". In this way they became privy to intimate secrets, which perhaps originally accounted for the fact that some reached high rank. Even so, like other disabled persons, they were more often rejected by the public.[50]

Some eunuchs, not necessarily hermaphrodites, consider themselves as being neither male nor female, but rather as belonging to a "third sex", and in certain societies they are expected to dress in this manner.[51] Yet, while most eunuchs retain their men's clothing, some cross-dress because they have always felt themselves to be women in every possible way, except for the presence of what they consider as an unwanted anatomical anomaly. In fact, they may so greatly desire to be like women that they contemplate "surgical" castration. Not all actually go to such lengths, since the operation is expensive, as well as painful and dangerous. Such persons, who are now medically classified as "trans-sexuals",[52] are often affected by some disorder of chromosomal sex and the resultant hormonal effects may differ from those of the Anarieis, who, like those suffering from haemochromatosis today, express no wish to be "surgically" castrated.

True "trans-sexuals" are common in every part of the world and

---

[50] See, for example, Lucian, *Eunuchus* 6, 8, 10 in *Luciani Opera*, ed. M. D. Macleod, III (Oxford 1980) 47, for a second century AD discussion as to whether eunuchs by birth should be allowed to teach philosophy in Greek society. However satirical the author's intention, he is clearly reflecting a prevalent view, when one participant maintains that they should be excluded even from the temple and all other public places, since a eunuch is "neither a man nor a woman but something hybrid and monstrous, alien to nature".

[51] As among the *xanith* of Oman, see U. Wikan, *Behind the Veil in Arabia* (Baltimore 1982).

[52] See H. I. Kaplan, B. J. Sadock, *Modern Synopsis of Comprehensive Textbook of Psychiatry* IV, 4th edn. (Baltimore 1985) 434–435.

always appear to have been so. In India, for example, they are known as *hijras* or "natural" eunuchs and as such are considered as outcasts. Thus many still live in communities of their own, often including a "transvestite" brothel which is run by a "madam" of their kind; and all come under the "patronage" and care of a specific goddess at some temple.[53] Under these auspices they can undergo castration or even perform the operation on themselves. They tend to possess a flamboyant and extrovert nature: manifested in their female dress and adornments. Hence, they have always earned their bread as "female" entertainers of all kinds (accomplishments also utilised by shamans). While prostitution and begging often play a prominent part, they may be practised on behalf of the temple. [. . .]

Little is known of the true roles of pagan sanctuaries in Western Asia and Europe. Certainly many of the deities concerned were credited with protective or medical functions.[54] In certain temples the apparently "female" devotees may well have been cross-dressing eunuchs, along the lines of the "Galli" of the ancient Near East, whose cult extended throughout the Roman Empire. These are said to have castrated themselves in mad, religious frenzy and then dedicated their lives, as temple-servants or beggars, to Attis (perhaps one of their predecessors) or, more often, to the goddess Cybele.[55] Yet, it seems probable that some, if not all, of these votaries were in fact sterile trans-sexuals. Under the influence of alcohol or drugs to still the pain, they had willingly castrated themselves, because they desired to be women, in form as well as in spirit.[56] [. . .]

It thus seems possible that in the ancient Near East certain sanctuaries protected eunuchs of particular types. While Cybele may have cared for trans-sexuals, Aphrodite (or her Near Eastern equivalent) was responsible for those such as the Anarieis, resulting from inborn "nature" and disease. [. . .]

[53] J. Shortt, "The Kojahs of Southern India", *Journal of the Anthropological Institute of Great Britain* 2 (1873) 402–407; P. F. Fawcett, "On Basivis", *Journal of the Anthropological Society of Bombay* 2 (1891) 322–353. On the modern Indian version, see T. McGirk, "Altered states", *The Independent Magazine*, 22.5.93, 28–33.

[54] In the first century AD sick slaves were confided to the care of Asklepios on the Tiber Island in Rome. This must certainly have included medical care. See M. Besnier, *L'Ile Tibérine dans l'antiquité* (Paris 1902) 207. The sanctuary was eventually replaced by true hospitals, which exist on the site to this day.

[55] Ovid, *Fasti* IV, 179–246; Lucian, *De Syria Dea* 44: 15, 27, 32 (see note 50 above); H. Graillot, *Le culte de Cybèle . . . à Rome* (Paris 1912) 287–319; Frazer (see note 24 above). In a Greek inscription found in the Near East, a Gallus boasts of the money he has raised by begging for a temple of the Dea Syria: see C. Fossey, "Inscriptions de Syrie", *BCH* 21 (1897) 39–65.

[56] See Josephus, *Jewish Antiquities* IV 290–291 [40], who, although totally unsympathetic to the rites of the "Galli", yet attributes their sex-changes to "the effeminacy of their soul": thus apparently recognising that they are not simply religious fanatics.

## CONCLUSION

Herodotus, Aristotle and the author of the Hippocratic PA all describe the so-called Enarees or Anarieis as members of a "Royal" group of "Scythian" nomads, who were hereditarily afflicted by a "feminine disease". PA discusses in great detail the cause and progress of this physical illness, whereby "many" of these people eventually became cross-dressing eunchs, although in this case "surgical" castration is not mentioned.

Until now any "medical" interpretation of this "disease" has largely been rejected or ignored. It is considered that these people are homosexuals of some kind, or that they are self-castrating votaries of a deity, or, according to the most popular view, that they served as the "shamans" of the "Scythians". Yet, when taken together, the ancient accounts present a true-to-life picture of an endemic form of a hereditary disease now known as haemochromatosis. Among other manifestations, it may culminate in total impotence and eunuchism. The condition occurs only in persons with a genetically-determined defect in the mechanism which controls the absorption of iron; particularly if they are exposed to an excess of iron in their diet. Venesection is still the main treatment today. Unlike certain other types of "natural" eunuch, such sufferers express no desire for castration. It is postulated that among the "Scythians" only the "Royal" clan possessed this deleterious trait: for apparently they alone were affected when, around the eighth century BC, the "Scythians" migrated to the iron-rich regions to the north and the east of the Black Sea.

Even if their aetiological inferences are not necessarily correct, the observations of these ancient authors are thus remarkably shrewd and the interaction of "natural" innate and environmental factors are rightly stressed in PA. However, in addition to these "rational" considerations, this author not only maintains that this disease, like all others, is divine, but also nowhere denies that in this case a sin against some deity was the ultimate cause of the condition. According to Herodotus the "Scythians" believed it to have been inflicted upon them for ever by the goddess Aphrodite, after their ancestors plundered her temple at Ashkelon in the seventh century BC.

It is tentatively suggested that certain ancient Near Eastern temples served as sanctuaries for the disabled, including eunuchs of various kinds, some of whom were never castrated, while others even castrated themselves. The temple at Ashkelon may have sheltered cross-dressing eunuchs (perhaps even those afflicted with haemochromatosis), who were then observed by the "Scythian" attackers. As the number of Anarieis gradually increased, their condition became attributed to this ancestral sin. But while Aphrodite engendered their illness, as it steadily progressed according to the workings of "nature", she offered them protection as well.

# Intellectual Chronology

This list includes ancient texts, images, and objects singled out for discussion in the chapters of this book as well as significant or influential modern works of scholarship. (We have added brief descriptions of the more unfamiliar of these.) Many ancient dates are approximate only.

BC

| | |
|---|---|
| 6000–3000 | Neolithic "Mother Goddess" figurines |
| 725 | Homer, *Odyssey* |
| 725–700 | Courtyard houses at Zagora on Andros |
| 700 | Hesiod, *Works and Days* |
| 430–420 | Herodotus, *Histories* |
| 425–350 | Hippocratic Corpus |
| 425 | Aristophanes, *Acharnians* |
| 411 | Aristophanes, *Lysistrata, Thesmophoriazusae* |
| 408–406 | Euripides, *Bacchae* |
| 393–392 | Aristophanes, *Ecclesiazusae* |
| 400–380 | Lysias 1 |
| 385–371 | Xenophon, *Oeconomicus, Memorabilia, Symposium* |
| 384–378 | Plato, *Symposium* |
| 350 | Plato, *Laws* |
| 345 | Aeschines, *Against Timarchus* |
| 340–330 | Funerary *lekythos* for Theophraste, Athens |
| 335–322 | Aristotle, *Generation of Animals, Nicomachean Ethics, Politics* |
| 185 | Plautus, *Casina* |
| 56 | Cicero, *In Defence of Caelius* |
| 30 | Cornelius Nepos, *Lives* |
| 23 | Restoration of Temple of Apollo Sosianus, Rome |
| 20 | Villa of the Farnesina, Rome |
| 2 | Temple of Mars *Ultor*, Forum of Augustus, Rome |

AD

| | |
|---|---|
| 40 | Seneca the Elder, *Controversiae, Suasoriae* |
| 60 | Persius, *Satires* |
| 95 | Quintilian, *Training in Oratory* |
| 100–150 | Soranus of Ephesus, *Gynecology* |
| 150–200 | Artemidorus, *On Dreams* |
| 450 | Caelius Aurelianus, *On Chronic and Acute Diseases* |
| 1672 | Christoph Rahnisch, *De cura virginum apud veteres* (introduces idea of the seclusion of Greek women) |
| 1689 | Johan Philipp Pfeiffer, *Opus Antiquitatum Graecarum gentilium sacrarum, politicarum, militarium et oeconomicarum* (first refers to the Oriental seclusion of Greek women) |
| 1699 | John Potter, *Archaeologia Graeca, or The Antiquities of Greece* (includes influential account of seclusion of Greek women) |
| 1762 | Jean-Jacques Rousseau, *Émile* (praises ancient separation of spheres of men and women) |
| 1787 | C. de Pauw, *Recherches philosophiques sur les Grecs* (develops idea of Oriental seclusion of Greek women) |
| 1788 | Christoph Meiners, *Geschichte des weiblichen Geschlechts I* (argues that Greek women were secluded as early as Homer) |
| 1796 | K. A. Böttiger, "Waren die Frauen in Athen Zuschauerinnen bei den dramatischen Vorstellung?," *Die Teutscher Merkur* (reprinted in J. Sillig [ed.], *Kleine Schriften* [Dresden and Leipzig 1837]: 295–307) (denies Athenian women attended the theatre) |
| 1824 | F.-K. Forberg,"Apophoreta" (appendix to *Hermaphroditus*) (collects Greek and Roman texts on sexual activity) |
| 1830 | Friedrich Jacobs, *Beiträge zur Geschichte des weiblichen Geschlechtes* (argues that Greek women were neither denigrated or secluded) |
| 1861 | J. J. Bachofen, *Das Mutterrecht* |
| 1861 | Henry Maine, *Ancient Law* |
| 1864 | Denis-Numa Fustel de Coulanges, *La cité antique* |
| 1877 | Lewis H. Morgan, *Ancient Society* |
| 1884 | Friedrich Engels, *The Origin of the Family, Private Property and the State* |
| 1925 | A. W. Gomme, "The position of women in Athens in |

the fifth and fourth centuries BC," *Classical Philology* 20 (1925): 1–25

1928  Paul Brandt, *Sittengeschichte Griechenlands* (long the standard discussion of ancient Greek sexual life)

1935  Euios Lênaios, *Aporrhêta* (the Greek erotic vocabulary)

1938  Theodor Hopfner, *Das Sexualleben der Griechen und Römer* I (ancient views on the anatomy and physiology of the genitals)

1951  H. D. F. Kitto, *The Greeks*

1956  Marie Delcourt, *Hermaphrodite*

1964  K. J. Dover, "Eros and nomos (Plato, *Symposium* 182A– 185C)," *Bulletin of the Institute of Classical Studies*, 11 (1964): 31–42

1975  Sarah B. Pomeroy, *Goddesses, Whores, Wives, and Slaves: Women in Classical Antiquity*

1975  Jeffrey Henderson, *The Maculate Muse: Obscene Language in Attic Comedy*

1976  Michel Foucault, *Histoire de la sexualité. I. La volonté de savoir*

1978  K. J. Dover, *Greek Homosexuality*

1990  D. M. Halperin, J. J. Winkler, and F. I. Zeitlin (eds), *Before Sexuality: The Construction of Erotic Experience in the Ancient Greek World*

1995  Maud W. Gleason, *Making Men: Sophists and Self-Presentation in Ancient Rome.*

# Further Reading

The Greeks and Romans saw gender in the same places we see sex—everywhere. Under the circumstances, it is virtually impossible to avoid reading further on this book's subjects. Necessarily selective in any case, what follows is further restricted to work in English. More material may be found in the notes to the Introduction.

The fullest collection of ancient texts on sexual activity is still F.-K. Forberg, "Apophoreta" (first published in 1824 as an appendix to his *Hermaphroditus*); it is most accessible in the edition with English translation by Viscount Julian Smithson (Manchester 1884). Greek and Roman sex manuals are discussed by H. N. Parker, "Love's body anatomized: the ancient erotic handbooks and the rhetoric of sexuality," in A. Richlin (ed.), *Pornography and Representation in Greece and Rome* (New York and Oxford 1992): 90–111, and H. King, "Sowing the field: Greek and Roman sexology," in R. Porter and M. Teich (eds), *Sexual Knowledge, Sexual Science: The History of Attitudes to Sexuality* (Cambridge 1994) 29–46. R. W. Hooper, *The Priapus Poems* (Urbana and Chicago 1999), collects and translates an important Latin genre. J. M. Snyder, *Lesbian Desire in the Lyrics of Sappho* (Columbia 1997), discusses a single celebrated author. Catherine Johns, *Sex or Symbol: Erotic Images of Greece and Rome* (Austin 1982), is witty and well illustrated. M. F. Kilmer, *Greek Erotica on Attic Red-Figure Vases* (London 1993), engages cultural and interpretative issues whose relevance extends beyond the genre he catalogues. Much essential source material on gender is translated in M. R. Lefkowitz and M. R. Fant, *Women's Life in Greece and Rome*, 2nd edn (Baltimore 1992).

The introduction (3–20) to D. M. Halperin, J. J. Winkler, and F.I. Zeitlin (eds), *Before Sexuality: The Construction of Erotic Experience in the Ancient Greek World* (Princeton 1990)—itself an important collection—includes a good brief account of modern scholarship on ancient sexuality. J. Blok offers a more extended overview of work on gender since the nineteenth century in "Sexual asymmetry: a historiographical essay," in J. Blok and P. Mason (eds), *Sexual Asymmetry: Studies in Ancient Society* (Amsterdam 1987): 1–57. (The work of Schnurr-Redford and Katz excerpted in this volume takes the story back into the seventeenth and eighteenth centuries.) A number of review articles survey more recent work: M. Arthur-Katz, "Sexuality and the body in ancient Greece," *Metis*, 4 (1989): 155–79; M. Golden, "Thirteen years of homosexuality (and other recent work on sex, gender and the body in ancient Greece)," *EMC*, 35 (1991): 327–40; D. Cohen, "Sex, gender and sexuality in ancient Greece," *Classical Philology*, 87 (1992): 145–60; R. M. Karras, "Active/passive, acts/passions: Greek and Roman sexualities," *AHR*, 105 (2000): 1250–65. *The Garden of Priapus: Sexuality and Aggression in Roman Humor* has been enhanced by the introduction (xiii-xxxiii) on trends in the study of ancient sex and gender which Amy Richlin has added to her second edition (New York 1992). Mary Beard, "Re-reading (Vestal) virginity" (in R. Hawley and B. Levick [eds], *Women in Antiquity: New Assessments* [London and New York 1995]: 166–77), affords an unusual glimpse of a scholar reviewing and revising her own influential account of gender ("The sexual status of Vestal Virgins," *Journal of Roman Studies,* 70 [1980]: 12–27).

For the language of sex, see J. Henderson, *The Maculate Muse: Obscene Language in Attic Comedy* (New Haven 1975), and J. N. Adams, *The Latin Sexual Vocabulary* (Baltimore 1982). Special studies are devoted to homosexuality (K. J. Dover, *Greek Homosexuality*, 2nd edn [Cambridge, MA 1989]); C. A. Williams, *Roman Homosexuality: Ideologies of Masculinity in Classical Antiquity* [New York and Oxford 1999]). For sources, see T. K. Hubbard (ed.), *Homosexuality in Greece and Rome* (Berkeley and Los Angeles 2003). Devotees of heterosexuality must make do with the article by Holt Parker in the latest edition of the *Oxford Classical Dictionary* (1996: 702–3). Similarly, Sarah Pomeroy's pathbreaking *Goddesses, Whores, Wives and Slaves: Women in Classical Antiquity* (New York 1975)—still stimulating—soon had many successors (for example, E. Fantham, H. P. Foley, N. G. Kampen, S. B. Pomeroy, and H. A. Shapiro, *Women in the Classical World: Image and Text* [New York and Oxford 1994]) but had to wait twenty years for comparable work on men and masculinity (M. W. Gleason, *Making Men: Sophists and Self-Presentation in Ancient Rome* [Princeton 1995]; K. Bassi, *Acting Like Men: Gender, Drama and Nostalgia in Ancient Greece* [Ann Arbor 1998]), and Suzanne Dixon's *The Roman Mother* (London and Sydney 1988) has yet to find a worthy mate. Otto

Brendel's long article, "The scope and temperament of erotic art in the Greco-Roman world" (in T. Bowie and C. V. Christenson (eds), *Studies in Erotic Art* [New York 1977]: 3–107), is a classic. Contemporary work on sexuality and gender concentrates on some particularly problematic intersections: rape (S. Deacy and K. F. Peirce [eds], *Rape in Antiquity* [London 1997]), medical science (L. Dean-Jones, *Women's Bodies in Classical Greek Science* [Oxford 1994]; H. King, *Hippocrates' Woman: Reading the Female Body in Ancient Greece* [London and New York 1998]; R. Flemming, *Medicine and the Making of Roman Women: Gender, Nature and Authority from Celsus to Galen* [Oxford 2000]), and prostitution (J. Davidson, *Courtesans and Fishcakes: The Consuming Passions of Classical Athens* [London 1997]; T. A. J. McGinn, *Prostitution, Sexuality and the Law in Ancient Rome* [New York 1998]). Foucault's influence is assessed in D. Larmour, P. A. Miller, and C. Platter (eds), *Rethinking Sexuality: Foucault and Classical Antiquity* (Princeton 1998), is evident in its most attractive form in J. J. Winkler, *The Constraints of Desire: The Anthropology of Sex and Gender in Ancient Greece* (New York 1990), and is subjected to a (politically in)corrective by B. S. Thornton, *Eros: The Myth of Ancient Greek Sexuality* (Boulder 1997). In a world where most roads lead to Greece, the collection edited by Judith P. Hallett and Marilyn B. Skinner puts Rome back on the map (*Roman Sexualities* (Princeton 1997).

# Bibliography

Adams, B. D. 1985. "Age, structure and sexuality: reflections on the anthropological evidence on homosexual relations": In E. Blackwood (ed.), *Anthropology and Homosexual Behaviour (Journal of Homosexuality*, 11.3–4): 19–33.

Adams, J. N. 1982. *The Latin Sexual Vocabulary*. Baltimore.

Adams, J.N. 1984. "Female speech in Latin comedy", *Antichthon*, 18: 43–77.

Ahl, F. 1988. "*Ars est celare artem* (art in puns and anagrams engraved)." In J. Culler (ed.), *On Puns*. Oxford: 17–43.

Ajootian, A. 1997. "The only happy couple: hermaphrodites and gender." In A. O. Koloski-Ostrow and C. L. Lyons (eds), *Naked Truths: Women, Sexuality, and Gender in Classical Art and Archaeology*. London and New York: 220–42.

Alston, R. 1998. "Arms and the man: soldiers, masculinity and power in Republican and Imperial Rome." In L. Foxhall and J. Salmon (eds), *When Men Were Men: Masculinity, Power and Identity in Classical Antiquity*. London and New York: 205–23.

Antonaccio, C. M. 2000. "Architecture and behavior: building gender into Greek houses," *Classical World*, 93: 517–33.

Ardener, S. (ed.) 1993. *Women and Space: Ground Rules and Social Maps*. Oxford.

Arthur-Katz, M. 1989. "Sexuality and the body in Animal Greece," *Metis*, 4: 155–79.

Arvanitopoulos, A. 1928. *Graptai stelai Demetriados-Pagason*. Athens.

Aubert, J.-J. 1989. "Threatened wombs: aspects of ancient uterine magic," *GRBS*, 30: 412–49.

Bachofen, J. J. 1861. *Das Mutterrecht*. Repr. Basel 1948.

Bakhtin, M. 1981. *The Dialogic Imagination*. Trans C. Emerson and M. Holquist. Austin.

Balsdon, J. P. V. D. 1979. *Romans and Aliens*. Chapel Hill.

Bassi, K. 1997. "Orality, masculinity and the Greek epic," *Arethusa* 30: 315–40.

Bassi, K. 1998. *Acting Like Men: Gender, Drama and Nostalgia in Ancient Greece*. Ann Arbor.

Beard, M. 1980. "The sexual status of Vestal Virgins," *Journal of Roman Studies*, 70: 12–27.

Beard, M. 1995. "Re-reading (Vestal) virginity." In R. Hawley and B. Lewick (eds), *Women In Antiquity: New Assessments*. London and New York: 166–77.

Beard, M. and Henderson, J. 1997. "With this body I thee worship: sacred prostitution in antiquity," *Gender and History*, 9: 480–503.

Berger, E. 1968. *Antike Kunstwerke*. Kassel.

Bieber, M. 1949. "Eros and Dionysos in Kerch vases." In *Commemorative Studies in Honor of T. L. Shear*, *Hesperia* Supplement 8. Princeton: 31–8.

Blok, J. 1987. "Sexual asymmetry: a historiographical essay," in Blok and P. Mason (eds), *Sexual Asymmetry: Studies in Ancient Society*. Amsterdam: 1–57.

Bloomer, M. 1995. "Schooling in persona." Paper presented at a conference on "Creating Roman Identity: Subjectivity and Self-Fashioning in Latin Literature." Held 9 September 1995, University of California, Berkeley.

Bloomer, M. 1997. "Whose speech? Whose history? A preface to the history of declamation." In T. Habinek and A. Schiesaro (eds), *The Roman Cultural Revolution*. Cambridge: 199–215.

Boardman, J. 1992. "The phallos-bird in archaic and classical Greek art," *Revue archéologique*: 227–42.

Bonfante, L. 1989. "Nudity as a costume in classical art," *American Journal of Archaeology*, 93: 543–70.

Bonner, S. 1949. *Roman Declamation in the Late Republic and Early Empire*. Liverpool.

Bonner, S. 1977. *Education in Ancient Rome*. Berkeley.

Borgeaud, P. 1988. *The Cult of Pan in Ancient Greece*. Trans. K. Atlas and J. Redfield. Chicago.

Boswell, J. 1982–3. "Revolutions, universals, and sexual categories." In R. Boyers and G. Steiner (eds), *Homosexuality: Sacrilege, Vision, Politics*. Saratoga Springs, NY. = *Salmagundi*, 58–9: 89–113.

Brandes, S. 1981. "Like wounded stags: male sexual ideology in an Andalusian town." In S. Ortner and H. Whitehead (eds), *Sexual Meanings: The Cultural Construction Of Gender and Sexuality*. Cambridge: 216–39.

Brandt, P. 1928. *Sittengeschichte Griechenlands*. Zurich.

Brandt, P. (pseud. "Hans Licht") 1932. *Sexual Life in Ancient Greece*. Trans. J. H. Freese. London.

Breccia, E. 1922. *Alexandrea ad Aegyptum: A Guide to the Ancient and Modern Town and its Graeco-Roman Museum*. Bergamo.

Bremmer, J. 1984. "Greek maenadism reconsidered," *ZPE*, 55: 267–86.

Bremmer, J.N. 1999. "Transvestite Dionysos", *Bucknell Review*, 43: 183–200.

Brendel, O. 1977. "The scope and temperament of erotic art in the Greco-Roman world." In T. Bowie and C. V. Christenson (eds), *Studies in Erotic Art*. New York. 3–107.

Brisson, L. 1997. *Le sexe incertain: androgynie et hermaphroditisme dans l'Antiquité gréco-romaine*. Paris.

Brown, B. 1957. *Ptolemaic Paintings and Mosaics and the Alexandrian Style*. Cambridge, MA.

Brown, B. 1974. "The painted seals of Demetrius," *American Journal of Archaeology*, 78: 161.

Brown, P. 1990. "Bodies and minds: sexuality and renunciation in early Christianity." In D. M. Halperin, J. J. Winkler, and F. I. Zeitlin (eds), *Before Sexuality: The Construction of Erotic Experience in the Ancient Greek World*. Princeton, 479–93.

Brückner, M. 1888. "Von den griechischen Grabenreliefs," *SAWW*, 116: 514–20.

Brumfield, A. 1981. *The Attic Festivals of Demeter and their Relation to the Agricultural Year*. New York.

Burkert, W. 1983. *Homo Necans: The Anthropology of Ancient Greek Sacrificial Ritual and Myth*. Trans. P. Bing. Berkeley.

Butler, J. 1990. *Gender Trouble: Feminism and the Subversion of Identity*. New York.

Bynum, C. W. 1986. "The body of Christ in the later Middle Ages: a reply to Leo Steinberg," *Renaissance Quarterly*, 39: 399–439.

Bynum, C. W. 1987. *Holy Feast and Holy Fast: The Religious Significance of Food to Medieval Women*. Berkeley.

Calame, C. 1999. *The Poetics of Eros in Ancient Greece*. Trans. J. Lloyd. Princeton: 65–88.

Campese, S., Manuli, P., and Sissa, G. (eds) 1983. *Madre materia: sociologia e biologia della donna greca*. Turin.

Cantarella, E. 1991. "Moicheia: reconsidering a problem." In M. Gagarin (ed.), *Symposion 1990: Papers on Greek and Hellenistic Legal History*. Cologne: 289–96.

Caplan, P. (ed.) 1987. *The Cultural Construction of Sexuality*. London.

Carettoni, G. 1973. "Nuova serie di grande lastre 'Campana'," *BdA*, ser. 5, 58: 75–87.

Carpenter, T. 1986. *Dionysian Imagery in Archaic Greek Art: Its Development in Black-Figure Vase Painting*. Oxford.

Carpenter, T. H. and Faraone, C. A. (eds) 1993. *Masks of Dionysus*. Ithaca, NY, and London.

Chase, G. 1924. *Greek and Roman Sculpture in American Collections*. Cambridge, MA.

Clairmont, C. 1970. *Gravestone and Epigram: Greek Memorials from the Archaic and Classical Period*. Mainz.

Clairmont, C. 1972. "Gravestone with warriors in Boston," *Greek, Roman, and Byzantine Studies*, 13: 49–58.

Clarke, J. R. 1998. *Looking at Lovemaking: Constructions of Sexuality in Roman Art 100 BC–AD. 250*. Berkeley and Los Angeles.

Cohen, D. 1987. "Law, society and homosexuality in classical Athens," *Past and Present*, 117: 3–21.

Cohen, D. 1991. *Law, Sexuality and Society: The Enforcement of Morals in Classical Athens*. Cambridge.

Cohen, D. 1992. "Sex, gender and sexuality in ancient Greece," *Classical Philology*, 87: 145–60.

Cohen, D. and Saller, R. 1994. "Foucault on sexuality in Greco-Roman antiquity." In J. Goldstein (ed.), *Foucault and the Writing of History*. Oxford: 35–59.

Cohen, E. E. 2000. "'Whoring under contract': the legal context of prostitution in fourth-century Athens." In V. Hunter and J. Edmondson (eds), *Law and Social Status in Classical Athens*. Oxford: 113–48.

Cohn-Haft, L. 1995. "Divorce in classical Athens," *Journal of Hellenic Studies*, 115: 1–14.

Cole, S.G. 1984. "Greek sanctions against sexual assault," *Classical Philology*, 79: 97–113.

Cole, S. G. 1992. "*Gynaixi ou themis*: male and female in the Greek *leges sacrae*," *Helios*, 19: 104–22.

Cole, S. G. 1993. "Procession and celebration at the Dionysia." In R. Scodel (ed.), *Theater and Society in the Classical World*. Ann Arbor: 25–38.

Conkey, M. W. and Tringham, R. E. 1995. "Archaeology and the Goddess: exploring the contours of feminist archaeology." In D. C. Stanton and A. J. Stewart (eds), *Feminisms and the Academy*. Ann Arbor: 199–247.

Conze, A. 1893–1922. *Die attischen Grabreliefs*. Berlin.

Corbeil, A. 1990. "Political humor in the late Roman Republic: Romans defining themselves." Diss. Berkeley.

Corbeil, A. 1996. *Controlling Laughter: Political Humor in the Late Roman Republic*. Princeton.

Cornwall, A. and Lindisfarne, N. 1994. "Dislocating masculinity: gender, power and anthropology." In A. Cornwall and N. Lindisfarne (eds), *Dislocating Masculinity: Comparative Ethnographies*. London and New York: 11–47.

Crifò, G. 1999. "'Prodigium' e diritto: il caso dell'ermafrodita," *Index*, 27: 113–20.

Cyrino, M. S. 1998: "Heroes in d(u)ress: transvestism and power in the myths of Herakles and Achilles," *Arethusa*, 31: 207–41.

Czaja, M. 1974. *Gods of Myth and Stone: Phallicism in Japanese Folk Religion*. New York and Tokyo.

Daraki, M. 1985. *Dionysos*. Paris.

Davidson, A. I. 1986–7. "How to do the history of psychoanalysis: a reading of Freud's *Three Essays on the History of Sexuality*." In F. Meltzer (ed.), *The Trial(s) of Psychoanalysis (Critical Inquiry*, 13): 252–77.

Davidson, A. I. 1987–8. "Sex and the emergence of sexuality," *Critical Inquiry*, 14: 16–48.

Davidson, J. 1997. *Courtesans and Fishcakes: The Consuming Passions of Classical Athens*. London.

Davidson, J. 2001. "Dover, Foucault and Greek homosexuality: penetration and the truth of sex," *Past and Present*, 170: 3–51.

De Martino, G. and Schmitt, A. 1985. *Kleine Schriften zu zwischen-männlicher Sexualität und Erotik in der muslimischen Gessellschaft.* Berlin.

De Vries, K. 1973. "East meets West at dinner," *Expedition*, 15: 32–39.

Deacy, S. and Peirce, K. F. (eds), 1997. *Rape in Antiquity*. London.

Dean-Jones, L. 1991. "The cultural construct of the female body in classical Greek science." In S. B. Pomeroy (ed.), *Women's History and Ancient History*. Chapel Hill and London: 111–37.

Dean-Jones, L. 1992. "The politics of pleasure: female sexual appetite in the Hippocratic Corpus," *Helios*, 19: 72–91.

Dean-Jones, L. 1994. *Women's Bodies in Classical Greek Science*. Oxford.

DeFelice, J. 2001. *Roman Hospitality: The Professional Women of Pompeii.* Warren Center, PA.

Delcourt, M. 1961. *Hermaphrodite: Myths and Rites of the Bisexual Figure in Classical Antiquity.* Trans. J. Nicholson. London. (Orig. pub. Paris 1956.)

Demand, N. 1994. *Birth, Death and Motherhood in Classical Greece.* Baltimore and London.

Demand, N. 2002. "Gender studies and history: participation and power." In S. M. Burstein, R. MacMullen, K. A. Raaflaub, and A. M. Ward (eds), *Current Issues and the Study of Ancient History*. Publications of the Association of Ancient Historians 7. Claremont, CA: 31–43.

Dessen, C. E. 1995. "The figure of the eunuch in Terence's *Eunuchus*," *Helios*, 22: 123–39.

Detienne, M. 1989. "Un phallus pour Dionysus." In G. Sissa and M. Detienne (eds), *La vie quotidienne des dieux grecs*. Paris: 253–64.

Deubner, L. 1932. *Attische Feste*. Berlin.

Deutsch, H. 1969. *A Psychoanalytic Study of the Myth of Dionysus and Apollo: Two Variants of the Son-Mother Relationship*. New York.

Devambez, P. 1955. "Le motif de Phèdre sur une stèle thasienne," *BCH*, 79: 121–33.

Devereux, G. 1967. "Greek pseudo-homosexuality and the 'Greek miracle'", *Symbolae Osloenses*, 42: 69–92.

Devereux, G. 1973. "Le fragment d'Eschyle 62 Nauck²: Ce qu'y signifie *chlounês*," *Revue des études grecques*, 86: 271–84.

Dixon, S. 1988. *The Roman Mother*. London and Sydney.

Dixon, S. 1992. *The Roman Family*. Baltimore and London.

Dodds, E. R. (ed.) 1944. *Euripides: Bacchae*. Oxford.

Dover, K. J. 1964. "Eros and nomos (Plato, *Symposium* 182A-185C)," *Bulletin of the Institute of Classical Studies*, 11: 31–42.

Dover, K. J. 1973. "Classical Greek attitudes to sexual behaviour," *Arethusa*, 6: 59–73.

Dover, K. J. 1974. *Greek Popular Morality: In the Time of Plato and Aristotle*. Oxford.

Dover, K. J. 1978. *Greek Homosexuality*. Cambridge, MA. (2nd edn 1989.)

duBois, P. 1984. "Sexual difference: ancient and modern," *Pacific Coast Philology*, 19.1–2: 43–9.

Dupont, F. 1985. *L'Acteur-roi, ou le théâtre dans la Rome antique*. Paris.

Edmunds, L. 1988. "Foucault and Theognis," *Classical and Modern Literature*, 8.2: 79–91.

Edwards, C. 1993. *The Politics of Immorality in Ancient Rome*. Cambridge.

Edwards, C. 1997. "Unspeakable professions: public performance and prostitution." In J. P. Hallett and M. B. Skinner (eds), *Roman Sexualities*. Princeton: 66–95.

Edwards, M. W. 1960. "Representation of maenads on archaic red-figure vases," *Journal of Hellenic Studies*, 80: 78–87.

Engels, F. 1884. *Der Ursprung der Familie, der Privateigentums und des Staats*. Zürich.

Evans, A. 1988. *The God of Ecstasy: Sex-Roles and the Madness of Dionysos*. New York.

Fantham, E., Foley, H. P., Kampen, N. B., Pomeroy, S. B., and Shapiro, H. A. 1994. *Women in the Classical World: Image and Text*. New York and Oxford.

Faraone, C. 1999. *Ancient Greek Love Magic*. Cambridge, MA.

Féray, J.-C. 1981. "Une histoire critique du mot *homosexualité*," *Arcadie*, 28. 325–8: 11–21, 115–24, 171–81, 246–58.

Fineberg, S. 1983. "Dionysus in the new democracy." Unpublished paper.

Fitzgerald, W. 1988. "Power and impotence in Horace's *Epodes*," *Ramus*, 17: 176–91.

Fitzgerald, W. 1992. "Catullus and the reader: the erotics of poetry," *Arethusa*, 25: 419–43.

Fitzgerald, W. 1995. *Catullan Provocations: Lyric Poetry and the Drama of Position*. Berkeley.

Flemming, R. 1999. "*Quae corpore quaestum facit*: the sexual economy of female prostitution in the Roman Empire," *JRS*, 89: 38–61.

Flemming, R. 2000. *Medicine and the Making of Roman Women: Gender, Nature and Authority from Celsus to Galen*. Oxford.

Forberg, F.-K. 1824. *Apophoreta*. Coburg. (Trans. J. Smithson, Manchester 1884.)

Foucault, M. 1978. *Histoire de la sexualité. 1. La volonté de savoir* (Paris 1976) = *The History of Sexuality. 1. An Introduction*. Trans. R. Hurley, New York.

Foucault, M. 1980a. "Introduction." In M. Foucault, *Herculine Barbin, Being the Recently Discovered Memoirs of a Nineteenth-Century French Hermaphrodite*. Trans. R. McDougall. New York: vii–xvii.

Foucault, M. 1980b. *Power/Knowledge: Selected Interviews and Other Writings 1972–77*. Ed. C. Gordon. Brighton.

Foucault, M. 1983. "On the genealogy of ethics: an overview of work in progress." In H. L. Dreyfus and P. Rabinow (eds), *Michel Foucault: Beyond Structuralism and Hermeneutics*. 2nd edn. Chicago: 229–52.

Foucault, M. 1985. *Histoire de la sexualité. 2. L'usage des plaisirs* (Paris 1984) = *The History of Sexuality. 2. The Use of Pleasure*. Trans. R. Hurley, New York.

Foucault, M. 1986. *Histoire de la sexualité. 3. Le souci de soi* (Paris 1984) = *The History of Sexuality. 3. The Care of the Self*. Trans. R. Hurley. New York.

Foxhall, L. 1989. "Household, gender, and property in classical Athens," *Classical Quarterly*, 39: 22–44.

Foxhall, L. 1991. "Response to Eva Cantarella". In M. Gagarin (ed.), *Symposion 1990: Papers on Greek and Hellenistic Legal History*. Cologne: 297–304.

Foxhall, L. 1994. "Pandora unbound: a feminist critique of Foucault's *History of Sexuality*." In A. Cornwall and M. Lindisfarne (eds), *Dislocating Masculinity: Comparative Ethnographies*. London and New York: 133–46.

Foxhall, L. 1995. "Monumental ambitions: the significance of posterity in ancient Greece." In N. Spencer (ed.), *Time, Tradition, and Society in Greek Archaeology: Bridging the "Great Divide"*. London: 135–49.

Foxhall, L. 1996. "The law and the lady: women and legal proceedings in classical Athens." In L. Foxhall and A. Lewis (eds), *Greek Law in its Political Setting*. Oxford: 133–52.

Foxhall, L. 1998. "Natural sex: the attribution of sex and gender to plants in ancient Greece." In L. Foxhall and J. Salmon (eds), *Thinking Men: Masculinity and its Self-Representation in the Classical Tradition*. London and New York: 57–70.

Foxhall, L. and Salmon, J. (eds) 1998a. *Thinking Men: Masculinity and its Self-Representation in the Classical Tradition*. London and New York.

Foxhall, L. and Salmon, J. (eds) 1998b. *When Men Were Men: Masculinity, Power and Identity in Classical Antiquity*. London and New York.

Frickenhaus, A. 1912. *Lenäenvasen*. Berlin.

Frontisi-Ducroux, F. and Lissarrague, F. 1990. "From ambiguity to ambivalence: a Dionysiac excursion through the 'Anakreontic' Vases." In D. M. Halperin, J. J. Winkler, and F. I. Zeitlin (eds), *Before Sexuality: The Construction of Erotic Experience in the Ancient Greek World*. Princeton: 211–56.

Fustel de Coulanges, N. D. 1864. *La cité antique: Étude sur le culte, le droit, les institutions de la Grèce et de Rome*. Paris.

Gardner, J. 1989. "Aristophanes and male anxiety—the defence of the *oikos*," *G&R*, 36 : 51–62.

Gilmore, D. (ed.) 1987. *Honor and Shame and the Unity of the Mediterranean*. Special Publication of the American Anthropological Association, 22. Washington, DC.

Gilmore, D. 1990. *Manhood in the Making: Cultural Concepts of Masculinity*. New Haven.

Gleason, M. W. 1995. *Making Men: Sophists and Self-Presentation in Ancient Rome*. Princeton.

Godelier, M. 1981. "The origins of male domination," *New Left Review*, 127: 3–17.

Gold, B. 1998. "'Vested interests' in Plautus' *Casina*: cross-dressing in Roman comedy," *Helios*, 25: 17–29.

Golden, M. 1984. "Slavery and homosexuality at Athens," *Phoenix*, 34: 308–24.

Golden, M. 1985. "*Pais*, 'Child,' and 'Slave.'" *L'Antiquité classique*, 54: 91–104.

Golden, M. 1991. "Thirteen years of homosexuality (and other recent work on sex, gender and the body in ancient Greece)," *EMC*, 35:327–40.

Goldhill, S. 1995. *Foucault's Virginity: Ancient Erotic Fiction and the History of Sexuality*. Cambridge.

Goodison, L. and Morris, C. (eds) 1999. *Ancient Goddesses*. Madison.

Gourevitch, D. 1984. *Le mal d'être femme*. Paris.

Grant, M. 1975. *Erotic Art in Pompeii*. London.

Greenblatt, S. 1980. *Renaissance Self-Fashioning*. Chicago.

Griffin, J. 1976. "Augustan poetry and the life of luxury," *Journal of Roman Studies*, 66: 87–104.

Grossberg, L., Nelson, C., and Treichler, P. A. (eds) 1992. *Cultural Studies*. New York.

Grubbs, J. Evans. 2000. "The slave who avenged her master's death: *Codex Justinianus* 1.19.1 and 7.13.1," *Ancient History Bulletin*, 14: 81–8.

Gunderson, E. 1996. "Contested subjects: oratorical theory and the body." Diss. Berkeley.

Gunderson, E. 1998. "Discovering the body in Roman oratory." In M. Wyke (ed.), *Parchments of Gender*. Oxford: 169–90.

Guyot, P. 1980. *Eunuchen als Sklaven und Freigelassene in der griechisch-römischen Antike*. Stuttgart.

Habinek, T. 1997. "The invention of sexuality in the world of Rome." In T. Habinek and A. Schiesaro (eds), *The Roman Cultural Revolution*. Cambridge: 23–43.

Hallett, J. P. 1977. "*Perusinae glandes* and the changing image of Augustus," *American Journal of Ancient History*, 2.2: 151–71.

Hallett, J. P. 1989a. "Female homoeroticism and the denial of Roman reality in Latin literature," *Yale Journal of Criticism*, 3.1: 209–27 (= J. P. Hallett and M. B. Skinner (eds), *Roman Sexualities*. Princeton 1997: 255–73).

Hallett, J. P. 1989b. "Women as 'same' and 'other' in the classical Roman elite," *Helios*, 16: 59–78.

Hallett, J. P. and Skinner, M. B. (eds) 1997. *Roman Sexualities*. Princeton.

Halperin, D. 1985. "Platonic *erôs* and what men call love," *Ancient Philosophy*, 5: 161–204.

Halperin, D. 1986. "Plato and erotic reciprocity," *Classical Antiquity*, 5: 60–80.

Halperin, D. M. 1990. *One Hundred Years of Homosexuality and Other Essays on Greek Love*. London and New York.

Halperin, D. M. 1998. "Forgetting Foucault: acts, identities, and the history of sexuality," *Representations*, 63: 93–120.

Halperin, D. M., Winkler, J. J., and Zeitlin, F. I. (eds) 1990. *Before Sexuality: The Construction of Erotic Experience in the Ancient Greek World*. Princeton.

Hamilton, R. 1992. *Choes and Anthesteria: Athenian Iconography and Ritual*. Ann Arbor.

Hanson, A. E. 1975. "Hippocrates: Diseases of Women 1," *Signs*, 1: 567–84.

Harris, E. 1990. "Did the Athenians regard seduction as a worse crime than rape?," *Classical Quarterly*, 40: 370–7.

Heller, T. C., Sosna, M., and Wellbery, D. E. (eds) 1986. *Reconstructing Individualism: Autonomy, Individuality and the Self in Western Thought*. Stanford.

Henderson, J. 1975. *The Maculate Muse: Obscene Language in Attic Comedy*. New Haven.

Henderson, J. 1987. "Older women in Attic comedy," *Transactions of the American Philological Association*, 117: 105–29.

Henderson, J. 1988. "Greek attitudes toward sex." In M. Grant and R. Kitzinger (eds), *Civilization of the Ancient Mediterranean: Greece and Rome*. 2. New York: 1249–63.

Henrichs, A. 1978. "Greek maenadism from Olympias to Messalina," *Harvard Studies in Classical Philology*, 82: 121–60.

Henry, M. 1985. *Menander's Courtesans and the Greek Comic Tradition*. Frankfurt.

Herdt, G. 1987. *The Sambia: Ritual and Gender in New Guinea*. Case Studies in Cultural Anthropology. New York.

Herter, H. 1938. "Phallos." In *Paulys Real-Encyclopädie der classischen Altertumswissenschaft*. Stuttgart, 19: 1681–1748.

Herter, H. 1960. "Die Soziologie der antiken Prostitution im Lichte der heidnischen und christlichen Schrifttums," *JAC*, 3: 70–111.

Herter, H. 1972. "Phallos," *Der kleine Pauly*, 4: 701–6.

Herzer, M. 1985. "Kertbeny and the nameless love," *Journal of Homosexuality*, 12.1: 1–26.

Herzfeld, M. 1985. *The Poetics of Manhood: Contest and Identity in a Cretan Mountain Village*. Princeton.

Hoffman, D. J. 1989. "Ritual license and the cult of Dionysus," *Athenaeum*, 67: 91–115.

Holst-Warhaft, G. 1992. *Dangerous Voices: Women's Laments and Greek Literature*. London and New York.

Hooper, R. W. 1999. *The Priapus Poems*. Urbana and Chicago.

Hopfner, T. 1938. *Das Sexualleben der Griechen und Römer*. 1. Prague.

Houby-Nielsen, S. 1997. "Grave gifts, women and conventional values in Hellenistic Athens." In P. Bilde, T. Engberg-Pedersen, L. Hannestad, and

J. Zahle (eds), *Conventional Values of the Hellenistic Greeks.* Aarhus: 220–62.

Hunter, V. 1989. "Women's authority in classical Athens," *Echos du monde classique,* 33: 39–48.

Jackson, S. 1990. "Myrsilus of Methymna and the dreadful smell of the Lemnian women," *ICS,* 15: 77–83.

James, S. L. (ed.) 1998. *Gender and Genre in Roman Comedy and Elegy* (*Helios,* 25.1). Lubbock.

Jameson, M. 1990a. "Domestic space in the Greek city state." In S. Kent (ed.), *Domestic Architecture and the Use of Space.* Cambridge: 92–113.

Jameson, M. 1990b. "Private space in the Greek city." In O. Murray and S. Price (eds), *The Greek City.* Oxford: 171–98.

Jameson, M. 1993. "The asexuality of Dionysus." In T. H. Carpenter and C. A. Faraone (eds), *Masks of Dionysus.* Ithaca, NY and London: 44–64.

Jameson, R. D. 1949. "Phallism." In *Standard Dictionary of Folklore, Mythology, and Legend.* New York, 2: 863–68.

Johansen, K. F. 1951. *The Attic Grave-Reliefs of the Classical Period: An Essay in Interpretation.* Copenhagen.

Johns, C. 1982. *Sex or Symbol: Erotic Images of Greece and Rome.* Austin.

Joshel, S. R. 1992. "The body female and the body politic: Livy's Lucretia and Verginia." In A. Richlin (ed.), *Pornography and Representation in Greece and Rome.* London: 112–30.

Kaempf-Dimitriadou, S. 1979. *Die Liebe der Götter in der attischen Kunst des 5. Jhr. v. C. Antike Kunst* Beiheft 11. Bern.

Karras, R. M. 2000. "Active/passive, acts/passions: Greek and Roman Sexualities," *AHR,* 105: 1250–65.

Katz, M. A. 1989. "Sexuality and the body in ancient Greece," *Metis,* 4.1: 155–79.

Katz, M. A. 1992. "Ideology and 'the status of women' in ancient Greece." In A.-L. Shapiro (ed.), *History and Feminist Theory.* Middletown, CT: 70–97 (= *History and Theory* Beiheft 31).

Katz, M. A. 1998. "Did the women of ancient Athens attend the theater in the eighteenth century?," *Classical Philology,* 93: 105–24.

Katz, M. A. 1999. "Women and democracy in ancient Greece." In T. M. Falkner, N. Felson, and D. Konstan (eds), *Contextualizing Classics: Ideology, Performance, Dialogue. Essays in Honor of John J. Peradotto.* Lanham: 41–68.

Keith, A. M. 1997. "*Tandem venit amor*: a Roman woman speaks of love." In J. P. Hallett and M. B. Skinner (eds), *Roman Sexualities.* Princeton: 295–310.

Keith, A. M. 1999. "Versions of epic masculinity in Ovid's *Metamorphoses.*" In P. Hardie, A. Barchiesi, and S. Hinds (eds), *Ovidian Transformations: Essays on the Metamorphoses and its Reception.* Cambridge: 214–39.

Keith, A. M. 2000. *Engendering Rome: Women in Latin Epic.* Cambridge.

Kellum, B. 1981. "Apollo vs. Hercules: The Temple of Apollo on the Palatine and the Battle of Actium," *American Journal of Archaeology*, 85: 200.

Kellum, B. 1997. "Concealing/revealing: gender and the play of meaning in the monuments of Augustan Rome." In T. Habinek and A. Schiesaro (eds), *The Roman Cultural Revolution*. Cambridge: 158–81.

Kelsen, H. 1942. "Platonic love," Trans. G. Wilbur, *American Imago*, 3: 3–110.

Kerényi, K. 1976. *Dionysos: Archetypal Images of Indestructible Life*. London.

Keuls, E. 1984. "Male–female interaction in fifth-century Dionysiac ritual as shown in Attic vase painting," *Zeitschrift für Papyrologie und Epigraphik*, 55: 287–97.

Keuls, E. C. 1985. *The Reign of the Phallus: Sexual Politics in Ancient Athens*. New York.

Keuls, E. C. 1995. "The Greek medical texts and the sexual ethos of ancient Athens." In P. J. van der Eijk, H. E. J. Horstmanshoff, and P. H. Schrijvers (eds), *Ancient Medicine in its Socio-Cultural Context*. 1. Amsterdam and Athens, GA: 261–73.

Kilmer, M. 1990. "Sexual violence: archaic Athens and the recent past." In E. Craik ed., *Owls to Athens: Essays on Classical Subjects presented to Sir Kenneth Dover*. Oxford: 261–7.

Kilmer, M. F. 1993. *Greek Erotica on Attic Red-Figure Vases*. London.

Kilmer, M. F. 1997. "Painters and pederasts: ancient art, sexuality and social history." In M. Golden and P. Toohey (eds), *Inventing Ancient Culture: Historicism, Periodization and the Ancient World*. London and New York: 36–49.

King, H. 1986. "Agnodike and the profession of medicine," *Publications of the Cambridge Philological Society*, 32: 53–75

King, H. 1994. "Sowing the field: Greek and Roman sexology." In R. Porter and M. Teich (eds), *Sexual Knowledge, Sexual Science: The History of Attitudes to Sexuality*. Cambridge: 29–46.

King, H. 1998. *Hippocrates' Woman: Reading the Female Body in Ancient Greece*. London and New York.

Kitto, H. D. F. 1951. The *Greeks*. Harmondsworth.

Klein, F. and Wolf, T. J. (eds) 1985. *Bisexuality: Theory and Research* (*Journal of Homosexuality*. 11.1–2).

Kockel, V. 1983. "Beobachtungen zum Tempel des Mars Ultor und zum Forum des Augustus," *MDAI(R)*, 90: 421–48.

Koestenbaum, W. 1991. "The queen's throat: (homo)sexuality and the art of singing." In D. Fuss (ed.), *Inside/Outside: Lesbian Theories, Gay Theories*. New York: 205–34.

Konstan, D. 1994. *Sexual Symmetry: Love in the Ancient Novel and Related Genres*. Princeton.

Kraemer, R. 1979. "Ecstasy and possession: the attraction of women to the cult of Dionysus," *Harvard Theological Review*, 72: 55–80.

Krenkel, W. 1981. "Tonguing," *WZ Rostock*, 30: 37–54.

Krenkel, W. 1990. "Transvestismus in der Antike," *WZ Rostock*, 39.9: 144–57.

Kron, U. 1996. "Priesthoods, dedications and euergetism: what part did religion play in the political and social status of Greek women?" In P. Hellström and B. Alroth (eds), *Religion and Power in the Ancient Greek World: Proceedings of the Uppsala Symposium 1993*. Uppsala: 139–82.

Kurke, L. 1997. "Inventing the *hetaira*: sex, politics and discursive conflict in archaic Greece," *Classical Antiquity*, 16: 106–50.

Kurtz, D. C. and Boardman, J. 1971. *Greek Burial Customs*. London.

Lacan, J. 1977. "The signification of the phallus." In J. Lacan, *Écrits*. Trans. A. Sheridan. New York: 281–91.

LaRocca, E. 1985. *Amazzonomachia: le sculture frontonali del tempio di Apollo Sosiano*. Rome.

Laqueur, T. 1986. "Orgasm, generation, and the politics of reproductive biology," *Representations*, 14: 1–41.

Lardinois, A. and McClure, L. (eds) 2001. *Making Silence Speak: Women's Voices in Greek Literature and Society*. Princeton.

Larmour, D., Miller, P. A., and Platter, C. 1998. "Situating *The History of Sexuality*." In D. Larmour, P. A. Miller, and C. Platter (eds), *Rethinking Sexuality: Foucault and Classical Antiquity*. Princeton: 3–41.

Lawler, L. 1927. *The Maenads: A Contribution to the Study of Dance in Ancient Greece*. Rome.

Leeman, A. D. 1963. *Orationis Ratio: The Stylistic Theories and Practice of the Roman Orators, Historians, and Philosophers*. Amsterdam.

Lefkowitz, M. R. 1996. "Women in the Panathenaic and other festivals." In J. Neils (ed.), *Worshipping Athena: Panathenaia and Parthenon*. Madison: 78–91.

Lefkowitz, M. R. and Fant, M. R. 1992. *Women's Life in Greece and Rome*. 2nd edn. Baltimore.

Leipoldt, J. 1954. *Die Frau in der antiken Welt und im Urchristentum*. Leipzig.

Lênaios, E. 1935. *Aporrhêta*. Thessalonica.

Lieber, E. 1993. "The Hippocratic 'Airs, Waters, Places' on cross-dressing eunuchs: 'natural' yet also 'divine.'" In R. Wittern and P. Pellegrin (eds), *Hippokratische Medizin und antike Philosophie: Verhandlungen des VIII. Internationalen Hippokrates-Kolloquiums in Kloster Banz/Staffelstein vom 23. bis 28. September 1993*. Hildesheim: 451–76.

Ling, R. 1990. "Street plaques in Pompeii." In *Architecture and Architectural Sculpture in the Roman Empire*. Oxford University Committee for Archaeology Monograph, 29. Oxford: 51–66.

Lissarrague, F. 1987. "Dionysos s'en va-t-en guerre." In C. Bérard, C. Bron, and A. Pomari (eds), *Images et société en Grèce ancienne: l'iconographie comme méthode d'analyse*. Lausanne: 111–20.

Lissarrague, F. 1990. "The sexual life of satyrs." In D. M. Halperin, J. J. Winkler, and F. I. Zeitlin (eds), *Before Sexuality: The Construction of Erotic Experience in the Ancient Greek World*. Princeton: 53–81.

Lissarrague, F. 1998. "Satyres chez les femme." In P. Veyne, F. Lissarrague, and F. Frontisi-Ducroux, *Les mystères du gynécée*. Paris: 179–98.

Lizzi, R. 1995. "Il sesso e i morti." In F. Hinard (ed.), *La mort au quotidien dans le monde romain: Actes du colloque organisé par l'Université de Paris IV (Paris–Sorbonne 7–9 octobre 1993)* Paris: 49–68.

Loraux, N. 1981. "Le lit, la guerre," *L'Homme*, 21: 37–67.

Loraux, N. 1986. *The Invention of Athens: The Funeral Oration in the Classical City*. Trans. A. Sheridan. Cambridge, MA.

Loraux, N. 1990. "Herakles: the super-male and the feminine." In D. M. Halperin, J. J. Winkler, and F. I. Zeitlin (eds), *Before Sexuality: The Construction of Erotic Experience in the Ancient Greek World*. Princeton: 21–52.

Loraux, N. 1992. "What is a goddess?" In P. Schmitt Pantel (ed.), *A History of Women in the West. 1. From Ancient Goddesses to Christian Saints*. Trans. A. Goldhammer. Cambridge, MA: 11–44.

Loraux, N. 1995. *The Experiences of Tiresias: The Feminine and the Greek Man*. Trans. P. Wissing, Princeton.

MacDowell, D. M. 1986. *Spartan Law*. Edinburgh.

MacMullen, R. 1983. "Roman attitudes to Greek love," *Historia*, 32: 484–502.

Maine, H. 1861. *Ancient Law: Its Connection with the Early History of Society and its Relation to Modern Ideas*. London.

Manuli, P. 1980. "Fisiologia e patologia del femminile negli scritti ippocratici dell'antica ginecologia greca." In M. Grmek (ed.), *Hippocratica: Actes du Colloque hippocratique de Paris (4–9 septembre 1978)*. Colloques internationaux du Centre National de la Recherche Scientifique, 583. Paris: 393–408.

Manuli, P. 1983. "Donne masculine, femmine sterili, vergini perpetue: la ginecologia greca tra Ippocrate e Sorano." In S. Campese, P. Manuli, and G. Sissa (eds), *Madre materia: Sociologia e biologia della donna greca*. Turin: 147–92.

Marder, T. 1979. "Context for Claude-Nicholas Ledoux's *Oikema*," *Arts*, 54.1: 174–6.

Marks, M. C. 1978. "Heterosexual coital position as a reflection of ancient and modern cultural attitudes." Diss., SUNY. Buffalo.

Mason, P. 1984. *The City of Men: Ideology, Sexual Politics, and the Social Formation*. Göttingen.

Maurizio, L. 1995. "Anthropology and spirit possession: a reconsideration of the Pythia's role at Delphi," *Journal of Hellenic Studies*, 115: 69–86.

McClure, L. 1999. *Spoken Like a Woman: Speech and Gender in Athenian Drama*. Princeton.

McGinn, T. 1998. *Prostitution, Sexuality and the Law in Ancient Rome*. New York.

McNally, S. 1978. "The maenad in early Greek art," *Arethusa*, 11: 101–36.

Meinder, C. 1788. *Geschichte des weiblichen Geschlechts*. 4 vols. Hannover.

Mendelsohn, D. 1996. "The stand: expert witnesses and ancient mysteries in a Colorado courtroom," *Lingua Franca*, 6: 34–46.

Merriam, A. 1887. "Painted sepulchral stelai from Alexandria," *American Journal of Archaeology*, 3: 259–68.

Meskell, L. 1995. "Goddesses, Gimbutas and new age archaeology," *Antiquity*, 69: 74–86.

Michon, E. 1905. "Lécythe funéraire en marbre de style attique: Musée du Louvre," *Monuments et Mémoires (Fondation Piot)*, 12: 177–99.

Mihailov, G. 1970. *Inscriptiones Graecae in Bulgaria repertae*. 2nd edn. Academia Litterarum Bulgarica. Institutum Archaeologicum. Series Epigraphica No. 10. Sofia.

Miller, M. 1989. "The *ependytes* in classical Athens," *Hesparia*, 58: 313–29.

Miller, M. C. 1999. "Reexamining transvestism in archaic and classical Athens: the Zewadski stamnos," *American Journal of Archaeology*, 103: 223–53.

Montserrat, D. 1996. *Sex and Society in Graeco-Roman Egypt*. London and New York.

Montserrat, D. 2000. "Reading gender in the Roman world." In J. Huskinson (ed.), *Experiencing Rome: Culture, Identity and Power in the Roman Empire*. London: 153–81.

Moodie, T. Dunbar 1987–8. "Migrancy and male sexuality in the South African gold mines," *Journal of Southern African Studies*, 14: 228–56.

Moore, T. 1991. "*Palliata togata*: Plautus, *Curculio* 462–86," *American Journal of Philology*, 112: 343–62.

Morgan, L. H. 1877. *Ancient Society*. Chicago.

Morris, I. 1999. "Archaeology and gender ideologies in early archaic Greece," *Transactions of the American Philological Association*, 129: 305–17.

Moxnes, H. 1997. "Conventional values in the Hellenistic world: masculinity." In P. Bilde, T. Engberg-Pedersen, L. Hannestad, and J. Zahle (eds), *Conventional Values of the Hellenistic Greeks*. Aarhus: 263–84.

Murray, S. O. 2002. "Gender-mixing roles, gender-crossing roles, and the sexuality of transgendered roles." *Reviews in Anthropology*, 31: 291–300.

Negbi, M. 1995. "Male and female in Theophrastus's botanical works," *Journal of the History of Biology*, 28: 317–32.

Nevett, L. 1994. "Separation or seclusion? Towards an archaeological approach to investigating women in the Greek household in the fifth to third centuries B.C.", in M. Parker Pearson and C. Richards (eds), *Architecture and Order*. London and New York: 98–112.

Nevett, L. 1995. "Gender relations in the classical Greek household: the archaeological evidence", *ABSA*, 90: 363–81.

Nevett, L. 2002. "Continuity and change in Greek households under Roman rule: the role of women in the domestic context." In E. N. Ostenfeld (ed.), *Greek Romans and Roman Greeks*. Aarhus: 81–97.

Nielsen, T. H., Bjertrup, L., Hansen, M. H., Rubinstein, L., and

Vestergaard, T. 1989. "Athenian grave monuments and social class," *Greek, Roman, and Byzantine Studies*, 30: 411–20.

Nilsson, M. 1952. "Dionysos Liknites," *Bulletin de la Société Royale des Lettres de Lund*, 1–18.

Noshy, I. 1937. *The Arts in Ptolemaic Egypt: A Study of Greek and Egyptian Influences in Ptolemaic Architecture and Sculpture*. London.

Oliensis, E. 1997. "The erotics of amicitia: readings in Tibullus, Propertius and Horace." In J. P. Hallett and M. B. Skinner (eds), *Roman Sexualities*. Princeton: 151–71.

Olsen, B. A. 1998. "Women, children and the family in the late Aegean Bronze Age: differences in Minoan and Mycenaean constructions of gender," *World Archaeology*, 29: 380–92.

Osborne, R. 1993. "Women and sacrifice in classical Greece," *Classical Quarterly*, 43: 393–405.

Osborne, R. 1997. "Law, the democratic citizen and the presentation of women in classical Athens," *Past and Present*, 155: 3–33.

Osborne, R. 1998. "Sculpted men of Athens: masculinity and power in the field of vision." In L. Foxhall and J. Salmon (eds), *Thinking Men: Masculinity and its Self-Representation in the Classical Tradition*. London and New York: 23–42.

Otto, W. 1965. *Dionysus: Myth and Cult*. Trans. R. B. Palmer. Bloomington.

Padgug, R. A. 1979. "Sexual matters: on conceptualizing sexuality in history," *Radical History Review*, 20: 3–23.

Parke, H. 1977. *Festivals of the Athenians*. London.

Parker, H.N. 1992. "Love's body anatomized: the ancient erotic handbooks and the rhetoric of sexuality." In A. Richlin (ed.), *Pornography and Representation in Greece and Rome*. New York and Oxford:. 90–111.

Parker, H. N. 1997. "The teratogenic grid." In J. P. Hallett and M. B. Skinner (eds), *Roman Sexualities*. Princeton: 47–65.

Parker, H. 1996. "Heterosexuality." In *Oxford Classical Dictionary*, Oxford: 702–3.

Parker, R. 1983. *Miasma: Pollution and Purification in Early Greek Religion*. Oxford.

Patterson, C. B. 1998. *The Family in Greek History*. Cambridge, MA.

Paul, G. M. 1982. "*Urbs capta*: a sketch of an ancient literary motif," *Phoenix*, 36: 144–55.

Payer, P. J. 1984. *Sex and the Penitentials: The Development of a Sexual Code 550–1150*. Toronto.

Peek, W. 1955. *Griechische Vers-Inschriften*. Berlin.

Petersen, W. L. 1986. "Can *arsenokoitai* be translated as 'homosexuals'?," *Vigiliae Christianae*, 40: 187–91.

Pfuhl, E. 1901. "Alexandrinische Grabreliefs," *MDAI (A)*, 26: 268–70.

Phillips, E. 1973. *Greek Medicine*. London.

Pingiatoglou, S. 1981. *Eileithyia*. Würzburg.

Pomeroy. S. B. 1975. *Goddesses, Whores, Wives and Slaves: Women in Classical Antiquity.* New York.

Pomeroy. S. B. 1984. *Women in Hellenistic Egypt from Alexander to Cleopatra.* New York.

Poster, M. 1986. "Foucault and the tyranny of Greece." In D. Hoy (ed.), *Foucault: A Critical Reader.* Oxford: 205–20.

Pottle, F. A. (ed.) 1950. *Boswell's London Journal 1762–1763.* London and New Haven.

Powell, A. 1999. "Spartan women assertive in politics? Plutarch's *Lives* of Agis and Cleomenes." In S. Hodkinson and A. Powell (eds), *Sparta: New Perspectives.* London: 393–419.

Price, S. 1990. "Anacreontic vases reconsidered," *Greek, Roman, and Byzantine Studies,* 31: 133–75.

Pugliese-Carratelli, G. 1948. "*Tabulae Herculanenses,*" *Parola del Passato,* 3: 105–84.

Rapp, A. 1872. "Die Mänade im griechischen Cultus, in der Kunst und Poesie." *Rheinisches Museum für Philologie,* 27: 1–22 and 562–611.

Raval, S. 2002. "Cross-dressing and 'gender trouble' in the Ovidian corpus." *Helios,* 29: 149–72.

Reed, J. D. 1995. "The sexuality of Adonis," *Classical Antiquity,* 14: 317–47.

Reinsberg, C. 1989. *Ehe, Hetärentum und Knabenliebe im antiken Griechenland.* Munich.

Reutersvard, O. 1971. *The Neo-Classic Temple of Virility and the Buildings with a Phallic Shaped Ground-Plan.* Lund.

Rhodes, P. J. 1981. *A Commentary on the Aristotelian* Athenaion Politeia. Oxford.

Richardson, T. E. 1984. "Homosexuality in the *Satyricon,*" *Classica et Mediaevalia,* 35: 105–27.

Richlin, A. 1991. "Zeus and Metis: Foucault, feminism, classics," *Helios,* 18: 160–80.

Richlin, A. 1992a. "Julia's jokes, Galla Placidia, and the Roman use of women as political icons." In B. Garlick, S. Dixon, and P. Allen (eds), *Stereotypes of Women in Power.* New York: 63–91.

Richlin, A. 1992b. *The Garden of Priapus: Sexuality and Aggression in Roman Humor.* 2nd edn. New York.

Richlin, A. (ed.) 1992c. *Pornography and Representation in Greece and Rome.* New York and Oxford.

Richlin, A. 1992d. "Reading Ovid's rapes." In A. Richlin (ed.), *Pornography and Representation in Greece and Rome.* London: 158–79.

Richlin, A. 1992e. "Roman oratory, pornography, and the silencing of Anita Hill," *Southern California Law Review,* 65: 1321–32.

Richlin, A. 1993. "Not before homosexuality: the materiality of the *cinaedus* and Roman law against love between men," *Journal of the History of Sexuality,* 3: 523–73.

Richlin, A. 1995. "Making up a woman: the face of Roman gender." In D. Eilberg-Schwartz and W. Doniger, *Off with her Head! The Denial of Women's Identity in Myth, Religion and Culture*. Berkeley: 185–213.

Richlin, A. 1996. "How putting the man in Roman put the Roman in romance." In N. Hewitt, J. O'Barr, and N. Rosebaugh (eds), *Talking Gender: Personal Journeys and Political Critiques*. Chapel Hill: 14–35.

Richlin, A. 1997a. "Towards a history of body history." In M. Golden and P. Toohey (eds), *Inventing Ancient Culture: Historicism, Periodization and the Ancient World*. London and New York: 16–35.

Richlin, A. 1997b. "Carrying water in a sieve: class and body in Roman women's religion." In K. L. King (ed.), *Women and Goddess Traditions: In Antiquity and Today*. Minneapolis: 330–74.

Richlin, A. 1997c. "Pliny's brassiere." In J. P. Hallett and M. B. Skinner (eds), *Roman Sexualities*. Princeton: 197–220.

Richlin, A. 1997d. "Gender and rhetoric: producing manhood in the schools." In W. J. Dominik (ed.), *Roman Eloquence: Rhetoric in Society and Literature*. London and New York: 90–110.

Richlin, A. 1999. "Cicero's Head." In J. I. Porter (ed.), *Constructions of the Classical Body*. Ann Arbor: 190–211.

Riemann, H. 1940. *Kerameikos: Ergibnisse der Ausgrabungen. 2, Die Skulpturen vom 5. Jahrhundert bis in Römische Zeit*. Berlin.

Riggsby, A. M. 1997. "'Public' and 'private' in Roman culture: the use of the *cubiculum*," *JRA*, 10: 38–56.

Robinson, T. M. 1981. Review of Dover 1978. *Phoenix*, 35: 160–3.

Roscoe, W. 1996. "Priests of the goddess: gender transgression in ancient religion," *History of Religions*, 35: 195–230.

Rose, G. 1993. *Feminism and Geography: The Limits of Geographical Knowledge*. Minneapolis.

Rouselle, A. 1980. "Observation féminine et idéologie masculine: le corps de la femme d'après les médecins grecs," *Annales (ECS)*, 35: 1089–115.

Rousselle, A. 1988. *Porneia: On Desire and the Body in Antiquity*. Trans. F. Pheasant. Cambridge, MA.

Roy, J. 1997. "An alternative sexual morality for classical Athens," *Greece and Rome*, 44: 11–22.

Roy, J. 1999. "*Polis* and *oikos* in classical Athens," *Greece and Rome*, 46: 1–18.

Rubin, G. 1975. "The traffic in women: notes on the 'political economy' of sex." In R. R. Reiter (ed.), *Toward an Anthropology of Women*. New York: 157–210.

Russell, B. F. 1998. "The emasculation of Antony: the construction of gender in Plutarch's *Life of Antony*," *Helios*, 25: 121–37.

Said, E. 1979. *Orientalism*. New York.

Santoro L'hoir, F. 1992. *The Rhetoric of Gender Terms: "Man, "Woman" and the Portrayal of Character in Latin Prose*. Leiden.

Sartre, M. 1985. "L'homosexualité dans la Grèce ancienne," *L'Histoire*, 76 (March): 10–17.

Schaps, D. M. 1982. "The women of Greece in wartime," *Classical Philology*, 77: 193–213.

Schaps, D. M. 1998. "What was free about a free Athenian woman?," *Transactions of the American Philological Association*, 128: 161–88.

Scheidel, W. 1995/6. "The most silent women of Greece and Rome: rural labour and women's life in the ancient world," *Greece and Rome*, 42: 202–17, 43: 1–10.

Schmaltz, B. 1970. *Untersuchungen zu den attischen Marmorlekythen*. Berlin.

Schmaltz, B. 1983. *Griechische Grabreliefs*. Darmstadt.

Schmitt, Pantel, P. 1992. "The difference between the sexes: history, anthropology and the Greek city." In M. Perrot (ed.), *Writing Women's History*. Trans. F. Pheasant. Oxford: 70–89. (Orig. pub. 1984.)

Schnapp, A. 1981. "Une autre image de l'homosexualité en Grèce ancienne," *Le Débat*, 10: 107–17.

Schnurr-Redford, C. 1996. *Frauen im klassischen Athen: Sozialer Raum und reale Bewegungsfreiheit*. Berlin.

Schöne, A. 1987. *Der Thiasos: Eine ikonographische Untersuchungen über das Gefolge des Dionysos in der attischen Vasenmalerei des 6. und 5. Jhr. v. Chr.* Göteborg.

Schweitzer, B. 1941. "Krieger in der Grabkunst des fünften Jahrhunderts," *Die Antike*, 17: 35–48.

Scott, J. 1986. "Gender: a useful category of historical analysis," *AHR*, 91: 1053–75.

Seaford, R. 1984. *Euripides: Cyclops*. Oxford.

Sealey, R. 1990. *Women and the Law in Classical Greece*. Chapel Hill.

Segal, C. 1982. *Dionysiac Poetics and Euripides' Bacchae*. Princeton.

Seidler, V. 1987. "Reason, desire, and male sexuality." In P. Caplan (ed.), *The Cultural Construction of Sexuality*. London: 82–112.

Shapiro, H. A. 1991. "The iconography of mourning in Athenian art," *AJA*, 95: 629–56.

Siems, A. K. (ed.) 1988. *Sexualität und Erotik in der Antike Welt*. Darmstadt.

Simon, E. 1963. "Eine Anthesterien-Skyphos des Polygnotos," *Antike Kunst*, 6: 6–22.

Simon, E. 1969. *Die Götter der Griechen*. Munich.

Simon, E. 1983. *Festivals of Attica: An Archaeological Commentary*. Madison.

Skinner, M. B. 1979. "Parasites and strange bedfellows: a study in Catullus' political imagery," *Ramus*, 8: 137–52.

Skinner, M. B. 1987. "Greek women and the metronymic: a note on an epigram by Nossis," *Ancient History Bulletin*, 1: 39–42.

Skinner, M. B. 1993. "*Ego mulier*: the construction of male sexuality in Catullus," *Helios*, 20: 107–30.

Skinner, M. B. 1996. "Zeus and Leda: the sexuality wars in contemporary classical scholarship," *Thamyris*, 3.1: 103–23.

Skinner, M. B. 1997. "Introduction: *quod multo fit aliter in Graecia ...*" In J. P. Hallett and M. B. Skinner (eds), *Roman Sexualities*. Princeton: 3–25.

Slater, P. 1968. *The Glory of Hera: Greek Mythology and the Greek Family*. Boston.

Slater, W. 1978. "Artemon and Anacreon: no text without context," *Phoenix*, 32: 185–94.

Snyder, J. M. 1997. *Lesbian Desire in the Lyrics of Sappho*. Colombia.

Sommerstein, A. H. 1955. "The language of Athenian women." In F. De Martino and A. H. Sommerstein (eds), *Lo spettacolo delle voci*. Bari: 2.61–85.

Sourvinou-Inwood, C. 1987a. "Erotic pursuits: images and meanings," *Journal of Hellenic Studies*, 107: 131–53.

Sourvinou-Inwood, C. 1987b. "Menace and pursuit: differentiation and the creation of meaning." In C. Bérard, C. Bron, and A. Pomari (eds), *Images et société en Grèce ancienne: l'iconographie comme méthode d'analyse*. Lausanne: 41–58.

Sourvinou-Inwood, C. 1990. "Myths in images: Theseus and Medea as a case study." In Lowell Edmunds (ed.), *Approaches to Greek Myth*. Baltimore: 395–445.

Spain. D. 1992. *Gendered Spaces*. Chapel Hill.

Speier, H. 1932. "Zweifiguren-Gruppen im fünften und vierten Jahrhundert vor Christus," *MDAI(R)*, 47:1–94.

Stambaugh, J. E. 1988. *The Ancient Roman City*. Baltimore.

Steinberg, R. H. 2000. "The nurturing male: bravery and bedside manners in Isocrates' *Aegineticus*," *Greece and Rome*, 47: 172–85.

Stevenson, W. 1995. "The rise of eunuchs in Greco-Roman antiquity," *Journal of the History of Sexuality*, 5: 495–511.

Stigers, E. S. 1981. "Sappho's private world." In H. P. Foley (ed.), *Reflections of Women in Antiquity*. New York: 45–61.

Stone, L. 1981. *Costume in Aristophanic Comedy*. New York.

Strazzulla, M. 1990. *Il principato di Apollo: mito e propaganda nelle lastre "Campana" dal tempio di Apollo Palatino*. Rome.

Stumpp, B. 1998. *Prostitution in der römischen Antike*. Berlin.

Stupperich, R. 1977. "Staastsbegrabnis und Privategrabmal im klassischen Athen." Diss. Westfalischer Wilhelms Universität.

Sussman, L. A. 1984. "The elder Seneca and declamation since 1900: a bibliography," *Aufstieg und Niedergang der römischen Welt*, 32.1: 557–77.

Sutton, R. 1981. "The interaction between men and women portrayed on Attic red-figure pottery." Diss. University of North Carolina, Chapel Hill.

Talalay, L. E. 1994. "A feminist boomerang: the Great Goddess of Greek pre-history," *Gender and History*, 6: 165–83.

Tatum, J. 1983. *Plautus: The Darker Comedies*, Baltimore.

Taylor, R. 1997. "Two pathic sub-cultures in ancient Rome," *Journal of the History of Sexuality*, 7: 319–71.

Thornton, B. 1991. "*Idolon theatri*: Foucault and the classicists," *CML*, 12: 81–100.

Thornton, B. S. 1997. *Eros: The Myth of Ancient Greek Sexuality*. Boulder, CO.

Tortzen, C. G. 1991. "Male and female in Peripatetic botany," *Classica and Mediaevalia*, 42: 81–110.

Traina, A. 1998. "L'ambiguo sesso: il c.63 di Catullo." In N. Criniti (ed.), *Commune sermioni: società e cultura della "Cisalpina" dopo l'anno mille*. Brescia: 189–98.

Triantaphyllopoulos, J. 1988. "Virginité et défloration masculine." In B. G. Mandilaras (ed.), *Proceedings of the XVIII International Congress of Papyrology, Athens, 25–31 May 1986*. 2. Athens: 327–33.

Tripp, C. A. 1975. *The Homosexual Matrix*. London.

Trumbach, R. 1977. "London's sodomites: homosexual behavior and western culture in the 18th century," *Journal of Social History*, 11: 1–33.

van Wees, H. "A brief history of tears: gender differentiation in archaic Greece." In L. Foxhall and J. Salmon (eds), *When Men Were Men: Masculinity, Power and Identity in Classical Antiquity*. London and New York: 10–53.

Vedder, U. 1988. "Frauentod-Kriegertod im Spiegel der attischen Grabkunst den 4. Jhr. v. Chr.," *MDAI(A)*, 103: 161–91.

Vedder, U. 1989. "'Szenenwechsel'—Beobachtungen an zwei Grabstelen in Cambridge (Mass.) und Athen." In H.-U. Cain, H. Gabelmann, and D. Salzmann (eds), *Festschrift für Nikolaus Himmelmann*. Mainz: 169–77.

Veeser, F. 1989. *The New Historicism*. Berkeley.

Veneri, A. 1986. "Dionysos." In *LIMC*, 3.1.414–19.

Vernant, J.-P. 1980–1. "Étude comparée des religions antiques," *ACF*, 81: 391–405.

Veyne, P. 1978. "La famille et l'amour sous le haut-empire romain," *Annales (ESC)*, 33: 35–63.

Veyne, P. 1982. "L'homosexualité à Rome," *Communications*, 35: 26–33.

Veyne, P. 1985. "Homosexuality in Ancient Rome." In P. Ariès and A. Béjin (eds), *Western Sexuality: Practice and Precept in Past and Present Times*. Trans A. Forster. Oxford: 26–35.

Vidal-Naquet, P. 1981. "The black hunter and the origin of the Athenian ephebia." In P. Vidal-Naquet, *The Black Hunter*. Baltimore and London: 106–28.

Vidler, A. 1990. *Claude-Nicolas Ledoux*. Cambridge, MA.

Wagner-Hasel, B. 1989. "Frauenleben in orientalischer Abgeschlossenheit?: Zur Geschichte und Nutzanwendung eines Topos," *Die altsprachliche Unterricht*, 32.2: 18–29.

Waldner, K. 2000. *Geburt und Hochzeit des Kriegers: Geschlecterdifferenz und Initiation in Mythos und Ritual der griechischen Polis*. Berlin.

Wallace, M. B. 1970. "Notes on early Greek grave epigrams," *Phoenix*, 24: 95–105.

Wallace, R. W. 1997. "On not legislating sexual conduct in fourth-century Athens." In G. Thür and J. Vélissaropoulos-Karakostas (eds), *Symposion 1995*. Cologne: 151–66.

Wallace-Hadrill, A. 1988. "The social structure of the Roman house," *Publications of the British School at Rome*, 56: 43–97.

Weeks, J. 1977. *Coming Out: Homosexual Politics in Britain, from the Nineteenth Century to the Present*. London.

Weeks, J. 1980. "Capitalism and the organization of sex." In Gay Left Collective (ed.), *Homosexuality: Power and Politics*. London: 11–20.

Westphal, C. 1870. "Die conträre Sexualempfindung, Symptom eines neuropathischen (psychopathischen) Zustandes," *Archiv für Psychiatrie und Nervenkrankheiten*, 2: 73–108.

Wilhelm, A. 1937. "SUMMEIXIS," *Anzeiger der Österreichischen Akademie der Wissenschaften in Wien*, 74: 39–57.

Williams, C. A. 1999. *Roman Homosexuality: Ideologies of Masculinity in Classical Antiquity*. New York and Oxford.

Winkler, J. J. 1990a. "Laying down the law: the oversight of men's sexual behavior in classical Athens." In J. J. Winkler, *The Constraints of Desire: The Anthropology of Sex and Gender in Ancient Greece*. New York: 45–70.

Winkler, J. J. 1990b. "Unnatural acts: erotic protocols in Artemidoros' Dream Analysis." In J. J. Winkler, *The Constraints of Desire: The Anthropology of Sex and Gender in Ancient Greece*. New York: 80–98.

Winkler, J. J. 1990c. *The Constraints of Desire: The Anthropology of Sex and Gender in Ancient Greece*. New York.

Wolters, P. 1892. "Boiotikaí archaiotêtes," *AE*: 214–40.

Wolters, P. and Friederichs, C. 1885. *Die Gipsabgüsse antiker Bildwerke in historischen Folge erklärt*. Berlin.

Women and Geography Study Group of the IBG 1984. *Geography and Gender*. London.

Wright, R. 1997. *A Scientific Romance*. Toronto.

Wyke, M. 1987. "The elegiac woman at Rome," *Proceedings of the Cambridge Philological Society*, 33: 153–78.

Wyke, M. 1995. "Taking the woman's part: engendering Roman love elegy." In A.J. Boyle (ed.), *Roman Literature and Ideology: Ramus Essays for J. P. Sullivan*. Bendigo: 110–28.

Zanker, P. 1983. "Der Apollontempel auf dem Palatin." In K. de Fine Licht (ed.), *Città e architettura nella Roma imperiale. Analecta Romana Instituti Danici*, Supplement 10. Copenhagen: 21–40.

Zanker, P. 1990. *The Power of Images in the Age of Augustus*. Trans. A. Shapiro. Ann Arbor.

Zeitlin, F. 1982. "Cultic models of the female: rites of Dionysus and Demeter," *Arethusa* 15: 129–57.

Zeitlin, F. 1996. *Playing the Other: Gender and Society in Classical Greek Literature*. Chicago.

# Index

active/passive, 6–8, 125, 140–8, 151–2,
160–1, 177–8, 260–3, 285, 339–41, 345
Adams, J. N., 5
adultery, 58, 70, 110, 117–18, 156, 158, 163,
177, 181, 286; *see also moikheia*
Aeneas, 280, 285–6, 288
Aeschines, 123, 153–4, 155–6, 157, 159, 217
Aeschylus, 47, 52, 123, 319
agriculture, 15, 172–3
Alcibiades, 66
Alexandria, 33, 56, 59, 60, 229, 230
Anacreon, 64, 325
Andrén, Anders, 273
*ankhisteia*, 169, 171, 173, 176
Anthesteria, 299, 325–6
Antisthenes, 126
Antony, Marc, 8, 208, 279–80, 285
Aphrodite, 60, 79, 112, 114, 121, 152, 290,
324–5, 353, 365–9
Apollo, 172–3, 276–80, 289, 322
archaeology, 14, 264–73, 307–18
Archilochus, 84, 115, 119
Ariadne, 325–7, 333
Aristophanes, 44, 52, 81, 115, 116, 118,
126–8, 157, 161–2, 166, 172, 180, 244,
247, 254, 260, 293, 322, 329
Aristotle, 15, 45, 107, 116, 154–6, 158,
160–2, 164, 166, 173, 174, 178, 186–8,
190–1, 195–201, 241, 355, 360, 366
Arretine ware, 230–8
Artemidorus, 65, 148–9
Athena, 17
Athens, 3, 4, 5, 11, 15, 16, 26–7, 30–1, 32–5,
37, 40, 41, 44–56, 58, 61, 71, 72, 80, 89,
93, 107, 109, 118–19, 125–6, 138–44,
147–8, 151–66, 167, 172, 175, 230, 243–5,
254–63, 265–7, 271, 325–6, 328, 332
Augustine, 60
Augustus, 14, 208, 221, 222, 230, 236, 276,
279–81, 283–6, 288

Bacchylides, 144
Bachofen, J., 4, 19, 315

Bailey, F. G., 152
Bakhtin, M., 286
Basil of Caesarea, 103
Becker, W. A., 37–8
Beloch, K. J., 32
bodies, 5, 7–9, 83–90, 121–2, 132, 143,
147–8, 150, 183–201, 211, 212, 214–15,
224, 231–5, 322, 337, 342, 347, 354–5,
358, 361–2
Böttiger, K. A., 36–7
Boswell, John, 138
boys, 2, 8, 9, 84, 122–3, 144–5, 147, 153–66,
170, 177, 179–81, 188, 205–6, 210, 214–15,
225, 227, 228, 230, 238, 296–300, 320
Brandt, Paul (Hans Licht), 6
breasts, 188–91, 200
Brendel, O., 230
Brown, Peter, 10
Butler, Judith, 204, 327

Caelius Aurelianus, 131–2
Caelius Rufus, M., 205
Caryatids, 283, 288
Cato the Elder, 62, 65, 207
Catullus, 227
Chandler, Richard, 26
childbirth, 4, 17, 170, 172, 193, 253–63, 317
Christianity, 10, 34, 57–8, 60, 62–3, 67, 70,
74, 89, 90, 110–13, 115, 126
Cicero, 40, 95, 105–8, 212, 215–17, 219, 220,
243
*cinaedi*, 11n., 339, 345
class, 15, 17, 75–7, 79, 92, 101, 102, 125–6,
221–2, 230, 238, 272, 363
Clement of Alexandria, 69, 82, 327
Cleopatra, 279–80
clothing, 87–90, 101–2, 223–4, 226–7, 228,
234, 248–51, 255, 256, 260, 261, 301,
321–3, 334–42, 344, 346, 355, 357, 360,
364, 366–8
Columella, 213–14
concubines (*pallakai*), 66, 69–70, 107, 109,
121, 127

397